MICHEL ROUX

The Essence of French Cooking

Quadrille
PUBLISHING

PHOTOGRAPHY BY LISA LINDER

Notes

All spoon measures are level unless otherwise stated:
1 tsp = 5ml spoon; 1 tbsp = 15ml spoon.

Egg sizes are given where they are critical, otherwise use medium eggs, preferably organic or free-range. Anyone who is pregnant or in a vulnerable health group should avoid sauces that use raw egg whites or lightly cooked eggs.

Use fresh herbs, sea salt and freshly ground black pepper unless otherwise suggested.

If using the zest of citrus fruit, buy organic, unwaxed fruit.

Timings are for fan-assisted ovens. If using a conventional oven, increase the temperature by 15°C (1 Gas mark). Use an oven thermometer to check the temperature.

MICHEL ROUX

The Essence of French Cooking

Contents

Introduction

Before I begin, with the benefit of my seventy years' experience, I would like to take you by the hand and lead you on an exploratory tour of France's natural riches. Without such a tour, it would be difficult, if not impossible, for me to explain and describe to you our limitless diversity of food and produce; a diversity that is unique to the world and that has for centuries enabled us to devise and create a whole host of dishes, from the most simple to the most sophisticated.

L'Hexagone – as France is often called owing to its shape – is surrounded by the Atlantic Ocean to the west, the English Channel to the north and the Mediterranean to the south. The country boasts numerous assets: a temperate climate, countless micro-climates, incredibly fertile soil. It is criss-crossed by several large, magnificent rivers, with hundreds of tributaries, rivulets and streams, not forgetting the lakes, canals, lagoons and even the Camargue delta. The landscape is varied, with never-ending stretches of fields, vineyards, mountains, highlands, hills and forests, and relatively few cities, towns and villages.

Time and again, I have crossed from east to west and north to south, avoiding the motorways, preferring to take the scenic route along *routes nationales* or better still *routes départementales* and lanes, travelling at a speed that allows me to admire the rich, vibrant landscapes. I have taken the time to stop in villages, or picnic in a field, wood or forest. I have also been lucky enough to travel the coast in small fishing boats, discovering *la belle France* from another perspective. It is a land that embraces many different cultures and offers a huge diversity of landscape, tradition and regional identity, as well as one of the richest, most delectable and varied cuisines of the world.

The ingredients – their quality, variety and abundance – lie at the core of French cooking. There are so many to discover as you travel through the country, too many to describe here, but I would like to draw your attention to some of my favourites.

Of the various beef cattle breeds, Charolais is the most distinguished and prized, representing around 40% of French beef livestock. It is mainly found in the centre of France and in the Vendée, and is characterised by its white coat and rounded, pale horns. As for the bulls, they weigh in at over a tonne… The quality of flavour in the marbled meat of the Charolais, with its lean and succulent texture, delights even the most exacting palettes. I am proud to be a Charolais!

There are, of course, other well-known breeds, including Limousin, with its handsome mahogany coat and lighter patches around the muzzle and eyes, and the increasingly popular Blonde d'Aquitaine, with its attractive yellow coat. When driving on smaller roads, I often slow down to try to identify the breed from a distance. If I am fortunate, I will catch sight of a Parthenais, a breed highly prized for its tender, succulent meat of great finesse, or a silvery grey Gascon, or even an Aubrac, which is the favourite among many Michelin-starred chefs, thanks to its highly scented and distinctively flavoured meat.

France is the second largest producer of milk in Europe after Germany, and there are around a dozen dairy breeds. The most widespread is Prim'Holstein, which is easily recognisable by its large black and white markings and has a very high milk yield.

As for sheep, there are over 60 breeds in France, including some reared specifically for ewes' milk. I love to cook suckling lamb, spring lamb and even mutton – in a flavourful stew. For dairy use, Lacaune is the most common breed; the milk is used to make various cheeses, of which the most renowned is Roquefort.

France is the biggest producer and consumer of goat's milk in Europe. Found mainly on rugged terrain, goats are lively, agile and inquisitive creatures. I love to spit-roast kid meat to serve on the bone with young, early vegetables in spring. It is delicious and full of flavour, succulent almost to the point of being juicy. On the Saint-Tropez peninsula (where I have my house, a former *bergerie*, or sheepfold) and in the surrounding countryside, a number of goat-herders graze their flocks. The forest owners are always happy to have the herds roaming through their woods, as it's the most efficient method of clearing the ground. The goat's milk goes into making hundreds of different types of cheese, and I always take great pleasure in going to fetch my *petits chèvres frais* from my friend Gérard who keeps goats in the Maures nature reserve.

There are only a few breeds of pig in France, with the most well-known being those found in Auvergne, Ventoux and the Southwest. Their meat is highly prized and in great demand for use in charcuterie, something for which the French public has a marked penchant, consuming and exporting it in great quantities.

I have cooked in all corners of the globe and have never come across poultry of an equivalent quality to that found in France. Brittany is the main region for poultry rearing and Bresse chickens are renowned for their flavour. Whether chickens, pigeons, ducks, geese, guinea fowl, turkeys or little quail, the flavour of French poultry is outstanding. For this reason, I have always imported it for my restaurant The Waterside Inn, notably Challans ducks, with their plump and flavourful breasts, chubby little pigeons from Carnau or Charentes, as well as firm-fleshed Bresse chickens, which imbue the kitchen with distinctive mouth-watering aromas as they cook. The French really love game too. All varieties of furred game are popular, from wild boar and venison to hare, and numerous game birds, large and small, are cooked for the table.

The North Sea, the Atlantic and the Mediterranean – not forgetting the oyster parks that you find all along the French coasts – offer an incomparable array of fish and shellfish. In terms of quantity, quality and choice, the wealth of seafood in France is the envy of neighbouring countries – from the small, freshly landed sardines, which are so delicious cooked over hot coals, to the more imposing tuna that can be served raw or very lightly cooked.

France's mosaic of climates and micro-climates and diverse topography support numerous favourable growing areas, such as Brittany, the Loire valley, Aquitaine and Midi-Pyrénées, as well as the Rhône-Alpes and Provence. More particularly, it is the area around the city of Nantes, on the central west coast of France, that has thrived as a market garden area *par excellence* for more than a century, providing us with beautiful and delicious varieties of vegetables, salads and aromatic herbs. Every conceivable vegetable that you come across in Europe today can be found in this 'great garden' of France, before being dispatched to Rungis market and distributed to supermarkets and local markets, or exported to other European countries.

Bees and other pollinators play a vital role in the management and production of fruit trees. Languedoc-Roussillon, the lower Rhône valley, the Eastern Pyrénées, Provence and the Southwest have between them a total of 150,000 hectares of orchards, to which should be added the countless fruit trees planted in so many private properties. As with vegetables, every imaginable fruit can be found growing in these orchards. For my desserts, I use all the seasonal fruits that I can. Among my favourites are the first cherries, apricots and, of course, peaches, especially the white variety, with its sublime flavour and colour. As for winter fruits, I eagerly look forward to the arrival of apples and pears, so that I can create my *tartes Tatin*.

French farmers, fishermen and market gardeners supply Rungis, one of the biggest wholesale markets in the world, with fresh produce. It is situated in the southern suburbs of Paris and nicknamed the belly of France. Its location, with direct access to or within easy reach of Orly airport, the A6 motorway and the railway network, means that the produce can be transported away to all corners of the globe extremely quickly, so preserving its freshness and quality of flavour. Rungis also largely supplies the local markets that flourish all over France, their aromas and visual displays delighting the discerning consumer and professional customer alike. This traditional market network also plays an important part in the continuous evolution and ongoing endurance of French cuisine, be it regional, classic or contemporary. Thank you and *bravo* to everyone involved in the professions cited above who make it possible for us to achieve the unrivalled brand that is *la cuisine française*.

I have visited over 60 countries during my career, but only in France have I encountered such a wealth of resources and diversity of produce of every sort. This cornucopia partly explains the breadth and depth of French cuisine, but it is the family tradition of handing down from generation to generation, like a flaming torch, a first-class, authentic platform of knowledge that accounts for the prestigious reputation that French culinary art has gained. The same vein runs through the professional sector to which I belong.

From the beginning of the 1960s and through to the 1990s, thousands of young chefs from Japan, the USA, Australia, South Africa, Spain, England and other countries came to France to hone their skills in 2- and 3-star Michelin restaurants and in the greatest French pâtisseries, in order to garner expertise and knowledge that they then took back to their respective countries. It was this process that gave rise to the emergence of culinary standards abroad equal to those in some French establishments. Similarly, a great many young French chefs, pâtissiers, bakers, chocolatiers, maîtres d'hôtel and sommeliers have emigrated and are spreading French gastronomy across the world.

The inspiration for writing this book is a personal reflection that dates from my childhood and that has remained with me throughout my life, to the point of becoming a raison d'être. This project represents a considerable proportion of my life's work, and I am setting it down on paper as I have lived it daily in the kitchen. One of the toughest jobs for me was to choose, among the thousands of dishes I have made, which ones to include. Classic dishes with a touch of modernity are those I consider to be among my favourites, so they feature strongly. Some of the more ordinary dishes, such as terrine de pâté de campagne, salad of dandelion leaves with lardons, or cream of mushroom soup, for me embody the essence of French cooking as much as tournedos Rossini, dodine of duck or bouillabaisse do. So I have deliberately mixed the grand and humble; they all share their roots in our heritage and in authentic French cuisine.

I have created this book over the course of three years, working with a small, close-knit team who have understood with exceptional sensitivity, how to integrate and work with my demands and requirements. In particular, photographer Lisa Linder, throughout our travels in the various regions of France that we visited, always knew exactly how to capture, at the precise moment, the perfect angle and quality of light in order to convey my dishes perfectly.

In essence, the pleasure of creating this book offered me a double invitation to travel: to all the regions of France, and back in time, and I would like to invite you to share with me the same sentiments and passion of that journey that I experienced.

Soups

Soupe à l'Oignon à la Normande

Popular throughout France since Roman times, onion soup is regarded as simple fare, although Louis XV apparently enjoyed it at his hunting lodge, using champagne as the base liquor. In the Lyon area, it is made with Macon or southern Burgundy white wine. My mother, who was from Normandy, always used cider, the inexpensive, typical drink of the region, and one that I enjoyed from a very early age.

Peel the onions and slice them thinly. Heat 40g of the butter in a fairly deep frying pan over a medium heat, add the onions and sweat for 2 minutes, then increase the heat and cook until golden. Add 150ml of the cider and the bouquet garni and simmer for 5 minutes, then take off the heat and set aside.

Melt the remaining 30g butter in a saucepan, add the flour and cook over a gentle heat, stirring constantly with a whisk for 2 minutes, to create a lightly coloured roux. Add the stock and bring to the boil, still stirring with a whisk, then reduce the heat to low and cook for 15 minutes.

Add the onions and the cider they were cooked in and simmer for a further 15 minutes, skimming the surface every few minutes. Add salt and pepper to taste and set aside to keep warm.

Meanwhile, preheat the grill. Toast the bread slices on both sides until golden. Divide the remaining cider between 4 ovenproof bowls, then ladle in the onion soup and top with the cream. Arrange the croûtes over the surface of the soup, sprinkle with Gruyère and toast under the grill for 1–2 minutes until melted. Serve immediately, while piping hot.

Serves 4

400g onions

70g butter

250ml sweet or medium cider

1 small bouquet garni

30g plain flour

650ml chicken stock (page 248), or
   buy good-quality fresh stock

24 slices of baguette, cut about 3mm
   thick on the diagonal

70ml double cream

30g Gruyère, freshly grated

Salt and freshly ground pepper

Variation

You could use white wine in place of the cider, but it won't be quite the same. If you do not have any chicken stock to hand, use a good-quality ready-made stock rather than water.

Minestrone au Pistou

This delicious soup can be served throughout the seasons, even in the height of summer. The pistou, or pesto introduces Mediterranean flavours – reminiscent of Nice for some, or of Italy, specifically Genoa, for others. It's not practical to make the pistou in a smaller quantity, but you can store the rest in the fridge and use it for another meal – serve with pasta, risotto or simply on slices of beautifully ripe tomatoes.

Pod the broad beans and peas and set aside separately. Peel the carrot, potato and turnip. Cut these and the leek, celery and courgette into 5–7mm dice; keeping each vegetable separate.

Pour the cold water into a large pan, salt lightly and add the clove-studded onion and the bouquet garni. Bring to the boil over a medium heat, then lower the heat and simmer for 20 minutes.

Add the carrot, leek and celery dice to the pan and cook over a gentle heat for 15 minutes. Add the potato, turnip, green beans, broad beans and diced tomatoes and cook for 15 minutes over a medium heat. Finally, add the courgette, peas and macaroni and cook until the macaroni is done. Remove the bouquet garni and onion and keep the minestrone hot, if you intend to serve it imminently.

To make the pistou, put the garlic, pine nuts and a pinch of salt in a food processor or mortar and process or crush with a pestle to a purée. Add the basil and process or grind to a purée again. Add the Parmesan and process or stir in for 30 seconds. Finally, pour in the olive oil in a thin, steady stream, with the food processor on the slowest speed or whisking constantly with a balloon whisk in the mortar, as you would for mayonnaise, until the oil is completely absorbed. Season generously with pepper.

Serve the minestrone in a large tureen with the pistou and grated Parmesan on the side.

Variation
In winter, you can use more root and seasonal vegetables, such as celeriac, Jerusalem artichokes, kale, etc. Broad beans and peas are more appropriate for spring and summer.

Serves 6–8

200g tender broad beans in small pods

100g tender peas in small pods

100g carrot

100g potato

100g turnip

1 small leek, well washed

1 tender celery stalk

100g courgette

4 litres water

1 medium onion, peeled and studded
    with 2 cloves

1 bouquet garni

100g green beans

200g plump tomatoes, peeled, deseeded
    and diced

100g elbow macaroni

Salt and freshly ground pepper

75g Parmesan, freshly grated, to serve

Pistou

4 garlic cloves, peeled

50g pine nuts

40 basil leaves

75g Parmesan, freshly grated

200ml olive oil

Velouté aux Champignons de Paris

CREAM OF MUSHROOM SOUP

With its distinctive flavour and velvety texture, this is one of my favourite soups. Champignons de Paris date back to Louis XIV, and were introduced by the king's gardener, Jean-Baptiste de la Quintinie. These days they are grown in the caves of Saumur in Anjou, quarried from the pale local limestone, known as tufa, which was used to build the impressive castles and churches of the Loire Valley. Saumur is also the equestrian capital of France, which explains why horse manure compost is used for growing these mushrooms.

Melt the butter in a pan over a gentle heat. Add the shallots and sweat for 1 minute, then add the mushrooms and a little salt and increase the heat slightly. As soon as the liquid released from the mushrooms has evaporated, add the wine and cook for 3 minutes. Add the stock, garlic and bouquet garni and cook over a medium heat for 20 minutes.

Add the cream and simmer for 10 minutes, then remove the bouquet garni. Blend in a food processor or blender for 2 minutes, then strain through a fine chinois. Add salt and pepper to taste and keep warm while you cook the croûtons.

Heat the clarified butter in a frying pan over a medium heat, add the bread cubes and colour evenly for 1–2 minutes, until golden and crisp. Drain in a sieve, then arrange in a single layer on several pieces of kitchen paper. Leave for 30 seconds, then transfer to a ramekin or small dish.

Serve the soup piping hot in shallow bowls or plates, with the warm croûtons on the side. For a playful gourmet touch, mix the cream with the lemon juice and parsley and swirl on top of the soup.

Champignons de Paris

These are used in hundreds of recipes, including the celebrated *chicken chasseur*, *blanquette de veau* and mushroom omelette. In summer, they are equally delicious served as an hors d'oeuvre, raw and finely chopped, mixed with fresh cream, loosened a little with lemon juice and generously seasoned with pepper.

Serves 4

30g butter

50g shallots, peeled and thinly sliced

400g firm, white button mushrooms, cleaned and thinly sliced

50ml dry white wine

500ml vegetable stock (page 250) or water

1 garlic clove, peeled

1 small bouquet garni

125ml double cream

50g clarified butter (page 266)

2 slices of white sandwich loaf, crusts removed and cut into small cubes

Salt and freshly ground pepper

To finish (optional)

60ml double cream

Squeeze of lemon juice

A little snipped flat-leaf parsley

Velouté de Châtaignes au Champagne — CREAM OF CHESTNUT SOUP

The Ardèche is the main area for sweet chestnuts in France. Over half of the country's produce is harvested in the region and chestnut festivals take place annually in Antraigues, Désaignes and Privas. A long time ago sweet chestnut trees were nicknamed 'bread trees', as the nuts were an important source of flour for bread-making in mountainous areas where cereals were difficult to grow. These days you are more likely to come across them on street corners in winter, roasted over coals and served piping hot in paper cones to passers-by.

Roughly chop the chestnuts. Melt the butter in a saucepan over a gentle heat, add the shallots and sweat for 1 minute, then add the celeriac and chestnuts, stir with a wooden spoon, and sweat without colouring for 2–3 minutes.

Pour in the champagne or sparkling wine, increase the heat and cook at a gentle boil for 2 minutes. Add the stock or water and simmer for about 20 minutes.

When the chestnuts are tender, add the milk and cream, season lightly with salt and simmer for 3 minutes. Transfer to a food processor or blender and blend for 2 minutes, then strain through a fine chinois. Adjust the seasoning with salt and pepper to taste.

Transfer the soup to a large tureen and serve piping hot.

Variations
Try adding a grilled and julienned chicken breast to this soup just before serving, or in the game season, a couple of partridge breasts, prepared in the same way.

Sweet chestnuts
I often use chestnuts as a stuffing for game, in particular pheasant and venison; or braise them whole to serve as an accompaniment; or poach them in milk to make a delicious purée. But my favourite way to enjoy them at the beginning of the season, is to cook them whole in their shells in my hearth embers, having first made an incision in each with a knife. Roasted in this way, they are also delicious eaten after a meal with a glass of port and knob of salted butter.

Serves 4–6

250g vacuum-packed cooked, peeled chestnuts, or 300g freshly cooked chestnuts, shelled and skinned (see page 235 for preparation)

30g butter

50g shallots, peeled and thinly sliced

60g celeriac, peeled and diced

75ml champagne or sparkling white wine

600ml chicken stock (page 248) or water, or buy good-quality fresh chicken stock

50ml milk

50ml double cream

Salt and freshly ground pepper

Soupe de Potiron WINTER SQUASH SOUP

This is a staple of home-cooking all over France, where squash and pumpkins are known by varying regional terms: *potiron*, *citrouille*, *courge*, etc. Spices can be added in moderation (a little curry powder, perhaps), but it's up to you… I love it just as it is.

Preheat the oven to 160°C/Gas 3. Cut the squash into large cubes, reserving the seeds.

Wash the reserved squash seeds in cold water to remove the sticky matter clinging to them. Drain and pat dry between sheets of kitchen paper. Sprinkle lightly with fine salt, then spread the seeds out on a baking sheet. Place in the oven to dry out for about 1 hour, until lightly coloured and crunchy. Set aside.

Cut the onions, leek, carrot and celery into mirepoix (2–3cm cubes).

Melt the butter in a large saucepan. Once hot, add the squash cubes and mirepoix vegetables and cook over a brisk heat, stirring every minute or so, until lightly coloured. Add the stock and thyme sprig, salt very lightly and cook over a medium heat for 30 minutes.

Add the cream and simmer for 5 minutes. Transfer the soup to a blender and process for 2–3 minutes until very smooth, then strain through a fine chinois into a clean pan. Adjust the seasoning, adding salt and pepper to taste.

If finishing the soup with cream, whip it lightly and mix with the lemon juice. Divide the steaming hot soup between warmed soup dishes or bowls. Using a spoon, drizzle the semi-whipped cream, if using, decoratively onto each portion. Sprinkle the toasted seeds on top or serve them in a separate dish for guests to help themselves.

Serves 8

750g winter squash or pumpkin flesh

100g onions, peeled

40g leek (white part only), well washed

50g carrot, peeled

40g celery stalk, de-stringed

75g butter

750ml vegetable stock (page 250) or
  chicken stock (page 248)

1 thyme sprig

250ml double cream

Salt and freshly ground pepper

To finish (optional)

100ml whipping cream

Juice of 1 lemon

Variations
• For an elegant finish, add a few finely sliced raw scallops to the steaming hot soup at the last moment.
• For a more unusual presentation, you can serve the soup in the hollowed-out squash: Cut off the top of the squash with a sharp knife, to create a lid, then scrape out the flesh from the inside using a spoon, to use for the soup. To warm the squash shell, put it in the oven preheated to 100°C/Gas ¼ for the last 20 minutes of the soup's cooking time. Pour the soup into the squash shell to serve.

Soupe de courgettes au parfum de curry

This summery soup has a subtle hint of curry and is delicious hot or cold. You can replace the chicken stock with vegetable stock, or even water, depending on the flavour you want to achieve. The crisp courgette flowers are an attractive garnish, if you are able to source some; omit them and the courgette batons if you are serving the soup cold.

For the crisp courgette flowers, if serving, preheat the oven to 100°C/Gas ¼. Open out each flower, remove the pistil in the middle and place each flower flat on a baking sheet lined with a sheet of silicone or baking parchment. Using a brush, dab very lightly with olive oil and sprinkle lightly with salt. Place a sheet of silicone or baking parchment on top of the flowers, then a second baking sheet, to act as a press. Place in the oven for about 2 hours, until the flowers are dry and crisp. Remove to a wire rack to cool, then set aside the cooled flowers in a dry place, to prevent them going soft.

For the soup, trim the ends of the courgettes, then cut into large dice (leave the skins on). Heat the olive oil in a pan over a medium heat, then add the onion and leek and sweat for 1 minute, without letting them colour.

Add the diced courgettes, garlic and curry powder and sweat for 4–5 minutes, stirring from time to time with a wooden spoon, without letting the vegetables take on any colour.

Add the chicken stock and potatoes, with a pinch of salt, and cook over a medium heat for 15 minutes, until the potatoes are just cooked.

Transfer the contents of the pan to a food processor or blender and process for 1–2 minutes to a creamy consistency. Strain through a fine chinois into a clean pan; keep hot until ready to serve.

For the courgette batons, heat the grapeseed oil in a deep, heavy pan to 160–170°C. Add the batons and fry until lightly crisp. Transfer to kitchen paper to drain, using a skimmer, and spread out slightly to keep them crisp.

Season the soup with salt and pepper to taste, then serve very hot in bowls and offer the batons and crisp flowers separately.

Serves 6–8

500g small or medium firm courgettes

2 tbsp olive oil

1 medium onion, peeled and thinly sliced

60g leek (white part only), well washed and thinly sliced

1 medium garlic clove, peeled and chopped

1 tsp Madras curry powder

500ml chicken stock (page 248), or buy good-quality fresh stock

60g potatoes, peeled and cut into large dice

Salt and freshly ground pepper

To serve

6 courgette flowers (optional)

A little olive oil, if using flowers

250ml grapeseed oil, for deep-frying

100g baby courgettes, cut into small batons

Variation
In season, you can replace the courgettes with asparagus, using the same ingredients and method as the main recipe. Add 100ml double cream to the soup just before serving, and serve with croûtons, made by frying small cubes of sliced bread in clarified butter (page 266) until crisp and golden brown.

Soupe de Poissons et sa Rouille

FISH SOUP WITH ROUILLE

My *soupe de poisson* is made with rockfish flavoured with saffron, and is similar to the kind found in Nice or Marseille. All the Mediterranean countries have their own versions, made with local fish and seafood. In this country, rockfish can be replaced by haddock, cod, pollock, halibut, flounder, coley, langoustine and/or mussels; a selection of four varieties is enough to make a very good fish soup.

Scale, gut and trim all the fish, cut the larger ones in half, then wash all of them in very cold water and drain. Preheat the oven to 160°C/Gas 3.

Heat the olive oil in a large cooking pot over a gentle heat. Add the leeks, onions, garlic, tomatoes, bouquet garni and fennel and sweat for 5 minutes. Add the fish and crabs, if using, increase the heat and stir constantly with a wooden spoon for 15 minutes. Pour in the boiling water and bring to the boil. Add the saffron and dried orange zest, lower the heat and simmer for 40 minutes. Meanwhile, dry the baguette slices in the oven for 20 minutes or so until crisp.

Remove the bouquet garni and pass the soup through a mouli, pressing the fish and vegetables through. Strain through a chinois, pushing down with the back of a ladle. Season generously with salt and pepper and keep hot.

Transfer the piping hot soup to a large soup tureen and serve at once, in deep plates or shallow bowls. Offer the crisp bread slices separately, with the garlic cloves on the side for anyone who likes to rub them with garlic. Serve the rouille in a bowl.

Serves 10

1.5kg small rockfish, such as scorpion fish, weevers, wrasse, combers, pagres, girelles, bavèques, etc.

1–2 conger eel heads or tails

50ml olive oil

2 medium leeks (white part only), washed and thinly sliced

150g onions, peeled and thinly sliced

3 garlic cloves, peeled and crushed

500g properly ripe tomatoes, roughly diced

1 medium bouquet garni

1–2 fennel sprigs

10 green shore crabs, rinsed in cold water (optional)

3.5 litres boiling water

3g (½ tsp) saffron threads

Dried zest of 2 oranges (see page 267)

Salt and freshly ground pepper

To serve

20 thin slices of baguette

4–5 garlic cloves, peeled

1 quantity rouille (page 257)

Bisque de Homard

'Bisque' refers to a soup with a shellfish base, of any variety – lobster, crab, etc. The name would seem to derive from the place where it was first made: the Bay of Biscay. But a second theory is that it comes from the term *bis-cuit* (twice cooked): the pieces of shellfish are first sautéed in their shell, and then simmered with aromatics and white wine. I'll let you decide...

Cut the leek, carrot, celery and fennel into mirepoix (2–3cm cubes). Heat the oil in a large, heavy-based saucepan (ideally a copper one). When it is hot, add the lobster heads and claws and, using a skimmer, stir over a brisk heat until the shells have turned a good dark red colour. Add the mirepoix vegetables and cook for 3 minutes, stirring a few times.

Sprinkle over the Cognac and flambé (set alight with a long match). When the flame has died down, add the tomato purée, chopped tomatoes, crushed peppercorns and wine and cook over a medium heat for 5 minutes. Now pour in the fish stock, stir well, bring to the boil and skim. Add the bouquet garni, lower the heat and leave to cook at a bare simmer for 30 minutes. Discard the bouquet garni.

Using a slotted spoon, transfer the shells and cooking juices, a quarter at a time, to a food processor and process on a low speed until the shells are crushed. Strain through a fine chinois, pressing down on the mixture with a ladle to extract as much liquid as possible. (The bisque can be prepared ahead to this stage and refrigerated or frozen; defrost in the fridge overnight before finishing if frozen.)

Melt the butter in a small pan, add the flour and cook, stirring, over a medium heat for 2 minutes, without colouring. Heat the strained bisque in a saucepan, whisking in the roux at the same time. As it comes to the boil, add the cream. Lower the heat and simmer for 5 minutes, stirring with a whisk occasionally.

Taste the bisque and adjust the seasoning with a pinch of cayenne, salt and pepper and then add the lemon juice. Divide between soup dishes and drop a spoonful of crème fraîche onto each. Finish with a scattering of chervil sprigs, and vegetable pearls if you wish.

Variations
• If you ever come across little live green, or shore crabs, then you can use them to make a crab bisque, in exactly the same way as for lobster in this recipe.
• If you can't find raw lobster heads and claws, buy two 500–600g lobsters. Separate the claws and head from the tail to use in the bisque, and simmer the tail for 5–6 minutes in fish stock. You can either add little pieces of the tail to the bisque or slice it into medallions, mix with a little mayonnaise and serve with cherry tomatoes as a starter.

Serves 8

100g leek (white part only), well washed

100g carrot, peeled

100g celery stalk, trimmed

100g fennel bulbs, trimmed

50ml grapeseed or groundnut oil

600g raw lobster heads and claws, fresh or frozen, roughly chopped

30ml Cognac

30g tomato purée

100g very ripe tomatoes, chopped

10 white peppercorns, crushed

200ml dry white wine

1.5 litres fish stock (page 249)

A bouquet garni (20g tarragon, 20g dill, 5g thyme and 2 bay leaves tied together)

25g butter

25g plain flour

200ml double cream

Juice of ½–1 lemon, to taste

Cayenne, salt and freshly ground pepper

To finish

100ml crème fraîche

Chervil sprigs

Vegetable pearls (scooped with a melon baller, from courgettes, turnips, etc., and blanched), optional

Consommé de Volaille, Royale de Tomates

CHICKEN CONSOMMÉ

This is a lovely delicate soup, ideal as a *mise en bouche* for a dinner of several courses to follow. Conveniently, all the components can be cooked a day or two in advance. You can make the *royale* using leeks, truffle, asparagus, etc. It's a bit like an ice cream; you get to choose the flavour.

Put the hen into a cooking pot in which it fits comfortably, cover generously with cold water and add the roasted chicken necks and wings. Bring to the boil over a medium heat, then immediately reduce the heat so the water is at 80–90°C and cook for 30 minutes, skimming as necessary. Now add the carrots, celery, leeks, onion, bouquet garni and coarse salt and cook gently for 1½ hours, at 80–90°C, skimming occasionally.

Carefully lift out the hen, necks, wings and vegetables, disturbing the liquid as little as possible, to preserve the consommé's clarity. Discard the vegetables, necks and wings. Place the hen on a dish, cover with a damp tea towel and set aside. Carefully strain the consommé through a muslin-lined chinois into a large bowl and set aside. Preheat the oven to 150°C/Gas 2.

To make the tomato royale, very lightly brush a small oval dish or 2–3 ramekin dishes with the grapeseed oil. Put the tomato purée, egg yolks and 2 tbsp of the cooled consommé in a bowl and mix with a small balloon whisk, without overworking it. Season with salt and pepper and strain the mixture through a muslin-lined sieve or chinois into the dish(es). Stand in a roasting tray and pour in enough hot water to come halfway up the dish(es). Cook in the oven for 10–15 minutes, until just set. Remove the dish(es) from the tray and leave to cool, then refrigerate for at least 6 hours.

To clarify the consommé, mix the egg whites with the chopped chicken breast in a large saucepan, then add the tomatoes and tarragon. Pour on the cooled consommé and bring to the boil over a medium heat, stirring with a wooden spoon every 5 minutes and taking care that the chicken doesn't stick to the pan. When it is nearly reaching the boil, lower the temperature so the liquid is at 80–90°C and cook for 20 minutes. Carefully strain through a muslin-lined sieve or chinois into a clean pan, add salt and pepper to taste and keep hot.

To serve, remove the breasts from the poached bird, discard the skin and cut the meat into small batons. Arrange 4–6 batons in each warm soup plate, then use a melon baller to scoop out balls of tomato royale; distribute between the bowls. Drain the perles Japon or tapioca and divide between the bowls. Pour on the hot consommé, garnish with chervil and serve.

Serves 6–8

1 boiling hen, 1.75–2kg

300g chicken necks and wings, roasted in a hot oven until well browned

250g carrots, peeled and cut into rounds

½ head of celery, stalks halved

250g leeks, well washed and finely sliced

1 onion, peeled, halved and each half studded with a clove

A bouquet garni

10g coarse salt

1 tsp grapeseed oil

50g tomato purée

2 egg yolks, plus 4 whites

350g chicken breasts, skinned and finely chopped

250g tomatoes, cut into pieces

10g tarragon leaves, snipped

30g perles Japon, or tapioca, cooked in boiling water for 5 minutes, then set aside in cold water

Salt and freshly ground pepper

Chervil sprigs, to garnish

Starters

Artichauts à la Barigoule

BRAISED BABY ARTICHOKES

The success of this dish lies in the tenderness and freshness of the small artichokes, which should have been picked only a short time before you buy or cook them. They are lovely as a starter but also good as an accompaniment to roast fish, such as John Dory (see page 99).

Put the lardons in a saucepan, cover with cold water and bring to the boil, then lower the heat and cook for 1 minute to blanch.

Gently pick off the outside leaves from each artichoke. Using a small knife, cut through the stalk about 2cm from the base, then cut about 2cm down from the tip of the leafy ends. Using a small spoon, scoop out the choke found in the middle of the heart, concealed by the leaves. Use a small knife to trim the leaves a little at the top and any part at the base of the leaves that seems woody. Pare the stalk back with the knife to leave just the tender part.

Rinse the artichokes under cold running water and transfer them to a bowl of water with the lemon juice added until ready to cook. Make sure you leave them in the acidulated water for no longer than the time it takes to sweat the other vegetables.

Heat the olive oil in a flameproof casserole over a gentle heat. Add the carrot, fennel, celery, onions, garlic, thyme, bay and lardons. Sweat for 2–3 minutes, then add the artichokes and lemon juice. Cook, stirring occasionally, for 1–2 minutes, then add the white wine and cook for another 5 minutes.

Now add the chicken stock with a pinch of salt and a little pepper. Cover and cook over a very gentle heat for 10–15 minutes, until the artichokes are tender, or for just 5 minutes if you like them to have some crunch.

Using a slotted spoon, transfer the artichokes, flavouring vegetables and lardons to a warm dish, leaving the liquor behind. Place the casserole over a lively heat and reduce the liquor by half. Adjust the seasoning with salt and pepper and pour the reduced liquor over the artichokes. Serve warm or cooled to room temperature.

Serves 4

50g semi-salted belly pork, cut into lardons

8 small (poivrade) artichokes

Juice of ½ lemon

2 tbsp olive oil

60g carrot, peeled and cut into small dice

50g fennel bulb, trimmed and cut into small dice

60g very tender celery stalk, cut into small dice

8 baby white onions, peeled and halved

1 garlic clove, peeled and crushed

2 thyme sprigs

2 bay leaves

Juice of ½ lemon

100ml dry white wine

100ml chicken stock (page 248), or buy good-quality fresh stock

Salt and freshly ground pepper

Variation

Very tender, young artichokes can, once they have been prepared from raw in the same way as for the main recipe, be sliced raw into very fine slivers and drizzled with olive oil and lemon juice, sprinkled with salt and pepper and topped with shavings of Parmesan and a few extremely fresh, raw anchovy fillets… an absolute treat for the taste buds and the ultimate in simplicity.

Salade Niçoise

There are innumerable different versions of this dish but this is the way I have always made mine, from the days of my first visits to the Côte d'Azur. If I can't find perfect lettuce, I use a mixture of mesclun and rocket instead, and I sometimes add small cubes of cucumber. Do not refrigerate any part of the salad at any stage, except possibly the eggs.

Put the eggs in a saucepan, cover with cold water and bring to the boil over a medium heat. As soon as the water boils, lower the heat and simmer for 6 minutes, then drain and cool in cold water.

Meanwhile, soak the anchovy fillets in milk for 5 minutes to remove the excess salt. Drain and split them in half lengthways.

Boil the new potatoes in their skins until just tender; drain. Cook the green beans in boiling salted water for a few minutes until al dente, then drain.

Peel the eggs and cut them in half lengthways. Scoop out the set yolks and transfer to a bowl. Crush the yolks, using the back of a spoon, then incorporate 1 tsp of the olive oil and season with salt and pepper to taste. Transfer to a piping bag fitted with a 6mm fluted nozzle.

Pipe the yolk mixture into the empty egg white halves, to create a rosette effect. Wrap a halved anchovy fillet around each piped yolk, reserving the rest, and place in the fridge until ready to serve.

To make the vinaigrette, put 2 pinches of fine salt and 2 turns of the pepper mill in a bowl and add the wine vinegar. Mix with a small whisk, then whisk in the remaining olive oil. Set aside until needed.

Using a small knife, remove just the top of the marmande tomato, then scoop out the seeds inside using the back of a spoon. Sprinkle salt and pepper lightly into the tomato shells and set aside.

Peel the cooked potatoes, ideally while they are still warm. Cut each one into 4 or 6 wedges, put into a bowl with the green beans and pour over two-thirds of the vinaigrette. Mix gently.

Separate the lettuce heart into leaves, discarding any tougher outer leaves. Rinse, dry, then arrange in a large, shallow dish. Put the marmande tomato in the middle and surround with the potatoes, beans and tomato wedges. Arrange the filled egg halves and remaining anchovy fillets on the salad.

Scatter the olives and tarragon leaves on top, then trickle over the remaining vinaigrette. Sprinkle a little coarse salt over the tomato wedges and serve.

Serves 4

2 medium eggs

4 plump anchovy fillets in oil

A little milk

6 small new potatoes

100g green beans, sliced lengthways if large

4 tbsp olive oil

1½ tbsp red wine vinegar

1 large ripe marmande tomato, peeled

1 flavourful, firm lettuce heart

2 ripe, firm medium tomatoes (ideally Saint Pierre), peeled, deseeded and cut into wedges

12 medium black olives, or 20 small Niçoise olives

2 tarragon sprigs, leaves picked

Salt (coarse and fine) and freshly ground pepper

Salade de Pissenlits aux Lardons

SALAD OF DANDELION LEAVES WITH LARDONS

I've always loved the firm texture of dandelion leaves and their hint of bitterness. These leaves are tender in spring, which is the best time to gather them from meadows and the foothills of mountains. This is a humble salad that our grandmothers would have made using pan-fried lardons or back fat, to which they added a trickle of vinegar and pieces of stale bread. It dates back to around the time of the First World War and is a poor man's dish that has evolved into a more refined one, to the extent that dandelion leaves are now cultivated, in their original green as well as yellow forms.

Wash the dandelion leaves in very cold water and remove any outer leaves, if necessary. Split the base of each leaf in two and remove a little of the stalk. Drain, dry in a salad spinner and arrange on a large shallow serving dish or in a salad bowl.

For the croûtes, preheat the oven to 180°C/Gas 4. Place the baguette rounds on a large baking tray and toast in the oven until golden, then rub each one with the cut surface of the garlic and set aside.

Remove the rind from the belly pork. Cut the pork into slices, about 5mm thick, then into lardons about 5mm long. Put into a saucepan, cover with cold water and bring to the boil, reduce the heat to low and simmer for 2 minutes to blanch. Refresh in cold water, drain and pat dry with kitchen paper.

For the vinaigrette, put 2 pinches of salt into a small bowl with a grinding of pepper and 1½ tbsp of the wine vinegar. Stir with a fork to combine, then add the oil, stirring all the time with the fork.

Trickle the vinaigrette over the dandelion leaves and toss lightly. Add the lardons to a hot, dry, non-stick frying pan and cook over a lively heat for 1 minute to colour all over, then add the remaining ½ tbsp vinegar, stir well and immediately pour over the dandelion leaves. Arrange the croûtes on top and serve at once.

Serves 4

300g dandelion leaves, a mixture of green and yellow

16 slices of baguette, about 3mm thick

1 garlic clove, peeled and halved

150g piece of lightly smoked belly pork

2 tbsp red wine vinegar

4 tbsp groundnut oil

Salt and freshly ground pepper

Variations

Adding one or two roughly chopped hard-boiled eggs and some capers with the lardons will transform this salad into a more substantial starter, while still retaining its original character. You could also make this salad with frisée instead of dandelion leaves, but it will not have the same flavour.

Légumes Provençaux à l'Anchoïade

BASKET OF PROVENÇAL VEGETABLES WITH ANCHOÏADE

The time to best appreciate this dish is in spring or early summer, when the young, tender vegetables are at their most delicious. Depending on what is available, you can substitute some of the vegetables for others, without detracting from the overall appearance and flavour of the dish. For example, white or red chicory from northern France is a lovely addition.

For the anchoïade, soak the anchovy fillets in cold water for 30 minutes to remove some of their salt.

Meanwhile, prepare each vegetable as appropriate, by trimming, paring or peeling with a swivel peeler, then rinse them all in very cold water. Leave whole, halve or quarter as appropriate. Remove the white membranes and seeds from the peppers.

Arrange the vegetables in a large wicker basket, or in a huge, flared salad bowl. Cover with a very damp tea towel and set aside until ready to serve.

To make the anchoïade, drain the anchovy fillets and thoroughly wipe dry with a tea towel, then put into a mortar or small food processor with the garlic. Grind or process to a smooth, homogeneous purée. Start to incorporate the oil a little at a time, still working with the pestle or with the motor running, until you have a very smooth mixture. Add the vinegar and season very lightly with salt if necessary, and with pepper to taste. Transfer to a large bowl.

To serve, place the basket or bowl of vegetables in the middle of the table for guests to help themselves. Serve with the anchoïade, slices of crusty bread and a bowl of olives.

Anchoïade

Originally from Provence, but now enjoyed all along the Côte d'Azur and as far as Languedoc Roussillon, anchoïade is a deliciously savoury dip. It should be served cold in summer, with young, tender crudités, but can also be spread on toasted pieces of bread and served with an aperitif; in which case, a white wine from Cassis would make a perfect match. Served warm in winter with raw seasonal vegetables, peeled and cut into matchsticks, anchoïade is known as *fondue occitane*.

(Illustrated on previous page)

Serves 6–8

8 small, tender (poivrade) artichokes

2 bunches of radishes

250g broad beans in pods

1 medium, firm, white cauliflower

300g baby carrots (in a bunch)

8 medium, firm button mushrooms

4 medium, very tender fennel bulbs

4 yellow, red or green peppers

12 salad onions, with greenery

2 small, firm cucumbers

2 hearts of firm, crisp celery

2 stems of cherry tomatoes on the vine

2 beef tomatoes

1 fresh spring garlic bulb (if available)

Anchoïade

250g fresh, lightly salted anchovy fillets

2 garlic cloves, peeled and crushed

150ml olive oil

2 tbsp wine vinegar

Salt and freshly ground pepper

To serve

Crusty bread and green or black olives

Croustades d'Escargots en Habit Vert

SNAIL CROUSTADES WITH PARSLEY AND CREAM SAUCE

These are good to eat and simple to make. To enhance the presentation, you can confit 8 cherry tomatoes in a little olive oil at 140°C for 5 minutes, then arrange a couple in each croustade, mixed in with the snails.

Roll out the pastry on a lightly floured surface to a 2–3mm thickness and cut out 4 rounds, using a 10cm diameter plain or fluted pastry cutter. Use the rounds to line 4 croustade or tart moulds, 6–7cm in diameter and 1.5cm tall. Prick each pastry base twice with a fork and rest in the fridge for 20 minutes. Preheat the oven to 180°C/Gas 4.

Line each pastry case with a circle of greaseproof paper and fill with ceramic baking beans or dried beans, then bake for 10–15 minutes, until the pastry is cooked. Remove the paper and beans, then put the pastry cases back in the oven for 2 minutes to dry and cook the bases. Unmould each pastry case and set aside on a wire rack.

Bring a pan filled with lightly salted water to the boil. Set aside 4 parsley sprigs for presentation, then drop the remaining parsley into the boiling water, blanch for 2 minutes, and drain.

Heat the cream in a sauté pan over a medium heat. As soon as it boils, add the drained parsley and cook for 2 minutes. Pour the cream and parsley mixture into a food processor or blender and process for 2–3 minutes, until you have a very smooth, slightly runny purée. Strain through a fine sieve, using a pestle to push the mixture through. Transfer to a small pan; keep hot.

Heat the butter in a frying pan and, as soon as it is foaming and has a nutty aroma, add the snails. Add salt and pepper to taste and remove from the heat. Divide the parsley and cream sauce between the pastry cases, then arrange 6 snails on each. Arrange the reserved parsley sprigs over the snails and serve at once.

Serves 4

120g quick puff pastry (page 263)

Flour, for dusting

100g de-stemmed flat-leaf parsley sprigs

300ml double cream

40g butter

24 snails, in a jar or tin, rinsed in cold
   water and thoroughly drained

Salt and freshly ground pepper

Brandade de Morue

The roots of this dish can be traced back to two places: the Basque country, where it first appeared in the early 16th century (as salt cod purée made using potato, and used to stuff piquillo peppers); and Nîmes, which has an equal claim on the dish in the form of a salt cod purée mixed, originally, with potatoes browned in the oven. My interpretation is closer to this second version, which has itself evolved over time.

Serves 6–8

1kg semi-dried salt cod fillet

500ml cold milk

500ml water

2 bay leaves

1 thyme sprig

4 garlic cloves, peeled

300ml light, fruity olive oil

Juice of 1 lemon

24 slices of baguette, cut about 3mm thick on the diagonal

Generous pinch of Espelette pepper (optional)

Salt and freshly ground pepper

Black olives, to serve

Soak the salt cod in cold water to cover generously for 24 hours, changing the water every 6 hours or so.

Split the soaked salt cod fillet in two and put into a saucepan with 300ml of the milk, the 500ml cold water, bay leaves and thyme sprig. Over a gentle heat, bring the liquid to 80–90°C and poach the fish at this temperature for 6 minutes. Drain the fish and cover it with a generously dampened tea towel.

Rub the insides of a cast-iron or enamelled pot with the garlic cloves, dipping them in fine salt from time to time to help crush them against the sides of the pot and use up the entire cloves. Bring the remaining 200ml milk just to the boil in a pan, then remove from the heat and leave to cool until tepid.

Remove the skin and any bones from the salt cod and flake it into the pot. Place over a very gentle heat and work the cod with a wooden spoon, crushing it against the sides of the pot until it turns into a rough purée, about 3–4 minutes.

Now add half the olive oil in a thin stream, as you would to make mayonnaise, stirring constantly with the wooden spoon, then do the same with half of the tepid milk. Alternate the remaining oil and milk, adding both until the salt cod has absorbed all of both liquids. Add the lemon juice and season with salt and pepper to taste.

Toast the bread slices until golden. Transfer the salt cod purée, or brandade, to a serving dish, ideally a dark rustic bowl. Sprinkle with the Espelette, if using, and serve with the croûtes and some olives on the side. A glass of rosé is the perfect complement.

Variations

During the black truffle season, a few slivers of truffle added to the brandade with the warm milk will add a grander note. You could also top the brandade with a few fine shavings of Parmesan and serve it with a rocket or mesclun salad.

Soufflé aux Moules · MUSSEL SOUFFLÉ

This is an unusual soufflé that will delight anyone who enjoys
the fruits of the sea presented in a different way. All of the
components can be prepared several hours before assembling
the individual soufflés, making the task easier.

Cut the carrot, onion, celery and fennel into mirepoix (2–3cm dice). Put half
the butter in a deep pan (large enough to fit all the mussels) and melt over a
medium heat. Add the vegetables and sweat over a gentle heat for 5 minutes,
stirring from time to time. Add the wine, stirring to deglaze, increase the heat
and cook over a medium heat for 3–4 minutes.

Add the mussels to the pan, increase the heat to high and cover the pan with
a tight-fitting lid, moving the mussels around every minute or so. As soon as
all the shells have opened, about 3–4 minutes, remove from the heat and tip
the mussels into a strainer placed over a bowl to catch the juices. Strain the
juices through a chinois and set aside. Take the mussels out of the shells and
remove their frilly skirts, then set aside the 20 most attractive mussels (to use
in the sauce for serving alongside the soufflés).

Put the remaining mussels in a food processor with 2 tbsp of the cooking
juices and blitz to a soft, slightly runny purée, 1–2 minutes. Transfer to a bowl,
cover with cling film and set aside. Measure another 100ml cooking juices
and set aside for the sauce (for serving).

For the velouté, melt the remaining 40g butter in a saucepan, add the flour
and cook for 2 minutes, stirring constantly with a whisk, to make a roux.
Add 300ml of the mussel cooking juices (making up the quantity with a
little fish stock if necessary), then add the saffron and bring to the boil over
a gentle heat, stirring with the whisk. Lower the heat and simmer for 2–3
minutes, still stirring. Remove from the heat and add half the lemon juice, the
egg yolks and a grinding of pepper. Mix well with a whisk, cover with cling
film and set aside.

Preheat the oven to 180°C/Gas 4. Brush the insides of 4 individual soufflé
dishes, about 10cm in diameter and 6.5cm tall, with the softened butter.
Sprinkle half the chives into the moulds, tilting them to distribute the chives
evenly over the base and sides.

To make the sauce for serving, put the reserved 100ml mussel cooking juices
in a small pan over a medium heat and let bubble to reduce by half. Add
the cream and 40g of the mussel purée and reduce until the sauce is
thick enough to coat the back of a spoon. Remove from the heat, add the
20 reserved mussels, the remaining lemon juice and some pepper to taste;
keep warm until needed.

Using a hand-held electric or balloon whisk, in a clean bowl, whisk the egg
whites with a pinch of salt until holding their shape but not too firm.

Serves 4

1 carrot, peeled

1 onion, peeled

2 celery stalks, trimmed

½ fennel bulb, trimmed

80g butter

250ml dry white wine

1.5kg live mussels, cleaned
  (see page 80)

40g plain flour

A little fish stock (page 249), if needed

Small pinch of saffron threads

Juice of 1 lemon

3 egg yolks

10g chives, finely snipped

100ml double cream

6 egg whites (240g in total)

20g Gruyère, freshly grated

Salt and freshly ground pepper

For greasing the moulds

40g butter, softened

Put the velouté in a large bowl with the remaining soft mussel purée, making sure both are warm. Using a balloon whisk, gently incorporate one-third of the whisked egg whites, then the Gruyère and remaining chives. Add the rest of the egg whites and gently fold into the mixture, using a large metal spoon or rubber spatula, taking care not to overwork it.

Divide the mixture between the 4 dishes and lightly smooth the tops with a palette knife. Stand in a shallow baking dish lined with greaseproof paper or foil and pour near-boiling water (at about 80°C) into the dish to come halfway up the sides of the dishes. Bake in the oven for 8 minutes, until well risen.

Serve the soufflés as soon as they come out of the oven with the sauce presented separately. At the table, make a small hole in the middle of each soufflé with a spoon and pour in a little of the sauce and mussels.

CHARCUTERIE… a simple and natural delight

Of all the many disciplines of French cooking, charcuterie is unique in its use of just one meat ingredient – pork – as a base for all of its preparations. From nose to tail, every part of the pig, including the rind, is used, wasting nothing in its methodical, economical and meticulous process that produces the most delicious results and gives the greatest pleasure to those who love to snack on cured meats, in other words the whole of France. It was following the arrival of one Louis-François Drône, who settled in Paris during the Second Empire under Napoleon III, that charcuterie acquired greater renown, thanks to the new manufacturing methods that he introduced. From that time on, charcuterie started to appear on gala dinner menus.

Every village in France has always had among its food traders a pork butcher, as well as one or two bistros or family-run restaurants. As the son and grandson of a Charollais pork butcher, I had the privilege of being born over the family shop. From dawn, the daily cooking preparations emitted the most enticing aromas that found their way up through the floors of the house and into my bedroom. And so I had a personalised alarm call that roused me out of bed with great speed… my belly calling, you might say. Sadly, this very demanding and low-status trade no longer attracts enough young people, and many pork butchers are disappearing or offering mediocre charcuterie products, bought in from a curing factory and not anything like as good as those made in the small kitchen found at the back of the shop.

I am always on the look-out, since there are now only several hundred, rather than thousands, of pork butchers who sell their own products, and who take pride in what they make. Some have even earned the coveted title of Meilleur Ouvrier de France Charcutier, which guarantees the excellence of their products.

Probably because of my origins, I adore charcuterie and enjoy everything from a simple pâté de campagne (such as the one on page 51) to chicken pâté en croûte (see page 53), a more sophisticated dish intended for a feast day table. Alain, my son, beguiles me with his velvety black pudding, spiced to perfection and embellished with apples cooked in butter, and with his rabbit rillettes served on toasted croûtons, which he makes from time to time at The Waterside Inn.

On market days, as soon as I get back to the house I love to grab a bite to eat – a little jambon persillé or a few slices of andouille and salami, perhaps, as well as a portion of pâté de campagne. Butter is there at the party too, along with a few baby cornichons and a good crusty baguette. I wash it all down with a chilled red wine from the Loire, such as Bourgueil, Chinon or Saumur Champigny.

For picnics, I favour my chicken pâté en croûte, which will survive a journey as well as hot weather, along with a few slices of cured ham that I eat with a large, round pain de campagne. For a lunch occasion or smart dinner, I like to start with my dodine de canard (on page 56), or maybe a ballotine of chicken. In short, charcuterie brings momentary pleasures throughout the day. For optimal flavour, it is vital you remove it from the fridge at least 15 minutes before serving.

During my regular visits to Paris, I take charcuterie to my family and friends, always buying it from the small shop belonging to Gilles Verot (3 rue Notre Dame des Champs, Paris 6ème), a place overflowing and imbued with authentic charcuterie, all made by Mr Verot and his team. It takes me back to my childhood and reminds me of our homemade charcuterie. I remember shelves bowed under the weight of all manner of pâtés, hams on the bone, galantines, stuffings, cooked dishes such as bouchées à la Reine and stuffed tomatoes… However long the queue on the pavement outside the shop, I await my turn patiently while contemplating the joy that Mr Verot brings to the epicurean such as me.

Clockwise (from top left): Rosette de Lyon;
terrine de boeuf; terrine de lapin en gelée;
andouille; saucisson à l'ail; jambon crus du pays

Terrine de Pâté de Campagne

This is a delicious, rustic coarse-textured terrine, made with inexpensive, flavourful cuts of meat, including some liver. Fine slices of pork back fat are typically used to line the terrine. Once cooked and thoroughly cooled, the pâté can be glazed with a chicken gelée (as shown) an hour or two before serving, to enhance its appearance if you like, but this is by no means essential…

Put the pork neck in a dish, sprinkle with the wine, cover and leave to marinate in the fridge for 12 hours.

Melt the butter in a small pan, add the shallots and garlic and sweat over a low heat for 3 minutes. Drain and set aside to cool.

Pass the pork liver and back fat through a meat mincer fitted with a medium plate. Change to a coarse plate and pass the marinated pork through it. Put all the ground meat into a large mixing bowl and stand the bowl in a larger bowl of crushed ice cubes to which you have added a little very cold water.

Using a wooden spoon, mix the meats together, then add the eggs and stir well. Add the shallot and garlic mixture, the thyme, quatre-épices, cream, salt and pepper. Stir until thoroughly combined.

Line a terrine, 20 x 15cm and 8cm deep, with the sliced back fat. Fill the dish with the meat mixture, doming the surface slightly. Arrange a few back fat slices in a lattice pattern on top of the pâté and refrigerate for about 12 hours.

Preheat the oven to 170°C/Gas 3. Stand the terrine in a shallow oven dish lined with greaseproof paper and pour just-boiled water into the dish to come halfway up the terrine. Cook in the oven for 70 minutes, then check the terrine by inserting a trussing needle into the centre; it should feel warm, verging on hot. (Or insert a meat probe into the centre; it should register 55°C.)

Transfer the terrine from the bain-marie to a wire rack and place a small plate on top of the pâté. Place a 500–750g weight on top of the plate and leave to cool completely. Refrigerate for at least 48 hours before serving. If required, coat the surface with chicken gelée an hour or two before serving and return to the fridge. This pâté will keep well in the fridge for up to 10 days.

To serve, remove the plate and weights and present the pâté in its dish at the table. I like to offer gherkins, pickled baby white onions and slices of pain de campagne on the side.

Serves 12–14

500g pork neck (or shoulder), cut into strips

50ml dry white wine

30g butter

100g peeled shallots, finely chopped

5g peeled garlic, very finely chopped

250g pork liver, cut into strips

250g pork back fat, cut into strips

2 eggs, lightly beaten

3g (1½ tsp) thyme leaves, chopped (ideally flowering thyme)

2g (½ tsp) quatre-épices

50ml double cream

8–10g fine sea salt

5g (1 tsp) freshly ground pepper

To line the dish and finish

200g pork back fat, cut into fine slices, about 1cm wide

Chicken gelée (page 248), optional

Variation
For a delicious game pâté, replace the pork liver with wild duck meat or venison.

Pâté de Volaille en Croûte aux Trompettes de la Mort

CHICKEN PÂTÉ EN CROÛTE WITH MUSHROOMS

Dating back in France to the Middle Ages, pâté en croûte was probably first produced in Lorraine, and it is still most popular in the northeast of the country. It can be made with rabbit, game, duck, veal, and of course chicken, and may be very elaborate in appearance, depending on the mould you use.

Slice the chicken breasts into strips the thickness of your little finger and set aside a couple of the best looking ones. Put the rest in a bowl with the 200g strips of back fat, the belly pork and chicken livers. Sprinkle with the wine and Armagnac, cover with cling film and refrigerate for 12 hours.

Remove from the fridge and pass the chilled pieces of meat through a mincer, using the coarse setting. Place back in the bowl and add the cream, egg and egg yolk, salt, pepper and thyme. Mix well, cover with cling film and set aside in the fridge.

Use 30g of the butter to grease the insides of a 23cm long, 14cm wide (at its widest part) and 9cm tall hinged, oval, raised pie mould. Place in the fridge.

Wipe the trompettes de la mort using a slightly damp tea towel, to clean off any traces of sand or dirt, then trim the stalks if necessary, using a small knife. Cook in a frying pan over a medium heat with 40g of the remaining butter for 2–3 minutes. Salt lightly and set aside in a colander.

Heat 30g of the remaining butter in a small frying pan over a medium heat, add the 2 reserved strips of chicken breast and cook for 1 minute, without letting them colour, then set aside on a plate. Melt the remaining 20g butter in the pan, then brush over the chicken strips. Roll the strips in chopped parsley so that they are generously coated; set aside in the fridge.

Shape three-quarters of the pastry into a ball and roll out on a lightly floured surface to a round. Use your thumbs to form the pastry round into an oval coracle, or boat shape, then dust the inside with flour and fold it over on itself, in half. Roll out to the size and shape of the pâté mould, dusting the inside with flour from time to time. Open it out into a boat shape again and, using your fist placed inside the 'boat', work the dough gently to adjust its shape and size to fit the mould perfectly.

Transfer the pastry to the buttered mould and make sure that it is properly attached to the base and sides of the mould by taking a small floured plug of pastry and pressing it lightly into the corners, any patterned recesses, and onto the base.

(continued overleaf)

Serves 8–10

850g boneless chicken breasts, skinned

200g pork back fat, derinded and cut into strips, plus 150g fine slices

150g belly pork with plenty of fat, derinded and cut into strips

100g chicken livers, cleaned and trimmed

75ml sweet white wine, ideally Jurançon

50ml Armagnac or Cognac

150ml double cream

1 egg, plus 1 egg yolk

5g (1 tsp) fine salt

3g (½ tsp) freshly ground pepper

7g (1 tbsp) thyme leaves

120g butter

100g trompettes de la mort mushrooms or chanterelles

20g flat-leaf parsley, chopped

900g pâte à pâté (page 263)

Flour, for dusting

20 pitted green olives

300ml chicken gelée (page 248)

To glaze

1 egg yolk mixed with 2 tsp milk

Line the pastry case with the 150g back fat slices so that they overhang the edges slightly. Mix the cooled trompettes de la mort and the olives into the pâté mixture, then place a 4cm layer of the mixture in the base. Lay the parsley-coated strips of chicken down the length of the pâté mixture. Fill with the remaining pâté mixture and bring the ends of the back fat over to cover the mixture.

Roll out the remaining pastry on a lightly floured surface to make a lid to fit the mould. Brush the top ridge of the pastry in the mould with egg glaze and place the pastry lid on top of the (back fat covered) pâté. Make sure that the pastry lid and sides are properly sealed together, then cut off the excess pastry using a small knife. Pinch the edges all round using a thumb and forefinger, then refrigerate for at least 2 hours.

Preheat the oven to 180°C/Gas 4. Place the mould on a baking sheet, brush with egg glaze and use the tip of a knife to score lines in an attractive pattern. Stick one or two pastry leaves cut from the pastry trimmings on top and glaze these too. Using the tip of a knife, make a small hole in the middle and insert a small cylinder of foil, or chimney.

Cook in the oven for 20 minutes, then lower the setting to 160°C/Gas 3 and cook for a further 55 minutes. Check that it is cooked by inserting a trussing needle or skewer into the foil chimney and down through the filling; it should come out hot for it to be perfectly cooked.

Transfer the pâté to a wire rack and set aside to cool for 2 hours. Carefully unmould it while it is still warm, by undoing the hinges and removing the sides of the mould. Once cold, which will be about 3 hours after it has come out of the oven, transfer to the fridge for 20 minutes.

Make a cone out of greaseproof paper and insert it into the hole that the foil funnel was in. Pour the semi-set chicken gelée in through the cone and refrigerate for at least 24 hours before serving. This pâté will keep well in the fridge for up to 10 days.

To serve, cut off the end that is mostly pastry, then cut into slices at the table, on the diagonal if you like, using an extremely sharp knife. The aromas wafting up as you carve will be an added pleasure for your guests.

Variation

You can replace the chicken with rabbit, using the same method and substituting the olives for hazelnuts. The results will be just as delicious.

Escalopes de Foie Gras Chaudes aux Citrus
WARM ESCALOPES OF FOIE GRAS WITH CITRUS FRUITS

One of the finest delicacies, where all the elements of the dish can be prepared in advance, leaving just the foie gras to be pan-fried at the last minute, once your guests are seated. I adore the acidity of the citrus fruits, which cuts through the richness of the foie gras and accentuate its flavours.

Pare 8 wide strips of zest from the oranges using a swivel vegetable peeler, then cut the strips into long, thin julienne. Blanch the julienne in boiling water for 30 seconds, then refresh, drain and set aside.

Using a sharp, flexible knife, cut all the pith and the remaining zest from the oranges, then release the segments by sliding the knife between the membranes into a bowl. Squeeze the membranes and pulp over the bowl to extract the rest of the juice; set aside. Reserve the pulp and membranes.

Remove the zest and pith from the limes, and release the segments in the same way. Reserve the pulp and membranes.

Heat the Armagnac in a saucepan, then flambé using a long match, standing back. As soon as the flames have died down, add the stock and reserved citrus pulp and membranes. Cook over a low heat for 15 minutes. Add the juice from the orange segments with the Curaçao and cook for 10 minutes.

Scoop the pulp from the passion fruit into the pan and cook gently for about 5 minutes, still over a gentle heat, then remove from the heat and strain through a fine chinois. Add the lemon juice, then whisk in the butter a little at a time. Add salt and pepper to taste, cover with cling film and keep warm.

To cook the foie gras, preheat 1 or 2 non-stick dry frying pans for 1 minute (you want to cook it all at once). Separate the larger lobe from the smaller one. Using a small knife, remove the green part where the bile duct is located. Cut the smaller lobe into 4 slices and the larger lobe into 8 slices. Sprinkle salt on both sides.

Place the foie gras in the very hot frying pan(s) and cook over a medium heat for 1 minute, then turn using a palette knife and cook on the other side for 1 minute, if you like your foie gras pink. If you prefer it *à point*, cook each side for an extra 30 seconds. Drain the foie gras on kitchen paper for a few seconds before serving.

Arrange 3 or 4 slices of foie gras on each warm plate, grind over some pepper and, working quickly, arrange a border of orange segments, with the lime segments scattered over the foie gras. Pour the sauce generously over each slice of foie gras, sprinkle with orange zest julienne and serve at once.

Serves 4–6

3 oranges, washed in cold water and wiped dry

2 limes

100ml Armagnac or Cognac

300ml veal stock (page 249), or buy good-quality fresh stock

1½ tbsp Curaçao or Grand Marnier

2 passion fruit, halved

Juice of ½ lemon

30g butter

1 fresh duck foie gras, 400–500g, thoroughly chilled

Salt and freshly ground pepper

Dodine de Canard

BONED DUCK WITH A PISTACHIO AND TRUFFLE STUFFING

This impressive boned whole duck filled with a tasty pork
and duck stuffing flavoured with pistachios and truffle makes
a wonderful centrepiece for a special meal. Boning the duck
requires some skill and dexterity, but you could always ask
your butcher to do it for you. The dodine can be prepared
ahead – it keeps well in the fridge for up to 10 days before
being cut into. Brioche toasts are the perfect accompaniment.

To bone the duck, place it on a board and cut off the feet, if they are still
attached, 1.5cm above the joint, then cut off the wing tips at the joint. Lift up
the skin at the neck and, using a small, very sharp knife, detach the wishbone
from the meat and remove it.

Put the duck breast side down, then, using a very sharp boning knife, cut
through the skin from end to end down the middle of the back. Slide the
knife between the meat and the carcass and rib cage bones, working down
one side of the duck and then the other to release the meat. Make sure that
the skin stays attached to the meat and take particular care not puncture it
anywhere with the knife as you work. Remove the carcass and set aside for
another use (such as stock).

Use the knife to scrape the thigh bone free of its fat and meat, then do the
same for the drumsticks, making sure that the skin stays attached to the
meat. Using secateurs or a hacksaw, cut the femurs off the drumsticks 2cm
above the joint. Set the bones aside with the carcass. Cut or saw off the
wings in the same way, 3cm above the joint.

Put the boned duck skin side down, flat on a board. Remove any visible
sinew or tendons from the thighs and breasts, sprinkle saltpetre and sugar,
if using, over the meat, and rub both in thoroughly with your fingertips (wear
gloves to do this, to protect your hands from the saltpetre, or rinse them
thoroughly afterwards).

Transfer the duck to an oval dish, skin side down, and pour the port over
the meat. Fold the duck over on itself and leave to marinate in the fridge for
12 hours.

For the stuffing, cut the pork fillet, livers, back fat and duck meat into small
pieces and place in a large bowl. Add the salt and pepper and sprinkle in the
60ml port. Stir with a wooden spoon until evenly combined, then cover with
cling film and refrigerate for 12 hours.

Remove the stuffing mixture from the fridge and pass it through a mincer,
using the medium setting, into a large bowl placed over crushed ice.

(continued overleaf)

Serves 8–10

1 oven-ready duck (Dombes or
    Aylesbury), about 2kg

1 tsp each saltpetre and caster sugar
    (optional)

50ml ruby port

Stuffing

300g pork fillet, trimmed

300g duck (or chicken) livers, trimmed

200g pork back fat, derinded

150g skinless duck breast

10g (2 tsp) salt

3g (½ tsp) freshly ground pepper

60ml ruby port

2 eggs

125ml very cold double cream

1 tsp groundnut oil

10g pistachio nuts

1 truffle, about 20g, ideally raw, brushed,
    then cut into small dice

To serve

Juice of 1 lemon

Small bunch of watercress, washed and
    stems removed

Add the eggs, mix well with a wooden spoon, then incorporate the chilled cream a little at a time.

To test for seasoning, heat the oil in a small frying pan over a gentle heat, add about 30g stuffing mixture and cook for 2 minutes. Turn and cook the other side for 2 minutes, then remove from the pan and leave to go cold. Once cold, taste the mixture for seasoning and adjust the stuffing as necessary. Blanch the pistachios in boiling water for 1 minute, then drain and peel away the skins. Finally, mix the diced truffle and pistachios into the stuffing.

Take the duck from the fridge and place skin side down, flat on the work surface. Distribute the stuffing over the duck, spreading it out well to cover all the meat. Bring the outsides of the duck up to re-create its original form. Stitch the skin together where it meets using a trussing needle and kitchen string, and tie string around the middle in 3 places, not too tightly, to help maintain its shape as it cooks. Put the duck into a roasting tin, into which it fits snugly, and refrigerate for 3–4 hours.

Preheat the oven to 190°C/Gas 5.

Cook the duck in the oven for 15 minutes, then lower the setting to 150°C/Gas 2 and cook for a further 35–40 minutes, using a large spoon to baste it with its cooking juices every 5–10 minutes. Remove from the oven and set aside to cool a little for 30 minutes, still in the roasting tin, then carefully remove the duck, using a large palette knife, to a large oval serving dish. After 4 hours, cover with cling film and refrigerate for 48 hours.

Take out of the fridge and carefully remove the stitching string, as well as the pieces around the duck holding its shape, making sure you don't damage the skin as you do so. Wrap tightly in cling film and keep in the fridge until ready to serve.

To serve, cut off a few slices, on a slight diagonal, and place the duck on an oval dish with the cut slices arranged in front. Squeeze some lemon juice lightly over the watercress and arrange it around the duck. Slice the duck at the table in front of your guests.

Pistachio nuts

Pistachios, which grow on small, bush-like trees, have a sweet taste and can be eaten raw like almonds, or toasted; I personally adore them. Originating in the Middle East and Central Asia, they were introduced to Europe by the Romans, and to France in the 17th century, when they were known as 'Persian almonds'. I sometimes use them in my champagne sauce, to serve with poached fish, and also in my pistachio crème brûlée – a signature dish at the Waterside Inn that I created some 30 years ago.

Eggs

Oeufs en Cocotte aux Crevettes Grises

EGGS EN COCOTTE WITH BROWN SHRIMPS

Here is a dish from our great-grandmothers' kitchens…
Originally simply eggs cooked in the oven in a stoneware
dish, with the addition of a little cream, some snipped parsley
or tarragon, salt and pepper, this dish has been developed
creatively over the years, incorporating all kinds of flavouring
ingredients. Even special cocotte moulds are now available.
All the ingredients can be prepared ahead, ready to pop the
eggs into the oven as soon as your guests are at the table.

Set aside 4 attractive whole shrimps for serving. Peel the rest of the shrimps
and separate the heads from the tails. Put the tails into a bowl.

Put the shrimp heads and the butter into a small food processor or mortar
and process or pound for 2 minutes to create a shrimp butter. Using a pestle,
press the butter through a very fine sieve and add the cayenne.

Preheat the oven to 180°C/Gas 4. Very generously grease 4 cocotte moulds
or ramekins, about 6cm in diameter and 4cm deep, using the shrimp butter.

Break an egg into each dish and divide the shrimp tails between them,
placing them around the yolk. Season lightly with salt and pepper and spoon
the cream on top of the shrimps.

Stand the moulds in a shallow ovenproof dish lined with greaseproof paper.
Pour near-boiling water (at 80°C) into the dish to come halfway up the moulds,
and bake for 5–6 minutes, depending on how soft you like your eggs.

Meanwhile, heat the clarified butter or oil in a frying pan over a medium heat.
Add the bread cubes and cook for 30–45 seconds. Drain the croûtons in a
chinois or sieve, then mix with the capers.

As soon as the cocotte dishes come out of the oven, sprinkle the croûtons
and capers over the surface, with a little parsley, then position a whole shrimp
on the edge of each dish. Place on plates and serve at once.

Serves 4

48 brown shrimps, rinsed in cold water

60g softened butter

Pinch of cayenne

4 eggs

2 tbsp double cream

75g clarified butter (page 266) or
   50ml grapeseed oil

2 slices of white sandwich loaf, crusts
   removed, cut into 5mm dice

24 capers

2 tsp snipped flat-leaf parsley

Salt and freshly ground pepper

Variations

During the mushroom season, for a delicious alternative, try replacing the shrimps with
a few chanterelles, sautéed first in butter. Or substitute the shrimps with a concasse
of tomatoes, when they are at their seasonal best and bursting with flavour, adding a
touch of shredded basil. In both cases, use plain butter to grease the moulds.

Oeufs Brouillés aux Pointes d'Asperge et au Crabe

SCRAMBLED EGGS WITH ASPARAGUS AND CRAB

There are hundreds of different ways to serve scrambled eggs, depending on the season, but this is a sublime combination. I created this dish at the beginning of the 1980s and Egon Ronay, the leading food critic of the time, was very taken with it. If using live crabs, you can put them in the freezer for 30 minutes before cooking to sedate them.

If using live crabs, cook them in a large pan of lightly salted boiling water for 8 minutes. Drain and set aside to cool.

Once cold, separate the legs and claws from the body. Gently crack open the claws using a small mallet or the flat side of a large chef's knife, so that they stay whole, and set aside, covered with cling film. Crack open the legs and set aside with the claws.

Separate the bodies from the shell without damaging the latter, which will be used for serving. Rinse the shells thoroughly and set aside.

Extract the white meat from the body and place in a bowl. Spoon the brown meat into a second bowl, add 1½ tbsp of the cream and mix it in with a fork. Season with salt and pepper to taste, and set both bowls of crab meat aside in a cold place.

Peel the asparagus spears using a swivel peeler and trim the stalks to leave the top 6cm. Cook in lightly salted boiling water for 3–4 minutes, depending on how firm you like them. Drain and set aside in a dish until ready to serve.

Melt the butter in a sauté pan over a gentle heat. Break the eggs into a bowl, season with salt and pepper and beat lightly with a fork. Pour the eggs into the pan and cook, stirring gently and almost continuously with a wooden spoon. For just set but still very creamy eggs, this will take 3–4 minutes, and for a firmer consistency 5–6 minutes. As soon as the eggs reach the desired consistency, add the remaining 2½ tbsp cream and adjust the seasoning.

Place the crab shells on a platter and divide the white crab meat between them, then arrange 4 asparagus spears to the side of each, with the tips pointing upwards. Spoon the scrambled eggs into the shells and place a crab claw on top. Arrange the crab legs in the corners of the platter.

Top the scrambled eggs with a spoonful of the brown meat mixture and a sprinkling of chives. Serve at once; it will be a warm rather than hot dish, as scrambled eggs can never be very hot.

Serves 4

4 medium crabs, about 400g each, preferably live (or already cooked)

4 tbsp double cream

16 medium asparagus spears, preferably a mixture of green and white

80g butter

8 eggs

10g chives, cut into short lengths

Salt and freshly ground pepper

Piperade

This is without doubt the most famous dish to come out of the Basque country, and neighbouring Béarn has willingly embraced it. Its composition has evolved over time, according to tastes, places and passing generations. Tomatoes, onion, peppers and Bayonne ham all feature in the simple dish – known and loved the world over – yet bread, once integral, has totally disappeared from the recipe and the inclusion of eggs appears to be fairly recent. As well as a starter, piperade is ideal served as a lunch, with a green salad and good bread.

Remove the stalks from the peppers and cut them in half, then remove the white membranes and seeds. Cut into wide strips and use a swivel peeler to remove the fine, shiny outer skin. Cut the peeled strips into large dice.

Heat the olive oil in a large open pan, preferably a sauté pan, over a low heat. Add the onions and sweat for 5 minutes, without letting them colour. Add the garlic and diced peppers, cover and cook for a further 5 minutes, still over a gentle heat.

Now add the tomatoes, a little salt and pepper and the thyme sprig, and cook, uncovered, over a medium heat for about 15 minutes, giving everything a stir every 2–3 minutes. Once the water released from the tomatoes has evaporated, remove from the heat, adjust the seasoning to taste with salt and pepper, and set aside to keep hot.

Preheat the grill. Break the eggs into a bowl, add salt and pepper to taste, then beat lightly. Put the pan of vegetables over a medium heat and, as soon as it is bubbling, pour in the eggs and stir the mixture with a wooden spoon every 30 seconds, as you would for scrambled eggs. The moment the mixture reaches the consistency of a soft purée, remove from the heat.

Divide the piperade between 4 plates and arrange a slice of ham over each. Place under the grill for 20 seconds, to warm the ham, then serve at once.

Serves 4

400g peppers, preferably green

4 tbsp light olive oil

250g onions, peeled and chopped

2 garlic cloves, peeled and chopped

600g ripe tomatoes, peeled, deseeded and diced

1 thyme sprig

8 eggs

4 very thin slices of Bayonne ham, or other cured ham

Salt and freshly ground pepper

Variation

If you are a fan of Espelette peppers, then feel free to add a little – fresh or dried – to the piperade; the hint of spice enhances this egg dish perfectly.

Oeufs Pochés à la Florentine
EGGS FLORENTINE

A great classic dish, perfect for brunch, lunch or a light supper and popular with everyone. Depending on appetites, you might need to allow a couple of eggs per person.

First make the sauce. Melt the butter in a small pan over a low heat, add the flour, stir with a whisk and cook for 2 minutes. Pour in the cold milk, mix with the whisk and bring to the boil over a medium heat, stirring with the whisk. When it reaches the boil, reduce to a very gentle heat and cook for 5 minutes, stirring constantly.

Mix the egg yolks and cream together and add to the sauce. Cook, stirring, for 30 seconds, then remove from the heat and add the 50g grated cheese. Season with salt, pepper and nutmeg to taste. Cover the surface with cling film and set aside; keep warm.

To cook the spinach, melt half the butter in a frying pan over a high heat. As soon as it is foaming, add half the spinach, sprinkle with a pinch each of sugar and salt, and stir the spinach for 1 minute so that it cooks evenly. Tip into a colander and repeat with the remaining butter and spinach.

Put the cream into a pan and mix in the spinach, add a generous pinch of nutmeg and set aside in a warm place, covered with cling film.

Fill a medium saucepan about two-thirds full with cold water (do not salt it). Add the vinegar and bring to the boil. Break an egg into a small ramekin and carefully tip it into the area of water where it is bubbling. Repeat at once with the remaining 3 eggs. As soon as they are poached to your liking, 2–3 minutes, drain one by one, transferring them to a tea towel and trimming with a small knife to remove excess white that will have spread a little on cooking. Preheat the grill.

Divide the spinach between warmed individual egg dishes. Place a poached egg in the middle of each dish, coat generously with the Mornay sauce and sprinkle with the 30g grated cheese. Brown under the hot grill until a light nutty colour, then serve.

Variations
You can serve these eggs as tarts, in pre-cooked puff pastry cases. Of course, there are endless ways to serve poached eggs. I often replace the spinach in this recipe with mushrooms, finely chopped and sautéed in butter (forestière).

Serves 4

60g butter

400g spinach, stems removed, washed and well drained

2 pinches of sugar

50ml double cream

2 tbsp white wine vinegar

4 eggs

Mornay sauce

20g butter

20g plain flour

350ml milk

2 egg yolks

30ml double cream

50g Comté or Emmenthal cheese, freshly grated, plus 30g to finish

Salt, freshly ground pepper and freshly grated nutmeg

Omelette aux Tomates Cerise et Parfum de Basilic

There is no limit to the fillings you can put into an omelette, but I prefer to keep to simple combinations of flavours. If the filling is too complex and overly flavoured, it tends to overpower the flavour of the eggs. You can, if you like, brush the top of the cooked omelette with a touch of clarified butter, which will give it an appetising sheen.

Preheat the oven to 160°C/Gas 3. Heat the olive oil and garlic in a small frying pan over a gentle heat for 2 minutes, then remove from the heat. Using a brush, generously daub the cherry tomatoes with the garlic oil, then arrange on a small grill rack placed on a baking sheet. Sprinkle with a little salt and cook in the oven for 20 minutes. As soon as they come out of the oven, transfer the tomatoes to a shallow dish and set aside.

Heat the grapeseed oil in a small pan to 150°C. Drop the whole basil leaves into the hot oil for 30 seconds, then use a skimmer to remove them from the oil to a piece of kitchen paper. Salt lightly and set aside in a warm place.

Break the eggs into a bowl, season with salt and pepper and beat lightly with a fork. Heat the clarified butter in a 20cm frying pan, preferably non-stick, over a lively heat. As soon as the butter is very hot, pour in the eggs and leave to cook for 5–10 seconds so that they can set a little on the bottom.

Using the side of a fork, bring the set edges towards the middle and stir continuously, very gently shaking the pan with the other hand until the egg is cooked to your liking. A fairly runny, or *baveuse* omelette, will take 30–40 seconds, a lightly set, or *à point* omelette, will take 1 minute and a firm omelette 1 minute 30 seconds.

To semi-fold the omelette, give a small, sharp jerk of the wrist towards you with the pan at a slight tilt, then fill the omelette with the cherry tomatoes, sprinkle with the snipped basil and finish by folding the omelette right over itself. Turn out at once onto an oval dish, sprinkle the fried basil leaves over the top and serve immediately.

Serves 2

1 tbsp olive oil

1 garlic clove, peeled and finely chopped

10 ripe cherry tomatoes, washed, drained and de-stemmed

100ml grapeseed oil

10 basil leaves, plus an extra 4 finely snipped leaves

6 eggs

20g clarified butter (page 266)

Salt and freshly ground pepper

Variation

For a different but equally lovely filling, substitute the tomatoes and basil with finely sliced courgette, sautéed first in olive oil for a few minutes and sprinkled with chopped flat-leaf parsley.

Quiche Lorraine

This famous tart, named after the region where it originated in Northeast France, has stood the test of time. It should be served just warm or hot, but not piping hot or its flavours will be lost on the palate. Some purists won't hear of using Comté or any other cheese… but I'm standing by my inclusion of both cheese and lardons.

Butter the inside of a tart ring, about 24cm in diameter and 3.5cm high, place on a small baking tray and set aside in the fridge. Roll out the pastry on a lightly floured surface to a round, 3mm thick. Roll the pastry around the rolling pin and unravel it over the tart ring. Press the pastry into the ring using your index fingers and thumbs, making sure it is properly attached to the ring, then set aside in the fridge for 20 minutes. Preheat the oven to 180°C/Gas 4.

Cut off any excess pastry above the top of the ring, using a small knife. Prick the base with a fork in a dozen or so places, then line the base and sides with greaseproof paper. Fill with ceramic baking beans, rice or dried beans and cook in the oven for 15 minutes.

Lift out the paper and baking beans or rice. Brush the insides of the pastry case with the beaten egg and return it to the oven for 5 minutes, for the base to dry out. Remove from the oven and set aside to cool down, with the pastry case still in the ring.

For the filling, heat the groundnut oil in a frying pan over a medium heat, add the lardons and cook for 1 minute, then set aside in a small sieve.

Put the eggs, egg yolks and cream in a bowl and mix with a whisk, without overworking. Add the nutmeg, some salt and pepper and the Kirsch, if using.

Distribute the lardons and cheese over the base of the pastry case. Pour the egg and cream mixture into the case almost to the top of the ring, and transfer to the oven (at 180°C/Gas 4) for 20 minutes. Lower the oven setting to 160°C/Gas 3 and cook for a further 20 minutes.

Check the filling is cooked by inserting a trussing needle or skewer into the centre; it should come out clean and shiny, with no trace of filling on it. As soon as the quiche is cooked and out of the oven, lift the tart ring up and off the quiche, taking care not to damage it.

To serve, use a large palette knife to slide the quiche onto a round plate, or serve it on the baking tray. Use a sharp knife to cut it into slices at the table.

Serves 8–10

20g butter, to grease

300g flan pastry (page 262)

Flour, for dusting

½ egg, beaten

Filling

2 tsp groundnut oil

100g salted belly pork, rind removed, cut into small lardons, blanched and refreshed

3 eggs, plus 6 egg yolks

600ml double cream

Pinch of freshly grated nutmeg

1½ tbsp Kirsch (optional)

100g Comté cheese, freshly grated

Salt and freshly ground pepper

Variation

To make a tarte flambée, a distant cousin of this quiche, very finely slice 2 large onions and mix with 200ml double cream and the juice of 1 lemon. Add a generous sprinkling of thyme leaves and season with salt and pepper. Spread this mixture over a puff pastry base 3–4mm thick, sprinkle with a few drops of olive oil and cook in a hot oven at 200°C/Gas 6 for 12–15 minutes. Serve straight from the oven, scattered with a few shavings of smoked pork if you like.

Shellfish

Noix de Coquilles Saint Jacques au Vermouth — SCALLOPS IN VERMOUTH

For this delicate dish, it is essential to cook the scallops to perfection. Poach them for no more than a minute, depending on their size, to ensure they don't turn rubbery. And serve them warm, even hot, but not piping hot. If you can't find scallops in their shells, simply serve them in little eared dishes.

Preheat the oven to 160°C/Gas 3.

Hold a scallop shell flat side uppermost and insert a rigid knife blade between the two shell halves, running the knife carefully against the flat side in order to separate the scallop from the flat shell. Lift off the flat shell, then slide a spoon or small palette knife under the scallop in the concave shell to detach and remove it from the shell. Using your thumb, separate the scallop and coral from the surrounding skirt and stomach sac, and remove the small sinew that attached the scallop to the shell. Rinse under cold running water, pat dry and repeat with the remaining scallops.

Blanch the leeks in boiling water for 2 minutes, drain, refresh in cold water, drain and set aside. Bring the Noilly Prat to the boil in a sauté pan and reduce by one-third. Turn the heat to low and add the shallot with the scallops and corals. Poach for 1 minute, turning the scallops after 30 seconds. Transfer the scallops and corals to a bowl, cover with a dampened piece of kitchen paper and set aside. Put the concave shells in the oven to heat up for 2–3 minutes.

Reduce the cooking liquid over a medium heat by one-third, then stir in the cream. Remove from the heat and gradually add the butter, in pieces, gently shaking the pan so that the butter mixes in perfectly to create a sauce.

In a small pan, mix a quarter of the sauce with the leeks and snipped dill, season to taste with salt and pepper and keep warm over a gentle heat.

Arrange the seaweed, if using, on serving plates. Sit the warmed shells on top and divide the leek mixture between them. Top with the scallops and corals and pour some sauce generously over the scallops and lightly over the corals. Place a dill sprig on each and serve at once.

Serves 4

8 fresh scallops, preferably in their shells

2 medium leeks (white part only), well washed and sliced into fine julienne

150ml Noilly Prat

30g shallot, peeled and very finely chopped

2 tbsp double cream

60g butter

10g dill leaves, snipped, plus 4 sprigs to garnish

Salt and freshly ground pepper

Handful of seaweed (optional), to serve

Variation

When scallops are extremely fresh, they can be served raw. Simply slice them into fine rounds, sprinkle lightly with olive oil and lemon juice and season with salt and pepper. A few young and tender salad leaves served alongside will give you a delicious, elegant starter that is also very quick to prepare.

Huîtres Gratinées OYSTERS GRATINÉES

The French are the most prolific consumers of oysters in the world and oyster cultivation is an important industry. They can be sweet, firm with a crunch, fine and briny, firm and tender, or even meaty, depending on the variety and locality. There are two types of oyster in France: *creuse* (cupped) and *plate* (flat). The flat belon variety is cultivated exclusively in Brittany, but oyster beds are also plentiful in Normandy, the Loire, Poitou-Charentes and Aquitaine. I enjoy these oysters with a glass of Chablis, Muscadet or Alsace Pinot Blanc.

Using an oyster knife, open each oyster, catching the juices in a bowl; discard the flat, upper shell. Slide the blade of the knife under each oyster to release it from the shell, and place the oysters in a medium saucepan. Rinse the concave shells, then set aside in a warm place, ready to use for serving.

Pour the reserved oyster juices onto the oysters in the pan and place over a gentle heat. Poach at 50°C for 30 seconds, then, using a fork, carefully turn each one over individually and set aside to cool in the cooking juices.

For the sauce, blanch the shallot in boiling water for 30 seconds, refresh in cold water, drain and pat dry. Melt the butter in a pan over a low heat. Add the shallot and sweat for 1 minute, then add the wine, increase the heat and reduce by half. Pour in the double cream, mixing with a balloon whisk, then add the curry powder and reduce by half again over a low heat. Add the juices from the oysters and season with salt and pepper to taste, then cover the surface with cling film and set aside in a warm place.

Cut the courgette into long julienne, ideally using a mandoline. Blanch in salted water for 30 seconds, then drain, season to taste and set aside; keep warm.

Preheat the grill. Spread rock salt in a layer in a shallow heatproof dish, then arrange the cleaned oyster shells on top, wedging them together slightly.

Lightly whip the single cream with the egg yolk. Divide the courgette julienne between the shells, then top with the oysters. Give the sauce a quick blast of heat, then remove from the heat and mix in the whipped cream mixture.

Coat the oysters generously with the sauce, sprinkle very lightly with breadcrumbs and place under the grill for 1 minute, until turning just very lightly golden on top. Serve straight away.

NOTE The oysters will vary in size, depending on the time of year. Two is usually enough as an *amuse bouche*; for a starter I would serve six each.

Serves 4 as an *amuse bouche*

8 Portuguese or native oysters, size 2

30g peeled shallot, finely chopped

30g butter

200ml dry white wine, ideally Graves

150ml double cream

A good pinch of Madras curry powder

1 small, long courgette, about 80g

50ml single cream

1 egg yolk

10g breadcrumbs, ideally fresh

Salt and freshly ground white pepper

Coarse rock salt, for serving

Mouclade d'Aunis

MUSSELS IN A CREAMED CURRY SAUCE

The first spices were landed several hundred years ago in the
Charente region, with its many ports that include La Rochelle
and Brouage. Curry powder was among them, and soon found
itself at home with the ubiquitous onion, and with the mussels
of Bouchot, farmed in the Vendée, next to Charente. And
so this humble dish for fishermen was born. I enjoy it with
a pilaf or steamed rice, mixed with little diced red pepper,
and a glass of white Bordeaux Graves or Touraine Sauvignon,
or a light red from the Rhône Valley, such as a Gigondas.

Scrape the mussels clean, if necessary, using the back of a small knife.
Remove their beards, then rinse under cold water to clean. Drain well.

Put the mussels and wine in a large saucepan, cover with a tight-fitting lid
and place over a very lively heat for 3–4 minutes, stirring every minute or so
with a skimmer. The mussels are cooked as soon as they have opened; take
care not to overcook them. Drain in a sieve placed over a bowl, to catch all
the cooking juices. Place a tea towel dampened with cold water over the
mussels and set aside.

Decant the strained cooking juices (about 400ml), and reserve for the sauce.

Melt the butter in a sauté pan over a low heat. Add the onion and cook for
1 minute, then add the curry powder and flour. Cook over a low heat, stirring
with a wooden spoon, for 4–5 minutes. Pour in the slightly cooled reserved
juices, stirring, and bring to the boil, still over a gentle heat. Add the bouquet
garni and cook over a very low heat for 20 minutes.

Meanwhile, shell the mussels, cover with cling film and set aside.

Remove the bouquet garni from the sauce, add the cream and increase the
heat. Simmer, stirring from time to time, for 5 minutes, then season with salt
and pepper to taste. Add the shelled mussels to the pan and reheat them
in the sauce over a medium heat for 1–2 minutes. Serve in shallow bowls,
making sure everyone has a spoon, for the sauce.

Variation

For moules au gratin, cook the mussels in the same way, omitting the curry powder.
Pour the sauce over the mussels in a gratin dish, sprinkle with a little grated Comté
or Parmesan and place under a hot grill for 30 seconds. Serve at once.

Serves 4

2kg live mussels, ideally Bouchot or
    rope-grown

300ml dry white wine

60g butter

1 large onion, peeled and finely chopped

1 tbsp Madras curry powder

40g plain flour

1 medium bouquet garni

300ml double cream

Salt and freshly ground pepper

Homard à l'Américaine Lobster Américaine

The exact origin of this classic dish is uncertain, although it is decidedly French. Sauce américaine is time-consuming but it can be prepared a day or two in advance, then reheated over a very gentle heat to serve. I like to accompany this with a pilaf, adding some diced lobster meat (saved from the sauce) and sautéed diced red pepper to the rice. Put the lobsters in the freezer for 30 minutes before cooking to sedate them.

Fill a large saucepan with cold, lightly salted water and bring to the boil. Plunge all 3 lobsters into the boiling water and cook for 1 minute, then immediately transfer to a bowl of cold water with ice cubes added to cool quickly. After 2 minutes, drain and set aside the 2 smaller lobsters.

For the sauce, separate the head from the tail of the large lobster and remove the claws, separating them into pieces along the joints. Cut the tail into medallions and crack open the claws. Cut the head in half lengthways and remove and discard the gravel pocket (that contains impurities), found next to the antennae, as well as the membranes.

Remove the tomalley and coral to a bowl, add the softened butter, mix with a fork and set aside.

Sprinkle the cayenne over the lobster pieces. Heat the 100ml grapeseed oil in a large sauté pan over a high heat. As soon as it is very hot, add the lobster pieces and cook for 4 minutes, until bright red, turning them with tongs after 2 minutes. Use a skimmer or slotted spoon to remove the lobster pieces from the pan; set aside. Pour off all but 1 tbsp of the cooking oil.

Add the diced carrot and shallots, with the garlic, to the same sauté pan and sweat over a gentle heat until softened. Return the lobster pieces to the pan, sprinkle over the Cognac and flambé. As soon as the flame has died down, pour in the wine, fish stock, tomatoes, bouquet garni, tarragon and a touch of salt. Increase the heat and bring to the boil, then lower the heat and cook gently for 15 minutes.

Lift out the lobster claws and tail medallions and set aside (to add to the pilaf, if serving). Cook the sauce for a further 20 minutes over a gentle heat, skimming if necessary.

Add the coral-tomalley butter, stirring with a whisk, then add the cream, if using. Strain the sauce through a chinois, pressing with the back of a ladle to extract as much sauce as possible. If you prefer a fine rather than rustic sauce, transfer to a food processor and process for 1 minute until smooth. Keep hot until needed.

(continued overleaf)

Serves 2

2 live lobsters, about 600g each

50ml grapeseed oil

Sauce américaine

1 live lobster, 800g–1kg

40g butter, softened

Pinch of cayenne

100ml grapeseed oil

1 medium carrot, peeled and diced

2 shallots, peeled and diced

2 garlic cloves (unpeeled), bashed

50ml Cognac

300ml dry white wine

300ml fish stock (page 249), or buy
   good-quality fresh stock

250g very ripe tomatoes, peeled,
   deseeded and diced

1 medium bouquet garni

2 tarragon sprigs, snipped

70ml double cream (optional)

Juice of ½ lemon

Salt and freshly ground pepper

To serve

Bunch of flat-leaf parsley

Preheat the oven to 220°C/Gas 7.

Split the 2 smaller lobsters in half lengthways. Crack the claws without detaching them from the body. Remove and discard the gravel pocket next to the antennae, the membranes and the antennae. Brush the meat and shells with the 50ml grapeseed oil and salt lightly.

Heat a large ovenproof sauté pan, add the lobster halves, meat side down, and colour for 2–3 minutes, then turn them over and transfer the pan to the oven for 10 minutes.

To serve, place a lobster half on each plate, add the lemon juice to the sauce américaine and serve it on the side. Give a turn of the pepper mill over the tail, place a small bunch of parsley on both plates and serve piping hot.

Mousse de Homard LOBSTER MOUSSE

This delicately flavoured mousse is used for my turban of salmon and sole (on page 114) and in my Dover sole recipe (on page 108).

Cook the lobsters as described on page 83, but for 30 seconds only, refresh in iced water, then drain. Remove the tails and claws. Crack open the claws and extract the meat. Remove the membrane from the tail, then use a spoon to scoop out the meat. You should have about 400g meat in total.

Put the lobster meat into a food processor or blender, add the egg whites, salt and cayenne and process for 2 minutes, until homogeneous; do not overwork. Using a pestle, push the mixture through a sieve into a bowl set over crushed ice. Now work in the cream a little at a time, until the mixture is very soft, even slightly runny.

Test the consistency by forming a small quenelle with 2 spoons. Drop this into a little just simmering, salted water, poach for 3 minutes, then drain. It should have a delicate but slightly firm consistency.

Cover with cling film and refrigerate until needed, for up to 2 days; stir before use.

Makes about 650g

2 live lobsters, about 600g each

2 egg whites

15g fine salt

2 pinches of cayenne

220ml double cream, well chilled

Gratin de Crabe aux Saveurs des Îles GRATIN OF CRAB

This gently spiced, delicate dish has hints of sweetness and fruit, the crab meat harmonising beautifully with the pineapple. Basmati or fragrant Thai rice makes a perfect accompaniment. If using live crabs, you can put them in the freezer for 30 minutes before cooking to sedate them.

If using live crab(s), fill a saucepan big enough to fit it (or them) with cold water, add the 20g salt and bring to the boil over a lively heat. Add the crab(s) and cook for 20 minutes, then remove from the water and set aside in a cool place, or in cold water with a few ice cubes added.

Once they are cool, using a small mallet or the flat side of a large knife, break open the legs and large claws. Detach the body from inside the shell, then extract and set aside all the white meat, taking care to eliminate any fragments of shell, and the cartilage. Using a spoon, scoop out the brown crab meat from the body, which will be used in the sauce.

Peel the pineapple and cut the most tender part of the flesh into large julienne. Set aside, keeping the pieces of skin and the tougher core section for the sauce.

Melt the butter in a medium pan, then add the shallots, carrot, orange and grapefruit, and the pineapple skin and core. Sweat over a medium heat for 4 minutes, stirring with a wooden spoon every minute or so, then add the bouquet garni, brown crab meat and harissa. Add the wine and cook over a gentle heat for 20 minutes.

Remove the bouquet garni and transfer the sauce to a food processor or blender. Process for 30 seconds, then strain through a chinois into a pan, pressing the mixture down with the back of a small ladle. Reduce the sauce by half over a medium heat. Preheat the grill to medium hot.

Add the cream, white crab meat and pineapple julienne to the reduced sauce and bring to the boil over a medium heat. Lower the heat and simmer for 1–2 minutes, then add salt and pepper to taste. Remove from the heat and stir in the hollandaise. Transfer the mixture to a lightly buttered shallow gratin dish and brown under the grill for 1–2 minutes. Serve at once.

Serves 4

1 or 2 live crabs, or freshly cooked, about 1.6kg in total

20g coarse salt

1 dwarf pineapple, about 300g

50g butter, plus extra to grease

60g shallots, peeled and cut into small dice

1 carrot, peeled and cut into small dice

1 orange, peeled and cut into dice

1 grapefruit, peeled and cut into dice

1 medium bouquet garni

1 level tsp harissa paste

500ml sweet white wine

250ml double cream

2 tbsp sauce hollandaise (page 254)

Salt and freshly ground pepper

Calamars Farcis à la Marseillaise

STUFFED SQUID MARSEILLAISE STYLE

I adore this simple, classic dish, which epitomises the Côte d'Azur, in particular Marseille and the surrounding area. It is delicious and delicate, and imbues the kitchen with its aromas as it is cooking. A little bottle of good olive oil can be served on the side.

Put the bread cubes in a bowl, pour on enough milk to cover them and set aside to soak.

Rinse the squid well in cold water and wipe the pouches dry inside and outside. Using a knife, separate the tentacles from the pouches and finely chop the tentacles. Set the pouches aside.

Heat 20ml of the olive oil in a pan, add the chopped tentacles and cook over a medium heat for 2 minutes. Now, at 2-minute intervals, add the following ingredients in the order listed: onions, tomatoes, garlic, parsley and the soaked bread cubes (lightly squeezed to remove excess milk).

Remove from the heat, mix well and set aside for 5–10 minutes, until the mixture has cooled a little. Add the eggs and extra yolk, the cayenne and a generous pinch of salt. Transfer this stuffing mixture, which should be evenly combined, to a bowl, cover with cling film and set aside until cool.

Preheat the oven to 180°C/Gas 4. Brush an ovenproof dish (that will hold the squid in a single layer) with the remaining 10ml olive oil.

Fill the squid pouches three-quarters full with the stuffing mixture, without over-cramming them, then sew up the opening of each using a trussing needle and kitchen string. Arrange them in the oiled ovenproof dish.

For the cooking stock, heat the olive oil in a pan over a medium heat, add the onion, garlic and bay leaves and sweat for 2 minutes. Add the wine and reduce by half, still over a medium heat. Remove from the heat, add a little salt and pepper, then strain the slightly cooled stock over the squid.

Transfer the dish to the oven and cook for 30 minutes, basting with the cooking stock every 10 minutes. Preheat the grill to high.

As soon as the dish comes out of the oven, sprinkle the breadcrumbs over the top of the squid and place under the grill for about a minute, to lightly brown the crumbs. Present the stuffed squid in the cooking dish, using a large spoon to serve it into warm shallow bowls.

Variation

Add 150g spinach to the stuffing mixture: roughly chop and sweat the spinach with a dash of olive oil for 1 minute, then add it as the last ingredient to the stuffing mixture.

Serves 4

100g stale crustless bread, cut into cubes

About 100ml cold milk

8 cleaned baby squid with tentacles attached, about 150g each (prepared weight)

30ml olive oil

2 medium onions, peeled and finely chopped

200g tomatoes, peeled, deseeded and finely diced

2 garlic cloves, peeled and finely chopped

20g flat-leaf parsley, chopped

2 eggs, plus 1 egg yolk

Generous pinch of cayenne

20g dried white breadcrumbs

Salt and freshly ground pepper

Cooking stock

35ml olive oil

1 medium onion, peeled and finely chopped

1 garlic clove, peeled and crushed

2 bay leaves

100ml dry white wine

Langouste à la Parisienne

Elegant, impressive and delectable, this is another masterpiece of classic French cuisine. Most of the component parts can be prepared and cooked the day before, so avoiding any last-minute stress. You can sedate a langouste (also known as spiny lobster or seawater crayfish) in the same way as a lobster, by putting it in the freezer for 30 minutes before cooking.

For the court bouillon, put all the ingredients into a cooking pot long and wide enough to fit the langouste and its board (see below). Bring to the boil, lower the heat and cook gently for 20 minutes.

Lay the langouste belly down on a small wooden board and tie it to the board with a few turns of kitchen string, so that it keeps it shape as it cooks. Lower into the simmering court bouillon and cook at 85–95°C for 10 minutes. Remove from the court bouillon, cover with a dampened tea towel and set aside to cool for 2 hours.

Set the court bouillon pot over a medium heat and reduce by two-thirds. Meanwhile, lightly brush the truffle to clean. Remove the court bouillon from the heat, add the truffle and leave to poach in the residual heat for 10 minutes.

Meanwhile, soak the gelatine in a shallow dish of cold water to soften.

Remove the poached truffle from the pan and place under the tea towel with the langouste. Strain the court bouillon through a fine chinois into a small bowl. Immediately drain the gelatine leaves, squeezing out excess water, then add to the reduced court bouillon, stirring to dissolve. Chill over crushed ice to thicken (this is for an aspic glaze to finish the langouste).

Preheat the oven to 180°C/Gas 4.

Using a serrated bread knife, cut the crusts from the loaf. Now cut out a wedge shape of bread to make a stand for the langouste, to enhance the presentation, by cutting diagonally down through the loaf from end to end, then trimming it so that you end up with a piece 18cm long and 6cm wide, 5cm high at the taller end and 5mm high at the shorter end. Brush the back and 3 exposed sides of the bread base with the clarified butter, then place on a baking sheet and bake in the oven for 15 minutes, until it has dried out and taken on a very light colouring. Transfer to a wire rack and set aside to cool.

For the garnish, cook the carrot and turnip dice, beans and peas separately in boiling salted water for 2–3 minutes so that they keep a firm, almost crunchy texture, then refresh in cold water, drain and pat dry. Mix them with 100g of the mayonnaise and season with salt and pepper to taste. Cover with cling film and set aside.

Using a very sharp knife, cut a little off the bottom of each tomato to create a stable base, then cut off the top third and set aside.

(continued overleaf)

Serves 6–8

1 live, stout, pink langouste (800g–1kg), from Brittany or Ireland

1 fresh black truffle, 40–50g

4 sheets of leaf gelatine

1 small white sandwich loaf

100g clarified butter (page 266)

Salt and freshly ground pepper

Court bouillon

4 tbsp white wine vinegar

2 carrots, peeled and cut into rounds

1 medium onion, peeled and thinly sliced

1 bouquet garni, with leek (white part)

8 black peppercorns, crushed

¼ head of celery

10g coarse salt

3 litres water

Tomato garnish

30g finely diced carrot

30g finely diced turnip

20g fine green beans, chopped

20g petit pois

250g mayonnaise (page 256)

6–8 small tomatoes, with stalks

To serve

150g samphire

Using a teaspoon, scoop out the insides of the tomatoes, sprinkle inside lightly with salt and pepper and fill generously with the chopped vegetable and mayonnaise mixture. Replace a top on each and set aside in the fridge.

Place the cooked langouste on a board and snip off the string to remove the smaller board. Put the langouste on its back and, with the tips of a pair of scissors, cut down the length of the membrane found on both sides under the tail. Remove the membrane, then gently free the whole piece of tail meat from the shell, without breaking it, and without the head separating from the back shell. Cut the tail meat into 8–10 pieces, then place on a wire rack set over a tray and refrigerate for 5–10 minutes.

Slice the truffle into slivers, to give the same number of neat, attractive slices as you have of tail meat. Remove the tail meat slices from the fridge and brush with the semi-set aspic, to glaze, then place a truffle slice on each. Refrigerate for 10 minutes, then brush for a second time with the aspic to glaze and place back in the fridge. Brush the head, antennae, legs and all over the emptied out shell with the aspic, then place in the fridge.

To serve, blanch the samphire for 1 minute, refresh in cold water and drain well. Place the bread base lengthways on a rectangular serving platter. Lay the langouste shell on the bread base with the head end on the higher part. Put the samphire at the head end, to partially cover the bread base.

Arrange the slices of tail meat on the shell, starting at the head end and overlapping them slightly until you reach the tail end. Arrange the filled tomatoes around the tail and serve the remaining mayonnaise on the side. Put the dish in the middle of the table and let your guests appreciate your masterpiece before savouring it. Gourmands will enjoy the meat found inside the head that they can help themselves to, using a lobster pick.

Variations
• You can also serve hard-boiled eggs alongside the baby tomatoes as part of the garnish; mash the yolks with some mayonnaise, then pipe back inside the whites.
• Langouste *à la russe* calls for the same preparation, but the slices of tail meat are coated in mayonnaise rather than aspic.

Truffles
Black truffles (*Tuber melanosporum*) are regarded as the black diamonds of French cuisine. They first made their appearance in the 14th century, on the tables of princes, including Charles V. Since then, they have made their way onto less prestigious tables, spreading the glory of French cuisine across the world. They are in fact fungi that grow in symbiosis on the roots of certain trees, including oak and hazel. They need alkaline soil conditions – chalk or limestone – and prefer the edge of a wood or a clearing, with direct light on the ground. They grow unseen, between 5 and 15cm below the surface. Dogs have largely replaced pigs as truffle hunters, not least because pigs had a tendency to eat them as they found them… I have had many opportunities to search out truffles with my friend Eric Jaumard and his dog in the southern Ardèche. Around 40% of French truffles come from the Vaucluse region, but they are also found in the Gard, Drôme and the Var. The season runs from around the beginning of December to the end of February and prices are exorbitant, varying between 800 and 1,500 euros per kilo. Over the last 30 years or so, truffle orchards (*truffières*) have been successfully planted in France as well as in other countries: New Zealand, Australia and the United States. In terms of flavour, eggs certainly make the best match for truffles.

Fish

Bouillabaisse

Introduced to Marseille by the Phocaeans, ancient Greeks from Asia Minor who founded the city in 600BC, this famous dish was originally a ragoût made from the unsold fish in the bottom of the fisherman's basket – too small and full of bones for anyone to buy. These days bouillabaisse is traditionally served first as the light and flavoursome liquid soup, with toasted croûtons and rouille, followed by the fish. The most important quality of these is utmost freshness, then a rapid, minimal cooking that preserves their flavours. It is a uniquely flavoured dish that has become a refined, elegant, but also rather costly one. You need to cook it for at least 10 people.

Scale, gut and trim all the fish, then cut into large sections if necessary, wash in very cold water and drain. Remove the innards, beak and quill from the squid, then clean, rinse and cut the squid into medium-sized pieces. Wash and drain the crabs, if using.

Heat the fish soup in a large earthenware or metal cooking pot over a medium heat. Meanwhile, cut the potatoes into slices, 3–4mm thick. Add to the soup with the olive oil and saffron and adjust the seasoning with salt and pepper, if necessary. Bring to the boil and cook for 5 minutes.

Start to add the firmer fleshed fish, such as conger eel, John Dory, scorpion fish, squid and crabs, if using, and keep it at a rapid simmer for 10 minutes. Add more delicately fleshed fish and simmer steadily for a further 10 minutes. Remove from the heat.

Use a skimmer to remove and drain the pieces of fish one by one. Working quickly, remove the skin, then the bones and transfer the fish to a large serving dish; keep hot.

Distribute a few potato slices between deep plates or shallow bowls, then add a variety of fish pieces. Carefully pour a ladleful of the very hot broth into each bowl (checking for any missed bones).

Serve at once, with the aïoli or rouille in a large bowl on the table and the crisp bread slices in a separate bowl, so that everyone can help themselves to more according to appetite.

Serves 10

2kg Mediterranean fish, such as conger eel, John Dory, weever, sea bass, scorpion fish, wrasse, white bream, hake, beaux-yeux, galinette, etc.

1 or 2 squid

1 or 2 small crabs (optional)

1 quantity fish soup (page 26)

500g potatoes, peeled

3 tbsp olive oil

2 pinches of saffron threads

1 quantity aïoli (page 256) or rouille (page 257)

20 thin slices of baguette, dried in the oven at 160°C/Gas 3 until crisp

Salt and freshly ground pepper

Rougets de Roche à la Vapeur, Sauce Vierge
STEAMED RED MULLET WITH SAUCE VIERGE

This dish is full of delicate marine flavours. Two types of red mullet flourish in the Mediterranean: the more delicate *rouget barbet de roche*, or rock red mullet, which is striped, and *rouget de vase*, or sand red mullet. Cooking red mullet calls for precision, as the delicate white flesh loses its finesse if it's even a fraction overcooked. It must also be very fresh, to avoid any hint of bitterness in the flesh found at the base of the fillets.

Using the blunt edge of a small knife, carefully remove the scales from the mullet. Using scissors, snip a small opening in the belly of each, then detach the gills using the tips of the scissors, drawing back the fins, and pull out the gills, along with the fins and guts. Gently rinse under cold running water and pat dry with kitchen paper.

Cut the potatoes into very fine slices, 2mm thick, and blanch in boiling salted water for 2–3 minutes. Drain and refresh under cold water.

One-third fill the base of a steamer with cold water and add a pinch of salt.

Arrange the potato slices in the top part of the steamer, cover with the sea lettuce, if using, and arrange the mullet on top. Put the lid on and bring the water to a gentle boil over a medium heat. Cook for 4–6 minutes, then remove from the heat and set aside.

Heat the oil in a small frying pan, add the basil leaves and fry for 1 minute. Remove with a slotted spoon to a layer of kitchen paper, to absorb the oil.

Meanwhile, warm the sauce vierge over a gentle heat for 1 minute.

Using a flexible fish slice, transfer the red mullet, potatoes and seaweed to a serving dish or to individual plates. Pour the sauce vierge to one side of the fish, sprinkle the basil leaves over the top and arrange the lemon wedges to one side. Serve immediately.

Variation
One of the simplest ways to cook red mullet is to fillet them, sprinkle the fillets with salt and pepper and place them on a baking tray brushed with olive oil, then cook for just a couple of minutes under a hot grill. Transfer the fillets to a hot plate, brush with green olive tapenade and serve with a warm rice salad.

Serves 4

4 extremely fresh red mullet,
  200–250g each

4 small ratte potatoes, or other small
  new potatoes, peeled

100g sea lettuce (edible seaweed)
  (optional)

50ml grapeseed or groundnut oil

16 basil leaves

½ quantity sauce vierge (page 254)

1 lemon, cut into 4 wedges

Saint-Pierre Rôti au Beurre à l'Échalotte
ROAST JOHN DORY WITH SHALLOT BUTTER

Although the flesh of John Dory is very firm, it is also subtle and delicate; many consider it to be the finest fish of all. In this recipe I coat the fish in a mixture of butter, shallot and paprika, so that the flesh is flavoured and basted as it roasts. Buy a super-fresh fish and roast it to perfection – as you remove the fillets, they should reveal a 'pink' bone. A simple accompaniment of boiled new potatoes is all you need.

To prepare the shallot butter, blanch the chopped shallots in boiling water for 2 minutes, then drain and refresh under cold water. Drain and pat dry with a tea towel. Mix the shallots with the butter, paprika and the juice of 1 lemon.

Cut the other lemon into 6 wedges and preheat the oven to 180°C/Gas 4.

Slide the blade of a fish filleting knife under the skin of the John Dory on its black skin side and remove the skin a little at a time, taking care not to damage the flesh underneath. Using scissors, trim the fish all around the edge, removing the gills and eyes, then remove the guts. Make an incision 5mm deep along the bone, to help with even cooking. Rinse in cold water and dab dry with a tea towel.

Spread a quarter of the shallot butter on a roasting tray big enough to fit the John Dory and 5–7cm deep. Season the John Dory and place white skin side down, skinned side up on the shallot butter. Spread the remaining butter over the top of the fish and cook in the oven for 25 minutes, using a spoon to baste the fish with the shallot butter every 5 minutes. Once cooked, remove from the oven and set aside to rest on its roasting tray for 5 minutes.

With the help of 2 palette knives, transfer the John Dory to a large oval serving dish, baste with a little of the cooking butter, arrange the lemon wedges around the fish and serve, with boiled new potatoes.

Serves 6

1 John Dory, 1.8–2kg

Salt and freshly ground pepper

Shallot butter

150g shallots, peeled and chopped

300g butter, softened

5g (1 tsp) medium-hot paprika

2 lemons

Variations
• Dill or basil can be used in place of shallot in the butter; simply snip the herbs and mix with the softened butter, then proceed as for the shallot butter.
• When in season, sauté some finely chopped ceps with a little garlic in olive oil, let cool, then use in place of the shallot butter, spreading them over and under the fish before baking. The ceps lend a deep, earthy flavour to the fish.

Bar Braisé sur lit d'Oseille

BRAISED SEA BASS ON A BED OF SORREL

A beautifully succulent dish, where the flavour of the fish has a purity you rarely achieve by any other means of cooking. The extraordinary whiteness of the flesh, and the accompanying vegetables, make it one of my favourite dishes.

Gut the sea bass via the gills and a small incision made at the base of the stomach. Descale it, working from the tail end towards the head. Trim, then rinse in cold water and lightly pat dry.

Preheat the oven to 220°C/Gas 7. Squeeze the juice from 1 lemon half and set aside; cut the other half in two. Melt 40g of the butter in a saucepan, add the vegetables and sweat lightly over a gentle heat for 3–4 minutes.

Put the bass on the rack of a fish kettle and place the rack in the kettle, then arrange the sweated vegetables around the fish. Add the bouquet garni and the 2 lemon pieces, lightly salt the fish and pour over the wine.

Place over a medium heat, and at the first signs of a simmer, when the liquid reaches 70–80°C, cover and transfer to the oven. Cook for 20 minutes, basting the fish every 7–8 minutes. As soon as it comes out of the oven, lift the rack out of the kettle and cover the fish with a dampened tea towel. Strain the braising liquid through a muslin-lined chinois into a saucepan and reduce over a high heat by about two-thirds to a jus. Remove from the heat and whisk in 30g butter. Add salt and pepper to taste and set aside to keep warm.

For the duxelles, finely chop the mushrooms using a large chef's knife. Heat 60g butter in a sauté pan, add the mushrooms and lemon juice and cook over a medium heat for about 5 minutes, stirring with a wooden spoon. Add salt and pepper to taste, then set aside to keep warm.

Heat the remaining 30g butter in a frying pan and, as soon as it is hot, add the sorrel and wilt down for 2 minutes, without letting it take on any colour, stirring with a wooden spoon. Set aside to keep warm, draining off any liquid, if necessary.

To serve, arrange the bass on a large oval dish. Remove the skin and spoon the braising jus over the flesh to coat. Encircle the bass with the sorrel on one side and the mushroom duxelles on the other, then serve at once.

Serves 6–8

1 very fresh sea bass, about 1.75kg, preferably line-caught

1 lemon

160g butter

2 medium carrots, peeled and finely chopped

2 medium onions, peeled and finely chopped

1 shallot, peeled and finely chopped

1 leek (white part only), trimmed, washed and finely chopped

1 bouquet garni

400ml dry white wine

400g button mushrooms

250g sorrel leaves, stalks removed, washed

Salt and freshly ground pepper

Variations

The same method can be used for braising other whole fish weighing 1.5–3kg, such as turbot (use a turbot kettle), pollock, rascasse (scorpion fish), etc. They each make a perfect dish for a special occasion.

Gigot de Lotte en Cocotte
CASSEROLE OF MONKFISH

This is one of my favourite ways to serve monkfish. If you are ever lucky enough to find small monkfish tails (about 300g), you can prepare them in the same way as a large tail, but only cook them for 6–8 minutes; they will be deliciously tender and succulent. During the chanterelle season, I use these delicate mushrooms in place of peppers; their flavour complements the monkfish beautifully.

Preheat the oven to 200°C/Gas 6, or a grill to high. Rub the peppers with the olive oil and either roast or grill until the skins are blistered and blackened, turning them once or twice so they char evenly. Transfer to a bowl, cover tightly with cling film and leave for a few minutes; the steam will help to lift the skins. Use your fingertips or a small knife to remove the skins. Keep the peeled peppers whole, but make a small opening at the stem end and scoop out the white membranes and seeds from inside.

Lower the oven setting to 180°C/Gas 4 (or preheat if you've used the grill for the peppers) and place a casserole inside to heat up.

Put the onions in a small pan, cover with water, add the 30g butter and a pinch of salt and cook until the water has evaporated. Set aside.

Put the lardons in a saucepan, cover with cold water, bring to a slow boil and blanch for 2 minutes. Drain and refresh in cold water, then drain again and put back in the pan with 20g of the clarified butter. Cook for 2 minutes to colour, then set aside with the peppers and onions.

Heat the remaining clarified butter in a frying pan over a medium heat. Pat the monkfish dry, season lightly with salt and add to the pan. Cook for 2 minutes on all sides until lightly coloured, then transfer with the peppers, onions and lardons to the warm casserole and cook in the oven for 10 minutes.

Meanwhile, blanch the mangetout for 30 seconds, refresh in cold water and drain. Lift the monkfish out of the casserole, gently stir the mangetout through the peppers, onions and lardons, then replace the monkfish on top. Cook in the oven for a further 5 minutes. Grind a little pepper over the monkfish and serve straight from the casserole.

Serves 4

2 medium peppers, ideally red

2 tbsp olive oil

8 cebette onions or small salad onions, peeled

30g butter

200g piece of lightly smoked bacon, rind removed, cut into large lardons

80g clarified butter (page 266)

1 monkfish tail, about 1kg prepared weight (skin and membrane removed)

150g mangetout, trimmed

Salt and freshly ground pepper

Variation
Cut the monkfish into thick steaks, pan-fry to colour on both sides, then cook for a few minutes in a Côtes du Rhône red wine that has been reduced by half. Serve the fish with Basque rice: Spanish rice flavoured with peppers, garlic and chorizo.

Duo de Rouget et Maquereau à l'Escabèche

RED MULLET AND MACKEREL ESCABECHE

This classic, cold dish has its origins in the Mediterranean region, and is greatly appreciated during the summer. Its success is determined by the freshness of the fish. You can use sardines, or other oily fish, to replace the mackerel.

Cut the heads off the fish, then gently rinse in cold water. Working on a board and using a filleting knife, fillet all the fish, starting with the mullet, which are more delicate than the mackerel, from the back to the stomach and following the line of the backbone. Trim and neaten the fillets, then cut the mackerel fillets in half (so the pieces are similar in size to the smaller whole mullet).

Score a 5mm deep incision in two places in the skin of each mackerel piece, to help the flesh, which is firmer than that of the mullet, to cook. Rinse all the fish pieces under cold running water, then drain and gently pat dry.

Heat half the olive oil in a large frying pan over a medium heat. Lightly salt the mackerel fillets and, as soon as the oil is hot, add the fillets flesh side down to the pan and cook for 1½ minutes. Remove and place flesh side down in a large, shallow dish. Wipe the frying pan clean and add the remaining oil. Cook the mullet fillets in the same way, for 1½ minutes. Arrange in the dish with the mackerel, alternating the two types of fish. Set aside. Wipe the frying pan clean.

For the marinade, use a canelle knife to score narrow, parallel lengthways grooves down the lemons, and do the same to the carrots, to create a fluted effect. Remove both ends of the lemons and cut into 2mm slices. Thinly slice the carrots into rounds.

Add the 50ml olive oil to the frying pan and place over a medium heat. Add the carrots and shallots and sweat for 2 minutes, stirring all the time, then add the remaining marinade ingredients. Bring to the boil, lower the heat and simmer for 3 minutes, then skim the surface if necessary and salt very lightly.

Pour the piping hot marinade over the fish fillets and cover with cling film, pierced in several places with the tip of a knife. Set aside to cool completely, then transfer to the fridge for at least 4–6 hours.

To serve, present the fish in the dish. The marinade is an integral part of the dish, so it's best served in shallow bowls, to accommodate a little marinade with the fish.

Serves 6

6 super-fresh red mullets, about
   350g each
3 super-fresh mackerel, about
   350g each
40ml mild olive oil
Salt

Marinade

2 lemons
120g carrots, peeled
50ml olive oil
80g shallots, peeled and thinly sliced
2 garlic cloves, peeled and crushed
2 tsp white peppercorns, crushed
2 generous thyme sprigs, crumbled
2 tsp coriander seeds, crushed
2 bay leaves
Generous pinch of cayenne
100ml good-quality white wine vinegar
400ml water

Dos d'Esturgeon Cuit à la Vapeur, Petits Blinis et Oeufs de Saumon

STEAMED STURGEON WITH BLINIS AND SALMON ROE

Sturgeon is not widely eaten, and is a relatively unfamiliar fish, but it's begging to be discovered. Deliciously silky and delicate, it is even better when served with blinis or potato cakes, which provide a good contrast in texture.

For the blinis, mix the wheat and rye flours together. Put the yeast in a large bowl, pour in the tepid milk, stir with a small whisk, then add 25g of the flour mixture with the bulgur wheat. Stir with a whisk, cover the bowl with cling film and leave to rest in a warm place at about 25°C for 2 hours.

Whisk the remaining 100g flour and the egg yolks into the mixture, then cover with cling film again and leave to rest in a warm place for another hour.

Whisk the egg whites with a pinch of salt to semi-firm peaks and fold into the blini mix with a spatula; do not overwork. Season with a little salt and pepper.

You will need to cook the blinis in batches. Heat a trickle of grapeseed oil in a non-stick frying pan over a medium heat. Drop generous spoonfuls of the mixture into the pan, leaving space in between, and cook for about 1 minute. Turn them over using a palette knife and cook for 1 minute more. Transfer the cooked blinis to a plate and repeat to cook the rest; you should have 8–12 blinis, depending on size. Set aside in a warm place, ready to serve.

Half-fill the base of a steamer with salted cold water. Place the firm white fish fillets in the top half, put the lid on and place over a medium heat. As soon as the water boils, lower the heat and steam for 4–5 minutes. Check the fish is cooked by inserting a trussing needle or point of a small knife into the thickest part of one of the fillets; if it passes through easily, the fish is cooked.

While the fish is cooking, whisk the cream to a ribbon consistency and fold in the juice of ½ lemon and some salt and pepper.

Transfer the cooked firm white fish to warm plates. Arrange the rocket around the fish and dress with olive oil, lemon juice, salt and pepper. Using 2 spoons, shape 4 large quenelles from the cream, one for each plate and top with the dill. Serve the blinis and salmon roe, with the samphire, if using, on the side.

Variation
Steamed sturgeon is also delicious served with a champagne sauce (page 108).

Serves 4

4 firm sturgeon, each 140g, skinned (by the fishmonger)

150ml double cream (at room temperature)

Juice of ½ lemon

Salt and freshly ground pepper

Blinis

60g wheat flour

65g rye flour

15g fresh yeast

250ml tepid milk (at 35°C)

2 tsp bulgur wheat

2 eggs, separated

2 tsp grapeseed oil

To serve

20g rocket leaves

3 tbsp olive oil

Juice of ½ lemon

4 dill sprigs or fennel top sprigs

40g salmon roe

50g samphire, blanched for 1 minute (optional)

Soles Soufflées Homardine

DOVER SOLE WITH LOBSTER MOUSSE

All the components of this impressive dish can be prepared
the day before, with the exception of the champagne sauce,
leaving just the soles to be braised at the last minute. Leaf
spinach and new potatoes are ideal accompaniments, and
a great wine, such as a young Château Grillet or a Corton
Charlemagne would be sublime. Remember to sedate the
lobsters by placing in the freezer 30 minutes before cooking.

Put one of the soles on a board, white skin side down. Using a small knife,
make a light incision into the skin at the end of the tail, then use the blade
of the knife to scrape the skin back a little towards the head end, to detach
the skin from the flesh by about 1–2cm. Holding a tea towel, or better still a
new scouring pad, pinch the detached piece of skin between your thumb and
index finger and pull the skin in one movement from the tail to the head end,
to remove it neatly in one piece.

Turn the sole over and gently scrape over the white skin with the back of
a knife. Using scissors, trim 1cm from all around the edge of the sole and
remove the head at the point the fillets begin, angling the scissors slightly
as you do so.

Using a sharp filleting knife, make an incision on the skinned side of the sole
the length of the backbone, stopping 2cm from the tail and from where the
head was. Slide the blade of the filleting knife into the incision and along
between the bone and fillets, stopping 2cm from the outside edge of the fillet
on both sides. This will create 2 flaps of fillet, still attached at the sides, that
when opened out reveal the whole bone.

Snip the ends of the bones down one side, using just the tips of the scissors
and taking care not to pierce right through the fish. Insert the tip of the knife
into this place under the bone, and slide the blade between the fillet and the
bone to release the bone from both fillets underneath. Snip down the bone
ends on the other side as you did for the first, then remove the entire bone
from the flesh; the sole is now boned but still intact.

Carefully rinse the filleted fish under a trickle of cold water, then gently dab
dry all over, especially the boned out insides. Repeat the procedure with
the second sole, then set both aside on a dish covered with cling film in the
fridge, ready to stuff.

Fill a large saucepan, big enough to take both lobsters, with lightly salted cold
water and bring to the boil. As soon as it boils, plunge the lobsters into the
water and par-cook for 4 minutes with the water just bubbling. Transfer them
straight away to a bowl filled with a mixture of cold water and ice cubes.

Serves 4

2 Dover soles, 600–700g each

2 lobsters, preferably live, about
  500g each

50g butter, to grease

600g lobster mousse (page 84)

½ egg white

500ml fish stock (page 249)

6 chervil sprigs

Salt and freshly ground pepper

Puff pastry half-moons (optional)

100g quick puff pastry (page 263)

Flour, for dusting

1 egg yolk mixed with 2 tsp milk, to glaze

Champagne sauce

50g butter

60g shallots, peeled and thinly sliced

60g button mushrooms, thinly sliced

400ml dry champagne

300ml fish stock (page 249)

350ml double cream

(continued overleaf)

After 10 minutes, separate the tails from the heads, then use scissors to remove the shell, and cut 4 nice-looking medallions from each piece of tail meat (they will only be one-third cooked). Set aside in the fridge, on a plate covered with cling film.

Lightly butter a shallow baking dish, large enough to fit both soles, using 30g of the butter, and place one sole skin side down in the dish. Pipe half the lobster mousse into the boned insides of the sole, using a piping bag without a nozzle. Bring the fillets back over the mousse, which will leave a gap of about 4cm in the middle, tapering to 1–2cm at either end. Smooth the top of the mousse using a palette knife. Brush a tiny bit of egg white onto one side of 4 lobster medallions and arrange brushed side down in a line on top of the mousse, pushing them very lightly into the mousse. Repeat with the other sole. Cover the dish with cling film and set aside in the fridge.

Preheat the oven to 190°C/Gas 5, if making the pastry half-moons. Roll out the pastry on a lightly floured surface to a 3–4mm thickness. Use a ridged pastry cutter to stamp out 4 half-moons, transfer to a lightly dampened baking sheet and refrigerate for 20 minutes. Brush the tops with the egg glaze, then use the tip of a knife to score a lined pattern on the top of each. Bake for 10–12 minutes, then transfer to a wire rack and keep warm.

For the champagne sauce, melt 20g of the butter in a pan, add the shallots and sweat for 1 minute without letting them colour. Add the mushrooms and cook over a gentle heat for 2 minutes, stirring with a spoon. Add the champagne, then reduce over a medium heat by one-third. Pour in the fish stock and reduce by half. Add the cream and cook until the sauce lightly coats the back of a spoon. Strain through a fine chinois into a second pan and, using a small balloon whisk, whisk in the remaining 30g butter to emulsify. Add salt and pepper to taste and set aside to keep warm.

Lower the oven temperature to 130°C/Gas ½ (if used for the half-moons, otherwise preheat it) and heat the 500ml fish stock in a pan, to boiling point. Butter a piece of greaseproof paper large enough to cover the soles, using the remaining 20g butter. Pour the hot fish stock around the outsides of the soles, place the buttered paper over the top and cook in the oven for 20 minutes, gently basting the fish every 6–7 minutes with the braising stock. Once they are cooked, remove from the oven and set aside in the baking dish for 5 minutes before serving.

To serve, use a large, wide palette knife to transfer both soles, one at a time, from the baking dish to a serving dish, holding them on the palette knife over a tea towel for 30 seconds to drain. Blend the champagne sauce in a food mixer for 30 seconds to lighten it, then pour some around the soles; serve the rest in a sauceboat. Arrange a pastry half-moon and a few chervil sprigs at either end of both fish, and serve immediately.

Variations

Salmon mousse can be used in place of lobster mousse, but it won't be quite as splendid. You can also stuff a whole turbot of around 1.25kg following the same idea; you would need to cook it for around 35 minutes, depending on size.

Dos de Saumon Grillé Argenteuil, Sauce Maltaise

GRIDDLED SALMON FILLETS WITH MALTAISE SAUCE

Salmon is a delicate fish that calls for a sauce and vegetable accompaniment that complement it well; this recipe, for me, achieves a perfect harmony.

Use a swivel peeler to pare the asparagus stems, then break the stems at the point where they naturally snap when bent. Divide into 3 small bunches with the tips aligned and tie together with kitchen string, but not too tightly. Trim the ends of each bunch so the stems are the same length, then set aside in a bowl of cold water.

Cut off the peel and pith from the oranges, using a flexible knife, then release the segments from their membranes and set aside in a bowl. If you are not serving the salmon rare, preheat the oven to 180°C/Gas 4.

Cook the asparagus bunches in boiling salted water for 6–8 minutes, or steam for 10 minutes, until the spears are cooked but still just firm to the bite. Once they are cooked, release the string.

Meanwhile, heat a ridged griddle pan over a high heat. Pat dry the salmon using kitchen paper, then brush each with a little oil. Very lightly salt the fillets and place them in the very hot pan. After 1 minute, give them a quarter-turn, then after another minute turn them over and cook as for the first side, giving them a quarter-turn after 1 minute. The salmon should now be cooked but still rare in the middle; if you prefer the fish pink all the way through, transfer to the oven for 3 minutes.

Place one salmon fillet on each plate and arrange some asparagus spears in a small mound to one side. Brush the asparagus with melted butter, then arrange some cucumber, if serving, on the other side. Grind a little pepper over the salmon, then arrange 3 orange segments on each fillet and a lemon segment on the edge of each plate. Serve the Maltaise sauce separately.

Variation

Anchovy or maître d'hôtel butter (with herbs and lemon juice) can replace the Maltaise sauce, but would be better matched with salmon cooked outdoors on a barbecue; place a round of the butter on top of each salmon fillet once it is cooked. The results will be delicious but not quite as delicate.

Serves 6

500g medium thickness asparagus
   spears (green or white)
2 oranges
6 middle-cut salmon fillets, about 180g
   each, skinned
1 tbsp light olive oil
60g butter, melted
Salt and freshly ground pepper

To serve

Cucumber braised in butter (page 196),
   optional
1 lemon, cut into 6 segments
Maltaise sauce (page 254)

Darne de Turbotin Grillé Sauce Choron

GRIDDLED TURBOT STEAKS WITH SAUCE CHORON

The 'darne' refers to a specific cut of the turbot. The fish is sliced in half, following the backbone, then each half is cut into 2–3cm thick steaks on the bone. These are then cooked with or without the skin. Turbot prepared in this way and lightly griddled on the bone is quite simply sublime. The flesh is firm, flavoursome, a touch iodised, and even succulent as you reach the bone. The potato roses and Choron sauce add a touch of sophistication.

To make the potato roses, peel and wash the potatoes and cut each in half lengthways. Using a plain 5cm pastry cutter, cut out a round of potato 4cm high from each potato half. Use a knife to pare each round into a cone shape. Hold one of the potato cones in one hand and, using a speed peeler, gently follow the angle of the potato without stopping at all, until you have a long, fine uninterrupted strip of potato, stopping when you reach 1cm from the middle. Starting with the end you began peeling, very carefully roll up the potato strip on the work surface into a rose shape, and insert a wooden toothpick through the middle so that it keeps its shape. Repeat with the remaining 3 potato halves to make 4 roses.

Heat the grapeseed oil to 170°C in a deep frying pan or small saucepan, drop 2 potato roses in and cook for 4–5 minutes, until golden and crisp, turning them once after 2–3 minutes. Using a skimmer, remove them from the oil and set aside to drain on kitchen paper, sprinkle with salt and repeat with the remaining 2 roses. Carefully remove the toothpicks before they cool down.

Meanwhile, heat a griddle pan until very hot. Lightly brush each turbot steak with olive oil. Wipe the surface of the pan with a lightly oiled piece of kitchen paper, then add the turbot steaks. Give them a quarter-turn after 3 minutes, then turn them all over and do the same to the other side after 2–3 minutes. Remove the turbot to a warm plate, cover with foil and set aside.

Heat the butter in a frying pan over a medium heat, add the spinach with the sugar and cook until just wilted. Season with salt and pepper to taste, and set aside in a bowl.

Divide the spinach between 4 plates and arrange the turbot steaks on top. Place a lemon half topped with a chervil sprig and a potato rose to the side. Spoon a little sauce on top of the fish and serve at once, with the rest of the sauce on the side.

Serves 4

2 large King Edward or Agria potatoes

250ml grapeseed oil

4 turbot steaks, about 200g each, skinned

1 tbsp light olive oil

40g butter

100g spinach leaves, stalks removed, washed and well drained

Pinch of caster sugar

2 lemons, halved, pointed ends sliced off

4 chervil sprigs

½ quantity Choron sauce (page 255)

Salt and freshly ground pepper

Turban de Saumon et de Sole, Mousse de Homard

TURBAN OF SALMON AND SOLE WITH LOBSTER MOUSSE

This is a dish that requires skill and mastery. You can serve a champagne sauce on the side if you like, but the dish is elegant and delectably smooth enough not to need it. I serve it either with wilted spinach or, as here, with carrots turned in the shape of elongated olives and cooked in butter and water, because their colour complements the salmon. I suggest that you make the turban at least once before serving it to guests, to ensure that you are confident it will turn out well.

Using a sole fillet knife, carefully lift off the sole fillets then, still with the knife, remove the skin and rinse the fish in very cold water. (Alternatively, this can be done by your fishmonger.) Place the fillets between sheets of cling film and, using the flat side of a large cook's knife, tap down very lightly on each fillet individually. Using a knife, trim the fillets so that they are a neat, long triangular shape with a point. Set aside in the fridge.

Using a sole fillet knife, remove the salmon skin and any greyish meat found at the centre of the fillet. Cut 7 escalopes 4–5mm thick, making sure they are more or less the same size and shape as the sole fillets, trimming each again until they are precise and neat. Set aside in the fridge.

Brush the insides of a savarin (ring) mould, about 18cm in diameter and 4cm deep, with some of the melted clarified butter. Set aside in the fridge for 5 minutes. Preheat the oven to 100°C/Gas ¼.

Gently pat the fish fillets dry, one by one, using a tea towel. Place a sole fillet in the buttered savarin mould with the wider end hanging outside the mould and the pointed end over the inside edge of the mould. Next place a salmon fillet in the same way, so it is touching the sole fillet, and continue in this fashion, alternating the salmon and sole, until the inside of the mould is completely lined with fish. (You might have some of each fish left over that can be used in another dish.)

Lightly salt the fish lining the dish. Put the lobster mousse into a piping bag fitted with a large plain nozzle and pipe it evenly into the mould, to come to the top. Bring the fish fillets hanging over both sides of the mould back over the mousse and, using your fingertips, press them lightly down.

Cover the entire mould with a circle of buttered greaseproof paper, then a circle of foil on top, making sure the foil is flattened onto the top of the mould.

Serves 6–8

2 Dover soles, about 600–700g each

½ salmon fillet from the middle of the salmon, about 500–600g

60g clarified butter (page 266), melted

300g lobster mousse (page 84)

Salt

To serve

Buttered carrots or spinach (see above)

Place the covered mould in a shallow baking dish and pour hot water at about 60°C to come halfway up the mould. Transfer to the oven and cook for 20 minutes. Insert a trussing needle into the middle of the turban to test the mousse; if the needle comes out clean and shiny, the turban is cooked. Remove from the oven and transfer the mould from the baking dish to a wire rack. Leave to rest for 5–6 minutes before unmoulding.

To unmould the turban, carefully remove the foil and greaseproof paper from the top. Use kitchen paper to very gently dab the top of the turban to remove the small quantity of water produced by the fish and mousse during cooking. Place a round serving dish on top of the mould and invert. Very gently remove the mould and brush just a hint of melted clarified butter over the top, to revive the colours and add shine to the fish.

Fill the centre of the turban with buttered carrots or spinach and serve straight away; this is not a dish that can wait.

Poultry & Game

Fricassée de Pintadeau au Riesling et Girolles

GUINEA FOWL COOKED WITH RIESLING AND CHANTERELLES

This dish is from Alsace, where Riesling is produced. Guinea fowl is often replaced by the ubiquitous chicken, but I adore guinea fowl. It has a stronger flavour than chicken, somewhat reminiscent of partridge, though less pronounced, and it deserves greater recognition. In this delicate dish, the creamy, tarragon sauce complements the meat perfectly. Serve with an Alsace Riesling or Pinot Gris, of a young vintage.

Put the onions and butter in a small pan, cover with cold water, add a pinch of salt and cook over a medium heat for 15 minutes. Remove from the heat and set aside, leaving the onions in their cooking water. Preheat the oven to 200°C/Gas 6.

Cook the broccoli stems in boiling salted water for 2 minutes, then refresh in cold water and drain. Cover with cling film and set aside.

Trim the chanterelle stalks with a small knife, then use a damp tea towel to gently wipe away any traces of sand or earth. Heat 40g of the clarified butter in a frying pan over a lively heat, add the chanterelles, salt lightly and sauté for 3–4 minutes. As soon as they have released their liquid, transfer to a bowl and cover with cling film, perforated in several places.

Heat the remaining clarified butter in an ovenproof pan set over a lively heat. Sprinkle the guinea fowl pieces and carcass with salt and add to the pan. Colour on all sides, then transfer the pan to the oven and cook for 15 minutes. Lift the guinea fowl pieces out of the pan into a dish (leaving the browned carcass pieces in the pan), cover with foil and set aside. Pour off the fat.

Add the shallots, thyme, bay and tarragon stalks to the carcass pieces in the pan. Deglaze with the wine over a high heat, then reduce by two-thirds. Pour in the stock and reduce by half, then add the cream and cook over a gentle heat until the sauce lightly coats the back of a spoon. Strain through a chinois into a large sauté pan and season with salt and pepper to taste.

Add the pieces of guinea fowl to the sauce, along with the onions, broccoli and chanterelles, making sure each is well drained. Bring to the barest simmer over a gentle heat, then add the lemon juice and two-thirds of the tarragon leaves and immediately remove from the heat. Tip the contents of the pan into a shallow serving dish, sprinkle with the remaining tarragon leaves and serve, with bread to mop up the delicious juices.

Serves 4

12 baby white onions, peeled

30g butter

300g tenderstem broccoli spears, trimmed

200g chanterelles

80g clarified butter (page 266)

1 guinea fowl, about 1.6kg, cut into 8 pieces, carcass and neck chopped and reserved

3 shallots, peeled and thinly sliced

2 thyme sprigs

2 bay leaves

2 tarragon sprigs, leaves stripped and stalks reserved

500ml Alsace Riesling white wine

300ml chicken stock (page 248), or buy good-quality fresh stock

300ml double cream

Juice of ½ lemon

Salt and freshly ground pepper

Coq au Vin

This is a dish stemming from *la France profonde*, served on the ritual 'killing the cock' feast day. These days, it's often easier to find a female bird than a male one, in which case a chicken will only need cooking for about 1¼ hours. I like to serve it with boiled potatoes and a fine red Burgundy with a little age.

Put the pieces of bird in a large dish with the bouquet garni, carrot, onion and garlic and pour over the wine. Cover with cling film and leave to marinate in the fridge for at least 12 hours.

Take the dish from the fridge and strain all the ingredients, reserving the bouquet garni, vegetables and marinade. Thoroughly pat dry the pieces of bird, one by one, and sprinkle with salt on all sides.

Heat 60g of the clarified butter or oil in a large cooking pot over a lively heat, add the pieces of bird and colour on all sides until deep brown. Remove from the pot and set aside in a dish.

Add the carrot, onion and garlic from the marinade to the fat in the pot and sweat over a gentle heat for 5 minutes, then add back the pieces of bird. Sprinkle over the eau-de-vie or marc de Bourgogne and flambé, using a long match to ignite it and standing well back. As soon as the flame has died down, sprinkle over the roasted flour and stir, using a large wooden spoon.

Pour the reserved marinade and stock into the pot, increase the heat and bring the boil, stirring right down to the bottom of the pot from time to time with the wooden spoon. As soon as it reaches a boil, reduce to a light simmer, add the reserved bouquet garni and cook, uncovered, over a gentle heat for 1½ hours, skimming the surface from time to time.

Meanwhile, heat 30g of the butter in a small pan. As soon as it is foaming, add the baby onions with the sugar and colour evenly over a medium heat, then add water to cover and a small pinch of salt and cook, still over a medium heat, until the cooking water has evaporated. Set aside in a bowl.

Melt the remaining 80g butter in a large frying pan and, as soon as it is foaming, add the mushrooms and half the lemon juice, salt lightly and cook, stirring every minute or so, until the liquid released from the mushrooms has evaporated. Set aside in a dish.

Heat the remaining 30g clarified butter in a frying pan, add the lardons and cook for 2 minutes to colour, then drain and set aside in a bowl.

When the bird has been cooking for 1½ hours, check to see if it is done: the flesh should be slightly firm but the tip of a knife should penetrate with minimal resistance. If not, cook for a further 30 minutes. Once it is cooked, take the pieces of bird from the pot, place in a large dish and set aside, covered with a very damp tea towel.

Serves 6–8

1 young cock, about 2kg, cut into 6 pieces

1 medium bouquet garni

1 large carrot, peeled and cut into thick rounds

1 large onion, peeled and quartered

½ head of garlic (split horizontally)

1 litre fine-quality red Burgundy wine, ideally Côtes de Nuits

90g clarified butter (page 266)

50ml eau-de-vie or marc de Bourgogne

50g roasted plain flour (see page 267)

300ml chicken stock (page 248) or veal stock (page 249), or buy good-quality fresh stock

110g butter

20 baby salad onions, peeled

Pinch of sugar

400g button or field mushrooms, peeled, gently wiped and cut into 4 or 6 pieces, depending on size

Juice of 2 lemons

200g piece of streaky bacon, derinded, cut into big lardons and blanched

150g black pudding (optional, see note)

20g flat-leaf parsley, chopped

Salt and freshly ground pepper

Strain the cooking sauce through a chinois into a large pan and reduce over a medium heat until it lightly coats the back of a spoon. Add the lardons, baby onions and mushrooms and cook over a gentle heat for 5 minutes.

If you are using the blood, pour about 50ml into the sauce, agitating with a wooden spoon and making sure the liquor doesn't boil. Alternatively, skin the black pudding and break into small pieces, then add these a little at a time to the sauce, which will balance the flavour. Add salt and a generous grinding of pepper.

Put the pieces of bird back into the sauce to reheat, without letting it boil, for 5 minutes, until they are properly hot through, then add the remaining lemon juice. Transfer everything to a large tureen, sprinkle generously with the parsley and serve piping hot.

NOTE If possible, for an authentic coq au vin, buy an older 2–3 years old cock, weighing 2.5–3.5kg, direct from a farm and ask for its blood. This larger bird will serve 8, so cut into 8 rather than 6 pieces. As blood is rarely available these days, black pudding is used here to lend a similar flavour.

Variations
• Coq au Riesling can be made along the same lines, but using dry Riesling in place of Burgundy.
• The mushrooms can be substituted for morels, when in season.
• Omit the blood/black pudding, and serve with fresh pasta rather than boiled potatoes.

La Poule au Pot

There are numerous ancient versions of this recipe, especially when it comes to the composition of the stuffing, and mine is closest to the Béarn style. For centuries families served this unique dish on feast days.

To make the stuffing, melt the butter in a small pan over a gentle heat, then add the onions and garlic and sweat for 2 minutes. Transfer to a bowl and leave to cool.

Cut the chicken livers into small pieces, dice the ham and put both into a large bowl. Add the remaining stuffing ingredients, mix well, then incorporate the cooled onions and garlic. Season very generously with salt and pepper.

Fill a cooking pot big enough to accommodate the hen and all the vegetables two-thirds full with cold water. Add the chopped hen carcass and bring to the boil over a lively heat.

Put the boned-out hen on a board, skin side down. Sprinkle salt lightly over the flesh and arrange the stuffing in the middle. Bring the skin and meat up over the stuffing to meet. Stitch the skin together using a trussing needle and kitchen string, to re-create the hen's original form, then tie kitchen string around the bird in 3 places to hold it together, not too tightly.

Rub the stuffed hen all over with the half lemon, then lower it into the pot of boiling water and carcass. Wash all the vegetables, except the garlic, and add them to the pot. Cook at a bare simmer (about 90°C), for 1½ hours. Add the ginger, if using, 5 minutes before the end of cooking.

To make the sauce, lightly whip the cream to a ribbon consistency and mix in the horseradish and lemon juice, with salt and pepper to taste.

Using a large skimmer, remove the hen from the pot and place in a shallow serving bowl. Carefully snip off all the string, then turn the hen onto its back. Surround with the vegetables and strain some of the cooking liquid through a chinois over the top.

Portion the chicken and vegetables into warm shallow bowls and serve with the horseradish sauce.

Variation

A mixed meat pot au feu can be made along the same lines, but without the stuffing, and using chicken and beef knuckle, cheek, tongue and marrow bones. It needs to be cooked for 2–3 hours with whatever vegetables are in season (it's more of a wintry dish). Serve with the horseradish sauce and strong Dijon mustard.

Serves 4–6

1 boiling hen, 1.75–2kg, boned, carcass reserved and chopped into pieces

½ lemon

20g fresh root ginger slices (optional)

Salt and freshly ground pepper

Stuffing

30g butter

200g onions, peeled and chopped

3 garlic cloves, peeled and chopped

4 chicken livers, trimmed

200g Bayonne ham, or other cured ham

300g sausagemeat

10g parsley, stalks removed, chopped

1 egg

Vegetable garnish

2 leeks, white only, halved lengthways

6 small salad onions

6 small potatoes, peeled

½ Savoy cabbage, cut into 3 pieces

½ head of celery, cut into 3 pieces

3 carrots, peeled and halved

3 turnips, peeled and quartered

1 head of garlic, cut across the middle

Sauce

50ml double cream

30g grated fresh horseradish, or from a jar

Juice of ½ lemon

Vol-au-Vent Blancs de Volaille et Champignons — CHICKEN AND MUSHROOM VOL-AU-VENT

All the components of this classic dish can be prepared several hours in advance and assembled at the last minute. You can add lamb's or calf's sweetbreads to the filling, cooked and cut into large dice or slivers of black truffle, when in season.

Line a large baking sheet with baking parchment and place in the fridge to chill. Roll out the pastry on a lightly floured surface to a 75 x 24cm rectangle, 2.5–3mm thick. Using the tip of a small knife, and a tart ring as a guide, cut out 3 rounds of pastry, 22cm in diameter. Using a palette knife, transfer them to the chilled baking sheet and chill for 20–30 minutes. Meanwhile, preheat the oven to 180°C/Gas 4.

Transfer one pastry round to a small baking sheet and brush lightly with egg glaze. Place a 16cm tart ring on another pastry round and cut through the pastry, following the ring. Remove the inner round of pastry. Using a palette knife, lift the outer ring on top of the glazed pastry round. Lightly glaze the pastry ring and cover with the third pastry round. Chill for 10 minutes.

Score the side of the vol-au-vent all the way round, to a depth of 1mm. Brush the whole surface of the vol-au-vent with egg glaze. Now, with the tip of a knife, mark a 4cm border on the top by scoring quarter-circle lines. Score a lattice pattern on the pastry inside the border, which will become the lid.

Bake in the oven for 20 minutes, then lower the oven setting to 170°C/Gas 3 and cook for a further 25 minutes. Remove from the oven and use the tip of a knife to cut out the lid. Carefully lift it off, then scoop out and discard the undercooked pastry inside. Transfer the vol-au-vent case to a wire rack and set aside. Reduce the oven temperature to 130°C/Gas ½.

Put the chicken breasts in a saucepan with the lemon, carrot, onion, bouquet garni and a pinch of salt. Just cover with water, bring to a simmer over a low heat and poach gently (at about 80°C) for 6 minutes. Let cool in the liquid.

In a small saucepan, cook the mushrooms in a little of the chicken poaching liquid over a medium heat for 1 minute. Set aside, in the liquid.

Heat up the sauce allemande. Drain the chicken, discard the skin and cut the flesh into fine slices. Drain the mushrooms and add to the sauce with the chicken and pickled tongue. Heat gently, stirring, and adjust the seasoning.

To serve, warm the vol-au-vent case in the low oven for 5 minutes, then transfer to a warm serving dish. Spoon the chicken and mushroom filling into the case. You can add the pastry lid, to sit at an angle on top, if you like.

Serves 6–8

750g quick puff pastry (page 263) or
   all-butter shop-bought puff pastry

Flour, for dusting

1 egg yolk, mixed with 2 tsp milk and
   a pinch of salt, to glaze

Filling

3 medium boneless chicken breasts
   (skin on)

½ lemon

1 carrot, peeled and cut into rounds

1 medium onion, peeled and sliced
   into rings

1 bouquet garni

150g button mushrooms, wiped clean

1 quantity sauce allemande (page 253)

200g pickled beef tongue, cut into strips

Salt and freshly ground pepper

Variation

For a delicious seafood version, make a Champagne sauce using fish stock (page 108) and use a combination of cooked mussels, prawns, langoustine tails, scallops and a little crabmeat for the filling.

Poulet Sauté à la Bohémienne

SPICY SAUTÉED CHICKEN WITH TOMATOES AND PEPPERS

The origin of this dish from Provence/Vaucluse dates back to the time when a large community of gypsies from Eastern Europe settled near Sainte-Marie de la Mer, hence the inclusion of paprika, which is so popular in their homeland. It's a wonderfully flavoursome winter dish, best served simply with boiled rice.

Sprinkle all the chicken pieces liberally with paprika and lightly salt them. Heat the oil in a flameproof casserole over a medium heat. Add the chicken pieces and colour evenly until almost browned, then reduce the heat to very low and cook for 15 minutes.

Meanwhile, detach the stalks from the peppers, cut in half lengthways and remove the white membranes and seeds. Cut the flesh into wide strips, then use a swivel peeler to take off the skin. Blanch the onion in boiling water for 1 minute, then drain.

Add the peppers, tomatoes, fennel and onion to the chicken, cover and cook over a gentle heat for 25 minutes. Transfer the chicken pieces from the pot to a dish and set aside.

Deglaze the casserole with the wine and reduce by half over a medium heat, then add the stock and cook over a gentle heat for 10 minutes. Taste and adjust the seasoning with salt and pepper. Put the chicken pieces back into the sauce and heat gently for 5 minutes, so that they reheat and absorb the flavours of the sauce. Add the lemon juice.

Transfer to a shallow serving dish, sprinkle with the parsley and serve.

Serves 4

1 chicken, about 1.6kg, cut into 8 pieces

2½ tbsp paprika

2½ tbsp groundnut oil

400g peppers, preferably red

1 onion, peeled and cut into small dice

200g tomatoes, peeled and cut into
  thick slices

½ fennel bulb, cut into small dice

100ml dry white wine

75ml veal stock (page 249), or buy
  good-quality veal or chicken stock

Juice of 1 lemon

1 tbsp chopped parsley

Salt and freshly ground pepper

Oie Braisée à la Flamande

BRAISED GOOSE

Southwest France may be famous for its geese and foie gras but this family dish originated in the North of France. It is a taste sensation when the bird is young (around 6 months). The vegetables are 'turned' for an authentic presentation.

Preheat the oven to 190°C/Gas 5. Remove the wishbone from the goose. Heat half the lard or goose fat in an oval flameproof casserole large enough to fit the goose, then add the bird and colour on all sides.

Add the carrot, onion, celery, parsley, thyme and juniper berries and cook over a medium heat for 5 minutes, then pour in 300ml of the stock. Transfer to the oven and cook, uncovered, for 1½ hours, basting every 15 minutes with the cooking juices.

Meanwhile, prepare the stuffed cabbage balls. Blanch the largest dozen or so cabbage leaves for a minute, then drain, pat dry and lay out on a board. Blanch the bacon slices for a minute, then drain. Grease a medium-small roasting dish with the butter.

Mix the sausagemeat with the egg, season with salt and pepper, then divide between the cabbage leaves. Fold each leaf over to enclose the filling and create a small ball shape, and squeeze each lightly. Place in the buttered roasting dish, placing the bacon slices in between the balls.

Turn the carrots, turnips and potatoes to shape them into large olive shapes with a knife, or simply cut into chunks. Poach the cooking sausage in gently simmering water at 90°C for 30 minutes.

Meanwhile, pour 200ml of the stock over the cabbage balls and place the dish in the oven alongside the goose. Cook for 25 minutes.

Cook the carrots and turnips separately in some of the chicken stock over a medium heat for about 20 minutes, until tender. At the same time, cook the potatoes in lightly salted water for about 20 minutes until tender. Drain the vegetables and set aside to keep hot.

Once the goose is cooked, transfer it to a large dish, breast side down, partially cover with foil and set aside to rest in a warm place. Remove some of the fat from the roasting juices using a small ladle, then reduce the juices over a lively heat to a flavourful jus. Season to taste and strain.

Drain and slice the sausage. Untruss the goose and place on a large oval serving dish. Arrange all the vegetables around the goose, with the cabbage parcels, bacon pieces and sausage slices. Pour half of the jus over everything and serve the rest in a gravy boat. Carve the goose at the table.

Serves 6–8

1 ready-to-cook young goose, 3–4kg

100g lard or goose fat

1 large carrot, peeled and diced

1 large onion, peeled and diced

2 celery stalks, trimmed and diced

20g parsley stalks

Few thyme sprigs

10 juniper berries, crushed

1 litre chicken stock (page 248), or buy good-quality fresh stock

1 saucisson à cuire (cured cooking sausage), about 800g

Salt and freshly ground pepper

Stuffed cabbage balls

1 Savoy cabbage, leaves separated

250g piece of streaky bacon, cut into 12 slices

60g butter

250g sausagemeat

1 egg

Turned vegetables

2 large carrots, peeled

5 medium turnips, peeled

5 medium potatoes, peeled

Canard Rôti à l'Orange
ROAST DUCK WITH ORANGE

This prized dish is among the great classics of French cuisine. You need to invest a little time in its preparation, but it will reward you in return. I like serving it at Christmas, as it makes a lovely festive centrepiece. Depending on appetites, you may wish to cook two ducks, serving half a duck each.

Using a sharp knife, remove the wishbone from the duck, drawing back the skin at the neck end to locate it. Cut the wings off at the main joint and reserve with the wishbone. Season the inside of the duck; set aside.

Heat the clarified butter in a pan over a lively heat. Add the duck (or chicken) necks, wings and wishbone and cook, turning, until lightly coloured. Add the shallots with the sugar and cook, stirring occasionally, until they are a light caramel colour. Deglaze with the wine vinegar, stirring well to scrape up the sediment, and continue to stir for 1 minute over the heat.

Pour in the orange juice. As soon as it boils, lower the heat to medium and reduce the liquor by half. Add the stock and cook for 15 minutes at a bare simmer, skimming from time to time, until the sauce is thick enough to lightly coat the back of a spoon. Preheat the oven to 200°C/Gas 6.

Meanwhile, prepare the kumquats for the garnish. Rinse and pierce each one with a skewer in a few places. Dissolve the sugar in the water in a small pan and bring to the boil over a medium heat. Add the kumquats to the syrup, lower the heat and poach for 5 minutes. Set aside until almost cooled, then poach for a further 5 minutes, at a bare simmer. Set aside.

Strain the sauce through a fine chinois, season to taste, cover and keep warm.

Place the duck in a roasting tin. Cook in the oven for 25 minutes for pink, or 30 minutes for à point, lowering the setting to 180°C/Gas 4 after 10 minutes and basting the duck every 5–10 minutes.

Meanwhile, finely pare the zest from one of the oranges, using a swivel peeler, then cut into fine julienne. Blanch in boiling water for 2 minutes, then refresh in iced water. Segment the zested orange, discarding all pith and membrane; set aside. Use a zester to score several parallel grooves in the skin of the second orange, cut the orange in half, then cut each half into fine slices.

Once the duck is cooked to your liking, remove the thighs. Lay the duck breast side down on a plate, partially cover with foil and leave to rest in a warm place for 10 minutes. Return the thighs to the oven for 10 minutes.

To serve, thread the kumquats onto a small skewer. Place the duck on a serving dish and stick the skewer into its fleshy back end. Arrange the orange segments and half slices around the duck. Sprinkle the orange julienne on top, put the bunch of watercress into the cavity at the back end and pour on a little of the sauce. Pass the rest of the sauce around in a gravy boat.

Serves 4

1 duck, ideally Challans, about 1.8kg

200g duck necks and wings, chopped (or chicken if you can't find duck)

50g clarified butter (page 266)

80g shallots, peeled and thinly sliced

100g caster sugar

60ml red wine vinegar

400ml freshly squeezed orange juice

100ml veal stock (page 249) or chicken stock (page 248), or buy good-quality fresh stock

2 oranges

Salt and freshly ground pepper

To garnish

4 small kumquats

75g caster sugar

750ml water

Small bunch of watercress, stalks removed, washed

Cailles en Cocotte à la Vigneronne
CASSEROLE OF QUAILS WITH NOISETTE POTATOES

As this dish cooks, it will imbue your kitchen with heavenly aromas. Quails can often be more tender and succulent than chicken, and the cooking juices are so delicious – perfect for mopping up with bread.

Preheat the oven to 220°C/Gas 7. Wrap each quail in 2 vine leaves then a slice of barding fat. To hold these in place, tie kitchen string around each quail in two places, but not too tightly. Sprinkle lightly with salt.

Blanch the lardons for 1 minute, then drain. Heat half the oil with 20g of the butter in a flameproof casserole over a medium heat. Add the quails and brown them all over. Add the lardons, then a minute later add the carrot, celery, shallot, thyme and bay leaves. Cook for 2 minutes, then pour the Armagnac over the quails and flambé, using a long match to ignite it and standing well back.

When the flame has died down, place the casserole, uncovered, in the oven and cook for 12 minutes, turning the quails after 5 minutes. Once cooked, remove the string and untruss the quails, keeping the vine leaves and barding fat intact. Place breast side down on a plate, cover with foil and set aside in a warm place.

Scoop out the lardons and add to the quails. Put the casserole over the heat and deglaze with the wine. Reduce by one-third over a medium heat, then add the stock and simmer over a low heat for 6 minutes. Add salt and pepper to taste. Strain through a fine chinois, then pour back into the casserole.

Sprinkle the sugar into a non-stick frying pan and, over a lively heat, cook the sugar to a caramel. Immediately add the grapes and heat them in the caramel for 2–3 minutes, then add to the liquor in the casserole. Return the quails and lardons to the casserole and keep hot until ready to serve.

For the noisette potatoes, peel the potatoes and use a melon baller to scoop out balls. Blanch these in boiling salted water for 1 minute, then drain. Heat the remaining oil and butter in a frying pan, add the garlic and cook until coloured, then add the potato balls and cook for 6–8 minutes, stirring every 2 minutes. Keep warm.

To serve, put the casserole on the table. Serve one quail per person, moving the vine leaf aside a little to expose the breast, and cutting down the length of the breastbone so that your guests can remove the meat from the carcass more easily. Serve the noisette potatoes separately so that they stay crisp.

Serves 4

4 ready-to-cook quails, wishbone removed

8 vine leaves, ideally fresh, or from a jar, rinsed and dried

4 thin slices of barding fat (pork back fat)

100g semi-smoked belly pork, cut into small lardons

4 tbsp grapeseed oil

60g butter

1 medium carrot, peeled and diced

1 small celery stalk, diced

1 shallot, peeled and diced

1 thyme sprig

2 bay leaves

2 tbsp Armagnac

150ml red wine, ideally Pinot Noir

150ml chicken stock (page 248), or buy good-quality fresh stock, or use water

30g caster sugar

200g red or green grapes, peeled and deseeded

Salt and freshly ground pepper

Noisette potatoes

250g large potatoes

2 garlic cloves (unpeeled), smashed

Variation
Use small quarters of caramelised apple in place of the grapes, and cider or medium-sweet white rather than red wine to deglaze the casserole.

Grouse Rôtie, Pommes Soufflées
ROAST GROUSE WITH POTATO WAFFLE NESTS

Grouse is the king of all game. You could cut the preparation time here by 30 minutes by not making the pommes soufflées nests… but they are divine, so it's up to you. A full-bodied red from the Rhône Valley, such as a Châteauneuf-du-Pape or even a Madiran, would be wonderful with this dish.

For the farce à gratin, put the lard in a small frying pan and melt over a brisk heat. When it is very hot and melted, add the shallot, thyme and livers and cook for 20 seconds. Pour over the Cognac and flambé, using a long match to ignite it. When the flame has died down, add salt and pepper, then transfer to a bowl and leave to cool. When cool, pass the mixture through a fine sieve.

Preheat the oven to 200°C/Gas 6, for the grouse.

Cut 4 croûtons from the bread slices, ideally using a heart-shaped cutter. Toast the croûtons under the grill and, once cold, mound the farce à gratin onto each to cover them completely, forming a domed shape. Set aside.

Place the grouse in a roasting tin big enough to fit all 4 birds, sprinkle lightly with salt and roast in the oven for 20 minutes for very pink, 25 minutes for medium-rare and 30 minutes for well done. Baste them at least twice as they cook with the barding back fat (which will partially render as it cooks). Once cooked, remove the grouse from the oven and untruss them, then cover with foil and leave to rest in a warm place for 3–5 minutes.

Cook the Brussels sprouts in boiling salted water for 6–8 minutes.

Meanwhile, for the jus, gently heat the stock in a pan, then incorporate 30g of the butter, stirring all the time. Transfer to a sauceboat; keep warm.

Drain the sprouts. Heat the remaining 70g butter in a frying pan until hot and foaming, then add the sprouts and cook, stirring occasionally, for 10 minutes. Add salt and pepper to taste.

Reheat the farce à gratin croûtons in the warm oven for 5 minutes, or until heated through but not beginning to turn dry.

Meanwhile, for the polonaise, heat the butter in a frying pan. As it starts to foam, add the breadcrumbs and cook for 2–3 minutes, depending on whether you prefer it soft or crisp. Add the lemon juice and serve in a small warm dish.

Place a grouse on each plate and serve whole, but cutting into the breast with a very sharp knife to make the task, or the pleasure of enjoying the breast meat on the bone, easier. Add a warm farce à gratin croûton, some sprouts and a few watercress leaves, then serve at once with the potato waffle nests filled with pommes soufflées, if using, and the polonaise, bread sauce and jus on the side.

(Illustrated on previous page)

Serves 4

4 young grouse, wishbones removed, generously barded with very thin slices of back fat, trussed and ready to roast

250g Brussels sprouts, trimmed

100ml veal stock (page 249) or light game stock (page 250), or buy fresh stock

100g butter

½ bunch of watercress

Salt and freshly ground pepper

Farce à gratin croûtons

75g lard, cut into small dice

1 shallot (20g), peeled and chopped

1 thyme sprig

4 grouse livers or 2 large chicken livers

1 tbsp Cognac

2 slices of white bread

Polonaise

120g butter

100g fresh breadcrumbs

Juice of ½ lemon

To serve

Potato waffle nests (see right), optional

Souffléed potatoes (page 201), optional

Bread sauce, ½ quantity (page 253)

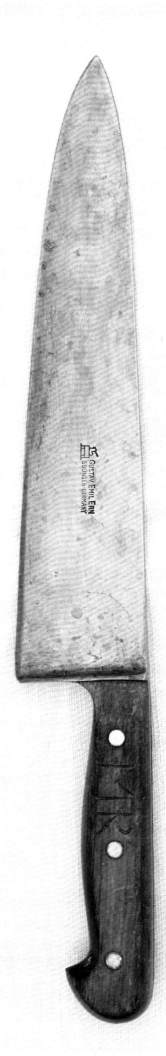

Nids de Gaufrettes

POTATO WAFFLE NESTS

Peel 250g potatoes (suitable for frying, such as Agria or Lovers), then rinse under cold water. Slice lengthways using a mandoline fitted with the julienne blade, giving a quarter-turn between each slice to give a waffle effect. You will need 24 waffle slices in total to make 4 nests.

Heat 1 litre grapeseed or groundnut oil in a deep fryer to 160°C.

Cut each waffle slice using an oval pastry cutter, about 5 x 7cm, rinse in cold water and pat dry between sheets of kitchen paper. Arrange 5 waffle slices inside a *moule à frire* (small wire basker mould), from the base towards and up the sides, overlapping one over another, then place another waffle slice in the base of the mould. Place the top of the *moule à frire* on top of the waffle slices so the nest stays intact as it cooks.

Immerse in the hot oil for 2–3 minutes, until the potatoes have taken on a good colour. Remove from the oil and lift off the top. Gently remove the potato waffle nest from the mould and set aside in a warm place while you repeat the process to make a further 3 nests.

(Illustrated on page 135)

Chartreuse de Faisan
PHEASANT CHARTREUSE

This is a flagship dish of French cuisine that I love preparing for friends. The classic recipe is made in a round dish but I do it in a rectangular or oval dish for ease of serving. You need time and patience, but it isn't a costly dish to make and you can prepare some of the components a few hours in advance of assembling. Use your artistic flair when cutting and arranging the vegetables so they look attractive when the dish is served. A game jus (page 267) can be served on the side if you like, although the dish is succulent enough without it.

Using a large knife, cut the cabbage into quarters and remove the outer, darker green leaves. Cook the cabbage quarters in a large pan of boiling salted water for 5 minutes, then refresh and drain well.

Heat 1½ tbsp of the oil in a sauté pan over a lively heat, add the 6 pieces of pheasant and cook, turning, until coloured all over. Remove from the pan and set aside. Preheat the oven to 200°C/Gas 6.

Season the hen pheasant lightly with salt. Place in the same sauté pan over a medium heat and colour evenly on all sides, then transfer to the oven and cook for 20 minutes. Set aside for 5 minutes, then remove the legs and breasts. Using a large, heavy knife, cut the carcass into 3 or 4 pieces. Set aside with the 6 browned pieces.

Cut each pheasant breast into 3 pieces and the legs into 2 pieces. Bone the thighs and reserve the drumsticks with the carcass and browned pheasant pieces. Wrap the breast and thigh meat in foil and set aside. Lower the oven temperature to 160°C/Gas 3.

Remove the core from the outside leaves of the cabbage quarters, then heat the duck or goose fat or lard in an ovenproof pan, add the cabbage and colour lightly. Arrange the pieces of the older pheasant and the drumsticks and the carcass pieces from the younger one among the cabbage quarters and season lightly with salt. Cover and cook in the oven for 1 hour, turning the cabbage every 20 minutes, until it is braised and has absorbed the pheasant flavours. Increase the oven temperature to 180°C/Gas 4.

Using a swivel peeler, peel the carrot and turnip, then using a mandoline or fine blade knife, slice both into 2–3mm strips. Cut each strip into rectangles about 4 x 6cm. Blanch the carrot for 3 minutes and the turnip for 2 minutes in boiling salted water, then refresh and set aside on a plate.

Cook the Morteau sausage in barely simmering water for 30–40 minutes, depending on its thickness. Drain, then remove the skin and cut the sausage into slices 3mm thick. Set aside on a plate.

Serves 4

1 Savoy cabbage, about 700g

2 tbsp grapeseed oil

2 pheasants, 1 older bird cut into 6 pieces and the other younger, preferably a hen, barded and ready to roast

100g duck or goose fat, or lard

1 large carrot

1 large turnip, preferably a long variety

1 Morteau sausage

4 Toulouse sausages

30g clarified butter (page 266), melted

Salt and freshly ground pepper

Heat the remaining oil in a frying pan and brown the Toulouse sausages over a medium heat for 5–6 minutes, turning so they colour evenly, then cut them into 4mm thick slices. Set aside on a plate.

To assemble the chartreuse, line the sides and base of an oval or rectangular terrine mould or dish, about 24cm long, 14cm wide and 8cm deep, with cling film, leaving a generous overhang. Place the carrot and turnip rectangles alternately with the hen pheasant pieces and both types of sausage slices across the base and sides, using the breast meat first and then the thigh.

Fill the middle of the dish with the braised cabbage (discard the pheasant pieces they were cooked with) and add pepper to taste. Pressing firmly on the cabbage, adjust the pheasant and sausage slices so that all the ingredients stick together well. Bring the excess cling film up over the terrine to cover well. Cover with foil, then place in a roasting dish.

Pour enough just-boiled water into the roasting dish to come two-thirds of the way up the sides of the terrine, and cook in the oven for 1 hour. Remove from the oven and keep warm until ready to serve, at most 20 minutes.

To serve, remove the foil and open up the cling film. Place an oval serving dish on top of the dish and, using a tea towel to protect your hands, invert the dish and unmould the chartreuse onto the serving dish. Remove all the cling film, then brush a little clarified butter all over the surface of the terrine, to add shine. Serve immediately; this is not a dish that can sit around.

Variations

You can replace the pheasant with partridges, or even wild pigeons. The chartreuse can also be made with just vegetables, using celeriac and potatoes (boiled first) in place of the meat. In this case, caramelise some sliced onions and use with the cabbage.

Perdreaux Lautrec PARTRIDGE LAUTREC

This was created in honour of the great French painter and printmaker of the end of the 19th century, Toulouse-Lautrec. He was loved and admired by the inhabitants of Paris, in particular of Montmartre, and the dish's creation was a tribute paid to him by a chef of the period. Serve a green vegetable on the side, such as French beans or spinach.

Push 2 metal skewers diagonally through each flattened out partridge, entering through the plump part of the thigh and coming out through the top of the opposite wing, to keep the partridge flat.

For the Maître d'hôtel butter, mix the butter with the parsley and lemon juice and season with a little salt and pepper.

Preheat a ridged griddle pan or light a barbecue.

Using a brush, daub oil over the birds, sprinkle lightly with salt and cook over a medium heat, on the griddle or barbecue, for 8–10 minutes on each side, depending on whether you like them pink or medium-rare, giving them a quarter-turn every 2–3 minutes to achieve a criss-cross pattern.

Once cooked, cover with foil and set aside to rest for 5 minutes. Lightly oil the mushrooms and cook on the griddle or barbecue for 1–2 minutes on each side, then transfer to a dish and dot with the flavoured butter.

Gently warm the stock. Using a tea towel to protect your hands, remove the skewers from the birds and place them flat on warm serving plates. Grind a little pepper over them and pour the stock in a circle around the birds. Arrange the hot mushrooms on the plates, squeeze a little lemon juice over each and serve at once.

Serves 3

3 young partridges, split open down the
   back with a pair of kitchen scissors
   and lightly flattened

75ml grapeseed or groundnut oil

9 medium button mushroom caps

4 tbsp veal or feathered game stock,
   such as pheasant or partridge (page
   250), or buy good-quality fresh stock

1½ lemons

Salt and freshly ground pepper

Maître d'hôtel butter

75g butter, softened

10g flat-leaf parsley, chopped

Juice of ½ lemon

Variation

When figs are in season in September and October and bursting with flavour they are a delicious addition to this dish. Cut a few fresh figs into 4 or 6 wedges and cook in the oven (preheated to 200°C/Gas 6) alongside the whole partridges for 15–20 minutes, adding a sprinkling of port as they come out of the oven.

Lapin Sauté à la Moutarde
SAUTÉED RABBIT IN MUSTARD

In this lovely dish, the mustard permeates into the rabbit meat as it cooks, losing its strength but keeping its taste, and lending a beautifully mellow depth of flavour to the rabbit. This is one of my favourite dishes from my childhood; we ate any leftovers cold the following day with an escarole salad.

Preheat the oven to 220°C/Gas 7.

Heat 60g of the clarified butter in a flameproof casserole over a medium heat. Lightly salt the rabbit pieces, add to the casserole and cook until evenly browned all over. Remove to a wire rack and set aside for 4–6 minutes.

Meanwhile, blanch the vegetables separately: the carrots for 1 minute; celeriac for 3 minutes; white onions for 2 minutes. Add the carrots, celeriac, garlic, onions and thyme to the same casserole and sweat for 3 minutes.

Meanwhile, blanch the tomato for 1 minute, deseed and cut into fine slivers, then add to the casserole and cook for a further 2 minutes.

Using a brush, daub the rabbit pieces generously on all sides with the Dijon mustard, then sprinkle breadcrumbs all over. Place the rabbit pieces in the casserole on top of the sweated vegetables and transfer to the oven. Cook, uncovered, for 15 minutes.

Take the casserole and lift out all the rabbit pieces except the thighs. Put the casserole back in the oven and cook the thighs for a further 5 minutes. Meanwhile, blanch the mangetout for 2 minutes.

Remove the casserole from the oven and add the mangetout, with the reserved pieces of rabbit. Stir lightly with a wooden spoon so that the vegetables underneath are mixed with the rabbit. Remove the thyme, taste and adjust the seasoning. Sprinkle the snipped tarragon over the top.

If serving the rabbit liver and kidneys, cut the liver into 4 pieces and halve the kidneys. Cook them in a frying pan with the remaining, very hot clarified butter for 15 seconds, turning after 5 seconds. Season lightly with salt and transfer to a small bowl.

Bring the rabbit casserole to the table. Serve the liver and kidneys separately on the side.

Serves 4

80g clarified butter (page 266)

1 farmed rabbit, about 1.5kg, cut into 8 pieces (reserving the liver and kidneys separately, optional)

2 carrots, peeled and cut into batons

1 medium celeriac, peeled and cut into 8 half-moon segments

8 small white onions, peeled

4 garlic cloves (unpeeled), halved

2 thyme sprigs

1 ripe, medium tomato

100g strong Dijon mustard

30g fresh, fine white breadcrumbs

100g mangetout, trimmed

1 tbsp snipped tarragon leaves

Salt and freshly ground pepper

Variation

The rabbit can be cooked as for *blanquette de veau*, in a sauce made with one-third dry white wine and two-thirds chicken stock over a gentle heat for about 1½ hours. Replace the carrot, celeriac and tomato with button mushrooms. Double the quantity of small onions and omit the mangetout. Thicken the sauce with cream and egg yolk off the heat just before serving. Serve with spinach, lightly cooked in butter.

Selle de Chevreuil, Sauce Grand Veneur ROAST SADDLE OF VENISON

This is one of the most regal of game dishes – intensely flavoured but with a delicate finesse. A Côte Rôtie Syrah from the Rhône Valley, with its spiced notes, would be a perfect match. The sauce poivrade can be made a day ahead.

Put the venison saddle and all the marinade ingredients in a container large enough to fit everything. Turn to coat the meat with the marinade, then cover with cling film and refrigerate for 2 hours.

Using a large kitchen fork or tongs, remove the saddle from the marinade, pat dry with a tea towel, wrap in cling film and put back in the fridge. Leave everything else in the marinade for a further 6 hours.

Preheat the oven to 200°C/Gas 6.

To make the sauce poivrade, strain the marinade through a sieve placed over a large dish, reserving all the flavouring ingredients in the sieve. Put the grapeseed oil in a roasting tin, add the bones from the marinade and transfer to the oven to brown for 40 minutes, turning them every 10 minutes.

Heat the clarified butter in a frying pan over a high heat, add the diced vegetables from the marinade and cook until lightly caramelised. Add the wine vinegar and stir to deglaze then, after 1 minute, add the marinade liquid and reduce by half.

Tip into a saucepan and add the browned game bones, both bouquet garnis (one from the marinade), the cracked white peppercorns and game or chicken stock. Bring to the boil, then lower the heat and cook at a bare simmer for 1 hour, skimming the surface from time to time.

Strain the sauce through a fine chinois, return to the pan and reduce by one-third. When it has reduced enough to coat the back of a ladle, strain again through a chinois and set aside until needed.

Increase the oven temperature to 220°C/Gas 7.

Put the venison saddle in a roasting tin, brush the surface liberally with the clarified butter and sprinkle lightly with salt. Cook in the oven, allowing 25 minutes for rare, or up to 35 minutes for *à point*, turning the saddle halfway through cooking.

While the saddle is in the oven, prepare the chestnut purée (see overleaf). Once the venison is cooked, transfer it to a wire rack set over a plate to catch any juices and set aside to rest in a warm place, loosely covered with foil.

(continued overleaf)

Serves 6–8

1 venison saddle, about 2kg, skin and
   membrane removed

40g clarified butter (page 266)

Salt and freshly ground white pepper

Marinade

500ml red wine

50ml red wine vinegar

1 tbsp groundnut oil

1 medium carrot, peeled and diced

½ medium onion, peeled and diced

1 small celery stalk, diced

1 small bouquet garni

1 clove

2 unpeeled garlic cloves, bashed

10 white peppercorns, cracked

400g game bones, preferably venison,
   cut into small pieces

Sauce poivrade

30ml grapeseed oil

40g clarified butter (page 266)

30ml red wine vinegar

1 medium bouquet garni

10 white peppercorns, cracked

600ml game stock (page 250) or chicken
   stock (page 248), or buy fresh stock

For the chestnut purée, put the chestnuts in a pan with the chicken stock. Bring to the boil and cook for 3–4 minutes. Add the cream and cook over a gentle heat for a further 3–4 minutes. Season with a little salt and white pepper and transfer to a food processor or blender. Process for 2 minutes, to a smooth purée. Keep warm in a bain-marie until needed.

For the Grand Veneur sauce, heat the sauce poivrade and add any juices from the resting meat. As soon as it boils, whisk in the redcurrant jelly and cream. Simmer for 2–3 minutes, then add salt and white pepper to taste.

To serve, slice the venison saddle on a carving board at the table, using a very sharp knife. Arrange on warm plates and serve the chestnut purée, Dauphine potatoes and Grand Veneur sauce separately.

Variations

Before roasting you can stud the saddle with small lardons, soaked first in cognac. The venison can be served without the sauce: cook it on a bed of diced carrot and onion, with thyme, bay and juniper berries, add 100ml each of red wine and water, plus a dab of redcurrant jelly, to the deglazing juices. This is quicker and results in a very digestible, though less indulgent sauce. An accompaniment of seasonal wild mushrooms, or button mushrooms, sautéed in a frying pan with shallots and parsley, can be served on the side.

Chestnut purée

150g cooked chestnuts, tinned or
    vacuum packed
100ml chicken stock (page 248), or
    buy good-quality fresh stock
100ml whipping cream

Sauce Grand Veneur

1 tbsp redcurrant jelly, melted
1 tbsp double cream

To serve

Dauphine potatoes (page 200)

Daube de Sanglier WILD BOAR STEW

The success of this dish, much appreciated by game lovers, lies in selecting a boar between 6 months and a year old; an older animal, between 2 and 4 years, will not have the same flavour or be as tender. The choice of vegetables is a matter of individual taste, but personally I adore celeriac as an accompaniment, and I can't resist Lyonnaise potatoes…

Trim the wild boar of sinew and excess fat, then cut into roughly 3cm cubes.

For the marinade, cut the vegetables into mirepoix (2–3cm cubes). Heat the olive oil in a pan over a medium heat, add the carrot, onions, celery and garlic and sweat for 5 minutes. Add the wine and the remaining ingredients (do not add salt). Bring to the boil, then reduce the heat to low and simmer gently for 45 minutes. Strain through a fine chinois into a bowl and leave to cool.

Put the pieces of wild boar into a large bowl or dish. Pour over the cooled marinade, cover with cling film and place in the fridge for 3 hours. After this time, strain through a colander, reserving the marinade. Pat dry the cubes of wild boar with a tea towel and salt lightly. Heat the olive oil in a frying pan over a lively heat, add the wild boar and colour on all sides.

Put the pork rind fat side down in the base of a flameproof casserole, add the wild boar and pour over the marinade and stock. Bring to the boil over a lively heat and, as soon as it boils, reduce to a gentle heat and cook, uncovered, at about 90°C, for 45 minutes.

Meanwhile, put the celeriac wedges in a sauté pan with the butter and lemon juice, cover with a little cold water, salt very lightly and cook over a medium heat for 35–40 minutes.

In the meantime, peel the potatoes and cut into 5mm slices. Heat the olive oil in a frying pan, add the potato slices and cook, stirring every 5 minutes or so, for 20 minutes, then add the onion and a little salt and pepper. Cook for a further 15 minutes, stirring occasionally, until nicely golden and cooked. Once cooked, keep the celeriac and potatoes warm.

Remove the wild boar from the casserole to a plate, cover and keep hot. Strain the cooking juices through a fine chinois into a pan and reduce over a lively heat until the sauce coats the back of a spoon. Add the boar back to the sauce and heat through for 2–3 minutes, without letting it boil. Transfer to a large, shallow serving dish and arrange the celeriac around the edge. Sprinkle the Lyonnaise potatoes with the parsley and serve separately.

NOTE The orange zest should be dried in a low oven at 100°C/Gas ¼ for 6 hours to intensify the flavour.

Serves 4

1.2kg fillet of young wild boar

50ml light olive oil

250g pork rind

200ml veal stock (page 249)

Salt and freshly ground pepper

Marinade

1 carrot, peeled

2 medium onions, peeled

1 celery stalk

50ml light olive oil

3 garlic cloves (unpeeled)

750ml red wine, preferably Languedoc or Roussillon

20 black or white peppercorns, crushed

10 juniper berries, crushed

1 medium bouquet garni

Dried pared zest of 1 orange (see note)

Lyonnaise potatoes and celeriac

1 celeriac, peeled and cut into 8 wedges

100g butter

Juice of ½ lemon

750g potatoes

50ml light olive oil

1 onion, peeled and thinly sliced

10g flat-leaf parsley, chopped

Meat

Tournedos Rossini

Properly executed, this is a French gastronomy beef dish *par excellence*. It was originally created by the famous Parisian chef Marie-Antoine Carême for the Italian opera composer Rossini. It comprises a fillet steak cut from the centre of the tenderloin (*tournedos*), fried in butter and served on a bread croûte. Topped with a slice of hot foie gras and slivers of black truffle, the steak is accompanied by an exquisite truffle sauce.

Have the fillet steaks ready at room temperature.

For the croûtes, from the bread slices, cut 4 rounds, 6cm in diameter, and 4 triangles, about 8cm tall and 4cm across the base. Heat 150g of the clarified butter in a frying pan over a medium heat. Fry the bread rounds for 1 minute on each side until golden, then remove to a plate lined with kitchen paper to drain. Repeat with the bread triangles. Set the croûtes aside.

Bring the sauce périgourdine to the boil in a saucepan, then add the chopped truffles and remove from the heat. Cover and set aside to infuse. Just before serving, reheat the sauce very gently, add the 20g butter and agitate the pan in a forwards and backwards motion to incorporate the butter.

Heat the remaining clarified butter in a frying pan over a medium heat. Season the steaks lightly with salt, add to the pan and cook on both sides and around the edge for about 4 minutes in total for rare or 6 minutes for *à point*. Transfer to a rack and set aside to rest in a warm place while you cook the foie gras.

Heat a dry frying pan, preferably non-stick, over a medium heat. Sprinkle the foie gras slices with salt and cook for 1–2 minutes on each side, until golden on the outside and still lightly pink in the middle. Using a fish slice, transfer to a plate lined with kitchen paper and season with pepper.

To serve, lay a croûte on each plate and place a steak on top. Add a light grinding of pepper, then place a foie gras slice on each steak and top with a truffle sliver. Dip the bases of the triangular croûtes in the sauce périgourdine and stand upright on the plates, next to the steaks. Pour a spoonful of sauce on top of each steak and serve straight away, with the rest of the sauce in a sauceboat. Salsify is a delicious winter accompaniment.

Variation

In summer, I love a simply grilled or pan-fried *tournedos*, served not with a sauce but alongside a ratatouille – a velvety rich and delicious accompaniment just bursting with Mediterranean flavours (see page 199). And, of course, I like to serve it all with a glass of chilled Provençal rosé.

Serves 4

4 fillet steaks, 180–200g each (cut from the centre of the fillet)

½ good-quality thin-sliced white sandwich loaf

200g clarified butter (page 266)

100ml sauce périgourdine (page 251)

40g black truffles, finely chopped, plus 4 good slivers, ideally raw

20g butter

4 slices foie gras, about 70g each

Salt and freshly ground pepper

Filet de Boeuf à la Bisontine

In this superb classic recipe, the meat is threaded with pieces of lard, which keeps it succulent as it cooks, and the tongue, or ham, which contributes a subtle, barely definable flavour. Slices of black truffle can also be used in the same way, for a sublime flavour. The beef is accompanied by little potato nests filled with cauliflower purée and braised chicory.

Using a larding needle threaded with a baton of back fat and starting at one end, pierce into the side of the fillet to a depth of 1cm and round the edge of the fillet, emerging after 3cm, and leaving a 1.5cm length of fat at both the needle's place of entry and exit. Continue in the same way around the fillet, alternating with the batons of tongue and leaving a 2cm space between each. Once the row is complete around the fillet, start a second row, staggering the strips of fat and tongue with the first row. Continue until the fillet is barded along its entire length. Place on a dish, cover with cling film and refrigerate.

For the potato nests, generously butter 4 tartlet moulds, 8cm diameter, with the softened butter, then chill for 15 minutes. Preheat the oven to 180°C/ Gas 4. Place a scoop of Duchesse potato (30–40g), in each mould, then use your thumb to flatten it onto the insides of the mould, up to the top of the rim.

Stand the moulds on a baking sheet and cook in the oven for 15 minutes, until lightly coloured. If any are puffed up, place an empty tart mould on top and press down lightly. Let cool until just warm, then carefully unmould the potato cases, with the help of a small palette knife. Place on a wire rack; keep warm.

Heat the clarified butter in a frying pan (ideally ovenproof), over a medium heat. Season the fillet of beef with salt and colour in the pan on all sides for 3 minutes. Transfer the pan to the oven (or transfer to a roasting tin) and cook for 15 minutes for rare and 20 minutes for à point, basting the fillet with the cooking juices and turning it over after 8 minutes.

Transfer the fillet to a wire rack, partially cover with foil and leave to rest for 5–10 minutes. Meanwhile, skim off most of the fat from the pan and deglaze with 50ml water. Reduce by half and strain this (tiny drizzle of) jus through a sieve into a small pan.

Fill the potato cases with the hot cauliflower purée. To serve, cut generous slices of fillet and serve with the jus trickled over each slice. Garnish with chervil and accompany with the cauliflower purée-filled potato cases and braised chicory.

Serves 4

150g pork back fat, derinded and cut into small batons, 5–6cm long

1 fillet of beef, centre cut, about 800g trimmed weight

120g pickled beef tongue (preferably) or cooked ham, cut into small batons, 5–6cm long

50g clarified butter (page 266)

Salt

Chervil sprigs, to garnish

To serve

40g butter, softened

150g Duchess potatoes (page 200)

½ quantity cauliflower purée (freshly prepared and hot, page 187)

4 braised chicory (freshly prepared with out orange juice and hot, page 188)

Daube de Boeuf à la Beaujolaise

This is an ideal family dish; the wine cooks for long enough to leave no trace of alcohol, so children can enjoy it too. It is also delicious prepared with sections of flavourful oxtail.

Cut the beef into roughly 4cm cubes. Put all the marinade ingredients into a large dish, add the cubes of beef, cover and refrigerate for at least 12 hours.

Drain the meat in a sieve placed over a dish, to catch the liquor, then pat the beef pieces dry, reserving all the flavouring ingredients in the sieve. Preheat the oven to 150°C/Gas 2.

Heat 70g of the clarified butter in a frying pan over a lively heat. Brown the beef in batches, on all sides, salt lightly and place in a flameproof casserole. When it is all browned, pour the Cognac into the pan and flambé with a long match, standing well back. When the flame has died down, sprinkle in the roasted flour, stir with a wooden spoon, then pour the reserved liquor and stock over the meat. Add the calf's foot, if using, and the bouquet garni from the marinade, then bring to the boil over a medium heat, stirring occasionally.

Meanwhile, in the frying pan used to fry the beef, sweat the reserved vegetables from the marinade for 3 minutes, then add to the casserole. When it comes to the boil, put the lid on and cook in the oven for 3 hours.

In the meantime, gently boil the potatoes in salted water for 15–20 minutes, until just cooked. Take off the heat and set aside, in their cooking water. In another pan, heat another 30g clarified butter over a medium heat, then add the baby onions and sugar. As soon as they have coloured lightly, cover with a little cold water and cook over a low heat for 20 minutes. Remove from the heat and set aside in their cooking water.

Blanch the lardons and drain. Heat another 30g clarified butter in a frying pan, add the lardons and cook for 2 minutes, then remove from the pan and drain on kitchen paper. In another frying pan, heat the 60g butter, add the mushrooms and lemon juice and cook until the mushrooms give out their liquid, about 5 minutes, stirring occasionally. Set aside in a bowl.

Cut 6 triangles from the bread slices. Heat the remaining 70g clarified butter in a frying pan, add the bread triangles and cook for 30–60 seconds, until golden. Turn and brown the other side, then set aside on kitchen paper.

When the daube is cooked, remove the bouquet garni, garlic and calf's foot, if used, and skim off excess fat from the surface, if necessary. Drain the onions and add to the daube with the lardons and mushrooms. Simmer over a medium heat for 3–5 minutes, then adjust the seasoning with salt and pepper.

Pour the contents of the casserole into a very large tureen or deep serving dish. Arrange the potatoes around the edge and place the croûtons over the surface of the daube. Sprinkle with chopped parsley and serve.

Serves 6

1.4kg beef cheeks, chuck or skirt steak, trimmed of sinew and excess fat

200g clarified butter (page 266)

100ml Cognac

50g roasted plain flour (see page 267)

1 litre veal stock (page 249)

½ calf's foot, blanched (optional)

12 small new potatoes, peeled

18 baby onions, peeled

Pinch of sugar

300g belly pork, with plenty of fat layers, rind removed, cut into large lardons

60g butter

18 button mushrooms, wiped clean

Juice of ½ lemon

3 medium-thick slices of white sandwich loaf

20g flat-leaf parsley, finely chopped

Salt and freshly ground pepper

Marinade

1 large onion, peeled and cut into mirepoix (2–3cm cubes)

1 large carrot, cut into mirepoix (2–3cm cubes)

½ head of garlic, cut in half horizontally

1 medium bouquet garni

6 black peppercorns, crushed

1.5 litres red wine, ideally Beaujolais

30ml light olive oil

Escalopines de Veau Normande

This was always a favourite dish of our mother, who was herself from Normandy. The marriage of apple, veal, cream and Calvados is simply sublime. Spinach subrics served alongside will further enhance this great classic, from one of the most beautiful regions of France.

Peel the apples with a swivel peeler and remove the cores using an apple corer, reserving the peelings and core. Cut each apple into 8 segments, put into a bowl, add half the lemon juice and mix to coat the slices.

Melt 40g of the butter in a saucepan over a medium heat, add the apple segments with the sugar and cook, stirring, for 5–6 minutes, until golden; they should be cooked but still with a slight crunch. Set aside in a bowl in a warm place.

Put another 30g of the butter in the same pan, add the shallots and sweat over a gentle heat, then add the apple peelings and cores. After 3 minutes, pour in the Calvados and flambé with a long match, standing well back. When the flame has died down, add the stock and cook over a medium heat for 5 minutes. Add the cream and let bubble for 5 minutes, then strain through a fine chinois and add salt and pepper to taste. Keep hot.

Heat another 40g butter in a frying pan over a medium heat until melted and foaming. Add the mushrooms and remaining lemon juice. Salt lightly and cook, stirring, for several minutes until the mushroom juices have evaporated. Transfer to a bowl.

Heat the clarified butter in a large frying pan over a lively heat. Season the veal escalopes lightly on both sides with salt and pan-fry over a high heat for 1 minute on each side for rare, or 1 minute 30 seconds for *à point*. Transfer to a wire rack placed over a dish.

To serve, place 2 veal escalopes and a few watercress leaves on each plate, then arrange the mushrooms in a small mound and the apples in a semi-circle around the meat. Pour half the sauce over the meat and offer the rest in a sauceboat. Serve at once, with the spinach subrics separately on a plate.

Serves 4

2 slightly tart, firm apples, such as Cox or Gala

Juice of 1 lemon

110g butter

2 generous pinches of caster sugar

2 shallots, peeled and thinly sliced

50ml young and fruity Calvados

100ml chicken stock (page 248), or buy good-quality fresh stock

75ml double cream

250g small button mushrooms, wiped clean

60g clarified butter (page 266)

8 veal escalopes, 5–7mm thick, preferably cut from a boned rack of veal

Salt and freshly ground pepper

To serve

½ bunch of watercress, trimmed

8 spinach subrics with mushrooms (page 192), optional

Carré de Veau Orloff VEAL ORLOFF

This is an extremely distinguished dish, dating back to the 19th century and created by the great chef Urbain Dubois, who was in Prince Orloff's service. A Pinot Noir wine, such as a Nuits-Saint-Georges or Vosnes-Romanée would be an excellent choice to serve with this magnificent dish.

For the duxelle, trim the mushroom stalks with a small knife and wipe the mushrooms with a damp cloth. Chop finely on a board, using a large knife. Melt the butter in a frying pan over a medium heat, then add the mushrooms and lemon juice. Season lightly with salt and cook, stirring from time to time with a wooden spoon, until the mushroom juices evaporate and produce a 'dry duxelle'. Set aside on a plate covered with cling film, pierced in several places with the tip of a knife.

For the soubise, cut the onions into very thin slices and blanch for 3 minutes, then drain but don't refresh. Melt the butter in a pan, add the onions and sweat over a medium heat for 6–7 minutes without letting them colour, stirring with a wooden spoon every minute or so. Add the water and a pinch of salt, cover with a lid and cook over a gentle heat until the onions are soft and cooked down completely, about 30 minutes. Transfer to a food mixer and blend for 2 minutes, to give a nicely smooth and homogeneous purée. Set aside in a bowl covered with cling film, pierced in several places with the tip of a knife.

For the béchamel, melt the butter in a pan over a gentle heat, then add the flour and stir with a balloon whisk. Cook the roux for 2 minutes, then stir in the milk and bring to the boil, stirring constantly with the whisk. Lower the heat and cook at a simmer for 3 minutes, stirring all the time. Remove from the heat and whisk in the egg yolks. Add salt and pepper to taste and set aside in a bowl covered with cling film, pierced in several places with the tip of a knife. Preheat the oven to 180°C/Gas 4.

Brush the veal all over with the grapeseed oil and sprinkle lightly with salt. Place a roasting tin over a medium heat, add the veal rack and brown on all sides. Transfer to the oven and roast for 1 hour, basting with the cooking juices and turning the rack over every 15 minutes.

Meanwhile, turn the carrots with a knife into large olive shapes, place in a pan and add a little cold water to just cover them. Add 50g of the butter and a small pinch of salt and cook, uncovered, over a medium heat until the water evaporates. Set aside with a lid on, to keep warm.

Blanch the lettuces whole for 2 minutes, then refresh in cold water and drain. Cut into quarters and press down on them to extract any water. Melt the remaining 100g butter in a large frying pan over a medium heat, add the lettuces and increase the heat so that they colour lightly, then sprinkle very

(continued overleaf)

Serves 8–10

1 rack of veal, with 5 ribs, trimmed of sinew and excess fat, bones cut back and scraped (2.5–3kg prepared weight)

2 tbsp grapeseed oil

4 medium carrots, peeled

150g butter

3 large, firm lettuces

50g Parmesan, freshly grated

1 large black truffle, ideally fresh, about 80g, brushed, trimmed and cut into fine slivers

Salt and freshly ground pepper

Duxelle

800g firm button mushrooms

50g butter

Juice of ½ lemon

Soubise

1.5kg large onions, peeled

150g butter

150ml water

Béchamel

15g butter

20g plain flour

200ml milk

3 egg yolks

lightly with salt and turn them over using a palette knife to colour the other side. Transfer to a plate and cover with cling film, pierced with a knife tip.

Once cooked, set the rack of veal aside in a warm place to rest, covered loosely with foil.

Mix half the onion soubise with the mushroom duxelle. Mix the béchamel with the remaining soubise and add the grated Parmesan. Preheat the oven grill.

On a board, use a very sharp knife to cut the meat from the rack of veal, in one piece (it should be pink in the middle) but leaving a 5mm thickness of meat at either end (which will hold the replaced slices of veal in place, like bookends). Slice the removed piece of meat into 1cm thick slices.

Cover one of the end pieces of meat still on the rack with some duxelle and place 2 truffle slivers on the duxelle. Cover the first slice of meat generously with duxelle, then stick the slice against the end piece, with the uncovered side against the truffle slices. Put 2 truffle slivers on the duxelle of the first slice, then place the next slice of meat against this, with duxelle spread on the other side, and continue until all the slices are replaced on the bones between the end slices, with duxelle and truffle slivers between each, and so that the rack is now back in its original form.

Preheat the oven grill. Slide the rack onto a baking tray and coat generously with the béchamel-soubise mixture. Place under the hot grill for 1–2 minutes, until nicely glazed and lightly browned.

Either serve the veal from its original roasting dish or transfer to an oval platter. Spoon the glazed carrots and braised lettuces around the veal and serve at the table, giving one duxelle- and truffle-covered slice to each guest.

Côtelettes d'Agneau à la Rouennaise

LAMB CUTLETS ROUEN STYLE

This delicious regional dish has its origins in the famous Rouen duck with duck liver sauce. It is the sauce that contributes the somewhat rustic character, as it is thickened with chicken livers and imbued with the flavours of Calvados, onions and shallots. Fondant potatoes (page 201) and simply boiled green beans would be ideal accompaniments.

For the croûtes, using a heart-shaped cutter, stamp out 4 hearts from the bread slices. Heat the clarified butter in a frying pan over a medium heat and, as soon as it is nice and hot, add the pieces of bread. Turn them after 45–60 seconds, and once they turn golden on the other side, transfer to a tray lined with kitchen paper and set aside.

Reduce the stock by one-third in a wide pan set over a medium heat.

Heat 40g of the butter in a saucepan over a gentle heat, then add the onions and shallots and sweat for 2 minutes, stirring. Season lightly with salt and set aside in a bowl.

Heat the grapeseed oil in a sauté pan over a high heat. Season the lamb cutlets very lightly with salt, then add to the pan and cook for 2 minutes. Turn them over and cook for a further 2 minutes for pink, or 3 minutes for *à point*. Transfer to a small wire rack placed over a large plate, cover with foil and keep warm. Mix the sieved livers with the Calvados.

Tip off most of the fat from the sauté pan, then deglaze with the reduced stock, add the onions and shallots and cook over a lively heat for 5 minutes. Remove from the heat and, immediately, use a small balloon whisk to incorporate the liver and Calvados mixture. Mix in the remaining 20g butter, and add salt and pepper to taste. Keep the sauce hot, without letting it boil, until ready to serve.

Put the watercress bunch in the middle of a round, shallow serving dish. Sprinkle lightly with salt, then arrange the lamb cutlets around the watercress, with the bones pointing towards the middle to meet in a crown shape. Pour a generous serving of sauce over the cutlets, then arrange the croûtes towards the top of the cutlet bones and serve at once.

Serves 4

150ml veal stock (page 249) or chicken stock (page 248), or buy good-quality fresh stock

60g butter

100g onions, peeled and finely chopped

50g shallots, peeled and finely chopped

2½ tbsp grapeseed oil

8 lamb cutlets, loin or neck end, fat trimmed and bones scraped clean

4 chicken livers, chopped, then pushed through a fine sieve

2 tbsp Calvados

Salt and freshly ground pepper

Croûtes

4 thin slices of white sandwich loaf

60g clarified butter (page 266)

To serve

Small bunch of watercress, stalks removed, washed

Carré d'Agneau Rôti à la Niçoise

ROAST RACK OF LAMB WITH NIÇOISE VEGETABLES

A dish full of Mediterranean flavours – delectable, light and bursting with sunshine – as well as quick and easy to prepare.

Preheat the oven to 200°C/Gas 6. Tie the rack of lamb in 5 or 6 places to hold it in shape and brush all over with some of the clarified butter. Heat a frying pan over a medium heat and colour the meat on all sides. Transfer to a roasting dish.

Heat the remaining clarified butter in the same pan, still over a medium heat, then add the carrots, onion, garlic, thyme and bay and sweat for 2 minutes. Add the sweated vegetables to the roasting tin and cook in the oven for 10 minutes for very pink lamb, 15 minutes for *à point*, or 20 minutes for well done meat.

Meanwhile, for the vegetables, turn the potatoes into large olive shapes and cook in salted water until tender. Blanch the beans for a few minutes until just tender.

When the lamb is ready, transfer it to a dish, partially wrap in foil and keep warm. Skim a little excess fat from the roasting tin, place over a medium heat and deglaze with the wine. Reduce the juices by one-third, then add 100ml water and reduce by half. Season with salt and pepper to taste and strain through a fine chinois; keep warm.

Heat the butter for the vegetables in a saucepan over a gentle heat. As soon as it has melted, add the garlic, then after 1 minute add the tomatoes and potatoes. Increase the heat to medium and, after 4 minutes, add the green beans. As soon as everything has heated through, add the olives, season with salt and pepper to taste, remove from the heat and set aside.

Cut the lamb into cutlets. Serve on hot plates with a little of the cooking juices. Arrange the vegetables in a serving dish, place the lemon slices and anchovy fillets, if using, over the top and serve at once, as this dish goes cold very quickly.

Variation

The roast rack of lamb can be served with seasonal vegetables, depending on the time of year, rather than Niçoise vegetables. I like serving it with braised chicory with orange (page 188) in winter, or with artichokes Clamart (page 183) in spring.

Serves 2

1 x 6-bone rack of lamb, bone ends
    trimmed and excess fat removed

60g clarified butter (page 266)

2 medium carrots, peeled and diced

1 large onion, peeled and diced

4 garlic cloves (unpeeled)

4 thyme sprigs

1 bay leaf

100ml dry white wine

Salt and freshly ground pepper

Niçoise vegetables

150g small new potatoes

75g green beans, trimmed and sliced
    lengthways if large

60g butter

2 garlic cloves, peeled and very
    finely chopped

200g tomatoes, peeled, quartered
    and deseeded

8 black olives, pitted

1 lemon, peel pared off, cut into rounds

4 tinned anchovy fillets in oil (optional)

Baron d' Agneau Rôti

ROAST BARON OF LAMB

The baron is one of the most spectacular butcher's cuts. Comprising both legs and the saddle, it is impressive and I've always loved preparing it. Even if you do so only once in your life, I urge you to cook a baron of lamb. It's a unique experience. If you happen to have a large spit, you can cook the lamb on it, which is a marvellous sight to behold. A top wine from Pauillac or Saint-Julien would be a wonderful complement to this excellent dish.

Make sure your butcher has removed all the fine layer of skin covering the saddle, which would be tough when cooked, and tied the baron with kitchen string in several places to keep its shape.

Wrap the saddle end of the baron in several layers of cling film and immerse it saddle-end down in a bucket filled with ice, keeping the legs clear of the ice; leave for 20 minutes. This will rapidly chill the flesh on the saddle, where it is less dense than the leg end and would, if not started at a lower temperature, overcook in the time the legs took to cook, which is about double the time of the saddle.

While the saddle is chilling, preheat the oven to 200°C/Gas 6 for at least 20 minutes. Remove the cling film from the saddle. Use a brush to daub the baron generously with the warm clarified butter, sprinkle very lightly with salt and place in a large roasting tin, 3–5cm deep.

Cook in the oven, basting with the cooking juices after 30 minutes, then arrange the carrot, onion and celery mirepoix around the lamb. Return to the oven and baste again with the cooking juices after 20 minutes. Add the garlic cloves, bay, thyme and 100ml water, to moisten the vegetables liberally, and cook for a further 50 minutes, basting the lamb with its juices every 10–15 minutes. The total cooking time for a 7–8kg baron will be 1½ hours for very pink and 1¾ hours for medium-rare.

Once cooked, remove the baron to a board, cover with foil and leave to rest for 10–15 minutes for the meat to relax. Deglaze the roasting tin with the wine over the heat and leave to simmer for 6–7 minutes with the vegetables. Strain through a fine chinois, add salt and pepper to taste and set aside to keep hot.

To serve the baron, remove the string, place the bunch of watercress in the gap between the legs and carve the lamb at the table in front of your guests, giving a slice or two of leg and saddle to each. Serve with your choice of vegetables and the jus on the side.

(Illustrated on previous page)

Serves 12–16

1 baron of lamb, from a 70–150 day-old, milk-fed spring lamb, 7–8kg; or, though less ideally, from a 6–9 month-old grass-fed lamb, 12–14kg (which would serve 20–24)

200g warm clarified butter (page 266)

500g carrots, peeled and cut into large mirepoix (3–4cm cubes)

300g onions, peeled and cut into large (mirepoix 3–4cm cubes)

200g celery stalks, cut into large mirepoix (3–4cm cubes)

1 head of garlic (cloves separated and unpeeled)

6 bay leaves

12 thyme sprigs

100ml water

200ml dry white wine

Salt and freshly ground pepper

Bunch of watercress, stalks removed, washed, to garnish

Gigot de Sept Fleures

'SEVEN-HOUR' LEG OF LAMB

A dish of Auvergne heritage, although the people of Lyon and Bordeaux also lay claim to its origins. It's another food with its roots in the countryside, a peasant dish that would have been put on to cook in the dying heat of the oven, at a temperature no higher than 100–140°C, and left there all night. Lamb in those days would have in fact been mutton, which needed to be cooked for as long as seven hours, if not longer – hence the title of this recipe. The lamb we buy today doesn't take as long to reach melting tenderness.

Preheat the oven to 150°C/Gas 2. Season the lamb all over with salt. Heat the oil in a large frying pan over a medium heat, add the lamb and brown on all sides for 3–4 minutes.

Place the pork rind skin side up in the base of a large flameproof casserole, preferably oval, and place the browned lamb on top. Set the frying pan used to brown the lamb over a medium heat, add the onions, carrots and garlic and sweat for 2–3 minutes. Deglaze with the white wine and cook for 2 minutes, then transfer everything to the casserole containing the lamb.

Add the stock, bouquet garni, the reserved leg bone, cloves and potatoes and place the casserole over a medium heat. Bring to the boil, then put the lid on and check it is properly closed, and remove from the heat.

In a small bowl, mix the flour with 2 tbsp cold water, using your fingertips, to make a wet paste. Stick this luting paste around the edge of the lid and top edge of the casserole, to create a hermetic seal.

Transfer to the oven and cook for 5 hours, then remove and set aside at room temperature for 10 minutes or so, before breaking the paste seal, which will have turned hard. Remove the lid, taking care that the steam that escapes doesn't burn you, take out the bouquet garni and adjust the seasoning with salt and pepper.

Using 2 skimmers, carefully transfer the leg of lamb to a shallow serving dish and remove the string keeping it in shape. Arrange the vegetables from the cooking dish around the lamb, adding some of the cooking juices as well, and serve the remaining juices in a warm jug.

Serve the lamb using a spoon and fork; slices will not be possible.

Serves 6–8

1 large leg of lamb, about 2.5kg, with the central bone removed and reserved, tied in 4 or 5 places with kitchen string to hold its shape

2½ tbsp grapeseed oil

Piece of fresh pork rind, about 300g

3 medium onions, peeled and cut into mirepoix (2–3cm cubes)

6 medium carrots, peeled and cut into large sections

1 head of garlic, cut in half horizontally

300ml dry white wine

400ml veal stock (page 249) or chicken stock (page 248), or buy good-quality fresh stock

1 large bouquet garni, with a sprig of rosemary added

2 cloves, crushed

1kg medium potatoes, peeled and washed

60g plain flour

Salt and freshly ground pepper

Navarin d'Agneau Printanier
NAVARIN OF LAMB

This is a classic of true French cuisine that several regions of France, including Paris, claim as their own. It is a rich-tasting sauce-based dish, but is still light and is always popular. It's also very good reheated.

Preheat the oven to 180°C/Gas 4. Heat the clarified butter in an ovenproof sauté pan that has a lid. Sprinkle some salt and the sugar over the pieces of lamb and add to the pan. Brown over a lively heat until coloured all over, then transfer immediately to a colander.

Add the carrot and onion mirepoix to the same sauté pan and sweat over a gentle heat for 5 minutes, without letting them colour. Add the flour and cook for 3–4 minutes, stirring with a wooden spoon over a gentle heat. Pour in the wine, increase the heat, stir and simmer for 5 minutes.

Now add the stock, garlic, diced tomatoes and the bouquet garni. Bring to the boil, then add all the lamb pieces back to the pan, cover and transfer to the oven for 50–60 minutes. Check the lamb is cooked: the pieces should feel tender when prodded gently with a finger, and the tip of a knife should slide in with no resistance.

Remove the pieces of lamb one at a time from the pan and place in a dish, then cover with a very damp tea towel. Reduce the cooking liquid in the pan over a medium heat to a semi-syrupy consistency. Strain through a fine chinois, add salt and pepper to taste and place the pieces of lamb back in the reduced juices. Keep hot, at around 70–80°C.

Cook the baby carrots, turnips, onions and potatoes separately in lightly salted boiling water. As soon as they are cooked, drain well and mix in with the lamb.

Pod the peas and broad beans and cook in boiling water for 1–2 minutes, then drain and keep warm.

Serve the lamb in a copper or earthenware dish, adding the peas, broad beans and parsley leaves to the top of the dish at the last moment.

Serves 4

60g clarified butter (page 266)

20g caster sugar

1 shoulder of new season lamb, boned and cut into 8 pieces

400g lamb middle neck on the bone, cut into 4 pieces

1 large carrot, peeled and cut into mirepoix (2–3cm cubes)

1 large onion, peeled and cut into mirepoix (2–3cm cubes)

30g plain flour

200ml dry white wine

1 litre chicken stock (page 248), or buy good-quality fresh stock

3 garlic cloves, peeled and crushed

2 large tomatoes, peeled, deseeded and diced

1 medium bouquet garni

8 baby carrots, peeled

8 baby turnips, peeled

12 baby white onions, peeled

8 small new potatoes, peeled

200g tender peas in pods

250g young, tender broad beans in pods

Salt and freshly ground pepper

A few flat-leaf parsley leaves, to serve

L'Agneau.

1. Collier.
2. Côte découverte.
3.4. Côtes première et seconde.
5. Filet. 6. Côte filet.

Cochon de Lait Rôti à la Broche

SPIT-ROAST SUCKLING PIG

One of the most delicious things you can eat, with some parts of the pig crisp (the crackling), some falling apart and tender (the shoulder or neck) and others, such as the legs, offering a denser texture, but all equally delectable. It's a truly visual, olfactory and gastronomic feast. Apples, leaf spinach and spinach subrics (page 192) are all good accompaniments.

About 20 minutes before you are ready to cook, preheat the rotisserie to medium or a large oven to 200°C/Gas 6. Using a boning knife, trim the inside of the pig's carcass to remove any innards, excess fat, nerves, veins, testicles and blood-stained areas. Use a small blowtorch to burn off any hairs still on the skin.

If cooking on the rotisserie, skewer the suckling pig onto the spit bar by inserting the bar through the back end and out through the mouth. Tie the hind feet together using flexible wire, then tie the feet to the bar, to stop the pig moving during cooking. Tie the front feet together in the same way, but tying them to the lower jaw of the pig to keep them from moving. Wrap the feet, tail and ears in foil, so that these places don't burn during cooking. If cooking in the oven, place the pig belly side down in a large roasting tin.

Generously brush the pig all over with clarified butter and sprinkle with salt and pepper. Place it on its spit on the rotation fixings of the rotisserie or in the oven and cook for 1¼–1½ hours, basting it with the cooking juices every 10 minutes. Once cooked, remove the pig from the spit or oven and rest for 20 minutes, in as warm a place as you can.

Meanwhile, peel the apples, cut into quarters and remove the cores. Put the apple pieces into a bowl with the lemon juice and mix to coat the pieces in the juice. Heat the butter in a large frying pan over a medium heat. As soon as it is very hot, add the sugar and apples and cook for about 15 minutes, moving them around the pan every 2–3 minutes, until lightly caramelised. Set aside to keep hot.

Serve the suckling pig whole on a large board. Set it on a table next to your guests and slice it in front of them. If you use a very sharp knife you will be able to serve all 12–16 guests within 15 minutes or so. It is essential you give each person a small serving of each different part of the animal. Serve the apples separately.

Serves 12–16

1 suckling pig, about 8kg

300g semi-set clarified butter (page 266)

Salt and freshly ground pepper

Apples

12–16 apples, ideally Cox

Juice of 2 lemons

150g butter

100g caster sugar

Variation

You can replace the suckling pig with a suckling lamb, but only if your rotisserie is substantial enough, as even the smallest lambs tend to weigh around 16–20kg. Increase the cooking time to around 1¾ hours.

Carré de Porc à la Bonne Femme

PORK LOIN with VEGETABLES

This flavoursome dish would often appear on the table in family homes on Sundays in the 1950s. It takes me back to when I was an apprentice pâtissier in rue de Belleville in Paris: towards midday, customers from the neighbourhood would bring us their pot of meat and vegetables, already browned, to finish cooking in the dying heat of our baker's oven, saving on their own gas or electricity.

Preheat the oven to 180°C/Gas 4. Heat the lard or butter in a round or oval flameproof casserole over a medium heat. Season the pork loin lightly with salt, add to the casserole and colour on all sides. Add the thyme and bay, cover and cook in the oven for 1¼ hours.

As soon as the pork is in the oven, melt the 100g butter in a large frying pan over a lively heat, add the potatoes, salt lightly and brown them for 5 minutes, turning them every 2 minutes. Add the onions and grapeseed oil and cook for a further 15 minutes, stirring every 5 minutes. When everything is nicely golden all over, after 20–25 minutes of cooking, add salt and pepper and transfer to the casserole with the pork, which will be midway through cooking. Cover again and cook in the oven for a further 40 minutes, the time remaining for the pork.

Once the casserole is out of the oven, remove the thyme and bay, replace the lid and set aside in a warm place for a few minutes before serving.

To serve, take the casserole to the table, sprinkle the parsley over everything, then take out the pork and cut into slices on a board, making sure each person has at least one bone. Spoon the browned vegetables around each slice of pork and eat at once.

Serves 4

60g lard or butter

1 bone-in pork loin, about 1.2kg, rind and a little fat removed, trimmed and tied in several places with kitchen string to hold its shape

2 thyme sprigs

4 bay leaves

100g butter

600g small new potatoes, peeled

24 baby onions, peeled

2½ tbsp grapeseed oil

20g flat-leaf parsley, finely snipped

Salt and freshly ground pepper

Choucroute à l'Alsacienne
ALSACE SAUERKRAUT

A big celebratory family dish that makes winter much more tolerable. Strong Dijon mustard is essential as a condiment. As with cassoulet, leftover sauerkraut reheats very well, and is possibly even better served the next day, if indeed there are any leftovers…

Add the pork knuckle, half-shoulder or blade, rack and pig's tails, if using, to a pan of boiling salted water and cook for 30 minutes, then drain.

Blanch the sauerkraut in boiling water for 2 minutes, then drain. Squeeze it a little at a time with your hands, to extract as much water as possible.

Wrap the bay leaves, juniper berries, garlic cloves, cloves and peppercorns in a piece of muslin and tie securely.

Melt the goose fat or lard in a large cooking pot over a gentle heat, then remove one-third to a small dish and set aside. Add the onion to the pot and sweat for 2 minutes, then add half the sauerkraut and arrange the pork knuckle, shoulder and rack and the pig's tails, if using, on top.

Add the bag of aromatics, cover with the remaining sauerkraut and pour over the wine, stock and reserved melted goose fat. Cover with a lid and cook over a gentle heat for 2 hours, keeping it at a light simmer.

About 40 minutes before the end of the cooking time, put the Montbéliard or Morteau sausages into a pan of cold water and cook over a gentle heat for 30 minutes. Add the Strasbourg or Frankfurter sausages and poach for another 10 minutes.

Meanwhile, 30 minutes before the sauerkraut is cooked, add the potatoes to a pan of lightly salted cold water and cook until tender. Lightly oil the black pudding slices and veal sausages and cook in a griddle pan for 5–6 minutes just before everything else is ready.

To serve, discard the aromatics. Cut the meats cooked in the sauerkraut into regular-sized pieces, and season with salt and pepper to taste. Transfer the sauerkraut to a large, warm, shallow serving dish and arrange the meat on top. Cut the Montbéliard or Morteau and the veal sausages into thick rounds, then arrange on top with the black pudding and the whole Strasbourg or Frankfurter sausages. Arrange the potatoes around the edge of the dish and serve, ideally keeping the serving dish on a plate heater placed in the middle of the table.

Serves 8

1 semi-salted pork knuckle

1 lightly smoked half-shoulder of pork, blade end

600g semi-salted rack of pork

4 pig's tails (optional)

2kg sauerkraut, preferably raw

2 bay leaves

10 juniper berries

4 garlic cloves (unpeeled)

4 cloves

8 peppercorns, crushed

150g goose fat or lard

1 large onion, peeled and chopped

500ml dry white Riesling wine

250ml chicken stock (page 248), or buy good-quality fresh stock

4 Montbéliard or 2 Morteau sausages

8 Strasbourg or Frankfurter sausages

1kg small potatoes, peeled

A little grapeseed oil

8 slices black pudding, 2cm thick

4 white veal sausages

Salt and freshly ground pepper

Cassoulet de Castelnaudary

A classic dating from the mists of time, served all over the Southwest of France, where every chef claims to have the definitive, authentic recipe. What everyone can be sure of is that it fills the whole kitchen with its glorious aromas as it cooks, and there's no denying its position as one of the beacon dishes of French cuisine.

Soak the dried beans in plenty of cold water for 6–12 hours.

Using the tip of knife, prick the Morteau sausage and put into a saucepan with the half pork knuckle. Cover with cold water and bring to the boil. Lower the heat and simmer gently for 30 minutes, then remove the sausage and set aside covered in a damp tea towel. Continue to cook the knuckle for a further 30 minutes, then take off the heat and set aside in its cooking water.

Drain the soaked beans and put into a large pan. Cover with plenty of cold water and add the carrot, onion, bouquet garni, 2 garlic cloves and the pork rind, if using. Bring to the boil, then reduce to a gentle simmer.

After 30 minutes, skim the surface, add a little cold water if necessary and transfer the knuckle from its cooking water to the pan. Cook, still at a very gentle simmer, for a further 30 minutes, skimming if necessary.

Meanwhile, colour the duck legs and pieces of lamb evenly all over in a frying pan set over a medium heat. Once they are nicely golden, remove the duck to a plate. Add the lamb to the beans and cook for a further 30 minutes.

Prick the Toulouse sausages in a few places with the tip of a knife and colour them evenly in the same frying pan, over a gentle heat. Set aside with the duck legs.

When the beans have been cooking for 1½ hours, add the tomatoes and crushed peppercorns and cook for a further 30 minutes. Add the duck legs and Toulouse sausages and cook for another 30 minutes, still over a very gentle heat. Preheat the oven to 160°C/Gas 3.

Remove the carrot, onion, bouquet garni, garlic and pork rind, if used. Peel the skins from the Morteau and Toulouse sausages and cut the sausages into slices. Dip the remaining garlic clove in fine salt and rub it all over the insides and base of an earthenware or ceramic shallow baking dish. Tip the beans and lamb, duck legs and knuckle into the dish. Taste and adjust the seasoning and arrange the sausage slices over the top, burying them slightly in the beans.

Mix the breadcrumbs with the parsley and scatter over the surface of the cassoulet. Cook in the oven for 20–30 minutes, until the topping is golden. Serve straight from the dish.

Serves 6–8

800g dried white haricot beans, ideally Tarbais

1 Morteau sausage, about 300g

½ raw, semi-salted pork knuckle, rinsed in cold water

1 large carrot, peeled

1 medium onion, peeled and studded with 2 cloves

1 medium bouquet garni

3 garlic cloves, peeled

1 piece of pork rind, about 200g (optional)

4 confit duck legs (tinned or vacuum-packed in their fat)

½ boned shoulder of lamb, cut into 4 pieces

2 Toulouse sausages

200g tomatoes, peeled, deseeded and chopped into fine dice (concasse)

10g black peppercorns, crushed

30g dried white breadcrumbs

20g flat-leaf parsley, chopped

Salt and freshly ground pepper

Foie de Veau Rôti aux Herbes

ROASTED CALF'S LIVER WITH HERBS

This is a Sunday dish for the family to share, and is a treat
for offal lovers. The liver is delicately smooth, with the herbs
lending just the right aromatic notes. Cauliflower purée
(page 187) or potatoes would make a perfect accompaniment.

Preheat the oven to 220°C/Gas 7.

Dry the caul fat thoroughly and spread out in a double layer on a work surface
lined with cling film. Mix the parsley, tarragon and thyme together and sprinkle
over the caul fat.

Gently pat dry the liver with kitchen paper, sprinkle all over with salt and
pepper and position it in the middle of the caul fat. Bring the caul fat up and
around the liver, so that it is well wrapped all over. Secure the caul fat by tying
kitchen string in 4 or 5 places, but not too tightly or the string will leave a
mark and prevent even cooking.

Heat the clarified butter over a medium heat in a large, ovenproof frying pan,
preferably oval, add the liver and cook for 2–3 minutes, until evenly coloured
all over.

Transfer to the oven and cook for 25 minutes for very pink, 30 minutes for
pink, or 35 minutes for *à point*, spooning the butter over the liver every
10 minutes as it cooks.

Once cooked, transfer to a wire rack placed over a dish, remove the string
and cover with foil. Keep warm for about 10 minutes before serving.

To serve, slice the liver on a board, not too thickly, ideally at the table. Serve
the watercress separately, in a small salad bowl, seasoned with olive oil,
lemon juice, salt and pepper.

Serves 6–8

250g pork caul fat, soaked in cold water

2½ tbsp chopped parsley

1 tbsp snipped tarragon

½ tbsp snipped thyme sprigs

1 good, firm calf's liver, about 1.2–1.4kg,
   trimmed of any visible sinew and veins
   if necessary

60g clarified butter (page 266), or
   60ml grapeseed oil

½ bunch watercress, stalks removed,
   washed

1 tbsp light, fruity olive oil

Juice of ½ lemon

Salt and freshly ground pepper

Variation
The calf's liver can be sliced raw, lightly floured and immediately cooked briskly in
a frying pan, as for a steak. I would recommend serving liver cooked in this way with
a well-seasoned tomato coulis (page 255).

Noix de Ris de Veau Braisées

BRAISED CALF'S SWEETBREADS

This offal dish, one of the great classics of French gastronomy, is one I am crazy about, to the point of dreaming about it in my 'chef's dreams'. In my view, sweetbreads should always be served braised and in their natural state.

Put the sweetbreads in a bowl of very cold water and set aside to soak for 4–6 hours, changing the water frequently.

Transfer the sweetbreads to a saucepan, cover with cold water, salt lightly and bring almost to a simmer over a medium heat. Blanch at 90°C for 5 minutes, taking care not to let the water boil. Refresh under a trickle of cold water for at least 20 minutes. Drain, then use your fingertips to remove the membrane, fat and veins partly covering them. Place between 2 damp tea towels, put a small board on top, and on top of this sit a 1–1.5kg weight, to lightly flatten them.

After about 1 hour, remove the weight, board and tea towels and set the sweetbreads aside in the fridge, on a dish covered in cling film, until ready to cook.

When ready to cook, rinse the morels in cold water with a splash of vinegar added. Drain and wipe dry. Heat the 60g butter in a sauté pan, add the morels and cook for 6–8 minutes, until tender.

At the same time, heat the clarified butter in a sauté pan over a medium heat. Mix the honey, lemon juice and thyme leaves together and brush the sweetbreads with the mixture, then add to the hot, but not burning hot, clarified butter in the pan. After 3–4 minutes, give them a quarter-turn over and cook for 3–4 minutes, then continue turning in this way until the surface is lightly golden and caramelised all over; they will be very soft in the middle and are now cooked. Set aside for 2–3 minutes on a wire rack, partially covered in foil, before serving.

Place a whole sweetbread on each plate and sprinkle with a light grinding of pepper. Serve at once, with braised artichoke hearts or baby artichokes (page 34), or stuffed mushrooms (page 190).

Variations

• In place of the morels, serve 4 artichoke hearts Clamart (page 183) or 4 stuffed mushrooms (page 190).
• After the sweetbreads have been pressed under the weights, cut them into slices about 1.5cm thick. Brush with melted butter, then cook on a ridged griddle pan over a medium heat for 1–2 minutes on each side. Serve with asparagus tips and sauce hollandaise (page 254), ideally flavoured with some truffle juice…

Serves 4

4 calf's sweetbreads, round part or 'heart' only, with a pearly white skin

200g fresh morels, halved

Splash of white wine vinegar

60g butter

80g clarified butter (page 266)

2½ tbsp delicately flavoured runny honey

Juice of ½ lemon

2 thyme sprigs, leaves only

Salt and freshly ground pepper

Rognons de Veau à la Bordelaise
CALF'S KIDNEYS À LA BORDELAISE

Rice pilaf would make the perfect partner for this delectable dish. Kidneys should be served pink, or even better very pink, as they will turn hard, almost rubbery, if well done or cooked *à point*. They are much celebrated for their flavour by gastronomes.

Cut the calf's kidneys in half lengthways, remove the outer coating, fat and transparent membrane surrounding them, then remove the sinews and the fatty part found in the middle of these. Cut the kidneys into fine slices, about 5mm thick, and set aside in a dish.

Poach the diced beef marrow in barely simmering salted water for 1 minute, then drain thoroughly.

Heat the clarified butter in a large frying or sauté pan over a very high heat. Season the kidneys lightly with salt, add to the pan and sauté for about 1½ minutes; they should be very pink. Drain in a sieve.

Melt the 20g butter in the same pan used for the kidneys over a gentle heat. Add the shallots and sweat for 1 minute, then add the wine, increase the heat to high and reduce by half. Add the stock and reduce by half, still over a lively heat. Add the peppercorns and reduce the heat to low.

Stir in the dissolved potato flour, using a small balloon whisk, and simmer for 2 minutes. Adjust the seasoning with salt and pepper, then add the kidneys to the sauce and, after 1 minute, the well-drained marrow dice. Immediately remove from the heat and serve at once, sprinkled with parsley.

Variation
To make veal kidneys with a mustard sauce, follow the main recipe but replace the veal stock with double cream, and the marrow with 50g strong Dijon mustard and 50g wholegrain Meaux mustard. Omit the potato flour and replace the parsley with finely chopped tarragon. Leaf spinach cooked briskly in butter and served on the side is perfect with this dish.

Serves 4

2 calf's kidneys, covered with a generous, very white coating of fat

100g beef marrow, cut into about 5mm dice

40g clarified butter (page 266)

20g butter

40g shallots, peeled and finely chopped

150ml dry white wine

200ml veal stock (page 249) or chicken stock (page 248), or buy good-quality fresh stock

10 white peppercorns, crushed

½ tbsp potato flour, dissolved in 1 tbsp cold water

20g parsley, finely snipped

Salt and freshly ground pepper

Vegetables

Fonds d'Artichauts Clamart

TURNED ARTICHOKE HEARTS WITH PEAS AND BABY ONIONS

This sublime accompaniment is also very good as a starter.
Clamart, on the outskirts of Paris, was in the past renowned
for its tender peas that were grown in the area. Things have
changed, and peas now come from the Loire valley, among
other places. But the classic Clamart term has persisted, with
any recipe garnished with peas defined in this way.

Fill a large saucepan with cold water and salt lightly. Mix the flour and vinegar together to a smooth paste, using a small balloon whisk, then add to the pan. Bring to the boil over a medium heat, stirring occasionally and thoroughly with the whisk. As soon as it boils, reduce the heat to a bare simmer.

Break off the stem of an artichoke and remove the hard, fibrous outside leaves from the base and sides. Using a small knife, cut back and trim the inside leaves and the base of the heart. Rub the base and sides of the heart with the half lemon, then cut off the top of the leaves, about three-quarters of the way from the top of the artichoke. Now pare back the dark green circumference at the base of the leaves, rub the newly exposed part with lemon, and set aside in a bowl of cold water. Repeat with the remaining 5 artichokes.

Plunge the prepared hearts into the simmering water and cook over a medium heat for 30–40 minutes, until tender. Test one by inserting the tip of a knife: it should go in with minimal resistance. Leave to cool in the liquor.

Once cooled, remove the chokes with your thumb. Arrange the artichoke hearts in a lightly buttered ovenproof dish and cover with lightly buttered greaseproof paper, ready to heat and serve. Preheat the oven to 160°C/Gas 3.

Put the halved baby onions in a small pan, add cold water to cover, then add 20g of the butter and a pinch of salt. Cook over a medium heat until tender, about 10 minutes. Take off the heat and set aside in the cooking liquor.

Put the dish of artichoke hearts into the oven to heat through for around 6–8 minutes. Meanwhile, cook the peas in a pan of lightly salted boiling water for 3–5 minutes, until just tender. Drain and transfer with the remaining 40g butter to a pan set over a low heat. Drain the onions and add these to the pan, heat through for 2–3 minutes, then sprinkle with the icing sugar.

Arrange a reheated artichoke heart on each plate, add a light grinding of pepper, fill generously with the pea and onion mixture and serve at once.

Serves 6

2 tbsp plain flour

1½ tbsp white wine vinegar

6 large, very tender artichokes,
   ideally Breton

½ lemon

60g butter, plus extra for greasing

6 baby white onions, peeled and halved

200g freshly podded peas (about 500g
   in pods)

1 tsp icing sugar

Salt and freshly ground pepper

Variation

Fill the artichoke hearts with baby cherry tomatoes, cooked to a mi-confit with a little oil and garlic, in place of the peas and onions. Sprinkle with breadcrumbs and place under a hot grill for 30 seconds.

Aubergines à la Catalane

This is a light, fresh vegetable dish from the Southwest with Mediterranean notes, and should be served only very slightly warm. It goes well with all fish, such as the steamed red mullet on page 96, and could also be served as a starter.

Preheat the oven to 180°C/Gas 4. Prick each aubergines in a dozen places with the tip of a small knife.

Spread the coarse salt out in a roasting dish and place the aubergines on top. Cook in the oven for 25–30 minutes, turning them once during cooking. Check they are done by pricking one of the aubergines in its thickest part with a skewer; it should slide in with just slight resistance.

While the aubergines are in the oven, cook the rice in lightly salted boiling water until tender. Cool under cold running water, then drain thoroughly.

Cut the peel and all pith from 2 lemons, then cut out the segments, from between the membranes; set aside. Squeeze the juice from the other lemon.

Once cooked, leave the aubergines to cool on their bed of salt, then remove to a board and cut both in half lengthways. Use a spoon to scoop out the flesh, leaving about 5mm lining the skins.

Roughly chop the aubergine flesh, tip into a bowl and mix in the lemon juice and rice. Roughly chop the hard-boiled egg whites and add them to the aubergine and rice mixture with all but 1 tbsp of the diced tomatoes, half the lemon segments, the olives and the olive oil. Toss to combine and season with salt and pepper to taste. Divide the mixture between the aubergine skins, without compressing it.

Arrange the filled aubergine halves on a serving dish. Sprinkle the egg yolks over the top, by pushing them through a small, medium-meshed sieve, held directly over the aubergines. Arrange the salad leaves down one side and garnish the dish with the remaining diced tomato and lemon segments.

Serves 4

2 nicely firm aubergines, about 250g each

200g coarse salt, for cooking

80g basmati rice

3 lemons

2 hard-boiled eggs, yolks and whites separated

200g ripe tomatoes, skinned, deseeded and cut into small dice

12 black olives, stoned and diced

4 tbsp olive oil

50g mesclun or other delicate salad leaves

Salt and freshly ground pepper

Purée de Chou-fleur Ivoirine
CAULIFLOWER PURÉE

I like to serve my cauliflower purée in its original leafy casing. It calls for an extra 10 minutes' preparation but the presentation is aesthetically pleasing and inviting.

If necessary, trim off some of the outside leafy parts of the cauliflower, without the outside structure becoming detached, to remove volume, then remove the base of the core. Insert the tip of a very sharp, pointed knife 1cm from the base of the cauliflower and cut using a left to right motion, or right to left, to liberate the base of the cauliflower.

Next, insert the knife into the top of the cauliflower, 5mm from the inside edge and cut all around, tilting the knife lightly towards the centre of the cauliflower and cutting as far as 1cm from the bottom of the cauliflower. The majority of the floret part, 70–80%, will now be detached from the sides. Rinse the emptied out base carefully in cold water and set aside.

Separate the white inside part of the cauliflower into large florets and wash in cold water. Put into a pan and add enough milk to cover. Add a pinch of salt and cook for 3 minutes over a medium heat, then drain well.

Heat the cream in a pan and, as soon as it reaches boiling point, add the cauliflower florets. Simmer for 5 minutes, then transfer the mixture to a food processor and blend for about 2 minutes, until you have a smooth purée. Add salt to taste, with a light grinding of pepper and the nutmeg. Set aside and keep hot until ready to serve.

Half-fill a couscoussier or steamer base with water, then add the lemon juice and a pinch of salt. Put the reserved cauliflower base in the steamer and steam for 10 minutes.

Using a skimmer, carefully transfer the steamed base to a serving dish, preferably shallow, and fill the inside with the cauliflower purée. Your guests may like to help themselves some of the outside casing, along with the purée.

Serves 4

1 cauliflower, about 600g, nicely white and with tender, healthy outside leaves
About 500ml milk
150ml double cream
Small knifetip of freshly grated nutmeg
Juice of 1 lemon
Salt and freshly ground white pepper

Variations

Pumpkins can be emptied out in a similar manner, with the pulp made into a purée and the shell used as a serving vessel, so turning an ordinary dish into a spectacular one. Aubergine purée can be served in a half aubergine skin, or a fennel bulb can be scooped out and filled with its purée, in a similar fashion.

Endives Braisées au Jus d'Orange
BRAISED CHICORY WITH ORANGE

This is a succulent vegetable dish with a citrussy flavour –
perfect to serve with fish such as salmon, or with white meat,
such as chicken, veal or guinea fowl.

Using a small knife, make a cross in the base of each chicory bulb, to help
them cook. Place in a saucepan and cover with cold water. Add 50g of the
butter, the lemon quarter and a pinch of salt and bring to the boil over a
medium heat. As soon as it boils, place a cartouche of greaseproof paper flat
on the surface and cook over a gentle heat for 1–1½ hours.

To check when they are cooked, insert the point of a knife into the plumpest
part of a chicory bulb; it should go in with minimal resistance. Tip the chicory
and cooking liquid into a dish, replace the cartouche over the surface and set
aside for at least 1 hour, or longer.

Heat the orange juice in a small pan and reduce over a medium-low heat by
two-thirds; set aside.

About 10 minutes before serving, drain the chicory and press each bulb
gently to extract some of the liquid held inside. Heat the remaining 30g butter
in a frying pan and, as soon as it is foaming, sprinkle in the sugar and add the
chicory. Cook to a light noisette colour, 2–3 minutes, then turn them over with
a fork and leave to colour in the same way on the other side for 2–3 minutes.
Add the reduced orange juice and cook over a gentle heat so that the chicory
absorbs nearly all the juice.

Arrange the chicory on 4 individual serving plates, pour over a little braising
juice from the pan, add a light sprinkling of pepper and serve at once.

Serves 4

4 firm, white chicory bulbs

80g butter

¼ lemon

Juice of 2 oranges

2 pinches of caster sugar

Salt and freshly ground pepper

Variations
• You can braise the chicory without orange juice and instead simply drizzle a little
of some veal or roast chicken juices over the top and sprinkle with chopped parsley,
just before serving.
• For a gratin, instead of braising the chicory, wrap each cooked chicory in a very fine
slice of ham, cover in a béchamel sauce, sprinkle with grated cheese and cook in the
oven preheated to 200°C/Gas 6 for 15 minutes.

*Clockwise (from top left): Carrots à la crème
(page 197); haricots blancs à la charcuterie
(page 191); braised chicory with orange (above);
spinach subrics with mushrooms (page 192)*

Champignons Farcis   STUFFED MUSHROOMS

You can stuff the mushrooms several hours in advance and then cook them in the oven 10 minutes before serving. The silky texture of the duxelle stuffing combined with the more fleshy texture of the whole mushroom makes this an original vegetable dish.

Preheat the oven to 200°C/Gas 6.

Wipe all the mushroom caps clean using a lightly dampened piece of kitchen paper, then remove the ends of the stalks of the small mushrooms with a small knife. Break off the stalks of the 4 large mushrooms and set aside with the small mushrooms. Using your finger, spread a little lemon juice over the caps of the 4 large mushrooms.

Heat 20g of the butter in a large frying pan over a gentle heat, then add the 4 large mushrooms and cook for 1 minute on each side. Season lightly with salt, then remove from the pan and set aside.

Using a large chef's knife, very finely chop the small button mushrooms and 4 large stalks.

Heat the remaining butter in the frying pan used for the large mushrooms. Add the shallot and sweat gently for 2–3 minutes to soften without colouring. Add the chopped mushrooms with the remaining lemon juice, season lightly with salt and cook over a medium heat for 2–3 minutes, until the liquid has evaporated, then add the cream and simmer for a further 1 minute. Add the chopped parsley with salt and pepper to taste, then transfer the mixture – or duxelle – to a bowl and set aside.

Once lightly cooled, divide the duxelle between the 4 large mushrooms, using a spoon to mound it into domes. Sprinkle with breadcrumbs, if using, and cook in the oven for 10 minutes.

Arrange the mushrooms around a piece of meat as a garnish, or serve them very hot on a separate plate as a vegetable side dish.

Serves 4

4 large, firm button mushrooms

100g small button mushrooms

Juice of ½ lemon

60g butter

1 medium shallot, peeled and finely chopped

3 tbsp double cream

1 tbsp chopped parsley

1 tbsp dried white breadcrumbs (optional)

Salt and freshly ground pepper

Variation

For a delightful starter, add some pancetta, cut into small dice, to the duxelle just before stuffing the mushrooms, and sprinkle with a mixture of breadcrumbs and grated Parmesan before baking.

Haricots Blancs à la Charcutière

A vegetable dish that always goes down very well, especially in autumn or winter, served alongside a roast leg of lamb or grilled pork chops, or with pan-fried medallions of monkfish.

Soak the dried beans in plenty of cold water overnight, or for 8 hours.

The next day, drain the beans, tip into a saucepan and cover generously with cold water. Peel one of the onions, stud with the clove and add to the pan with the carrot and bouquet garni. Bring to the boil over a medium heat, then lower the heat and cook gently, skimming the surface from time to time, for 2–3 hours, until the beans are tender to the bite (the cooking time will depend on the variety of bean used).

Remove the bouquet garni, carrot and onion, and transfer the beans and their cooking liquid to a bowl. Peel and chop the second onion. Melt the butter in the pan the beans were cooked in, add the chopped onion and sweat for 1 minute. Add the diced ham, followed by the beans and their cooking liquid, making sure there is just enough to moisten the beans. Simmer for about 15 minutes, then season with salt and pepper.

If you are using a breadcrumb topping, preheat the grill to high and mix the breadcrumbs with the parsley. Spoon the beans into bowls or a shallow dish, sprinkle with the breadcrumb mixture and grill for 1–2 minutes. Alternatively, simply sprinkle the beans with parsley and serve.

(Illustrated on page 189)

Serves 6

300g dried white Tarbais haricot beans, or coco or white Soissons beans

2 medium onions

1 clove

1 medium carrot, peeled

1 small bouquet garni

40g butter

100g piece of ham cooked on the bone, cut into large dice

1 tbsp dried white breadcrumbs (optional)

1 tbsp finely snipped flat-leaf parsley

Salt and freshly ground pepper

Variation

Grilled pork crépinettes, or Toulouse sausages, arranged over the top of the cooked beans just as you serve them, turn this vegetable into a particularly flavoursome dish, especially if you partially top the crépinettes or sausages with a semi-cooked concasse of tomatoes.

Haricots

The white *coco* haricot bean, plump and oval in shape, is produced in Brittany and has AOC 'controlled designation of origin' status, as coco de Paimpol. Its crunchy texture and flavour are reminiscent of hazelnut, and it is highly regarded and appreciated.
• The Tarbais bean has a fine, soft and milky flesh, with a balanced taste and low acidity. It is grown in the Midi-Pyrénées and was granted the label rouge (the highest quality label guaranteeing regional origin) in 1997.
• Soissons or Gros Jacquot white haricots are very large ivory-coloured beans with a delicate flavour. They are a gastronomic product of the Picardie region of northern France, grown in Aisne.

Subric d'Épinards et Champignons de Paris

SPINACH SUBRICS WITH MUSHROOMS

These are little gems of French cuisine. More than just a vegetable, they are a melt-in-the-mouth delicacy. You can cook them ahead of time and reheat them in a bain-marie for 10 minutes or so just before serving, but they will not have quite the same delicate perfection. A Chardonnay, such as Macon Villages or Saint-Veran, will bring a mellow smoothness to this elegant vegetable dish.

Brush the softened butter over the insides of 8 dariole moulds, about 4.5cm tall, 4.5cm diameter across the top and 3cm diameter at the base. Transfer to the fridge for 5 minutes, then repeat the process so that they are all generously buttered. Set aside in the fridge until needed.

Cook the spinach in a large pan of lightly salted boiling water for 3–4 minutes. As soon as it is cooked, drain and plunge into a bowl of iced water. After a few minutes, drain and squeeze the leaves between your hands to extract as much water as possible.

Heat the cream in a saucepan and, as soon as it boils, add the spinach and cook for 2–3 minutes over a medium heat, stirring constantly with a wooden spoon. Add the nutmeg with salt and pepper to taste.

Transfer to a food processor or blender and process for 3–4 minutes, until the mixture is perfectly smooth. Pass through a fine chinois into a bowl set over a bowl of ice and stir with a wooden spoon so that the mixture cools rapidly and so avoids oxidisation.

Mix the egg yolk with the whole egg in a bowl, then add to the spinach mixture. Stir in the eggs by agitating the mixture evenly and efficiently with a wooden spoon rather than with vigorous whisking, to avoid any air bubbles forming as the subrics cook.

Preheat the oven to 160°C/Gas 3.

Wipe the mushrooms clean, cut into thin 2mm slices and sprinkle with a few drops of lemon juice. Position the mushroom slices against the inside and base of the dariole moulds, making sure they stick well. Pour the creamed spinach mixture into the moulds, to come to the top, then cover each mould with a small piece of foil, to keep them watertight during cooking.

Arrange the moulds in a shallow baking dish lined with greaseproof paper or foil and pour hot water, at 60°C, into the dish to come halfway up the sides

Makes 8–10

40g butter, softened

350g spinach (not baby leaves)

170ml double cream

Knifetip of freshly grated nutmeg

1 egg yolk, plus 1 small egg (50–55g)

4 button mushrooms

Juice of ¼ lemon

20g clarified butter (page 266), melted

Salt and freshly ground pepper

of the moulds. Transfer to the oven and cook for 16–18 minutes. To check they are done, lift the foil covering the top of one of the moulds and insert a trussing needle, which will emerge clean and shiny if they are cooked to perfection. Transfer the moulds from the dish to a wire rack and set aside to rest for 3–5 minutes before unmoulding.

Invert the moulds very carefully, one by one, onto a serving dish, making sure they hold their shape as they come out. Brush a little clarified butter over each one and serve at once.

Variations
You can also make subric of carrot or pumpkin, following the same principle. Cook your chosen vegetable, then in the cream (as in the main recipe). Blitz in a food processor until smooth, then strain through a fine chinois and bind with eggs before cooking in a bain-marie as above. They will be delicious served alongside lamb or veal.

MAIRIE DE GASSIN
LIBERTÉ · ÉGALITÉ · FRATERNITÉ

Asperges Vertes
et
Asperges Blanches
11,95 €/kg

Fraises chers
de Carpentras
Barquette 500g
5,50 € la gte
19,00 € la 2

Fraises
Barquette
19,00 la
gte

Haricots
Verts
7 € le Kg
or: France

Oeufs de Nos poules
Cat. II
2,60 la boite de 6
or: France Besoforce

Cèpes à la Bordelaise

The cep, chanterelle and morel seasons are highlights
in the gourmet's calendar. I like to serve this cep dish with
a pan-fried rib-eye steak, or roast rib of beef.

Using a small knife, trim the cep stalks, then gently wipe the caps and stalks
with a damp tea towel, to remove all traces of grit and other impurities.

Heat the butter in a sauté pan over a medium heat, add the whole ceps and
lemon juice, cover with a lid and stew gently over a low heat for 5 minutes.
Drain in a colander, allow to cool a little, then wipe them gently one by one
with kitchen paper. Cut each on a slight bias into slices about 5mm thick.

Heat the olive oil in a frying pan over a lively heat, add the cep slices and
cook for 2–3 minutes, then reduce the heat and cook over a gentle heat for
6–8 minutes. Season with salt and pepper to taste, add the garlic and parsley
and cook for a further 1 minute. Serve straight away.

Serves 4

750g small ceps, with firm caps

50g butter

Juice of ½ lemon

50ml light olive oil

2 garlic cloves, peeled and finely
  chopped

20g flat-leaf parsley, finely snipped

Salt and freshly ground pepper

Concombre Étuvé au Beurre
CUCUMBER BRAISED IN BUTTER

You can spice this up a little if you like, by adding a pinch of
curry powder at the last minute, but if I am serving it with
chicken, I prefer the dish just as it is.

Peel the cucumbers and cut lengthways into quarters. Remove the seeds and
cut the flesh into 1.5cm lengths, if serving with a small fish or chicken, or 3cm
pieces if serving with a large piece of fish, a whole fish or large chicken. Using
a small knife, trim the pieces into the shape of large, elongated garlic cloves.

Blanch the cucumber in lightly salted boiling water for 30 seconds, then
refresh and drain. Heat 60g of the butter in a small sauté pan and, as soon as
it has melted, add the cucumber pieces and salt very lightly. Cover and sweat
over a gentle heat for 15–20 minutes, stirring every 5 minutes.

Once cooked, drain and add the remaining 40g butter to the pan. Turn the
cucumber in the butter to coat, add salt and pepper to taste and serve at
once, sprinkled with chervil, if using.

Serves 4

500–600g cucumbers, firm, fleshy and
  not too large (so with fewer seeds)

100g butter

15g chervil, finely snipped (optional)

Salt and freshly ground white pepper

Lentilles du Puy

A cooking sausage or piece of *petit salé* (cured pork) spare ribs or blade end of shoulder, cooked separately in water and mixed into the lentils at the end, turns this into a delicious main dish.

Put the lentils in a sieve and rinse in cold water, checking for small stones (occasionally found in lentils).

Put the water or stock in a saucepan. Add the lentils and all the remaining ingredients except the butter and seasoning. Bring to the boil over a medium heat, then reduce the heat to just the merest simmer. After 10 minutes, skim the surface and continue to cook for another 10 minutes, then salt very lightly and cook for a further 10 minutes, so 30 minutes in total.

Taste the lentils, which should be just cooked, and season with salt and pepper to taste. Take off the heat and stir in the butter in small pieces. Remove the bouquet garni, celery and onion, then serve.

Variations
You can perk up the lentils with some tomato concasse, added just before serving. Or, served cold and dressed with a vinaigrette, they make a delicious and simple starter; just add a little finely chopped onion and parsley to lift the flavours a little.

Serves 4–6

250g green lentils, preferably Puy

600ml water or chicken stock (page 248), or buy good-quality fresh stock

1 medium bouquet garni

1 medium carrot, peeled and cut into short lengths

1 medium onion, peeled and studded with 2 cloves

1 celery stalk, halved

30g butter

Salt and freshly ground pepper

Carottes à la Crème

This simple accompaniment goes beautifully with roast veal, pan-fried or roast guinea fowl, as well as with braised sea bass.

Cut the carrots into rounds or lengths on the diagonal and put into a saucepan. Add enough cold water to just cover, then add the butter, sugar and a pinch of salt. Cook over a medium heat until the cooking liquid has evaporated, about 15–20 minutes.

Add the cream and simmer over a gentle heat for a further 3 minutes. Season with salt and pepper to taste and serve at once.

Serves 4

400g medium carrots

30g butter

2 tsp caster sugar

4 tbsp double cream

Salt and freshly ground pepper

(Illustrated on page 189)

Ratatouille

A culinary speciality of Nice dating back to around 1780, ratatouille is a ragoût of mixed vegetables cooked in light olive oil. When the vegetables are cooked to perfection – neither too soft nor too firm – it is one of the finest dishes of Provence – you could almost call it sunshine on a plate. I love it cold or hot, for lunch or dinner.

Rinse the aubergines and courgettes in cold water and trim off the ends of both. Cut the aubergines into roughly 1.5cm cubes, sprinkle lightly with salt and place in a dish. Set aside for 30 minutes to lightly degorge them. Cut the courgettes into roughly 2cm cubes and set aside.

Preheat the grill and brush the peppers with a little of the olive oil. Cook under the grill, turning frequently, until they blister and colour a little all over. Plunge into a bowl of iced water, then carefully peel off the skins, using your fingers or a small knife. Split them in half down the middle, remove the seeds and white parts, cut into small pieces and set aside in a bowl.

Heat one-third of the olive oil in a heavy-based flameproof casserole over a gentle heat. Add the onions and garlic and sweat for 2 minutes, stirring with a wooden spoon, then add the tomatoes and bouquet garni and cook over a medium heat for 15 minutes or so, stirring every 5 minutes. Add the peppers and courgettes, season lightly with salt and cook for 30 minutes.

Drain and dab dry the aubergines. Heat the remaining olive oil in a frying pan over a medium heat, add the aubergines and cook for 20 minutes, stirring once during cooking.

Tip the aubergines into the casserole, stir with a wooden spoon and leave to simmer over a gentle heat for 25–35 minutes, depending on the freshness of the vegetables, stirring every 5–10 minutes. The vegetables should be properly cooked but not to a mush; you should be able to discern the flavour of each one. Remove the bouquet garni and garlic and adjust the seasoning with salt and a generous amount of pepper. Serve straight from the casserole.

NOTE Ratatouille is very good reheated, often better in fact. A few beaten eggs cooked with any leftovers are also absolutely delicious.

Serves 4

300g aubergines

400g courgettes

200g peppers, preferably green or yellow, washed and wiped dry

200ml olive oil

200g onions, peeled and diced

½ unpeeled head of garlic (cut horizontally)

800g tomatoes, peeled, deseeded and cut into large dice

1 medium bouquet garni

Salt and freshly ground pepper

Pommes Duchesse DUCHESS POTATOES

These enriched potatoes can be piped around the edge of a dish, or in swirls on a baking tray and baked at 190°C/Gas 5 for 5–10 minutes, or shaped into nests (see page 153).

Preheat the oven to 180°C/Gas 4. Prick each potato several times with a fork or skewer. Place them on a baking tray, on a layer of salt, and bake in the oven for 1½–2 hours, depending on size, until soft when pierced with a knife.

Cut the baked potatoes in half and scoop out the fluffy flesh with a spoon; discard the skins. Pass the flesh through a sieve, fine mouli or ricer into a large bowl and add the butter, egg yolks and some seasoning. Mix thoroughly with a wooden spatula, then taste and adjust the seasoning. Serve as required (see above).

Serves 6–8

1kg Desiré or Maris Piper medium-large
potatoes, washed and patted dry

Coarse salt, for baking

50g butter, finely diced

3 egg yolks

Salt and freshly ground pepper

Pommes Dauphine DAUPHINE POTATOES

I like to serve these with game dishes, such as roast saddle of venison, as shown on page 145.

Put the potatoes in a pan, cover with cold water, add salt and bring to the boil. Cook for 20–30 minutes, depending on size. Drain well, then purée using a mouli fitted with the fine blade, or push through a fine sieve using a pestle.

Put the potato purée into a saucepan and dry it out over a medium heat for 1 minute, stirring with a wooden spoon. Remove from the heat and stir in the pieces of butter. Mix the warm potato purée with the warm choux paste, then add the nutmeg with salt and pepper to taste.

Shape the dauphine potatoes into large, neat quenelles, using 2 large spoons, or transfer to a piping bag fitted with a plain 1.5cm nozzle and pipe attractive, regular cylinder shapes, pressing the bag and using the back of a small knife to cut off each to the desired length. Arrange the shaped dauphine potatoes individually on a sheet of lightly oiled greaseproof paper.

Heat the oil in a deep fryer to 170–180°C. Using a small palette knife, transfer 4–6 dauphine potato quenelles or cylinders to the hot oil, sliding them in gently. Cook for 3–5 minutes, until golden brown. Use a spider skimmer to remove them from the oil and onto kitchen paper to drain. Repeat with the remaining piped or quenelle shapes. Serve at once.

Serves 4–6

750g potatoes, Bintje or a similar variety,
peeled and washed

50g butter, cut into small pieces

¼ litre freshly made (still warm) choux
paste (page 264)

Knifetip of freshly grated nutmeg

1 litre grapeseed oil, plus extra for
greasing

Salt and freshly ground pepper

Pommes de Terre Fondantes

FONDANT POTATOES

These potatoes are succulent, flavoursome and rich, without being greasy, hence the name *fondant* (meltingly tender).

Using a swivel peeler or small knife, peel the potatoes and wash in cold water. Cut 2 lengthways slabs, 1.5cm thick, from each and trim with a small knife into even oval shapes. Arrange these side by side in a heavy-based sauté pan. Add just enough cold water to cover, then dot the butter over the surface. Add a little salt and pepper, the garlic cloves and thyme sprigs.

Cook over a very high heat until all the water has evaporated, and until the potatoes on the bottom just turn a light nutty colour. Remove from the heat at once and place on a cool surface, which will help the potatoes to release from the base of the pan. Leave for 5 minutes, then use a palette knife to turn each potato piece over, and place back over a medium heat. Cook for 3–5 minutes, until the undersides of the potatoes have coloured lightly. Remove from the heat, discard the garlic and thyme, then serve.

Serves 4

2 large potatoes, ideally Bintje or Belle de Fontenay, about 350–400g each

150g butter, in small pieces

2 garlic cloves (unpeeled)

2 thyme sprigs

Salt and freshly ground pepper

Pommes Soufflées

SOUFFLÉED POTATOES

Perfect with game dishes, these crisps are delightful served in potato waffle nests (page 137), as shown on page 135.

Peel the potatoes, rinse in cold water and slice lengthways into 5mm slices, using a mandoline. Cut each slice to shape using an oval pastry cutter about 3 x 6cm (or bigger if they do not need to fit inside potato waffle nests). Dab the slices lightly with water, but don't wash them.

Pour a 6cm depth of oil into a heavy-based saucepan and heat to 130°C. Do the same in a second heavy-based pan but heat the oil to 170°C. Add a maximum of 5 or 6 potato slices at a time to the 130°C oil. Fry for 2–3 minutes, moving the pan in a forwards and backwards motion as they cook, so that the potato slices do not float on the oil and are covered at all times. As soon as little pockets of air appear on their surface, use a spider skimmer to transfer the potato slices to the second pan of oil at 170°C and cook until they have puffed up nicely and turned golden on both sides.

Transfer to a plate lined with kitchen paper and set aside; keep warm. Repeat with the rest of the potato slices and sprinkle with salt just before serving.

Serves 4

250g potatoes suitable for frying, ideally Agria or Lovers

About 1.5 litres grapeseed or groundnut oil

Gratin Savoyard

POTATO GRATIN SAVOYARD

As the name indicates, this farmhouse dish was created in the Savoie region. Originally, the potatoes were cooked in beef stock, and the local cheese Beaufort was used. In the last thirty years or so, many cooks, myself included, have replaced the beef stock with cream, which doesn't interfere with the flavour of the potato. And I use Comté cheese, which has more flavour than Beaufort. It goes very well with roast lamb or beef and is just as good reheated – in a low oven at 130°C/Gas ½ for 30 minutes.

Peel the potatoes using a swivel peeler, wash them and use a mandoline to cut them into even, not too thick slices, about 2–3mm. Spread them out on a clean surface, sprinkle generously with salt, rub them together well, then rearrange them in a pile and set aside for 10 minutes.

Preheat the oven to 160°C/Gas 3.

Dip the half garlic clove in fine salt, then use it to rub the insides of a shallow baking dish, either a Le Creuset type or earthenware.

Put the cream and milk in a large saucepan and heat over a medium heat. Add a grinding of pepper, then the nutmeg. As soon as the cream is warm, squeeze the potatoes in small handfuls to extract the water, then add them to the cream. Bring to the boil over a medium heat, stirring with a wooden spoon every minute. Cook for a further 2 minutes, stirring constantly.

Remove from the heat, add the grated cheese, then tip everything into the baking dish and spread out evenly; the gratin needs to be 5–6cm deep. Cook in the oven for 45 minutes, then remove and set aside in a warm place.

Serve within 20 minutes of removing from the oven, either as it is at the table, so that everyone can serve themselves using a large spoon, or serve out portions in the kitchen using a plain 5–7cm pastry cutter, placing these on small, individual dishes.

Variation
The more familiar classic dish of dauphinois potatoes is made in exactly the same way, but without cheese; it is better suited to serving with fish dishes.

Serves 4–6

650g medium potatoes, such as
  Charlotte, Bintje, etc.

½ garlic clove

500ml double cream

4 tbsp milk

Pinch of freshly grated nutmeg

150g Comté, Gruyère or
  Emmenthal cheese, grated

Salt and freshly ground pepper

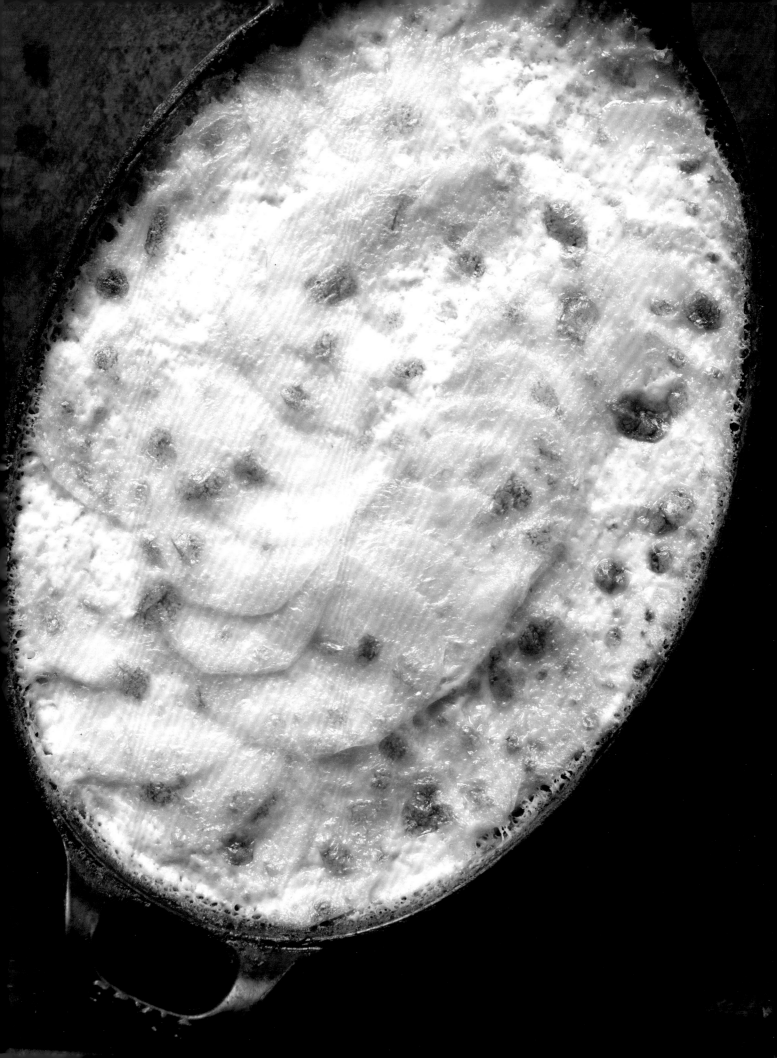

FOR CHEESE LOVERS... an exploratory guide

The origins of cheese stretch back to antiquity, although it is likely that what was called 'cheese' at that time was far from being the product we are familiar with today. It is surprising to note that at the end of the Middle Ages there were already some 50 varieties of cheese in France, with individuals using their wherewithal and local resources to make cheese intended for personal consumption. This explains in part why France has such a wonderful wealth and variety of cheeses.

These days, no other country produces such a palette of more than 500 different cheeses, all of exceptional quality and offering everything from mild to stronger flavours, a range of consistencies from fresh white cheeses, to soft unpasteurised and hard pasteurised cheeses. Some are eaten while still young, while others will spend three, six or even 24 months, depending on their size and type, in an ageing cellar or cave (*cave d'affinage*). Most French people, including me, would not consider ending a meal without indulging in a little piece of cheese...

The locally distinctive regions of our country, its moderate climate and the varied grasslands mean that dairy cows, which give an average of 20–30 litres of milk per day, sheep (½–1 litre per day) and goats (2–5 litres per day), all produce milk with unique characteristics, which in turn result in cheeses of multiple different flavours.

Added to all this is the *savoir-faire* of small and medium producers, who use their expertise to transform their everyday milk into their own idiosyncratic cheeses, putting pride and love into an activity they perform all their lives.

Some of the finest of these cheeses will find their way to master *affineurs* who, in their ageing caves, will bring them to the optimal point of ripening before selling them to their clientele at the perfect eating stage.

There are three very distinct cheese categories (*appellations*) that are important to be aware of when selecting your cheese, with a significant price differential. The first one is of course the best and most expensive, with industrially produced cheeses the least flavourful and the cheapest:

- Farmhouse (*fermier*) cheeses: This label signifies that the milk is processed on the farm where it is produced within 24 hours at most from being milked. These cheeses could be described as nature's legitimate heirs; all made using untreated milk, they are 100% representative of the *terroir* that nurtured them. They are full of flavour, unpredictable and occasionally pungent, especially if the animals feed on tall grasses rather than hay. These are my favourite cheeses and I adore them...
- Artisanal cheeses: These are made from milk produced on several farms from a local radius of neighbouring parishes and villages. They are often made by small enterprises, using untreated milk. They are generally archetypal in flavour and their quality is reliably good, but they are not on a par with the pre-eminent *fermier* cheeses.
- Industrial cheeses: This is the biggest category. The cheeses are made largely using pasteurised milk and are often intended for large-scale distribution. Of a standardised flavour, they keep longer and are ideal for pre-slicing and packaging to sell on self-service shelves. It's a vast manufacturing market that has never held any attraction for me.

A good cheese platter comprises four to six cheeses from different *terroirs* and a range of varieties, but if possible all with the AOP (Appellation d'Origine Contrôlée) label. Ideally you should follow the seasons and try to buy cheese from a *maître-fromager*, who will be happy to advise you, or seek guidance from a book written by such an expert. It is essential to serve cheese at room temperature, meaning it should never be cold.

I like to match some cheeses with certain fresh fruits (grapes, pears, apples or figs), or with dried fruits and nuts at the start of the year (especially walnuts, hazelnuts and dates), or with crudités (celery, cucumber, chicory and fennel go especially well with blue cheese), or sometimes with a condiment (such as honey, quince paste or chutney).

For bread, I favour *baguette de tradition*, with plenty of crust and a fairly neutral flavour that gives prominence to all the fragrances and flavours of the cheese, as well as neutrally flavoured crackers. If you would like to serve a more original bread, then walnut, raisin, almond or hazelnut bread pair well with a number of cheeses.

In terms of drinks, depending on the strength and type of cheese, my choice veers towards, amongst others, Gewürztraminer, red wine, white Burgundy, whisky, *vin jaune* (a Jura wine similar to sherry), Sauternes, Port, even beer. It's up to each individual to sample and discover the different combinations that will seduce…

As a guide, here are some happy marriages that I have discovered:

- Morbier served with a Chardonnay and eaten with baguette and dried fruit

- Comté goes particularly well with *vin jaune* or whisky, and with walnut or hazelnut bread

- Camembert is excellent accompanied by cider or red wine, as well as crackers or baguette

- Goat's cheese, such as Chabichou or Charolais, makes a fine match with a wine from the Loire or a Burgundy Chardonnay, and with a dried fruit or multigrain bread

- Maroilles, with its characteristic odour and strong flavour of the *terroir*, can be enjoyed at its best with beer and crackers, or even wholemeal bread

- Munster, a wonderful AOC cheese from Alsace with a lingering spicy taste, is particularly delicious sprinkled with cumin seeds and eaten with bread or crackers

- Roquefort, my favourite, which I regard as the king of cheeses, is best savoured with Port or Sauternes, and baguette or Duchy Original Organic Oaten biscuits

Last but not least, the golden rule: avoid putting cheese in the fridge, as it has a detrimental effect on the flavour. Store cheeses, loosely wrapped in waxed paper (not cling film), in a cool larder.

Saint-Nectaire (above left);
Fougerous (below left);
Mimolette (above)

Desserts

Tarte aux Pommes

Filled with a vanilla-scented apple compote and topped with wafer-thin slices of apple arranged in a beautiful rosette, this is the classic French apple tart that has stood the test of time. In Alsace, the compote is often replaced with crème pâtissière (see page 259), which is equally good. I sometimes use rough puff pastry rather than the usual shortcrust for this tart, as it gives a lighter, crisper crust.

Lightly butter a 24cm fluted loose-based tart tin, 3cm deep. Roll out the pastry on a lightly floured surface to a 3mm thickness for shortcrust, or 2.5mm for quick puff. Drape it over a rolling pin and unfurl it carefully into the prepared tin. Press it evenly onto the base and sides of the tin and, using your thumb and index finger, press the edges up into an even ridge that sits slightly proud of the rim. Slide the tin onto a baking sheet and rest in the fridge for 20 minutes.

Peel, halve and core the apples, then cut each half into wafer-thin (2mm thick) slices. Put the 50ml water into a saucepan and add the vanilla pod, butter and about one-third of the total apples, selecting the smallest slices. Simmer gently over a low heat until the apples are completely cooked. Remove from the heat, pick out the vanilla pod and whisk the apples to make a compote. Set aside to cool. Meanwhile, preheat the oven to 200°C/Gas 6.

Prick the pastry case base with a fork in 8–10 places. Spoon the cooled apple compote over the base. Arrange a ring of apple slices in an overlapping circle on the compote inside the edge of the tart case. Then create another overlapping circle inside the ring, arranging the apple slices in the opposite direction (as shown). Cut the remaining apple slivers into smaller pieces to fill the space in the centre; the apple compote should be completely covered.

Bake the tart in the oven for about 35–40 minutes, until the pastry and apples are cooked and lightly coloured. Set aside to cool for 20 minutes or so before unmoulding the tart.

While still warm, brush the apples with the warm, melted quince jelly or sugar syrup to glaze. The tart is best served warm.

Serves 8

60g butter, plus extra to grease

300g flan pastry (page 262) or 250g quick puff pastry (page 263)

Flour, for dusting

8 dessert apples, ideally Cox (about 1kg in total)

50ml water

1 vanilla pod, split lengthways

80g quince jelly, melted, or 80ml sugar syrup (page 266)

Apple turnovers

Any leftover pastry and trimmings can be used to make apple turnovers. Roll out the pastry into a long strip, about 3mm thick. Place generous spoonfuls of apple compote down one half, 6–8cm apart. Brush egg glaze around each mound of apple and bring the other half of the pastry over to cover the filling. Use a pastry cutter to cut out individual turnovers and press the pastry edges together to seal. Brush egg glaze over the tops and score a pattern with a small knife, then bake in the oven at 180°C/Gas 4 for 15 minutes.

Les Cerises Glacées à la Montmorency

GLAZED POACHED CHERRIES WITH VANILLA ICE CREAM

The marriage of good red wine with black cherries, so simply cooked, is absolutely delicious. Vanilla ice cream makes a perfect accompaniment, both visually and in terms of flavour.

Pour two-thirds of the wine into a saucepan, add the cinnamon stick, orange zest and half the sugar. Slowly bring to the boil over a medium heat, then lower the heat and simmer to reduce for 10 minutes. Remove from the heat and set aside.

Put the remaining sugar in a non-stick frying pan and melt over a medium heat. As soon as it turns a light caramel colour, add the cherries, increase the heat and cook for 5 minutes, stirring all the time. Pour the remaining wine over the cherries and cook for another 2 minutes, then transfer the cherries and caramel to the pan containing the reduced wine.

Poach the cherries over a medium heat for 10 minutes, then drain, reserving the poaching wine. Pour this back into the pan and reduce by one-third. Pour this reduced wine over the cherries, remove the orange zest and set aside to cool; do not refrigerate.

For the vanilla ice cream, churn the crème anglaise in an ice-cream machine for about 20 minutes. As soon as it becomes firm, transfer to a container in the freezer.

Divide the cooled cherries and reduced poaching wine between individual bowls. Sprinkle lemon zest julienne over each portion and serve a scoop of vanilla ice cream to each guest.

Montmorency cherries

Belonging to the sour cherry family, Montmorency cherries, or *griottes* (also called *gaudrioles*), have a slightly acidic taste and a soft, pinkish, almost translucent flesh. Nowadays they are nearly impossible to find in their town of origin, Montmorency, some ten miles to the north of Paris, but they are still grown around the nearby districts of Soissy-sous-Montmorency and Saint-Prix. They are also grown in Michigan, USA, and Ontario, Canada.

Serves 4

750ml red Burgundy wine, ideally Pinot Noir

1 small cinnamon stick

Pared zest of 1 orange

150g caster sugar

400g very ripe Montmorency or other sour black cherries, stoned

½ quantity vanilla crème anglaise (page 258)

Pared zest of 1 lemon, cut into julienne and blanched

Clafoutis aux Figues à la Bourdaloue FIG CLAFOUTIS

Here the red flesh of the figs contrasts beautifully with the golden clafoutis batter. The figs must be properly drained and dabbed dry after poaching, so that only a little of their juices escape as they cook, allowing the batter to cook correctly.

Pour the red wine into a sauté pan, add 300g of the caster sugar and the cinnamon stick, and place over a medium heat. Very gently rinse the figs and, using a small knife, remove a little of the stalk.

As the wine comes to the boil, add the figs and poach over a gentle heat (at about 80°C), for 20–30 minutes, depending on their ripeness. Remove from the heat and leave the figs to cool in the wine. Once cold, carefully drain in a sieve or colander set over a jug to catch the liquor. Pour this back into the pan and reduce over a medium heat by half. Strain through a fine chinois into a bowl and leave to cool, then refrigerate.

For the clafoutis batter, pour the milk and cream into a pan and set over a gentle heat. Break the eggs into a bowl, add 150g of the remaining sugar and work very lightly with a balloon whisk. Add the flour and ground almonds and whisk well.

As soon as the milk and cream mix comes to the boil, pour it onto the egg mixture, whisking all the time. Once combined, set aside to cool, stirring with the whisk from time to time. Meanwhile, preheat the oven to 190°C/Gas 5.

Use the butter to grease the base and sides of a 24cm ceramic tart dish, about 3cm deep, then dust the remaining 20g sugar over the base. Very carefully dab the figs dry with a tea towel, then arrange them over the base of the dish. Pour the clafoutis mixture into the dish and cook in the oven for 40 minutes, lowering the setting to 180°C/Gas 4 after 20 minutes.

Once cooked (the middle softer than the edge), transfer to a wire rack to cool down. When it is still just warm, brush the tops of the figs with a little of the red wine reduction, then serve using a tart slice, with the help of a large spoon. If you like, serve the remaining chilled wine reduction separately, in small liqueur glasses.

Variations

When quetsche plums are in season, you can use these in place of the figs, keeping the stones in so that they retain their shape in the clafoutis, and replacing the cinnamon with a generous pinch of quatre-épices. Or replace the figs with sweet cherries, to make a classic *clafoutis aux cerises*.

Serves 8

1 litre red wine, preferably Bordeaux

470g caster sugar

1 cinnamon stick

12–14 ripe figs (depending on size), preferably red

120ml milk

120ml double cream

4 eggs

30g plain flour

30g ground almonds, sieved unless very fine

30g butter

Tarte des Demoiselles Tatin aux Poires PEAR TARTE TATIN

The classic Tarte Tatin is of course made with apples, and is sublime, but when pears are in season I can't resist this juicy and flavourful version. The pears partially absorb the flavour of the star anise, and the sugar-butter mixture, which turns to a caramel-butter on cooking, is divine. A glass of Sauternes will only enhance your enjoyment of this lovely dessert.

Cut the top off one pear, with the stalk still attached and set aside. Peel all 4 pears, cut them in half from top to bottom and remove the cores. Put the pear halves in a large bowl with the lemon juice, gently moving them in the juice to coat and prevent them from turning brown.

Coat the base of a 24cm diameter, 7cm high tatin pan, or ovenproof sauté pan, evenly with the butter. Scatter over the sugar, so that the butter is all covered and add the star anise, spacing them evenly. Now arrange the pear halves rounded side down on the sugar with the reserved pear top in the centre, stalk down.

Roll out the pastry on a lightly floured very cold surface to a round, about 3mm thick. Prick the pastry in 5 or 6 places with a fork, then loosely roll the pastry onto the rolling pin and unfurl it over the pears, to cover them. Using scissors, trim the excess pastry overhanging the dish to leave just 1–2cm overhanging. Place in the fridge for 20 minutes.

Preheat the oven to 220°C/Gas 7. Place the tatin pan directly over a lively heat for 5 minutes, then lower the heat to medium. After about 15 minutes, use a small palette knife to lift the pastry edge a little and check that the butter-sugar mixture is boiling nicely. As soon as it has turned a glossy amber, transfer to the oven. Cook for 10 minutes, then reduce the oven setting to 180°C/Gas 4 and cook for a further 20 minutes. Remove from the oven and rest on a wooden board in a warm place for 2 minutes.

Holding a dry tea towel, invert a heatproof shallow serving dish over the pastry. Turn the tatin pan and dish over sharply and deftly, keeping your forearm covered with the tea towel to protect it from any escaping hot caramel. The pastry is now underneath and the pears on top. If necessary, adjust them and the star anise into place with a fork. Serve at once.

Variation
Replace the pears with (not too ripe) mangos, reducing the butter and sugar quantities by a third. Once the Tatin is turned out, scoop passion fruit seeds and juice over the top, to bring out the mango flavour even more.

Serves 4

4 medium pears, not too ripe

Juice of 1 lemon

120g butter, softened

200g caster sugar

5 star anise

220g quick puff pastry (page 263)

Flour, for dusting

Pommes au Four Meringuées
BAKED APPLES WITH MERINGUE

This is one of my favourite family desserts from my childhood. My mother used to make it for us using the plentiful apples she would pick in the orchards of her native Normandy. It is one of the easiest desserts to make – and inexpensive – perfect to round off an autumn or winter meal. It isn't essential to pipe the meringue, you can simply spoon it around the apples. Try using bananas, sprinkled with lemon juice, instead of apples if you like, halving the baking time.

Preheat the oven to 200°C/Gas 6. Butter an ovenproof dish, using 60g of the butter. Remove the stalk from the apples and scoop out the core with an apple corer. Make an incision with the tip of a knife round the middle of each apple, to help with cooking.

Arrange the apples in the buttered dish and divide the remaining butter between their cavities. Dust with the sugar and bake for 50–60 minutes, depending on the size of the apples and variety used. They are cooked when the tip of a knife penetrates easily.

While the apples are in the oven prepare the meringue, following the instructions for meringue italienne on page 265.

When the apples are ready remove them from the oven and set aside for 5–10 minutes, keeping the oven at 200°C/Gas 6.

Put the meringue into a piping bag fitted with a large fluted nozzle and pipe the meringue around the apples. Return the dish to the oven for 3–5 minutes, until the meringue colours lightly.

As you remove the dish from the oven, brush the tops of the apples with the melted redcurrant jelly or apricot jam. Serve at once, from the baking dish.

Variation

I sometimes replace the redcurrant jelly or apricot jam with a warm crème anglaise, to which I add raisins (ideally Corinthe), which I have first blanched and then soaked in rum. This makes an ideal dessert for a weekend in the country, next to the fire…

Serves 8

160g butter, softened

8 medium, not too ripe dessert apples, ideally Cox or Granny Smith

80g caster sugar

Meringue

360g caster sugar

30g liquid glucose (optional)

6 medium egg whites

To glaze

200g redcurrant jelly, or sieved apricot jam, melted

Galette des Rois ALMOND GALETTE

This is a classic dessert made to celebrate Epiphany in France. Tradition calls for everyone to 'find the king': one or two beans are hidden in the galette, representing the king and queen. The person who finds the first bean is crowned king or queen, depending on who has found it. It is customary for that person to offer round the second galette, while the second person to find a bean offers round the drinks.

Divide the pastry into two pieces, one about 200g and the other about 300g. On a lightly floured surface, roll out the smaller piece of pastry to a round, about 2.5mm thick and 24cm in diameter, giving it a quarter-turn several times as you do so. Now loosely roll the pastry around the rolling pin and unfurl it onto a baking sheet.

Using a palette knife, spread the frangipane over the pastry, leaving a 3–4cm border round the edge. Brush the pastry border with egg glaze.

Roll out the second piece of pastry in the same way, to a 25cm round, about 3mm thick. Place this thicker round on top of the first and, with your fingertips, press the edges together so that the two rounds of pastry are properly fused together. Transfer to the fridge for 30 minutes. Preheat the oven to 200°C/Gas 6.

Place a 22cm tart ring or pithiviers cutter over the galette and, using a small knife, cut off the excess pastry on the outside, which will give about 125g trimmings. Using a knife with a flexible blade, flute up the sides of the pastry by lightly scoring the pastry all around, which will help the pastry rise evenly as it cooks.

Brush egg glaze over the top of the galette and, using a small, very sharp, pointed knife, very lightly score neat, regular incisions into the pastry. Start by making pairs of small parallel lines, 2mm apart, with each pair about 3cm apart, then long lines in between to give a wheat-ear effect.

Bake for about 30 minutes, then remove from the oven and increase the temperature to 220°C/gas mark 7. Dust the surface of the galette with a veil of icing sugar, then put back in the oven for 1–2 minutes, until the icing sugar has melted to a shiny glaze. Transfer to a wire rack and allow to cool slightly.

Serve the galette whole on a large plate and cut into slices, using a serrated knife. It is at its best served warm.

Variation

For a Pithiviers, fill the galette more generously with frangipane and mark a radial pattern on top of the pastry. Serve with chilled crème anglaise.

Serves 6

500g quick puff pastry (page 263)

Flour, for dusting

100g frangipane (page 264)

1 egg, mixed with 2 tsp milk and a pinch of salt, to glaze

Icing sugar, for dusting

Soufflé Harlequin

The exquisite appearance and flavours of this soufflé will delight your guests. I prepared it for the Meilleur Ouvrier de France (Best Craftsman of France) competition in 1976.

Using a brush, butter the insides of 4 individual soufflé dishes, 10cm in diameter and 6.5cm high, with the softened butter. Place the 50g sugar in one dish and tip and rotate it so that the sugar coats all of the inside, then invert it over the next dish, tapping the base so that the excess sugar falls out. Repeat with the remaining dishes to coat.

You will need to make a divider to keep the vanilla and chocolate quarters separate. To do this, cut out 2 strips of thin, rigid cardboard the length to fit the diameter of the dishes exactly, with both just taller than the dish and one slightly taller than the other. Cut up the centre of the taller one almost to the top and slide this piece right down onto the shorter one, so the bases are level and it forms a cross. You can use one divider for all 4 dishes.

For the vanilla crème pâtissière, put the milk, cream and vanilla pod in a pan over a medium heat. Put the egg yolks, sugar and cornflour in a bowl and whisk together for 1 minute. As soon as the milk and cream mixture comes to the boil, pour it onto the yolks, whisking all the time. Pour back into the pan and simmer for 30 seconds, whisking constantly. Remove the vanilla pod, pour into a bowl and cover with cling film.

For the chocolate crème pâtissière, put the milk and cream in a pan over a medium heat. Put the egg yolks, sugar, cornflour and cocoa powder in a bowl and whisk together for 1 minute. As soon as the milk and cream mixture comes to the boil, pour it onto the yolk mixture, whisking all the time. Pour back into the pan and simmer for 30 seconds, whisking constantly. Remove from the heat and add the chocolate. Mix well with a whisk, pour into a bowl and cover with cling film.

Put a baking sheet inside the oven and preheat the oven to 200°C/Gas 6.

It is important to use precise quantities, so measure 220g of the vanilla crème pâtissière and put into a large bowl. Measure 220g of the chocolate crème pâtissière and place in another large bowl. Both should be either warm or hot; they must not be cold.

Using electric beaters, whisk the egg whites to soft peaks, then add the 120g sugar and whisk to semi-firm peaks. Whisk one-sixth of the whites into the vanilla crème pâtissière, then, using another whisk, another sixth into the chocolate crème pâtissière. Divide the remaining whites evenly between the two mixtures and mix gently, using a rubber spatula and without overworking.

Fill a large piping bag with a 2cm opening (and no nozzle) with the vanilla mixture and another with the chocolate mixture. Brush the cardboard divider lightly with oil and place it in one of the prepared dishes.

(continued overleaf)

Serves 4

For the dishes

50g butter, softened

50g caster sugar

2 tsp grapeseed oil

Vanilla crème pâtissière

220ml milk

65ml double cream

1 vanilla pod, split lengthways

2 egg yolks

20g caster sugar

18g cornflour

Chocolate crème pâtissière

220ml milk

65ml double cream

2 egg yolks

20g caster sugar

18g cornflour

25g dark cocoa powder, sifted

40g good-quality dark chocolate, 70% cocoa solids (ideally Valrhona), finely chopped

To assemble

12 egg whites

120g caster sugar

To finish

Icing sugar

Pipe vanilla mixture into two opposite quarters to come to the very top, then pipe the chocolate mixture into the other two opposite quarters.

Carefully remove the divider and place it in the next dish, then repeat the procedure to fill the remaining 3 dishes. Using a small palette knife, even out the tops of the soufflés, taking care not to mix the colours, then transfer to the preheated baking sheet in the oven. Lower the oven setting to 180°C/Gas 4 and cook for 7 minutes.

As soon as they come out of the oven, sift a very light dusting of icing sugar over the soufflés, place on individual serving plates and serve at once.

Crêpes Suzette

A great classic of luxury hotels all over France, and even of 3-star Michelin restaurants, throughout the 1950s and '60s. Sadly, because part of its preparation takes place in the dining area, and few maître d's are inclined to offer it to their guests, this beautiful dessert is gradually disappearing, but you can still enjoy it at the Waterside Inn, witnessing the deft expertise of our Director, Diego Masciaga.

For the crêpe batter, put the flour, sugar and salt in a bowl. Using a small balloon whisk, add the eggs one at a time, adding a third of the milk with each. Whisk well to mix, then whisk in the remaining milk, the cream and the Curaçao. When the mixture is smooth and homogeneous, cover the bowl with cling film and set aside in a warm (but not hot) place for at least 1 hour.

For the sauce, wash the oranges, wipe dry and rub the sugar lumps against their skins, so that they absorb the maximum orange fragrance. Whisk the softened butter and sugar together, using a small balloon whisk, then add the Curaçao and sugar lumps.

Put a small knob of clarified butter in a non-stick frying pan, about 16cm in diameter. Heat the pan over a medium heat, then ladle in a little crêpe batter and swirl it over the base of the pan, by moving the pan to and fro and giving it a light circular motion with the wrist. After 30–45 seconds, with the help of a palette knife, turn the half-cooked crêpe over, and finish cooking to a nice golden colour on the other side.

Transfer to a flat plate and cook the remaining crêpes in the same way, until all the mixture is used up, taking care to butter the pan a little between every 2 or 3 crêpes, and interleaving the cooked crêpes with small circles of greaseproof paper to prevent them from sticking together.

Squeeze the juice from the oranges into a frying pan (ideally copper-based and stainless-steel lined). Set over a high heat and reduce the juice by half.

Transfer the pan to a spirit or gas flambé lamp placed in the middle of the table, as you would for a fondue. Mix the buttery sauce into the orange juice and bring to a low boil. One at a time and working quickly, spread each crêpe out in the sauce, flip it over with a fork and fold into 4 triangles. Serve 3 crêpes to each guest to eat straight away, to enjoy them at their best.

Serves 6

Crêpes

125g plain flour

15g caster sugar

Small pinch of salt

2 eggs

300ml milk, boiled and cooled

75ml double cream

2 tsp Curaçao

30g clarified butter (page 266)

Sauce

1½ oranges

6 sugar lumps

180g butter, softened

180g caster sugar

2½ tbsp Curaçao

Mousse au Chocolat

Some chocolate mousse recipes use a crème anglaise base, but I find that too rich, which is why I favour this still rich, but not cloyingly so, version. An almond tuile would go beautifully as an accompaniment. Good-quality chocolate is essential; choose the variety according to the intensity of flavour required – the higher the cocoa solids the more intense the flavour.

Heat the milk in a pan until boiling. Remove from the heat and add the pieces of chocolate, mixing them in well using a balloon whisk. Once the mixture is smooth, add the egg yolks, whisking constantly for 2–3 minutes. Pour the mixture into a large bowl and set aside for 10 minutes, stirring every 2–3 minutes with a whisk.

Using electric beaters, whisk the egg whites to semi-firm peaks, then add the sugar and whisk on a fast setting for a further 2–3 minutes. Using a balloon whisk, gently fold one-third of the whisked whites into the chocolate mixture, then use a rubber spatula to fold in the remaining whites, taking care not to overwork it. As soon as the mixture is homogeneous, pour it carefully into a serving bowl and refrigerate for at least 4 hours before serving.

For the chocolate curls to decorate, if required, melt the 100g chocolate in a bain-marie, stirring a few times. As soon as it has melted, pour it onto a very cold, completely dry marble surface. Use a palette knife to spread out the melted chocolate until it begins to show the first signs of setting. Immediately hold a long-bladed knife at a 30° angle and push it away from you, gradually turning the angle of the knife up to 90° as you do so. The sharper the angle, the smaller the chocolate curls.

Scatter the chocolate curls on top of the mousse, if using, and serve using a large spoon to scoop out portions. The mousse should be chilled but not ice-cold. A glass of Pineau des Charentes or Maury-du-Roussillon will contrast the bitter sweetness of the chocolate perfectly.

Variation

White chocolate mousse scented with kaffir lime zest is also delicious. Off the heat, add the finely grated zest of a kaffir lime to the just-boiled milk and leave to infuse for a minute or so before whisking in finely chopped, good-quality white chocolate, along with 1 sheet of leaf gelatine, pre-soaked in cold water. Continue as for the main recipe.

Serves 8

300ml milk

300g good-quality dark chocolate,
   55–75% cocoa solids (ideally Valrhona),
   cut into small pieces

3 egg yolks

6 egg whites

90g caster sugar

Chocolate curls (optional)

100g good-quality dark chocolate
   (as above)

Vacherin Royal

For me, a vacherin needs to be assembled just before serving, with the ice creams churned only an hour beforehand, so that it is exceptionally silky and smooth. You can vary the fruit for the sorbet as you wish – try raspberry, melon or passion fruit, for example. For an extra touch of decadence, serve with a demi-sec Champagne, ideally rosé, or Loire valley Vouvray.

Preheat the oven to 100°C/Gas ¼. On a 40 x 60cm piece of baking parchment draw three 20cm diameter circles in pencil. Turn the parchment over and place on a baking sheet the same size as the parchment.

Prepare the meringue, following the instructions for Meringue française on page 265. Put the meringue mixture into a piping bag fitted with a plain 7–8mm nozzle and pipe meringue onto one of the circles, starting at the centre and working out in a spiral, making sure there is no space between the piped lines of coil, until the circle is entirely covered. Repeat with the other two circles, then pipe small balls around the edge of these two meringue rounds, to decorate (these will be the top and base).

Place in the oven for 2 hours, then turn the oven off and leave the meringue bases inside for 20–30 minutes. Take out and leave until nearly cold, then detach from the paper and place on a wire rack. Leave in a dry place until ready to assemble. (These keep well for several days in airtight containers.)

Set aside 8–10 of the best strawberries. To make the sorbet, hull the rest and put into a food processor or blender with the sugar syrup. Process for 1 minute, then strain through a chinois. Add the lemon juice and churn the mixture in an ice-cream machine for about 20 minutes, until set. Transfer the sorbet to a suitable container and freeze.

Clean the ice-cream machine. Churn the vanilla crème anglaise in the same way, until firm, then transfer to a suitable container in the freezer. Churn the pistachio crème anglaise and freeze in the same way.

To assemble, very lightly dust the decorated border of one of the meringue circles with cocoa for the vacherin base and place on a chilled large plate. Spread the pistachio ice cream on top, using a large spoon. Arrange the pistachios, if using, around the piped border at regular intervals. Place the plain meringue circle on top. Spoon the strawberry sorbet on top and arrange the reserved strawberries around the edge. Finally, place the second decorated meringue circle on top of the sorbet.

Put the vanilla ice cream into a large piping bag fitted with a 1.5cm fluted nozzle and pipe it on top of the vacherin to form a dome. Arrange mint sprigs decoratively around the dome and place little sprigs of redcurrants around the edge of the plate. Serve at once.

(Illustrated on previous page)

Serves 8–10

Meringue

5 medium egg whites

150g caster sugar

150g icing sugar, sifted

Sorbet

400g perfectly ripe strawberries

150ml sugar syrup (page 266)

Juice of 1 lemon

Ice creams

¼ litre vanilla crème anglaise (page 258)

¼ litre pistachio crème anglaise
  (page 258)

To assemble

2 tsp good-quality cocoa powder

20 skinned pistachios (optional)

10 small mint sprigs

50g redcurrant sprigs

Sabayon au Champagne Brut
CHAMPAGNE SABAYON

Originally the Italian zabaione, sabayon first appeared in France in the 16th century, thanks to Catherine de Medici bringing it with her from Italy when she married the future king Henry 2nd of France. Marvellously rich and silky, it comes in various flavour guises – sweet and savoury – and is well known around the world.

Two-thirds fill a saucepan large enough to hold the base of a round-bottomed heatproof bowl with warm water, and place over a gentle heat. Pour the champagne or sparkling wine into the bowl, then add the egg yolks, stirring constantly with a balloon whisk. Still whisking, shower in the sugar.

Whisk continuously for 8–10 minutes, making sure that the water temperature in the pan increases steadily but moderately. At this stage, the sabayon will be a light ribbon consistency. Check the temperature in the centre of the sabayon using a kitchen thermometer, and whisk constantly until this core temperature reaches a maximum of 55–60°C.

Remove the pan from the heat and continue to whisk; the sabayon should have a very thick ribbon consistency, with a foamy, glossy and creamy texture. Remove the bowl from the pan and fill 4 cocktail or burgundy wine glasses with the sabayon. Serve immediately, because sabayon won't tolerate being left to stand.

NOTE Sponge fingers would pair very well with this sabayon; pipe the mixture into thumb-width lengths, using a plain piping nozzle, and cook as described in the recipe for pear charlotte (page 238).

Variation
You can make this sabayon using Sauternes instead of champagne, but reduce the sugar to 40g, to compensate for the sweetness of Sauternes.

Serves 4
100ml champagne brut or dry
  sparkling wine
3 egg yolks
60g caster sugar

Gâteau Religieuse

Assembled into a pyramid tower and set on a pâte sablée base, this is a creation evocative of Antoine Carême's era, and takes some skill to prepare. These days, a religieuse is a small choux bun set atop a larger one – an example of rise and fall or merely just the passing of time, but here I am offering you a glimpse into the sumptuous past of French cuisine.

Fill a piping bag fitted with a 1.5cm plain nozzle with the choux pastry. Pipe 8 tapered éclair shapes, 11cm long, onto a baking sheet lined with baking parchment: squeeze the bag a little as you start to pipe so that each éclair starts 2.5cm wide, then gradually release the pressure as you pipe the length so that it finishes in a point about 1cm wide. On a second lined baking sheet, pipe a choux ring with an outside diameter of 5–6cm, and a 4cm diameter choux bun.

Preheat the oven to 200°C/Gas 6. Brush egg glaze over the tops of the éclairs, choux ring and bun, then use the back of a fork to very lightly indent the surface of the piped shapes. Bake in the oven for 20 minutes, then remove the choux ring and bun, reduce the oven temperature to 150°C/Gas 2 and cook the éclairs for a further 10 minutes. Transfer everything from the oven straight to a wire rack and set aside to cool.

As soon as the éclairs have cooled, use a 7mm nozzle to make an opening at both ends, another in the base of the bun, and two in the base of the choux ring, on opposite sides. Increase the oven temperature to 180°C/Gas 4.

Roll out the pastry on a lightly floured surface to a round, 3–4mm thick. Using a palette knife, transfer the round to a baking sheet. Place a ring or pithiviers marker on the pastry and cut round it with a sharp knife to give a 14cm diameter circle. Brush a 5cm margin around the edge of the pastry with the egg glaze, then lightly score a lattice pattern into the glazed area, using the back of a fork. Bake for 12 minutes, then remove from the oven and leave to cool on the baking sheet for 2 minutes, before sliding it onto a wire rack with the aid of a palette knife.

Put the almost cold meringue in a bowl and whisk in the butter 20–30g at a time, then whisk until very smooth. Set this buttercream aside.

Sift the cocoa powder into a small bowl and mix in 2 tsp warm water to make a smooth paste. Divide the crème pâtissière equally between 2 bowls. Lightly whisk half the dissolved coffee into one and half the dissolved cocoa into the other. Fill a piping bag fitted with a plain 7mm nozzle with the coffee crème pâtissière and pipe a very generous amount into 4 éclairs, through the openings at either end, and into the choux bun through the opening in the

(continued overleaf)

Serves 8

¼ quantity choux pastry (page 264)

1 egg yolk mixed with 2 tsp milk, to glaze

200g sweet flan pastry (page 262)

Flour, for dusting

300g meringue italienne (page 265), just cooled

200g butter, at room temperature

3 tbsp good-quality unsweetened cocoa powder

350g crème pâtissière (page 259)

3 tbsp instant coffee granules, dissolved in 1½ tbsp warm water

400g (½ tub) ready-made fondant pâtissier icing (pouring consistency, not ready-to-roll)

1 tbsp liquid glucose

base. Fill a second piping bag fitted with a 7mm nozzle with the chocolate crème pâtissière and fill the remaining 4 éclairs and the ring.

Divide the fondant icing equally between 2 small saucepans. Place one of the pans over a very gentle heat, 30°C maximum, and stir in the remaining dissolved coffee.

Spoon a very fine coating of coffee icing onto the tops of the coffee-filled éclairs, then use your index finger to spread out and smooth it evenly and meticulously, to achieve an attractive icing glaze. Transfer each iced éclair to a wire rack as you work, then ice the choux bun in the same way.

Repeat with the other pan of fondant and the remaining cocoa paste, to ice the remaining éclairs and ring. When both icings have cooled completely, about 20–30 minutes, you can start to prepare for assembling the religieuse.

Fill a piping bag fitted with a 7mm fluted nozzle with the buttercream. Take a clean, empty 75cl bottle, without its label and with a 7cm diameter base. Place the pâte sablée base on a round, flat serving dish. Place the bottle in the middle of the base.

Dip the thicker end of one of the coffee éclairs into a little of the liquid glucose, then place the éclair lightly on its end on the sablée, so that the thicker end sits 2cm from the bottle and the tapering end leans in to rest on the bottle higher up.

Arrange a chocolate éclair in the same way next to the coffee one, then continue with the remaining 6 éclairs, alternating flavours as you go. Pipe buttercream generously between each éclair, which will help hold the éclairs in place.

Very carefully lift out the bottle from the top and pipe buttercream over the tops of the éclairs. Place the chocolate ring on top, pipe buttercream over that, then place the coffee choux bun on top, finally piping a little buttercream on top to decorate. It is now ready to serve, and is a work of art that should be enjoyed first with the eyes, and then in its eating.

Mont-Blanc aux Marrons

CHESTNUT MONT-BLANC

Named after the famous snow-capped mountain in the French alps, which it resembles, this classic French dessert is, quite simply, delicious. The marriage of chestnuts, Chantilly cream and chocolate is one of the best. Little sablé biscuits would make a perfect accompaniment.

Using a small knife, remove the outer layer of skin from the chestnuts. Put them into a saucepan, cover with cold water and bring to the boil over a high heat. Drain and, before they cool, peel away the second layer of skin. As you work, place each skinned chestnut in a second pan and add the milk, salt, sugar and vanilla pod.

Place the pan over a gentle heat and cook for about 40 minutes. As soon as the chestnuts are cooked, drain them, discarding the milk (which will have evaporated down). Discard the vanilla pod and leave the chestnuts to cool, covered in cling film.

Generously brush the insides of a savarin mould (ideally) or génoise tin, about 18cm in diameter, with the clarified butter. If using a savarin mould, place it on a large plate. Chill the mould in the fridge for 10 minutes.

Place a medium mouli, or coarse-meshed sieve, over the chilled mould. Press the chestnuts through the mouli or sieve. Spoon up any extruded chestnut that has landed outside the mould or tin, and add this to the rest, making sure you don't compress the mixture. Refrigerate for at least 40 minutes.

Put the cold whipping cream and sugar syrup or icing sugar into a chilled bowl and whisk with a balloon whisk to a thick ribbon consistency. Put the whipped Chantilly cream into a piping bag fitted with a large, fluted nozzle.

To turn out the chestnut Mont-Blanc, invert a chilled dish over the mould or tin, hold them together and turn them in a brisk but careful movement, then lift off the mould to unmould the dessert onto the plate. Pipe the cream in a dome in the middle, if you've used a savarin mould. If you have used a génoise tin, use a spoon to scoop out a well in the centre of the chestnut and pipe Chantilly cream into the space.

Arrange the marrons glacés around the edge of the dish and gently push the chocolate curls into the Chantilly cream. Sprinkle the sugared violets or mimosas, if using, over the top and serve at once.

Serves 6

750g fresh chestnuts

600ml milk

Pinch of salt

120g caster sugar

1 vanilla pod, split in half lengthways

40g clarified butter (page 266)

Chantilly cream

300ml very cold whipping cream

30ml sugar syrup (page 266) or
   30g icing sugar

To finish

6 marrons glacés (shop-bought)

12 chocolate curls (see page 226),
   optional

50g sugared violet or mimosa flowers
   (optional)

Charlotte aux Poires Mêlée de Framboises
PEAR AND RASPBERRY CHARLOTTE

This is a proper charlotte, as it was taught to me by my friend
Jean Millet, Meilleur Ouvrier de France Pâtisserie 1961
(Best Pâtisserie Craftsman of France). You can offer a red
fruit coulis on the side but the finesse and purity of the pear
flavours make me hesitate to suggest you do.

You will need a charlotte mould, about 10cm in diameter across the base and
12cm diameter across the top, 10cm tall.

Preheat the oven to 220°C/Gas 7. Line a 60 x 40cm baking sheet with baking
parchment.

For the sponge biscuits, whisk the egg yolks and two-thirds of the sugar,
using an electric mixer fitted with a whisk, to a ribbon consistency. Whisk the
whites separately to semi-firm peaks, then add the remaining sugar gradually,
whisking constantly, until it reaches firm peaks. Using a balloon whisk,
incorporate one-third of the whisked whites into the yolks. Use a spatula to
fold in the remaining whites, without overworking, then gently shower in both
flours and fold in carefully until evenly incorporated.

Fit a piping bag with a 1cm plain nozzle and fill with the sponge mixture. Pipe
strips side by side down one width of the sheet (a little longer than the depth
of your mould), covering half the surface.

Pipe two rounds in a daisy pattern (see photograph on previous page) onto
the space next to the strips, the first 8cm in diameter, which will dress the top
of the charlotte, and the second 10cm in diameter and a little less thick than
the first, which will be the base. If your mould has different dimensions, pipe
to fit the correct diameters.

Dust all the piped biscuits with icing sugar, especially the smaller top round,
and leave to rest for 5 minutes, then dust again and place in the oven. Cook
for 8 minutes, then set aside on the baking sheet for 10 minutes. Carefully
invert the sheet over another baking sheet, lined with a dry tea towel, and
remove the parchment. Leave to cool completely.

Using a serrated knife, trim the ends of the biscuit strips so that when they
line the sides they will fit the exact dimensions of your mould.

Line the inside of the charlotte mould with cling film. Place the smaller daisy
round top side down in the base, then line the sides with the trimmed strips,
top sides against the mould, so that they meet neatly in a complete circle. Set
aside in a dry place until you are ready to assemble the charlotte.

Serves 8–10

Sponge biscuits

7 egg yolks

85g caster sugar

4 egg whites

35g plain flour, sifted

40g potato flour, sifted

Icing sugar, for dusting

Bavaroise

4 sheets of leaf gelatine

350ml poached pear syrup, or from a jar
  (see below)

35g powdered milk

10 egg yolks

60g caster sugar

100g freshly poached pears in vanilla
  syrup (or from a jar)

400ml whipping cream

100g meringue italienne (page 265),
  just cooled

60ml pear eau de vie

160g raspberries

4 mint sprigs, to finish

For the bavaroise, soak the leaf gelatine in a shallow dish of cold water. Meanwhile, heat the syrup (from the pears) and powdered milk together over a gentle heat, whisking continuously. Whisk the egg yolks and sugar together in a bowl until they reach a ribbon consistency. Pour the boiling syrup mixture onto the yolks, whisking all the time. Transfer to a saucepan and cook gently, stirring constantly with a wooden spoon and taking great care that it doesn't boil, as for a crème anglaise.

Remove the bavaroise mixture from the heat, immediately drain the gelatine and squeeze out excess water, then add to the mixture, stirring to dissolve. Strain the mixture through a fine chinois into a bowl placed over crushed ice and allow to cool, gently agitating the mixture with a spoon from time to time, until it has almost completely cooled.

In the meantime, dice the poached pear, drain well and pat dry. Whip the cream to a thick ribbon consistency.

Gently whisk the Italian meringue mixture, whipped cream and eau de vie into the bavaroise mixture, still over the crushed ice. Then, when the mixture begins to thicken nicely, mix in the diced pear and half the raspberries. Pour the semi-set mixture into the lined charlotte mould, cover with the larger biscuit base, top side down, and set aside in the fridge for at least 12 hours.

To serve, invert the charlotte mould over a round serving plate. Lift off the mould, gently peel off the cling film and dust the top with a hint of icing sugar. Arrange little bunches of raspberries with mint sprigs around the base.

NOTE As you can't scale down the ingredients for the sponge biscuits without compromising the end result, you will have about a quarter left over, which you can cut into little squares and serve with coffee as petits fours.

Variation

A winter version of this, which was all the rage in the 1960s, is hot apple charlotte, made with an apple compote flavoured with cinnamon and lined with strips of fried bread rather than sponge biscuit. It is best served with a warm crème anglaise.

(Pear charlotte illustrated on page 237)

Paris Brest

In 1910 a pâtissier from the Maisons-Lafitte area of Paris called Louis Durand, inspired by the bicycle race between Paris and Brest, created this dessert in the shape of a bicycle wheel. During my pâtisserie apprenticeship, I made several hundred of them, and Paris Brest remains one of my favourite desserts.

For the choux pastry, put the water, milk, butter, salt and sugar in a saucepan and bring slowly to the boil over a low heat. As soon as it boils, take off the heat and shower in the flour in one swift movement, then mix with a wooden spoon until smooth and homogeneous. Return to a medium heat and stir for about 1 minute to dry out the paste, then tip it into a bowl. Add the eggs one at a time, beating with the wooden spoon. Once they are incorporated, the mixture should be smooth and shiny, with a thick ribbon consistency.

The choux pastry is now ready to use. If you're not using it immediately, cover the surface with one-third of a beaten egg to prevent a crust from forming.

For the crème pâtissière praliné, soak the gelatine in cold water to cover for 5 minutes or so to soften. Whisk the egg yolks and one-third of the sugar together in a bowl to a light ribbon consistency, then whisk in the flour. In a pan, slowly heat the milk with the remaining sugar. As it approaches the boil, pour onto the egg and sugar mixture, stirring well. Pour the mixture back into the pan and bring back to the boil over a medium heat, whisking all the time. Cook, stirring, for 2 minutes, then remove from the heat.

Drain the gelatine leaves, squeeze to remove excess water and add to the hot crème pâtissière mixture to dissolve, along with the praline noisette, whisking all the time. Transfer to a bowl and set aside to cool.

Prepare the meringue, following the instructions for meringue italienne on page 265.

Preheat the oven to 200°C/Gas 6. Draw an 18cm circle on a piece of baking parchment placed on a baking sheet, then turn the paper over. Put the choux paste into a piping bag fitted with a 1.2cm plain nozzle. Pipe a thick ring around the outside edge of the circle, then pipe a second ring inside the first one, so that they are just lightly touching. Finally, pipe a coil on top of the piped rings, so it sits neatly on the join between the other rings.

Brush the piped choux with the egg glaze and sprinkle on the flaked almonds. Bake for 25 minutes, then prop the oven door slightly open by about 1cm, by placing a spoon handle in the top of the door, and bake for a further 25 minutes. The choux pastry should be cooked through and very slightly dry. Slide the choux ring onto a wire rack and leave to cool for 30 minutes.

Using a serrated knife, carefully cut the top off the cooled pastry crown and dust it generously with icing sugar.

Serves 8–10

Choux pastry

125ml water

125ml milk

100g butter, cut into large dice

Pinch of salt

1 tsp caster sugar

150g plain flour

4 eggs

Crème pâtissière praliné

2 sheets of leaf gelatine

6 egg yolks

125g caster sugar

40g plain flour

500ml milk

100g praline noisette (see right)

Meringue

80ml water

360g caster sugar

30g liquid glucose (optional)

6 egg whites

To finish

1 egg yolk, mixed with 2 tsp milk and a pinch of salt, to glaze

80g flaked almonds

20g icing sugar, for dusting

Using a balloon whisk, mix four-fifths of the cooled Italian meringue into the crème patissière praliné for 30 seconds, without overworking, then fold it through more gently with a spatula. Put into a large piping bag fitted with a 1.2cm ridged nozzle and pipe it generously into the choux crown base, to give a braid effect once it is topped (as shown).

Position the choux top over the filling, so that the piped filling moves gently towards the middle and outside of the ring. Chill in the fridge for at least 30 minutes or up to 1 hour before serving. Use a serrated knife to cut it into slices.

NOTE The classic filling for this choux ring is typically buttercream mixed with praline crème patissière but I find this too heavy, so I use praline crème patissière lightened with Italian meringue instead. You can buy praline noisette in specialist food stores, or prepare it yourself.

WINE, a source of joy, pleasure and humility…

I was fascinated from childhood by the 'robe', or colour, of a wine being poured into a glass, whether bright red, purple or really dark, or clear white, golden or rosé – from a pale petal colour to a stronger shade of pink. Nonetheless, I had to wait until I was 13 years old, to be allowed to try my first half glass of red wine, a Santenay Burgundy. The pleasure of that moment was far superior to the breakfast grape juice I was used to! It was a revelation and the beginning of a lifelong passion as important to me as my love for food and cooking.

I went on to experience my first wine tastings and my first purchase from the stands at the Foire de Paris, at the age of 19. I was very proud that with my meagre salary I could buy my mother a mixed case of six wines from Alsace, Burgundy and the Loire, which I carried back on the metro like a box of treasure tucked under my arm… At the age of 22, I began working for the Rothschild family and went on to discover the *premier cru* wineries. I was progressing 'from church to cathedral'. For five years, I had the privilege of regularly tasting a glass of Château Duhart-Milon, or of Carruades de Lafite, or Lafite-Rothschild and, on special occasions, a glass of Château Yquem that was offered alongside the dessert I had just served. Brought to me by Marcel, the butler, at the end of service it was the dregs, yet still a treat!

This inspired me, now more than 30 years ago, to buy an ancient vineyard on the St Tropez peninsula that I replanted with 2,200 Grenache vines. They give me a very good rosé and are leased into the care of Jean-Etienne and François Matton, my neighbours and owners of Château Minuty. It's a great joy to be able to offer and drink wine from my own vineyard on a daily basis…

In terms of volume, France is the third largest producer of wine in the world, close behind Italy and Spain, and produces the most agreeable *vins de soif* (light-bodied thirst-quenching wines) costing only a few Euros a bottle, as well as the magnificent *grands vins* worth several hundred Euros a bottle. It is worth mentioning that only some 50 grape varieties are authorised in French wine making and that only a dozen or so of these at most are used in blending white or red wine. By way of example, the main grape varieties used for Bordeaux reds are Cabernet Sauvignon, Merlot, Cabernet Franc, and sometimes a touch of Petit Verdot, and the percentages in the blend vary according to the *communes* and *appellations*, and whether they are from the 'left' or 'right' bank of the Gironde.

Two grape varieties are used for Burgundy wine, Pinot Noir for red and Chardonnay for white. The wines produced by these *terroirs* and their wine growers (*vignerons*) are those that without doubt I consider to be the most magnificent; I am completely in thrall to them. Beaujolais red wine, which is very enjoyable as an accompaniment to a snack or lunch, is made exclusively from Gamay grapes, and Moulin-à-Vent, the most highly rated Beaujolais, can rival the greatest Burgundies but at a fraction of the price.

There isn't room to list all the French wine-making regions and their grape varieties here, but there are a great number of specialist books on the subject, written by professionals – oenologists and Masters of Wine – and I strongly recommend you use one or more of them to further your knowledge of wine.

France produces a unique diversity of wines – red, white and rosé – all representative of the varied typicity of their *terroir*, grape variety and *vigneron*. The geology and chemistry of the soil both influence the aromas. Vine roots can reach as deep as 7 metres into the ground and, depending on the region and location, may penetrate limestone, clay, gypsum, minerals and/or volcanic lava, with stone and shingle on the surface. The landscape, the aspect, exposure to sun, drainage, climate and micro-climates, erosion, proximity to rivers or sea, and of course the grape variety selected hundreds of years ago, are all factors that contribute to determining the final quality of the wine.

Add to this the *vignerons* – men and women, whose appearance often mirrors the personality of their wine, who are always happy to offer a tasting in their cellar, whose eyes gleam and sparkle like their wines – and you have all the ingredients that generate the success of French wines.

In order to explore and gain a better understanding of wine, I strongly recommend wine tasting, engaging your senses to the full. The eye discerns the 'robe', which should be clear. Its hue will reveal the age of the wine: less intense or less bright would indicate a ten-year old wine, at least.

In swirling the glass, you release the aromas, which will be clean, fresh, intense or possibly questionable, even corked. You may also be able to detect in it aromas of citrus, spices, etc. To appreciate the taste, the final aspect, keep the wine in your mouth and roll it around your tongue, while sucking a little air through your teeth, to aerate it and disclose the aromas, flavours and in the case of a *grand vin*, its complexity, before spitting it out and assessing its length and persistence in the mouth, all signs of fine quality.

The ideal temperatures to serve wines are as follows: Champagne 10–12°C; dry white wine and rosé 12–14°C; red wine 16–18°C; Sauternes and Barsac, as well as other sweet wines such as *Vendanges Tardives* (late harvest), 10–12°C.

It is unnecessary to decant a wine unless there is sediment present, which happens in wines that are 20 years old or more. Decanting separates the wine from the sediment, but should not be done more than 30 minutes before serving otherwise the wine may start to oxidise.

Young *premier cru* or *grand cru* vintage wines, both red and white, benefit from aerating before drinking. Simply pour the wine into a decanter about 15 minutes ahead of serving to aerate them.

As for achieving harmony between French food and wine, both so revered the world over, how can this be accomplished? Of course, there are some guidelines that we all know – fish and shellfish are generally better served with a white wine, while meat, game and cheese are better with red, but there are no hard and fast rules. A light red can be an excellent accompaniment to fish, for example. When I am choosing wine to accompany different dishes, I marry common sense, personal taste and inspiration. As you will have discovered, throughout the recipes I have offered some suggestions of wines to serve with particular dishes. These are pairings I recommend because I have tried them and they work for me, but of course, the choice of a specific wine to serve with a particular food is a personal matter.

A final thought... have you considered creating your own wine cellar? It is never too late to realise the dream of having several dozen bottles within reach and under your own roof. Then, after a few years, why not a hundred or more? I have fulfilled this dream, through building up a collection little by little over the course of some 50 years. It is a tangible, but more importantly drinkable pleasure that can be shared with family and friends. Wine must and does live and breathe, and should, of course, be enjoyed.

Stocks
&
Sauces

Fond de Volaille Chicken Stock

This stock has many uses in the kitchen. I sometimes add half a knuckle of veal when preparing it, to make it extra rich and unctuous.

Put the chicken or carcasses into a large saucepan and cover with the cold water. Bring to the boil over a high heat, then immediately lower the heat and keep at a simmer.

After 5 minutes, skim the surface and add all the other ingredients. Cook gently for 1½ hours, without boiling, skimming whenever necessary to remove any impurities and fat floating to the surface.

Strain the stock through a fine-meshed chinois into a bowl and cool over ice. Refrigerate and use within 4 or 5 days, or freeze for up to 3 months.

CHICKEN GELÉE

First roast the chicken carcasses or wings: place in a roasting tray, trickle over 2 tbsp grapeseed oil and roast in the oven preheated to 180°C/Gas 4 for about 40 minutes, until coloured.

Transfer the roasted chicken carcasses and wings to a saucepan, cover with 2.5 litres cold water and continue as above, but simmer for 2 hours (i.e. an extra 30 minutes).

After straining, return the stock to the cleaned pan and simmer to reduce to 380ml, then cool over ice. Refrigerate and use within 4–5 days, or freeze for up to 3 months.

NOTES

For a beautifully clear gelée, you can clarify the chicken stock as for chicken consommé (page 30).

If the jellied stock seems a little soft, stir some pre-soaked leaf gelatine into the hot stock to dissolve; allow 1–2 sheets of leaf gelatine per 250ml stock.

Makes about 1.5 litres

1 boiling fowl, weighing 1.5kg, or an equal weight of raw chicken carcasses or wings, blanched and refreshed

2.5 litres water

200g carrots, peeled and cut into chunks

2 leeks (white part only), well washed and cut into chunks

1 celery stalk, coarsely chopped

1 onion, peeled and studded with 2 cloves

150g button mushrooms, thinly sliced

1 bouquet garni

Fond de Veau   VEAL STOCK

Veal stock forms the base for most brown sauces used for meat and poultry, and is sometimes used in fish sauces too.

Preheat the oven to 220°C/Gas 7. Put the veal bones and calf's foot in a roasting tin and roast in the oven for about 40 minutes, turning them from time to time with a slotted spoon, until well browned. Add the carrots and onion, mix together and cook for another 5 minutes.

Using the slotted spoon, transfer the entire contents of the roasting tin to a large saucepan or casserole. Pour off the fat from the roasting tin and deglaze with the white wine, scraping up all the sediment. Set over a high heat and reduce by half, then pour the wine into the saucepan.

Add the cold water and bring to the boil over a high heat. As soon as the liquid boils, lower the heat so that the surface is barely trembling. Simmer very gently for 10 minutes, then skim well.

Add all the other ingredients and simmer, uncovered, for 2½ hours, skimming as necessary. Strain the stock through a muslin-lined or fine-meshed chinois into a bowl and cool over ice. Refrigerate and use within 4 or 5 days, or freeze for up to 3 months.

Makes 1 litre

1.5kg veal bones, chopped

½ calf's foot, split lengthways, chopped and blanched for 5 minutes

200g carrots, peeled and cut into rounds

100g onion, peeled and roughly chopped

250ml dry white wine

3 litres water

1 celery stalk, thinly sliced

6 tomatoes, peeled, deseeded and chopped

150g button mushrooms, cleaned and thinly sliced

2 garlic cloves

1 bouquet garni, including a sprig of tarragon

Fumet de Poissons   FISH STOCK

Avoid cooking a fish stock for longer than the recipe suggests otherwise it will lose flavour and can also acquire a bitter taint. If your fish stock is destined for a red wine sauce, use red rather than white wine.

Rinse the fish bones and trimmings under running cold water, then drain. Melt the butter in a large saucepan, add the sliced vegetables and sweat over a low heat for a few minutes.

Add the fish bones and trimmings and allow to bubble gently for a few moments, then pour in the white wine. Let bubble until it has reduced by two-thirds, then add the cold water. Bring to the boil, then lower the heat, skim the surface and add the bouquet garni and lemon slices.

Simmer very gently for 25 minutes, skimming as necessary. About 10 minutes before the end of cooking, add the muslin-wrapped peppercorns.

Gently ladle the stock through a fine-meshed chinois into a bowl and cool over ice. Refrigerate and use within 2 or 3 days, or freeze for up to 3 months.

Makes 2 litres

1.5kg white fish bones and trimmings (from sole, turbot, brill, whiting, etc.), cut into pieces

50g butter

2 leeks (white part only), well washed and thinly sliced

75g onions, peeled and thinly sliced

75g button mushrooms, cleaned and thinly sliced

200ml dry white wine

2.5 litres water

1 bouquet garni

2 lemon slices

8 white peppercorns, crushed and tied in muslin

Fond de Gibier — GAME STOCK

This stock makes an ideal sauce for pan-fried venison. Deglaze the pan with port, add 1 tsp redcurrant jelly, then the game stock. Whisk in a knob of butter, season and serve.

Preheat the oven to 220°C/Gas 7. Heat the oil in a roasting pan, then put in the game carcasses or trimmings and brown in the hot oven for about 30 minutes, turning them from time to time with a slotted spoon. When the meat has browned, add the carrots, onions and garlic, mix together and cook for another 5 minutes.

With the slotted spoon, transfer all the contents of the roasting pan to a large saucepan or casserole. Pour off the fat from the roasting pan and deglaze with the red wine. Set over a high heat and reduce the wine by half, then pour it into the saucepan.

Add the cold water and bring to the boil over a high heat. As soon as the liquid boils, reduce the heat so that the surface barely trembles. Simmer for 10 minutes, then skim well and add all the other ingredients.

Simmer, uncovered, for 2 hours, skimming the surface as necessary. Strain the stock through a fine-meshed chinois into a bowl and cool over ice.

Once the stock has been strained, you can reduce it by one-third to give it more body. Like all stocks, it will keep well for several days in the fridge, or for up to 4 months in the freezer.

Makes 1.5 litres

3 tbsp groundnut oil

2kg furred or feathered game trimmings, carcasses, necks, wings, etc., cut into pieces

150g carrots, peeled and cut into rounds

150g onions, peeled and coarsely chopped

½ head of garlic (unpeeled), halved widthways

500ml red wine (preferably Côtes du Rhône)

2 litres water

500ml veal stock (page 249)

8 juniper berries, crushed

8 coriander seeds, crushed

1 bouquet garni, including 2 sage leaves and a celery stalk

Bouillon de Légumes — VEGETABLE STOCK

You can substitute your own choice of seasonal vegetables, varying the stock with flavourful, ripe tomatoes in summer, perhaps a few wild mushrooms in autumn (chanterelles add a particularly fine aroma), and so on.

Put all the vegetables, garlic, bouquet garni and wine in a saucepan and add 2 litres cold water. Bring to the boil over a high heat, then lower the heat and cook at a bare simmer for 45 minutes, skimming as necessary. After 35 minutes, add the muslin-wrapped peppercorns.

Strain the stock through a fine-meshed chinois into a bowl and cool over ice. Refrigerate and use within 4 or 5 days, or freeze for up to 3 months.

Makes 1.5 litres

300g carrots, peeled and cut into rounds

2 leeks, white part only, thinly sliced

100g celery stalks, thinly sliced

50g fennel bulb, very thinly sliced

150g shallots, peeled and thinly sliced

100g onion, peeled and thinly sliced

2 garlic cloves (unpeeled)

1 bouquet garni

250ml dry white wine

2 litres water

10 white peppercorns, crushed and tied in muslin

Sauce Périgourdine

This sauce is excellent served with little hot pies or pâtés en croûte, with beef tournedos or pan-fried saddle of lamb, and of course on pasta.

Bring the veal stock to the boil in a small saucepan and let it bubble over a medium heat to reduce until it is thick enough to lightly coat the back of a spoon.

Add the truffle juice and cook for another 5 minutes. Add the chopped truffles and let the sauce bubble briefly.

Take the pan off the heat and add the butter, a piece at a time, swirling and rotating the pan to incorporate it. Season the sauce with salt and pepper to taste and serve immediately.

Serves 6

400ml veal stock (page 249)

50ml truffle juice (bottled or ideally the cooking juices from fresh truffles)

20g truffles, finely chopped or sliced into discs

40g butter, chilled and diced

Salt and freshly ground pepper

Fond de Gibier à Plumes SAUCE FOR GAME BIRDS

This sauce has a lovely mild, gamey flavour, as it absorbs the savour of the carcasses during its brief cooking. Serve with roasted game birds.

Chop the game carcasses, place in a saucepan and heat them through, then add the Cognac and ignite it. When the flame has died down, pour in the red wine and let it bubble over a high heat to reduce by half.

Pour in the vegetable stock and add the juniper berries, thyme and bay leaf. Cook briskly until the liquid has reduced by half. Now add the cream, if using, and let bubble for another 3 minutes.

Pass the sauce through a fine-meshed chinois into a clean pan, reheat gently and season with salt and pepper to taste. Serve immediately.

Serves 4

Carcasses of 2 roasted wild duck or snipe, or 4 wood pigeons

50ml Cognac or Armagnac

150ml red wine

450ml vegetable stock (page 250)

5 juniper berries, crushed

1 thyme sprig

½ bay leaf

4 tbsp double cream (optional)

Salt and freshly ground pepper

Sauce Béchamel

Béchamel sauce goes well with vegetables, white meats, poultry and ham, and it forms the basis of many other sauces.

Makes 500ml

30g butter

30g plain flour

500ml milk

Freshly grated nutmeg (optional)

Salt and freshly ground white pepper

Melt the butter in a small, heavy-based saucepan over a low heat, then add the flour. Stir with a whisk and cook gently for 2–3 minutes to make a roux.

Pour the cold milk onto the roux, whisking as you do so, and bring to the boil over a medium heat, whisking continuously. When the sauce comes to the boil, lower the heat and simmer gently for about 10 minutes, stirring frequently. Season to taste with salt, white pepper and a little nutmeg if you wish, then pass the sauce through a fine-meshed chinois.

Either serve immediately or, if necessary, keep warm in a bain-marie, dotting a few flakes of butter over the surface to stop a skin from forming.

MORNAY SAUCE

Prepare the béchamel as above. Mix 3 egg yolks with 50ml double cream in a bowl, then pour the mixture into the béchamel, whisking all the time. Let the sauce bubble for about 1 minute, whisking continuously, then take the pan off the heat and shower in 100g finely grated Gruyère, Emmenthal or Cheddar. Stir until melted, then taste and adjust the seasoning. You can coat poached eggs, vegetables, fish or white meats with this sauce, then lightly brown them under a hot grill, or mix it with pasta to make a macaroni cheese.

PARSLEY SAUCE

Melt 20g butter in a saucepan over a low heat, then add 20g plain flour. Stir with a whisk, and cook gently for 2–3 minutes to make a roux. Pour 150ml cold milk onto the roux, whisking as you do so, then whisk in 350ml cooled chicken stock (page 248) or the cooking liquor from a boiled ham. Bring to the boil over a medium heat, whisking. Add 2 tbsp chopped parsley and simmer for 15 minutes. Season to taste with salt, pepper and nutmeg. Parsley sauce is especially good with boiled ham. It also goes well with Brussels sprouts, carrots or potatoes.

VELOUTÉ

Prepare the sauce as above, using cold fish, chicken or vegetable stock in place of the milk, depending on what you intend to serve the sauce with. Cook the sauce over a low heat for about 30 minutes, stirring occasionally with a whisk. Season with salt and pepper to taste. If required, the sauce can be enriched with cream.

Sauce Allemande

This light, silky sauce with its satisfying texture goes very well with poached poultry, sweetbreads and spinach ravioli.

Combine the shallots, white wine, crushed peppercorns and bouquet garni in a saucepan. Bring to the boil over a medium heat and bubble to reduce the wine by two-thirds.

Add the chicken stock and mushrooms and cook until the liquid has reduced by half. Pour in the cream and let the sauce bubble for 5 minutes, or until it is thick enough to lightly coat the back of a spoon.

Meanwhile, for the liaison, lightly whip the cream to soft peaks, then fold in the egg yolks and lemon juice.

Pour the liason mixture into the sauce, whisking to combine. Immediately turn off the heat, season the sauce with salt and white pepper to taste and pass it through a fine-meshed chinois. Serve at once.

Serves 6

60g shallots, peeled and finely chopped

100ml dry white wine

10 white peppercorns, crushed

1 bouquet garni, including a savory sprig

500ml chicken stock (page 248)

100g button mushrooms, sliced

200ml double cream

salt and freshly ground white pepper

For the liaison

100ml whipping cream

3 egg yolks

Juice of 1 lemon

Sauce à la Mie de Pain BREAD SAUCE

The perfect traditional sauce to accompany roast chicken, turkey, pheasant or grouse. Flavour with a little freshly grated nutmeg, if you like.

Melt the butter in a small saucepan, add the chopped onions and sweat gently for 1 minute. Pour in the milk, add the clove-studded onion and bring to a bare simmer. Cook gently, stirring occasionally, for 20 minutes.

Stir in the bread cubes and bring to the boil. Lower the heat and cook the sauce gently for 30 minutes, stirring occasionally with a wooden spoon.

Remove the studded onion, add the cream and let the sauce bubble gently for 5 minutes, whisking delicately. Season with salt and white pepper to taste and serve.

Serves 4

20g butter

60g onions, peeled and chopped

400ml milk

1 whole or ½ onion (about 60g), peeled and studded with 2 cloves

80g white bread, crusts removed, cut into cubes

50ml double cream

Salt and freshly ground white pepper

Sauce Hollandaise

This light, creamy emulsion sauce is sublime served warm with asparagus or steamed, poached or lightly grilled fish. It needs to be served as soon as it is made, or briefly held, covered, in a warm place.

Put the wine vinegar, 4 tbsp cold water and the crushed peppercorns in a small pan. Let bubble to reduce by one-third, then leave to cool completely. Add the egg yolks to the cold reduction and mix with a whisk.

Put the saucepan on a heat diffuser over a very low heat and continue to whisk, making sure that the whisk comes into contact with the bottom of the pan. Gradually increase the heat so that the sauce emulsifies progressively, becoming very smooth and creamy after 8–10 minutes. Do not allow the temperature of the sauce to rise above 65°C.

Off the heat and still whisking, pour in the tepid clarified butter in a steady stream. Season with salt to taste. At the last moment, stir in the lemon juice. Pass the sauce through a muslin-lined chinois, then serve immediately.

Serves 6

1 tbsp white wine vinegar

1 tsp white peppercorns, crushed

4 egg yolks

250g freshly clarified butter (page 266), cooled to tepid

Juice of ½ lemon

Salt

MALTAISE SAUCE

Zest 1 large or 2 small oranges (preferably blood oranges). Blanch the zest, refresh and chop very finely. Squeeze the juice and reduce in a small pan over a low heat by one-third, then add the zest and take the pan off the heat. Just before serving, whisk into the hollandaise together with the lemon juice. Season to taste and serve immediately. Delicious with poached salmon trout; also with asparagus and mangetout.

Sauce Vierge

I serve this sauce with steamed fillets of red mullet and sea bass, and fresh pasta – especially cappelletti filled with lobster or other shellfish.

Peel, deseed and dice the tomatoes and place in a bowl with the olive oil, lemon juice, herbs, garlic and coriander seeds. Mix gently and season with salt and pepper to taste.

Just before serving, warm the sauce slightly, to about 30–40°C.

Serves 6

80g tomatoes

200ml olive oil

Juice of 1 lemon

2 tbsp snipped basil leaves

1 tbsp snipped chervil leaves

1 garlic clove, peeled and finely chopped

6 coriander seeds, crushed

Salt and freshly ground pepper

Sauce Béarnaise

The classic accompaniment to a grilled steak, this is also a good accompaniment to a beef fondue.

Combine the wine vinegar, 2 tbsp tarragon, the shallot and peppercorns in a small, heavy-based saucepan and reduce by half over a low heat. Set aside to cool.

When the vinegar reduction is cold, add the egg yolks and 3 tbsp cold water. Set the pan over a low heat and whisk continuously, making sure that the whisk reaches right down into the bottom of the pan. As you whisk, gently increase the heat; the sauce should emulsify slowly and gradually, becoming unctuous after 8–10 minutes. Do not let it become hotter than 65°C.

Turn off the heat and whisk the clarified butter into the sauce, a little at a time. Season with salt and pepper to taste and pass through a fine-meshed chinois into another pan. Stir in the rest of the tarragon, the chervil and lemon juice. Check the seasoning and serve.

Serves 6

2 tbsp white wine vinegar

3 tbsp snipped tarragon

30g shallot, peeled and finely chopped

10 black or white peppercorns, crushed

4 egg yolks

250g freshly clarified butter (page 266), cooled to tepid

2 tbsp snipped chervil

Juice of ½ lemon

Salt and freshly ground pepper

CHORON SAUCE

Add 2 tbsp well-reduced cooked tomato coulis (see below) to the finished béarnaise. Excellent served with fish en croûte.

Coulis de Tomates

Flavourful ripe tomatoes are essential for this coulis, which is particularly good with grilled fish and shellfish. I also use it for pizzas and pasta dishes.

First peel the tomatoes: cut a shallow cross on the top of each one and cut out the core, then immerse the tomatoes in a bowl of boiling hot water for 10–20 seconds – just until the skin starts to split. Lift out with a slotted spoon and peel away the skins. Halve, deseed and dice the tomatoes.

Heat the olive oil in a large heavy-based saucepan. Add the onions and cook gently for 5 minutes to soften. Add the tomatoes, garlic and thyme, and cook slowly for about an hour to make a thick coulis.

Discard the thyme, whisk the coulis lightly and season with salt and pepper to taste. Leave to cool. The coulis can be kept in the fridge for several days, in a sealed jar with a film of olive oil covering the surface.

Serves 6

1kg tomatoes

50ml olive oil

150g onions, peeled and chopped

40g garlic, peeled and chopped

1 thyme sprig

salt and freshly ground pepper

Mayonnaise

Mayonnaise has many uses and is especially good with fish and seafood. It is also the basis for various other sauces.

Stand a mixing bowl on a tea towel on the work surface. Put the egg yolks, mustard and a little salt and pepper into the bowl and mix together with a balloon whisk.

Now slowly add the oil in a thin trickle to begin with, whisking continuously. As the mayonnaise begins to thicken, add the oil in a steady stream, still whisking all the time.

When the oil is completely incorporated, whisk more rapidly for 30 seconds until the mayonnaise is thick and glossy. Add the vinegar or lemon juice, then taste and adjust the seasoning as necessary.

Unless serving the mayonnaise straight away, cover and refrigerate until needed; it will keep for several hours.

Makes about 300g

2 egg yolks, at room temperature

2 tsp Dijon mustard

250ml groundnut oil (or use one-third olive oil; two-thirds groundnut oil)

2 tbsp white wine vinegar or lemon juice

Salt and freshly ground pepper

RÉMOULADE SAUCE

Finely chop 40g cornichons or gherkins, 20g capers and 1 anchovy fillet and fold into the mayonnaise with 1 tsp Dijon mustard and 1 tbsp each snipped flat-leaf parsley, chervil and tarragon, using a spatula. Season to taste. This piquant sauce is perfect for a cold buffet, with assorted cold meats or as a condiment for picnic food like pressed tongue and cold roast chicken.

AÏOLI

Infuse a pinch of saffron threads in 3 tbsp boiling water for 5 minutes or so. Rub 180g baked potato pulp, then 2 hard-boiled egg yolks through a sieve into a mortar. Add 4 crushed garlic cloves, 1 raw egg yolk and a pinch of salt. Crush together with the pestle. Add 200ml olive oil in a thin, steady stream, mixing continuously. When about half of the oil has been incorporated, add the saffron infusion. Incorporate the remaining olive oil, then season the aïoli with a good pinch of cayenne and salt to taste.

Rouille

This highly seasoned, piquant sauce is utterly Provençal in origin, and is usually served with fish soup or bouillabaisse. It should always be served cold. Hand it round separately in a sauceboat so guests can help themselves.

Boil or steam the potatoes until tender, then drain thoroughly and return to the pan. Toss over a medium heat for a few minutes to dry them out.

Peel the garlic clove and roll it in fine salt, then rub it round the inside of a bowl. Rub first the potatoes, then the hard-boiled egg yolks through a fine-meshed sieve into the bowl.

Stir with a spatula until well mixed, then gradually incorporate the olive oil, stirring continuously until very smooth. Season with salt and white pepper to taste and finally add the saffron.

Serves 6

250g potatoes, peeled

1 garlic clove

3 hard-boiled egg yolks

250ml olive oil

Pinch of saffron threads

Salt and freshly ground pepper

Vinaigrette

Orleans wine vinegar (*vinaigre d'Orléans*), which is made and aged in oak barrels, is my preferred choice for a vinaigrette. It is full-bodied and crisp, and has a perfect balance of acidity with no hint of acridity.

Put the mustard in a bowl with salt and pepper to taste. Whisk together, then pour in the vinegar as you whisk. Finally, add the oil in a steady stream, whisking all the time. Taste and adjust the seasoning, and add a few more drops of vinegar if you feel it is needed. Vinaigrette will keep for up to a week in the fridge, in a sealed jar or bottle.

Serves 4

1 tsp strong Dijon mustard

1 tbsp red or white wine vinegar, or cider vinegar

3 tbsp groundnut, sunflower or grapeseed oil

Salt and freshly ground pepper

Crème Anglaise

The classic accompaniment to so many desserts, this light, creamy custard can be flavoured to taste.

Put the milk, two-thirds of the sugar and the vanilla pod into a heavy-based saucepan and slowly bring to the boil.

Meanwhile, whisk the egg yolks and remaining sugar together in a bowl to combine smoothly. Continue to whisk until the mixture becomes pale and has a light ribbon consistency.

Pour the boiling milk onto the egg yolks, whisking continuously, then pour the mixture back into the saucepan. Cook over a low heat, stirring with a wooden spatula or spoon; do not let it boil or it may curdle. The custard is ready when it has thickened slightly – just enough to lightly coat the back of the spatula. When you run your finger through, it should leave a clear trace on the spatula. Immediately take the pan off the heat.

Unless you are serving the crème anglaise warm, pour through a fine-meshed chinois into a bowl set over crushed ice and leave to cool, stirring occasionally to prevent a skin from forming.

The custard will keep in a covered container in the fridge for up to 48 hours.

Makes about 750ml (6–8 servings)

500ml milk

125g caster sugar

1 vanilla pod, split lengthways

6 egg yolks

CHOCOLATE CRÈME ANGLAISE

Stir 60g melted good-quality dark, bitter chocolate, 70% cocoa solids (ideally Valrhona), into the milk as you warm it.

MINTED CRÈME ANGLAISE

Infuse the milk with a bunch of fresh mint instead of the vanilla. The freshness of this minted custard goes brilliantly with all berries. It is also excellent with chocolate ice cream and chocolate truffle cake.

PISTACHIO CRÈME ANGLAISE

Either use 40g pistachio paste or 200g skinned fresh pistachio nuts soaked in cold water for 24 hours, drained and crushed to a paste using a pestle and mortar. Pour one-third of the hot crème anglaise onto the pistachio paste, stirring with a whisk, then stir into the rest of the hot custard. Blitz in a blender for about 3 minutes, until very smooth. Pass through a fine-meshed chinois into a bowl, cool over ice and chill until ready to use. This unusual custard is superb with poached peaches and pears poached in Sauternes.

Crème Pâtissière

Crème pâtissière – or pastry cream – has many uses, including fillings for choux buns and sweet tarts.

Combine the egg yolks and one-third of the sugar in a bowl and whisk to a light ribbon consistency. Add the flour and whisk it in thoroughly.

In a saucepan, heat the milk with the rest of the sugar and the vanilla pod. As soon as it comes to the boil, pour it onto the egg yolk mixture, stirring as you go. Mix well, then return the mixture to the saucepan. Bring to the boil over a medium heat, stirring continuously with the whisk. Allow the mixture to bubble, still stirring, for 2 minutes, then tip it into a bowl.

To prevent a skin forming on the crème pâtissiére as it cools, dust the surface with a veil of icing sugar or dot all over with little flakes of butter. Remove the vanilla pod before using.

CHOCOLATE CRÈME PATISSIÈRE

Add 75g melted good-quality dark chocolate, 70% cocoa solids (ideally Valrhona), to the crème pâtissière before cooling.

Makes about 750g

6 egg yolks

125g caster sugar

40g plain flour

500ml milk

1 vanilla pod, split lengthways

A little icing sugar or butter

Sauce au Chocolat

This rich, velvety sauce is sublime spooned over vanilla or coffee ice cream, poached pears, profiteroles or meringues filled with whipped cream.

Chop the chocolate and place in a heatproof bowl. Set over a pan of gently simmering water, making sure the bowl is not touching the water, and let it melt slowly, stirring occasionally until very smooth. Take off the heat.

Combine the milk, cream and sugar in a saucepan, stir with a whisk and bring to the boil. Still stirring with the whisk, pour the boiling milk mixture onto the melted chocolate, then return the mixture to the pan and let it bubble over the heat for a few seconds, stirring continuously.

Turn off the heat and whisk in the butter, a little at a time, to give a smooth, homogeneous sauce. Pass it through a fine-meshed chinois. Serve at once or keep warm in a bain-marie until needed.

Serves 6

200g good-quality dark chocolate, 70% cocoa solids (ideally Valrhona)

175ml milk

2 tbsp double cream

30g caster sugar

30g butter, diced

Basics

Pâte à Foncer FLAN PASTRY

This pastry has a lovely crispness and is easier to work with than pâte brisée. It can be kept in the fridge for a week or in the freezer for up to 3 months.

Heap the flour on a clean work surface and make a well. Put the butter, egg, sugar and salt in the middle. With your fingertips, mix and cream the ingredients in the well.

Now, little by little, draw the flour into the centre and work the dough with your fingertips to a grainy texture. Add the cold water and mix it in until the dough begins to hold together.

Using the palm of your hand, push the dough away from you 4 or 5 times until it is completely smooth. Roll the pastry into a ball, wrap in cling film and refrigerate until ready to use.

Makes about 480g

250g plain flour

125g butter, cut into small pieces and slightly softened

1 egg

1 tsp caster sugar

½ tsp fine salt

40ml cold water

Pâte Sablée RICH SWEET FLAN PASTRY

This pastry is fragile and requires delicate handling but it melts in the mouth like no other pastry. If well wrapped, it will keep in the fridge for up to a week, or in the freezer for up to 3 weeks.

Heap the flour on a clean work surface and make a well. Put in the butter, icing sugar and salt. With your fingertips, mix and cream the butter with the sugar and salt, then add the egg yolks and work them in delicately with your fingertips.

Little by little, draw the flour into the centre and work the mixture delicately with your fingertips until you have a homogeneous dough.

Using the palm of your hand, push the dough away from you 3 or 4 times until it is completely smooth. Roll it into a ball, wrap in cling film and refrigerate until ready to use.

Makes about 650g

250g plain flour

200g butter, cut into small pieces and slightly softened

100g icing sugar, sifted

pinch of salt

2 egg yolks

Feuilletage Minute QUICK PUFF PASTRY

This quick puff pastry rises well – almost 75% as much as classic puff pastry and is much quicker to make. Tightly wrapped in cling film, it will keep for 3 days in the fridge, and for at least 4 weeks in the freezer.

Put the flour in a mound on a clean work surface and make a well. Put in the butter and salt and work them together with the fingertips of one hand, gradually drawing the flour into the centre with the other hand.

When the cubes of butter have become small pieces and the dough is grainy, gradually add the iced water and mix until it is all incorporated, but don't overwork the dough. Roll it into a ball, wrap in cling film and refrigerate for 20 minutes.

Flour the work surface and roll out the pastry into a 40 x 20cm rectangle. Fold it into three and give it a quarter-turn. Roll the block of pastry into a 40 x 20cm rectangle as before, and fold it into three again. These are the first 2 turns. Wrap the block in cling film and refrigerate it for 30 minutes.

Give the chilled pastry another 2 turns, rolling and folding as before. This makes a total of 4 turns, and the pastry is now ready. Wrap it in cling film and refrigerate for at least 30 minutes before using.

Makes 1.2kg

500g plain flour

500g very cold butter, cut into small cubes

1 tsp salt

250ml ice-cold water

Pâte à Pâté PASTRY FOR PÂTÉ EN CROÛTE

This is the pastry to use for pâté en croûte. It will keep in the fridge for a week, or in the freezer for 3 weeks.

Put the flour in a mound on a clean work surface and make a well. Place the salt and lard or butter in the centre. Use your fingertips to mix and soften the ingredients in the well, gradually drawing in the flour and mixing with your fingertips.

When the dough has a fine grainy texture, make a well in the middle. Slowly pour the egg yolk and water mixture into the well, mixing with your fingertips.

When the dough is well amalgamated, push it away from you 4 or 5 times with the heel of your hand to make it homogeneous. Roll into a ball, wrap in cling film and refrigerate until needed. If it is in the fridge for a while, take it out an hour before rolling out.

Makes 950g

500g plain flour

20g salt

200g lard (preferably) or butter, cut into small pieces and slightly softened

5 egg yolks mixed with 110ml cold water if using lard, 125ml if using butter

Pâte à Choux CHOUX PASTRY

Choux pastry expands dramatically on cooking, the outside becoming crisp and dry while the inside remains soft.

Combine the milk, water, butter, salt and sugar in a saucepan and set over a low heat. Bring to the boil and immediately take the pan off the heat. Shower in the flour and mix with a wooden spoon until completely smooth.

Return the pan to a medium heat and stir continuously for about 1 minute to dry out the paste, then tip it into a bowl. Add the eggs one at a time, beating with the wooden spoon.

Once the eggs are all incorporated, the paste should be smooth and shiny with a thick ribbon consistency. It is now ready to use. (If you're not using it immediately, brush the surface lightly with a little eggwash to prevent a crust forming.)

Makes about 500g

125ml milk

125ml water

100g butter, diced

½ tsp salt

1 tsp caster sugar

150g plain flour

4 eggs

Eggwash (1 egg yolk beaten with
   1 tbsp milk)

Frangipane ALMOND CREAM

This delicious almond cream is used as a filling for tarts and pancakes. For best results, use freshly ground almonds.

Sift the icing sugar and ground almonds together and set aside. In a large bowl, work the butter with a whisk until creamy. Still whisking, add the icing sugar and almond mixture, then the flour. When the mixture is evenly combined, incorporate the eggs one by one, whisking between each addition. You should now have a smooth, light cream. Stir in the rum, if you wish.

This cream will keep in an airtight container or bowl, covered with cling film, in the fridge for up to a week. Leave it at room temperature for 30 minutes before using.

Makes about 500g

125g icing sugar

125g ground almonds

125g butter, at room temperature

25g plain flour, sifted

2 large eggs

25ml rum (optional)

Meringue Française

I use this simple meringue to make individual meringues and for my Vacherin (page 230).

In a bowl, beat the egg whites with a balloon whisk until they form soft peaks.

Still whisking continuously, shower in the caster sugar, a little at a time, and continue to whisk for about 10 minutes, until the mixture is smooth and shiny, and holds firm points on the whisk when you lift it out of the mixture.

Shower in the icing sugar and fold it in with a spatula. The meringue is now ready to use.

Individual meringues

Using a tablespoon, shape the meringue into large quenelles and place on a baking sheet lined with baking parchment, or pipe them if you prefer. Cook in the oven at 110°C/Gas ¼ for 1¼ hours for small meringues, or allow an extra 5–10 minutes for larger ones. Switch off the oven and leave them to cool inside for several hours. They keep well for several days in an airtight container stored in a dry place.

Makes 350g

4 medium egg whites

125g caster sugar

125g icing sugar, sifted

Meringue Italienne

A sugar thermometer is essential for preparing this stable 'cooked' meringue. It can be kept in an airtight container in the fridge for up to 48 hours before use.

Pour the water into a heavy-based saucepan, add the sugar and glucose if using, and set over a medium heat. Bring to the boil, stirring occasionally and brushing down any crystals that form on the side of the pan, using a pastry brush moistened with water. Increase the heat and place a sugar thermometer in the boiling syrup to register when it reaches 110°C.

Still keeping an eye on the syrup, beat the egg whites until they hold peaks, either by hand or with an electric mixer. Stop cooking the syrup the moment it reaches 121°C. Take the pan off the heat and let the bubbling subside for 30 seconds. Pour the syrup onto the beaten egg whites in a thin, steady stream, whisking at low speed with the mixer or by hand until very firm.

When all the syrup has been absorbed, continue to beat at low speed for 15 minutes, until the meringue is almost completely cold (30–35°C). It is now ready to use.

Makes about 600g

80ml water

360g caster sugar

30g liquid glucose (optional)

6 medium egg whites

Sirop à Sorbet SUGAR SYRUP

This simple sugar syrup, also known as stock syrup, is used to make fruit sorbets and coulis.

Put the water in a saucepan, then add the sugar and glucose. Bring to the boil, stirring occasionally with a wooden spoon. Boil for 3 minutes, skimming the surface if necessary. Pass the syrup through a chinois and let it cool completely before using.

It can be kept in an airtight container in the fridge for up to 2 weeks.

Makes about 1 litre

650ml water

750g caster sugar

90g liquid glucose

Beurre Clarifié CLARIFIED BUTTER

This is used for making emulsified sauces like hollandaise and its derivatives. It is also excellent for cooking, as it can be heated to a higher temperature than ordinary butter.

Melt the butter over a very gentle heat and bring slowly to the boil. Skim off the froth from the surface. Carefully pour the liquid butter into a bowl, holding back the milky sediment in the bottom of pan. The clarified butter should be the colour of light olive oil.

It will keep in the fridge for 2 weeks.

Makes about 100g

120g unsalted butter

Suppliers

For my cooking as well as my food preparation, I have for years opted for Tefal brand, especially their non-stick or ceramic frying pans, and their smaller kitchen appliances such as beaters and mixers. As for chocolate, the crucial ingredient in my desserts, I have used Valrhona brand for many years. Valrhona has made great advances in the precise flavour of couverture chocolate, and their range of products is exceptional.

Glossary

Bain-marie This is literally a water bath, used to control the cooking of custards etc., and to keep delicate sauces warm. A bowl over a pan of simmering or hot water works as a bain-marie on the hob; in the oven a baking dish may be placed in a roasting pan containing hot water.

Bake blind To bake a pastry case, either partially or fully, before adding the filling. Line the pastry case with baking parchment or greaseproof paper and fill with ceramic baking beans or dried pulses before baking. The beans and paper are then removed and the tart returned to the oven to dry the base (or cook it fully if the filling won't be baked in the case).

Blanch To plunge an ingredient briefly into boiling water, usually for 30–60 seconds, then refresh in cold water to loosen the skin (of peaches, for example) or par-cook.

Bouquet garni A small bunch of herbs, typically parsley stalks, thyme sprigs and a bay leaf tied onto a piece of celery, used to flavour soups, stews, etc. during cooking and removed before serving.

Butter To brush a mould or baking sheet with melted or softened butter.

Caramelise To heat sugar until it dissolves and forms a caramel. Also used to describe cooking foods until their natural sugars – or an applied sugar topping – has browned.

Cartouche A circle of greaseproof paper or baking parchment with a small steam hole cut in the centre laid over the surface of fruit in a poaching liquid (or similar), to keep it immersed and lessen evaporation. To make one, fold the paper circle into segments, snip off the point and open out.

Chinois A conical sieve used for sieving a mixture to make it smooth.

Citrus zest, dried To dry lemon or orange zest, scatter on a baking sheet lined with baking parchment and dry in a low oven at 60–80°C for 1–2 hours.

Coulis A thin purée, usually of fruit mixed with a little sugar syrup, of a pourable consistency.

Crimp To pinch up the pastry border of a tart attractively with a pastry crimper or between your index finger and thumb.

Demi-glace/glace An intensely flavoured reduced stock, which lends a fuller flavour to sauces. For a demi-glace, reduce the stock by one-third. For a glace, reduce the stock by half.

Eggwash An egg yolk lightly beaten with 1 tbsp milk, used to lightly brush pastry dough before baking.

Foncer To line a mould or tin with rolled-out pastry.

Fold in To gently combine one mixture with another, using a rubber spatula or large metal spoon to cut through and turn the mixtures lightly and gently so they are combined with minimum loss of air and lightness.

Glaze To brush or dust the surface of pastry, filling (or other food) with something that gives colour and shine. Eggwash is often used as a glaze. Icing sugar is sometimes sprinkled over puff pastry, then caramelised in a very hot oven to form the glaze.

Infuse To flavour a liquid, such as a sugar syrup for poaching fruit, or milk for a custard, by immersing aromatics such as herbs, spices or vanilla pods to impart a subtle flavour and aroma. The liquid is usually gently warmed with the flavourings to just below the boil and left to stand for a while before straining out the flavouring ingredients.

Julienne Very fine strips – usually of citrus zest – or finely shredded herbs.

Jus A light gravy, made by deglazing the meat juices in a roasting pan with wine, then adding a cupful or two of water and reducing to a light gravy.

Knock back To return a risen yeasted dough to its original volume by lifting it with your lightly floured hand and quickly flipping it over 2 or 3 times.

Macerate To steep fruits in a syrup, sometimes including alcohol, to soften.

Mirepoix A mix of diced vegetables, typically celery, onion and/or leek and carrot, cut into 2–3cm dice, used as a flavouring base for sauces, soups etc.

Point, à To cook food, usually meat or game, to medium-rare.

Reduce To boil a liquor steadily to reduce and thicken it by evaporating some of the water.

Refresh To immerse food in cold water immediately after blanching or cooking to stop the cooking process, in order to preserve the colour and texture of the food.

Ribbon consistency Used to describe the texture of whisked cream or a whisked sponge mixture, when it is thick enough to leave a ribbon trail as the beaters are lifted from the bowl.

Roasting flour Toasting flour in the oven cooks out the raw taste, enabling the flour to lend a fuller, slightly nutty flavour to dishes it is added to. Scatter the flour on a baking sheet and roast at 180°C/Gas 4 for 5 minutes.

Toasting (or roasting) nuts Scatter the whole or chopped nuts on a baking tray and place in the oven at 180°C/Gas 4 for 10 minutes, or until evenly coloured, shaking occasionally.

Zest To pare orange, lemon or lime zest with a citrus zester very thinly, leaving behind all the bitter white pith.

Index

Dedication

'To all Roux scholars past and present, who I embrace as family'

Acknowledgements

I would like to thank every member of the team who was with me in the making of this stunning book:

Janet Illsley, project editor, who with calmness and persuasion knew how to steer my ship into harbour, against wind and tide;

Lisa Linder, photographer: this first encounter between two perfectionists has produced photographs that leave me full of admiration;

Elodie Rambaud, stylist, whose choice of fabrics, plates, dishes, glasses etc., was always spot on, providing the perfect vehicle for showcasing my cooking;

Lucy Gowans, art director and designer, who with intuition and talent knew how to coordinate the work of the team, and to get the best out of everyone;

Sally Somers, whose impeccable translation of all the text and recipes fills me with admiration;

Chris Lelliott, **Raj Holuss** and **Dario Grossini**, my former sous chefs, who took it in turns to accompany me on my trips to France, working alongside me at the photography sessions and contributing with such brilliance;

Claude Grant, who was always on hand to organise and type up my manuscript with equanimity, and to edit my French text expertly. Her contribution has been invaluable.

And finally, thank you to my wife, **Robyn Roux**, who checked the English version of my recipes at its various stages.

Editorial director **Anne Furniss**
Creative director **Helen Lewis**
Project editor **Janet Illsley**
Design and art direction **Lucy Gowans**
Translator **Sally Somers**
Photographer **Lisa Linder**
Stylist **Élodie Rambaud**
assisted by **Frankie Unsworth**
Photographer's assistant **Rita Platts**
Production **Aysun Hughes**, **Sarah Neesam**, **Vincent Smith**

First published in 2014 by
Quadrille Publishing Limited
Alhambra House,
27–31 Charing Cross Road,
London WC2H 0LS
www.quadrille.co.uk

Text © 2014 Michel Roux
Photography © 2014 Lisa Linder
Design and layout © 2014
Quadrille Publishing Limited
The rights of the author have been asserted.

Cataloguing in Publication Data: a catalogue record for this book is available from the British Library.
ISBN 978 1 84949 380 2
Printed in China

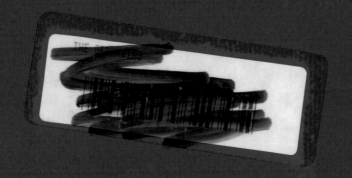

THE GERSHWINS

ROBERT KIMBALL
AND
ALFRED SIMON

DESIGNED
BY
BEA FEITLER

JONATHAN CAPE
LONDON
1974

First published in Great Britain 1974
Copyright © 1973 by Robert Kimball and
Alfred Simon

Jonathan Cape Ltd., 30 Bedford Square,
London WC1

ISBN 0 224 01014 X

Manufactured in the United States of America
First Edition

MUSIC AND LYRIC COPYRIGHTS

PHOTO CREDITS

PERMISSIONS

For Ira, with admiration, gratitude, and affection

ACKNOWLEDGMENTS

A book of this complexity owes much to the help of a great many people. We can never adequately express our gratitude to those whose devoted support and encouragement sustained us at every point in our work. First and foremost they are: Ira and Lee Gershwin, Frances and Leopold Godowsky, Jr., Arthur Gershwin, Emily Paley, Mabel Schirmer, and Kay Swift.

So many others in so many diverse ways also helped bring this book to life. We acknowledge with appreciation the contributions of the following: Harold Arlen, Fred Astaire, George Balanchine, Robert Baral, Irving Berlin, Eubie Blake, William Bolcom, Henry Botkin, Mario Braggiotti, Irving Caesar, Edgar Carter, Mary Corliss of the Museum of Modern Art Film Stills Archive, Jacques d'Amboise, Virginia Donaldson, Irving Drutman, Todd Duncan, Stan Friedman of the United Press International, Charles Gaynor, Leopold Godovsky III, John Green, Stanley Green, Kay Halle, William Hammerstein, E. Y. Harburg, Kitty Carlisle Hart, Arthur P. Hendrick, Edward Jablonski, Robert Jackson of Culver Pictures, Jane Reisman Jampolis, Eva Jessye, Abigail Kuflik Kimball, Tessa Kosta, Miles Kreuger, Burton Lane, Dan Langan, Lotte Lenya, June Levant, Lorna Levant, the late Oscar Levant, Howard Levine, Richard Lewine, Myrna Loy, Ian MacBey, Herman Meltzer, Terry Miller, Michael Montgomery, Emil Mosbacher, Warren Munsell, Paul Myers, Dorothy Swerdlove, Maxwell Silverman, Rod Bladel, Betty Wharton, Don Madison, Monte Arnold, Richard Buck, Frank Campbell and Jean Bowen of the Theatre and Music Collections of the New York Public Library, Melvin Parks, Maggie Blackmon, Charlotte LaRue and Marion Spitzer Thompson of the Theatre and Music Collection of the Museum of the City of New York, Marian Powers of *Time* magazine, Aileen Pringle, Louis A. Rachow and Carl Willers of the Walter Hampden Memorial Library of the Players Club, Lillian Reisman, Ann Ronell, Don Rose, Arthur Schwartz, Bobby Short, Andrea Simon, Anna Sosenko, Lawrence D. Stewart, Dorothea Swope, Rosamond Walling Tirana, Walter Wager of ASCAP, Fred Walker, Richard Warren Jr. and Joseph Fuchs of the Yale University Library, Edward Waters, William Lichtenwanger, Carroll Wade, Peter Fay and Wayne Shirley of the Music Division of the Library of Congress, and L. Arnold Weissberger.

Finally, we thank Tony Clark, Lesley Krauss, and Paul Hirschman for bringing exceptional talent and patience to the editing of this book.

CONTENTS

Composers, by tradition, are not a generous lot. Essentially, we are a breed of men and women concerned with the arrangement of the same seven notes. So with raw material in such short supply, we tend to be somewhat taciturn when it comes to assaying each other's work. We are "closet worshippers" of our colleagues' talents—and will often go to extremes to avoid having to pay them public compliment. I suspect there are even those among us who are tempted to give credence to the apocryphal anecdote about Beethoven getting the idea for his Fifth Symphony from the whistling of a street sweeper. We belong to a tightly knit but mutually exclusive brotherhood that could have given sibling rivalry its name.

So it ought to be with some misgivings that I attempt to set down my thoughts on George Gershwin and his music. In this case, however, I am delighted to break with tradition—something I've never been at pains to avoid—and pay my unreserved respects to a fellow composer. Indeed, one of my favorite memories of George Gershwin leads me to think that he himself would not necessarily find Richard Rodgers an odd choice to introduce these recollections:

George had an endearing appreciation of himself, an almost childlike delight in his own work that was quite contagious. When he had a new song he could hardly wait to marshal his friends for a first-time-anywhere recital. On this occasion we were weekend guests at the home of a friend in Westhampton. All was quiet and relaxed, when suddenly George announced (to no one's great surprise) that he had "a new composition." Without further introduction he sat down and played his just completed symphonic poem, "An American in Paris." I thought it was superb, and I raved about it. But a little later, as we were all on our way to the beach for a swim, George caught up with me and remarked with some puzzlement, "I never knew you were like that."

I was surprised and asked him what in the world he meant. Hastily, he clarified. "I didn't know you could like anyone else's stuff!"

Gershwin's "stuff" was marvelous, and I was crazy about it. I can hardly remember a time when I didn't know about him. He was just three years older than I, and our early careers followed much the same pattern. We were both in our teens when our first songs were published, and we both made our first marks writing music for revues. And we shared a great admiration and affection for Jerome Kern. George, in fact, is supposed to have insisted that he "paid Kern the tribute of frank imitation," but I don't for a moment believe it. George's style was uniquely his own from the very first. He owed a great deal to Kern, it's true. We both did. Kern was the father of the modern book musical, which Gershwin spent the greater part of his professional life helping to refine, and which is still my first working concern. But George never "imitated" anybody.

He loved to play the piano. He played marvelously—and at the least provocation. Performing was like a shot of adrenalin to George; he loved to be the life of the party, and could entertain for hours at a stretch, improvising on themes suggested by his "audience," or playing endless variations on themes of his own. Nor was his performing limited to the piano. He was a great storyteller, had a natural gift for dancing, and demonstrated no little talent as an actor. He liked being a star. I remember once going to a costume party at which he and I dressed as two of the Marx Brothers. George, of course, was the flamboyant Groucho. The occasion was preserved for posterity in a photograph which is included in the following pages.

If parties gave Gershwin an additional platform for his considerable talents and a forum for his original and intriguing ideas, they were also the perfect showcase for a personality that helped to give New York in the twenties so much of the character we have come to associate with those years. Some of the best parties of the decade were given by Jules Glaenzer, Vice President of Cartier's and supreme host to the celebrities of the day. The array of talent at one of those affairs almost amounted to an embarrassment of riches. Fred and Adele Astaire were regulars, as were Florenz Ziegfeld, Charlie Chaplin, and Noël Coward. Often George would be at one piano with Cole Porter at the other, and Gertrude Lawrence would sing while Bea Lillie clowned. Those were wonderful, vibrant parties, and George was almost always in attendance.

Perhaps my most vivid recollection of Gershwin was Christmas Eve of 1934. My wife Dorothy was expecting our younger child, Linda, as it turned out, and was having a difficult time of it. So she had been ordered to stay in bed until the baby's arrival. George must have known how the hours dragged for Dorothy, cooped up in a New York apartment during the gayest season of the year. So that night before Christmas he and composer Kay Swift burst in on us like two irrepressible magi, bearing a present that only George Gershwin could have given.

George and I—he in typically ebullient mood—carried Dorothy into the living room and settled her on the sofa. Our four-year-old daughter, Mary, in her pajamas, was romping around the lighted Christmas tree, a fire burned in the fireplace, and so did one on the end of George's ever-present big cigar.

When the scene was set to his satisfaction, George paused until the suspense in the room had mounted to a sufficient pitch and then he sat down at the piano and proceeded to play the entire score of *Porgy and Bess*. It was months before its Broadway première. He also sang his brother Ira's lyrics—in a funny high voice, to be sure—but with all the emotional depth of a Caruso, at least. The two songs that impressed us most on that special night were "Summertime," of course, and "Bess You Is My Woman Now." That was a Christmas we shall never forget.

My wife asked George once if he had ever taken art lessons; he was a prodigious painter. He told her that he enjoyed painting, painted "well enough," and he therefore saw "no reason to take lessons." I personally think it was a point of pride with him that he painted as well as he did without any formal training. He was fond of saying that had he pursued painting rather than music, he would have been just as accomplished an artist as he was a pianist and composer. The fact was that he had excellent—and instinctive—taste.

He owned a magnificent Chagall, long before Chagall was prized, and he collected some enviable Post-Impressionists, simply because they appealed to him, when they were priced at a fraction of their worth today. Undeniably, he had an eye for quality, just as he had an ear for it. George recognized the good in art as readily as he did in music—his own or anyone else's.

He could be absolutely objective about his work, and often discussed one of his paintings or songs as though Gershwin, the artist-composer, was not in the same room as Gershwin, the critic. Although he wanted the approval of his peers, he really sought their honest opinion, and I am sure he would not be affronted that I felt he made a mistake in writing *Porgy and Bess* as an opera, because I truly do not think it worked as such when the Theatre Guild produced it in 1935. The *recitative* device was an unfamiliar and difficult one for Broadway audiences, and it didn't sustain the story. It was when Cheryl Crawford revived it later as a musical play that it gained such overwhelming success and universal acceptance. And there is no question that it deserves every accolade it has received. Although I certainly remember all of his shows, the ones I recall with special warmth and nostalgia were the wonderful plays and films with the Astaires.

When George died so tragically and unexpectedly in Hollywood in 1937, I was out there working with my friend and collaborator, Larry Hart. George's passing came as a shock to all of us who knew him, of course, but to Ira Gershwin the blow was stunning both personally and professionally. The partnership of the two brothers had been so close that for a time it seemed as though Ira might not work again. But four years later he joined Kurt Weill to do the exciting and innovative *Lady in the Dark*. And he went on to write material for a number of very successful films and plays during the forties.

George was the gregarious, firebrand member of the Gershwin team, and it is interesting that with the enormous body of work he produced, from scores for the stage and films to concert and symphonic music, the best way to sum up George Gershwin's work is simply:

'S won-der-ful!_____

And it was Ira who wrote the perfect words.

INTRODUCTION BY JOHN S. WILSON

George and Ira Gershwin were as dissimilar as two brothers could be. Almost everything that one was, the other wasn't. And yet the various pluses and minuses of these two very distinct and individually creative men were so complementary, fitting together as snugly as the parts of a cleanly cut jigsaw puzzle, that, together, they formed a remarkably complete whole.

The whole that was the Gershwins was exemplified by the conjunction of their words and music. But it was not by any means limited to that. It involved almost every aspect of their radically different personalities. It was their very differences, in fact, that made each a supportive complement to the other in ways that might not have been possible with two people of more similar chemistry.

In appearance, work habits, living habits, outlook, interests — run down any list — they were opposites. George — open, exuberant, a party-goer, loving the spotlight, an irrepressible performer, restless and physically active. Ira — withdrawn, shy, a meditator, slow-moving, an underplayer. And yet they functioned together with the smoothness of a beautifully tooled piece of machinery.

George was a trim, solidly built man of medium height (5 feet 9½ inches). He had a relatively high forehead, emphasized in later years as his hairline began to recede, and a slightly prominent, underslung jaw usually held at a jaunty, challenging angle. The combination of these features gave his face an appearance of length.

Ira is something else. A bit shorter but broad-shouldered, so that he has a stocky appearance. On top of this rectangular frame, a head that is so equally proportioned that it seems almost square. In pictures of the two brothers, George is typically looking eagerly up and out, while Ira appears to be gazing at the ground or off to the side, avoiding whatever it is that is causing this attention to be centered on him.

"George is unabated enthusiasm, Ira is phlegmatic mistrust," wrote Isaac Goldberg, the Gershwins' first biographer, who knew both the brothers well. "George is propulsive, Ira, though by no means a lazybones, needs constant prodding — when there is no avenue of escape, he is capable of tremendous spurts of energy."

The dynamism of George's personality was inescapable. "Whenever he entered a room," Ira's wife, Lenore, once said of George, "he captured it instantly and completely, not because he was overbearing but because he had an irresistible, infectious vitality, an overwhelming personal magnetism beyond that of most of the greatest movie stars."

George was a natural athlete in the sense that he had the grace and coordination to do well in almost any sport that he tried. He was a golfer, a tennis player, a swimmer, a rider, a skier, and an avid Ping-Pong player. He played everything with flair and enthusiasm. Ira, as a boy, indicated that he might have much the same potential but in the more plodding, steady, persistent way that was typical of him. His youngest brother, Arthur, remembers Ira swimming from Coney Island to Brighton Beach, a long-distance swim. "If you ask Ira about this," Arthur added, "he may try to deny it because he's so modest. But I saw him do it."

George was conscious of a relationship between his fondness for physical activity and the kind of music he wrote. "I feel I was meant for hard physical work, to chop down trees, to use my muscles," he told Goldberg. "This composing is indoor labor, much of it, and it takes it out of a fellow like me. If I cared for the ballad type of song I could write reams of them now, full of sad sobs and moony languors. But it wouldn't be me. And later, when I'd get over my blues, I'd play them through and feel that they were written by somebody else. When I'm in my normal mood the tunes come dripping off my fingers. And they're lively tunes, full of outdoor pep."

This "outdoor pep," which is characteristic of George's most popular songs, struck Alec Wilder, a fellow composer, as an indication of George's aggressiveness as a writer. "His was the 'hard sell,' as opposed to the softer, gentler persuasiveness of, say, Kern or Irving Berlin," Wilder has declared.* "If I were to compare his songs with Kern's, I'd say Gershwin's were active and Kern's passive. The constant, and characteristic, repeated note found throughout Gershwin's songs is a basic attestation of this aggressiveness."

But Harold Arlen, whose career as a composer was strongly encouraged by George, thought what Wilder viewed as aggressiveness was an expression of George's bubbling good humor and his joy in sheer animal vitality. "He bubbled just as much as his music does," Arlen pointed out. "That is why I believe that anyone who knows George's work knows George. The humor, the satire, the playfulness of most of his melodic phrases were the natural expression of the man."

Abram Chasins, the pianist and author, who was a teen-aged neighbor and friend of George's, remembers the "incredible ease, joyous spontaneity, and originality at the piano" that he had even as a young man of twenty-one. "He was the only pianist I ever heard who could make a piano laugh, really laugh," Chasins recalled, ruefully adding that while *he* had his nose stuck to the music grindstone, "George was having a love affair with music: no regular piano practice, no slaving away at theory, harmony, counterpoint, orchestration or form."

That exuberant love affair with music, particularly his own music, persisted throughout George's life. Wherever a piano was available, George would sit down and play. Part of his joy in going to

*Wilder's *American Popular Song* (New York: Oxford University Press, 1972), a unique and penetrating analysis of songwriters and their songs, includes a long, critical examination of George Gershwin's songs.

parties was because of the opportunities they afforded him to play. What he played was usually Gershwin, and, of the available Gershwin, his favorites at any given moment were whatever songs he had most recently written — as often as not, material for a show that was still in rehearsal. "George's music gets around so much before an opening," George S. Kaufman once observed, "that the first-night audience thinks it's at a revival."

Yet for all the love of self-acclaim that this seeking-out of the spotlight might suggest, George was generous in his enthusiasm for other composers, known and unknown. He gave support, encouragement, and advice to many neophyte composers, helping to launch the careers of Harold Arlen, Arthur Schwartz, Vernon Duke, Kay Swift, and Dana Suesse. Ann Ronell met George when she interviewed him for her school paper at Radcliffe. When she later moved to New York, he got her a job as a rehearsal pianist for his current show, *Show Girl*. And when he expressed admiration for her song "Willow Weep for Me," she was so grateful that she dedicated the song to him.

On a different level, he used a weekly radio show in 1934 and 1935 to promote the songs of his leading contemporaries — Richard Rodgers, Jerome Kern, Cole Porter, Hoagy Carmichael, Irving Berlin, and others in the upper echelon of ASCAP members — although the program was called *Music by Gershwin*.

Ira, on the other hand, was as retiring as George was extroverted. He preferred to close himself into a private world focused primarily on words (and the thinking that either produced words or resulted from them). He was an omnivorous reader from his early childhood. His instinct was to reject anything that involved physical activity. "Phlegmatic," his brother called him, not in a pejorative sense but in admiration for the calm, unruffled way in which Ira went through life. After a consultation over a song when a new show was in preparation, George would hurry off to watch a rehearsal, but Ira preferred to go back to the hotel room — "to think things over."

When George completed "Bess, You Is My Woman Now" for *Porgy and Bess* he played it for the first time for Dr. Albert Sirmay, an old friend who was his editor at Chappell's, his publisher. Sirmay began to cry because, he explained afterward, the music was so lovely and so fitting. George immediately picked up a phone on the piano and, brimming with excitement, called Ira, who lived across the street, urging him to come right over.

"Why?" grumped Ira.

"Because something is happening here!"

What, Ira wanted to know, could be so important that he should leave his apartment, take an elevator to the street, cross the street, and take another elevator up to George's apartment?

When the brothers moved to California in 1936, Ira immediately settled into the relaxing pleasures of the temperate climate and the soothing distance from the irksome business pressures of New York. But George grew restless away from the competitive hustle and bustle he knew in the East.

"Ira Gershwin is probably the only man in Hollywood who underacts," Benjamin Welles observed in a *New York Times* report on Ira's life in California. "He lives with and moves among showmen, yet exhibits no overtones of the movie colony. He is so normal in his appearance and deportment that one suspects he lets off steam in his lyrics."

Much of this appearance of "normality," as opposed to Hollywood norms, was part of the facade (usually colored with dry wit) that Ira had erected early in life as a defense for his shyness and his reluctance to commit himself to physical activity. In the mid-twenties he was goaded by his brother-in-law to learn to drive and he actually got a license. But after one summer at the wheel, he never drove again, explaining that he could not stand the dirty looks he got from other drivers.

As befits a careful, reticent man, Ira is a careful and meticulous workman. He works his lyrics over and over, keenly sensitive to an inadequate phrase or a word that does not have quite the right sound or texture. It is not finished in his eyes — and ears — until it "feels right."

He usually starts with a title which either is a result of the over-all idea for the song or generates the idea. Because they are the starting point, good titles are invaluable to Ira. A good title may not always cross the mental horizon at precisely the appropriate moment, but none was ever discarded. Ira filed it away in the back of his mind for future reference.

From the title he goes to the final line of the chorus, which, as often as not, may repeat the title but with a twist, to give the song a sock ending. Then, pacing around the room, singing to himself (he normally writes lyrics after the tune has been composed), Ira goes back to the beginning and works his way to the foreordained end of the lyric.

While Ira worked in solitude, George's gregarious nature often led him to compose surrounded by socializing friends or members of his family. Occasionally, when the conflict between creativity and geniality became too great, George would move to the solitude of a hotel room, and even then his friends were apt to intrude on his work. But because he was constantly at the piano, whether actively composing or simply playing, usable phrases flowed through his fingers in a steady stream and he had the facility to develop them quickly, just as Ira could reach back into his storeroom of titles and ideas.

There was an evening in 1937 when they were working on the score for the film *A Damsel in Distress*. George, typically, was out at a party. Ira, typically, was home, reading. At one A.M. George returned from the party, took off his dinner jacket, and sat down at the piano.

"How about some work?" he said to Ira. "Got any ideas?"

"Well," said Ira, putting down his book, "there's one spot we might do something about a fog. . . . How about 'a foggy day in London' or maybe 'foggy day in London Town'?"

"I like it better with 'Town,'" replied George, and he started into a melody. An hour later the brothers had finished words and music for the chorus of "A Foggy Day (in London Town)."

"Next day the song still sounded good," Ira recalled, "so we started on the verse."

The admiration the two brothers had for each other was unlimited. George, as his friend Emil Mosbacher pointed out, "was obsessed with Ira and was always figuring out ways to get Ira to work because he respected Ira so much and needed him, too." Ira, for his part, stood in wonder "at the reservoir of musical inventiveness, resourcefulness and craftsmanship George could dip into."

Ira had a rare opportunity to observe this with some measure of detachment when the Gershwins were working on *Porgy and Bess* with Du Bose Heyward. The lyric-writing was divided between Ira and Heyward — Ira, as usual, writing lyrics to George's melodies, while Heyward reversed the process, writing a lyric which George set to music.

"All [Du Bose's] fine and poetic lyrics were set to music by George with scarcely a syllable being changed — an aspect of this composer's versatility not generally recognized," Ira recorded. "He takes two simple quatrains of Du Bose's, studies the lines, and in a little while a lullaby called 'Summer-time' emerges — delicate and wistful, yet destined to be sung over and over again. Out of the libretto's dialogue he takes Bess's straight, unrhymed speech which starts: 'What you want wid Bess? She's gettin' old now,' and it becomes a rhythmic aria; then he superimposes Crown's lines. 'What I wants wid other woman? I gots a woman,' and now is heard at once a moving and exultant duet. Not a syllable of Du Bose's poignant 'My Man's Gone Now' is changed as the composer sets it to waltz time, adds the widow's heart-rending wail between stanzas, and climaxes the tragic lament with an ascending glissando — resulting in one of the most memorable moments in the American musical theater.... George could be as original and distinctive when musicalizing words as when composing music that would later require words."

Recognition of George's "genius" (to use a word that was frequently applied to him) came early in his career and from both sides of the musical fence. In 1922, when "Swanee" and "I'll Build a Stair-way to Paradise" were his primary claims to fame (and before any of his "serious" works had been composed), Beryl Rubinstein, the concert pianist, used the word in a newspaper interview in which he said that "with Gershwin's style and seriousness, he is not definitely of the popular music school but is one of the really outstanding figures in this country's serious musical efforts."

Even earlier, when George was working as a $15-a-week staff pianist at Remick's, the songwriter Harry Ruby ("Three Little Words," "Who's Sorry Now," "Watching the Clouds Roll By") was impressed by George's earnestness, enthusiasm, and his passionate interest in the popular-music business. "Sometimes when he spoke of the artistic mission of popular music," Ruby said, "we thought he was going highfalutin'. The height of artistic achievement to us was a 'pop' song that sold lots of copies and we just didn't understand what he was talking about."

In fact, when George was only fourteen his unique qualities were being noted. His teacher, Charles Hambitzer, barraged with George's arguments that popular music could be an important art if a composer brought to it the same background and capabilities that might be applied to the composi-tion of a symphony or an opera, wrote in a letter, "The boy is a genius without a doubt. He wants to go in for this modern stuff, jazz and what not. But I'm not going to let him for a while. I'll see that he gets a firm foundation in the standard music first."

Gershwin, in appraising himself midway in his career at the end of the twenties, called himself "a man without traditions." "Music must reflect the thoughts and aspirations of the people and the time," he said. "My people are American. My time is today." And it was because he wrote to those specifications — to his people, to his time — possibly even more shrewdly than he himself realized, that his music found so responsive an audience.

Just how much "the time" when Gershwin was writing had to do with his popular success is em-phasized by Alec Wilder, who has pointed out that radio came along just as George's career was getting under way. "The enormous exposure provided by this medium had much to do with the public's enthusiasm for his songs," says Wilder, adding that both jazz musicians and dance-band arrangers liked his songs and, between the two, gave them much greater coverage than those of most other contemporary writers. In contrast, during the early years of Berlin's and Kern's careers, vaude-ville, primitive acoustical recordings, and stage productions were the only means of promoting their songs, and, Wilder notes, "neither of these men wrote as much to the liking of the [jazz] players and arrangers as did Gershwin."

Ira, meanwhile, was not receiving quite the glowing accolades that were heaped on George. In the fall of 1924, six months after George had startled the musical world with his *Rhapsody in Blue*, Ira was so little known that an English reviewer, covering the London opening of the Gershwins' *Primrose*, referred to Ira as George's sister (a twist that is whimsically perpetuated today by the popular singing team of Jackie Cain and Roy Kral, who introduce "They Can't Take That Away from Me" as "by George Gershwin and his sister, Ira"). But Ira has, in Benjamin Welles's phrase, "played the tortoise to George's hare—as the latter soared in leaps and bounds, keeping quietly along with him as if drawn by a magnet." And, in the process, gaining the admiration of such peers as Ring Lardner, who came out of *Let 'Em Eat Cake* remarking, "You can count on the fingers of one thumb the present-day writers of song words who could wear becomingly the mantle of W. S. Gilbert, or even the squirrel neckpiece of Ira Gershwin."

Lardner could scarcely have chosen a more complimentary comparison, from Ira's point of view, than Gilbert. The author of the *Bab Ballads* and the Savoy operas was, with P. G. Wodehouse, the idol of Ira's youth. And Ira's right to a place in such company was confirmed when his lyric to "The Babbitt and the Bromide" from *Funny Face* was included in an anthology of light verse edited by Louis Kronenberger, the only song lyric to find a place in the collection.

The Gershwin brothers were born within two years of each other—Ira on December 6, 1896, on the Lower East Side of Manhattan, George in Brooklyn on September 26, 1898. Their mother and father, Rose and Morris Gershovitz (which was changed first to Gershvin and then to Gershwin), each of whom had emigrated from Russia before their marriage in 1895, were as different in their personalities as their two older sons were in theirs.

Morris Gershwin, according to George, was "a very easy-going, humorous philosopher" who took things as they came—which was fortunate, considering his peripatetic career. He was, at the time of his marriage, a foreman in a factory that made fancy uppers for women's shoes. But in the next twenty years he moved his family (which was increased by the arrival of Arthur and Frances) no less than twenty-eight times as his occupations shifted—part owner of a Turkish bath on the Bowery, part owner of a restaurant on Third Avenue near 129th Street, part owner of another restaurant on the Lower East Side, owner of a cigar store, owner of a billiard parlor, of a bakery, even a venture into bookmaking at Belmont Park for what proved to be a disastrous month because, Ira has recalled, "too many favorites won."

In later years, when Morris Gershwin could bask in George's glory (somehow Ira's accomplishments usually came as a second thought to him), he became part of the poker-playing atmosphere of the Gershwin home, noted for his performances on comb and tissue. Rose Gershwin, on the other hand, was, in George's words, "nervous, ambitious and purposeful." She wanted her children to be educated, feeling that with an education they could at least become teachers. She opposed George's desire to become a musician, thinking of such a career in terms of a $25-a-week piano player. But she did nothing to stand in George's way when he left school to take his first job as a pianist.

However, her ambitions for her only daughter, who was known as Frankie, were somewhat different. After a successful appearance as a singer and dancer in a school recital at the age of eleven, Rose took Frankie to Philadelphia to break in an act which led to a road tour in *Daintyland* at $40 a week. This was not a career that Frankie pursued assiduously. A decade later she sang at Les Ambassadeurs in Paris, but when, in 1930, she married Leopold Godowsky, Jr., who became one of the inventors of the Kodachrome process a few years later, her professional career came to an end.

Arthur, the third Gershwin son, started out on violin, but soon gave it up. It was at a time when George had just begun to study piano. Arthur complained that George could take his lessons sitting down whereas violin lessons meant standing up. After abandoning the violin, Arthur became a stockbroker and, eventually, a pianist who played by ear — and, of course, sitting down.

The nature of the Gershwin household — its priority values — may be summed up most readily in the matter of Ira's name. As a boy, he was always known as Izzy and he assumed that his name was Isadore, although neither of his parents could remember what name they had given him when he was born. When he was thirty years old and applying for a passport, Ira found out for the first time that his name was legally Israel. (George was named Jacob, after his paternal grandfather, Yakov Gershovitz.)

Ira's memories of growing up are a kaleidoscopic succession of apartments and grade schools, some uptown in New York but mostly downtown. He remembers "horse-drawn streetcars on Delancey Street, their stoves hot in the winter; the trips with other kids to Chinatown to buy sugar cane at about a cent a foot; learning to swim in the mucky Harlem River; picking up some Italian phrases to serve as passwords in case you were ganged up on around Mulberry Street (a ploy which sometimes worked — and if it didn't you got at least a sock in the jaw and ran like hell); the laundry with a two-cent lending library sideline (in the back a wooden bench with three or four piles of nickel novels to exchange: the *Young Wild West*, *Pluck and Luck*, *Fred Fearnot* and *Liberty Boys of '76* series); then the discovery of the public library...."

Ira's choice of reading matter did not meet his parents' (i.e., his mother's) approval, so he kept his books stashed around the house, under rugs, behind pictures. They fired his fascination with words. By the time he was going to high school at Townsend Harris Hall, Ira was contributing a column, "Much Ado," to the *Academic Herald* (although officially he was one of its art editors), and later, at City College, he collaborated on a column in the weekly *Campus* called "Gargoyle Gargles" with E. Y. Harburg, who followed Ira's path to Broadway as a lyricist, notably for *Finian's Rainbow*.

These columns reflected Ira's admiration for F.P.A.'s "Conning Tower" in the *Evening Mail*, an admiration that went even further in Ira's private writing when, just before his twentieth birthday, he began keeping a diary in the manner of F.P.A.'s "Our Own Samuel Pepys." Ira's variant was "Everyman His Own Boswell," which recounted his life and thoughts as cashier at a Turkish bath by day (one of his father's business projects), occasional student at City College by night, and on visits to vaudeville, the theater, and the movies.

He was sending contributions both to F.P.A. and to Don Marquis, who ran a column in the *Sun*, with only occasional success. Seeking professional advice, he put a copy of a short satirical piece called "The Shrine" in the mailbox of Paul M. Potter, an English playwright who had dramatized *Trilby* and who lived in the hotel above the bath where Ira was working. Potter suggested that he send it to H. L. Mencken's *The Smart Set*, which accepted the story, printed it, and sent Ira the sum of one dollar in "full payment of all rights in America and Great Britain." This so inflamed Ira's creativity that he bombarded *The Smart Set* with further contributions, none of which was accepted.

Potter also gave Ira a piece of advice that proved much more valuable in the long run than his suggestion of *The Smart Set*. He "advised me to learn especially 'your American slang,'" Ira later recalled. "Seemed to think that a writer doesn't necessarily have to experience everything he writes about, but by being an attentive listener and observer, can gain a good deal by second-hand experience."

This was a thought that was eminently suited to Ira's natural tendency for non-involvement. But the opportunities to apply it profitably still eluded him. He worked briefly in the receiving department of Altman's department store. He had a trial as a reviewer for a theatrical paper, the New York *Clipper*, and wrote three brief reviews. His longest job was as treasurer of a traveling carnival, Colonel Lagg's Greater Empire Shows. But after several months the nomad life palled and Ira trudged home.

"I'm afraid I was pretty much of a floating soul," Ira says of this period in his life. "I couldn't concentrate on anything. I haunted the movies; I read without plan or purpose. To tell the truth, I was at a complete loss and I didn't care. It was at this moment, back from the carnival, that I first thought of becoming a writer of what they call 'lyrics.'"

George, meanwhile, had been moving along a line of development that was as direct as Ira's was vague. The first response to music that he remembered came when he was six years old, barefoot and in overalls, standing outside a penny arcade on 125th Street, "listening to an automatic piano leaping through Rubinstein's 'Melody in F.' The peculiar jumps in the music held me rooted," he recalled.

A year later, skating past Baron Wilkins's night club, he was fascinated by the jazz he heard being played by James Reese Europe's band.

But most of George's interests then lay in roller-skating, playing stick hockey, and fighting until, when he was ten and playing ball outside his grade school, he heard a violinist playing Dvořák's "Humoresque." It was, he said, "a flashing revelation." The violinist was one of his schoolmates, Maxie Rosenzweig, whose violin continued to charm listeners when he took to the concert stage as Max Rosen. The two boys became close friends, and, through Rosen, George first became aware of the world of music.

When he was twelve, his mother bought a second-hand upright piano, partly because her sister had one, partly with the idea of starting Ira on lessons. As soon as the piano had been hoisted up through the window of their second-floor apartment, George was at the keyboard playing a popular tune of the day. Ira, the reluctant one, was chained to the keyboard for a while ("He actually covered about thirty-two pages of Beyer's text before re-signing to his fate," George recalled. "Words came easier to him than music."), but the effort was abandoned when it became evident that George was the family's natural pianist.

George's first teachers were local ladies at fifty cents a lesson. But soon he had worked up to a teacher who could command $1.50 a lesson, and by 1913 he was studying with Charles Hambitzer, who was, George said, "the first great musical influence in my life."

While George responded to Hambitzer's ebullient, outgoing nature, Hambitzer quickly recognized George's potential and nursed it along. He introduced George to the music of Chopin, Liszt, and Debussy and sent him to Edward Kilenyi for instruction in harmony and theory. Both teachers encouraged George in experimentation as a composer, but Hambitzer's apparent intention was to develop him as a concert pianist. However, Hambitzer died of tuberculosis in 1918 at thirty-seven (one year younger than George was himself when he died) and George's motivation for a concert career apparently ended there.

When he was fifteen, after two years at the High School of Commerce, George gave up school to go to work for Jerome H. Remick and Co. as a pianist and song-plugger at $15 a week. A year later he made his public debut as both composer and pianist, an event quite unrelated to his work for Remick.

Ira, as a sideline to his work as diarist, poet, and epigrammatist had joined the Finley Club of New York City College and, in 1914, found himself on the arrangement committee for the club's annual entertainment. Exercising a committee member's nepotistic prerogatives, he got George a spot on the program as both soloist and accompanist. George's solo, listed on the program as simply "Piano Solo," was actually a modest and conventional tango. This was not, however, his first composition. That was an unpublished song called "Since I Found You" and, according to his friend and biographer Isaac Goldberg, who heard him play it, the fact that it was never published was "just as well."

In 1915, when George was seventeen, he got into a field which may prove to be a fertile means for exploring the roots of the Gershwin style. At Remick's he met Felix Arndt, who is now known primarily as the composer of "Nola" and who was a prolific creator of piano rolls. Through Arndt, George began making piano rolls, going out to East Orange, New Jersey, on Saturdays, where he would get $25 for cutting six rolls for the Standard Music Company's Perfection label — thus almost doubling his weekly salary at Remick's. By 1916 he was also making rolls for the Universal label. He continued to make piano rolls on into the twenties, using not only his own name (one of the earliest instances in which he changed Gershvin to Gershwin) but "Bert Wynn" — a pseudonym which was supposedly based on his fondness for Ed Wynn, the comedian — along with such less explainable pseudonyms as "James Baker" and "Fred Murtha." Altogether, he is believed to have made 125 piano rolls, of which 80 are thought to be still in existence.

After two years at Remick's, and with the added cachet of his work as a piano-roll artist, George was beginning to be known even in the nether world of black ragtime pianists. Eubie Blake remembers hearing about him shortly after he moved to New York from Baltimore in 1916. "James P. Johnson and Luckey Roberts told me of this very talented ofay piano player at Remick's," Eubie recalled, referring to the two top black pianists in New York at the time. "They said he was good enough to learn some of those terribly difficult tricks that only a few of us could master."

Along with this recognition of his skill as a pianist, George was also making his first steps as a published composer. He got nowhere trying to sell his songs to the obvious outlet, Remick's ("You're here as a pianist, not a writer," he was told). But in 1916 he managed to get a song published by Harry Von Tilzer Music Publishing Co.—"When You Want 'Em, You Can't Get 'Em; When You Got 'Em, You Don't Want 'Em," which had lyrics by Murray Roth and the longest title of George's career.

At this same time George made his first significant move toward the theater. He and Roth had written a song called "My Runaway Girl," which they hoped to get into a Shubert revue at the Winter Garden. They managed to get an audition with Sigmund Romberg, who was then the Shuberts' all-purpose composer. "My Runaway Girl" was never heard at the Winter Garden, but one among several ideas submitted to Romberg by George became "The Making of a Girl," with lyrics by Harold Atteridge, and was included in *The Passing Show of 1916*, which had a score that otherwise was completely by Romberg.

"It was now that the popular-song racket began to get definitely on my nerves," George once said. "Its tunes began to offend me. Or, perhaps my ears were becoming attuned to better harmonies."

One of the things that had attuned his ears to better harmonies had occurred a year or so before. At the wedding of his aunt at the Grand Central Hotel, George had been so taken by a tune he heard the orchestra playing that he rushed up to the leader to find out what it was. "You're Here and I'm Here," composed by Jerome Kern for *The Girl from Utah*, he learned. A little while later another tune sent him back to the bandstand to find out what *it* was. It was Kern again and another song from *The Girl from Utah*—"They Didn't Believe Me."

"Kern was the first composer who made me conscious that most popular music was of inferior quality," George said many years later, "and that musical-comedy music was made of better material. I followed Kern's work and studied each song that he composed."

Kern's was the siren song that lured George away from Remick's. He was not fully conscious of this when he told Mose Gumble, for whom he worked at Remick's, that he was quitting. When Gumble asked him what he was going to do, George admitted that he didn't know. "All I knew was that something was taking me away," he said later. "As I look back, it's very clear that I wanted to be closer to production music—the kind Jerome Kern was writing."

His first job away from Remick's, aside from a brief fling as accompanist to a vaudeville singer, Rita Gould (for which he used a variant of one of his piano-roll pseudonyms, George Wynne), was as rehearsal pianist for *Miss 1917*, a musical to which Jerome Kern had contributed along with Victor Herbert. The show had only a short run at the Century Theatre, but after it closed George continued to work at the Century as accompanist at the star-studded Sunday concerts that were held there.

At one of these concerts Vivienne Segal sang two songs that George had written with Irving Caesar, "There's More to the Kiss than the X-X-X" and "You-oo Just You." Through these two songs George came to the attention of Max Dreyfus, the perceptive head of Harms, the music publishers. It was Dreyfus who had discovered Jerome Kern a decade earlier and he was subsequently to add Vincent Youmans and Richard Rodgers to his stable of composers. He offered George $35 a week, the same salary that he had received as a song-plugger at Remick's and as a rehearsal pianist for *Miss 1917*. But there was a big difference: at Harms he was hired as a composer.

George Gershwin.
June 9, 1931.

"I feel that you have some good stuff in you," Dreyfus told the nineteen-year-old composer. "It'll come out. It may take months, it may take a year, it may take five years, but I'm convinced that the stuff is there. You have no set duties. Just stop in every morning, so to speak, and say hello. The rest will follow."

What followed immediately was the first song by George and Ira Gershwin to be heard, if only briefly, in a musical comedy. Ira, back from his tour with the carnival and installed once again at his old job at the baths, passed the time working at his new goal of becoming "a writer of what they call 'lyrics.'" One of these efforts, "The Real American Folk Song," was set to music by George. Nora Bayes, who was rehearsing in a show that would eventually be called *Ladies First*, had heard and liked the first of George's songs published by Harms, "Some Wonderful Sort of Someone," and was using it in *Ladies First*. And when she heard "The Real American Folk Song," she added that to the interpolated "concert" that was a customary feature of such musicals. The material in these concerts was changed frequently, however, and after eight or nine weeks "The Real American Folk Song" disappeared from the show. It was not to appear again until Ella Fitzgerald recorded it in the late fifties, arousing enough curiosity to induce Chappell to finally publish it forty years after it was written.

"Some Wonderful Sort of Someone," however, remained in the show. This song, with lyrics by Schuyler Greene, contained one of several hints of things to come that were appearing in George's tunes at this time. In this case, he used a phrase in the bridge, or middle section, which six years later was used to good advantage in the main theme of "Fascinating Rhythm."

George's next advance was to move from interpolated songs to a full score. The opportunity to do this — at least to do a partial score — came through Max Dreyfus. A man named Perkins asked Dreyfus for help in producing a revue. Perkins had several songs and special effects that he had brought from Paris, as well as lyrics which he had written himself for five more songs. Could Dreyfus suggest a composer for his songs?

It seemed an ideal opportunity for nineteen-year-old George Gershwin. Dreyfus not only recommended George but offered to pay for the show's orchestrations. The show, *Half Past Eight*, starred Joe Cook, who was a friend of Perkins, and included Cook's vaudeville troupe, as well as a twenty-five-piece Negro orchestra, a bicycle act, and several other people. It opened in Syracuse and, within a few days, it closed in Syracuse. All George got out of it was his fare back to New York. But at least he had seen for the first time on a billboard the words "Music by George Gershwin."

While *Half Past Eight* was going through its agonies in Syracuse, George was not totally unrepresented on Broadway. "You-oo Just You," the song by George and Irving Caesar that Vivienne Segal had introduced at the Century Theatre the year before, had been interpolated in *Hitchy-Koo of 1918*, and another Gershwin-Caesar collaboration, "We're Pals," went into *Dere Mable*, a show based on World War I's most famous letter writer. The song was produced on demand to fill a spot in the script for which the show's official composer had been unable to produce anything satisfactory.

The Caesar-and-Gershwin team was just getting up steam with these two songs. The big hit of 1919 was a lively one-step called "Hindustan," part of a fancy for pseudo-Oriental ideas that had been flourishing since "Poor Butterfly" was sung at the Hippodrome in New York three years earlier by Sophie Bernard. Caesar, a sharp-witted opportunist, suggested to George that they write a one-step but with an American flavor. George agreed. He saw the setting as "something like Stephen Foster's 'Swanee River.'"

The two men discussed the song over dinner at Dinty Moore's and continued to talk it out as they rode a bus up to the Gershwin family's apartment in Washington Heights, where they found the customary poker game in progress. Ignoring the players, George and Caesar went straight to the piano and started writing.

"In about fifteen minutes we had turned out 'Swanee,' verse and chorus," Caesar has recalled. "But we thought the song should have a trio and for a few minutes we were deciding about this addition. The losers in the game kept saying, 'Boys, finish it some other time' and the lucky ones urged us to complete the song right there and then. This we did, and old man Gershwin lost not a moment in fetching a comb, over which he superimposed some tissue, and accompanying George while I sang it over and over again at the insistence of the winning poker players."

Ned Wayburn, who was producing a revue at the Capitol Theatre, a lavish new Broadway movie palace that was to open in October, accepted "Swanee" for his production along with another Gershwin song, "Come to the Moon," for which Lou Paley, a close friend of George's, wrote the lyrics. "Swanee" was given the works by Wayburn. It was sung by Muriel DeForest and played by Arthur Pryor's band, one of the most popular ensembles of the day, while sixty chorus girls with electric lights glittering in their slippers danced on a darkened stage. But even with all this hoop-la, "Swanee" developed no strong reaction and it might have remained as unknown as "Come to the Moon" if Al Jolson, whose successful revue *Sinbad* was playing across the street at the Winter Garden, had not heard George play the song at a party. Jolson liked it and tried it out at one of his Sunday-night concerts at the Winter Garden. The response was so enthusiastic that he put it into *Sinbad,* a show which, like the first revue in which George had had one of his songs interpolated, *The Passing Show of 1916,* had a score that was largely by Sigmund Romberg.

Sparked by Jolson's dynamic performance, "Swanee" became, by any standard, a tremendous hit, a bigger hit than anything else Gershwin would write throughout his career, which, at this point, had scarcely begun. This was due, at least partially, to the fact that he never again wrote such a blatantly and blandly commercial song. "It's cheerful and aggressive," Alec Wilder admits in his analysis of "Swanee," "but without any distinction. Were it not known to be by Gershwin, I doubt if even the most observant authority could name the writer from the hundreds writing at that time."

The tremendous popular success of "Swanee" completely overshadowed what would otherwise have been *the* major event in 1919 for Gorge Gershwin: his first complete Broadway score.

The show was *La, La, Lucille,* a bedroom farce and the first production effort of twenty-nine-year-old Alex A. Aarons. Advised to get Victor Herbert to write the score, Aarons, who sub-titled his production "The New Up-to-the-Minute Musical Comedy of Class and Distinction," liked the fresh, original touches he heard in Gershwin's music and chose George instead. At the show's opening in Boston, J. B. Atkinson, assistant music and drama editor of the Boston *Evening Transcript* (later to be known as Brooks Atkinson when he became drama critic of the *New York Times*), found the music "vivacious and surprising of detail and...harmoniously pleasing."

The score was scarcely fresh Gershwin, although it was new to most listeners. For it, George salvaged "There's More to the Kiss than the X-X-X" from Vivienne Segal's Century Theatre performance, two songs from *Half Past Eight*, and a melody he had developed during his song-plugging days at Remick's. With lyrics by Arthur Jackson, it became "Nobody But You," which has proved to be the sturdiest survivor of the score, although "Tee-Oodle-Um-Bum-Bo" won the ears of such critics as Heywood Broun and Alan Dale.

One week after *La, La, Lucille* opened at Henry Miller's Theatre in New York at the end of May, George White, a dancer who had appeared in *The Passing Show* and the *Ziegfeld Follies*, opened a revue two blocks away which he hoped would compete with Ziegfeld's *Follies*. He called it the *Scandals*, and after a modest run of 128 performances White began planning a new edition for the following year. On the strength of the success of *La, La, Lucille* and with "Swanee" beginning to emerge as a tremendous hit, Gershwin went to see White about doing the score for the 1920 *Scandals* (the score for the first *Scandals* had been written by Richard Whiting, who had just arrived in New York from Detroit, where he had been manager of Remick's branch there).

Gershwin got the job, which paid $50 a week at the start and which developed into a long-term relationship as he turned out scores for the next five *Scandals*, using the revues as a secure foundation on which he could mature as a composer and lay the groundwork for the work which became his true legacy. While he was working on his first *Scandals* score, the second hesitant step toward formation of the team of George and Ira Gershwin occurred.

Since "The Real American Folk Song" two years earlier, George had worked with a variety of lyricists but never again with brother Ira. On this first *Scandals* score, his lyricist was Arthur Jackson, with whom he had done *La, La, Lucille*. In the midst of his work on the *Scandals*, George heard that *The Sweetheart Shop*, which had been playing successfully in Chicago and was moving to New York, needed a new song for Helen Ford. George and Ira hastily turned out "Waiting for the Sun to Come Out" and George got an audition with Edgar MacGregor, the producer. Ira, concerned that MacGregor might be a skeptical listener if he knew that George had pulled in his unknown brother as lyricist, suggested that the lyrics be credited to "Arthur Francis"—a combination of the names of their younger brother and sister.

When MacGregor heard the song, he liked it. But, he asked George, "Who's Arthur Francis?"

"Oh, he's a clever college boy with lots of talent," George replied blithely.

MacGregor agreed to pay $250 for the song and it went into the show. But *The Sweetheart Shop* did not find as warm a response in New York as it had in Chicago, and when, after it had been running a few weeks, George tried to collect the $250, MacGregor admitted that business was so bad that the show was about to close.

George was generous. "I'm working, so I don't mind not being paid myself if things are that tough," he said, "but the college boy really needs the money."

MacGregor promptly wrote out a check for $125, which, as Ira has pointed out, added to the $723.40 earned from sheet-music sales and $445.02 from phonograph records, kept the "college boy" going.

"Waiting for the Sun to Come Out" was Ira's first published song, not to mention the first published song by Arthur Francis, a name behind which he continued to hide until 1924, when he began putting his own name on lyrics because "all who knew me, knew me as a Gershwin anyway."

George's first two scores for the *Scandals*—the *Scandals* of 1920 and 1921—were serviceable if not significant. But the *Scandals of 1922* included two key Gershwin compositions. One was "I'll Build a Stairway to Paradise," which was used in the first-act finale—a vast production number called "The Patent Leather Forest," featuring a high stairway as wide as the proscenium, with the entire cast and Paul Whiteman's Palais Royal Orchestra onstage singing and playing. This Gershwin tune is usually pinpointed as the true beginning of what became recognized as the Gershwin style, as well as the real beginning of his career as a writer for the musical theater. Its particular effectiveness in 1922 was probably due in part, as Alec Wilder has pointed out, to "the non-jazz atmosphere of the musical theater of the early twenties."

"This song probably thrilled listeners familiar with the more polite melodies of Friml and Romberg," Wilder has declared. "Vincent Youmans…had already started on his own path with rich harmony and unmistakably native rhythms, but without neon arrows pointing at the blue notes. However, Gershwin's bald insistence here on notes which had been virtually the early jazz players' and blues singers' private property must have been delightfully shocking to the average theater-goer."

The song was an outgrowth of an early, unpublished collaboration between Ira and George, "A New Step Every Day." Buddy De Sylva, already an established lyric-writer by 1922 (he had written "April Showers" and "Avalon" and, teamed with Lew Brown and Ray Henderson, he would become one of the most successful songwriters of the twenties), told Ira that he saw the germ of an idea for a production number in the song's last line ("I'll build a staircase to Paradise/With a new step every day"). One evening at De Sylva's apartment, the Gershwin brothers and De Sylva created the new song, which salvaged from the original song only the line that had appealed to De Sylva—and, as Ira has noted, "even 'staircase' had become 'stairway.'"

While "Stairway to Paradise" became the surprise hit of the *Scandals*, Gershwin's other notable contribution to the 1922 edition was cut from the show after opening night. This was a one-act Negro opera, with libretto by De Sylva, called *Blue Monday*. Written in a five-day flurry of activity when producer George White, after holding back his approval, made a last-minute decision to use it as a second-act opener, and performed by white actors in blackface, *Blue Monday* drew some very disparate reactions. At the out-of-town opening of the *Scandals* in New Haven, one critic predicted that "this opera will be imitated in a hundred years." After the New York opening, Charles Darnton of the *World* called it "the most dismal, stupid and incredible blackface sketch that has probably ever been perpetrated." George White felt that it had an unduly depressing effect in the generally light-hearted atmosphere of the *Scandals* and dropped it after the New York opening.

Yet *Blue Monday* proved to be the first step toward two of Gershwin's greatest works—*Porgy and Bess*, the ultimate fulfillment of the Negro opera toward which Gershwin was reaching with *Blue Monday*, and *Rhapsody in Blue*, which was commissioned by Paul Whiteman (whose orchestra was in the pit at the *Scandals*) largely because of his memories of working with Gershwin on *Blue Monday.*

Whiteman, in fact, was so impressed by *Blue Monday* that he kept trying to bring it before the public. He revived it in 1925 under the title *135th Street,* orchestrated by Ferde Grofé, with Benny Fields and Blossom Seeley singing the leads, and Austin "Skin" Young, one of the singers in Whiteman's orchestra, in one of the lesser roles. He tried it again in 1936, but on neither occasion was it successful.

Aside from "I'll Build a Stairway to Paradise" and *Blue Monday,* Gershwin's only other memorable contribution to five editions of the *Scandals* was "Somebody Loves Me," sung by Winnie Lightner in the 1924 edition, the last *Scandals* for which Gershwin wrote a score. Although "Somebody Loves Me" remained popular for many years as a ballad sung or played at a moderate tempo, it survives now primarily as one of the most popular and resilient vehicles for jamming by jazz musicians.

During the *Scandals* years George was also busy with other things. One of his non-*Scandals* songs, "Do It Again," with lyrics by Buddy De Sylva, was interpolated in *The French Doll* in 1922 by Irene Bordoni, and has, like "I'll Build a Stairway to Paradise," been cited as one of the earliest evidences of the mature Gershwin style. The following year he went to England to write a score (undistinguished) for a revue, *The Rainbow,* which proved to be a disaster.

He returned to the States to make his first appearance on the concert stage as accompanist to Eva Gauthier in a program at Aeolian Hall. For "A Recital of Ancient and Modern Music for Voice," Mme. Gauthier had been prevailed upon by Carl Van Vechten to include a selection of American popular songs — "jazz," as they were considered then. Mme. Gauthier not only accepted the suggestion, but engaged George Gershwin as her accompanist for these songs — "Alexander's Ragtime Band," Jerome Kern's "Siren's Song," Walter Donaldson's "Carolina in the Morning," and three Gershwin songs: "I'll Build a Stairway to Paradise," "Innocent Ingenue Baby" (from *Our Nell*), and "Swanee." As an encore, she sang "Do It Again" twice, and George drew a small share of attention to himself by interpolating a phrase from *Scheherazade* in "Stairway to Paradise."

This appearance by George at Aeolian Hall on November 1, 1923, proved to be the prelude to a much more important performance there three months later. Paul Whiteman was planning a concert early in 1924 that would be a serious effort to present "jazz" in a concert hall. With George's *Blue Monday* still on his mind, Whiteman asked him to write something for the concert. George, busy on a score for *Sweet Little Devil* with Buddy De Sylva, forgot all about Whiteman's concert until, early in January, he read in the New York *Tribune* that he was at work on a jazz concerto for it. With the concert now scheduled for February 12 at Aeolian Hall, George felt he would be too busy working on *Sweet Little Devil* to write anything. But Whiteman convinced him that all he needed was a piano copy from which the arranger Ferde Grofé could develop an orchestration.

So, en route to Boston for the tryout of *Sweet Little Devil,* George began to work on the piece. "On the train," he said later, "with its steely rhythms, its rattlety-bang . . . I suddenly heard — and even saw on paper — the complete construction of the *Rhapsody* from beginning to end. I heard it as a sort of musical kaleidoscope of America — of our vast melting pot, of our unduplicated national pep, of our blues, our metropolitan madness. By the time I reached Boston I had a definite *plot* of the piece, as distinguished from its actual substance."

n his return from Boston, Gershwin spent a week writing most of the actual substance, handing pages over to Grofé for orchestration almost as he wrote them. By February 4 Grofé had completed his orchestration, Ira had contributed a title, *Rhapsody in Blue*, and Whiteman's band began early-morning rehearsals at the Palais Royal after they had finished their nightly performances there and the club had emptied. But even after five days of rehearsal George had not written the piano solo parts, which he was to play himself. Those blank pages in the score were improvised by George at the concert, which Whiteman billed as "An Experiment in Modern Music."

The program, as Hugh C. Ernst told the audience in an introductory talk, was intended to demonstrate "the tremendous strides which have been made in popular music from the day of discordant Jazz, which sprang into existence about ten years ago from nowhere in particular, to the really melodious music of today." To accomplish this, Whiteman had lined up an incredibly trivial group of selections demonstrating: Legitimate Scoring vs. Jazzing (using "Whispering" as the vehicle), Comedy Selections ("Yes, We Have No Bananas"), Flavoring a Selection with Borrowed Themes (Grofé's "Russian Rose," based on "The Volga Boat Song"), Semi-Symphonic Arrangements of Popular Melodies (three songs by Irving Berlin). The closest the program came to anything related to jazz was in an attempt to copy the Original Dixieland Jazz Band's "The Livery Stable Blues" (an example of Mr. Ernst's "discordant Jazz") and several solos by pianist Zez Confrey, including his popular "Kitten on the Keys." Not even a "Suite of Serenades" by Victor Herbert, specially commissioned by Whiteman, could offset the growing ennui of the expectant, celebrity-studded audience.

But finally George Gershwin darted out on the stage, took his place at the piano, glanced at Whiteman, and Whiteman signaled to Ross Gorman, his virtuosic clarinetist, whose skill with a glissando had inspired George to open his *Rhapsody* with an electrifying, rising sweep on the clarinet. Gorman produced the required electricity. The audience was suddenly all interested attention. At the conclusion of the piece, they burst into enthusiastic, sustained applause.

The critics were divided. Olin Downes in the *Times* wrote of "a new talent finding its voice and likely to say something personally and racially important to the world," while Lawrence Gilman wept "over the lifelessness of its melody and harmony, so derivative, so stale and so inexpressive." But *Rhapsody in Blue* opened up a new world to George Gershwin, and from then on he was involved simultaneously in the worlds of concert music and theater music.

George, however, had little time to relish the success of the *Rhapsody*. Whiteman repeated the concert twice within the next two months, once at Aeolian Hall, once at Carnegie Hall, but without George, who was working on his last *Scandals* score before taking off for England for another London show. Unlike the disastrous *Rainbow*, this second show, *Primrose*, was such a smash hit that George, for the first time, had the experience of having his full score published.

The score included some lyrics by Ira, who, as "Arthur Francis," while George had been turning out *Scandals* scores, had finally made his own mark in the theater. The first show for which Arthur Francis was hired to write lyrics for an entire score was *Two Little Girls in Blue*, a 1922 production which was also the first show for which Vincent Youmans composed a score. Earlier, Arthur Francis had written lyrics to brother George's music for *A Dangerous Maid*, but it did not survive a tryout in Pittsburgh. *Two Little Girls in Blue*, however, had a satisfying run of 226 performances and Arthur Francis went on to collaborate on individual songs with Lewis Gensler, Raymond Hubbell, Milton Schwarzwald, and others. For *Be Yourself*, written with Gensler and Schwarzwald, he proclaimed himself as Ira Gershwin for the first time. And when he had proclaimed himself in this fashion, the team of George and Ira Gershwin went into business in the fall of 1924, writing a score for a show that was to star the rising brother-and-sister team, Fred and Adele Astaire.

The show, *Lady, Be Good!*, which opened in December 1924, was George's (and Ira's, too, of course) first big hit on Broadway, the starting point for a succession of shows through the twenties and early thirties which, if not always as successful as *Lady, Be Good!*, were almost without exception dotted with provocative Gershwin songs. The almost-title song of *Lady, Be Good!* (the song, "Oh, Lady, Be Good" adds an "oh" to the show's title) has remained consistently popular down through the years, particularly with jazz musicians, although, since Walter Catlett first sang it in the show, practically no one has ever performed it as it was originally marked, in questionable grammar: "Slow and gracefully."

Lady, Be Good! also started the strange and steady hegira of one of the Gershwins' most brilliant songs, "The Man I Love." George had written the now familiar chorus as the verse of a song before he left for England to do *Primrose* early in 1924. But he was dissatisfied with the relationship of this verse to its chorus — the verse was more interesting than the chorus, giving the song a top-heavy, anticlimactic feeling. So he moved the verse into the chorus position, wrote a new verse, and Ira supplied lyrics.

On the boat coming back to the States from England, George, as usual, spent a great deal of the trip at the piano playing his own songs, particularly his new ones. Otto Kahn, the banker, who was a fellow passenger, was very much taken with "The Man I Love." Later, when he was approached to invest in *Lady, Be Good!*, Kahn refused. "With those actors and singers and that music, you don't need me," he said. "The show will make good beyond a doubt." But when he was reminded that "The Man I Love" was in the show, he relented and wrote out a check for $10,000 (without indicating whether he felt that the inclusion of "The Man I Love" meant that the success of the show might now be dubious).

When *Lady, Be Good!* opened its tryout run in Philadelphia, Adele Astaire sang "The Man I Love" in the opening scene. But she sang it for only a week. Producer Vinton Freedley insisted on dropping it because it was too static, slowing down the show almost before it had started. In those days the sheet music of a show's songs was printed and on sale in the lobby even at an out-of-town tryout. So when Lady Mountbatten, who had heard George playing "The Man I Love" in London, found that it had been published, she asked George to autograph a copy for her. She took it back to London, turned it over to the Berkeley Square Orchestra, one of her favorite bands, and soon "The Man I Love" was being played by orchestras all over London. From London it spread to Paris, where it became equally popular.

In 1927, when the Gershwins were writing a score for the first production of *Strike Up the Band*, Edgar Selwyn, the producer, insisted that "The Man I Love" be part of the score. It was first sung by Vivian Hart and Roger Pryor and later, toward the end of the show, reprised by Morton Downey as "The Girl I Love." *Strike Up the Band* opened in Long Branch, New Jersey, and then moved to Philadelphia, where, for a change, "The Man (Girl) I Love" was *not* cut from the show. Instead, the entire show died in Philadelphia.

Later that year, when the Gershwins were called on by Florenz Ziegfeld to give Sigmund Romberg and P. G. Wodehouse a helping hand on the score of *Rosalie*, a starring vehicle for one of the musical theater's brightest stars, Marilyn Miller, they found themselves faced with "The Man I Love" once again. Ziegfeld had obtained the rights to the song from Selwyn, and Ira set about rewriting his lyric to fit possible plot cues. He rewrote it at least twice, but "It certainly wasn't in the show opening night," he recalled. "For that matter, there were so many switches in the score that I can't recall Miss Miller ever even rehearsing it."

Max Dreyfus, the Gershwins' publisher, decided to give "The Man I Love" a boost on its own. Getting the brothers to agree to cut their sheet-music royalty one cent each, Dreyfus used the consequent savings for exploitation, an endeavor that began to pay off when Helen Morgan adopted it as one of the ballads she sang from her perch on top of a piano. A second version of *Strike Up the Band* was ready in 1929, and there was talk of giving "The Man I Love" a fourth fling at the musical theater. But by then it had become so popular on its own that it could no longer be incorporated in an otherwise new score.

To George, the fate of "The Man I Love" seemed quite reasonable. "The song is not a production number," he explained. "That is, it allows of little or no action while it is being sung. It lacks a soothing, seducing rhythm; instead it has a certain slow lilt that subtly disturbs the audience instead of lulling it into acceptance. Then, too, there is the melody, which is not easy to catch; it presents too many chromatic pitfalls. Hardly anybody whistles or hums it correctly without the support of a piano or other instrument."

The basic pattern of work and success for both George and Ira that developed in 1924 — an important serious work by George (*Rhapsody in Blue*), a successful musical comedy by both brothers (*Lady, Be Good!*) — continued on through the twenties and into the thirties.

In 1925 George's serious work was his *Concerto in F*; the musical comedy was *Tip-Toes*. The *Concerto* was commissioned by the New York Symphony Society at the suggestion of Walter Damrosch, the conductor. George began working on it during the summer while he was in London for the opening of *Tell Me More*, which he wrote with Ira and Buddy De Sylva (and which was originally titled *My Fair Lady* — thirty-one years too early). This show ran only 100 performances in New York, but did much better in London. George continued work on the *Concerto* through the fall while he was simultaneously writing scores for *Tip-Toes* (with Ira) and *Song of the Flame* (without Ira).

George conceived the *Concerto* as "a piece of absolute music." "The *Rhapsody*, as its title implied, was a blues impression," he said. "The *Concerto* would be unrelated to any program. And that is exactly how I wrote." To try out his new work, George got the Globe Theatre for an afternoon and brought in sixty musicians. With his friend Bill Daly conducting and himself at the piano, he ran through it, made a few revisions, and decided that it was finished.

The première, given at Carnegie Hall on December 3, 1925, with Walter Damrosch conducting and George as soloist, drew mixed reviews, with Lawrence Gilman finding it "conventional, trite, at its worst a little dull," while Samuel Chotzinoff saw Gershwin as an accurate reflection of contemporary America ("He is the present, with all its audacity, impertinence, its feverish delight in its motion, its lapses into rhythmically exotic melancholy").

The première of *Concerto in F* was just the start of an unusually busy month for George. It wound up with the New York opening of *Tip-Toes* on December 28, Paul Whiteman's first effort to revive *Blue Monday* as *135th Street* on December 29 at Carnegie Hall, and the first night of *Song of the Flame* on December 30.

For Ira, *Tip-Toes* represented a distinct advance in his craftsmanship. He was, he admitted later, not completely satisfied with his work on *Lady, Be Good!* "I had adequately fitted some sparkling tunes, and several singable love songs and rhythm numbers had resulted," he wrote in *Lyrics on Several Occasions*. "Yet I was a bit bothered by there being no lyric I considered comic. . . .*Tip-Toes* contained longer openings, many of the songs had crisp lines, and the first-act finale carried plot action for four or five minutes. And I liked the trio 'These Charming People.' . . . Up to then I'd often wondered if I could do a comedy trio like the ones P. G. Wodehouse came up with."

The score for *Tip-Toes* included, along with "Sweet and Low-Down" and "Looking for a Boy," a song that Alec Wilder considers "mint Gershwin"—"That Certain Feeling," a song that he says "is neat as a pin." Wilder was particularly interested to find that, of its thirty-two bars, only three contained syncopation. "This . . . brings to mind the curious paradox that though Gershwin is considered the great 'jazz' song writer, his songs show less syncopation than do those of many other contemporary writers," Wilder has observed. "This may imply that the native song is less distinguishable by its syncopation than by other, more rarefied elements. One of these is boldness ; another is wit. Still another is unexpectedness. Syncopation is only the obvious device."

Song of the Flame, which had an identical run with *Tip-Toes* (194 performances), was a departure from the usual Gershwin style—a traditional operetta to which George contributed only two songs that were entirely his own (the rest of the music was written in collaboration with Herbert Stothart, and by Stothart alone, plus a few authentic Russian folk songs).

The pattern of 1925—a new serious work, a musical-comedy success—was repeated in 1926, although the serious work this time was relatively minor Gershwin : five piano preludes composed for a concert at the Hotel Roosevelt at which George served as accompanist for the contralto Marguerite d'Alvarez. He added a sixth prelude when the concert was repeated in Boston, but only three have been published.

The main Gershwin event of the year, was *Oh, Kay!*, which brought Gertrude Lawrence to the United States in a musical comedy for the first time (she had made her American debut two years earlier in *Charlot's Revue*). Miss Lawrence was thinking over an offer from Florenz Ziegfeld when Alex Aarons and Vinton Freedley approached her to do *Oh, Kay!* The successful bait they used was the fact that George Gershwin was writing the score. And he did very well by Miss Lawrence, for she got to introduce "Someone to Watch over Me" and "Do, Do, Do." The score also included "Dear Little Girl," the only song Ira can remember having written lyrics for that did not get one handclap of applause. It went into the show at a matinee in Philadelphia amid utter silence and was dropped that evening. It was not published until forty-two years later, when, in 1968, it turned up in a Julie Andrews film, *Star*.

In 1927 the Gershwins were writing for Fred and Adele Astaire again, but this show, *Funny Face*, seemed doomed during its out-of-town tryouts. The book went through drastic revisions. Robert Benchley bowed out as a librettist, a role was written in for Victor Moore, and almost half of the

Gershwins' score was thrown out ("How Long Has This Been Going On?" turned up a year later in *Rosalie*). Despite this, the show proved to be a triumph for Ira, for it contained two of his most remarkable lyrics. "'S Wonderful" not only made brilliant use of the sibilant sounds created by slurring "it's" down to "'s" and attaching it to adjectives, nouns, pronouns at random, but it also got considerable distance from a mannerism that Ira had picked up from the comedian Walter Catlett — shunning the "-tion" or "-sion" ending on "emotion,""devotion," "fashion," and "passion" to get "emosh," "devosh," "fash," and "pash."

Alec Wilder cites this song as "the perfect illustration of the great strength of Ira Gershwin's lyrics." "The lyric in this case is much stronger and more memorable than the tune," Wilder points out. "The tune is memorable, granted — but it is so, I think, because of its association with the lyric. The device of the apostrophized ''s'... is the attention-getter.... Its shameless adherence to such a word as 'paradise' — ''s paradise' — does the trick."

After *Funny Face*, the tone of the Gershwins' musicals, with the exception of *Girl Crazy* in 1930, changed considerably. This period started with two uninspired and uninspiring experiences with Florenz Ziegfeld. Their first Ziegfeld show was *Rosalie* in 1928, for which they were called in to help out Sigmund Romberg. The Gershwins wrote seven of the show's fifteen songs, but four of the seven were leftovers from *Primrose, Oh, Kay!*, the first version of *Strike Up the Band*, and *Funny Face*.

The next year Ziegfeld got the Gershwins to do another show for him — *Show Girl*, an extravaganza that included the night-club team of Clayton, Jackson, and (Jimmy) Durante, Duke Ellington's orchestra, the Albertina Rasch Ballet, and Ruby Keeler, who had just married Al Jolson. Jimmy Durante brought along some of his own songs — "So I Ups to Him," "I Can Get Along Without Broadway," and "Who Will Be with You When I'm Far Away" — and the Gershwins' score included "Liza," which at the first few performances Jolson sang to his wife from the audience, running up and down the aisles. But to no avail. It was a box-office failure and George had to threaten to sue Ziegfeld in order to collect his royalties.

The last and greatest of the musicals the Gershwins did in the light-hearted, light-headed tradition of the 1920s was *Girl Crazy*, which opened in October 1930. Except for its plot line, which was ridiculous even by the standards of twenties musicals, *Girl Crazy* was a momentous achievement in every department. It provided a stage debut for Ethel Merman and a leading role for Ginger Rogers. It had an incredible line-up of songs — "I Got Rhythm," "Embraceable You," "But Not for Me," "Sam and Delilah," "Bidin' My Time." Even the pit band was remarkable — conducted by Red Nichols, it boasted such jazz greats as Benny Goodman, Jack Teagarden, Glenn Miller, Jimmy Dorsey, and Gene Krupa.

For one song, "Bidin' My Time," Ira went all the way back to his college days for a poem he had written in 1916 to get the title. He had been keeping it for fourteen years on a list of possible titles. "Embraceable You" has a lyric which, like "'S Wonderful," is such an intrinsic part of the song that, as Alec Wilder has said, "Any Gershwin enthusiast is as aware of the words, 'Come to papa, come to papa, do!,' as they are of the repeated notes that make them singable."

By the 1930s, however, the day of the inane musical was passing. The Depression was turning the mood of the country in a different direction. And well before *Girl Crazy* the Gershwins were turning to more thought-provoking projects.

George had continued his serious writing. In the spring of 1928 he went on a trip that took him to London, Paris, Berlin, and Vienna, carrying with him the beginnings of a new orchestral work which he completed during the course of the trip. It was an evocative impression of an American visitor in Paris, strolling the city, listening to the street noise, absorbing the atmosphere — *An American in Paris*. Walter Damrosch conducted its première at Carnegie Hall, which took place on December 13, 1928. The next day the critics ran what had by now become their customary gamut of reaction to Gershwin's concert works — from "nauseous clap-trap, so dull, patchy, thin, vulgar, long-winded and inane that the average movie audience would be bored by it into open remonstrance" (*Telegram*) to "one of the genuine inspirations of our native music" (*Sun*).

Unlike *Concerto in F*, *An American in Paris* was almost immediately plucked from the concert hall and inserted in a Gershwin show, *Show Girl*, where it served as music for a ballet danced by Harriet Hoctor and the Albertina Rasch girls.

But even before George became involved with *An American in Paris*, he and Ira had been at work on a musical that would take them up a new theatrical path—satire. The vehicle was *Strike Up the Band*, with a bitingly cynical book by George S. Kaufman about war profiteers. It opened in Long Branch, New Jersey, in August 1927 and moved on to Philadelphia, where, after two weeks of dwindling attendance, it closed. The title song was the fifth march called "Strike Up the Band" that George wrote in a continuing effort "to get something better."

Two and a half years later producer Edgar Selwyn and the Gershwins tried *Strike Up the Band* for a second time, with Kaufman's book toned down by Morrie Ryskind and an essentially new score. The title song was retained (ironically, considering its satirical origins, "Strike Up the Band" has become widely accepted as a patriotic march), "I've Got a Crush on You" was picked up from *Treasure Girl*, and four bars of an aria-like melody in the original version were used as the basis of "Soon."

Although the book had been made bland enough to be more acceptable than Kaufman's (and the public outlook had undoubtedly become a bit more cynical between 1927 and 1930), the Gershwins' score retained its bite. In addition to the title song, George and Ira made full use of their mocking wit on such songs as "The Unofficial Spokesman," which pointed out that the way to get to the top in politics was to keep your mouth shut, and "A Typical Self-Made Man," which offered similar guidance for getting ahead in business.

"Strike Up the Band" gave the Gershwins a taste of a new form of theater that they relished. The brothers went joyously to work again, with both Kaufman and Ryskind writing a libretto, to create *Of Thee I Sing*, a satirical exploration of the American political scene, focusing on the Presidency and Congress. For the first time the Gershwins deviated from their customary work habit — George writes a tune, then Ira fits a lyric to it. This time the lyrics and the music were to be an integral part of the plot development, using recitatives, arias, finalettos along with more traditional musical-comedy songs. So Ira sketched out his ideas first and George then provided a setting.

Normally, Ira's ideas centered on the lyrics. But on one significant occasion he had a musical thought. George was having trouble getting the appropriate melody for the opening campaign

Ira

by George.

song, "Wintergreen for President," when Ira remembered an unfinished project that he and George had worked on with Herbert Fields in the mid-twenties called *The Big Charade*. For it George had written a pseudo-medieval march, "Trumpets of Belgravia," to which Ira's lyrics had started out, "Trumpets of Belgravia/Sing ta-ra, ta-ra, ta-ra." Ira suddenly realized that these seven-syllable lines exactly fitted the seven syllables of "Wintergreen for President." He reminded George of this. George tried it out — and found the tune he was looking for.

Critical and audience response to *Of Thee I Sing* was overwhelming. George Jean Nathan called the show a "landmark in American satirical musical comedy" and Brooks Atkinson found it "funnier than the government and not nearly so dangerous." It played for 441 performances, the longest run achieved by any Gershwin show. It became the first American musical comedy to be published as a book (libretto and lyrics). And it set a precedent when it was awarded the Pulitzer Prize for "drama," there being no award for the musical theater. The decision to give it the "drama" prize meant that, just as George's music was omitted from the published book, he (and his music) were omitted from the Pulitzer award even though his score was an essential part of the satirical comment and the dramatic development of the production.

Two years later the same team of writers, composer, lyricist, producer (Sam H. Harris) and leading performers (William Gaxton, Victor Moore, and Lois Moran) tried to repeat the success of *Of Thee I Sing* with *Let 'Em Eat Cake*. But this time the satire failed to jell. The writers' angry vision of a fascist America emerged in a relentlessly dour and eventually vicious show (Alexander Throttlebottom, the bumbling, lovable Vice-President of *Of Thee I Sing*, was shown in the process of being guillotined). And yet to George Gershwin the largely contrapuntal score that he wrote seemed the best he had done — "the composer's claim to legitimacy," he called it.

The show was a quick failure. It was also the Gershwins' last joint venture into Broadway musical comedy.

Between the great successes of *Girl Crazy* and *Of Thee I Sing*, the Gershwins went to Hollywood to write the score for a film, *Delicious*. Their principal contributions turned out to be a song that had been written for an unproduced Ziegfeld show, *East Is West*, and George's *Second Rhapsody*.

The song had been known in *East Is West* as "Lady of the Moon." Subsequently Ira and Gus Kahn had rewritten it as "I Just Looked at You," but they had no outlet for it. When Ira got to Hollywood, he decided a spoof on the current rage for movie theme songs might be effective in *Delicious*. The exiled melody from *East Is West* had the properly "ballady" feeling for a theme song, so he used it as the basis for "Blah Blah Blah," which, even with the cynical injection of "blahs," managed to remain a very tender ballad.

While Ira was adapting something from their past for *Delicious*, George composed an orchestral sequence, identified in the film as "Manhattan Rhapsody," which became the basis for his *Second Rhapsody*. George developed the sequence into a full-scale serious composition because, as he told Isaac Goldberg, "Nearly everybody comes back from California with a Western tan and a pocketful of moving-picture money. I decided to come back with both those things, and a serious composition."

The result was known first as *Rhapsody in Rivets* because of its rhythmically descriptive opening, but it subsequently became the *Second Rhapsody*. There was some talk that Toscanini might give it a first performance; when this did not materialize, the première was given by Serge Koussevitzky with the Boston Symphony on January 29, 1932, in Boston. The critical reception there and in New York, where Koussevitzky conducted it a week later, was, as it always had been for George's serious work, sharply divided.

In February of that year, George went to Havana for a brief rest and became so interested in Cuban music — and the Cuban percussion instruments — that he immediately began sketching a work which he first called *Rumba* but which emerged on August 16 at an all-Gershwin program at Lewisohn Stadium in New York as *Cuban Overture*. To put Gershwin's use of Cuban percussion into perspective, it should be remembered that in 1932 the first Cuban song to become an American pop hit, "The Peanut Vendor," had just been introduced in the United States by Don Azpiazu's orchestra (which had only a limited, specialized following here) and Xavier Cugat's popularization of Cuban rhythms and Cuban percussion was still a year or two away.

Cuban Overture was George's last attempt at a major serious orchestral work. He wrote *Variations on "I Got Rhythm"* in 1934 and a *Suite from Porgy and Bess* in 1936. But after composing scores for two unsuccessful shows in 1933 — *Let 'Em Eat Cake* and *Pardon My English* (so horrendous that Jack Buchanan, its star, bought his way out of it at a price rumored to be $20,000) — George turned his creative efforts toward a subject that had been in and out of his mind for more than ten years, an American opera.

The initial seed had been planted in *Blue Monday,* the one-act "black opera" that he wrote for the *Scandals of 1922.* After George had emerged as a serious composer with *Rhapsody in Blue, Concerto in F,* and *An American in Paris,* there were some, among them Otto Kahn, who were thinking of George in terms of opera, something for the Metropolitan Opera House. George had thought about an opera based on *The Dybbuk* for the Metropolitan and earlier he had considered one based on the melting-pot life of New York.

But it was the Negro theme that basically attracted him, from *Blue Monday* through his reading, in 1926, of Du Bose Heyward's novel, *Porgy,* and the subsequent play by Heyward and his wife, Dorothy, in 1927. George first wrote to Heyward about a musical adaptation in 1926 in the first flush of excitement engendered by reading the book. But he did not follow up on the thought until 1932, and actual work on the project did not start for another two years.

In January 1934, when George and Heyward met in Charleston, Heyward had written the first scene for the projected opera based on *Porgy,* but George had not composed a note. When he finally got to work, the first song he composed was "Summertime." The basis for the lyric of the song had earlier been spotted in the script of the play by Heyward, who was writing both libretto and lyrics. This was the first time since *Lady, Be Good!* that George had gone to work on a full musical score without Ira. But Ira soon came into the picture both as an editor of Heyward's lyrics and as a full-fledged contributor of other lyrics. This three-way division of work developed because Heyward preferred to stay home in South Carolina and, until the summer of 1934, George was kept in New York by his weekly radio program, *Music by Gershwin,* sponsored by Feen-A-Mint, on which with full concert orchestra and guests he often featured the songs of his peers in addition to his own.

Heyward sent his lyrics north to George, who then set them to music (reversing his customary procedure with Ira) while Ira made whatever adaptations were necessary to bring words and music into line. But Ira became the lyric-writer when Heyward sketched a scene in which he felt the music was the key and should be composed before the words were written.

"Du Bose was a poet," Ira once recalled, "which I am not. He could do something like 'Summertime,' which is poetry. I don't like such a formal word, but it's true. Du Bose wasn't much good on a rhythm number, though, like 'It Ain't Necessarily So.'"

Heyward also recognized this difference. Ira wanted to help him get into ASCAP, admission to which then required the writing of five songs. Ira knew that Heyward's name was on only four songs not including those on which he collaborated with Ira, so he offered to allow Heyward to take credit for "It Ain't Necessarily So." "Ira, you're very sweet," said Heyward in rejecting the offer, "but no one will ever believe that I had anything to do with that song."

Porgy and Bess opened in Boston on September 30, 1935, and reached New York on October 10. The music critics, whose views had been so divergent on George's earlier invasions of "serious" music, were unconvinced by his incursion into opera. The thing that seemed to bother them most was George's failure to adhere to what they considered the proper style for opera. "The style is at one moment of opera and another of operetta or sheer Broadway entertainment," wrote Olin Downes in the New York Times as he complained of Gershwin's failure to use all the resources of the operatic composer.

So, after 124 performances at the Alvin Theatre (far more than it might ever have received at the Metropolitan Opera House), it went on a road tour that ended in Washington after only two months.

But this was a show that seemed to have a life of its own. It kept coming back and it kept becoming more and more important. The first step was a brief but successful six-week revival split between Los Angeles and San Francisco in 1938. In the fall of 1941, Cheryl Crawford tried out a streamlined version in Maplewood, New Jersey, removing the word "opera" from its descriptive billing and taking out the recitative that George had favored. In its new form, Porgy and Bess reopened in New York in January 1942 to an acclaim it had never received on its original opening (both Virgil Thomson and Olin Downes reversed their earlier negative views).

The revival continued in New York until September and then toured the nation for almost two years. Meanwhile the show was performed in 1943 in Copenhagen with an all-Danish cast. It reached Moscow in 1945, performed by the Stanislavsky Players; Zurich in the same year; Sweden in 1949.

The longest-lasting, most widely seen production of Porgy and Bess opened in Dallas in 1952. After setting a box-office record in 14 performances there, it moved on to triumphs in Chicago, Pittsburgh, and Washington. By the time it reached Washington, it had created such a tremendous impact that it was sent to Europe under the sponsorship of the State Department. Opening in Vienna in September 1952, it began an international triumphal tour that continued for six years. Berlin, London, and Paris saw it in 1952. In 1953 it returned to the States for a long New York run and a nationwide tour. Then, once again under the auspices of the State Department, it went back to Europe, into the Balkans, through the Near East to Africa, then to Spain, and to La Scala in Milan (the first opera by an American-born composer to play there, the first time any opera had been presented there for a full week, the first time the rule against applause during a new work was broken). The company crisscrossed Europe, jumped the ocean to Central America and South America, then back to Europe and through the Iron Curtain to Poland, Czechoslovakia, and the Soviet Union, where it played to capacity crowds in Moscow.

But George never knew of these triumphs. He took a four-week vacation in Mexico after the opening of *Porgy* and then turned his eyes toward Hollywood. He and Ira had some ideas for a Fred Astaire film, but Hollywood, they found, had some discouraging ideas about *them* — about George, at least. The trouble with George, according to Hollywood, was that he had written *Porgy and Bess*. As one agent put it, there was "an ill-founded belief that George Gershwin would only be interested in writing so-called 'high brow' material and would not be willing to write the *Lady, Be Good!* type of material." Another agent asked George for reassurance on this point, something he could show to producers. "Rumors about highbrow music ridiculous," George wired back. "Am out to write hits."

In actuality, George's "serious" writing had had an effect on his popular writing that was just the opposite of what Hollywood feared. "After having examined nearly all of George Gershwin's published songs," Alec Wilder concluded, "I would say that the writing of his more ambitious compositions did not cause his songs to become too complex for popular appeal. Paradoxically, his last songs became *less* rather than more complex."

So, after much dickering, the Gershwin brothers were signed to do *Shall We Dance* for Fred Astaire and Ginger Rogers and showed that they were far from losing their light touch as they wrote "They Can't Take That Away from Me," "Let's Call the Whole Thing Off," and "They All Laughed." From this they went right into another Astaire film, this one with Joan Fontaine, *A Damsel in Distress,* and a score that included "A Foggy Day" and "Nice Work If You Can Get It." And, with scarcely a breather in between, they moved on to a third film in less than a year, the *Goldwyn Follies.*

"We managed to finish five songs the first six weeks of our contract," Ira has said, recalling their work on the *Goldwyn Follies.* "The reason we worked this fast on the vocal contributions was to allow the composer to have the following six or eight weeks free to write a ballet for Zorina. As it turned out, our first six weeks were George's last six weeks of work; and 'Love Is Here to Stay' the last song he composed."

The first indication that something might be wrong with George occurred in February 1937, just before he started work on the *Goldwyn Follies.* Playing his *Concerto in F* with the Los Angeles Symphony, he suddenly found himself fumbling on some passages. At the same time he was aware of a smell of burning rubber. A physical check-up indicated no problems.

Early in June he began to experience frequent headaches. At the end of the month, after more extensive medical examinations revealed nothing, his coordination began to fail as the headaches increased in number and severity. On Friday, July 9, his condition deteriorated rapidly and he fell into a coma. He was rushed to a hospital, where the source of his problem finally became evident: a brain tumor.

It was decided to call in Dr. Walter E. Dandy, one of the country's leading brain specialists. But Dr. Dandy was on a yacht on Chesapeake Bay. The White House sent two destroyers to pick up the doctor and he was flown to Newark Airport, where a private plane was standing by to take him to California, but by the time he reached Newark, doctors in California had already begun to operate. George never awoke from the coma into which he fell on July 9. He died on the morning of July 11, 1937.

For Ira, there was some immediate picking up of the pieces to be done. With Vernon Duke, he completed the score for the *Goldwyn Follies*. In the next year or two he wrote a few songs with Jerome Kern and Harry Warren, but nothing came of them. Then in 1940 Moss Hart asked Ira to collaborate with Kurt Weill on a musical about psychoanalysis which was originally known as *I Am Listening* but later became *Lady in the Dark*. Weill, an exile from Hitler's Germany, had been gradually working his way into the American musical theater, first with *Johnny Johnson*, then with *Knickerbocker Holiday*, and Hart felt that Ira's long Broadway experience would serve as a creative complement to Weill's Continental experience.

Their work together on *Lady in the Dark*—which produced "My Ship," "This Is New," "Jenny," and "Tschaikowsky"—seemed to presage the beginning of a major lyricist-composer team. But although they did another show, *The Firebrand of Florence*, and a film, *Where Do We Go from Here?*, both in 1945, that initial promise was not realized.

Ira, however, continued to work with various composers at a comfortably casual pace that was more characteristic of him than the headlong rush of George's activities in which he had previously been swept up. With Jerome Kern he wrote the score for the film *Cover Girl* in 1944, a score that produced the song that sold more sheet music in a single year than any other of Ira's songs, "Long Ago and Far Away." He took one final stab at Broadway in 1946 when he collaborated with the producer of *Cover Girl*, Arthur Schwartz, on *Park Avenue*, a show about the unmating habits of high society which lasted for only 72 performances.

In the same year, with the help of Kay Swift, a composer who had been a close friend of George's, a new score by George and Ira Gershwin was created for a film, *The Shocking Miss Pilgrim*. William Perlberg, the producer of the film, had two composers in mind with whom Ira might work, but when both proved to be involved in other projects, Ira suggested that a score might be developed from material in George's notebooks and his unused manuscripts. Perlberg agreed and, with Miss Swift playing and then copying over a hundred themes, sketches, and completed tunes that Ira thought might be possibilities, he wrote the lyrics for a score that eventually included "For You, For Me, Forevermore" and "Aren't You Kind of Glad We Did?"

After two more films that were relatively insignificant—*The Barkleys of Broadway*, a 1949 Fred Astaire–Ginger Rogers film for which Harry Warren wrote the music, and *Give a Girl a Break* in 1953 with music by Burton Lane—Ira collaborated with his old friend Harold Arlen on *A Star Is Born* and *The Country Girl*, both in 1954. *The Country Girl* is remembered not for the Arlen-Gershwin score, but primarily because Grace Kelly won an Oscar for her performance. In *A Star Is Born*, however, Ira, Arlen, and Judy Garland collaborated to create one of the classic musical moments in film when Miss Garland sang Ira's lyrics and Arlen's music for "The Man That Got Away."

With "The Man That Got Away," Ira seems to have drawn the curtain on his career as a lyricist—seventeen years after the death of his brother, thirty-five years after his first characteristically self-effacing professional appearance as "Arthur Francis." Almost everything one was, the other wasn't. George and Ira, Ira and George—brothers as different as brothers can be.

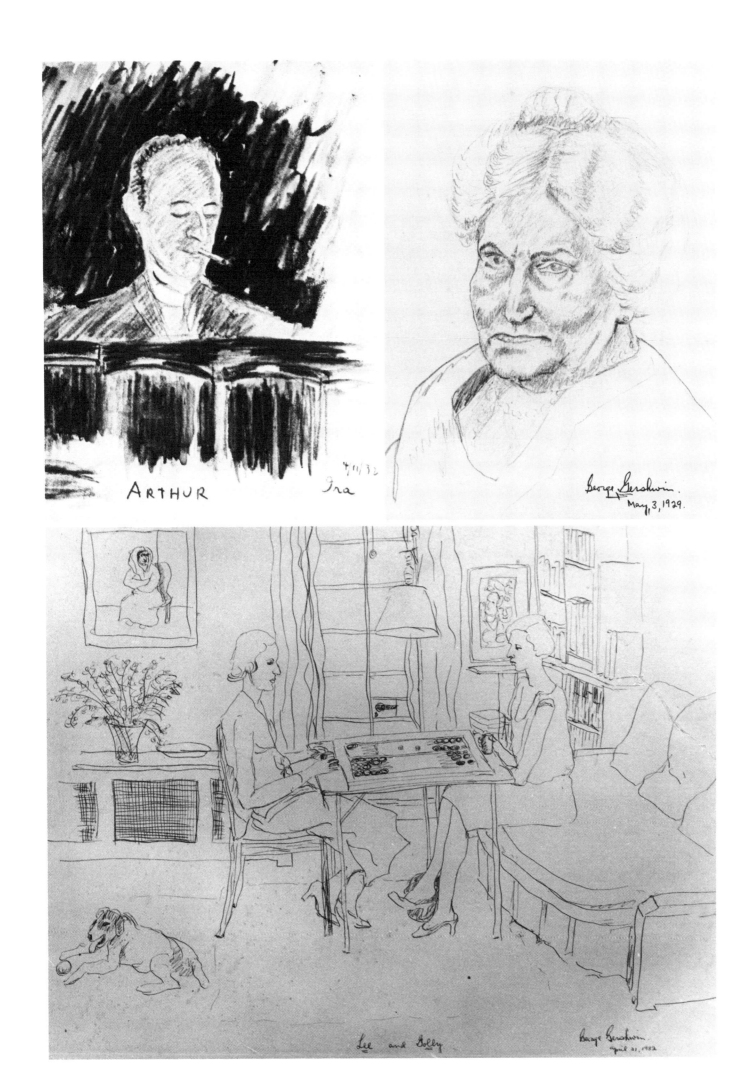

ARTHUR   Ira   4/11/32

George Gershwin.
May, 3, 1929.

Lee and Solly   George Gershwin.
April 21, 1932

THE GERSHWINS

Morris Gershovitz, later Gershwin, was the father of four children: Ira, George, Arthur, and Frances. Born in St. Petersburg (Leningrad), he emigrated from Russia in the early 1890s to escape compulsory military service. Ira: "Most of our early boyhood was spent on the Lower East Side of Manhattan, where my father engaged in various activities: restaurants, Russian and Turkish baths, bakeries, a cigar store and pool parlor on the 42nd Street side of what is now Grand Central Station, bookmaking at the Brighton Beach racetrack for three exciting but disastrous weeks.

"We were always moving. When my father sold a business and started another, we would inevitably move to the new neighborhood. George and I once counted over twenty-five different flats and apartments we remembered having lived in during those days."

Rose Bruskin, who had known her future husband in St. Petersburg, married him in America. George said of his mother: "Nervous, ambitious, and purposeful...She was never the doting type. Although very loving, she never watched every move we made. She was set on having us completely educated, her idea being that if everything else failed we could always become schoolteachers. She was against my becoming a musician, as she didn't want me to be a twenty-five-dollar-a-week piano player all my life, but she offered very little resistance when I decided to leave high school to take a job playing the piano for Remick. . . . She's what the mammy writers write about and what the mammy singers sing about. But they don't mean it; and I do."

The Gershovitzes' first home was on the the corner of Hester and Eldridge streets, where Ira was born on December 6, 1896.

George, the second child, arrived on September 26, 1898, at 242 Snediker Avenue, Brooklyn, between Sutter and Belmont avenues.

The house on Snediker Avenue had a front room, a dining room, a kitchen, and a maid's room on the ground floor; upstairs there were three or four bedrooms, one of which was rented to a Mr. Taffelstein for $3 a week.

The Gershwins paid $14 a month rent for the house. George's father was earning $35 a week as a skilled designer of uppers for women's shoes, an income that enabled Mrs. Gershwin to employ a maid.

Ira was the scholar of the family; George, a street kid from the first, was always getting into fights (note the scar over his right eye). Music was for sissies—"little Maggies," as George and his friends called them at this age. George liked sports—cat, hockey, and roller-skating —and became the skating champion of Seventh Street, where the Gershwins had moved by this time.

But George's put-down of things musical was street armor. He had really loved music since he was small: "One of my first definite memories goes back to the age of six. I stood outside a penny arcade listening to an automatic piano leaping through Rubinstein's 'Melody in F.' The peculiar jumps in the music held me rooted. To this very day I can't hear the tune without picturing myself outside that arcade on 125th Street, standing there barefoot and in overalls, drinking it all in avidly." Other favorites at that time were Sir Arthur Sullivan's "The Lost Chord" and "Loch Lomond."

George, not happy in school, was often in trouble with the teachers and school authorities. Once George

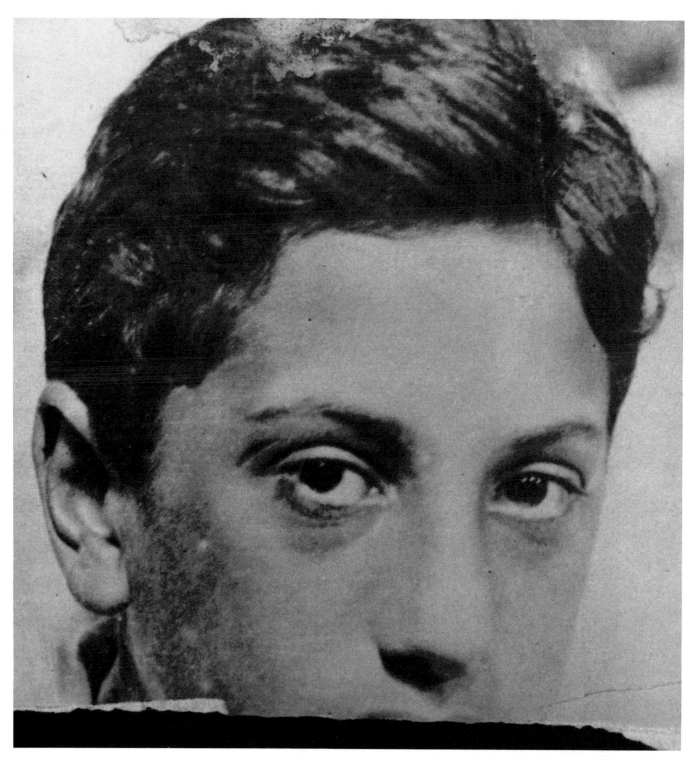

George.

George with his cousin Bernard Wolpin.

School picture, P.S. 25, Fifth Avenue and Second Street, 1912. George may be second from right in the next-to-last row.

wearing roller skates, was chased into a building by a gang of kids. The gang chased him upstairs, and George, still in his skates, careened into an elevator shaft and was knocked unconscious.

Around 1910 Rose Gershwin's married sister bought a piano and Rose had to have one too. E. Y. ("Yip") Harburg, the Gershwins' boyhood friend, claims to remember the day the secondhand upright was hoisted through the window into the front room of the Second Avenue flat. Ira: "My parents had in mind that I, as the oldest child, was shortly to start taking lessons. But the upright had scarcely been put in place when George twirled the stool down to size, sat, lifted the keyboard cover, and played an accomplished version of a then popular song. I remember being particularly impressed by his swinging left hand and by harmonic and rhythmic effects I thought as proficient as those of most of the pianists I'd heard in vaudeville." How had George learned all this? "He made it sound very simple: Whenever he had the chance, he'd been fooling around and experimenting on a player piano at the home of a schoolmate around the corner on Seventh Street." George remembered that Ira covered approximately thirty-two pages of Beyer's piano method before the musical palm was passed to George, who was to be the musician of the family.

But George's real conversion to music came about through a classmate at P.S. 25, Maxie Rosenzweig, who without knowing it kindled the spark one day when he played Dvořák's "Humoresque" on the violin at a school assembly. George hadn't even gone to the "entertainment," but he heard Max's playing through the assembly-hall window and "It was, to me, a flashing revelation of beauty," he recalled later. "I made up my mind to get acquainted with this fellow, and I waited outside from three till four thirty that afternoon, in the hopes of greeting him. It was pouring cats and dogs, and I got soaked to the skin. No luck. I returned to the school building. He had long been gone—must have left by the teachers' entrance. I found out where he lived and, dripping wet as I was, trekked to his house, unceremoniously presenting myself as an admirer. Maxie by this time had left; his family were so amused, however, that they arranged a meeting." George and Maxie (later known as Max Rosen) immediately became fast friends, wrestling, talking about music, playing hooky together. George wanted more than anything else to become Max's ac-

George with Sam Mesnik in the Catskills,
where he had a summer job playing the piano, 1915.

With Abraham Hirsch, about 1912.

companist. One day, however, came a crushing blow from his friend: Max told him flatly that he had better give up all thought of a musical career. "You haven't it in you, Georgie; take my word for it, I can tell!"

At any rate, George began piano lessons. Every neighborhood then had local piano teachers of varying gifts, and his first teacher, a Miss Green, seems to have been a garden-variety mentor who evidently did little else than take him through Beyer's. This wouldn't do; soon George tried out another local teacher, Mr. Goldfarb, who commanded three times as much per lesson ($1.50), and who appears to have taken a radically different approach to musical training. Goldfarb, who had composed a "Theodore Roosevelt March" and brandished published copies of it everywhere he went, concentrated exclusively on operatic potpourris of his own concoction and glossed over the usual catechism of scales, piano exercises, and easy pieces by the masters.

George began to attend concerts at nearby P.S. 63, where a school group called the Beethoven Society Orchestra had been set up. The official pianist of the ensemble was Jack Miller, but George must have played with the group at least once, as a photo of the Beethoven Society Orchestra published in the New York *World* shows him at the piano. By this time George was virtually living, breathing, and eating music, and, impressed by his enthusiasm, in 1912 Miller brought him to see his own teacher, Charles Hambitzer.

Hambitzer is without a doubt the man most responsible for shaping George's musical future. By all accounts, Hambitzer was no ordinary musician: a composer and pianist, he publicly performed the radical early piano works of Arnold Schoenberg and steeped the boy in the works of Debussy and Ravel, as well as the great classical piano literature. Through him George was initiated into the worlds of Bach, Beethoven, Liszt, and especially Chopin. Hambitzer must have been a remarkable man— a composer who wrote both popular and concert music. Most of it evidently disappeared at his death. But Hambitzer concentrated on teaching George the piano and soaking the boy in the literature of music and channeling his enthusiasm in the right directions. The catholicity of George's work is an extension of Hambitzer's philosophy; unfortunately, we will never know whether or not Hambitzer's own music had any stylistic influence on him.

Hambitzer's concentration on serious music was only part of George's early musical education. George played the piano at a school assembly at the High School of Commerce, which he entered in 1912, and found a summer piano job in the Catskills in 1913, where it is safe to say he played little Bach or Beethoven. He was still most interested in popular music: he admired Irving Berlin, and an early piece, "Ragging the Träumerei," was probably a response to Berlin's rag version of Mendelssohn's "Spring Song." However, as his first scrapbook shows, his early gods were Liszt and the great pianists who were then playing in New York—Josef Hofmann, Harold Bauer, Josef Lhevinne, and the composer-pianists Ferrucio Busoni and Leo Ornstein.

George *was* going to become a concert pianist, but it is interesting to note that his earliest known printed-program recital (1914) has George "Gershvin" (Ira's current rendering of the family name) playing popular music. (Behind the noncommittal designation of "Piano Solo," George managed to conceal a tango of his own composition but, as for "Vocal Selections by Chas. Stone and George Gershvin," what they were is anybody's guess.) George would soon quit the High School of Commerce, and embark on his first job in the music business as a song plugger for the Jerome H. Remick Music Company, a job he obtained with the help of his friend Ben Bloom. This was in May of 1914, and George Gershwin was only fifteen years old.

Ira, George, Arthur, and their cousin Rose Lagowitz at the postcard shop in Brighton Beach where Ira worked, 1912.

Ira at the postcard shop, 1912.
At Brighton Beach the Gershwins first saw the famous child vaudeville act, Fred and Adele Astaire.

Fred and Adele Astaire, about 1912.

RECOLLECTIONS OF FRED ASTAIRE

I would go to the various music publishers looking for material [in 1915], and George was a piano player demonstrating songs at Jerome H. Remick's. We struck up a friendship at once. He was amused by my piano playing and often made me play for him. I had a sort of knocked-out slap left hand technique and the beat pleased him. He'd often stop me and say, "Wait a minute, Freddie, do that one again."

I told George how my sister and I longed to get into musical comedy. He in turn wanted to write one. He said, "Wouldn't it be great if I could write a musical show and you could be in it?" That thought materialized only a few years later when Adele and I were in Lady, Be Good! *at the Liberty Theatre, New York, music by George Gershwin, lyrics by Ira Gershwin. I was fortunate later on to do several pictures with scores by George and his brother, Ira.*

From Steps in Time
(New York: Harper and Brothers, 1959)

Unlike George, Ira was a reader. Where George would go out in the street to see who was fighting and sometimes join in himself, Ira would stay inside, reading dime novels, the scourge of his epoch, books like *Liberty Boys of '76, Pluck and Luck, Fred Fearnot,* the Nick Carter mysteries, and similar classics. His parents reacted to his literary tastes much as conservative parents might today react to comic books, and Ira hid his detective novels all over the house, even behind the ancestral portraits.

In 1908 he began filling scrapbooks with bits from encyclopedias and his favorite columnists, especially Franklin P. Adams ("Always in Good Humor," a column later known as "The Conning Tower" and "The Diary of Our Own Samuel Pepys"). F.P.A.'s example led him, in 1916, to begin his own journal, *Everyman His Own Boswell,* and soon he was posing around the house, acting out his idea of how a fashionable eighteenth-century chronicler might behave. Ira was literally studying to be a writer in much the same way that his brother was studying to be a composer—by osmosis and imitation.

In 1910 he had wanted to be a journalist, and the simplest way to this was to found his own weekly (circulation: 1) entitled *The Leaf,* which he kept up for twenty-six weeks, drawing the cartoons (most of the Gershwin family had a gift for drawing), writing the stories, designing his own "advertisements," and laying it all out on laundry shirtcards. In 1913 he had become one of the four art editors on the school paper of Townsend Harris Hall, the *Academic Herald,* for which he and E. Y. ("Yip") Harburg were co-editors of a column called "Much Ado" and patterned after F.P.A.'s "Conning Tower." Later when both he and Yip entered City College they collaborated on a column in the college paper, *The Campus,* and Ira drew cartoons for the monthly humor magazine, *The Mercury.* But, like George, Ira was not to stay in school. After a year and a half of academic ups and downs, Ira was shunted to the night courses and presently abandoned school altogether.

School spirit—Ira in the last row.

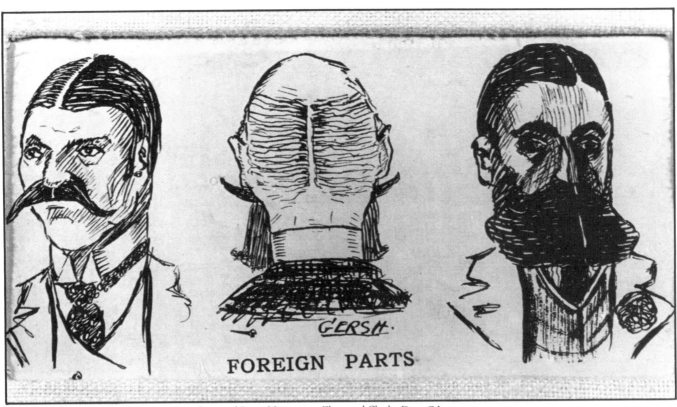

An early Ira Gershwin cartoon, showing the influence of James Montgomery Flagg and Charles Dana Gibson.

Ira in the second row, at left, in boater. Directly behind him is Yip Harburg.

I remember, I remember
Those peaceful, happy times
When we heard no music other
Than distant church-bell chimes.
That picture cannot now be drawn;
The flat wherein we dwell
Alas! Of late it has become
A throbbing torture cell.

I remember, I remember
The time when peace prevailed;
When no budding prima donna
Above "Lucia" wailed;
When the tenants living near us
No phonograph did own,
To drive me to insanity
With its metallic tone.

I remember, I remember
When no infernal chump
On a pianola, down below
Both day and night would pump.
Someone next door the bugle flares
He's blowing himself pink . . .
They're all to music taken, Woe!
I think I'll take to drink.
—Gersh

I got my first job with a musical concern when I was fifteen years old. A boy friend who was with the Remick Company told me of a vacancy for a piano player, one who could read notes readily, to play over songs to be tried out. I got the job at $15 a week and stayed there two years. All the time, however, I was working at my compositions.

George Gershwin
in an interview, December 1925

In February 1915 the Gershwin family moved to 108 West 111th Street, and probably it was in the same year that George began to make piano rolls. Ira remembers that every Saturday George would go out to East Orange, New Jersey, and make six rolls for $35. It was at this point that Gershvin became Gershwin once and for all; George had always admired Ed Wynn, the comedian, and so changed the "vin" ending to "win" in honor of his idol. When George submitted an early effort to his employer, he was flatly told that he had been hired by Remick's as a pianist, not a writer. In 1916

George in Atlantic City, about 1916.

the publisher Harry Von Tilzer took George's song "When You Want 'Em, You Can't Get 'Em—When You Got 'Em, You Don't Want 'Em," written with Murray Roth. Roth got $15 for it, but George wanted to wait for royalties and asked for an advance. Von Tilzer gave him a fiver out of his own pocket—the extent of George's earnings from the song.

———

George is working for Jerome H. Remick, music publisher; and receives every Saturday a little yellow envelope with $15 in it. He can get $25 with Maurice Abrahams, but he'll stick to Remick's as the work there is so much easier.

Ira in a letter to Harry Botkin
January 2, 1915
91 Second Avenue

George is playing in Atlantic City. He has had two of his songs published the past few months.

Ira, August 30, 1916
St. Nicholas Baths "Russian and Turkish"
Lenox Avenue at 111th Street

———

While taking occasional courses at City College, Ira worked as cashier at two hotel-and-bath establishments—first uptown on 111th Street, later down on Lafayette Street—that his father had acquired in a series of financial misadventures. In May 1917 Ira wrote a short satirical piece called "The Shrine" and, hoping for a professional opinion, stuck it in the letterbox of a guest at the Lafayette Baths, Paul M. Potter, the English playwright who had adapted *Trilby* for the stage. Potter suggested sending it to the *Smart Set*, H. L. Mencken's new magazine. Ira did so, and nothing happened until the following November, when Ira received first a letter of acceptance, then a check for $1, for "The Shrine."

Although Mencken's magazine had expressed interest in subsequent contributions, nothing else was ever accepted. On November 16 George mentioned to Ira that the New York *Clipper* was looking for a reviewer. Ira was "hired," on the basis of his wide experience in watching vaudeville acts, and he wrote three reviews which were published, but never paid for. But 1917 had not been a total loss; it was the year Ira first tried writing song lyrics.

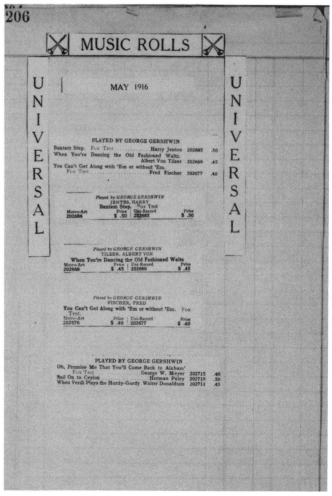

14

DIARY OF IRA GERSHWIN

I. GERSHVIN   108 W. 111

<u>May 5, 1917</u>. Evening to Finley Club where wasted an evening. Not wasted entirely, for supplied the "music" for some of the boys who wanted to dance. I cannot vouchsafe for their musical appreciation if they can stand the kind of music (?) I divinely played with 1 finger of the right hand & three of the left and almost my entire repertoire consisting of Pink Lady waltz, a Spanish waltz (introducing a trill herenthere) and a few simple folk songs like "Singing Polly woodywoodle all the Way," "Annie Laurie" and such in the simplest of keys.

<u>May 6, 1917</u>. Evening donned my gray top shoes, silk socks, blue double-breasted suit, brown double-breasted vest, blue silk shirt, purple knitted tie, soft collar, green velour and dark coat. Home. Then with Art G., George, Harry B., Solly E. to Terrace Gardens on 58th Street. Then after meekly submitting to the hat check fee of 25¢ per head, and then to the devilish advances, machinations of the hat check boy & air duster (he never touches your coat with the whisk broom), we entered the large hall where about 800 temporary seats had been placed. About 9 o'clock the entertainment began, with the weest of tots in blonde curls doing an interpretive dance, barely able to sustain balance on one leg, 20 dancing and singing acts followed. No one act lasting over 5 minutes some half that. There were several pretty kids (the enter. was entirely given by little girls) and all were "cute." Frances' Russian dance was a riot. Her singing of M-I-S-S-I-S-S-I-P-P-I didn't get over as we had expected it to, probably on account of the audience's lack of appreciation for a song of this sort. Then with little Jeanette Luxemberg as the girl and Frances in a chic little Tuxedo, as the boy, they did a neat little double version of "So Long Letty" very charming indeed. Then after watching for a while dancers on the floor after the seats had been cleared Harry and I went down town to the baths!

<u>May 7, 1917</u>. Frances & Mamma have gone to Philly for a week's sojourn it being Frances' debut in an act for the general public.

<u>May 24, 1917</u>. Wrote a song yesterday called—title

YOU MAY THROW ALL THE RICE YOU DESIRE
Subtitle
BUT PLEASE FRIENDS, THROW NO SHOES.

THERE IS NOTHING THE MATTER; IT'S PERFECT

(written May 23, 1917—appeared in Don Marquis' column, "The Sun Dial," New York Sun, May 1917)

Mr. Marquis, Dear Sir: I have sent the following lyric to six different publishers and they all sent it back. Maybe you or some of your readers can tell me what is the matter with it as I am a young fellow and want to give the public what it wants. It goes as follows:

YOU MAY THROW ALL THE RICE YOU DESIRE

LYRIC BY I. B. GERSHWIN

The ceremony was over
    And all was happy and gay.
The blushing bride and her lover
    To the steps did wend their way.
Their young friends them had preceded
    And had formed a merry plot;
Although the older folks pleaded,
    The younger folks heeded them not.
But the bridegroom knew all about it,
    And he stood with haughty head,
He lifted his hand (you may doubt it)
    But 'tis true, these words he said.

Chorus:

"You may throw all the rice you desire,
    But please, friends, throw no shoes.
For 'twill surely arouse my ire,
    If you cause my wife one bruise.
Should you heed these words and don't fire,
    Then my friendship you won't lose.
You may throw all the rice you desire,
    But please, friends, throw no shoes."

A thrill o'er that throng so motley
    Went like a flash so quick;
And many young faces flamed hotly,
    Their consciences made them sick.
Many a spirit so reckless,
    Was beginning to meditate.
Persons with souls not so fleckless
    Their wrongdoings vowed to abate.
As their decades rolled by, they never
    Forgot that brave husband's part.

They behaved thereafter, forever,
  Like they knew, as follows, by heart:

Chorus:

"You may," etc.

Maybe it is a little old-fashioned, but I don't know, the old songs are the best, they say, and it points a moral. If any reader likes it and can write music to it I will go fifty-fifty with him.

                    Respectfully yours,
                    I. B. Gershwin

DIARY OF IRA GERSHWIN

May 27, 1917. In the evening with George to the Paleys and I introduced to Miss Strunsky, a charming miss.

May 28, 1917. A drearisome day. In afternoon sent a contribution to F.P.A. with return envelope enclosed. This was mailed at 5 P.M. At 7:45 this morning (Tuesday) I had it again. That certainly beats all return records as far as my stuff is concerned.

RECOLLECTIONS OF MABEL SCHIRMER

It was my uncle Herman Paley, a good musician and song writer at Jerome Remick's ("Cheer Up Father, Cheer Up Mother," "My Mother's Eyes," and "Billy"), who brought George home and into our family circle. Herman recognized George's creative gift, took him under his wing, and advised him to go to T. B. Harms, music publishers known for encouraging young talent.

Lou Paley, Herman's brother, was the literary member of the family. George and Lou became close friends immediately, and Lou wrote the lyrics to several of

At the home of Mabel Schirmer's aunt: Mabel at left, George next to her, and, at right, Emily Strunsky, who later married Lou Paley.

George's songs. It was a musical household, with Herman and George taking turns at the piano and George and Lou collaborating on songs.

During this period, I met George for the first time; it was the beginning of a devoted friendship.

DIARY OF IRA GERSHWIN

June 7, 1917. A LETTER FROM FRANCES
Dear Izzy, George and Arthur,

Feeling well and hope to hear the same from you. I only wish you could see daintyland. We got very big write-ups in the papers. Now I'll explain the act to you. The beginning is we all sit up on the piano and sing hellow folks hellow and two girls stand at the foot of the piano. Then a girl sings Let's All Be Americans Now. Then Honey sings Mississippi and a boy and girl sings and dances Honalua Hickie Boola Boo and a boy plays a violin then after him I come. And the girl who sang

first sings a song, and then Honey sings a number. After that we do a number together and sing There's A Long Long Trail. After that we go to the dressing room and wait for the next show. We play in this house four times a day. Then I go to the Hotel and go to bed, and that is the end of it tell Girdie to send my things out.

Frances

June 18, 1917. With George to the pictures and saw Charlie Chaplin in The Immigrant.

Sunday, July 22, 1917. A very hot day. For a long stroll in the morning about 11 o'clock. A stroll which took me thru most of that part of the Park bounded on the South by the Reservoir and the Tennis Grounds and on the North by 110th Street. . . . George and I to Civic Orchestra Concert. Eyes hurt and seated in last row, otherwise might have had an enjoyable evening of Wagner and Grieg and others, Robert Lortat was the piano soloist.

George Gershwin and Lou Paley.

July 24, 1917. With George in the evening to the Rialto where saw Olive Thomas, late of the Follies in a Triangle Picture entitled An Even Break *a trite story well handled.*

July 31, 1917. To Coney (Brighton rather) with Geo. Signs at Parkway Baths, "25¢ daily 50¢ Sundays." This being Tuesday and a weekday we paid the regulation price at 1.00 each. Some mob. Some heat. To Thomashefsky's bungalow where met Harry and Mickey Thomashefsky, M playing Kern's latest records for us then taking George and muh canoeing!

August 15, 1917. Saw Hitchy Koo *this afternoon.*

August 23, 1917. Saw Sudden Jim *at Loew's 116th St. Theatre with George.*

August 26, 1917. Hippodrome with Frances. Saw the new show Cheer Up.

September, 3, 1917. Labor Day. With Harry B. to see Rita Gould at Proctor's 58th Street Theatre. Her accompanist being no one other than George Gershvin alias George Wynne. . . . Her accompanist played thoroughly in accord with her presentations. His solo was the "Desecration Rag" at the 1st performance, where too long, was substituted, subsequently at the 2nd performance "California Sunshine."

October 19, 1917. George continues working at the Century Theatre as rehearsal pianist. He works quite hard but comes in contact with such notables as Jerome Kern, Victor Herbert, P. G. Wodehouse, Ned Wayburn, Cecil Lean and wife, Margot Kelly, Vivienne Segal, Lew Fields et al.

November 5, 1917. Worked and in the evening to see the opening of the long awaited Miss 1917. *A glorious show—entertaining every minute.*

November 18, 1917. Sunday. Home singing with George. Evening to Century where George played for Arthur Cunningham.

November 25, 1917. George played for Vivienne Segal who took him out for a bow.

Page of George's song notebook started while he was at Remick's.

December 18, 1917. George sold "You Just You" to Remick's. Written by George and I. Caesar.

I wrote a chorus for a melody of Geo's "You Are Not the Girl."

Visited the Century Concert twice.

George is writing songs at present with Lou Paley and Caesar and myself (a couple) and Praskin also.

January 20, 1918. On Sunday with George and Lou Paley to the Majestic Theatre, Brooklyn, where met Louise Dresser and husband Jack Gardiner. Miss Dresser, who with George as accompanist is trying out a new act, is decidedly congenial.

George and Lou have written a sextette number that is surefire.

Lou and George have about 10 splendid numbers which with the addition of say half a dozen more, could score and lyricize a musical comedy book, as artistically and entertainingly as any musical comedy I have seen.

"Beautiful Bird" is a number that George, Lou and I are working on. Hope it turns out to be a 2nd "Poor Butterfly."

February 10, 1918. George has been placed on the staff of T. B. Harms Co. He gets $35 a week for this connection, then $50 advance and a 3¢ royalty on each song of his they accept. This entails no other effort on his part than the composing, they not requiring any of his leisure for plugging nor for piano-playing. Some snap.

February 25, 1918. George opened with Louise Dresser at the Riverside. Her routine consisted of songs and stories. The songs were "My Gal Sal" by the late Paul Dresser (her brother), "Down by the Erie" from Cohan's Revue of 1916, "It's a Sure Sign" by Jerome Kern from Have a Heart, "Neighbors" by Jean Harvey and Herman Paley's "Cheer Up Father, Cheer Up Mother." The honors of the evening were shared by Miss Dresser and Pat Rooney and Marion Bent.

George played Baltimore, Boston and Washington with Louise Dresser. As yet his firm has altogether 4 or 5 of his numbers and they have been filed away for use when opportunity presents. At present he is rehearsal pianist at the New Amsterdam Roof Garden where the 1918 Ziegfeld Follies is in preparation.

May 22, 1918. Saw Rockabye Baby. I don't know of any musical comedy that has appealed to me more.

In March 1917 George gave up his pianist job at Remick's—he had been bitten by the theater bug the year before. Sigmund Romberg had called for musical

help on a quickie Shubert production, *The Passing Show of 1916*, and George took five song choruses to Romberg. One was accepted, Romberg added his own name as collaborator, and "Making of a Girl," with lyrics by Harold Atteridge, was brought out by G. Schirmer and earned its composer $7 in royalties. It clearly wasn't the royalties he was making that took George out of the song-plugging business, but his new interest in theater in all its forms. He wanted to get closer to it and concentrate more of his energies on composition.

Already a ragtime pianist and composer (his only 1917 publication was "Rialto Ripples," a rag piano solo written with Will Donaldson), George intensified his contacts with the best black ragtime pianists and composers around. "White" ragtime, as found in Irving Berlin, was entirely different in spirit from the creations of Luckey Roberts and James P. Johnson, great rag composers and players who befriended George in these years. And it was to Will Vodery, the black composer and arranger, that George often went for advice on how to get "closer to production music—the kind Jerome Kern was writing," as he later put it. (Vodery was later to orchestrate the Negro musical *Shuffle Along*, by Noble Sissle and Eubie Blake, that was to make syncopation and jazz dancing *de rigueur* on Broadway after 1921; he also orchestrated George's short opera *135th Street* in 1922.)

Another important influence on George at the time was the work of James Reese Europe, the black composer and conductor who organized the Clef Club, a pool of hundreds of black musicians that Europe had collected from all over the world to form large orchestras and smaller dance bands to play in various parts of the city, and especially in Harlem. To Europe, and his close friends and associates Vernon and Irene Castle, must go the credit for popularizing the fox trot, the dance rhythm of so many subsequent American popular songs.

Although later white songwriters—notably Harold Arlen—were to adopt Negro rhythms and melodic configurations into their musical styles, George Gershwin was certainly one of the earliest to seek out black music purely from personal interest. He soaked himself in it, and this early enthusiasm would contribute mightily to that special fusion of European and Negro elements that is the Gershwin style.

In 1918 Charles Hambitzer, George's first real teacher, died of tuberculosis and with his death went any remaining intention on George's part to become a concert pianist. Composition was to become more and more important in his mind—particularly composition for the theater.

Will Vodery.

VARIETY

$2 SHOW NOT WORTH WAR TAX

Syracuse, N.Y. Dec 11

It may be deemed unpatriotic to assist in beating the Government out of a war tax, but it is no exaggeration to say that Half Past Eight, Joe Cook's symposium which opened here Monday at the Empire Theatre, will not be, until it is completely reshaped, worth either the $2 or the 40 cents war tax, separately or collectively.

It is not Joe Cook's fault. He is, as usual, a splendid comedian. It is the fault of some gentleman who conceived the idea that the public will pay high prices to see a one-act vaudeville sketch stretched into a two-act imitation revue.

"The Clef Club Players consisting of 20 spades," as the program puts it, is an exceptionally good vaudeville number, but there can be too much of this upon occasion.

Sybil Vane, who sings four delightful songs, is another who is not to blame for the poor entertainment. She is a bright spot in an otherwise gloomy atmosphere.

What disappointed the Tired Business Man and the thing that he will never forgive is that while somehow the impression had been spread through the city that this was to be a girly show, there were only three of the fair sex in the entire production. This may have been responsible for some hissing as the curtain went down at 10:30. With a chorus, the play might have been possible.

Monday night's curtain rose at 8:45 and there was a generous intermission between the two alleged acts.

Cook at the opening performance explained there was no real reason for calling the show Half Past Eight. *He was right. It is said that* Half Past Eight *ran for nine months in London before being brought to America. Maybe this is so, but some sort of an apology should be offered for the fact that many of the vaudeville acts that go to make up the production never saw England. Miss Vane, who claims Wales is her home, is probably the only Britisher in the cast.*

Roy Stever and Mildred Lovejoy, who began their career as dancers in the Onondaga Hotel here, do a whirlwind dance that brought applause from old friends. Ruby Loraine as songster gets over fairly well. The Happy Tramps, Joe Melino and Jack Nichols, with their bicycle number, bring some laughs.

Perhaps the most glaring error in Half Past Eight *lies in the fact that no attempt has been made to draw the vaudeville turns together into a connected entertainment. But even if connected, the show would not be worth $2.*

Edward B. Perkins qualified for the title of "jazz" stage magnate when he directed a dress rehearsal Sunday of Half Past Eight, *which had its American premiere at the Empire Theatre Monday. Perkins, who isn't 30, is owner, manager and director of* Half Past Eight. *He "directed" the dress rehearsal from the orchestra pit, the balcony, the stage, and the gallery. Every time the cast thought they had him located he popped up at another place in the theatre.*

Perkins was in Paris one week before the armistice was signed. In the interval that has elapsed, Perkins hit the trail to America, bringing Half Past Eight, *which has run nine months in London.*

George Gershwin, who wrote the music for it, was also in Syracuse for the dress rehearsal and the opening.

Perkins graduated from Columbia University six years ago, and is the youngest international theatrical magnate in the world. If he keeps up his present speed, he'll be old inside of three months. Talking with Perkins is just as easy as interviewing Barney Oldfield when he's burning up the miles.

The show closed when several of the thirty-member cast refused to appear for the Saturday matinee performance unless paid. Appearances in Rochester and Chicago were also canceled. Perkins was stricken with grippe after working himself to a point of exhaustion.

After World War I Irving Berlin had severed his relations with the music-publishing firm Waterson, Berlin and Snyder. Before he established his own firm in 1919, he considered tying up with Max Dreyfus, head of T. B. Harms. One day he came to Dreyfus with a song called "That Revolutionary Rag" and asked if he wanted to publish it. Dreyfus said he was interested and Berlin told him he needed someone to take the song down for him. Dreyfus said, "I have a kid here who can do it."

The kid, George Gershwin, took the song down, made a lead sheet, and played it for Berlin, improvising to such a degree that Berlin hardly recognized his own song. Yet he could see the young man was a brilliant pianist. Gershwin had heard that Berlin was looking for a musical secretary and he said he would like the job.

Berlin replied that his plans were unsettled and asked him what he really wanted to do. Gershwin said he wanted to write songs. Berlin listened to some Gershwin songs (later to become part of a show, *La, La, Lucille*) and said, "What the hell do you want to work for anybody else for? Work for yourself!"

Sheet music of "Revolutionary Rag" by Irving Berlin. George Gershwin wrote down the song and provided the piano arrangement.

At an outing, August 1919, George is in the first row—one of the few smiling photographs.

LA, LA, LUCILLE (1919)

Every career needs a lucky break to start it on its way, and my lucky break came in 1919 when I was brought to Alex Aarons, a dapper young man who had made some money selling smart clothes and wanted to have a fling at producing a show. I was twenty years old at the time, and Arthur Jackson, the lyric writer, was the man who brought us together. After hearing a few of my tunes, Alex Aarons decided to engage me as composer for his first show, La, La, Lucille. This was very brave of him, because I was quite inexperienced at the time, never having written a complete score.

George Gershwin

Billed as "A New Up-to-the-Minute Musical Comedy of Class and Distinction," *La, La, Lucille* involved a dentist whose aunt has left him two million dollars, provided he divorce his wife, an ex–chorus girl. An out-of-town review by young Brooks Atkinson in the Boston *Transcript* pointed out that "the music is now vivacious and surprising of detail, and again harmoniously pleasing." "You-oo Just You" is the show's best-remembered song. The show closed on August 19 not for dwindling box-office receipts, but as a casualty of the actors' strike that paralyzed theater business across the country. The strike's settlement in September firmly established Actors Equity as a representative of theatrical performers.

RECOLLECTIONS OF IRVING CAESAR

Although George came from the East Side as I did, I met him for the first time at Remick's when it was on 46th Street. Remick's was an amazing place. There was always something happening. Performers would be there to hear new songs for their acts, and it was a real beehive of rehearsal activity. George was a much-sought-after accompanist there. They all loved to have George play the new songs for them. He was like a salesman exposing the inventory, and the songs were inventory. He was a great salesman because the way he played the piano was unique.

With Alex Aarons.

Soon we got to like each other because I'm quite musical. I don't play the piano, yet I'm a piano buff, and anyone who plays the piano well has me. So with George I used to make up titles just to have him sit down and go up and down the keys and see what he could strike from them, and he could work wonders. I wrote very fast and he wrote very fast. Very often I would invent or pretend that I had ideas for songs just so he would sit down and try to translate them into some musical theme. I always worked with him right at the piano. He was very viable and very adaptive. You see, George wrote with chords. His chordation was so interesting, so modern and remarkable, and out of his chordation came the melodies.

Well, occasionally, an idea lent itself and a song emerged. The first song was called, "You-oo Just You." We were really young then—very, very young. We walked into Jerome H. Remick's one day with that song and they took it. Well, Vivienne Segal had already introduced it in Charles Dillingham's Miss 1917 at the Century Theatre, so they gave us an advance of $500

Irving Caesar.

each. $500 way back in 1917! We ran home to our fathers and mothers, and what do you think they said? "Boys, you're too young. Bring a lawyer next time." And we would have given $500 to have the song published! We thought that was a lot of money for 1917.

Well, soon after that we wrote some songs for Good Morning, Judge, a musical with Charlie and Mollie King. One song, "I Was So Young, You Were So Beautiful," was quite off the beaten path for that period. It became a hit of sorts, and it brought us to the attention of the publishers. However, by that time, 1919, George had been signed up by Max Dreyfus; I was signed up a little later. We then found most publishers accessible to us.

There was a big hit at the time called "Hindustan," a one-step ("Hindustan, where I came to rest my tired caravan"). So I said to George, "Why don't we write an American one-step? George, let's go up to your house and write it." The idea came quickly, and we wrote "Swanee" very fast up at the Gershwin house on 144th Street. George's father heard it right in the middle of his card game and he went out of the room and came back with a comb wrapped up in tissue paper and he played it and it sounded like a kazoo, and that was the first arrangement the song had. It was sheer inspiration. We wrote "Swanee" in about fifteen minutes or less.

One day we played the song at a rehearsal of the Ziegfeld Frolic up at the New Amsterdam Roof, where George was the rehearsal pianist. We played it to entertain the girls who happened to be up there, and Ned Wayburn heard it and said he'd like to use it in his Demitasse Revue, which was to open the new Capitol Theatre. So we gave it to Ned Wayburn along with another song of George's called "Come to the Moon," which he wrote with Lou Paley.

Funny thing about "Swanee." It was received with great enthusiasm, but it wasn't a hit right off the bat. The Capitol opening was tremendous, and it was the largest theater in the world at that time. Sixty girls danced to "Swanee"; they had electric lights in their shoes. Arthur Pryor's band played it. Seventy in the band. Everyone on the stage sang it. Everyone applauded. There were thousands of copies in the lobby—but they didn't sell.

George and I would hang around the lobby every night and hide behind posts, hoping against hope somebody would start the ball rolling. Occasionally we would try to start the ball rolling and we bought our own music.

We thought maybe a line would queue up if we started buying copies, but nothing happened.

One day Al Jolson gave a midnight party after a show at the Winter Garden. I was away at the time, so I didn't get in on that residual. George was invited up by Buddy De Sylva, with whom he also wrote songs. Buddy was a great friend of Jolson's and asked George to play for Jolson. At that party George played "Swanee," among several other numbers, and Jolson at once adopted it and introduced it within three or four days, and the rest is history. Jolson made "Swanee" a hit, the biggest hit song George ever had. If Jolson hadn't performed it with that great warmth he had, it probably wouldn't have happened. Now everybody knows the song, and when I sing "Swanee" when I do personal appearances, the audience starts singing it with me at once. Yet some people think George and I were Southerners because we wrote "Swanee." But at the time we wrote it we scarcely had been south of 14th Street. . . .

George's family were very practical people. After he achieved his success, they realized there was a future in the thing. You know how parents are—they always like to see their sons go into some legitimate enterprise—but it didn't take long for them to realize that George's was legitimate enough.

I was lucky to latch on to him. Since there were ten composers for one lyric writer, George welcomed me around him. He wanted his tunes wedded to words. I kept after him with titles. I pushed and prodded as much as I could, and I might have helped a little bit by creating an atmosphere of excitement around him and by breathing a certain enthusiasm into his early work—you could put it that way. And we were lucky. We were kids when we wrote "You-oo Just You" and "I Was So Young, You Were So Beautiful" and "Yankee Doodle Blues" and of course "Swanee."

George was very sweet and very soft and quite sensitive, but he had great faith and confidence in his music, and that was as it should be. There was nothing modest about him. I don't mean that he was overbearing, but he had self-confidence, and rightly so. For when George sat down at the piano, there was no one who could move you as George would. It was very difficult to put your finger on his talent because it lapsed over into the serious field, but there's no doubt that he blazed a trail for all popular musicians. His was a unique talent. He was in a class by himself! Isn't that enough?

Next to Al Jolson.

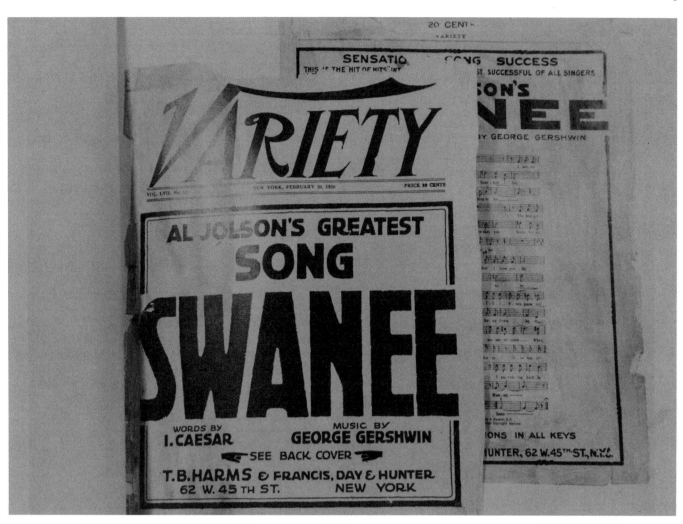

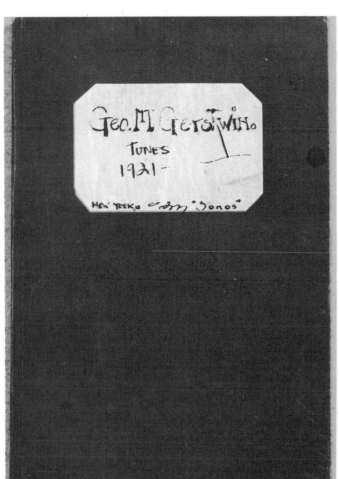

Cover of George's earliest surviving song notebook.

Ira and George joined ASCAP at the same time.

Early sketches for "Yankee Doodle Blues,"
later lyricized by Irving Caesar and introduced by Al Jolson.

"Anything for You" was used in George's *A Dangerous Maid*,
which opened and closed out of town in 1921.

Three fragments. "G.T." means Good Tune.
The words on the left side of the page in Ira's hand were intended
for the last fragment. *(Facing.)*

Ira with Vincent Youmans, his collaborator on
the successful *Two Little Girls in Blue* (1921).

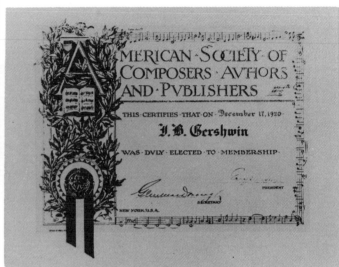

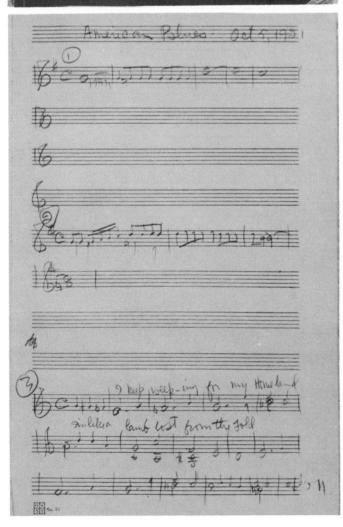

27

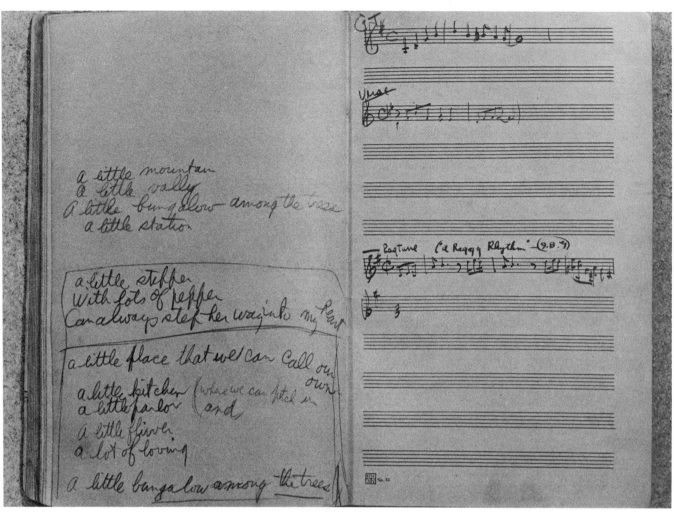

PARTY SONG OF THE EARLY 1920S

MISCHA, JASCHA, TOSCHA, SASCHA

Verse 1:

*We really think you ought to know
That we were born right in the middle
Of Darkest Russia.
When we were three years old or so,
We all began to play the fiddle
In Darkest Russia.
When we began,
Our notes were sour—
Until a man
(Professor Auer)
Set out to show us, one and all,
How we could pack them in, in Carnegie Hall.*

Refrain 1:

*Temp'ramental Oriental Gentlemen are we:
Mischa, Jascha, Toscha, Sascha—
Fiddle-lee, diddle-lee, dee.
Shakespeare says, "What's in a name?"
With him we disagree. -
Names like Sammy, Max or Moe
Never bring the heavy dough
Like Mischa, Jascha, Toscha, Sascha—
Fiddle-lee, diddle-lee, dee.*

Verse 2:

*Though born in Russia, sure enough,
We're glad that we became relations
Of Uncle Sammy.
For though we play the high-brow stuff,
We also like the syncopations
Of Uncle Sammy.
Our magic bow
Plays Liszt and Schumann;
But then you know
We're only human
And like to shake a leg to jazz.
(Don't think we've not the feelings everyone has.)*

Refrain 2:

*Temp'ramental Oriental Gentlemen are we:
Mischa, Jascha, Toscha, Sascha—
Fiddle-lee, diddle-lee, dee.
High-brow He-brow may play low-brow
In his privacy.
But when concert halls are packed,
Watch us stiffen up and act
Like Mischa, Jascha, Toscha, Sascha—
Fiddle-lee, diddle-lee, dee.*

Irene Bordoni.

DO IT AGAIN!

I was in the office of Max Dreyfus, my publisher, one day when Buddy De Sylva walked in. De Sylva said jokingly to me, "George, let's write a hit!" I matched him by saying "O.K.!" I sat down at the piano and began playing a theme, which I was composing on the spot. . . . Buddy listened for a few minutes and then began chanting this title "Oh, Do It Again!" which he had just fitted to my theme. Some time later my friend Jules Glaenzer, who is one of the most famous hosts on two continents, was giving one of his usual parties. Let me tell you who was there. There was Paul Whiteman, John McCormack, Charlie Chaplin, Georges Carpentier, then training for his fight with Dempsey—there were the Duncan Sisters, Nora Bayes, Zez Confrey, Fred and Adele Astaire, Alex Aarons, Fanny Brice, Marilyn Miller, William Rhinelander Stewart, Noël Coward, Vincent Youmans, Florenz Ziegfeld, and Irene Bordoni. This was a typical Glaenzer party. It was here that I played my newest song, "Do It Again!," whereupon Irene Bordoni rushed across the room and cried, "I must have that song! It's for me!" Needless to say, Irene got what she wanted, and sang the song in a show called The French Doll.

George Gershwin

RECOLLECTIONS OF EMILY PALEY

Lou's brother Herman Paley was the first person in our group to know George and it was Herman who introduced him to Lou. Lou, who was about ten years older than Ira, was an inspiring teacher of English at Stuyvesant and Seward Park high schools.

Lou and George wrote a number of songs together and, as their friendship grew, Lou guided George's reading and became his literary mentor. I can't swear to this, but I think Lou may have been the first person to tell George about DuBose Heyward's novel, Porgy. I also know they talked about The Dybbuk as a possible opera.

George played the piano at our wedding in June 1920. After Lou and I were married we lived at 18 West Eighth Street where, for many years, we had open house on Saturday nights. This was during Prohibition and we served tea, cookies and lichee nuts and played Twenty Questions. Among the people who came often were: my sister Leonore, my brother English, Dr. Alvan Barach, who invented the oxygen tent, Sam Behrman, Pamela Bianco, Marc Blitzstein, Arthur Caesar, Philip Charig, Buddy De Sylva, Howard Dietz, Lew Gensler, John Huston, Sam Jaffe, Dorlé Jaumel, Oscar Levant, Joe Meyer, Dr. Norman Pleshette, Edward G. Robinson, Josefa Rosanska, Morrie Ryskind, Mabel Schirmer, Dick Simon, Morris Strunsky, Vincent Youmans, and many others.

Ira never missed a Saturday and George came often. His playing was always a highlight of those evenings. Our house was even a testing ground for George's dates. If one of George's girls didn't like the atmosphere, he gave her up.

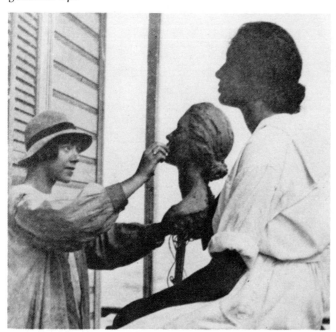

Emily Paley sitting for sculptress Minna Harkavy, c. 1920.

OUR NELL (1922)

This show, once called *Hayseed*, was billed as a "musical mellowdrayma." The setting was old New England, and the plot satirized the "And the Villain Still Pursued Her" type of play. The reviews were favorable, and the songs, especially "Walking Home with Angeline" and "Innocent Ingenue Baby," the latter written in collaboration with William Merrigan Daly, had a certain dash and charm.

Unhappily, George invested and lost much of his money in the show, but one lasting benefit was the forging of a lifelong friendship with Bill Daly, who on musical matters was as close to George as anyone was.

Among Those Seen and Seeing at "ZIEGFELD'S MIDNIGHT FROLIC"

Pick them out for yourself. Paul Whiteman and Helen Morgan are "down center." To the left are Mayor Walker, Dr. Copeland, Lillian Gish, George Jean Nathan, Peggy Joyce, Fanny Brice, Lew Fields, Richard Barthelmess, Irene Delroy, Ray Dooley, Walter Kingsley, Robert Benchley and "Wynn" (the artist who takes responsibility for these).

To the right of Paul Whiteman and Helen Morgan are Mr. Ziegfeld, Billie Burke, Louise Brooks, Ina Claire, Gertrude Lawrence, Noel Coward, Beatrice Lillie, Sam Harris, John Murray Anderson, Irene Bordoni, Will Rogers and Eddie Cantor. The Midnight Frolic—if any one needs to be told—takes place atop the New Amsterdam Theatre.

OPENING WEDNESDAY EVENING, FEBRUARY 6
AT 11:30

**ZIEGFELD
MIDNIGHT
FROLIC**

(Atop of the New Amsterdam Theatre, 42nd St. West of B'way)

Presenting World's Most Famous After-Theatre Diversion

**DUNCAN SISTERS
HELEN MORGAN**

TAMARA GEVA, PAUL GREGORY, CHARLOTTE AYRES, MALINOFF and CO.—And

PAUL WHITEMAN

(In Person)
Directing His Twenty-six Piece Concert and Dance Orchestra

ZIEGFELD GLORIFIED GIRL NUMBERS
Songs and Special Numbers by Dorothy Fields and James McHugh
Staged by Sammy Lee

DANCING——ENTERTAINMENT——RESTAURANT
(INFORMAL)

Make Your Reservations for the Midnight Frolic
at Box Office—During Intermission

Mon., Eve., Feb. 18—First American Appearance
MAURICE CHEVALIER

Idol of Paris and London—Newest Paramount Star
(By Arrangement with Jesse L. Lasky)

"THE MEETING PLACE OF THE WORLD"

At the close of World War I the musical stage offered a bewilderingly varied array of entertainment.

European operetta was still dominant, but there were also farce comedies, extravaganzas, burlesque, vaudeville, musical comedies and the revue, which in the early 1920s successfully challenged the European operetta for supremacy on the American musical stage.

European light opera, set among exotic locales in distant times, raised musical standards and paved the way for the work of John Philip Sousa, Victor Herbert, Rudolf Friml, Sigmund Romberg, most significantly, and Jerome Kern. It was Kern whose work was the crucial bridge in the transformation of our musical theater to a more distinctly American style.

Musical comedy had emerged in the 1870s out of farce comedy and quickly produced such talented individuals as Nate Salsbury, Harrigan and Hart, Charles Hoyt, Weber and Fields. George M. Cohan kept the American vernacular tradition alive during the period of European operetta domination. And in time he was joined by the syncopated offerings of Irving Berlin and the intimate sophistications of the Princess Theatre shows of Guy Bolton, P. G. Wodehouse, and Jerome Kern.

The revue, with varied sequences representative of the heterogeneity of urban life, had developed from the minstrel shows, variety, the music-hall tradition, burlesque, and vaudeville to become, in the hands of Florenz Ziegfeld, nothing less than an American institution. At a time when the American woman was struggling for the right to vote and be recognized as equal to men under our laws, Ziegfeld, borrowing a soupçon from the divertissements of the French *Folies-Bergère*, sought to glorify the American girl in a theatrical framework of song, dance, humor, and spectacle. Grandiose in design and extravagant in execution, the annual *Ziegfeld Follies*, which began in 1907, were the creation of a man with a remarkable eye for beauty and exquisite taste.

George White, who had worked for Ziegfeld as a dancer with Ann Pennington, began a revue series of his own in 1919. Dissatisfied with the score for his 1919 edition, White employed George Gershwin to write the music for his 1920 edition at a salary of $50 a week. The *Scandals* placed more emphasis on dancing, comedy, and music than the *Follies* did, and White, although he was loath to admit it, was glad to have Gershwin as his regular composer, especially after the success of "Swanee."

Although George produced few memorable songs for the *Scandals*, where he remained as composer for five

IDOL DREAMS

SECOND ANNUAL EVENT

GEORGE WHITE'S SCANDALS OF 1920

WITH ANN PENNINGTON

Book By ANDY RICE & GEORGE WHITE
Music By GEORGE GERSHWIN
Lyrics By ARTHUR JACKSON
Staged by GEORGE WHITE & WILLIE COLLIER
Scenery By LAW STUDIOS

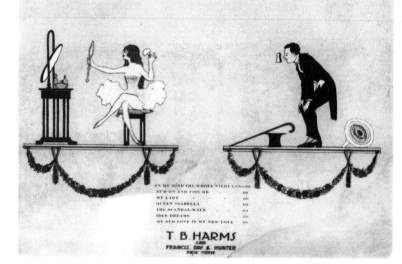

ON MY MIND THE WHOLE NIGHT LONG..........60
TUM ON AND TUNE ME..........60
MY LADY..........60
QUEEN ISABELLA..........60
THE SCANDAL-WALK..........60
IDLE DREAMS..........60
MY OLD LOVE IS MY NEW LOVE..........60

T. B. HARMS
AND
FRANCIS, DAY & HUNTER
NEW YORK

E. Hornstein

SOMEBODY LOVES ME

GEORGE WHITE'S SCANDALS

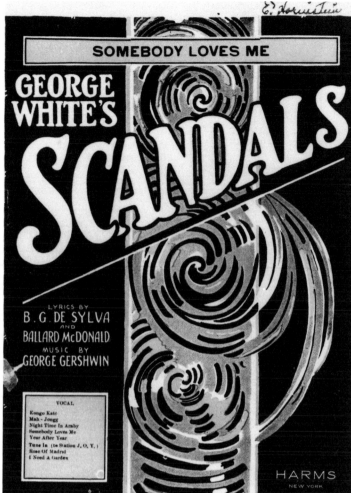

LYRICS BY
B. G. DE SYLVA
AND
BALLARD McDONALD
MUSIC BY
GEORGE GERSHWIN

VOCAL

Kongo Kate
Mah - Jongg
Night Time In Araby
Somebody Loves Me
Year After Year
Tune In (to Station J. O. Y.)
Rose Of Madrid
I Need A Garden

HARMS
NEW YORK

MADE IN U. S. A.

CINDERELATIVES

FOURTH ANNUAL PRODUCTION

George White's Scandals

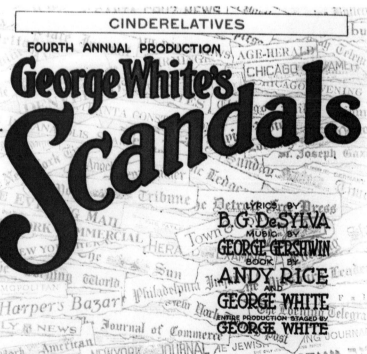

LYRICS BY
B. G. DeSYLVA
MUSIC BY
GEORGE GERSHWIN
BOOK BY
ANDY RICE
AND
GEORGE WHITE
ENTIRE PRODUCTION STAGED BY
GEORGE WHITE

Scenes by
The Law Studios
From Sketches by
John Wenger

VOCAL

ARGENTINA
CINDERELATIVES
I FOUND A FOUR LEAF CLOVER
OH, WHAT SHE HANG OUT
WHERE IS THE MAN OF MY DREAMS
I'LL BUILD A STAIRWAY TO PARADISE

HARMS
NEW YORK

WHERE IS SHE

FIFTH ANNUAL PRODUCTION

George White's Scandals

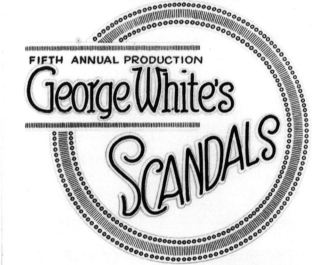

VOCAL

Lets Be Lonesome Together
Home Lights I Long To See
Where Is She
Life Of A Rose
You And I

LYRICS BY
B. G. DeSYLVA
MUSIC BY
GEORGE GERSHWIN
BOOK BY
GEORGE WHITE
ENTIRE PRODUCTION STAGED BY
GEORGE WHITE

SCENES BY
THE LAW STUDIOS
ART DIRECTOR
HERBERT WARD

HARMS
NEW YORK
MADE IN U.S.A.

editions (1920–1924), or for other musicals of that period, he developed his talents as a writer of varied and different types of songs.

For a revue, if there were flower costumes available, the composer wrote music for a song about flowers. If one of the writers produced a lyric about a current fad like Mah-Jongg or the development of the radio, the composer would oblige with a tune, for, like it or not, his contract called on him to do so. On the whole, George did what was required of him no better but certainly no worse than other revue composers. The very nature of the medium severely circumscribed the efforts of its creators.

For revues were a succession of numbers and sketches with little pretense to artistic unity. Yet, here a comedian could perfect and enrich his style. Here a show girl or dancing girl could win the plaudits she had always dreamed about and achieve the emoluments that had drawn her from tenement or small town. The songwriter, turning out love songs, production numbers, comedy songs, could—as George did—broaden his musical knowledge and enrich his melodic content, his harmonic palette, and his sense of rhythm. In songs like "Drifting Along with the Tide" from the 1921 *Scandals*, "I'll Build a Stairway to Paradise" from the 1922 version, and "Somebody Loves Me" from George's last effort for White, the 1924 *Scandals*, George wrote exquisitely with a distinctive personal stamp. Rising from a salary of $50 a week to $75 and finally $125 a week plus royalties, George asked White for a raise. When White refused him, George Gershwin was ready to write musical scores on his own.

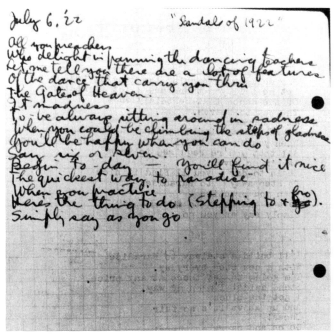

Ira's manuscript for the verse of "Stairway to Paradise."

GEORGE WHITE'S SCANDALS (1922)

Ann Pennington, dancing star of *George White's Scandals*.

(I'LL BUILD A) STAIRWAY TO PARADISE

This number was the first-act finale of George White's Scandals of 1922. It was called "(I'll Build a) Stairway to Paradise," with the subtitle "With a New Step Ev'ry Day." The word "step" in any title meant that the producer will give you just that—steps. Mr. White, Mr.

34

Ziegfeld, Mr. Wayburn—they all loved steps. And rightly so—it's the only way the entire chorus can be seen at once. "Stairway" was played in the show by Paul Whiteman's orchestra, and I'll never forget the first time I heard Whiteman do it. Paul made my song live with a vigor that almost floored me. Curiously enough, another piece, "I Found a Four Leaf Clover," was written to be the featured song or hit in the new show. But there was no stopping "Stairway to Paradise" once Whiteman got his brasses into it. Two circular staircases surrounded the orchestra on the stage, leading high up into theatrical paradise or the flies, which in everyday language means the ceiling. Mr. White had draped fifty of his most beautiful girls in a black patent-leather material which brilliantly reflected the spotlights. A dance was staged in the song, and those girls didn't need much coaxing to do their stuff to the accompaniment of Whiteman's music. Incidentally, my association with Whiteman in this show I am sure had something to do with Paul's asking me to write a composition for his first jazz concert. As you may know, I wrote the Rhapsody in Blue for that occasion, and there is no doubt that this was my start in the field of more serious music.

George Gershwin

Verse:

All you preachers
Who delight in panning the dancing teachers,
Let me tell you there are a lot of features
Of the dance that carry you through
The Gates of Heaven.

It's madness
To be always sitting around in sadness,
When you could be learning the Steps of Gladness.
(You'll be happy when you can do
Just six or seven.)

Begin today! You'll find it nice:
The quickest way to Paradise.
When you practice,
Here's the thing to know—
Simply say as you go:

Refrain:

I'll build a Stairway to Paradise,
With a new Step ev'ry day.
I'm going to get there at any price;
Stand aside, I'm on my way!
I got the blues
And up above it's so fair;
Shoes,
Go on and carry me there!
I'll build a Stairway to Paradise,
With a new Step ev'ry day.

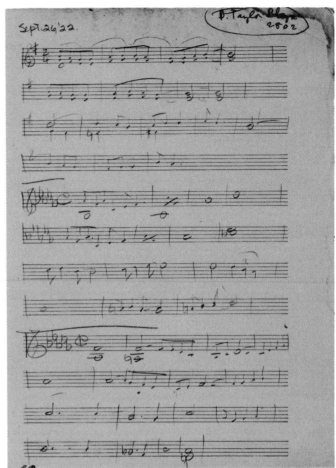

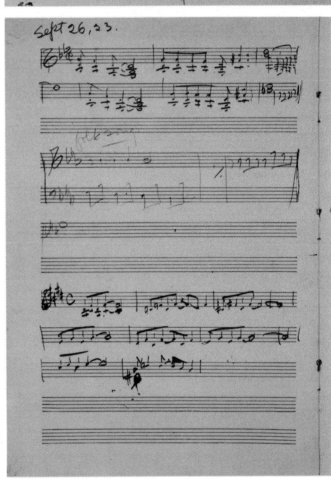

George's 24th birthday. This is the first page of a new notebook. The phone number was probably Deems Taylor's.

Written on George's 25th birthday.

SWEET LITTLE DEVIL (1924)

Even with a Gershwin score, and this time it was only so-so, *Sweet Little Devil* (known in its Boston tryout as *A Perfect Lady*) was simply another musical with a mistaken-identity plot. The charm of Constance Binney, who had started out as a dancer in musicals and then gone on to Hollywood, helped save it from early extinction. On opening night Miss Binney sent George a little calling card, on which she had written:

SWEET is the music you only can write
LITTLE the voice that attempts it to render
DEVIL take that, if the critics tonight
Will take their opinions of you from the sender.

RHAPSODY IN BLUE (1924)

I was summoned to Boston for the première of Sweet Little Devil. I had already done some work on the rhapsody. It was on the train, with its steely rhythms, its rattle-ty-bang that is often so stimulating to a composer . . . I frequently hear music in the very heart of noise. And there I suddenly heard—and even saw on paper— the complete construction of the rhapsody, from beginning to end. No new themes came to me, but I worked on the thematic material already in my mind, and tried to conceive the composition as a whole. I heard it as a sort of musical kaleidoscope of America—of our vast melting pot, of our unduplicated national pep, of our metropolitan madness. By the time I reached Boston I had a definite plot of the piece, as distinguished from its actual substance.

George Gershwin

Paul Whiteman and his Palais Royal Orchestra.

In January 1924 Ira opened a copy of the New York *Herald Tribune* and found that George was supposedly at work on a jazz symphony for Paul Whiteman. It is true that Whiteman had requested a score for his concert in Aeolian Hall on February 12, a concert intended to show the "straight" musicians that jazz was respectable music. But Gershwin had virtually forgotten the request and had no intention of writing a jazz symphony. When he saw the announcement, however, he went ahead with the project and completed his score of his *Rhapsody* in three weeks. It was Ira who, inspired by a visit to an art gallery, thought up the title. Whiteman's arranger Ferde Grofé orchestrated the *Rhapsody* in ten days, and the première went off as advertised—a well-publicized event and a resounding popular and critical success.

What happened in Aeolian Hall the afternoon of February 12, 1924, when Paul Whiteman presented George Gershwin's *Rhapsody in Blue* at his much-heralded "Experiment in Modern Music" concert, was of enormous importance to the future of American music—but not because it introduced jazz to the concert hall. Many similar events preceded it, and James Reese Europe's 1912 Clef Club Concert in Carnegie Hall holds a much stronger claim to the distinction so often bestowed on Whiteman's 1924 spectacular.

Yet the Whiteman concert and, especially, the *Rhapsody in Blue* deserve credit for introducing what Rudy Vallee aptly called a kind of "symphonized syncopation" to the musical cognoscenti, by presenting it in a concert hall, home ground for serious musicians.

The Aeolian Hall concert succeeded in its attempt to give respectability to what it called jazz. Gershwin and other American composers and working musicians would thereafter find it much easier to secure outlets and financial support for their creations and performances.

The *Rhapsody in Blue*, however, is not jazz, not even jazz dolled up. For George Gershwin, eclectic as he was, was not really a composer of jazz music. Although he indicated that the *Rhapsody* was scored for "jazz band and piano," even the most cursory examination of the *Rhapsody* reveals it to be a work of symphonic music that owes far more to the influence of Tchaikovsky and Liszt, both unquestionably skilled syncopators, than of Buddy Bolden or King Oliver.

Ironically, the barnyard simulations in the *Livery Stable Blues*, which opened the concert, were much closer to the essence of jazz than the *Rhapsody in Blue* was, although Whiteman mistakenly presented *Livery Stable* as a grotesque burlesque of the "real jazz" of the *Rhapsody*. It is true that there is real jazz in the stunning seventeen-note opening clarinet glissando that clarinetist Ross Gorman hurled at the Aeolian Hall audience. And it is true that the *Rhapsody* has occasional bursts of syncopation, polyrhythm, exotic instrumental effects, and even blue notes—flatted thirds, fifths, and sevenths. Yet these are really ornamentations to a work whose audacity, verve, and, above all, gorgeous melodies are akin in spirit and quality to the Russian music George Gershwin heard in his formative years.

And it is precisely because the *Rhapsody*'s form and melodic and harmonic content were recognizable and did not rile its sensibilities that the musical establishment could sanctify it. From that February day on, it soared swiftly and far beyond the confines of Aeolian Hall to a public that had been prepared for it by the musical ministrations of Whiteman and other musicians.

We should not forget that Whiteman's musicians were top professionals. They could play! Nor should we overlook the fact that when Gershwin played the *Rhapsody* he played it in a much freer, more open, more heavily accented and contrasted—yes, even jazz-like—style than has been achieved by subsequent performers. The two abridged recordings Gershwin and Whiteman made together of the *Rhapsody* have a dash and sparkle that virtually every later performance has lacked.

Although to some people the *Rhapsody* mistakenly represents the very essence of jazz, it lives on more importantly as a wonderfully varied, zestful work by a young musical genius who was still absorbing all kinds of music when on that train ride to Boston he found the inspiration for the *Rhapsody*.

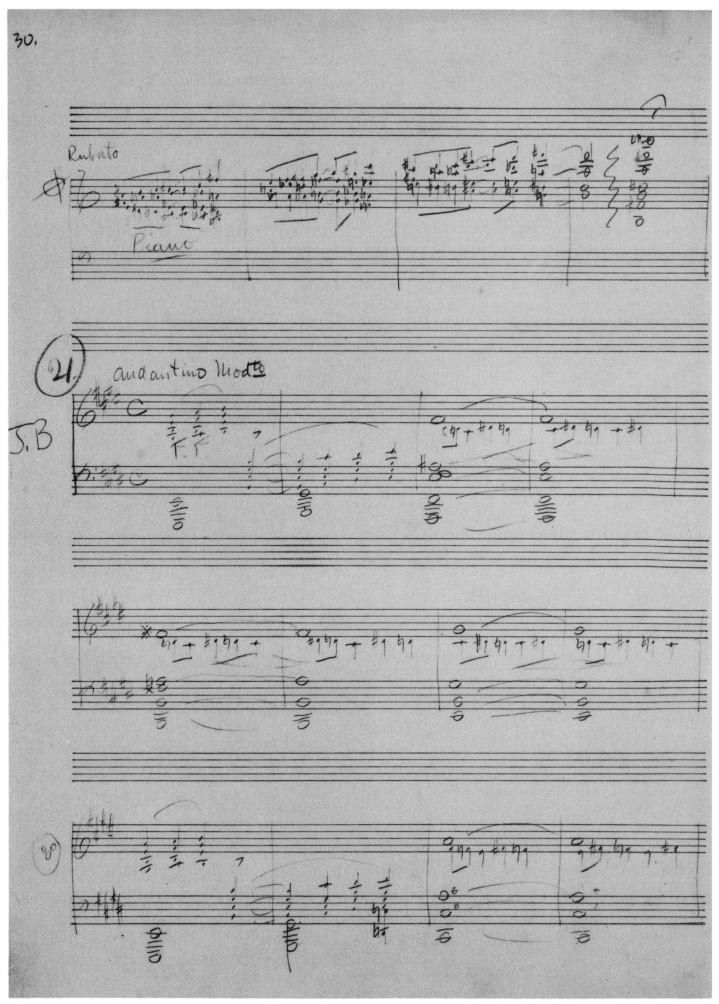

The piano transition into the slow theme of *Rhapsody in Blue*, perhaps the most famous theme in all American music. J.B. means Jazz Band. This is a page of George's fair-copy piano score. Ferde Grofé orchestrated both the original jazz-band arrangement and the later orchestral version.

10 Berkeley St. W. 1.
July 8 1924 London.

Dear Em-Son,

Just on my way to
dine with Miss Wiborg, who lives
just around the corner. Having a
few minutes however, I am writing
this small note to tell you how
nice everything seems this year as
compared with last. Alex Aarons
his wife and I have one of the
cheeriest flats I've seen anywhere.
It looks over Devonshire Gardens,
and makes a comfortable place for
me to work in.

Among the notables who
have been in it since our invasion
are Prince George, Otto Kahn,
Lord ~~Arthur~~ Berners,

the Earl of Lathom & several
others.

The new show goes into rehearsal
in two weeks. I hope to have it
about finished by then. I am
most optimistic about this show
because the book seems so
good — to say nothing of the
score. We also have the best
comedian in England to produce
the laughter. If the show is
only half way decent it will
be produced in America soon
after its London presentation
which makes it doubly in
teresting.

The weather has been
great —————— for London.

3.

It has been very cool.
Saw Brookes beat Hunter
the American, in the tennis
matches at Wimbledon. It
was a tough match.

Played golf for the eighth
time in my life on Sunday
& tied Guy Bolton for 15
holes. He thought I was a
golf genius. I believe I shall
it up professionally. That's a
good way to knock off some
heiress.

Wasn't in London more
than a week when I wrote a
number called "I'll have a house

in Berkeley Square. I'll have a
cottage at Kew" which Alex
says is more English than any
tune Paul Rubens ever wrote!
Desmond Carter wrote the
lyric. He is a promising young
lyricist.

I wish you would drop
me a line sometime. (Sat nyte)
My regards to the gang
& please let me know all
about them.

Yours for some
English hits

George.

LADY, BE GOOD! (1924)

Abe Erlanger's Liberty Theatre on 42nd Street was the site of the moderately heralded opening of *Lady, Be Good!* This show, the first producing venture of the newly formed team of Alex Aarons and Vinton Freedley, was noteworthy for two reasons: outstanding performances by Fred and Adele Astaire, and a superb score by George and Ira Gershwin. The shopworn musical-comedy formulas weathered the evening intact, but the quality of the songs, their originality and excellence, their complexity and sophistication in rhythm, harmony, and lyric-writing, raised musical-comedy writing to new heights and provided a standard of achievement for the musicals that would follow. The sculptor Isamu Noguchi wrote that Gershwin had "that rare gift of being able to transfix in such a slender song as 'Oh, Lady, Be Good' the timely, yet timeless image of an era, poignant still."

| LETTER FROM IRA |
| TO LOU AND EMILY PALEY |

HOTEL SYLVANIA
Locust and Juniper Streets
Philadelphia, Pa.

Wednesday
Nov. 26, 1924

Dear Lou and Em,

It is Wednesday 3 A.M. in room 917 at the above hotel and I was just about to pop off to bed when I bethought me I ought to send you word and music of what was what—(tho I say it who shouldn't (what I mean is, I have only received a couple of postcards from you), however—)

I was down to 8th Street some three weeks ago, and all was and were well. They told me you had sent a long letter and all was and were well with you, to say the least. Details were lacking, but I'm guessing wrong if you're not having a good time. I hope that last sentence makes sense but I can't be bothered at this hour. . . .

Winter Garden Theatre
DRURY LANE, W.C.2
:: Licensed by the Lord Chamberlain to ::
GEORGE GROSSMITH and J. A. E. MALONE

Every Evening at 8.15   Matinées: Thursday and Saturday at 2.30

GEORGE GROSSMITH & J. A. E. MALONE
present
HEATHER THATCHER
PERCY HEMING   MARGERY HICKLIN
and
LESLIE HENSON
in a New MUSICAL COMEDY in Three Acts

PRIMROSE
BOOK by GEORGE GROSSMITH and GUY BOLTON
LYRICS by DESMOND CARTER
MUSIC by GEORGE GERSHWIN
(By arrangement with ALEX A. AARONS and VINTON FREEDLEY)

Characters in the Order in which they Appear:

Jason	Mr. ERNEST GRAHAM
Freddie Falls	Mr. CLAUDE HULBERT
May Rooker	Miss VERA LENNOX
Sir Benjamin Falls	Mr. GUY FANE
Joan (his Ward)	Miss MARGERY HICKLIN
Hiliary Vane (a Novelist)	Mr. PERCY HEMING
Hon. Mrs. Warrender	Miss RUTH TAYLOR
Toby Mopham	Mr. LESLIE HENSON
Michael	Mr. THOMAS WEGUELIN
Manager of Hotel	HAROLD BRADLEY
Pinkie Peach (Mdme. Frazeline) ..	Miss HEATHER THATCHER
Lady Sophia Mopham	Miss MURIEL BARNBY
Pritchard	Miss SYLVIA HAWKES

Villagers, River Girls, Sports Girls, Sportsmen, Visitors, &c.:

Emily and Lou.

The Astaires do their famous run-around dance.

Well, Lady, Be Good! looks pretty good. I enclose a couple of clippings. . . . We did great business last (our first) week—over $21,000, but the show needs lots of fixing, the first half hour being very slow. I don't think it can be remedied either, before we open in New York City next Monday Dec. 1, at the Liberty (sounds like little Jerry). Still, I think it will take for a nice few months anyway. We wrote about twenty two or three numbers and have about half that in now, as the show was an hour or more too long opening night. They are:

(I)

1. Hang on to Me (Fred & Adele)
2. End of a String (Scene Opening)
3. Fascinating Rhythm (Fred & Adele & Ukulele Ike)
4. So Am I (Adele & Alan Edwards—very cute number)
5. Lady Be Good (Catlett & Girls)
6. Finale

(II)

1. Opening Chorus (6 Little Rainy Afternoon Girls)
2. We're Here Because (2 minor people)
3. Half of It Dearie Blues (Fred & his girl)
4. Juanita (Adele & Boys)

5. Leave It to Love (A number which goes in tomorrow replacing "Man I Love")
6. Ukulele Ike's Specialty (He sings 3 or 4 numbers—the first 2, "Little Jazz Bird" and "Singin Pete" by the Gershwins)
7. Carnival Dance by Company
8. Swiss Miss (Yodel #)
9. Finale.

My lyrics will be all right, I suppose, but it's too bad I couldn't get some of the niftier-lyric'd songs in, like "M.Y.T. Sascha," "Oil-Well," "Bad Bad Men," "Wonderful How Love Can Understand."

George played at Carnegie Hall Nov. 15 with Whiteman and ran away with the concert as far as the criticisms went. The critics suddenly discovered that they loved classical music again and proceeded to high-hat jazz in their reviews. But where the Rhapsody was concerned they were very enthusiastic. Ernest Newman knocked the concert but was delighted with the Rhapsody and expressed himself in no uncertain terms. . . . Geo. plays it here in Philly tomorrow with P. Whiteman at the Academy of Music. Incidentally tomorrow is Thanksgiving Day and with the holiday matinee Lady, Be Good should play to $9,000 on the day which means $90 for Ira which is not so bad. . . .

Be Yourself left for the road last week, not having done so well for 12 weeks. Scandals leaves next week after a six months run. Primrose is doing well in London —S.L. Devil not so good on the road. George has several offers to do London shows, Saxe (English producer here now) insisting that he leave with him next week. But G. needs a rest and I don't think he will leave until the middle of January. . . .

George is in New York at this writing attending to some new orchestrations for the show. He returns tomorrow for the Whiteman concert. . . .

Honestly you must forgive me: it is now 4:10 by my Waltham, and I'm not responsible for anything I've written.

I've been pretty busy here the past 10 days, writing songs and rewriting verses & choruses.

Well, old boy and girl, you see how it is. It is now 4:15 and they are probably preparing breakfast in the hotel kitchen.

Write me a long letter, telling me all sorts of things, and asking me all sorts of questions.

And with all sorts of love to you both, I pop off.

Iz.

Starring Adele and Fred Astaire.

OH, LADY,
BE GOOD!

Verse 1:

Listen to my tale of woe,
It's terribly sad, but true:
All dressed up, no place to go,
Each ev'ning I'm awf'ly blue.
I must win some winsome miss;
Can't go on like this.
I could blossom out, I know,
With somebody just like you.
So—

Refrain 1:

Oh, sweet and lovely lady, be good.
Oh, lady, be good to me!
I am so awf'ly misunderstood,
So, lady, be good to me.
Oh, please have some pity—
I'm all alone in this big city.
I tell you
I'm just a lonesome babe in the wood,
So, lady, be good to me.

Verse 2:

Auburn and brunette and blonde,
I love 'em all, tall or small:
But somehow they don't grow fond,
They stagger but never fall.
Winter's gone and now it's Spring!
Love! Where is thy sting?
If somebody won't respond,
I'm going to end it all,
So—

Refrain 2:

Oh, sweet and lovely lady, be good.
Oh, lady, be good to me!
I am so awf'ly misunderstood,
So, lady, be good to me.
This is tulip weather—
So let's put two and two together.
I tell you
I'm just a lonesome babe in the wood,
So, lady, be good to me.

THE MAN I LOVE

This tune [as] written . . . didn't quite click. Soon I realized that the verse was better than the chorus. So, I discarded the chorus. In went the verse as the chorus of a new song. I wrote another verse to fit this new chorus

(Left) "Once upon a time I wrote a show called *Lady, Be Good!*
Now, in that score, as in all self-respecting musical comedies, there was
a theme song—the title number. Well, Walter Catlett,
the comedian, sang this song. Walter was a funny man,
and, like a lot of comedians, even his voice was funny
—in fact, it was terrible. And what he did
to 'Lady, Be Good' was nobody's business."—George Gershwin

THE MAN I LOVE

The first edition of "The Man I Love" sold about 1,000 copies.

and my brother Ira set the words. . . . Well, about this time we did a musical comedy, Lady, Be Good! featuring those delightful performers, Fred and Adele Astaire. Imagine my discomfort when the tune received such a lukewarm reception in Lady, Be Good! that we felt obliged to take it from the play.

But my spirits rose again shortly after this when Lady Mountbatten asked me for a copy of the song to take back to England. Soon Mountbatten's favorite band, the Berkeley Square Orchestra, was playing "The Man I Love." Of course, they had no orchestral arrangement, so they "faked" an arrangement—that is, they played the song by ear. It wasn't long before all the dance bands in London had taken up "The Man I Love"—also in faked or ear arrangements. Paradoxically enough, I now had a London song hit on my hands without being able to sell a single copy! You see, we had retired the sheet-music edition of the song when I put it into Lady, Be Good! But I now felt that "The Man I Love" was worthy of a place in any score I might write, so in 1927, when we brought out the first version of the musical comedy Strike Up the Band, this melody was again introduced. And again the melody met with scant success! Apparently "The Man I Love" just lacked that thing, so far as theater presentation was concerned. . . . How-

ever, its out-of-the-theater popularity continued to grow, and after considerable success in London and Paris, "The Man I Love" was sung in New York by an artist who has been almost directly responsible for its American success. I refer to that remarkable personality, Helen Morgan.

George Gershwin

Verse:

When the mellow moon begins to beam,
Ev'ry night I dream a little dream;
And of course Prince Charming is the theme:
The he
For me.
Although I realize as well as you
It is seldom that a dream comes true,
To me it's clear
That he'll appear.

Refrain:

Some day he'll come along,
The man I love;
And he'll be big and strong,
The man I love;
And when he comes my way,
I'll do my best to make him stay.

He'll look at me and smile—
I'll understand;
And in a little while
He'll take my hand;
And though it seems absurd,
I know we both won't say a word.

Maybe I shall meet him Sunday,
Maybe Monday—maybe not;
Still I'm sure to meet him one day—
Maybe Tuesday
Will be my good news day.

He'll build a little home
Just meant for two;
From which I'll never roam—
Who would? Would you?
And so all else above,
I'm waiting for the man I love.

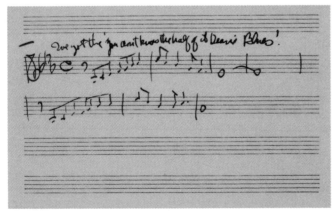

Sketch of the opening musical phrase.

THE HALF OF IT, DEARIE, BLUES

Verse:

(He) Each time you trill a song with Bill
Or look at Will, I get a chill—
I'm gloomy.
I won't recall the names of all
The men who fall—it's all appall-
 ing to me.
Of course, I really cannot blame them a bit,
For you're a hit wherever you flit.
I know it's so, but dearie, oh!
You'll never know the blues that go
Right through me.

Refrain (A):

I've got the You-Don't-Know-the-Half-of-
 It-Dearie Blues.
The trouble is you have so many from whom
 to choose.
If you should marry
Tom, Dick, or Harry,
Life would be the bunk—
I'd become a monk.
I've got the You-Don't-Know-the-Half-of-
 It-Dearie Blues!

Refrain (B):

I've got the You-Don't-Know-the-Half-of-
 It-Dearie Blues.
Will I walk up the aisle or only watch from the pews?
With your permission
My one ambition
Is to go through life
Saying, "Meet the wife."
I've got the You-Don't-Know-the-Half-of-
 It-Dearie Blues!

Verse:

(She) You dare assert that you were hurt
Each time I'd flirt with Bill or Bert—
You brute, you!
Well, I'm repaid: I felt betrayed
When any maid whom you surveyed
Would suit you.
Compared to you, I've been as good as could be;
Yet here you are—lecturing me!
You're just a guy who makes me cry;
Yet though I try to "cut" you, I
Salute you.

Refrain:

I've got the You-Don't-Know-the-Half-of-
 It-Dearie Blues.
Oh, how I wish you'd drop an anchor and end
 your cruise.
You're just a duffer
Who makes me suffer;
All the younger set
Says your heart's to-let.
I've got the You-Don't-Know-the-Half-of-
 It-Dearie Blues!

The step was a complicated precision rhythm thing in which we kicked out simultaneously as we crossed back and forth in front of each other with arm pulls and heads back. There was a lot going on, and when George suggested traveling, we didn't think it was possible.

It was the perfect answer to our problem, however, this suggestion by hoofer Gershwin, and it turned out to be a knockout applause puller. George threw me a couple for my solo routine, too. I liked to watch him dance. It made me laugh.

From Steps in Time
(New York: Harper and Brothers, 1959)

FASCINATING RHYTHM

Verse:

Got a little rhythm, a rhythm, a rhythm
That pit-a-pats through my brain;
So darn persistent,
The day isn't distant
When it'll drive me insane.
Comes in the morning
Without any warning,
And hangs around me all day.
I'll have to sneak up to it
Someday, and speak up to it.
I hope it listens when I say:

Refrain:

Fascinating Rhythm,
You've got me on the go!
Fascinating Rhythm,
I'm all a-quiver.

What a mess you're making!
The neighbors want to know
Why I'm always shaking
Just like a flivver.

Each morning I get up with the sun—
Start a-hopping,
Never stopping—
To find at night no work has been done.

I know that
Once it didn't matter—
But now you're doing wrong;
When you start to patter
I'm so unhappy.
Won't you take a day off?
Decide to run along
Somewhere far away off—
And make it snappy!

Oh, how I long to be the man I used to be!
Fascinating Rhythm,
Oh, won't you stop picking on me?

Adele Astaire introduced "The Man I Love" in Philadelphia. The photo is inscribed, "For *My* George—with love, Adele."

RECOLLECTIONS OF FRED ASTAIRE

During the final rehearsals of the "Fascinating Rhythm" number just before we were ready to leave for the opening in Philadelphia, Adele and I were stuck for an exit step. We had the routine set but needed a climax wow step to get us off. For days I couldn't find one. Neither could dance director Sammy Lee.

George happened to drop by and I asked him to look at the routine. He went to the piano. We went all through the thing, reaching the last step before the proposed exit, and George said, "Now travel—travel with that one."

I stopped to ask what he meant and he jumped up from the piano and demonstrated what he visualized. He wanted us to continue doing the last step, which started center stage, and sustain it as we traveled to the side, continuing until we were out of sight off stage.

The first eight bars were composed in London, when I was there putting on a show. . . . When I returned to New York, I played this theme for my brother Ira. He mulled it over for a while and then came through with a perfect title for the theme. However, it wasn't all as easy as that, for the title covered part of the first bar only, and there was many a hot argument between us as to where the accent should fall in the rest of the words. You see, the theme repeated itself, but each time on a new accent. . . . If you saw the show, you remember that "Ukulele Ike" sang the verse and chorus, followed by a miraculous dance by Fred and Adele Astaire. The song was played by an orchestra which featured Ohman and Arden in the pit—so—who could ask for anything more?

George Gershwin

Frances Gershwin.

RECOLLECTIONS OF FRANCES GERSHWIN GODOWSKY AND LEO GODOWSKY

<u>Leo</u>: I told the Bohemians about George after hearing Whiteman play his music at the Palais Royale around 1922 or 1923. We planned a concert to introduce his music to serious musicians. It was a sad managerial experience. I worked like a dog. The thing was a tremendous success. Kneisel and Goldmark gave me the responsibility. The serious musicians who comprised the Bohemians were shocked, but they were enchanted. Whiteman embraced Goldmark. Everybody embraced everybody. And I, the kid who did all the work, didn't get thanked from anybody.

My father always admired George. He was very much impressed with him not only as a composer but as a pianist as well.

<u>Frankie</u>: Ira used to help me with my homework. I'd leave my compositions that I had written for school in his room, and the next morning I'd wake up and find in red ink he'd written, "You don't put who, you put whom here"—you know, all the corrections. He was very sweet about it. And in my arithmetic. So the big contact I had with Ira in my youth was through my homework. By the time I was old enough to be aware of what George and Ira were doing, they were already on their way.

George was always very conventional. When I was about sixteen, the word darn was very popular, but George wouldn't allow me to use the word. He was just like the older brother in that sense. He once slapped me because I used the word darn.

He was very sweet about reactions to his music. I'd say, "Gee, I don't like that phrase in there." He'd say, "You don't? Do you like it better this way?" We just took that for granted in our household. My mother could say the same thing to him and he would take it that way. It was a wonderful quality. He might come back to what he wanted to do, but he would listen.

<u>Leo</u>: He was absolutely without any conceit whatsoever. People who didn't know him thought he was terribly conceited because he had an innate confidence which was very sensible, justified, completely justified. He knew his talents. He knew his strengths.

<u>Frankie</u>: When he moved to his new apartment on 72nd Street, he said to Kate, our aunt, about our grandmother: "She's so nice. I think I'm going to give her a big party." This was his spirit.

My father had a sort of Russian-Jewish accent. He was a real shnook. He was a darling person. But George would go to parties and tell stories of my father and sometimes would even use a little accent my father would use. He had no false pride about things like that. I must confess when I was a very young girl I was sensitive about it when I introduced my friends. I was just a little bit ashamed sometimes about the way my father sounded.

I used to admire George so much that he had such confidence in himself that this didn't matter and he would take my father places with him. He had no false sense of social values.

But he was difficult in other ways. You couldn't cross him. If you crossed him about something, he didn't like it at all. If he said something and I said, "Well, George, I don't know if I agree with you"—I was eighteen or nineteen or twenty—"What do you mean," he would say, "you don't agree with me?" He could be difficult that way and very clever, too. I used to think he'd make an awfully good lawyer. He would get angles in an argument that cornered you.

When we'd dance, he loved to trick me into rhythms by going off beat and trying to catch me. I had been a dancer and had a very good sense of rhythm, but he was a beautiful dancer. George used to come home after rehearsals with Fred Astaire and would show me the steps he'd learned from Fred. He did it beautifully because he was so well coordinated.

Yes, my mother was unhappy when he made music his work. She thought one son should be a doctor, one son a lawyer—the usual thing, especially in Jewish families. But George was making a living, and by the time Ira was doing it, they didn't object—they understood it a little more. My mother was against it, for George, but she didn't make it so strong that he didn't do it. Yet he would have done it anyway; he had a will of his own.

Then, of course, my mother was very proud of George. She was Mrs. Gershwin. She'd go to restaurants and they'd have to give her special seats and all that. She took it upon herself to have all the honors.

George was very sweet to my mother. He used to come up all the time after he had his own place and bring ice cream. He had a passion for ice cream. He used to bring a lot for everybody, although he would sit down and eat much of it himself. And he'd always send gifts when he was away.

After a date I used to come home to our house at 316 103rd Street and on each floor something different would be going on. To the left of the entrance hall was what had once been a small ballroom. In the middle of that room was the Ping-Pong table, and when I walked in I could see from the overhanging lights a line of peo-

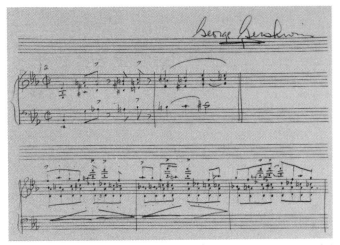

Manuscript of a piano study based on "Fascinating Rhythm" to be included in *George Gershwin's Song-Book* (1932). It is in George's hand and probably dates from 1931—although George may have worked it out, as he did with other variations in the *Song-Book*, at an earlier date for playing at parties.

To "George Gershwin from George" (Duke of Kent, son of King George V)

ple standing around the wall watching intense Ping-Pong tournaments going on. Then I'd walk up to the second floor and there were my parents' bedroom and a little sitting room and the large living room with two pianos where George used to play four hands with Bill Daly, the conductor. And when I came up my mother would be having friends in the living room.

Then I would go up to the third floor. Ira and Leonore

had a suite on that floor, where they would be entertaining. I also had a bedroom on that floor.

George had the fourth floor for himself. He had his music room and a little study and his bedroom there, and he would have his friends over and ask them if they liked the new things he had composed.

The whole house was so alive. Each floor had different color and different personalities.

George had some wonderful parties. He had a house-warming party in the big music room on the second floor when he bought that house. I remember F.P.A. showing slides of different people he had taken, and Katharine Cornell, and Norma Shearer. It was just overwhelming. I remember just sitting off in a corner watching these people, not knowing them, but being overwhelmed.

People would call George if they wanted to come to see him. We had an elevator in the house so they could go directly to the fourth floor, where George would see them.

It was George who brought vegetables into our house because my mother just never paid any attention to these things. He became very conscious of food and what was good for one.

At night we'd all gather down in the kitchen, which was beneath the dining room in the basement of the house. George loved cornflakes. While we all sat around, George would have a big bowl of cornflakes and milk.

Of course, Ira always worked during the night. He would get to bed at six or seven in the morning, then sleep most of the day. He said he liked to work when everything was quiet outside.

George's ability was such that he'd write a song sometimes in just a few minutes. There were very few things he'd have to struggle over. With Porgy and Bess it was different.

When he wrote songs for the shows, he had no routine. He'd get up in the morning after breakfast and he'd go to the piano and a few songs would happen. He'd go to a party and write a song. He'd suddenly play something and say, "This is a nice phrase," and then he would develop it. It all came easily to him.

Ira was a great perfectionist and would work all night on one word sometimes, and there were times when George in five minutes would have a song.

I'll never forget "Fascinating Rhythm"—when George wrote that tricky rhythm. I remember Ira saying, "George, what kind of a lyric can you write for that?" George shook his head. Ira asked again and produced what our father called "Fashion on the River."

TELL ME MORE! (1925)

Tell Me More!, with lyrics by Ira and B. G. De Sylva, opened in the spring of 1925, minus Vinton Freedley and Ohman and Arden at the paired pianos. Out of town Tell Me More! was known as My Fair Lady, perhaps named for the beautiful blonde leading lady, Phyllis Cleveland. Ironically, the original title was thought not commercial enough for Broadway. Certainly My Fair Lady didn't describe Lou Holtz, whose low dialect comedy highlighted the show. Tell Me More! had a modest run into the summer. The critics were more taken with the songs (including one called "Why Do I Love You," whose title would be used two years later in the Kern-Hammerstein Show Boat) than they were with the story. Sample gag line: "I hope," cried Andrew Toombes, "you're stranded on a desert isle with a crossword puzzle and without a dictionary."

WHY DO I LOVE YOU

ALFRED AARONS'
NEW MUSICAL PRODUCTION

My Fair Lady

BOOK BY
FRED THOMPSON & WILLIAM K. WELLS

LYRICS BY
B. G. DeSYLVA
AND
IRA GERSHWIN

MUSIC BY
GEORGE GERSHWIN

STAGED BY
JOHN HARWOOD
DANCES STAGED BY
SAMMY LEE

LETTER FROM IRA
TO LOU AND EMILY PALEY

501 West 110th Street
New York City.
June 8th, 1925.

Dear Lou and Em (and vice versa),

If you haven't heard from me up to now, it's your own fault. That novel, which you modestly called a letter, discouraged me. Ev'ry (excuse it, please—that comes from writing songs) —Every time I wanted to write you (and I have wanted to write almost every other day for the past six months), a vision of fourteen pages of type-writing floated before me. In the time it would have taken me to write a not altogether unworthy response (that is, of course, if I could), I could have done two shows. Well, the answer is, I didn't write, and Tell Me More! was the result. However, after seeing some weekly box office statements of the same, I know I should have written you. If business doesn't improve, I doubt if I'll be able to keep the Lily Wolfs from the door.

I certainly have missed you. For a dozen Saturday nights after you left, I found myself in the Subway, Southward bound. Rather sheepishly I would get off at Times Square, after realizing there was no Saturday Night.—Well, I've had a letter and post cards. That's something.

I got a cable from George the other day saying he was in Paris at the Hotel Chambord. I hope you've seen him. However, as there's the possibility that you weren't in Paris last week, I'll go ahead on the assumption that you haven't, and will tell you all there is to tell on a 95 degree Sunday afternoon, following a week of 95 degree days. . . .

But honestly, I'm having the time of my life on this trip. Yesterday, for instance, I saw the Altman Collection at the Metropolitan Museum, of which no doubt you have heard, and last Sunday I saw the collection at St. John's Cathedral, also of which no doubt you have heard. (If this is humor, make the most of it.) And the theatres! Seventy-two "legitimate" houses for plays about illegit—well, you know how they are in New York. The only drawback is that it is all a trifle expensive. Last night, to give an example, at a place called Moore's (quaint place), I had lamb chops for which they charged me $1.85—but lamb chops! But $1.85. But hang the expense! Yom Kippur Time is nearing, and the natives

tell me the festival is well worth while watching.

Jules Glaenzer is in both Paris and London at the same time.

The De Sylvas and the Genslers have taken a house on the Sound for the Summer, where Bud and Lew are to write a new piece for Schwab and Mandel.

Boy! what a Saturday Night you can have in Paris soon!

Josie,
Rose,
Henrietta (sailed a couple of days ago),
George (if he hasn't left),
Moss of the Gotham (sailed last week for Paris),
Vincent Youmans (	"	"	"	"	"),
Mable (or is it Mabel?) and Bob,
Bela Blau (sails in a couple of weeks—for Budapest, but that doesn't matter),
Fred Jackson (sailed yesterday),
Dukelski,
Foch,
Poincaré, and
Golly.

Baby! How I'd like to be there! How the 20 questions will quest! How the cross-words will be pacified! Save a place and a package of Tareytons for me, will you? I can see it now—Emily serving tea, and Morrie Ryskind just arriving at 2 A.M. There is little to add.

Still—

Irving Caesar has been back some five weeks. If you didn't know, he had been to London and Berlin with Max Dreyfus. What with Arthur writing scenarios, and Irving collecting from 5 companies of Nanette, the Caesars needn't worry about hot Summers or cold Winters.

Morrie Ryskind left his job about 4 months ago and is free lancing, while Phil Charig has been signed up by Harms, while Paul Lannin is still conducting Lady, Be Good! and Bill Daly conducting the Scandals which opens tomorrow and has been written by Bud, Lew Brown and Ray Henderson. . . .

Let's see.

I've been to see Jim and Lillian, Lee and Helen several times. All well.

About my going over. I don't think so. I have it from Freedley that Aarons returns the end of June, and I suppose George'll come back with him, and as George and I are to do a show for the firm to be produced in September, we'll have to get busy as soon as ship docks.

You'd better come back quickly if you want to see Lady. Business all over town has taken a nose dive, and while Lady *hasn't* been affected as much as most, still if it doesn't improve in the coming soon—*there's* no telling. However, if despite this injunction you remain where you are, I won't blame you.

Other than expecting to work with George, I have no plans for the Summer. I may go to camp for a week or so towards the end of the month.

I can go with an easy conscience, as we sold the house June 1st (coming out just a little ahead), and there will be no more rent or deposit slips to make out. Maybe when George returns, he and I will go with Schotzie and Behrman to a place in N.H. they recommend.

I hear you'll be back before September. I hope so. Write me and let me know how the last laps are. Remember me to Rose, Josie, Alice, Henry, Mrs. Eisen, Mable(el) and Bob.

Heaps and oodles of love to you. I have spoken.

Iz.

——————

Time magazine, founded by Henry Luce and Britton Hadden in 1923, appeared with Speaker of the House of Representatives Joseph Cannon on the cover of Vol. I, no. i. The issue sold 9,000 copies. Gradually adding circulation and influence, *Time* featured cover photos in black and white of individuals it believed were significant figures of the day.

ERNEST HUTCHESON

Ernest Hutcheson (1871–1951), Australian-born composer, pianist, and author, was from 1911 to 1944 head of the Piano Department of the Chautauqua Institute.

My personal friendship with George Gershwin, which began when he was "plugging" at the Palais Royal, is one of my most happy memories. . . . It was my good fortune that when he sought a quiet summer retreat to compose the Concerto in F, I was able to provide him with a studio at Chautauqua, New York. It was understood among the piano pupils that his room there was inviolable until four o'clock every afternoon. Promptly at that hour, however, a group of students invaded the room, when George would good-naturedly play and sing to them for a treasured hour. George was a wonderful friend and companion; ever reliable, sympathetic, and unshakably well-tempered.

From The Literature of the Piano
(New York: Alfred A. Knopf, Inc., 1948)

The first American-born musician to appear on the cover of *Time*.

George with Ernest Hutcheson at Chautauqua, New York, summer of 1925.

CONCERTO IN F (1925)

About a year after I wrote Rhapsody in Blue, *Walter Damrosch asked me to write something for his New York Symphony Orchestra. This showed great confidence on his part, as I had never written anything for symphony before. I started to write the Concerto in London, after buying four or five books on musical structure to find out what the concerto form actually was! And, believe me, I had to come through—because I had already signed a contract to play it seven times. It took me three months to compose this Concerto, and one month to orchestrate it. Because it was my first symphonic work, I was so anxious to hear it that I engaged fifty-five musicians to*

read it for me. Charles Dillingham generously gave me the use of the Globe Theatre for this private tryout. Mr. Damrosch, Ernest Hutcheson, and several other musician friends were there, and you can imagine my delight when it sounded just as I had planned.

The first movement employs the Charleston rhythm. It is quick and pulsating, representing the young enthusiastic spirit of American life. It begins with a rhythmic motif given out by the kettle drums, supported by other percussion instruments, and with a Charleston motif introduced by bassoons, horns, clarinets, and violins. The principal theme is announced by the bassoon. Later a second theme is introduced by the piano.

The second movement has a poetic, nocturnal tone. It utilizes the atmosphere of what has come to be referred to as the American blues, but in a purer form than that in which they are usually treated.

The final movement reverts to the style of the first. It is an orgy of rhythm starting violently and keeping to the same pace throughout.

George Gershwin

Among the telegrams received by George Gershwin at the première of his *Concerto in F:*

WONDERFUL ACHIEVEMENT GRAND MASTERFUL GLAD TO BE YOUR PAL KEEP IT UP GEORGE YOU DESERVE EVERYTHING I AM SHAKING YOUR HAND IN SPIRIT FROM THE BOTTOM OF MY HEART

SIGMUND ROMBERG

I HOPE YOUR CONCERTO IN F IS AS GOOD AS MINE IN F SHARP SERIOUSLY GEORGIE I AM ROOTING HARD FOR THE SUCCESS AND GLORY YOU SO RICHLY DESERVE

IRVING BERLIN

DEAR GEORGE WE ARE WISHING FOR A TRIUMPH

EMILY AND LOU

UNDERSTAND CON CONRAD HELPED YOU WRITE AND ORCHESTRATE NEW CONCERTO IF SO I CANNOT HANDLE AUSTRALIAN RIGHTS

ALEX A. AARONS

NIZE BABY EAT OP ALL THE MUSIC LOVERS HEARTS

QUEENIE SMITH

ALL MY BEST WISHES DEAR GEORGE FOR THE MOST TREMENDOUS SUCCESS

NOEL

THE GREAT LEE WISHES THE GREAT GERSHWIN THE GREATEST SUCCESS OF HIS CAREER

THE GREAT SAMMY LEE

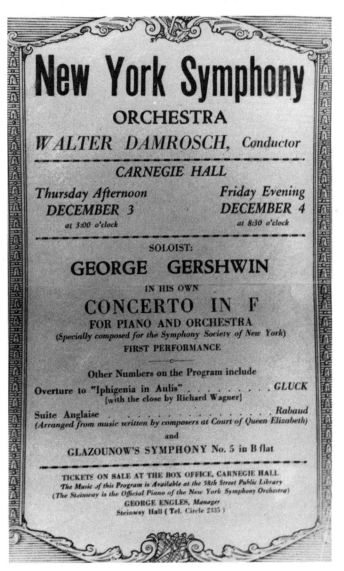

New York Symphony

ORCHESTRA

WALTER DAMROSCH, Conductor

CARNEGIE HALL

Thursday Afternoon
DECEMBER 3
at 3:00 o'clock

Friday Evening
DECEMBER 4
at 8:30 o'clock

SOLOIST:

GEORGE GERSHWIN

IN HIS OWN

CONCERTO IN F

FOR PIANO AND ORCHESTRA
(Specially composed for the Symphony Society of New York)

FIRST PERFORMANCE

Other Numbers on the Program include

Overture to "Iphigenia in Aulis" . . . . GLUCK
[with the close by Richard Wagner]

Suite Anglaise . . . . Rabaud
(Arranged from music written by composers at Court of Queen Elizabeth)
and

GLAZOUNOW'S SYMPHONY No. 5 in B flat

TICKETS ON SALE AT THE BOX OFFICE, CARNEGIE HALL
The Music of this Program is Available at the 58th Street Public Library
(The Steinway is the Official Piano of the New York Symphony Orchestra)
GEORGE ENGLES, Manager
Steinway Hall (Tel. Circle 2335)

Conferring on *135th Street*. Left to right: Deems Taylor, Ferde Grofé, Paul Whiteman, Blossom Seeley, and George.

TIP~TOES (1925)

1925 and 1926 saw the great Florida land boom, during which hundreds of thousands of Americans flocked to the state, frantically buying property at exorbitant prices in the expectation of selling it later for a fantastic profit. Eventually the bubble burst, but while it lasted it influenced all aspects of our popular culture. Songs were written about Florida, shows had their locales set there. Everything bright and hopeful was Florida.

The Gershwins' modest contribution to the craze was *Tip-Toes*, their 1925 show for Aarons and Freedley. The setting was Palm Beach, and the hero (Allen Kearns) was a glue king with a $7,000,000 fortune. The heroine (Queenie Smith) and her two conniving uncles (Andrew Toombes and Harry Watson, Jr.) were a trio of stranded vaudevillians. One of the secondary roles was played by Jeanette MacDonald and somehow it all ended early enough for commuters to catch the 10:47 to Scarsdale. Alexander Woollcott called it Gershwin's best score to date. "It was of course Gershwin's evening, so sweet and sassy are the melodies he has poured out for this *Tip-Toes*, so fresh and unstinted the gay, young blood of his invention."

Ira too was pleased with his own progress in lyric-writing. *Tip-Toes*, Ira recalled, "contained longer openings, many of the songs had crisp lines, and the first-act finale carried plot action for four or five minutes." Ira received praise in a fan letter from a distinguished fellow lyricist:

When, the other night at the Guild's menagerie, Joe Meyer told me a departing guest was Ira Gershwin, I should have brushed aside your friends, grasped you by the hand, and told you how much I liked the lyrics of Tip-Toes, but, probably because the circus clowns inspired a speedy retreat from a too acute consciousness, I had imbibed more cocktails than is my wont, and so when the coffee-loving Mr. Meyer pointed you out, all I could say, "Zat so!"

Your lyrics, however, gave me as much pleasure as Mr. George Gershwin's music, and the utterly charming performance of Miss Queenie Smith. I have heard none so good this many a day. I wanted to write you right after I had seen the show, but—well I didn't rush up to you at the Guild Circus either.

It is a great pleasure to live at a time when light amusement in this country is at last losing its brutally cretin aspect. Such delicacies as your jingles prove that songs can be both popular and intelligent. May I take the liberty of saying that your rhymes show a healthy improvement over those in Lady, Be Good!

You have helped a lot to make an evening delightful to me—and I am very grateful.

Thank you! And may your success continue!

Lorenz Hart

SWEET AND LOW-DOWN

Verse:

There's a cabaret in this city
I can recommend to you;
Peps you up like electricity
When the band is blowing blue.
They play nothing classic, oh no! down there;
They crave nothing else but the low-down there.
If you need a tonic,
And the need is chronic—
If you're in a crisis,
My advice is:

Refrain:

Grab a cab and go down
To where the band is playing;
Where milk and honey flow down;
Where ev'ry one is saying,
"Blow that Sweet and Low-Down!"

Busy as a beaver,
You'll dance until you totter;
You're sure to get the fever
For nothing could be hotter—
Oh, that Sweet and Low-Down!

Philosopher or deacon,
You simply have to weaken.
Hear those shuffling feet—
You can't keep your seat—
Professor, start your beat!

Come along, get in it—
You'll love the syncopation!
The minute they begin it,
You're shouting to the nation:
"Blow that Sweet and Low-Down!"

Queenie Smith, star of *Tip-Toes* (1925).

"That Certain Feeling"—Queenie Smith and Allen Kearns.

THAT CERTAIN FEELING

Verse 1:

(He) Knew it from the start,
Love would play a part,
Felt that feeling come a-stealing
In my lonesome heart.
It would be ideal
If that's the way you feel,
But tell me is it really real?
You gave me

Refrain 1:

That certain feeling—
The first time I met you.
I hit the ceiling,
I could not forget you.
You were completely sweet;
Oh, what could I do?
I wanted phrases
To sing your praises.

That certain feeling—
The one that they all love—
No use concealing
I've got what they call love.
Now we're together
Let's find out whether
You're feeling that feeling too.

Verse 2:

(She) I have symptoms, too,
Just the same as you.
When they centered, when they entered
In my heart, I knew.
Brighter is the day
Since you've come my way;
Believe it when you hear me say:
You gave me

Refrain 2:

That certain feeling—
The first time I met you.
That certain feeling
I could not forget you.
I felt it happen
Just as you came in view.
Grew sort of dizzy;
Thought, "Gee, who is he?"
That certain feeling—
I'm here to confess, it
Is so appealing
No words can express it.
I cannot hide it,
I must confide it:
I'm feeling that feeling too.

58

"When to the lisping of a hundred tapping feet in 'Sweet and Low-Down' a forest of trombones suddenly added their moan, then the Liberty Theatre quietly but firmly went mad."—Alexander Woollcott, New York *World* / (Overleaf) George in the mid-20s; the girl is unidentified.

THESE CHARMING PEOPLE

Verse 1:

*(Hen) We must make it our ambition
To live up to our position
As we take our places in society.*

*(Al) When those million dollar blokes pass,
I will never make a faux pas;
I will show them I am full of pedigree.*

*("Tip-Toes") And the lady isn't born yet
Who can beat me at a lorgnette,
When I'm honoring the op'ra at the Met.*

*(All) So if you're not social winners,
Don't invite us to your dinners—
We must warn you we'll be awful hard to get.*

Refrain 1:

*We'll be like These Charming People,
Putting on the ritz,
Acting as befits
These charming people:
Very debonair,
Full of savoir-faire.
I hear that Mrs. Whoozis
Created quite a stir:
She built a little love-nest
For her and her chauffeur.
If these people can be charming,
Then we can be charming, too!*

Verse 2:

*(Hen) Please recall, if you've forgotten,
That my father was in cotton,
And my family is truly F.F.V.*

*(Al) Merely social climbing varmints!
Ours was made in undergarments,
So you see before you one who's B.V.D.*

*("Tip-Toes") If that's pedigree, enjoy it!
My old man came from Detroit,
So I'll have you know that I am F.O.B.*

*(All) In our veins there runs the true blood!
When we mingle with the blue blood,
The Four Hundred will become Four Hundred Three.*

Refrain 2:

*We'll be like These Charming People,
Putting on the ritz,
Acting as befits
These charming people:
Very debonair,
Full of savoir-faire.
It seems that Mr. Smythe-Smythe
Had no children, till
Some twenty-seven turned up
To listen to the will.
If these people can be charming,
Then we can be charming too!*

SONG OF THE FLAME (1925)

Song of the Flame opened on December 30 to a warm critical reception. Walter Winchell reported, "It is a colossal and gorgeously spectacular production....Resplendent mountings and costumes, added to the magic of Herbert Stothart's and George Gershwin's rich musical score, swept the new production to the top of the current and imposing list of operettas." The book and lyrics were by Otto Harbach and Oscar Hammerstein II.

RECOLLECTIONS OF TESSA KOSTA

George Gershwin was particularly friendly toward me, I think, because I knew of a young lady he was keen about. George made several trips to Rochester to see her and she also came to New York to see him. For a while I thought it might be a serious romance. I liked George. Although we had very little contact with him during rehearsals, he did, as I recall, play for us a few times. He was very attractive, easy to work with, and cooperative in every way. I remember George saying that I should be complimented that I was going off to star in the tour after Broadway. Actually, they didn't think of replacing me because I don't think they could find anyone else who could sing against ninety Russians in the chorus.

Arthur Hammerstein had heard me in another show before he hired me for Song of the Flame. In those days we had no hidden microphones in the footlights, and musicals required people who could sing.

Herbert Stothart, a talented composer who also wrote music for the show, was the conductor. He loved to drown out everybody with the orchestra. He practically ruined the girls' voices with all the extra brass he was featuring. One day Hammerstein went backstage after Stothart had just drowned me out, and started swearing at Stothart. "What the hell are you trying to do? If I can't hear Kosta, I can't hear anybody!"

Mabel Schirmer.

"We've had no particularly thrilling news till the famous George arrived.... We met him at the station and escorted him home in triumph. He promptly got comfortably installed in our guest room and we began to talk —well, you can imagine the excitement, the joy of having him all to ourselves....

Our days consisted of breakfast together... then lying around the house, playing the piano, the Victor, and our vocal chords till about 2 or 3 P.M. .... The evenings we usually spent with other people.... George saw a lot of Eddie Knopf, Irving Berlin, Michael Arlen and many other acquaintances. We went to a French musical show, Pas sur la Bouche, which gave George some ideas about the Paris musical comedy stage—such ideas that he walked out in the middle of the 2nd Act because his bed at our house was more comfortable to sleep in than the theatre seat.... An evening at the Prize Fights was really a great success—best fights George had seen in years. An afternoon at the Steeplechase racing in the Bois de Boulogne was satisfactory in that having lost on every race previous, we made a comeback on the last one that recouped nearly all our losses. . . .

One evening we had quite a lot of fun by inviting George Antheil and his wife to dinner. Eddie Knopf and a Miss Bamberger, a friend of his, also present. Antheil is that young super-radical composer Mabel has written you about. He tried to give George an idea of his stuff but since most of it is scored for 16 grand-player-pianos, with an obligato by a boiler-factory, why I suppose it wasn't a very fair test. Then our George played excerpts from different things—Show numbers, Rhapsody and Concerto. . . . a pleasant evening was had by all. . . .

So after a splendid week we accompanied George to London. We went on a Saturday. The next afternoon Paul Whiteman gave his first concert in Albert Hall— sold out and a popular success—tho' the critics didn't take it very seriously or if they did they were generally unfavorable. George had two faults to find about the concert. First, Whiteman murdered the Rhapsody by playing it in a lot of crazy tempi that were nothing at all like the original performances. . . . Secondly, during the concert someone stole George's hat and overcoat which were hanging up in the back of the box we were in. So I had to lend him my cane so that the poor boy wouldn't look absolutely naked walking around the streets. Eventually he

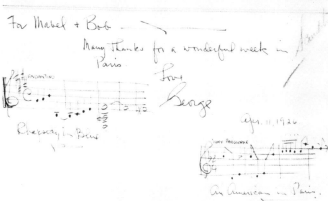

Photograph inscribed to Mabel and Bob Schirmer.

64

the tunes and since that night all the orchestras in London play nothing but Lady, Be Good! music, for you know they have up till now prevented them from playing the music in the hotels and dancing places in order not to have it get stale before the show opened. When the Astaires drove up before the show the police had to break a way thru the crowd to let them get to their dressing-room. When it was over the audience sat in their seats for a full 10 minutes after the final curtain—speeches by the Astaires and Billy Kent—the greatest enthusiasm you can imagine—every entrance and exit was greeted by literal cheering such as I have only heard previously at football and baseball games. It will be packed for at least a year....

After the show he took us to a party given by Sir Alfred Butt at the Embassy Club (most fashionable night club of London). Sir Alfred and Lady Butt, Lord Lathom, many other prominent people, members of the cast, and the Astaires themselves were at the party.... We left about 2 A.M., but George was up till 8 we heard! Some evening.

RECOLLECTIONS OF KAY SWIFT

In the early years I was a terrible snob about musical-comedy music and didn't like any at all. I liked blues, spirituals, fast music, but not musical comedy. It never would have occurred to me to write any. One day long before I met George my brother came to our house and put on some records of "Stairway to Paradise" and "Do It Again!" They seemed to me vastly different from anything else I'd heard. I thought, "Well, that's not like any other show music anybody's writing." It reflected the way I felt that things should be unpredictable. They were patently predictable at that time until George's music. I thought that one had to have this element of surprise in all music, any music. Shoot for the top. Why not? When I heard those records his music seemed fresh and new, instantly identifiable. I loved the verse of "Stairway to Paradise" and the whole thing was so alive. It had so much vitality.

I met him when he was brought to my apartment by Marie Rosanoff, who was a marvelous cello player. She brought Jascha Heifetz, Sam Chotzinoff, Pauline Heifetz. George came with Pauline, and Ira came along. It was great fun. That was quite a bit before Oh, Kay! 1925, I believe.

There was a period of three or four months during

found an old hat, he ordered a new overcoat and Mabel and I gave him as a parting token of esteem a handsome cane with rhinoceros horn handle—all the rage in London now.

That evening (Sunday) we witnessed the dress rehearsal of the Rhapsody in Blue as a ballet—done at the Midnight Follies Cabaret in the Hotel Metropole. The following evening the first performance took place, which we also attended as George's guests. Truly the Rhapsody makes a splendid ballet—a Greek classic idea—nymphs and satyrs, Pan etc., all the costumes and lighting in bright blue. The orchestra only has 11 pieces—the pianist stumbled thro the solo passages, the clarinetist cracked at the top of that opening upward slide, the trombone blew sour notes from time to time—but in spite of everything it was very effective indeed and made a big hit.

Wednesday night was the opening of Lady, Be Good! —It was a triumph.... Everyone went away whistling

Kay Swift.

With Estelle Brody in London.

alive, and he was not in the least embarrassed the way some composers are. I'm an old easy-embarrasser myself.

He heard his music simultaneously through his and yours and anyone else's ears. In fact, he would sit right down in this room while we were talking and be doing something on the piano and he would not be a bit embarrassed whether we listened or did not listen. He wasn't uptight about it at all in any way. It was amazing.

He played with exactly the same enthusiasm if he played for people who would appreciate it or anyone who would listen to it. It was an electric experience. It was plain to see that something important was happening. That great strong quality of excitement would prevail on everyone. I've seen people who were very old or little kids just get up and walk over to the piano, and they hadn't expected to—they were hypnotized. It was like the Pied Piper.

He was enthusiastic about other people's music. I never saw a composer who cared that much about everybody else's music. He could think his way into the point of view of any composer who he thought was good at all. He was very enthusiastic about Hoagy Carmichael's music. We bought a copy of the "Washboard Blues" and played it seven or eight times right then and there. He loved it.

The shows were always much more of a headache because there were such changes. He was very anxious that the show as a whole be successful. He didn't think of the music as standing out, because he was too good a showman. And knew well there was no use having a great score if it bombed.

He didn't go into great guilt about anything. He'd just fix it if he didn't like it. He'd try it different ways. He'd say, "I think I like this ending better than that one," and he would try it out on people. He was very open-minded. I'm sure Ira will back me up on this.

I love to hear Ira sing. I love to see him dance. He does a little dance. He would sing and do a little turn around with his eyes shut. Entirely beguiling.

which I didn't see him at all. I had just met him once. He came to a party and played for a long time and then said, "Well, I've got to go to Europe now." And I thought that was rather charming.

I remember George with much the most impact from the spring of 1926, when he'd come back from Europe.

He and his music were all of a piece—he was exactly like his music. And he had the face, personality, and the looks, and he moved exactly the way you'd expect from his music. I never saw anyone who was more like his music. As a matter of fact, I think people are like their work. I once met Ravel when he came over and wanted to meet Gershwin. He looked exactly like his music. You knew he'd written it.

George was somebody I'd rather hear play than anybody. He went right to the piano and sat down with joy. The first thing, I think, was "Kickin' the Clouds Away" and then some things from Tip-Toes, "Looking for a Boy" and "That Certain Feeling," and "The Man I Love." He used to play a chorus very brilliantly and then transpose to a lower key where he could sing it. He was always able to give an idea of the song, whether it was in Ezio Pinza's range or Lily Pons'. He would always sort of manage. He'd do it so it would make you want to imitate him if you did it again yourself.

Sometimes he would sit down and say, "I started a little theme something like this," and he'd play it and it would be very interesting. Immediately it would be

(Facing) Ira, Frankie, Mama, and Papa Gershwin.

(Overleaf) "In front of our family's hotel in Belmar, New Jersey, June 1926. My mother gave us a party for our sixth wedding anniversary. George decided that we should all be photographed. First he grouped us all exactly where he wanted us. Then he put himself in front."—Emily Paley
Front row: Marjorie Paley, Morris Strunsky, Elsie Payson, Howard Dietz, Cecelia Hayes, Arthur Caesar, Emily Paley, Phil Charig, Leonore Gershwin, Ira, George Backer, and Harold Goldman.
Second row: Cecelia Ager, Mrs. Bela Blau, Mischa Levitzki, Henrietta Malkiel Poynter, Jim Englander, and Anita Keen.
Third row: Milton Ager, Lou Paley, Bela Blau, S. N. Behrman, Mrs. Arthur Caesar, English Strunsky, Harold Keyserling, and Barney Paley.
Standing, extreme right: Albert Strunsky, proprietor of the hotel and father of Emily, Leonore, and English.

George with Josefa Rosanska.

George's derrière, Lou, Josie, and Emily.

George and Lou.

Leonore, Ira, and Emily.

Lee.

George.

OH, KAY! (1926)

During its preparation, *Oh, Kay!* was known variously as *Mayfair*, *Miss Mayfair*, and *Cheerio!* It reunited Guy Bolton and P. G. Wodehouse on the book and starred Gertrude Lawrence, who had captivated New York in *André Charlot's Revues* of 1924 and 1925. Since most theatergoers were all too familiar with speakeasies and bootleggers, they enjoyed almost any entertainment that dealt with Prohibition. Such gags as "Don't criticize a bootlegger's English if his Scotch is all right" dotted the libretto, for which George and Ira wrote what was probably their best and most successful score to date.

Percy Hammond remarked in the *Herald Tribune* that "all of us simply floated away on the canoodling notes of 'Maybe' and were brought back to Broadway by such flesh and bony anthems as 'Fidgety Feet' and 'Clap Yo' Hands.'" "Someone to Watch Over Me," which Gertrude Lawrence sang to a rag doll, "wrung the withers of even the most hardhearted of those present."

Gertrude Lawrence and Victor Moore, "Ain't It Romantic."

DO, DO, DO

Verse:

(He) *I remember the bliss*
Of that wonderful kiss.
I know that a boy
Could never have more joy
From any little miss.

(She) *I remember it quite;*
'Twas a wonderful night.

(He) *Oh, how I'd adore it*
If you would encore it. Oh—

Refrain:

Do, do, do
What you've done, done, done
Before, Baby.
Do, do, do
What I do, do, do
Adore, Baby.

Let's try again,
Sigh again,
Fly again to heaven.
Baby, see
It's A B C—
I love you and you love me.

I know, know, know
What a beau, beau, beau
Should do, Baby;
So don't, don't, don't
Say it won't, won't, won't
Come true, Baby.

My heart begins to hum—
Hum de dum de dum-dum-dum,
What you've done, done, done
So do, do, do
What you've done, done, done
Before.

Verse 2:

(She) *Sweets we've tasted before*
Cannot stand an encore.
You know that a miss
Who always gives a kiss
Would soon become a bore.

(He) *I can't see that at all;*
True love never should pall.

(She) *I was only teasing;*
What you did was pleasing. Oh—

Refrain 2:

Do, do, do
What you've done, done, done
Before, Baby.
Do, do, do
What I do, do, do
Adore, Baby.

Oscar Shaw and the girls in *Oh, Kay!* (1926).

Gertrude Lawrence and the boys performing the title song of *Oh, Kay!* (1926).

Oscar Shaw, Gertrude Lawrence, and Victor Moore.

Let's try again,
Sigh again,
Fly again to heaven.
Baby, see
It's A B C—
I love you and you love me.

(He) You dear, dear, dear
Little dear, dear, dear,
Come here snappy
And see, see, see
Little me, me, me
Make you happy.

(She) My heart begins to sigh—
Di de di de di-di-di,
So do, do, do
What you've done, done, done
Before.

SOMEONE TO WATCH OVER ME

Verse:

There's a saying old
Says that love is blind.
Still, we're often told
"Seek and ye shall find."
So I'm going to seek a certain lad
*   I've had in mind.*
Looking ev'rywhere,
Haven't found him yet;
He's the big affair
I cannot forget—
Only man I ever think of with regret.
I'd like to add his initial to my monogram.
Tell me, where is the shepherd
*   for this lost lamb?*

Refrain:

There's a somebody I'm longing to see:
I hope that he
Turns out to be
Someone who'll watch over me.

I'm a little lamb who's lost in the wood;
I know I could
Always be good
To one who'll watch over me.

Although he may not be the man some
Girls think of as handsome,
To my heart he'll carry the key.

Won't you tell him, please, to put on
*   some speed,*
Follow my lead?
Oh, how I need
Someone to watch over me.

"In the second act of *Oh, Kay!* the glamorous Gertrude Lawrence had the stage to herself to sing 'Someone to Watch over Me.' It was all very wistful, and, on the opening night, somewhat to the surprise of the management, Miss Lawrence sang the song to a doll. This doll was a strange-looking object I found in a Philadelphia toy store and gave to Miss Lawrence with the suggestion that she use it in the number. That doll stayed in the show for the entire run."—George Gershwin

George began 1927 with a series of performances of the *Concerto in F* that received predictable reviews: there was almost universal praise for George as a pianist and, with few notable exceptions, criticism of the work itself for falling between the realms of pure jazz and pure symphonic music. Yet audiences everywhere responded favorably and orchestras continued to program the piece and were always eager to have George's presence on their programs.

After his exhausting round of appearances, George went on a skiing trip to Canada's Laurentian Mountains with his friend Jules Glaenzer, the affable, social-lion vice-president of Cartier's, whose parties attracted the so-called elite of business, café society, and the theater and music worlds. After a brief vacation in Palm Beach, George appeared with the Cincinnati Symphony under Fritz Reiner in March. Once again he was soloist in the *Concerto in F.*

In an effort to find a quiet place in which to work, away from the frenetic bustle of New York, the Gershwins (George, Lee, and Ira) rented a house in Ossining, New York, where they received visits from such friends as Emily and Lou Paley and Mabel and Bob Schirmer. It was in Ossining that the brothers wrote the first version of *Strike Up the Band.*

On the farm in Ossining.

Watercolor of Lee by Ira—Ossining. April 23, 1927.

(Facing) Ira, Mabel, George, and Emily.

George.

The newlyweds—Mr. and Mrs. Ira Gershwin.

(Facing) Mabel and George.

Emily and George.

FUNNY FACE (1927)

Aarons and Freedley were delighted by the success of *Lady, Be Good!* and decided to try another musical starring the Astaires. This time they engaged drama critic Robert Benchley to collaborate on the show. The script was so weak, however, that Benchley bowed out, saying, "Gosh, how can I criticize other people's shows if I've had anything to do with this?" Other writers were engaged, a new comedy character was created (to be played by Victor Moore), and the title, originally *Smarty*, was changed to *Funny Face*. After an extended tryout, with many revisions and changes in the score, the show opened the new Alvin Theatre in New York City (its name derived from the first syllables of each producer's first name) on November 22, 1927. In Wilmington, Delaware, the week before, the show had grossed a slim $6,000. Opening week at the Alvin, however, grossed $44,000.

Benchley was chided by the other aisle-sitters for "having concocted a musical comedy plot about stolen jewelry, after long since showing his critical teeth in *Life* whenever such a plot by another came along." In his *Life*

review on December 3, 1927, Benchley remarked ruefully: "Every once in a while we drop in at *Funny Face* to count the house and figure out how much money we lost (it is well up in the four figures already) and we are putting it with the money we didn't put on Tunney and are planning to buy a town car with it."

'S WONDERFUL

Now, in song lyric writing, sound is one of the most important things, and I don't think anybody surpasses my brother, Ira, when it comes to inventing song titles. He fancies abbreviation. For example, "Sunny Disposish" and "'S Wonderful." And don't ever let Ira hear you say "It's Wonderful." Just "'S wonderful, 'S marvelous."

George Gershwin

Verse:

(He) *Life has just begun:*
Jack has found his Jill.
Don't know what you've done,
But I'm all a-thrill.
How can words express
Your divine appeal?
You could never guess
All the love I feel.
From now on, lady, I insist,
For me no other girls exist.

Refrain:

'S wonderful! 'S marvelous—
You should care for me!
'S awful nice! 'S Paradise—
'S what I love to see!
You've made my life so glamorous,
You can't blame me for feeling amorous.
Oh, 's wonderful! 'S marvelous—
That you should care for me!

Verse:

(She) *Don't mind telling you,*
In my humble fash,
That you thrill me through
With a tender pash.
When you said you care,
'Magine my emosh;
I swore, then and there,
Permanent devosh.
You made all other boys seem blah;
Just you alone filled me with AAH!

Refrain:

'S wonderful! 'S marvelous—
You should care for me!
'S awful nice! 'S Paradise—
'S what I love to see!
My dear, it's four leaf clover time;
From now on my heart's working overtime.
Oh, 's wonderful! 'S marvelous—
That you should care for me!

(Facing) Betty Compton, Adele Astaire, Gertrude McDonald, and Fred Astaire.

ALEX A. AARONS AND VINTON FREEDLEY
PRESENT
FRED AND ADELE ASTAIRE
IN THE
NEW MUSICAL COMEDY

Smarty

MUSIC BY
GEORGE GERSHWIN
BOOK BY
FRED THOMPSON
AND
ROBERT BENCHLEY
LYRICS BY
IRA GERSHWIN
DANCES AND ENSEMBLES BY
ROBERT CONNOLLY
BOOK DIRECTED BY
EDGAR MacGREGOR

What Am I Gonna Do
The World Is Mine
'S Wonderful
Let's Kiss And Make Up
How Long Has This Been
Going On

NEW WORLD MUSIC
HARMS

82

HIGH HAT

Verse:

(Solo) When a fellow feels he's got to win
  a girlie's handie,
He will send her loads of flowers, books
  and tons of candy.
(Chorus) The overhead is big;
Oh, how they make us dig!
(Solo) No use stepping out that way,
  the thing to do is lay low;
You can't win by treating her as if
  she wore a halo.
(Chorus) What is your solution?
Tell us if you can.
(Solo) Here's my contribution to man:

Refrain:

(Solo) High hat!
You've got to treat them high hat!
Don't let them know that you care;
But act like a frigidaire—
You'll win them like that,
(Chorus) Stand pat!
Put on your gayest cravat,
(Solo) But keep your feet on the ground.
Oh boy! How they'll come around!
Just treat them high hat!

"High Hat": Fred Astaire's first routine featuring top hat and tails.

(Overleaf) Golfing with Adam Gimbel and Everett Jacobs
at Palm Beach, Florida.

(Overleaf, right) With producer Edgar Selwyn.

RECOLLECTIONS OF EMIL MOSBACHER

In 1910, when Emil Mosbacher was thirteen years old, he delivered newspapers for the New York Commercial. Since his route included many Wall Street brokerage houses and he was fascinated by and quickly absorbed what he saw, he soon found employment there and within a few years had achieved great success.

Now seventy-six, the still trim and vigorous Mosbacher was one of George Gershwin's closest friends.

George was friendly with Everett and Randy Jacobs, who, in turn, were friendly with the producers Aarons and Freedley. The Jacobs brothers had money, and I would bet even money—I didn't say I'd lay five to one—that the Jacobs boys invested a lot in the Aarons-and-Freedley shows.

It was through the Jacobs brothers that I met George. I think it was around 1927, soon after George returned from opening a show in England, I had a country place in White Plains, near Armonk, and George and I soon became friends.

I loved being with George, partly because his life was so different from mine. I enjoyed that different world very much. I never met a person who had more feeling for people than George did. There was no phoniness about it, and he never did anything intentionally, of which I am aware, to hurt anyone.

God knows, he loved his family; I never knew a person more devoted to his family than George was. And George loved no one more than he loved Ira. He was

With Emil Mosbacher.

obsessed with Ira and always figuring out ways to get Ira to work because he respected Ira so much and needed him too.

Yet, because George liked parties and always had to be the life of the party, he couldn't understand why Ira preferred to stay home. There was one party that really bothered George—he talked about it for months. It occurred at the Kit Kat Club in London. The Prince of Wales was there, but not Ira. George would complain that "it was good enough for the Prince of Wales but not good enough for my brother." Ira was shy, had a wife he loved, and didn't need the limelight or all that lionizing.

I never saw George as nervous on opening nights as he was in a golf tournament. Every time he'd win a match, he'd come to me the next morning and moan, "I hope I lose today. I'm so nervous that I can't sleep." He was never that way about a show.

George was a low-nineties golfer. He was strong from all that piano playing—you know, he wasn't a finger player, he was an arm player—but George was a slicer. He always wanted me to teach him to keep his head from moving on his swing. He wanted me to join a golf club on Long Island that he'd paid $5,000 to join, but I wouldn't do it. So he joined my club, Quaker Ridge, so we could play together.

We went to Canada one time with two golf pros to watch the Canadian Open. Even there George was after me to help him improve his game. Now, I could play pretty close to guys like Johnny Farrell and, on a good day, even Gene Sarazen. I would try to get George to take lessons from them, but those guys always put the responsibility right back on me—and since they were nice enough to play golf with me, I was stuck.

George could drive about two hundred yards off the tee, but it was really less because he lost distance from his slice. George was at his best pitching and putting, and he was a pretty good putter, especially on sand greens, where the roll was slower. We played with a lot of guys, including Howard Hughes, who was a pretty good golfer himself.

Golf was relaxation for George and he always wanted to break eighty. Sometimes when we played alone or were with a group of friends, I used to kick George's ball ahead to help him break eighty. If George was talking to someone, I would kick the ball about six feet nearer to the cup without his knowing. Once or twice he caught me, and he'd say, "My ball went—" And I'd cut him off, I wouldn't let him finish his sentence. "George," I'd say, "that's no way to talk."

ROSALIE (1928)

Rosalie was a curious juxtaposition of operetta, musical comedy, revue, and extravaganza, built around the magical presence of Marilyn Miller. The score was a collaboration between Sigmund Romberg and George Gershwin; the idea made Alexander Woollcott "think we shall soon have a novel written by Harold Bell Wright and Ernest Hemingway." Woollcott added: "I can report in a large freehanded way, however, that Brother Romberg has written his usual thunderous choruses which you enjoy while they are being roared at you and forget by the time you reach the lobby. Brother Gershwin has written at least two jaunty songs which follow you further up the street."

The show drew its inspiration from the recent well-publicized visit to New York of Queen Marie of Romania. Another leading character in the show was modeled after Charles Lindbergh.

In *Rosalie* the most appealing ingredients are the most home-grown. The show was most successful where the Gershwins' musical comedy, Ziegfeld's and Urban's extravaganza, the Glorified American Girl, and Miss Miller worked together. These served to accentuate the archaic nature of the operetta elements and helped to weaken the spell that operetta had exerted on theatergoers for so many years. *Rosalie* ran for 335 performances, perhaps because of good luck generated by its name—which was that of Ziegfeld's mother.

A rehearsal of *Rosalie* in late 1927: Jack Donahue, Marilyn Miller, George, Sigmund Romberg, and Florenz Ziegfeld.

"There comes a time once in every two or three years when the vast stage of that playhouse [the New Amsterdam Theatre] begins to show signs of a deep and familiar agitation. Down in the orchestra pit the violins chitter with excitement and the brasses blare. The spotlight turns white with expectation. Fifty beautiful girls in simple peasant costumes of satin and chiffon rush pellmell onto the stage, all squealing simple peasant outcries of 'Here she comes!' Fifty hussars in fatigue uniform of ivory white and tomato bisque march on in columns of four and kneel to express an emotion too strong for words. The lights swing to the gateway at the back and settle there. The house holds its breath. And on walks Marilyn Miller."—Alexander Woollcott, New York World, January 11, 1928

HOW LONG HAS THIS BEEN GOING ON?

Verse 1:

(He) As a tot, when I trotted in little velvet panties,
I was kissed by my sisters, my cousins and my aunties.
Sad to tell, it was Hell—an Inferno worse than Dante's.
So, my dear, I swore, "Never, nevermore!"
On my list I insisted that kissing must be crossed out.
Now I find I was blind, and, oh lady, how I've lost out!

Refrain 1:

I could cry salty tears;
Where have I been all these years?
Little wow,
Tell me now;
How long has this been going on?

There were chills up my spine,
And some thrills I can't define.
Listen, sweet,
I repeat:
How long has this been going on?

Oh, I feel that I could melt;
Into heaven I'm hurled—
I know how Columbus felt
Finding another world.

Kiss me once, then once more.
What a dunce I was before!
What a break—
For heaven's sake!
How long has this been going on?

Verse 2:

(She) 'Neath the stars at bazaars often I've
had to caress men.
Five or ten dollars then I'd collect from all those
yes-men.
Don't be sad, I must add that they meant
no more than chessmen.
Darling, can't you see 'twas for charity?
Though these lips have made slips, it was never really
serious.
Who'd 'a' thought I'd be brought to a state that's so
delirious?

Refrain 2:

I could cry salty tears;
Where have I been all these years?
Listen, you—
Tell me, do:
How long has this been going on?

What a kick—how I buzz!
Boy, you click as no one does!
Hear me, sweet,
I repeat:
How long has this been going on?

Dear, when in your arms I creep—
That divine rendezvous—
Don't wake me, if I'm asleep,
Let me dream that it's true.

Kiss me twice, then once more—
That makes thrice, let's make it four!
What a break—
For heaven's sake!
How long has this been going on?

To Sarah,
Best love
Marilyn

RECOLLECTIONS OF MABEL SCHIRMER

Since my husband and I lived in Europe, mostly in Paris, during the five years after the Rhapsody in Blue, we saw George only on his trips to Europe in 1926 and '28 and on a brief visit we made to the States in 1927. I felt that he took his fame quite casually and handled it with considerable grace. I never felt he was impressed at all with the celebrities he met.

As you can see from the inscribed photo [page 63] he already had written part of the opening phrase of An American in Paris at the time he visited us in Paris in April 1926, over two years before the piece was finished. We had him practically all to ourselves that trip because he was living with us and it was just great.

He told me that in New York he had met Ravel, who had given him a letter of introduction to Nadia Boulanger. I went with him to see Nadia, who said she would not take him as a pupil because he had a natural musical talent that she wouldn't dare disturb for anything.

We often went shopping together and George was wonderful about getting gifts for his whole family. I remember we went to Rodier's, where he bought some beautiful scarves. The most fun of all came when he went shopping for taxi horns. We walked all along the Avenue of the Grande Armée, where all the automobile shops used to be. We went to every shop we could find to look for taxi horns for An American in Paris. He wanted horns that could sound certain notes. After he left Paris, George wrote asking me to find more, and I did.

RECOLLECTIONS OF FRANCES GERSHWIN GODOWSKY

When George took me along on the trip to Europe in 1928, I felt like Cinderella. It was the first time something had happened to me, as I was a very modest little

A party for Maurice Ravel's fifty-third birthday: Oscar Fried, conductor, Eva Gauthier, the party's hostess, Ravel, Tedesco, conductor of the San Carlos orchestra, and George.

girl. George was very proud, pleased, and sweet, like a nice older brother. During that time I met Leo, Papa Godowsky, and Mrs. Godowsky. Ira and George loved to play poker. I didn't play poker and Leo said he didn't care to, and so he used to take me to a café and we'd sit and talk. I was so shy that I didn't have any idea he was interested in me.

I remember a big night for George at the Kit Kat Club and a party at Elsa Maxwell's where someone asked George to accompany me. Cole Porter was there and he finally persuaded George to let me appear in his revue at Les Ambassadeurs. George played for me at the opening night and it was so informal in this formal place that it was just like being at home. I remember the piano was on a little raised ledge; I sat down on a step. It was a wonderful trip on which the whole world opened up to me.

GEORGE GERSHWIN

Feb. 28, 1928.

Dear Mabel:

Received your letter, and glad you are going to be excited. This letter may not reach you until after I cable you the time of our departure, arrival, etc. but I thought I might let you know about some possibilities of our plans.

We sail on the Majestic on March 10th, going straight to London, and expect to stay in London from a week to ten days. Then we are coming to Paris, and from the on our plans are rather vague. I expect that we will stay in Paris for about two weeks and then go someplace where the climate is right, and where I can do some work. If, however, I find somebody to study with in Paris, I may take a place on the outskirts of Paris and stay there most of the time.

Ira and Lee are going to travel around more than I am and see some of the sights, but their plans are also indefinite. (Lee wants me to tell you that she is bringing over with her shoes, stockings, brassieres and records for you).

If I go to the south of France, the kind of place I would like to take would be a house surrounded by a few cottages, where we could all live together and yet be separated if I wanted to work. In looking over some of the places, as you are doing, I wish you would keep this in mind. Also, I'd like to find, when I get to Paris, a valet who speaks several languages, and possibly drives a car.

I am looking forward to this trip more than any other I have ever taken, because it is the first time I have ever gone abroad without having to put on a show, and I will much more time to myself.

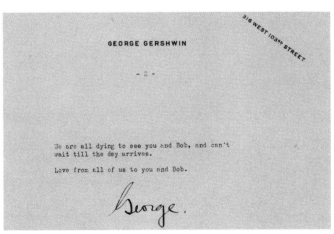

GEORGE GERSHWIN

- 2 -

We are all dying to see you and Bob, and can't wait till the day arrives.

Love from all of us to you and Bob.

George.

THE GERSHWINS' 1928 EUROPEAN TRIP

March 9, the day before sailing, was marked by a visit to Harms, the Gershwins' publisher, and discussions about a new musical for Ziegfeld based on *East Is West* and tentatively titled *Ming Toy*. That evening Lee and George joined Emily and Lou and many others at a farewell party given by Kay and Jimmy Warburg that lasted until five A.M. Later that morning the Gershwins, George, Ira, Lee, and Frankie, embarked on the *Majestic* for a trip to Europe that was to last until the middle of June. Also on board was the lyricist Leo Robin, who, like Ira, was making his first trip abroad. Lee's friend Henrietta Malkiel would join the group later in Paris.

The Atlantic crossing was relatively uneventful: breakfast at one P.M., shuffleboard, reading, and hearts. George played the piano for violinist Albert Spalding and met Dr. Rosenbach, the eminent book collector, who was a friend of Jerome Kern's. Ira read novels and kept a diary because he felt guilty about taking such a long vacation and having no work to show at the end of it.

DIARY OF IRA GERSHWIN

March 15, 1928. At about 5:30 George played in the lounge of the restaurant (having been asked by a girl last night). He played for over an hour to an audience of about 30, all very enthusiastic, especially Spalding and his accompanist—Benoit. . . . In lounge until 1 o'clock George Copeland playing for the few people there at that hour. Then George Gershwin played with his usual success, people coming in from on deck to hear him.

The ship arrived in England on March 16 and the next day George called Gertie Lawrence, the brothers visited Chappell, their English publisher, and then woke up their friend Phil Charig, who had written songs with Ira for *Americana* in 1926 and for an English production, *That's a Good Girl*, which was about to begin its tryout tour. The 18th was devoted to sightseeing, and on the 19th the group saw *That's a Good Girl* starring Jack Buchanan and Elsie Randolph. On the 20th George received visits from Vladimir Dukelsky (Vernon Duke), Desmond Carter, an English lyricist who had written with him in the past, and author Guy Bolton. Ira continues:

92

Frankie.

Lee and Ira, 1928.

George's last passport.

March 20, 1928. Walked (George and I) to 52 Maddox Street where we found Phil [Charig] and Leo [Robin] (they had preceded us) looking at a new Mercedes. Told us it belonged to Vince Youmans who had got in from Paris yesterday. Went upstairs and found Vince and Max Dreyfus. Pretty soon Kern came in with Russ Bennett. It was strictly a Harms affair. George, Leo, Phil, Dreyfus, Kern, Bennett, Youmans and myself. To hotel. Then as George went to Lady Mountbatten's for dinner, Phil, Leo, Frankie, Lee and I went out to dinner without him—to Kettner's.... Vince told us this day that he was going to do East Is West which is very strange as we thought we were going to do it.

March 21, 1928. George . . . told us he had spoken with the Prince of Wales for 20 minutes last night at the Embassy Club.

On the 22nd Ira reported that he had met Arnold Bennett and Frederick Lonsdale, while George and Frankie had gone to the George Gershwin Night at the Kit Kat Club and to the opening of the Noël Coward show *This Year of Grace*. On the 23rd, after Frankie and George had dinner with Noël Coward, all the Gershwins went to see *This Year of Grace*, George and Frankie for the second time. Ira's reaction: "All in all, a great production for one man to do."

March 24, 1928. At 5 to George's room where met Lady Mountbatten and a Mr. Murphy [Gerald?]. Kern dropped in, also Bolton & [Lee] Ephraim. Dinner at Gertie Lawrence's in hotel. Gertie & [Bert] Taylor—host and hostess—we didn't dress (the 4 of us) as we'd been in George's room too late but the others did of course— (there was also Mr. and Mrs. [André] Charlot and a girl friend of Gertie's). A lovely meal with plenty of wine and cocktails, smoked salmon, consommé, filet of sole, duck, apple sauce, asparagus, sweet, coffee, cigars, brandy—swell. If Ziegfeld were king he'd change the name of the country to Lox—Glorifying the Smoked Salmon & Featuring Filet of Sole. After dinner to our rooms, dressed—put on my new white tie & to His Majesty's [where Oh, Kay! was ending its successful London run]. Got in late, towards end of 1st Act—"Do! Do! Do!" was on. Sat in box. After Kern & others had told us show was poor, it came as an agreeable surprise to find we rather liked it—wasn't bad at all, though Gertie did clown too much. In finale she cried a little, it was real, too—and had to make a speech. Back stage, where Taylor was drenching everyone with magnums of

champagne. Home—packed—Goodbye to Phil. Looking forward to tomorrow and Paris. To bed about 4 A.M.

PARIS

Arriving in Paris on March 25, the Gershwins were met at the Gare St. Lazare by Bob and Mabel Schirmer and Josefa Rosanska. The Majestic Hotel would be their base for the next four weeks. On the 27th Ira found Josie and the Kolisch Quartet in George's room per-

Inscribed photograph from Lady Mountbatten.

forming chamber music by Arnold Schoenberg and Franz Schubert. The noted composer Alexander Tansman, who was almost like an official host to George while he was in Paris, was also present.

On the 29th George and Ira visited Salabert, their French publisher, where the general manager, Fekerte, volunteered to help George locate rare first editions of all of Claude Debussy's piano works. During the day Ira managed to get lost for several hours.

On March 31 the *Rhapsody in Blue* was performed by the Pasdeloup Orchestra, conducted by Rhené-Baton, with the piano part divided by Wiener and Doucet. Ira described the concert and its aftermath in his diary.

March 31, 1928. Although the performance was a

Inscribed photograph from Alexander Tansman, Paris, March 1928.

distorted one, at its conclusion the house was full of cheers and bravos. George expecting catcalls had left quickly for the bar to wait for us, but when I saw Wiener on the platform looking anxiously over the audience and gesticulating to Baton, I knew they wanted to see George (how they knew G. was in the audience was a mystery to me as we had only heard about the concert that morning). I called him and he was rushed to the stage where he received a small ovation. An encore was announced and of all things Wiener and Doucet played a verse and three choruses of "Do! Do! Do!" from Oh, Kay! This went with great éclat and the audience wanted more. It was the first time I ever heard of an encore by soloists at a symphony program. In the lobby, later, Baton apologized for the performance, saying they hadn't had much time for rehearsing the Rhapsody, that they had to use the stock [jazz band] arrangements, that he had no orchestral score and had to use a piano copy, etc. Anyway, despite the poor rendition, the reception was thrilling.

April 2, 1928. Found George being interviewed by a reporter, Wales, of the Herald. After 10 minutes of this another reporter came in. Phillips of the Tribune. Both wanted George's plans, etc. Had lunch. Later in after-

noon [Dimitri] Tiomkin and Albertina Rasch came in. Told George of the all-Gershwin concert that would be given by him in June at the Opera House. . . . Met Fritz Kreisler at Carlton.

April 3, 1928. 1st real sunshiny day. Mabel up & went shopping with George while Leo Godowsky took Lee, Frankie & myself to the Louvre. Stayed about an hour doing the wing nearest the river, mostly Italian primitives, Da Vincis, Hals, Van Dycks, Rubens, Tintorettos. A Memling near the entrance I loved. Whistler's mother. etc. etc. . . . Had dinner in hotel room with George, Frankie & Lee. Then the 4 of us with Mabel to Tansman's apartment where were E. Robert Schmitz & wife, [Jacques] Ibert & wife, Tiomkin, Albertina Rasch, a couple of other composers and wives and 3 critics. George played about 2 hours without stopping to the success and enthusiasm he is accustomed to. . . .

April 6, 1928. Strike Up to be done next year. Dukelsky came in for an hour or so. Argued with George about parts of American in Paris. Saying that George was 1928 in his musical comedies and in most of his concert music but in latter he allowed himself to become somewhat saccharine in spots.

In afternoon George and I walked along Avenue Kléber, bought a lot of fruit, a quart bottle [of] Cointreau & quart bottle of wonderful Spanish port—all for $6. Walked to Trocadero, then over bridge to Eiffel Tower. There was quite a line but we joined it and in 15 minutes were in the elevator along with some 50 others, all French excepting for about a dozen Germans, and an English tutor with 2 boys. It was 8 Francs apiece to le sommet. . . . I had never been so high up in a structure (22 stories or so was my highest in N.Y.) and it was terrific. I was afraid to walk the few feet to the railing, but finally did. George complained of peculiar sensations in his stomach & other portions. The view of course is magnificent. We walked around, kidding one another, but really greatly impressed. After 5 minutes or so we took it more casually and leaned over the railings. I must say the other visitors seemed to take it very naturally, one couple making love, the girl giving the man what we called as kids, "feels." George had a caricature made for 25 F—not bad. Then down in the elevator to the 2nd landing from which we decided to walk. It was 26 flights down to the 1st landing and 12 down from there —38 in all and boy how my legs trembled when we finally got to the street. It took me 3 blocks walking to get them straightened out.

On April 8 the Gershwins, minus George, visited Versailles, while George went to visit Prokofiev with Vernon Duke. In the evening Ira noted in his diary that they "walked through Montmartre for a while. One girl hung on to George until Lee and I walked up when she disappeared." On the 13th Ira noted that "I lost $8.20 to George at Casino, but outside of that 4/13 wasn't bad. Weather lovely." On the 14th there was a party at Albertina Rasch's. "Fray & Braggiotti played & then George—big hit as usual."

RECOLLECTIONS OF MARIO BRAGGIOTTI

When I was about seventeen, I went from Boston, Massachusetts, to Paris to study music at the Conservatory of Music, and there I met a young fellow student named Jacques Fray. We formed a piano-duo team and we were perhaps the first to play both classical and popular in the same program.

When we were in Paris, we heard about the young American composer George Gershwin coming to the French capital to get the atmosphere and write An American in Paris. Gershwin was a hero of Jacques' and mine, and we wanted to meet him.

So we went to his hotel one morning and boldly knocked on his door. He opened it. He was in his dressing gown, and his hair was all kind of up in what I call the composer's style. I said, "Mr. Gershwin, my name is Mario and this is Jacques. We are music students and we just would like to meet you." "Well, boys, that's fine," he said, "come right in." He was very welcoming. There was a Steinway piano right in the middle of his room and I noticed on the piano a collection of taxi horns —from those old-fashioned taxis they used in the Bataille de la Marne. There were about twenty of them lying there. I hadn't been to New York in a few years, so I thought this was some new American eccentricity or fad. I didn't know what to make of it.

"Oh," he said, "you're looking at these horns. Well, in the opening section of An American in Paris I would like to get the traffic sound of the Place de la Concorde during the rush hour, and I'd like to see if it works. I've written the first two pages of the opening. Jacques, you take this horn—this is in A flat. Mario, you take this—it's in F sharp. Now, I'll sit down and play, and when I go this way with my head, you go 'quack, quack, quack' like that in that rhythm."

So we took the horns, and there we stood, nervous and excited, and for the first time we heard the opening bars

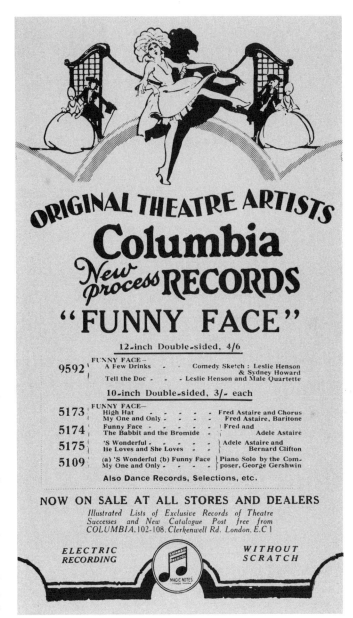

Fray and Braggiotti were the duo pianists for many of these recordings.

of An American in Paris—a lanky American walking down the Champs-Elysées. He captured the atmosphere, the feeling, the movement, the rhythm so perfectly.

Well, when we came to the horn parts, he nodded and we came in. That was the first and last time that I ever played French taxi horns accompanied by such an illustrious composer.

And with that our friendship with George Gershwin began. He said, "Boys, I'd like to hear you play." So we went to Jacques Fray's apartment. He had one of those Pleyels with a keyboard at each end with the crossed wires. We played some of Gershwin's songs and he said, "Boys, how would you like to play in my new show in London? We are opening there in a couple of months. The name of it is Funny Face, starring Fred and Adele Astaire." We didn't know who Fred and Adele Astaire were, but we said, "It sounds terrific," and it was our first job. We went to London and had another

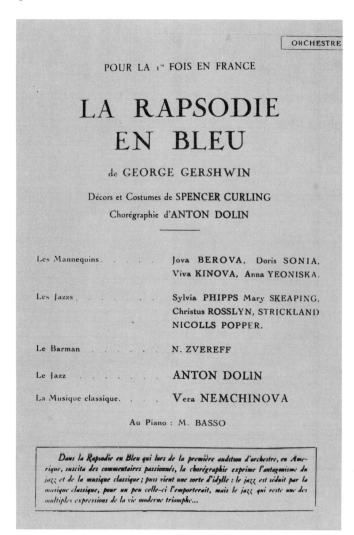

Pleyel piano with the crossed wires, raised and even with the stage.

It was a fantastic opening night, I remember. Those were the plush days. It ran for a year and we became very friendly with Fred and Adele.

DIARY OF IRA GERSHWIN

On April 15, 1928, while Ira played poker and enjoyed an excursion to Longchamps, George and Alexander Tansman visited M. and Mme. Rhené-Baton.

April 16, 1928. After dinner the girls & George dressed—I wore my blue serge and the 4 of us to the Theatre des Champs Elysees on Avenue Montaigne to see the Ballet Russe of Anton Dolin, an Irishman [performing La Rhapsodie en Bleu de George Gershwin]. The theatre is one of the loveliest I've ever seen —it was finished in 1913—and has much more charm than the Ziegfeld. . . . A jazz band of 5 girls played in the bar during the 3 entr'actes.

April 21, 1928. Up at 10 to American Express. . . .

Walked a bit. In afternoon Cole Porter, the Tansmans & Sam Dushkin to lunch in our salon. Very nice. Porter asked me if Frankie cared to go on stage. I said "Ask her." "Of course," said Frankie. So Porter called up the manager of his show, Revue des Ambassadeurs, and made an appointment for 10 P.M. Then he played some of his new songs—good. . . . Evening at 8:30 the 4 of us to Albertina Rasch's where with the Godowskys we had a fancy Russo-French meal ending with a floating pudding of which I had two portions. George & Frankie left about 10 o'clock to see the French manager. They returned [to Mme. Rasch's] about 1 A.M. with a contract. "How much?" "Might have been better," said George. But when I saw it I hardly believed it—$200/wk for an unknown. We all celebrated by having more drinks & music until 3 when we left for the Majestic.

BERLIN

On April 22 the Gershwins (minus Frankie, who had stayed in Paris) and Henrietta Malkiel left Paris for Berlin. Arriving on the 23rd, they went to the Hotel Esplanade. "At 8 o'clock we (George, Lee & I) walked a few blocks to the Bechstein Salle where Josie [Rosanska] was to play. . . . She played Bach, Chopin, Alban Berg, De Falla, Ravel & Stravinsky. . . . I thought, and so did George, that she had played exceptionally well and her program was most interesting." On April 24 George had his first meeting with the German composer Kurt Weill. The next day he had lunch with Franz Lehar, the great operetta composer. That evening the Gershwins enjoyed a Yiddish musical, *Die Reise Benjamins des Dritten.* On the 26th they traveled to Potsdam to visit the palace where Frederick the Great lived as a boy, and in the evening saw the classic Russian film *Ten Days That Shook the World.*

VIENNA

On the 27th the Gershwin party left Berlin for Vienna. They were met by operetta composer Emmerich Kálmán, who took them all to a gala luncheon at Sacher's, where a jazz band played *Rhapsody in Blue.* Later they went to see *The Duchess of Chicago* and passed an agreeable evening with Kálmán, a most congenial host.

April 29, 1928. Breakfast in room. Kálmán called for him at 1 and George played for him for an hour. To

J. G. M. + Mme. Rhene Baton, Tansma

George with M. and Mme. Rhené-Baton and Alexander Tansman.

Café Sacher, Vienna, April 28, 1928. On banquette, from left to right: Ira, Lee, George, Emmerich Kálmán, Henrietta Malkiel. In front: librettists Grünwald and Brammer, and two newsmen.

Kálmán's for lunch. [Ferenc] Molnár and Dr. [Albert] Sirmay. Saw Jonny Spielt Auf.

April 30, 1928. After breakfast Lee and I for a walk, a short one because it was raining. Back to Hotel and in dining room found George with Dick Simon and the author of a new book Dick was to publish, a book about a deer [Bambi]. . . . In evening were visited by Dick Simon, Josie, Henry, Madame Pohlner, Lady Zernier, Fredie Groeble. The 1st 4 and George went out to a new wine garten and returned about 11:30, a bit cockeyed.

> FROM A LETTER FROM
> RICHARD SIMON
> TO HIS BROTHER ALFRED

May 2, 1928

On Sunday evening after I returned to the hotel, there was a note from Henrietta Malkiel that she was in town with the Gershwins, in the same hotel in fact, and would I look them up.

So on Monday morning I met G.G. ("bluebeard") in the lobby of the Bristol. He seemed delighted to see me, and we arranged to have lunch and dinner. G.G., [Felix] Salten, Henrietta and I lunched at the Bristol, and after lunch George (if I may refer to him as such, and since we call each other by our so-called Christian names, why not?) and I went to the concert hall to hear a demonstration of John Hays Hammond Jr.'s piano with an organ effect. Only pretty good. But to show you what popularity George has, Hammond insisted on sending him one of his grand pianos when he returned to New York. G. told me also (another example) that at the end of the trip across the Atlantic, among other presents he received was a large box which contained a separate present and a separate letter for each day the boat was on the water. . . .

Then we returned to the Bristol where he has a suite including a Grand Piano. He played me quite a large

George, Count Felix Von Luckner, Gene Tunney, Max Schuster, Robert Ripley, Dick Simon, Sidney Lenz, Hendrik van Loon, and Hubert Wilkins.

portion of a piece he's working on now, a symphonic poem entitled An American in Paris—*and boy if the slow movement theme isn't going to throw the public for a row of W.C.'s then I'm just tone deaf. It has "The Man I Love" backed off the boards by several kilometers. It's called the Homesickness Theme. He is using regular taxi horns in the orchestra. The first performance is supposed to take place in Paris on May 25th, and if I can possibly be there to hear it, I most certainly will be. George tells me that "The Man I Love," having been released for popular consumption, will not appear in any show, but that* Strike Up the Band *will probably be put on in New York. By the way, you'll be interested to know that G.G. likes "The Man I Love" best of all the tunes he has written.*

In the evening a party of us went to a Heurigen. . . . Speaking of Wiener Wälzer, I could just see George's mouth water when we came in. They are not only played by the orchestra, but the crowd hums along. . . . George wasn't at all anxious to go. He wasn't feeling especially well, wasn't shaved and felt he had to work. But we dragged him into a taxi, and after he was there for a few minutes, stomach, shave and work were completely forgotten. He told me he was glad we kidnapped him. After we returned, about 12, he started working again.

DIARY OF IRA GERSHWIN

May 2, 1928. Breakfast in room, then for a walk with Lee. While looking at a window a couple stopped near us, the woman pointing to Lee, said to the man, "Now there's a well dressed Viennese woman."

May 3, 1928. George to lunch with Lehár. George meets Alban Berg.

May 5, 1928. Kálmán came up, then half an hour later George & Josie returned from Kolisch's where they had heard Alban Berg's string quartet with Berg one of the auditors.

On May 6 George returned to Paris for the opening of *La Revue des Ambassadeurs,* Cole Porter's floor show in which Frankie was a featured performer. The show had a gala opening on May 10 with the cream of café society in attendance. Frankie sang Gershwin songs and for the opening was accompanied by brother George, who gallantly put aside his personal opposition to Frankie's stage career for the occasion.

From Alban Berg, May 5, 1928, with a quotation from his *Lyric Suite.*

Inscribed photograph from Franz Lehár, Vienna, May 3, 1928.

Also on May 6, Lee, Ira, and Henry left Vienna for Budapest, where Lee was taken ill. They managed to get back to Vienna, but could not return to Paris in time for Frankie's opening. Upon Lee's recovery they motored to the Riviera and spent several days at Antibes. Driving back through the French countryside, they reached Paris on May 22.

May 22, 1928. At the Villa Majestic we found George, then Frankie, who told us she was out of the

With Leo Reisman at the Paris Opéra.

show with many others because practically nothing could be heard above the dishes, and they were going in for a visual, rather than aural show. George was getting along nicely with the American in Paris. *In the evening we went to a big party at the Tiomkins; where were Jules Glaenzer & frau, Russell Bennett and likewise, [Maurice] Chevalier, a host of painters, writers, musicians & critics (Mabel, Josie, Franzl, Henry [Vladimir] Golschmann, [Lazare] Saminsky, Dukelsky, Tansman, [Arthur] Honegger). George, as usual knocked them for a goal and we left about 3:30.*

May 24, 1928. Saw Mabel, [Samuel] Dushkin, Golschmann at George's suite. George got a cable from Ray Goetz about the Diaghilev Ballet wanting American in Paris *but he had already promised N.Y. to Damrosch—Philly to Stokowski. (The other day, George, alone in his room, called the waiter and said, "Salmon—you know, saumon, lox, fish"—here he made motions as if swimming—"Fish, rouge" the waiter nodded, "oui monsieur!" hurried out and in 10 minutes returned with lobster.)*

LEO REISMAN

Leo Frank Reisman (1897–1961) was the leader of what Jerome Kern called the "string quartet of dance orchestras," one of the finest musical groups to grace the air waves, recording studios, and posh New York and Boston night spots of the 1920s, '30s, and '40s. Born in Boston, this classically trained violin prodigy was admired for his musicianship by Maurice Ravel, Darius Milhaud, and Charles Martin Loeffler. Reisman was regarded with even greater fervor by Kern, Gershwin, Berlin, Coward, Arlen, and other musical-theater writers, both for his scrupulous regard for their own musical intentions and for his orchestra's elegant and refined performances of their songs.

On February 19, 1928, Reisman and an augmented orchestra gave Boston its equivalent of Paul Whiteman's historic Aeolian Hall concert with an evening of "symphonic" jazz that concluded, appropriately enough, with Gershwin's *Rhapsody in Blue.*

While on holiday in Paris, Reisman and his wife Lillian met George by chance at the Paris Opéra. Lillian Reisman recalls that during the next few May days they "lox-hunted" together through Parisian stores and restaurants in pursuit of the elusive smoked salmon that George loved and for which he had become homesick during his European trip.

DIARY OF IRA GERSHWIN

May 29, 1928. Performance of Concerto *with Tiomkin. George in a box with Elsa Maxwell. In the intermission I met Jules Glaenzer who blew me to champagne, my share of which was 20 francs. After the performance . . . we went to Laurent's on Avenue Gabriel where we found in the garden under an awning a crowd of 30 or so; let me see—Cole Porter, Clifton Webb, Mr. Honegger, Frances Hunter, Bea Lillie, Jules & Kendall (looking beautiful), Tansman, George and some countess, our hostesses Elsa Maxwell, Grace Moore, Fray & Braggiotti and others. Had supper and then all adjourned to the dance room where were two Steinways whereon Fray & Braggiotti played, then Porter, Lillie, Moore and George entertained in turn. We left about 2:30.*

RECOLLECTIONS OF VERNON DUKE

On May 29th, I took both Diaghilev and Prokofiev to hear Gershwin's piano concerto played by Dimitri Tiomkin at a concert in the Paris Opéra conducted by Vladimir Golschmann. Whether the fault lay with the French musicians, notoriously allergic to jazz, or with Mr. Tiomkin, an able pianist, but certainly no Gershwin, I cannot say. Diaghilev shook his head and muttered something about "good jazz and bad Liszt," whereas Prokofiev, intrigued by some of the pianistic invention, asked me to bring George to his apartment the next day. George came and played his head off; Prokofiev liked the tunes and the flavorsome embellishments, but thought little of the concerto (repeated by Gershwin), which, he said later, consisted of 32-bar choruses ineptly bridged together. He thought highly of Gershwin's gifts, both as composer and pianist, however, and predicted that he'd go far should he leave "dollars and dinners" alone.

From Passport to Paris *(Boston: Little, Brown and Company, 1955)*

DIARY OF IRA GERSHWIN

May 30, 1928. In evening took Mabel, Bob, Henry & Lee to Casenouve's. After dinner we drove to Dushkin's, 160 Rue de l'Université, where was a musical party: a Concerto for two violins by Bach, then Vladimir Horowitz played, then George. Nice formal people there and a nice formal party. Later Horowitz played his study on Carmen, *a marvelous technical ac-*

George, in Paris.

complishment. Dushkin also played Short Story & Blue Interlude *accompanied by George.*

May 31, 1928. To George's room after breakfast—found there Josie, the Quartet, the Tansmans and George playing for a critic who I learned was Ernest Newman of Berlin.

Had dinner in room. In evening to Mrs. Byfield, 179 Rue de la Pompe to a party given in honor of the Gershwins. We got there about 11 (Lee, Bob, Mabel & I); Frankie & Golschmann about 11:30 and George, who had been at a party at Baron Rothschild (which one I don't know), about 12. It was a large party, 200 easily being present and a mixture of Mayfair, the Rialto and Left Bank; Blythe Daly, Bea Lillie, Deems Taylor, Margot & Ernie Goldfinger, Helen Laidow, Fray & Braggiotti, some counts and barons, Nadia Boulanger, Dushkin, Russell Bennett, Orloff, George Slocombe, Arthur Moss, a couple of guys with monocles and dirty shirts, a band, 8 caterers, Madame Andre (Boskowitz), Tansmans, Man Ray, Lawrence Vail, Sylvia Beach, the

Tiomkins, Mike Shepard, Dersow, Mrs. Marx, Josie, Kolisch, Alex Aarons & Gilbert Kahn & wives, Arthur Kober, Elsa Maxwell, etc. etc. Stayed until 4, drank lots of champagne and didn't feel it. A good party—very lively. The dawn was coming up as we got into a cab with Deems Taylor and Henry.

June 3, 1928. Went to George's room about 2 and found Lee, Mabel and Henry helping him pack to go to London. Alex [Aarons] came up and Tiomkin and Golschmann and Dagmar [Godowsky] and Dushkin and Riviere and the Tansmans and and and.

While George was in London with Alex Aarons and Gertrude Lawrence to discuss their fall show, Lee and Ira remained in Paris. On June 13 they began their return home, meeting George at Southampton. A gala dinner given by Gertrude Lawrence was the highlight of the voyage back to New York.

George arrived in New York on June 18, 1928, with most of the piano score of *An American in Paris* already sketched out, but, as usual, it proved impossible to work quietly in his New York apartment. Fortunately, he was able to use Kay and Jimmy Warburg's cottage at Bydale, and there on November 18 he completed the orchestral score of *An American in Paris*.

TREASURE GIRL (1928)

Treasure Girl was the 1928 Alvin-Gershwin show. The score was good, but *Treasure Girl* did poorly at the box office and, as Ira Gershwin recalled, "after a couple of months took us all to Cain's Warehouse [the scenery graveyard]." This time Gertrude Lawrence was trapped in an idiotic story about a treasure hunt. "The probable reason for the demise of this show," added Ira, "was that Gertrude Lawrence . . . was here cast as one so avid for money and position that she even double-crossed her favorite young man. Not even [Gertrude] could overcome the, shall we say, bitchiness of the role." Clifton

Webb, Mary Hay, and Walter Catlett were among those present in this, the last of the so-called "smart" Gershwin musicals of the late twenties.

I DON'T THINK I'LL FALL IN LOVE TODAY

Verse 1:

(She) Just think of what love leads to:
Maybe to marriage—maybe divorce.
(He) Into a jam love speeds two;
It may be Nature's course,
But we mustn't be
Like the other sheep.
(She) Better far if we
Look before we leap.
(Both) Perhaps it's better after all
If we don't answer Nature's call.

Refrain 1:

(He) Who knows if we'd agree?
You like you and I like me.
I don't think I'll fall in love today.
(She) When evening shadows creep,
I like dancing—
(He) I like sleep.
I don't think I'll fall in love today.
(She) Still it might be fun to bring
Your carpet slippers;
When the dinner bell would ring,
I'd serve a can of kippers.
(He) Don't you know how to cook?
(She) I could look in a book.
(He) I don't think I'll fall in love today.

Verse 2:

(He) Love is a fever chronic;
We can avoid it—why take a chance?
(She) Safer to be platonic;
Why burn up with romance?
(He) Adam without Eve
Happiness had known,
So suppose we leave
Well enough alone.
(She) Imagine signing up for life,
Then finding peas roll off his knife.

Refrain 2:

(He) D'you sleep with window shut?
(She) Window shut.
(He) Charming, but—
I don't think I'll fall in love today.
(She) Did you pick that cravat?
(He) I did that.
(She) Here's your hat.
I don't think I'll fall in love today.
(Both) It's as clear as A B C
We're not agreeing;
Incompatibility
The judge would be decreeing.
When all is said and done,
Seems we two will never be one.
Let's, oh, let's not fall in love today!

George with Gertrude Lawrence, *Treasure Girl* (1928).

Manuscript of "I've Got a Crush on You."

ROYALTY STATEMENT
FROM
HARMS, Inc.
62-64 WEST 45TH ST., N. Y.

To GEORGE GERSHWIN

Below will be found the number of copies sold, and the amount of royalty due, from publication ending December 31, 1928

NUMBER OF COPIES D	TITLES	SOLD	COPIES RETD.	RATE	AMOUNT	TOTAL
	TREASURE GIRL					
863	WHAT ARE WE HERE FOR					
1,477	WHERES THE BOY HERES THE GIRL					
1,536	OH SO NICE					
2,242	I DON'T THINK I'LL FALL IN LOVE TODAY					
2,347	GOT A RAINBOW					
3,599	FEELING I'M FALLING					
1,694	KRAZY FOR YOU			3¢	$412.74	
13,758						

"The big money."

MECHANICAL ROYALTY STATEMENT
FROM
HARMS
INCORPORATED
62-64 WEST 45TH STREET
NEW YORK

For GEORGE GERSHWIN

For the three month ending December 31, 1928

No. OF RECORDS OR ROLLS D	TITLES	AMOUNT	TOTAL
	TREASURE GIRL		
	FEELING I'M FALLING		
4,936	Columbia		
22,728	Victor		
27,664	at 2¢	553.28	
	GOT A RAINBOW		
22,728	Victor at 2¢	454.56	
94	De Luxe at 10¢	9.40	
	K-RA-ZY FOR YOU		
94	De Luxe at 2¢	1.88	
		1,019.12	
	25% of...........		$254.78

Most of the record sales from *Treasure Girl* were from the Ohman-and-Arden Victor recording.

Smith Far in Lead With Writers, Actors

Gov. Smith has all the breaks over Herbert Hoover in a straw vote reported to-day by Vanity Fair and taken among a hundred writers, artists and Broadwayites.

The poll stands as follows:

For Smith: F. P. Adams, Sherwood Anderson, Adele Astaire, Fred Astaire, Gertrude Atherton, Clara Bow, Clare Briggs, Heywood Broun, Charles Chaplin, Eddie Cantor, Irvin S. Cobb, Jane Cowl, Frank Craven, Jack Donahue, Ruth Draper, Finley Peter Dunne, John Erskine, Edna Ferber, Mrs. Fiske, Gilbert Gabriel, Norman-Bel Geddes, George Gershwin, John Gilbert, Alma Gluck, Rube Goldberg, John Golden, Texas Guinan, Helen Hayes, John Held jr., Arthur Hopkins, Sidney Howard, Owen Johnson, Robert T. Jones jr., George S. Kaufman, Alfred A. Knopf, Walter Lippmann, Anita Loos, John McCormack, W. O. McGeehan, Charles MacArthur, Kenneth Macgowan, Willard Mack, Edgar Lee Masters, H. L. Mencken, Edna St. Vincent Millay, Alice Duer Miller, Gilbert Miller, Helen Morgan, George Jean Nathan, Charles Norris, Dorothy Parker, Maxfield Parrish, Channing Pollock, Cole Porter, John Riddell, Ellery Sedgwick, R. E. Sherwood, Lee Simonson, Simeon Strunky, Deems Taylor, Charles Hanson Towne, Jim Tully, June Walker, John V. A. Weaver, Al Woods, Peggy Woods, Alexander Woollcott.

For Hoover: George Abbott, Bruce Barton, Robert C. Benchley, John Alden Carpenter, Frank Crane, Cecil B. De Mille, Corinne Griffith, Walter Hagen, Percy Hammond, Walter Hampden, Jesse Lasky, Neysa McMein, Frederick MacMonnies, Christopher Morley, Kathleen Norris, Edmund Pearson, Otis Skinner, Norma Talmadge, Booth Tarkington, Laurette Taylor, William T. Tilden 2d, Thornton Wilder, Helen Wills.

For Norman Thomas: Upton Sinclair.

Not Voting: George Ade, Ralph Barton, Willa Cather, Theodore Dreiser, Douglas Fairbanks, Robert Edmond Jones, Rockwell Kent, Marilyn Miller, Walter Winchell.

Vanity Fair's 1928 presidential election poll.

To my dear friend - Dick - Hoping we get together on that book with admiration.

George Gershwin

George Gershwin
Nov. 1929.

An American in Paris

An Orchestral Tone Poem

Piano Solo

Inscription to Dick Simon.

Portrait of the artist.

RECOLLECTIONS OF BURTON LANE

My folks used to take my brother and me down to Atlantic City over the Christmas and New Year holidays. About 1928 we went to a Jewish hotel for dinner and my father saw a piano, an upright, against the wall. He said, "Burt, play." I was a very shy young kid and I hated to be in the least bit pushy so I said, "If you sit near me, I'll play something." So he came over and he sat against the wall and I started to play. After a few minutes a woman came over and said, "Are you Lazarus Levy?" and my father said, "Yes." She said, "I'm Mrs. Gershwin. I'm George Gershwin's mother." She said, "I remember you. You used to own the building." (They ran a Turkish bath, the Gershwin family, and my father owned the property.) And she said, "Is this your son?" He said yes. And she said two things: "When he started to play, he sounded like my son George, and when I looked up, he looked like George from the back."

This was sort of confirmed many months later after I knew George. I was invited to a party at 103rd Street just off Riverside Drive. I got there and George hadn't come downstairs yet. There were some people there and they pulled me to the piano and I started to play. Suddenly somebody's hands went over my eyes from behind me and a voice said, "Guess who this is." I said, "I don't know who this is." It was a girl friend of George's thinking it was George who was playing.

After we came back from Atlantic City, Mrs. Gershwin called one Sunday and invited us over, and that's when I met George.

He had a show called Funny Face *playing, and in the pit were a marvelous two-piano team, Ohman and Arden. They gave it a great style when they played the syncopated repeated notes. It was very exciting. And before I knew George I had made a one-piano arrangement with what Ohman and Arden did with "'S Wonderful." When I was introduced to him as a budding young talent whom Mrs. Gershwin had been raving about, he said, "Let me hear you play." Well, I started to play "'S Wonderful" and I did those repeated notes in octaves. I started too fast, but I got through it, playing it faster than I had ever played it in my life. I was so nervous, and when I got through I remember George held up my hand and said, "Make a fist." He felt my wrist and said, "You know I couldn't play like that when I was your age. In fact, I can't do it now." And that was my introduction to George.*

George later asked me if I would be a rehearsal pianist for Of Thee I Sing. I told my father, and he thought the idea of my being a rehearsal pianist for another composer was terrible. He wouldn't let me do it. But I was flattered that George thought I was good enough, as I was nineteen years old.

In those days a show would go into rehearsal without a book or half a book. The second act would be written while they were in rehearsal. They seemed to waste so many wonderful tunes in shows that were meaningless. The books were the trouble. I'm sorry they made that impression on me. Otherwise I might have written more.

George and Ira—they have the biggest medley of songs I wish I'd written. I remember the first time I came to their house Oscar Levant was there. I used to love Ping-Pong. I played Oscar and I beat him and he got so mean that I said, "Let's play another game," and I let him win.

AN
AMERICAN
IN
PARIS
(1928)

It was well known in the music world that George was writing *An American in Paris.* Some people thought it had been commissioned by Ziegfeld as a ballet for one of his musicals. Others thought he was writing it for producer Ray Goetz. Conductor Leopold Stokowski wanted to conduct the premiere of the work, but when he heard that George had finally decided to offer it to Walter Damrosch he bowed out of the picture. George proved somewhat elusive to Damrosch, as the following correspondence indicates, but the friendship formed during their collaboration on the *Concerto in F* in 1925 helped bring the negotiations to a satisfactory conclusion.

Hôtel de France & Choiseul
May 4, 1928

Dear Gershwin:

I just hear that you are in Paris and want so much to see you. Can you lunch with me tomorrow Saturday at the Union Inter Allié, rue de Faubourg St. Honoré at one o'clock.

I expect to leave for Marienbad on Tuesday evening.

I would love to arrange with you to do your new work at a Philharmonic Symphony this winter!

Please telephone me your hotel here and if tomorrow does not suit let us make it Sunday or Monday.

Always cordially
Yours
Walter Damrosch

P.S. I'm practicing your concerto!

Damrosch also sent a telegram to George at the Hotel Bristol, Vienna, May 5, 1928.

On August 5 Damrosch invited George to visit him at Blaine Cottage, Bar Harbor, Maine, to discuss the work's progress. George replied:

I am glad to report that I have finished the first sketch of An American in Paris; *and in a day or two will have finished a two piano arrangement. The next move, of course, is the orchestration.*

Besides this I have the new Gertrude Lawrence show to finish. That goes into rehearsal in three weeks. With all this work you can see that it is difficult for me to designate the time when I can visit you. However, at the first opportunity that presents itself I shall wend my way Bar Harborwards.

Damrosch persevered:

August 21, 1928

Dear Gershwin:

Just a line to tell you that I am beset by numerous charming and altogether exquisite young creatures with "Is Mr. Gershwin coming to stay with you," "When is Mr. Gershwin coming," "Wonderful" etc. etc. So please do not forget your promise and of course bring the score, finished or unfinished, of An American in Paris *with you.*

With cordial greetings,

Sincerely yours,
Walter Damrosch

And again:

November 5, 1928

My dear Gershwin:

We have definitely decided on December 13th and 14th for the first performances of An American in Paris. Needless to say, I am looking forward eagerly to this event and would like to hear the score as soon as possible. You told me it would take about twenty minutes to perform. Is this fairly accurate?

Couldn't you come in some morning and play it over for me so that I can get your tempi and the proper spirit. If you could come for luncheon, not only I, but my wife, would be doubly pleased. How about some day next week?

With cordial greetings,
Your very young friend
Walter Damrosch

When *An American in Paris* was given its première performance at Carnegie Hall, December 13, 1928, the program notes were written by Deems Taylor:

You are to imagine an American, visiting Paris, swinging down the Champs-Elysées on a mild, sunny morning in May or June. Being what he is, he starts with preliminaries, and is off at full speed at once, to the tune of The First Walking Theme, a straightforward, diatonic air, designed to convey an impression of Gallic freedom and gaiety.

Our American's ears being open, as well as his eyes, he notes with pleasure the sounds of the city. French taxicabs seem to amuse him particularly, a fact that the orchestra points out in a brief episode introducing four Parisian taxi horns. These have a special theme allotted to them (the driver, possibly?) which is announced by the strings whenever they appear in the score.

Having safely eluded the taxis, our American apparently passes the open door of a café, where if one is to believe the trombones, La Sorella is still popular. Exhilarated by this reminder of the gay nineteen-hundreds, he resumes his stroll through the medium of the Second Walking Theme, which is announced by the clarinet in French with a strong American accent.

Both themes are now discussed at some length by the instruments, until our tourist happens to pass something. The composer thought it might be a church, while the commentator held out for the Grand Palais—where the Salon holds forth. At all events, our hero does not go in.

Instead, as revealed by the English horn, he respectfully slackens his pace until he is safely past.

At this point, the American's itinerary becomes somewhat obscured. It may be that he continues on down the Champs-Elysées; it may be that he has turned off—the composer retains an open mind on the subject. However, since what immediately ensues is technically known as a bridge-passage, one is reasonably justified in assuming that the Gershwin pen, guided by an unseen hand, has perpetrated a musical pun, and that when the Third Walking Theme makes its eventual appearance, our American has crossed the Seine, and is somewhere on the Left Bank. Certainly it is distinctly less Gallic than its predecessors, speaking American with a French intonation, as befits that region of the city where so many Americans foregather. "Walking" may be a misnomer, for despite its vitality the theme is slightly sedentary in character, and becomes progressively more so. Indeed, the end of this section of the work is couched in terms so unmistakably, albeit pleasantly, blurred, as to suggest that the American is on the terrasse of a café, exploring the mysteries of an Anise de Lozo.

And now the orchestra introduces an unhallowed episode. Suffice it to say that a solo violin approaches our hero (in soprano register) and addresses him in the most charming broken English; and, his response being inaudible—or at least unintelligible—repeats the remark. The one-sided conversation continues for some little time.

Of course, one hastens to add, it is possible that a grave injustice is being done to both author and protagonist, and that the whole episode is simply a musical transition. The latter interpretation may well be true, for otherwise it is difficult to believe what ensues; our hero becomes homesick. He has the blues; and if the behavior of the orchestra be any criterion, he has them very thoroughly. He realizes suddenly, overwhelmingly, that he does not belong to this place, that he is the most wretched creature in all the world, a foreigner. The cool, blue Paris sky, the distant upward sweep of the Eiffel Tower, the bookstalls on the quay, the pattern of horsechestnut leaves on the white, sun-flecked street—what avails all this alien beauty? He is no Baudelaire, longing to be "anywhere out of the world." The world is just what he longs for, the world that he knows best; a world less lovely—sentimental and a little vulgar perhaps—but for all that, home.

However, nostalgia is not a fatal disease—nor, in this instance, of overlong duration. Just in the nick of time

The opening passage from George's orchestration of the Homesickness Theme in *An American in Paris*.

the compassionate orchestra rushes another theme to the rescue, two trumpets performing the ceremony of introduction. It is apparent that our hero must have met a compatriot; for this last theme is a noisy, cheerful, self-confident Charleston, without a drop of Gallic blood in its veins.

For the moment, Paris is no more; and a voluble, gusty, wise-cracking orchestra proceeds to demonstrate at some length that it's always fair weather when two Americans get together, no matter where. Walking Theme number two enters soon thereafter, enthusiastically abetted by number three. Paris isn't such a bad place, after all; as a matter of fact, it's a grand place! Nice weather, nothing to do till tomorrow. The blues return, but mitigated by the Second Walking Theme—a happy reminiscence rather than a homesick yearning—and the orchestra, in a riotous finale, decides to make a night of it. It will be great to get home; but meanwhile, this is Paris!

Cincinnati, Ohio, February 28, 1929. Left to right: Roy Hornikel, manager of the Cincinnati Symphony, George, conductor Fritz Reiner, James Rosenberg, who played the taxi horns, and tenor Richard Crooks. The occasion, a Cincinnati Symphony concert featuring *An American in Paris*.

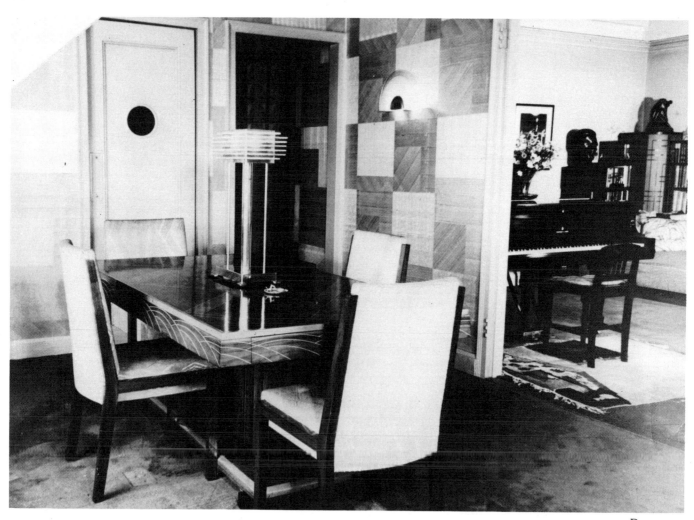

Dining room.

The bedroom.

A corner of the living room.

In George's penthouse apartment, 33 Riverside Drive, at 75th Street. George and Ira took adjoining penthouses there in 1929.

SHOW GIRL (1929)

East Is West having been postponed, Ziegfeld switched the Gershwins to a musical version of J. P. McEvoy's novel *Show Girl*, about the rise to stardom of a chorus girl named Dixie Dugan. Ira writes in *Lyrics on Several Occasions*:

For the new show Ziegfeld asked if I would mind collaborating with lyricist Gus Kahn, as he owed Gus a commitment. I welcomed the opportunity because Show Girl had to be done quickly to make a much too soon Boston opening date.

Including openings and finalettos and several songs written during rehearsal, George, Gus, and I wound up with twenty-seven musical items....

There was much musical entertainment in Show Girl. Of the twenty-seven items we wrote, fourteen were used. Then there was the ballet An American in Paris, *which opened the second act and ran at least fifteen minutes. Then there was a scene in which Duke Ellington and his band played a couple of their numbers; and another in which Clayton, Jackson, and Durante contributed several of their own specialties....Everything considered, I wouldn't be surprised if* Show Girl *set a record for sparseness of dialogue in a musical.*

Despite all the folderol, *Show Girl* was a box-office failure. Most people found it unbelievably heavy going. The show was an unhappy experience for the Gershwins, who had to threaten a lawsuit to obtain the royalties that Ziegfeld owed them—royalties Ziegfeld had lost in the stock market crash that occurred less than four months after *Show Girl* opened.

Show Girl (1929): Ruby Keeler with Clayton, Jackson, and Durante./(Page 114) Harriet Hoctor's ballet to *An American in Paris* in *Show Girl* (1929).

I MUST BE HOME BY TWELVE O'CLOCK

LYRICS BY IRA GERSHWIN AND GUS KAHN

Verse:

There is one at ev'ry party,
A girl with one thought in her dome.
Fun is fun, but she's that party
Who just keeps on saying,
"I gotta go home!"
She will dance till dawn is breaking;
But ev'ry chance, this speech she's making:

Refrain:

I'll say I'm having a hot time.
I'd stay, but I haven't got time.
I must be home by twelve o'clock!
That band is wicked but, brother,
You know I promised my mother.
I must be home by twelve o'clock!
Bup-a-rup-a-rup-pup!
What's the name of that song?
Hear the trumpet blowing!
Bup-a-rup-a-rup-pup!
I'll be getting in wrong,
I'm positively going!
Oh, good grief! It's three in the morning!
Once more I'm giving you warning,
I must be home by twelve o'clock!

LIZA

LYRICS BY IRA GERSHWIN AND GUS KAHN

Verse:

Moon shinin' on the river,
Come along, my Liza!
Breeze singin' through the tree-tops,
Come along, my Liza!
Somethin' mighty sweet
I want to whisper sweet and low,
That you ought to know, my Liza!
I get lonesome, honey,
When I'm all alone so long.
Don't make me wait;
Don't hesitate;
Come and hear my song:

Refrain:

Liza, Liza, skies are gray,
But if you'll smile on me
All the clouds'll roll away.

Liza, Liza, don't delay,
Come, keep me company,
And the clouds'll roll away.

See
The honey moon a-shinin' down;
We
Should make a date with Parson Brown.
So, Liza, Liza, name the day
When you belong to me
And the clouds'll roll away.

I'll never forget Show Girl because it was the greatest rush job I've ever had on a score. I was working on another show for Mr. Ziegfeld, when he suddenly decided to drop that one and produce Show Girl immediately. He often did those things. Mr. Ziegfeld called me down to his office one day and said, "George, I'm going to produce J. P. McEvoy's Show Girl and you must write the score for it. We go into rehearsal in two weeks!" I said, "But Mr. Ziegfeld, I can't write a score in two weeks. That's impossible." Mr. Ziegfeld smiled up at me and said, "Why, sure you can—just dig down in the trunk and pull out a couple of hits." Flo Ziegfeld had a way of getting what he wanted. . . . Well, the show went into rehearsal with half the score finished and about one-third of the book completed. . . . Mr. Ziegfeld said, "I would like to have a minstrel number in the second act with one hundred beautiful girls seated on steps that cover the entire stage." This minstrel number was to be sung and danced by Ruby Keeler. So we went to work on a minstrel number and wrote "Liza." The show opened in Boston—and I think the last scene was rehearsed on the train going up. The first act went along fine. The second act came and the attractive and talented Ruby Keeler appeared to sing and dance "Liza." Imagine the audience's surprise, and mine, when without warning Al Jolson, who was sitting in the third row on the aisle, jumped up and sang a chorus of "Liza" to his bride! Miss Keeler and he had just been married. It caused a sensation, and it gave the song a great start!
George Gershwin

Leabharlanna Contae Portláirge

RECOLLECTIONS OF
KAY SWIFT

Parties at the Glaenzers' were such fun I was willing to put up with the shushing. When George played they didn't talk. Nobody would move, except toward the piano, and everybody held his breath. You'd be in the middle of a sentence and Glaenzer would walk up to you and he'd say shush very loudly with his head right up to your face practically.

They were late parties. One wouldn't go there until after the theater, and then people who played in different shows would turn up. George would be there and I often went with him.

Everybody felt relaxed and happy at the Glaenzers'. Noël Coward would be there if he were in town. Cole, I'm sure, was there, and Dick Rodgers. On one occasion Dick said, "Let's write a little something for George." Many of George's friends did—and performed it for him at a subsequent party. I did a piano trio because that was what I was doing at the time. One of the themes became "Can This Be Love?"

George as Groucho at a costume party.

With conductor Willem van Hoogstraten at a rehearsal in Lewisohn Stadium, August 24, 1929. Two days later George made his debut as a conductor.

The "Four Marx Brothers," same party. Richard Rodgers is on the left.

STRIKE UP THE BAND (1930)

On Tuesday [January 14, 1930] Prokofiev and I went to the Strike Up the Band opening and later to a midnight party in Gershwin's honor at the Warburgs', where there was no room for nostalgia but where the music was better: George didn't leave the piano until the notices—all excellent—arrived, then resumed his recital with renewed vigor. At the party Pop Gershwin distinguished himself twice: when Russel Crouse asked him how he liked the show, he parried with: "What you mean how I like it? I have to like it."

From Passport to Paris *(Boston: Little, Brown and Company, 1955)*

In 1926 George and Ira joined with George S. Kaufman in creating a satire in the style of Gilbert and Sullivan that would lash out at the futilities of international politics, the League of Nations, and war itself.

Strike Up the Band opened in Long Branch, New Jersey, in August 1927, and *Variety* offered the following appraisal: "That it will be a commercial smash is doubtful, but it will unquestionably have a *succès d'estime*. . . . Satirical musical shows have never been a success in America, though the time may now be in sight." A few days later, when the show opened in Philadelphia, the critic of the *Inquirer* called it "a rollicking show, a veritable geyser of spontaneous comedy . . . a thoroughly refreshing departure from routine."

But the audience response was tepid. One night the creators were standing outside the theater in Philadelphia when a car pulled up and two elegantly dressed men with canes and monocles stepped out of the car. Ira Gershwin turned to George Kaufman and said, "It looks like Gilbert and Sullivan have come to fix up the show."

The show was not fixed then, however; it died in Philadelphia, and not till three years later was it resurrected with Morrie Ryskind as co-author of a toned-down plot. In some respects, the new *Strike Up the Band* was a typical Gershwin show with a high quota of good songs, but it was also a lampoon on war, American big business, politics, international relations, and Babbittry. The confidence of the Gershwins and their collaborators in the 1927 failure was vindicated by renewed critical praise and a six-month run following its Broadway opening in January 1930.

MADEMOISELLE IN NEW ROCHELLE

Verse:

(He) Little lady, as you stand before me,
You remind me
Of the little girl I left behind me.
Holding hands with you would never bore me;
What a torso!
Like my gal in New Rochelle, but more so!
(She) Sir, where do you get this "you and me" stuff?
(He) How about that "hands across the sea" stuff?
Sweetness, if you think you could adore me,
I'll forget about the gal back home.

Refrain:

I left my mademoiselle in New Rochelle,
But, what the hell!
You'll do as well.

I left my mademoiselle in New Rochelle,
But truth to tell,
You're twice as swell!

I love your lips!
Oh boy! what hips!
When I observe
Each lovely curve
Then I declare;
Yes, I can swear,
I'm glad I'm here "over there."

Oh, lady, if you could learn to play mam-mah
For zizz pa-pah,
Then, what the hell!
I'll never go back again to New Rochelle!

George at Lewisohn Stadium, New York, where for years all-Gershwin concerts were annual events and usually attracted record crowds.

(Overleaf) But what the hell! / You'll do as well."
Paul McCullough, Bobby Clark, and the chorus of
Strike Up the Band (1930).

"We don't know what we're fighting for—but we didn't know the last time!"
—Bobby Clark, Paul McCullough and the company of *Strike Up the Band*.

From *Strike Up the Band*.

STRIKE UP
THE BAND

Verse:

We fought in nineteen-seventeen,
Rum-ta-ta-tum-tum-tum!
And drove the tyrant from the scene,
Rum-ta-ta-tum-tum-tum!

We're in a bigger, better war
For your patriotic pastime.
We don't know what we're fighting for—
But we didn't know the last time!

So load the cannon! Draw the blade!
Rum-ta-ta-tum-tum-tum!
Come on and join the "Big Parade"!
Rum-ta-ta-tum-tum, rum-ta-ta-tum-tum,
Rum-ta-ta-tum-tum-tum!

Refrain:

Let the drums roll out!
(Boom boom boom!)
Let the trumpet call!
(Ta-ta-ra-ta-ta-ta-ta!)
While the people shout
(Hooray!)
Strike up the band!

Hear the cymbals ring!
(Tszing-tszing-tszing!)
Calling one and all
(Ta-ta-ra-ta-ta-ta-ta!)
To the martial swing,
(Left, right!)
Strike up the band!

There is work to be done, to be done—
There's a war to be won, to be won—
Come you son of a son of a gun—
Take your stand!

Fall in line, yea bo—
Come along, let's go!
Hey, leader, strike up the band!

SOON

Verse I:

I'm making up for all the years
That I waited;
I'm compensated
At last.
My heart is through with shirking;
Thanks to you it's working
Fast.
The many lonely nights and days
When this duffer
Just had to suffer
Are past.
Life will be a dream song,
Love will be the theme song.

Refrain:

Soon—the lonely nights will be ended;
Soon—two hearts as one will be blended.
I've found the happiness I've waited for:
The only girl that I was fated for.
Oh! Soon—a little cottage will find us
Safe, with all our cares far behind us.
The day you're mine this world will be in tune.
Let's make that day come soon.

Refrain 2:

Soon—my dear, you'll never be lonely;
Soon—you'll find I live for you only.
When I'm with you who cares what time it is,
Or what the place or what the climate is?
Oh, Soon—our little ship will come sailing
Home, through every storm, never failing.
The day you're mine this world will be in tune.
Let's make that day come soon.

Ferde Grofé, George, S. L. Rothafel ("Roxy"), and Paul Whiteman at the Roxy Theatre, New York.

The *Rhapsody in Blue* number from *King of Jazz*. When the film had its première at the Roxy Theatre in May 1930, George played in the stage show.

GIRL CRAZY (1930)

Girl Crazy was about as Western as West End Avenue. For its dialogue, characters, and point of view were really closer in spirit to Shubert Alley than to Custerville, Arizona, where a bevy of Broadway chorus girls romped on a dude ranch. Nevertheless, the show provided the backdrop for the Gershwins' most exuberant musical-comedy score to date. A spectacular debut by Ethel Merman, whose performance of "I Got Rhythm" is a Broadway legend; a comely ingenue named Ginger Rogers; the comic talents of Willie Howard and William Kent; and a pit orchestra, fronted by Red Nichols, that included such future jazz greats as Benny Goodman, Gene Krupa, Glenn Miller, Jack Teagarden, and Jimmy Dorsey all contributed to the show's success.

EMBRACEABLE YOU

Verse 1:

(He) Dozens of girls would storm up;
I had to lock my door.
Somehow I couldn't warm up
To one before.
What was it that controlled me?
What kept my love-life lean?
My intuition told me
You'd come on the scene.
Lady, listen to the rhythm of my heart beat,
And you'll get just what I mean.

Refrain 1:

Embrace me,
My sweet embraceable you.
Embrace me,
You irreplaceable you.
Just one look at you—my heart grew tipsy in me;
You and you alone bring out the gypsy in me.
I love all
The many charms about you;
Above all
I want my arms about you.
Don't be a naughty baby.
Come to papa—come to papa—do!
My sweet embraceable you.

Verse 2:

(She) I went about reciting,
"Here's one who'll never fall!"
But I'm afraid the writing
Is on the wall.
My nose I used to turn up
When you'd besiege my heart;
Now I completely burn up
When you're slow to start.
I'm afraid you'll have to take the consequences;
You upset the apple cart.

Refrain 2:

Embrace me,
My sweet embraceable you.
Embrace me,
You irreplaceable you.
In your arms I find love so delectable, dear.
I'm afraid it isn't quite respectable, dear.
But hang it—
Come on, let's glorify love!
Ding dang it!
You'll shout "Encore!" if I love.
Don't be a naughty papa,
Come to baby—come to baby—do!
My sweet embraceable you.

Refrain 3:

Dear lady,
My silk and lace-able you,
Dear lady,
Be my embraceable you.
You're the only one I love, yes, verily so!
But you're much too shy, unnecessarily so!
I'll try not
To be so formal, my dear.
Am I not
A man who's normal, my dear?
There's just one way to cheer me;
Come to papa—come to papa—do!
My sweet embraceable you!

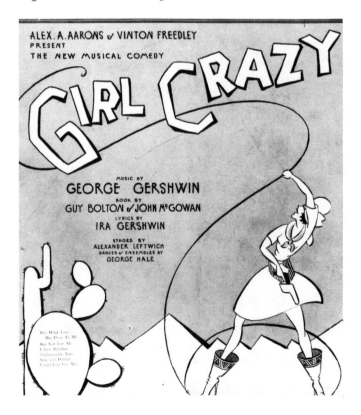

4

5

6

10

11

12

10122

No. "GIRL CRAZY"

White STUDIO

220 WEST 42ND STREET

NEW YORK

16

17

Ginger Rogers and the Foursome Quartet in *Girl Crazy* (1930).

BIDIN' MY TIME

Verse 1:

Some fellers love to Tip-Toe Through The Tulips;
Some fellers go on Singing In The Rain;
Some fellers keep on Paintin' Skies With Sunshine;
Some fellers keep on Swingin' Down The Lane—
But—

Refrain 1:

I'm Bidin' My Time,
'Cause that's the kinda guy I'm.
While other folks grow dizzy
I keep busy—
Bidin' My Time.

Next year, next year,
Somethin's bound to happen;
This year, this year,
I'll just keep on nappin'—

And—Bidin' My Time,
'Cause that's the kinda guy I'm.
There's no regrettin'
When I'm settin'—
Bidin' My Time.

Verse 2:

Some fellers love to Tell It To The Daisies;
Some Stroll Beneath The Honeysuckle Vines;
Some fellers when they've Climbed The Highest
  Mountain
Still keep a-Cryin' For The Carolines—
But—

Refrain 2:

I'm Bidin' My Time,
'Cause that's the kinda guy I'm—
Beginnin' on a Mond'y
Right through Sund'y,
Bidin' My Time.

Give me, give me
(A) glass that's full of tinkle;
Let me, let me
Dream like Rip Van Winkle.

He Bided His Time,
And like that Winkle guy I'm.
Chasin' 'way flies,
How the day flies—
Bidin' My Time!

BUT NOT FOR ME

Verse:

Old Man Sunshine—listen, you!
Never tell me Dreams Come True!
Just try it—
And I'll start a riot.
Beatrice Fairfax—don't you dare
Ever tell me he will care;
I'm certain
It's the Final Curtain.
I never want to hear
From any cheer-
Ful Pollyannas,
Who tell you Fate
Supplies a Mate—
It's all bananas!

Refrain 1:

They're writing songs of love,
But not for me;
A lucky star's above,
But not for me.

With Love to Lead the Way,
I've found more Clouds of Gray
Than any Russian play
Could guarantee.

I was a fool to fall
And Get That Way;
Heigh ho! Alas! And al-
So, Lackaday!

Although I can't dismiss
The mem'ry of his kiss—
I guess he's not for me.

Refrain 2:

He's knocking on a door,
But not for me;
He'll plan a two by four,
But not for me.

I know that Love's a Game;
I'm puzzled, just the same—
Was I the Moth or Flame . . .?
I'm all at sea.

It all began so well,
But what an end!
This is the time a Fell-
Er Needs a Friend:

When ev'ry happy plot
Ends with the marriage knot—
And there's no knot for me.

Alternative ending:

They ain't done right by Nell,
However, what the hell—
I guess he's not for me.

"Treat Me Rough"—William Kent and the girls (*Girl Crazy*, 1930).

"But Not For Me"—Ginger Rogers and Willie Howard (*Girl Crazy*, 1930). / (Overleaf) Ethel Merman and the girls (*Girl Crazy*, 1930).

I GOT RHYTHM

Verse:

Days can be sunny,
With never a sigh;
Don't need what money
Can buy.

Birds in the tree sing
Their dayful of song.
Why shouldn't we sing
Along?

I'm chipper all the day,
Happy with my lot.
How do I get that way?
Look at what I've got:

Refrain:
I got rhythm,
I got music,
I got my man—
Who could ask for anything more?

I got daisies
In green pastures,
I got my man—
Who could ask for anything more?

Old Man Trouble,
I don't mind him—
You won't find him
'Round my door.

I got starlight,
I got sweet dreams,
I got my man—
Who could ask for anything more—
Who could ask for anything more?

RECOLLECTIONS OF
FRANCES GERSHWIN GODOWSKY

My mother was very much against my marrying Leo because Leo didn't have any money. I had to meet him on the outside all the time. She had no faith in him whatsoever. My mother and father were leaving for Florida for the winter on November 2. George and Ira were leaving for California a few days later.

Leo came back from Europe the night of November 1, and when he heard that everyone was leaving, he said, "Look, let's get married tomorrow." I said, "That's impossible. My parents are leaving. My brothers are leaving. It just can't be done." Leo is the sort of fellow who doesn't say things can't be done. I said, "You can't get a license on a Sunday." He said, "You leave it to me, because they're all going to be gone for months. We want to get married anyway, and I don't like to have it happen without your family, as if I were doing it behind their backs."

About four in the morning I called him up at his hotel

and said forget the whole thing, it's just impossible. He said, "I'll manage it." Well, he got hold of Judge Botein and asked him where he could find out about a license. There was a place in the Bronx, so he trotted up to the Bronx and got the marriage license. Then we needed a wedding ring. So Leo had the jeweler meet me in the afternoon at Broadway and 103rd Street. He was described to me and I was described to him. This black limousine pulled up and I got into this car, met the man, and picked out the ring.

Meanwhile, everyone was meeting to say goodbye to my parents. Kay Swift, my uncle and my aunts, and of course Lee, Ira, and George. Now it is in the afternoon and we were at Botein's apartment, trying to find out who could marry us. This was a Sunday and many people were away. So Leo said, "Let's look up in the directory all the names of reverends in the neighborhood who might be Jewish." Finally we found someone, and now it was four P.M. and my parents were making a six-o'clock train. When he heard our names, he agreed to come because he was a music lover.

I was scared to tell my mother because she blamed her asthma a great deal on the fact I was going with Leo. Anyway, we went up to the apartment and told her, and there was really nothing she could do about it, as it was all arranged.

Then George came in. He walked from his penthouse roof into Ira's with a big cigar in his mouth and his pajamas and robe on. A little later these French doors opened and in walked this rabbi whom nobody knew— he had gone through George's apartment by mistake.

By this time my father had his watch in his hand and he said, "We've got to leave here, Rose, in a little while." He was so concerned about missing their train. Kay Swift had sent my mother some flowers, so she pinned them on me because I had no flowers. And George played the wedding march with this big cigar in his mouth. And the rabbi quickly started talking about harmony and rhythm, trying to use all the musical terms he could think of.

My father kept standing there with the watch in his hand, worrying about the train. And when the ceremony was over we all rushed out of Ira and Lee's apartment down to the station to see them off. Everybody was in such a panic about that train!

That night Bert Taylor, Gertie Lawrence's boy friend, was giving a tremendous farewell party for George and Ira, and that party became almost like a wedding reception for us because George went around saying, "What do you think? My sister just got married."

132

LETTER FROM IRA TO EMILY AND LOU PALEY

Hollywood, California
Friday. Jan. 16, 31.

Dear Lou & Em,

They played the American last night. That and Sacre gave them the biggest house of the season. George got his usual big reception. We gave them a small hand-out after the concert at our house.... And a very, very nice party it was.

The night before (Wednesday) we had dinner at the Eddie Mayers. They have Lionel Barrymore's house.... The night before that we were at Arthur Caesar's for dinner.... The night before that Guy [Bolton] took us out for dinner. The night before that, well, I don't remember, but we haven't had half a dozen meals since we've been here without two or more guests, or we've had dinner where we were guests.

George will need a couple more weeks to finish the rhapsody he's writing for our picture. As I may or may not have written you my end of the picture was finished weeks & weeks ago and I've had nothing to do but get up at noon, read the papers, see pictures, and dine in or out. A pleasure!

George is off today to spend the week-end at the Hamilton Fish ranch some 350 miles North, near Frisco. Lee and I are invited also but I must remain and try to break another 100. (I did a lousy 109 last week.) ... Girl Crazy will open here somewhere near the end of February but whether we'll remain for it or not, I don't know.

Next to pictures, sex is the big topic here, as elsewhere. It was cold here last night—must have been about 50.... Kern phoned us last night but our receiver was off, unfortunately. (He just got in yesterday and George had two tickets for him for the concert.) ...

Got a letter from Alex [Aarons] today, says he's not making any plans till he hears from us. I imagine we'll work on the Kaufman-Ryskind show first. If we get it well in hand before the Summer we probably can tackle one for him. Although, I think, George wants to return here in May when shooting starts on our picture....

Love and kisses.
Ira

DELICIOUS (1931)

The first film for which George and Ira collaborated on a full score, *Delicious* was a musical involving the romance of a Scottish immigrant (Janet Gaynor) and a rich polo player from Long Island (Charles Farrell). *Delicious* is set apart from the usual musical movie chiefly by the inclusion of an extended dream sequence and the one-minute use of a six-minute orchestral piece George had written for the film, later to be expanded into the *Second Rhapsody.*

DELISHIOUS

Verse:

What can I say—
To sing my praise of you?
I must reveal
The things I feel.
What can I say?
Each lovely phase of you
Just seems to baffle my descriptive powers
Four and twenty hours of ev'ry day.
What can I say?
What is the thing
I'd love to sing?
I've said you're marvelous;
I've said you're wonderful;
And yet that's not it.
Now let me see,
I think I've got it!

Refrain:

You're so delishious
And so caprishious;
I grow ambishious
To have you care for me.
In that connecshion
You're my selecshion
For true affecshion
For all the time to be.
Oh, I've had one, two, three, four, five, six, seven, eight,
Nine, ten girls before;
But now there's one, and you're the one,
The one girl I adore,
'Cause you're delishious,
And so caprishious,
If I'm repetishious,
It's 'cause you're so delishious!

Film star Aileen Pringle met George during the Gershwins' stay in California (November 1930–February 1931).

George wrote much of the *Second Rhapsody* at Aileen Pringle's Santa Monica home, and when he left California he inscribed another photograph to her: "For Pringie—this easterner will always look West with swell thoughts of you. George. Feb. 22, 1931." Next to his signature he drew the musical notation for the letter G. To this inscription he added the notes of the opening theme of the *Second Rhapsody*, part of which was used in the film *Delicious*.

Sketches of Pringie and George, 1931.

Pringie
by
Georgie Gershwin

"Pringie by Georgie Gershwin, Jan. 26, 1931."

RECOLLECTIONS OF ROSAMOND WALLING TIRANA

George Gershwin met Rosamond Walling at her cousin Emily Strunsky Paley's wedding. Beautiful, charming, and intelligent, she was the girl many thought George would and should marry, and indeed, George was among her fondest admirers. They were, by turns, romantic and platonic—a relationship between an irrepressible and sophisticated college girl who had grown up in diplomatic circles and a famous composer, twelve years her senior, who had left school at fifteen. Rosamond was confined to Swarthmore College in Pennsylvania most of the time, and George was busy pursuing his career, which often took him away from New York, but they saw one another whenever and wherever their divergent lives permitted. Rosamond's friends at Swarthmore loved to have her composer friend visit because he invariably gave them house seats to the new shows trying out in Philadelphia. And George enjoyed his fleeting contact with academic life, although his pleasure was tinged with regret for an experience that he himself had missed.

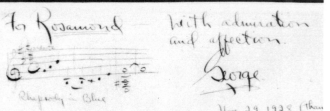

George photographed by Steichen, with an inscription to Rosamond Walling.

Throughout my childhood I'd come in from Greenwich, Connecticut, to be with my adored city cousins who lived in Greenwich Village—my Strunsky cousins. Once I did so in 1928 and found that the family was going to meet a boat: the Gershwins were returning from Europe. We all went to 103rd Street afterwards. There were many groups that I didn't know: a pinochle game of Mr. Gershwin's downstairs, pianos and noises upstairs, eating, greeting everywhere. Feeling very much a country cousin, I rode myself up and down in the elevator cage. George got in too, eventually.

"I've been looking for you," he said. Then, as always, because he admired my capacity, "Aren't you hungry?"

"Perhaps some pickles?"

"With a touch of pastrami and salami and two or three pounds of raw beef, a quart of milk and an onion. Come, we'll find something to nibble on. And then there's a surprise for you. I brought you a present from France. In fact, two presents."

The first present was the first "modern art" object in my life. It was a fine cigarette case, in black and white, with an eggshell inlay in cubist design. I was thrilled, especially at the recognition of my dignity—a cigarette case!

He fastened the second treasure on my left wrist. It was very delicate—emeralds, rubies, and little pearls set in old gold.

"I found it in an antique store in Paris. It reminded me of you—it looks as if it has a Russian soul."

George was always the youngest of the young to the whole world; but there were twelve years that made him seem very old to me then.

I don't remember our first meeting, but George told me it was at the wedding of my beautiful cousin Emily to Lou Paley, whom George admired and loved. George was eighteen, I was seven, and the man I held a torch for was Emily's brother, English, who was nine. George remembered years later that the young couple—us—were found asleep in a closet, plastered with champagne.

As for George, he always loved our Emily with the perfect feeling that Emily evokes. "Emily," he would say, "is as beautiful inside as out—her beauty comes from within." He believed that Fate, his Fate, arranged all things, big and little. George was too young when Emily was a grown-up girl; the right person for him would come along someday. He told me that at the wedding he figured out that I had possibilities, as Emily's cousin. When I was sixteen, Emily's sister, Leonore, married Ira Gershwin. After a while George decided that as I was the

Rosamond Walling.

Rosamond.

closest he could get to our adored Emily, I might turn out to be the right wife for him.

George was all for marriage, and was quite sure that he would marry someday. As soon as possible. A good girl, preferably at least half Jewish, and with sense, like his mother. He liked the fact that my mother was Anna Strunsky. My father was a tall, gray-eyed Anglo-Saxon, William English Walling. "It's nice about your father, because I like the English and Southerners and Westerners," George said. "But thank God your mother is Jewish." "Don't be so Anglo-Saxon" came later; but he liked the idea of the combination.

Whenever I could get away from Swarthmore College, I'd join George in New York, or Atlantic City, or Philadelphia. I would stay with Leonore and Ira, as George was always absolutely correct in his behavior—in fact, fastidious.

I went to rehearsals and openings and great events with George: when he first conducted at Lewisohn Stadium, on August 26, 1929, and the Carnegie Hall première of An American in Paris, on December 13, 1928.

George's idea of marriage held no charm for me. "Let's have four children to begin with," George

would say, "and bring them up in the country. Greenwich, if you like. You can teach them to ride. We'll get six horses to start with."

This absolutely lacked charm for me: I hoped never to see Westchester County again, and didn't get around to wanting children for a good ten years.

When he felt romantic—which did happen as time went on and I grew older and we were alone in various paradises—he never in any way tried to influence me. Given a moon, June, and myself in blue (because of the Rhapsody, of course), we might go for a long walk, holding hands, and sometimes dancing—he'd tap-dance at the slightest provocation—conversing on all sorts of subjects in delicious agreement. George might stop me and say, "You could be good for my stomach," or "My friends like you," or "If you could learn to keep your stockings straight and get those run-down heels changed, you might be glamorous. But not in that dress. It's terrible. The skirts are longer now, haven't you read? Tomorrow I'll make you a deal. You help me get some paints and I'll get you something that covers your knees."

So it happened. I insisted on an inexpensive black dress on sale on 57th Street, and a black linen hat. George went nuts in the paint store. He bought a huge empty box and filled it with a complete assortment of Grumbacher or Malfa oils, whichever cost most, in the biggest tubes. Then he chose sable brushes, a palette, and some big canvas boards. We walked all the way back to his new apartment—the one with the balcony at 33 Riverside Drive. George and Ira always drew and painted in water color. I don't remember whether George had worked in oils before. I had always painted and, as I knew absolutely nothing about music, was very happy at George's deep interest in painting.

I nearly married him when he moved to 33 Riverside Drive, because he said I could have the downstairs apartment and we'd make an inside staircase; so I would have privacy and could paint. It was a temptation, but I did not approve of the decorating job in the end. Too finished for me.

We made hay in separate fields while the sun shone, waiting for me to acquire some sense and years. We spent what time we could together and we wrote letters in between.

But I did not marry George Gershwin. Despite his heavenly eyes, he never made me feel needed. He didn't need me. He had reached the dizzy heights of fame and fortune without me. He would go on to always greater achievement. Sometimes I wanted to dedicate my life to helping him; but often I did not like the idea of missing romance. "It's your Russian soul," he'd say. "You want a poor painter or poet or scholar to suffer with." He knew that a poor painter or poet or scholar my own age seemed more glamorous to me.

The memories are as clear as yesterday's. Even now, how much to remember! A delightful time to remember!

LETTERS FROM GEORGE TO ROSAMOND WALLING

July 12, 1931

Dear Far-away Rosamond—

By this time I imagine you are settled comfortably in jolly London & perhaps already trying on your court dress. The Prince has probably danced with you at the Embassy & has pronounced you America's most beautiful girl. (If he hasn't he should have.) You are simply crazy about England & tall Englishmen & think English women, while attractive, dress abominably. My imagination is working most freely today.

About 2 weeks ago I engaged 56 men to try & play my new rhapsody. The N.B.C. people very kindly gave me their studio B for the occasion & I invited a few of my friends. I will not bore you with a long description of the rehearsal except to tell you it sounded better than I had hoped it would....

Everett [Jacobs] called me the other day to ask me to go with him to Europe on the first of August. How I wish I could. I have missed Europe quite much & now that you're there the only thing that keeps me from going with Ev is the show I must write for Aarons & Freedley.

Frankie & Leo left for Rochester where they shall reside for the next two years. I shall miss my sister very much as I have great fondness for her as a person as well as the usual brotherly love. I hope she will be happy there & I think there is a good chance for it as Leo is a most interesting fellow & will take her mind off Rochester....

The east penthouse at 33 Riverside Drive sends love & best wishes but the west penthouse sends best wishes & love.

George

August 3, 1931

Dear Rosamond—

How lucky you are to be where you are. Away from hot, depressing America where high temperatures & low stocks seem to hold sway over a helpless people....

Yesterday—between 5 & 6 o'clock I played the sec-

ond movement of my concerto under W. Damrosch's baton at N.B.C.'s studio. We broadcasted on a short wave length to Germany. It was very exciting & I am glad the performance was so good. Next Monday I am playing Rhapsody in Blue at the Stadium. And who do you suppose I got to conduct for me? None other than my good-looking Irish pal Bill Daly. It will be his first performance as symphony conductor & we're all excited about it....

Sept. 5, 1931

Dearest Rosamond—

. . . I gave up smoking 3 months ago & not one puff of smoke has passed through these lips. I may start smoking again someday if only to live up to those caricatures of me with a corona-corona in my face.

To-night I am going to Otto Kahn's country place for the week-end. Recently he asked about you & I told him everything. You certainly have made an indelible impression on my friends. Only last night Billy Seeman said you were the nicest girl he had ever seen me with. Often when I think of you I get a desire to fly over to where you are, swoop down like an eagle & steal you & bring you to a big rock on a mountain & there have you all to myself. And I may do it someday.

My parents got back from the country recently & I am glad to tell you my mother is much better than she was. She still suffers from sinus trouble but thank God she hasn't any of those horrible nights that caused her such misery for the past year. Pop as usual, goes along uncomplainingly, taking things as they come—the happy philosopher.

Ira & I have begun working on a George Kaufman book—a satire on "Politics & Love"—called Of Thee I Sing. It is most amusing & we are looking forward to writing a score for it.

Out in California they have begun shooting our picture Delicious. Over the telephone the other day they told me great things were expected of this picture. Let's hope their expectations will be fulfilled. It may mean another picture contract next year, which would be pleasing to Ira & me....

Albert Coates wants me to come to Europe in February to play while he conducts in London, Paris, Berlin, Barcelona & Moscow. I'm trying to arrange to do it. It will be easy if I become the eagle that I threatened, earlier in this letter, to become. Much love to you dear Rosamond.

George

RECOLLECTIONS OF KAY SWIFT

George was always an enthusiast, steamed up with the essentials of anything. A play would do it. A painting.

Riding. He did it well. He smoked a cigar at the same time and I told him it doesn't go with riding a horse. An instructor somewhere up the Hudson had said to him while he was learning, "Tummy in, tummy out. Tummy in, tummy out." That was how you trotted. Sounds like something Gilbert and Sullivan would write.

Dancing was just natural with him. He didn't take any lessons. He was a free spirit, but very conventional where his family was concerned—although he was always blazing ahead. He would say, "Frankie pull your skirt down." Ira was always more reticent.

He didn't have that self-image that most people have that gets between one and what one is doing. George always put all of himself into everything he was doing. He always had complete concentration.

I think he was very logical in the way he would know just when to bring the first theme to a close, to develop, to return to the first and to have it then in contrapuntal form running one against the other.

The film Rhapsody in Blue made George into a person who was always in a hurry and who had to make time. No, it was not like that at all. It was all done in a joyful way, not in a driven way. The only thing I saw was a joyous delight in whatever he was doing and doing it completely, not breaking off and doing something else. Just seeing it to an appropriate end.

For the time being he turned to painting and turned back to music, and it was all rhythmic. It was never chopped off, abrupt. Never.

Of Thee I Sing had a wonderful opening night. Beatrice Kaufman and I gave a party. The critics came and read their reviews. I've never heard of such a thing before. I was running everywhere and Alice Duer Miller said, "Stop running. It will all be all right."

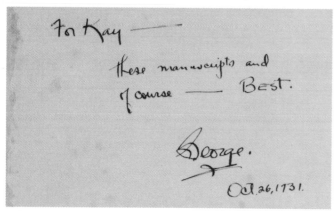

The inscription for the manuscripts of *George Gershwin's Song Book*, which George dedicated to Kay Swift.

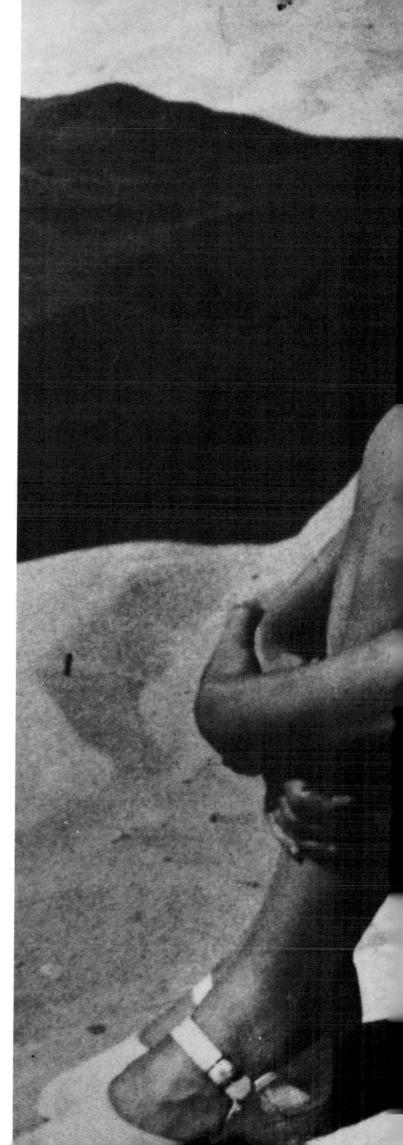

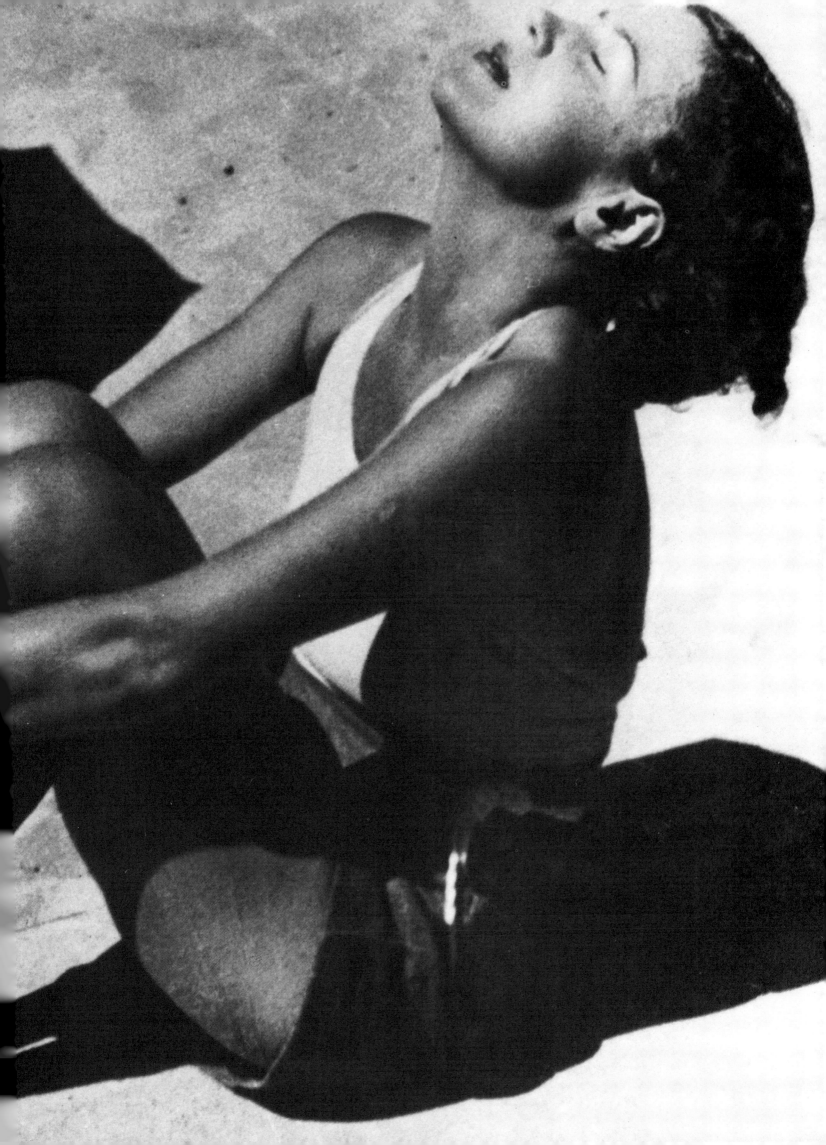

With *Of Thee I Sing* collaborators George S. Kaufman (left) and Morrie Ryskind (right).

OF THEE I SING (1931)

As a follow-up to *Strike Up the Band*, George S. Kaufman and Morrie Ryskind took as their target the United States government—the election of a President, the insignificance of being Vice-President, the Supreme Court, and national politics. Though the plot was far more genial than the serious business of *Strike Up the Band*, the authors nevertheless filled the proceedings with brilliant and devastating pokes at the foibles of government. Even the Depression didn't escape ribbing, but the satire was so deft that the show was rapturously received. Brooks Atkinson in the *New York Times* raved about the score, adding that the show itself was "funnier than the government, and not nearly so dangerous." The public seemed to agree and supported it for 441 performances on Broadway.

RECOLLECTIONS OF ALFRED SIMON

Since my early teens it had been my ambition to become involved in some way with the musical theater. And so, when Of Thee I Sing *was about to go into rehearsal in the autumn of 1931, I summoned up enough courage to ask George if I could be of assistance as pianist or in any other way. He told me that a rehearsal pianist had already been engaged, and that the conductor of the orchestra, Charles Previn (André's uncle, incidentally), would also be playing. Most composers, faced with such a question, would have let it go at that. Not George, however. Sensing my disappointment, he kindly and generously suggested that I drop in at the Music Box at any time to watch rehearsals—that I might, indeed, learn a lot just by observing.*

I jumped at this marvelous opportunity, and, as things turned out, I was soon put to work at the 46th Street Theatre around the corner, playing piano mostly for the dancers, headed by young George Murphy, who later made good in Hollywood and then in Washington. Day after day, I'd pound chorus after chorus of "Love Is Sweeping the Country," "Because, Because" and "Hello, Good Morning." Over at the Music Box headquarters, the principals and vocal ensemble were rehears-ing other songs, and sometimes I'd be called over there to help out. This was much more intricate (and of course less familiar) music to play than the dance numbers. George, conducting from the orchestra pit, right behind me, corrected me from time to time, saying "Not quite so fast" or "That should be an A flat."

George enjoyed playing piano during rehearsals just as much as he did at parties. Late one afternoon, after an exhausting rehearsal, some friends who came to call for him at the theater asked if he wouldn't play something before they left. Whereupon he went into an absolutely dazzling set of variations on "Liza." These, obviously, were improvisations; certainly it was a breathtaking musical experience for everyone there.

The three stars of that original Of Thee I Sing *cast were remarkably like the characters they played. William Gaxton, somewhat brash but affable, was a fine choice for the breezy Wintergreen. Lois Moran was a total delight as Mary. Most inspired of all was the casting of Victor Moore as Alexander Throttlebottom. Moore, a timid, top-heavy, lovable man, with a tentative manner, would arrive at the theater even on the sunniest days with an umbrella in hand. After taking off his coat and hat, he would walk to the edge of the stage, bend down slowly, and carefully place the umbrella near the footlights.*

Since my association with Of Thee I Sing *was primarily a musical one, these recollections have dealt mostly with George. Ira, reticent by nature, preferred to leave most decisions to his brother, although he was at the theater during most of the rehearsals. In contrast to the*

William Gaxton as John P. Wintergreen and Victor Moore as Alexander Throttlebottom, *Of Thee I Sing* (1931).

active George, who was always up on the stage, or in the orchestra pit, or in the back of the theater listening, Ira would remain seated in one of the front rows, just watching or conferring with his co-authors or with various members of the production staff.

The trials, intrigues, and storms that attend practically every Broadway musical during its preparation were notably absent in Of Thee I Sing, certainly insofar as one of my inexperience could notice. Rehearsals during the first five weeks always ended before midnight, and it was only during the final week that they sometimes went beyond that. It's also traditional for songs to be added, or dropped, or shifted from one scene to another, during the course of a tryout, but this show was so expertly planned that, except for some minor changes within musical sequences, the score was virtually intact when I heard it on the opening night in New York.

WHO CARES?

Verse:

(He) Here's some information
I will gladly give the nation:
I am for the true love—
Here's the only girl I do love.

(She) I love him and he loves me
And that's how it will always be—
So what care we about Miss Devereaux?

(Both) Who cares what the public chatters?
Love's the only thing that matters.

Refrain 1:

Who cares
If the sky cares to fall in the sea?
Who cares what banks fail in Yonkers
Long as you've got a kiss that conquers?
Why should I care?
Life is one long jubilee
So long as I care for you—
And you care for me.

Refrain 2:

Who cares
If the sky cares to fall in the sea?
We two together can win out;
Just remember to stick your chin out.
Why should I care?
Life is one long jubilee
So long as I care for you—
And you care for me.

Refrain 3:

Who cares
If the sky cares to fall in the sea?
Who cares how history rates me
Long as your kiss intoxicates me?
Why should I care?
Life is one long jubilee
So long as I care for you—
And you care for me.

LOVE IS SWEEPING THE COUNTRY

Verse:

Why are people gay
All the night and day,
Feeling as they never felt before?
What is the thing
That makes them sing?

Rich man, poor man, thief,
Doctor, lawyer, chief
Feel a feeling that they can't ignore;
It plays a part
In ev'ry heart,
And ev'ry heart is shouting "Encore!"

Refrain:

Love is sweeping the country;
Waves are hugging the shore;
All the sexes
From Maine to Texas
Have never known such love before.

See them billing and cooing
Like the birdies above!
Each girl and boy alike,
Sharing joy alike,
Feels that passion'll
Soon be national.
Love is sweeping the country—
There never was so much love!

Patter:
Spring is in the air—
Each mortal loves his neighbor;
Who's that loving pair?
That's Capital and Labor.

Florida and Cal-
ifornia get together
In a festival
Of oranges and weather.

Boston upper zones
Are changing social habits,
And I hear the Cohns
Are taking up the Cabots.

Cities are above
The quarrels that were hapless.
Look who's making love:
St. Paul and Minneap'lis!

Refrain:

Love is sweeping the country;
Waves are hugging the shore;
All the sexes
From Maine to Texas
Have never known such love before.

See them billing and cooing
Like the birdies above!
Each girl and boy alike,
Sharing joy alike,
Feels that passion'll
Soon be national.
Love is sweeping the country—
There never was so much love!

Opening, Act I, *Of Thee I Sing* (1931).

Wintergreen: "All that I can say of Mary Turner / Is that I love Mary Turner."
Wintergreen (William Gaxton), Mary Turner (Lois Moran).

Victor Moore, as the Vice-President, accompanies a guided tour of the White House.

OF THEE I SING (BABY)

Verse:

From the Island of Manhattan to the Coast of Gold,
From North to South, from East to West,
You are the love I love the best.
You're the dream girl of the sweetest story ever told;
A dream I've sought both night and day
For years through all the U.S.A.
The star I've hitched my wagon to
Is very obviously you.

Refrain:

Of thee I sing, baby—
Summer, autumn, winter, spring, baby.
You're my silver lining,
You're my sky of blue;
There's a lovelight shining
Just because of you.

Of thee I sing, baby—
You have got that certain thing, baby!
Shining star and inspiration,
Worthy of a mighty nation—
Of thee I sing!

…one of those rare shows in which everything clicked just right. After the opening there was little or no "fixing" to do.…One show that I'm more proud of than any I have written. I don't suppose it's hard to guess which one it is, and there's no suspense about it, I might as well tell you the name—it is Of Thee I Sing. This is the only musical comedy ever to be awarded a Pulitzer Prize. You remember what my father said when the prize was given. He said, "That Pulitzer must be a smart man."

George Gershwin

Wintergreen: "Twins! That's a little more than I counted on!"

(Overleaf) Guests at Rube Goldberg's fifteenth wedding anniversary celebration, October 23, 1931. Those identified include: (1) Mrs. Charles McAdams, (2) Billy De Beck, (3) Mrs. M. Malone, (4) Roy Long, (5) Roy Howard, (6) James Quirk, (7) O. O. McIntyre, (8) Lynne Overman, (9) Mrs. Walter Trumbull, (10) Mrs. Billy Seeman (Phyllis Haver), (11) Mrs. William De Beck II, (12) Mrs. Arthur William Brown, (13) Mrs. James Quirk (May Allison), (14) Walter Trumbull, (17) Mrs. Rube Goldberg, (18) John Golden, (19) Rube Goldberg, (20) Groucho Marx, (21) Sam Harris, and (22) George Gershwin.

On vacation in Havana, February 1932, after performances of the *Second Rhapsody*. With unidentified man, Adam Gimbel, Everett Jacobs, Bennett Cerf.

LETTER FROM SERGE KOUSSEVITZKY OCTOBER 28, 1929

Dear Mr. Gershwin,

I have seen Mr. Doukelsky [sic], who has told me of your wish that I should give performances to some of your compositions.

I will gladly do it, but, first of all, may I ask you to compose a piece special for the Boston Orchestra?

Next season is the 50th Anniversary of the Boston Symphony Orchestra and we would much appreciate it if you write a piece for the occasion.

I would be pleased to hear from you soon and to know if it suits you.

With best regards.

Sincerely yours
Serge Koussevitzky

Koussevitzky conducted the world première of Gershwin's *Second Rhapsody*, January 29, 1932, in Symphony Hall, Boston. George was soloist with the Boston Symphony.

RECOLLECTIONS OF EMIL MOSBACHER

George was in Cuba in 1932 with Everett Jacobs, Bennett Cerf, and Danny Silverberg, and he sent me a cable in Palm Beach to come over, but I didn't want to leave my family. At night they had to sleep with a mosquito netting over the bed. I finally went over for a few days, and there were George and Bennett chasing after the same girl, each trying to keep it from the other. When he returned from Cuba, George wrote and orchestrated the Cuban Overture at our home.

George always wanted to build a home out near my place in Westchester. He used to come up to use my teahouse room to finish his compositions. The teahouse room was in a great old fieldstone house, and George, once he got started on a piece, would work from seven in the morning until two the next morning. He'd work all day at the teahouse, but every so often he would come over to eat. The help would always spoil him; they always spoil bachelors.

Kay would often come up to visit him when he was working. I don't know if you realize the class of this girl or the home that Kay left, the home where she gave the parties after the openings. Oh, she had the place loaded with class.

George had such great admiration for her, and they both talked to me about marriage—separately, mind you —and I had one answer to both of them. I said that I wasn't going to open my mouth, I wasn't that crazy.

From George I'd get it every day. He was nuts about her. You know, she used to work night and day to help George with his orchestrations. Anyway, like George's, my admiration for her is so great that I always want the best for her.

Looking over the score of the *Second Rhapsody* with Serge Koussevitzky, conductor of the Boston Symphony Orchestra.

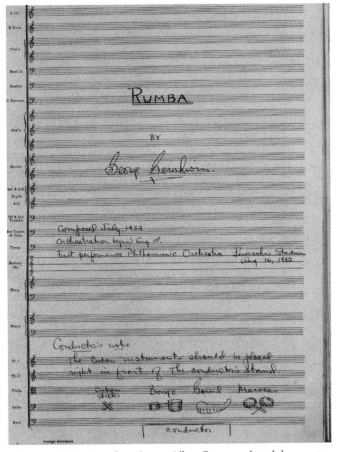

Title page of George's orchestral score. Albert Coates conducted the première. The title was later changed to *Cuban Overture.* George was especially proud of his engraved and monogrammed music paper.

Rose and Morris Gershwin in Florida, 1932.

A portrait of George by Henry Botkin.

Sketch by George of Henry Botkin.

RECOLLECTIONS OF HENRY BOTKIN

When I saw George's new apartment on Riverside Drive, I said, "George, the walls are bare! How about some paintings?" He said, "Fine. How do we start?" Just like that. I said, "George, I tell you what. We'll make it our business to go around to the galleries and see a lot of painters' work who we don't even know. Make a note of the painters you like and when I get back to Paris I can get them." And I said something else: "You know, in order to appreciate someone else's painting, do a little shmeering on your own." And I'll be damned. The next day when I came over, there was George with the canvas and paints all going. From the very beginning it was amazing! You could sit right down with George and he'd be making a pen-and-ink drawing which almost looked like it was a half-Matisse, half-Picasso. He had a knack. George had a way of valuing his painting and his music as an interchangeable phenomenon. They sprang, he felt, from the same Freudian elements, one of sight and the other of sound, the first to be shaped by a brush, the other with a goose bow. Isn't that amazing? He first stopped composing to paint, and then he finally stopped painting to compose. George never had the opportunity to carry on as a painter. He was always on the run. But if he ever had a time to paint for six months or even three months solid, he would have done surprisingly well.

Once he got started, I couldn't keep him away. We would go into some gallery—and I'm not speaking of a little gallery but a big one. Do you think he was satisfied in seeing the show that hung on the walls? No! When he went through there they had to open the whole place and pull everything out. He just couldn't wait. He wanted more, and more, and more. He had good judgment too.

George was so keyed up about his painting! He would come home about three or three-thirty in the morning after playing a long concert. I had set up a sort of studio for him, and he would say, walking over to his easel, "You know, Henry, there is something about this picture that bothers me." And he would stay up until about five o'clock sometimes, painting. He'd put the painting on his dresser just before he went to bed so when he'd wake up around one in the afternoon the next day he would see it with a fresh eye and see if it was what he had set out to do.

George was unbelievable about painting and collecting. If he were alive today, he would have had the house hung with nothing but the best. If you wanted to make George happy—and, God knows, who didn't?—you wouldn't say about his music, "The last thing you wrote, George, was simply beautiful." No, he wasn't interested. But if you said, about a painting of his, "That's beautiful. Did you just do that?" that would do it.

When I look back, I don't know how I had the knowledge to buy. I must have bought over two hundred paintings with George. Even with my Boston training, I was quite conservative, but I had lived in Paris for seven years.

PARDON MY ENGLISH (1933)

What can be said of a musical comedy that had five librettists, five directors, three orchestrators, a huge cast, numerous song changes, and a title that caused one critic to describe *Pardon My English* as a "poolroom drama"? Ira described it as "...a headache from start to finish. The Great Depression was at its deepest when we were asked to do the score for the show. Along with business, employment, and the stock market, the theater too was in terrible shape; and I felt we were lucky enough to be making a living from *Of Thee I Sing*. In addition, I disliked enormously the central notion of the project—duo-personality or schizophrenia or whatever the protagonist's aberration was supposed to be; so why toil and moil for six months on something we didn't want or need? However, loyalty to producer Aarons, who was broke and who told us if we didn't do the score his potential backers would back out, induced us to go ahead." Among those who fled or fell from the wreckage were Jack Buchanan (imported from England at a salary of $3,000 a week), Ona Munson, directors Ernst Lubitsch and George S. Kaufman, and authors Morrie Ryskind and Jack McGowan. The latter, however, permitted his name to be used as the show's director. The actual staging was done mostly by the beleaguered Vinton Freedley (who had come to Aarons' aid to save him from total ruin), dance director George Hale, and composer George himself.

Ira: "Herbert Fields was the only one brave enough to allow himself to be billed as librettist....Whatever business we did, including one good week in Boston, was primarily due to our leading comic, Jack Pearl, whose Baron Munchausen ('Vas you dere, Sharlie?') on the air attracted some of his radio audience to the theater. Opening night in New York, I stood among the few standees, but only for the first twenty minutes. A bad cold and a lukewarm audience had me home by nine thirty....I've never known of any theatrical failure where, sooner or later, an author or the stage-manager or one of the backers or some member of the cast didn't reminisce to the effect that there were some pretty good things in it. So, I must add: there were a couple of pretty good songs, like 'Isn't It a Pity?' and 'My Cousin in Milwaukee,' and a couple of pretty good comedy scenes in *Pardon My English*, olav hasholom."

Kay Swift remembers that both George and Ira were suffering from terrible colds, brought on by exhaustion from too much work in a hopeless cause. Nevertheless, she states enthusiastically that the Gershwin score was one of the best the brothers wrote.

A sad footnote to *Pardon My English* was that it marked the end of the producing team of Alex Aarons and Vinton Freedley, and this hurt the Gershwins, who were devoted to them and always grateful for their early sponsorship.

LET 'EM EAT CAKE (1933)

In his book *Lyrics on Several Occasions*, Ira Gershwin wrote: "If *Strike Up the Band* was a satire on War, and *Of Thee I Sing* one on Politics, *Let 'Em Eat Cake* was a satire on Practically Everything. Straddling no fence, it trampled the Extreme Right one moment, the Extreme Left the next. Kaufman and Ryskind's libretto was at times wonderfully witty—at other times unrelentingly realistic in its criticism of the then American scene." In *Let 'Em Eat Cake*, the sequel to *Of Thee I Sing*, Wintergreen and Throttlebottom are defeated for re-election, and head a revolution to overthrow the government. The public evidently found the issues too close to home, and *Let 'Em Eat Cake* closed after two and a half months.

Its score is perhaps the most inventive among all the Gershwins' musical comedies; in it one almost feels them rankling at the restrictions of the form. The *Let 'Em Eat Cake* overture is particularly adventurous, recalling in its opening some of the orchestral color and near-atonal harmonies of Alban Berg's *Wozzeck*.

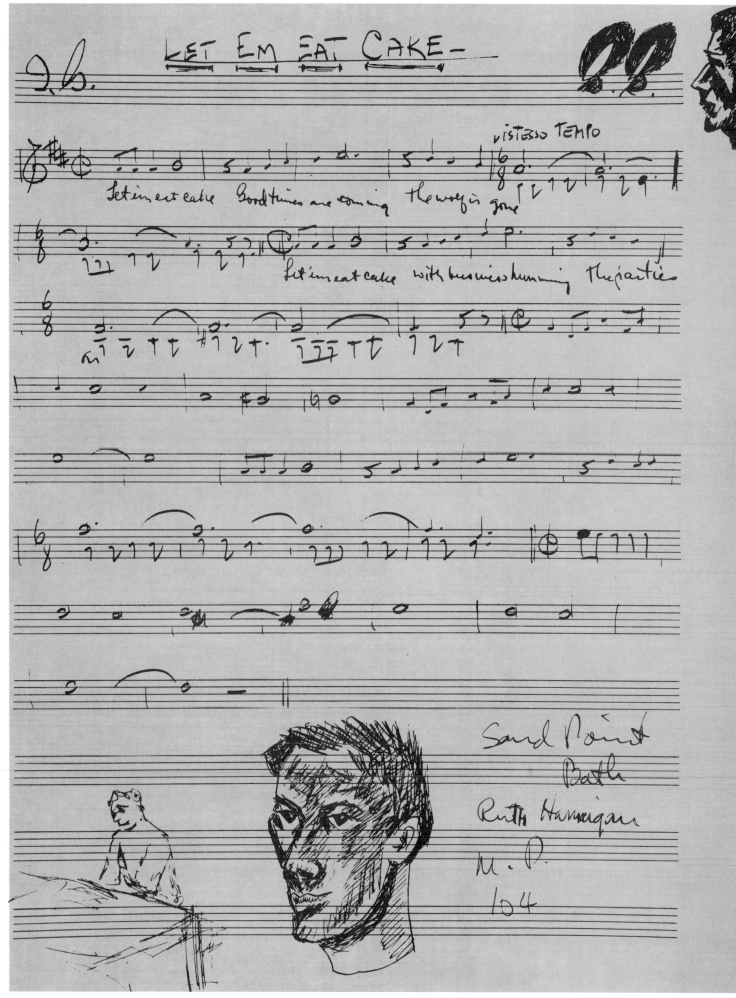

An early version of the title song. The doodles are George's.

The marquee of the Imperial Theatre in late 1933, the heart of the Depression.

Next door at the Music Box Theatre, Irving Berlin's *As Thousands Cheer*, one of the best revues ever staged, was beginning a run of 400 performances. It was Marilyn Miller's last show; she died April 7, 1936. / (Below) Back of the Imperial Theatre. The cars and streets were cleaner then.

MINE

Verse:

(Wintergreen) My good friends, don't praise me!
I owe it all to the little woman,
This little woman, my little woman.
She's the reason for my success.
Why when I think how we suffered together—
Worried together, struggled together,
Stood together together,
I grow so sentimental I'm afraid
I've got to burst into song.

(Ensemble) Please do!
We'd love to know how you feel about her
And how she feels about you.

Refrain:

(Wintergreen) Mine, love is mine,
Whether it rain or storm or shine.
Mine, you are mine,
Never another valentine.
And I am yours,
Tell me that I'm yours;
Show me that smile my heart adores.
Mine, more than divine,
To know that love like yours is mine!

Patter:

(Ensemble comes downstage
and sings the counter-melody
directly to audience)

The point they're making in the song
Is that they more than get along;
And he is not ashamed to say
She made him what he is today.
It does a person good to see
Such happy domesticity;
The way they're making love you'd swear
They're not a married pair.
He says, no matter what occurs,
Whatever he may have is hers;
The point that she is making is—
Whatever she may have is his.

(Ensemble repeats patter
as simultaneously the Wintergreens
repeat their refrain. Then Omnes:)

Mine, more than divine,
To know that love like yours is mine!

(Facing) Victor Moore as Throttlebottom: "Would you mind telling my newsdealer not to send any more papers?" Gaxton watches as Moore awaits a guillotine that never falls in *Let 'Em Eat Cake* (1933).

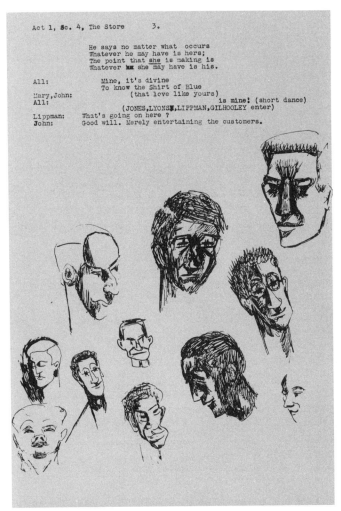

George doodled on the script too.

UNION SQUARE

Refrain:

Our hearts are in communion
When we gather down on Union
Square, heigh ho.
When whiskers are unshaven
One can always find a haven
There, heigh ho.
Though some may prefer the charming Bronnix,
Though some sing of dainty Sutton Place,
'Tis here we discover all the tonics
That cure all the problems of the race.
On boxes they put soap in
How we love it in the open
Air, heigh ho.
We may not fill our stomics,
But we're full of economics
Down on Union Square,
Down here on Union Square.

Patter:

(Kruger) Conditions as they are
Cannot go very far;
The world must move and we are here to move it.
The Brotherhood of Man
Is crying for a Plan,
So here's my Plan—I know you can't improve it!

(Henchmen) Conditions as they are
Can not go very far;
So—listen to his Plan
For man.

(Kruger) Down with one and one make two,
Down with ev'rything in view!
Down with all majorities;
Likewise all minorities!
Down with you, and you, and you!

(Ensemble) Down with one and two make three!
Down with all of us, says he.

(Kruger) Somehow I abominate
Anything you nominate.

(Henchmen) Ev'rything from A,B,C to X,Y,Z.

(Kruger) That's the torch we're going to get the
    flame from!
If you don't like it, why don't you go back where
    you came from?

(Ensemble—to one another) If you don't like it, why
    don't you go back where you came from?

(Kruger—with repeats from Ensemble)
Let's tear down the House of Morgan!
House of Morgan!
Let's burn up the Roxy organ!
Roxy organ!
Down with Curry and McCooey!
And McCooey!
Down with chow mein and chop suey!

And chop suey!
Down with music by Stravinsky!
By Stravinsky!
Down with shows except by Minsky!
Up with Minsky!

(Ensemble) Happiness will fill our cup,
When it's "Down with ev'rything that's up!"

(Kruger) Down with books by Dostoyevsky!
Dostoyevsky!
Down with Boris Thomashefsky!
Thomashefsky!
Down with Balzac! Down with Zola!
Down with Zola!
Down with pianists who play "Nola"!

(All dance to opening four bars of "Nola")

Down with all the Upper Classes!
Upper Classes!
Might as well exclude the Masses!
'Clude the Masses!
Happiness will fill our cup
When it's "Down with ev'rything that's up!"

(They are all pretty excited by now)

So down with this, and down with that!
And down with ev'rything in view!
The hell with this, the hell with that!
The hell with you, and you, and you!

(To one another)

(One Group) The hell with who?

(Second Group) The hell with you!

(Third) The hell with whom?

(Fourth) The hell with youm!

(All square off. A free-for-all follows.
Policeman enters, blows whistle.
The grounded ones get up, flick dust off.
All, Policeman included, saunter off singing:)

Refrain:

Our hearts are in communion
When we gather down on Union
Square, heigh ho.
When whiskers are unshaven
One can always find a haven
There, heigh ho.
Though some prefer the charming Bronnix,
Though some sing of dainty Sutton Place,
'Tis here we discover all the tonics
That cure all the problems of the race.
On boxes they put soap in,
How we love it in the open
Air, heigh ho.
We may not fill our stomics,
But we're full of economics
Down on Union Square,
Down here on Union Square.

Let 'Em Eat Cake (1933) starred William Gaxton, Lois Moran, and Victor Moore.

Phillip Loeb and ensemble sing "Down with Everything That's Up." / (Overleaf) In Nassau, 1933—Ira, Lee, George, with Ellen and Irving Berlin.

Tour Celebrating the Tenth Anniversary of "Rhapsody in Blue"

presenting

GEORGE GERSHWIN
Composer · Pianist

JAMES MELTON, *Tenor*
and the
REISMAN SYMPHONIC ORCHESTRA
CHARLES PREVIN, *Conductor*
IN A PROGRAM OF GERSHWIN SUCCESSES
(Program subject to change)

1. CONCERTO IN F...Gershwin
   The "Concerto in F" is of thirty minutes' duration and was published in 1925. The usual rhythmic effects are conveyed throughout the work which is unmistakably Gershwin. It has been played by Walter Damrosch, the Boston Symphony, the Philharmonic Orchestra under Mengelberg and Van Hoogstraten; the Milwaukee Orchestra, the Minneapolis Orchestra under Verbrugghen; the Cincinnati Orchestra and the Pasdeloup Orchestra of Paris.
   MR. GERSHWIN

2. (a) SWANEE
      DO IT AGAIN (Sam and Delilah)
      LADY BE GOOD
   (b) MINE ....Gershwin
   (c) STRIKE UP THE BAND
   ORCHESTRA

3. (a) HILLS OF HOME...........................Oscar Fox
   (b) HOME ON THE RANGE........................David Guion
   (c) CARRY ME BACK TO THE LONE PRAIRIE.......Carson Robinson
   MR. MELTON

4. RHAPSODY IN BLUE...Gershwin
   The famous "Rhapsody in Blue," the foundation stone of Gershwin's reputation, is the first of the composer's work in the larger forms. Jazz and nobility of thematic material stalk through the Rhapsody in alternating moods and the difficulty of the piano part is matched by its brilliance. This is a work which any audience will enjoy from beginning to end.
   MR. GERSHWIN
   INTERMISSION

5. AN AMERICAN IN PARIS..Gershwin
   Deems Taylor wrote an analysis of "An American in Paris" which follows: "By its composer's own confession, 'An American in Paris' is an attempted reconciliation between two opposing schools of musical thought. It is program-music in that it engages to tell an emotional narrative; to convey, in terms of sound the successive emotional reactions experienced by a Yankee tourist adrift in the City of Light. It is absolute music as well, in that its structure is determined by considerations musical rather than literary or dramatic. The piece, while not in strict sonata form, resembles an extended symphonic movement in that it announces, develops, combines and recapitulates definite themes. Only, whereas the ordinary symphonic movement is based upon two principal themes, 'An American in Paris' manipulates five."
   ORCHESTRA

6. (a) SOMETIMES I FEEL LIKE A MOTHERLESS CHILD ..Arr. by Frank Black
   (b) G'WINE TO HEB'N............................Jacques Wolfe
   (c) SHORTNIN' BREAD............................Jacques Wolfe
   JAMES MELTON

7. "I GOT RHYTHM," Variations (New)...............Gershwin
   MR. GERSHWIN

8. "WINTERGREEN FOR PRESIDENT" from "Of Thee I Sing".....Gershwin
   ORCHESTRA

9. MEDLEY (a) FASCINATING RHYTHM
           (b) MAN I LOVE
           (c) LIZA ....Gershwin
           (d) I GOT RHYTHM
   MR. GERSHWIN

Steinway Pianos Used

George with Leo Reisman in George's apartment. The music on the rack is the *Concerto in F.*

Program for the concert tour. Charles Previn conducted in place of the injured Leo Reisman, who had suffered a broken hip.

CONCERT TOUR (1934)

In late 1933 George wrote the *Variations on "I Got Rhythm"* while he was on a Palm Beach holiday with Emil Mosbacher. The work, dedicated to Ira, was premiered in Boston on January 14, 1934, at the first stop of George's whirlwind tour in which he played 28 concerts in 28 days with the Leo Reisman Orchestra conducted by Charles Previn. The tour, which also featured tenor James Melton, was a huge critical success and a remarkable testament to George's prodigious physical stamina. George played the *Concerto in F*, the *Rhapsody in Blue*, *Variations on "I Got Rhythm,"* and several of his songs at each of the concerts on the barnstorm, which took him to many American cities he had never seen before. Unfortunately, it also took him into some auditoriums that were not large enough to recoup the cost of the concerts. George, who waived any fee for the tour and received only his train fare and expenses, had to kick in over $5,000 of his own to help cover the deficit.

ITINERARY

GEORGE GERSHWIN
WITH THE LEO REISMAN ORCHESTRA. CHARLES PREVIN, CONDUCTOR,
AND JAMES MELTON, TENOR SOLOIST

Sun., Jan. 14	Symphony Hall	Boston, Mass.
Mon., Jan. 15	City Hall Auditorium	Portland, Me.
Tues., Jan. 16	Memorial Auditorium	Worcester, Mass.
Wed., Jan. 17	City Auditorium	Springfield, Mass.
Thurs., Jan. 18	Lincoln Auditorium, Central High School	Syracuse, N.Y.
Fri., Jan. 19	Massey Hall	Toronto, Canada
Sat., Jan. 20	Music Hall, Public Auditorium	Cleveland, Ohio
Sun., Jan. 21	Orchestra Hall	Detroit, Mich.
Mon., Jan. 22	Shrine Theater	Fort Wayne, Ind.
Tues., Jan. 23	Auditorium	Milwaukee, Wis.
Wed., Jan. 24	West High School	Madison, Wis.
Thurs., Jan. 25	Auditorium	St. Paul, Minn.
Fri., Jan. 26	The Coliseum	Sioux Falls, S.D.
Sat., Jan. 27	Technical High School	Omaha, Neb.
Sun., Jan. 28	Convention Hall	Kansas City, Mo.
Mon., Jan. 29	Shrine Auditorium	Des Moines, Iowa
Tues., Jan. 30	Masonic Auditorium	Davenport, Iowa
Wed., Jan. 31	The Odeon	St. Louis, Mo.
Thurs., Feb. 1	English Opera House	Indianapolis, Ind.
Fri., Feb. 2	Memorial Auditorium	Louisville, Ky.
Sat., Feb. 3	Taft Auditorium	Cincinnati, Ohio
Sun., Feb. 4	Auditorium Theater	Chicago, Ill.
Mon., Feb. 5	Memorial Hall	Dayton, Ohio
Tues., Feb. 6	Syria Mosque	Pittsburgh, Pa.
Wed., Feb. 7	Academy of Music	Philadelphia, Pa.
Thurs., Feb. 8	Constitution Hall	Washington, D.C.
Fri., Feb. 9	Mosque Auditorium	Richmond, Va.
Sat., Feb. 10	Academy of Music	Brooklyn, N.Y.

"Self-Portrait in a Checkered Sweater" by George Gershwin (1936)

"George
in an Imaginary
Concert Hall"
by David Siqueiros
(1935)

F. GODOWSKY

(Top, left) "Leonore" by C. W. Anderson (1925); (bottom, left) "Nadia—A Pastel by Her Mother" by Frances Gershwin Godowsky (1955); (top, center) "My Studio —Folly Beach" by George Gershwin (1934); (bottom, center) "Charlie's Lawn" by Ira Gershwin (1932); (top, right) "Emily" by George Gershwin (1933); (bottom, right) "Mother" by George Gershwin (1936)

"Self-Portrait in an Opera Hat" by George Gershwin (1932)

"My Grandfather" by George Gershwin (1933)

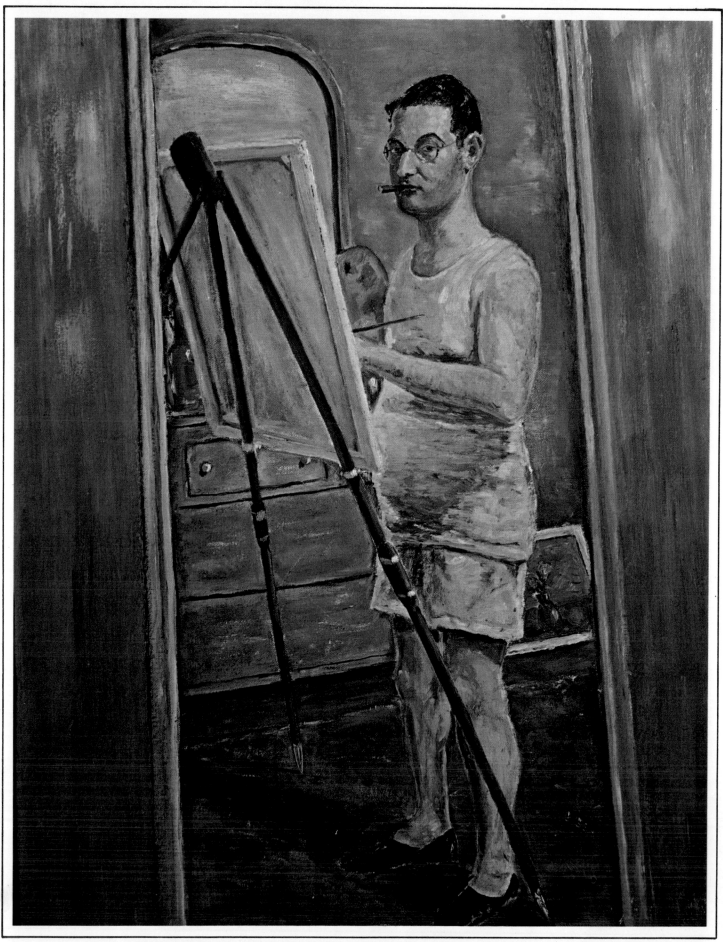

"My Body" by Ira Gershwin (1932)

Near the end of the arduous tour with the Reisman Orchestra—Richmond, Virginia, February 9, 1934.

At a party, 1934.

George with Mabel Schirmer at a party given by newscaster Boake Carter.

```
BAW493 12=US SARATOGASPRINGS NY 6 820P

HIP HARBURG,CARE LIFE BEGINS CO=
    SHUBERT THEATER=


YIP HOPE A BIG SUCCESS FOR YOU STARTS AT EIGHT FORTY TONIGHT=
    GEORGE GERSHWIN.
```

RECOLLECTIONS OF HAROLD ARLEN

I met George long before Ira and Yip and I collaborated on Life Begins at 8:40. I think it was in New Haven, although it may have been Philadelphia or Boston, when George and Ira were attending tryouts of Strike Up the Band. At the same time Ruth Selwyn was producing a show called the 9:15 Revue, to which many composers and lyricists each contributed one or two songs. My song "Get Happy" was sung by Ruth Etting as the first-act finale. It had lots of girls on a beach dancing to Busby Berkeley choreography, and there were some great, great men of jazz in the pit, fellows like Benny Goodman, Red Nichols, and Joe Venuti. The number came off very well.

One day a man came down the aisle; it was George, who was there because he and Ira also had a song in the show. He told me that "Get Happy" was "great, absolutely great," and that was a pretty encouraging way for our friendship to begin. In time I got to know him better. One night we walked home together from Lindy's. George lived on East 72nd Street and Ira lived in an apartment across the street. We went up to George's, where I played and then George played eight-, ten-, twelve-bar phrases. Whenever George wanted to play, I'd get off the stool. Hearing him play the piano is one of my most cherished memories.

George was a guy with a delicious talent who was always eager to learn. His own piano style was very staccato, and especially when he played his own songs he hated to use pedals. I, on the other hand, can't play without them. But you do need pedals for songs like "Bess, You Is My Woman Now."

George had great energy, love of hard work, and delight in other writers' work if they had merit. He was always analyzing. I remember George saying that if one melody seems to sound like another, don't use a lyric that reveals it.

George was famous, but he was also strongly criticized in his time. One day when I walked him home, he kept complaining, "What do they want me to do? What are they criticizing me for?" This was at the time of the radio shows he did for Feen-A-Mint. People forget that was in 1934 and the depression was still on. Those were bad times, and what George was doing on his radio show was helping all of us.

As a person, George was easy to be with, just as easy as can be. He was a very hamisch man, nothing phony about him. He knew he had it, and he celebrated it.

RECOLLECTIONS OF KITTY CARLISLE

I met George originally on a radio show that Rudy Vallee was conducting, an all-Gershwin program. I sang "The Man I Love," and George played for me. I was

Kitty Carlisle in Hollywood.

frightened to death, and George took me aside and said, "Come on now, we'll rehearse." That was so dear. He must have seen my terror, and so we rehearsed—and that's how I got to meet George Gershwin.

Then he used to take me to parties. I remember the first party I ever went to with George, at Elsa Maxwell's. It was frightfully glamorous. Everyone was there. Gertrude Lawrence sang, George played, and I sang—frightened out of my wits. I was in my first show in New York, Champagne Sec, and I was bug-eyed.

George was a good dancer and had a charming apartment on 72nd Street, which he ran extremely well. I used to go there quite often when he was orchestrating Porgy and Bess. He would orchestrate after dinner and I would sit there very admiringly. Once in a while he would say, "Just sing this for me so I can hear how it sounds"—from Porgy and Bess or something else he was working on. I realized later that this is what George would use as blandishments for ladies. I wasn't helping him a bit! It's like fireflies—they light up to attract the opposite sex. Well, this was George lighting up. I got on to it much later when one day he came to see me with a waltz that he played for all the ladies. He always said he had a piece he had written just for them. I don't know how I found out, but again this was one of his blandishments.

George was studying with Schillinger and would come over to see me after his lesson. I was living at the Ritz Tower then, and he would come running up with all his notations, of which I didn't understand anything. He would want to repeat what he had just learned to someone else because that is how you remember. This wasn't blandishments. I was very flattered.

George took me to the one and only prize fight I have ever been to, way up in the Bronx somewhere. He kept poking me in the ribs. I came out with my whole side black and blue.

I went to California, and when I came back, George took me to Porgy and Bess. Then we had dinner, Passover, and Oscar Levant was there. Oscar did the service in Hebrew, but in a sort of jazz version. Fascinating, absolutely fascinating.

I remember when George was going to do a concert at the Stadium one summer, I asked him whether he was going to practice. He said no, he didn't practice. What! You know the old saying: the first day you know you haven't practiced, by the third day your manager knows it, and by the fourth day your audience knows it. Then I realized that George didn't have to practice. He played the piano all the time. He not only played at home, but he played at everyone else's house too. Wherever he went. But it was very attractive. Everyone knew he was a genius, so they were very flattered to have George play on their piano.

One day George just called up Steinway and got them to loan me a small grand piano. I had it for years. And then one day Steinway called up and said they thought I should either buy it or give it back, and so of course I bought it.

Was his music the most important part of his life? I don't know. I think he wanted to get married. I know he wanted to get married. How important it was to him I don't know. He was very fussy about whom he wanted to marry.

George was so dear. He had everything, but there was something terribly vulnerable about him. People felt very protective about him. Why I don't know. He was successful, he was good-looking, women adored him, he had money. He had everything, but yet there was something vulnerable, childlike. He needed approval. Yes, maybe that's it. And you felt it. That was part of his charm. Enthusiasm—that was part of his charm too. And his enthusiasm was terribly boyish for a man who was that successful. He had an enormous sense of enjoyment and enthusiasm which he infused into everything he did. And enormous energy, and there's nothing quite as sexy as energy, is there? What else is there?

George exercised regularly and employed a trainer to help him keep in shape.

170

On February 19, nine days after his return to New York, George began a series of radio programs sponsored by Feen-A-Mint. These were presented as fifteen-minute shows twice a week from February 19 to May 31 and then as thirty-minute shows once a week from September 23 to December 23. Gershwin played Gershwin and featured songs by other composers of theater and popular music, making a show that is still memorable to those who heard it. George paid tribute to men who had influenced his own career (Sousa, Friml, Herbert,

Richard Rodgers and Lorenz Hart.

Ann Ronell.

John Green.

Jerome Kern.

W. C. Handy.

Herman Hupfeld.

Hoagy Carmichael.

Ferde Grofé.

Howard Dietz.

Handy, Kern, and Berlin), his contemporaries (Rodgers, Porter, Youmans, Henderson), younger composers (Green, Dana Suesse, Morton Gould, Vernon Duke, Harold Arlen), and many more, some of whom appeared as guests. Preparing the shows was time-consum-

ing and often difficult, but the remuneration was substantial—reportedly $2,000 a week. When people later chided George for having appeared on a show sponsored by a laxative, he replied, "Without Feen-A-Mint, I would not have been able to write *Porgy and Bess*."

Vernon Duke.

Vincent Youmans.

John Philip Sousa.

Morton Gould.

Victor Herbert.

Ray Henderson.

Arthur Schwartz.

Dorothy Fields.

Milton Ager.

PORGY AND BESS (1935)

Edwin Du Bose Heyward was born into an aristocratic Charleston, South Carolina, family on August 31, 1885. He left school early to take a job on the waterfront. At eighteen Heyward was stricken with polio and during his recovery began writing—poetry at first and later novels and plays.

In 1921, he met Dorothy Kuhns, a young dramatist, whom he married the following year. With her wide knowledge of the theater, Dorothy was to be Heyward's most successful collaborator.

In 1924 Heyward wrote his first book and greatest success, *Porgy*. The idea for the story he found in a newspaper article about a maimed black man who committed murder at the height of passion. Heyward drew upon his early experience on the waterfront, re-creating the teeming life of Catfish Row. In 1926 George Gershwin read *Porgy* and immediately wrote Heyward about his wish to compose an opera based on it. It was not until nine years later, however, that Heyward and Gershwin collaborated on *Porgy and Bess*.

It is astonishing today how innovative the treatment of black life in *Porgy* was. Heyward wrote not out of pity for an exploited race, nor with any desire to propagandize; rather it was his intention to dramatize a way of life which he found strange and admirable and worthy of serious artistic expression.

In March 1932 George again wrote Du Bose Heyward of his desire to set *Porgy* to music. They had met in 1926 at the time of the original Theatre Guild production of the Heywards' play. When Heyward informed George that the operatic rights to *Porgy* were "free and clear," George then informed Heyward that it would take at least a year for him to write the music for the opera.

In the meantime, Jerome Kern and Oscar Hammerstein II became interested in making *Porgy* into a musical for Al Jolson, and Jolson was eager to use *Porgy* as a vehicle. George, though he was fond of Jolson and appreciated his talents, was not wild about the idea. But he felt that an immediate Jolson *Porgy* would not conflict with an eventual operatic version by Gershwin.

Du Bose and Dorothy Heyward.

Evidently, Jolson decided not to pursue the *Porgy* project, and so Heyward began working on the libretto for George. A letter dated November 12, 1933, shows Heyward struggling with the job of rethinking his own play. It was here that one of George's favorite ideas, the opening Jazzbo Brown piano sequence (usually cut from productions), first saw the light of day:

I am offering a new idea for opening of scene as you will see from the script. The play opened with a regular riot of noise and color. This makes an entirely different opening, which I think is important. What I have in mind is to let the scene, as I describe it, merge with the overture, almost in the sense of illustration, giving the added force of sight and sound. I think it would be very effective to have the lights go out during overture, so that the curtain rises in darkness, then the first scene will begin to come up as the music takes up the theme of jazz from the dance hall piano. The songs which I have written for this part will fall naturally into the action and mood of the separate flashes of negro life.

Heyward invited his collaborator down to Charleston for a visit. George answered on the 25th:

Dear Du Bose:
I am leaving with my friend, Emil Mosbacher, the night of December second—next Saturday—for Charleston, arriving there sometime on the third.

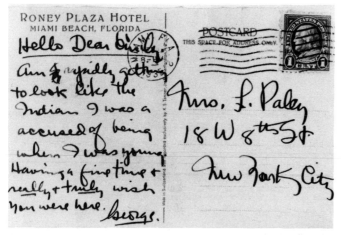

I expect to stay two or three days and then leave for Florida. I hope you can arrange it so as to spend most of the time with me. I would like to see the town and hear some spirituals and perhaps go to a colored cafe or two if there are any....

From the beginning Ira was a collaborator on *Porgy and Bess*. The lyrics to Act I are by Heyward, the lyrics to Acts II and III are by Ira and Heyward. Ira's greater experience as a lyric writer was of enormous help to Heyward, whose own unique contribution to *Porgy and Bess* included the lyrics to "Summertime" and "My Man's Gone Now." The collaboration was a fruitful and amicable one for all concerned, and Heyward himself later wrote of his experience in working with George.

RECOLLECTIONS OF DU BOSE HEYWARD

I imagine that in after years when George looks back upon this time, he will feel that the summer of 1934 furnished him with one of the most satisfying as well as exciting experiences of his career. Under the baking suns of July and August we established ourselves on Folly Island, a small barrier island ten miles from Charleston. James Island with its large population of primitive Gullah Negroes lay adjacent, and furnished us with a laboratory in which to test our theories, as well as an inexhaustible source of folk material. But the most inter-

esting discovery to me, as we sat listening to their spirituals, or watched a group shuffling before a cabin or country store, was that to George it was more like a homecoming than an exploration. The quality in him which had produced the Rhapsody in Blue in the most sophisticated city in America found its counterpart in the impulse behind the music and bodily rhythms of the simple Negro peasant of the South.

The Gullah Negro prides himself on what he calls "shouting." This is a complicated rhythmic pattern beaten out by feet and hands as an accompaniment to the spirituals and is indubitably an African survival. I shall never forget the night when, at a Negro meeting on a remote sea-island, George started "shouting" with them. And eventually to their huge delight stole the show from their champion "shouter." I think that he is probably the only white man in America who could have done it.

From George Gershwin,
edited and designed by Merle Armitage
(London: Longmans, Green and Co., Ltd., 1938)

LETTER FROM GEORGE TO HIS MOTHER

Wednesday

Dear Mother,

The place down here looks like a battered, old South Sea Island. There was a storm 2 weeks ago which tore down a few houses along the beach & the place is so primitive they just let them stay that way. Imagine, there's not one telephone on the whole Island—public or private. The nearest phone is about 10 miles away.

Our first three days here were cool, the place being swept by an ocean breeze. Yesterday was the first hot day (it must have been 95° in town) & it brought out the flys [sic], and knats [sic], mosquitos. There are so many swamps in the district that when the breeze comes in from the land there's nothing to do but scratch.

If you're thinking of coming down here, consider these nuisances as I'd hate to have you make the trip & then be uncomfortable. I know you like your comforts.

We wear nothing but bathing suits all day long & certainly enjoy that part of it.

Du Bose Heyward is coming down tomorrow to spend 2 weeks & I hope to get some work done on the opera.

I'm glad I didn't bring Tony as it would have been a little hot for him. I think you should send him up to Mosbachers, if you leave town.

Please write me & I'll let you know what happens. Hope you are well & that I'll see you soon. Love to yourself and Arthur.

Your George

George and two young friends.

to Emil + Gertrude —
     I might have just as good a time
away from you — but I strongly doubt it.
     Love, George.
                    +
                    Palm Beach.
                       1935

LETTER FROM GEORGE TO EMILY PALEY

July 11, 1934

Dear Emily—

I've thought about you a good deal, also. In fact, we probably exchanged thoughts mental-telepathy fashion. Your letter which arrived yesterday was so welcome. It really set me up. So sweetly worded, so sincerely felt, your letter was like seeing & talking to you. The trip down here was a very good thing in many ways. Firstly, I've thought a good deal about my present and future plans, & have come to a few decisions. Secondly, the place itself is very different from anything I've seen or lived in before & appeals to the primitive man in me. We go around with practically nothing on, shave only every other day (we do have some visitors, you know), eat out on our porch not more than 30 feet from the ocean at high tide, sit out at night gazing at the stars, smoking our pipes. (I've begun on a pipe.) The 3 of us, Harry, Paul & myself discuss our two favorite subjects, Hitler's Germany & God's women. We are in truth, Yankees from the North, always suspected a little by the southerner as being a bit slick.

Lonesomeness has crept in and hit me quite a few times, but that is to be expected. Paul & Harry have also been bitten, so I suppose that should be a bit consoling.

I've finished one scene of the opera & am now working on the second. It's been very tough for me to work here as the wild waves, playing the role of a siren, beckon to me every time I get stuck, which is often, and I like a weak sailor turn to them causing many hours to be knocked into a thousand useless bits.

I've seen & heard some grand negro sermons & when I see you I shall tell you all about them. Also remind me to tell you how we found ourselves in an auto in 4 feet of the Atlantic. Also, how we discovered a turtle's egg nest & found it to contain 164 eggs about the size of a silver dollar. Also about the beauty contest which takes place Sat. night when I will be the judge.

Give all my best to dear Lou & tell him I only played golf twice and shot an 85 the second time. My regards to your family & the gang.

Love,
George

P.S. We are driving home starting Monday. Stopping off various places. Home Saturday.

(Facing) Inscribed to the Mosbachers.

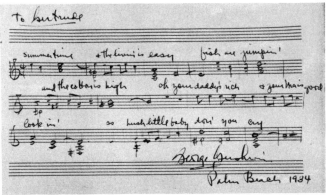

An early version of "Summertime," inscribed to Mrs. Emil Mosbacher.

Du Bose and Ira.

RECOLLECTIONS OF KAY HALLE

Kay Halle, writer and radio commentator, is a member of the family that owns Halle's, the famous Cleveland department store. While living in London in 1931, she became a close friend of the late Sir Winston Churchill, about whom she has written several books. She lived in New York in the mid-1930s and among her friends there was George Gershwin.

———

When George was writing Porgy and Bess, *he went down to South Carolina and wrote me that he had gone to a church and had heard the spiritual "Doctor Jesus, Lean Down from Heaven and Place a Belly Band of Love Around Me." This gave him inspiration, which he also received from going down by the shore and seeing the turtles coming out of the water. He became totally absorbed in the atmosphere around him.*

One day George called me up and said come over and have lunch because I've got another contender for the role of Porgy. It was Todd Duncan. He sang, among other things, Mussorgsky's "Song of the Flea" and George was so relieved because so many of the people whom he heard while he was casting the opera felt they had to perform Negro music even if it wasn't suited to their own style of singing. Then George gave him "Bess, You Is My Woman Now" and Todd sang it. At the end my sister, who was with me, and I looked at each other and saw George look at Todd and heard him say, "Todd, you are Porgy!"

While he was writing the score, George did a lot of work with a Hammond organ in order to try to simulate the full effect of the opera if it were orchestrated. During this period George had an arrangement with Gloria [Braggiotti] and myself. After we'd get home from dates we would call him up, and if he hadn't eaten, we'd go to a delicatessen and bring him snacks and listen to him play the new things he had worked out. Night after night we used to bring him salami and brown bread.

Throughout his work on Porgy, George was very restless. He couldn't stay in the country because, he said, the calibration of the bees, the crickets, and the birds and other sounds would conflict with what he was trying to do. The country seemed to disturb him, and he never stayed there very long.

For some reason he loved my piano. I had a baby grand that had been picked out by Mr. Fred Steinway after it had been approved by Artur Rubinstein. In fact, our family store in Cleveland was one of the few department stores in the country where you could buy a Steinway. Anyway, George loved that piano. And George and I had an arrangement with the man at the desk of the Elysée Hotel, where I lived. If I was out and George wanted to come in, he always could have the key to my room.

One night I came in after a dinner about eleven o'clock and as I walked up the stairway to my apartment, I heard the piano. I tiptoed in. George turned, saw me, and said, "Sit down, I think I have the lullaby." I knew he had been working very hard to get the lullaby and that he had done several versions that didn't suit him. And so he sang in this high wailing-wall voice "Summertime," and it was exquisite. We looked at each other and the tears were just coursing down my cheeks and I just knew that this was going to be beloved by the world.

RECOLLECTIONS OF WARREN MUNSELL

Warren Munsell was Theatre Guild Production Manager for Porgy and Bess.

George had an idea of opening the opera with a piano

scene in a café. It was never in the production. We had to cut it because, as I told George, it would mean a completely different set and the cost would be too great. George took the decision well—he was very agreeable to work with—and said, "Okay, that means we start with the lullaby, and that's some lullaby."

The show was too long in Boston, and I got into trouble with our subscribers because I booked the show there for only one week. There were to be forty-two musicians in the pit, but the Guild was already frightened at the cost of the show. Yet the show cost less than $50,000 to produce, and some of the Guild members invested in the show. Years later they more than got their money back.

RECOLLECTIONS OF EMIL MOSBACHER

We went down to Palm Beach one winter so George could orchestrate Porgy and Bess there. We rented a glorious home there, the Schiff house. My wife, Gertrude, and our three children were there, and so was George.

One morning he came to me—this time it wasn't the golf—and he said, "I'm afraid the Theatre Guild might not go through with Porgy." The Guild had scared George by telling him it might cost $75,000 to $100,000, which would be too much. Now, by this time I'm wrapped up in it. I said, "George, please don't louse things up. Handle it my way. Go to the telephone and tell the Theatre Guild lawyer that I, Emil Mosbacher, will put up half the money for the show. George, I bet you $100 I won't get any part of it, because as soon as they hear I'm ready to come in on that scale, they'll go ahead with the show and do anything to keep me out." I could have put up the dough. The money was there. But I knew the psychology of the thing—when one person makes a bid, that creates other bids. I really didn't want to invest in the show, but I would have done it to help George if it meant the difference between doing it and not doing it.

When George was living with us in Palm Beach that month, I'd say, "George, so-and-so called." Some top person, not café society. That person wanted to give a party and wanted George to play. George would say, "I'll have to play the piano"—but he always wanted to play the piano and I felt his protests were a lot of crap. He'd say, "Come on over with me." I didn't want to go. And he'd go, and play all night, and come home and complain like hell the next day.

It was the same thing when we would go to Saratoga for the races or the time we went to the Kentucky Derby.

George didn't want to make the trip to Louisville, but a group got a private railroad car with a bar and a piano and George played all the way down and back and loved it.

George worked in spells. It was all right for him to fault Ira, but George didn't start things either until the pressure of a deadline was on him—and then he'd work like hell.

When he worked on Porgy and Bess, he told me he'd always wanted to produce his own shows. I told him, "Please, George, don't produce. It will louse up your music." But he harped on it a great deal. I said, "George, you'll have all the income you'll ever need with ASCAP." But George would say, "I cast all the shows, why shouldn't I produce them?"

RECOLLECTIONS OF TODD DUNCAN

I had sung opera—at an all-Negro opera in the Mecca Temple on 55th Street. In 1934 Olin Downes had told Gershwin that he must hear me and a woman, Abbie Mitchell, who had sung Santuzza to my Alfio. Mecca Temple was packed.

George Gershwin was then going around the country looking for his Porgy. When they told him that I was teaching in a university, he said he didn't want any university professor to sing. But he'd been going to different night clubs all over the country—he told me that he heard a hundred Negro baritones in a year's time—so he called me and asked if I would come sing for him.

I just wasn't very interested. I was teaching in a university in Washington, and I thought of George Gershwin as being Tin Pan Alley and something beneath me. So I told him that I couldn't come this Sunday because I was singing in a little church where I was soloist, and I refused the wonderful man whom I came to love and revere. I said I could come the next Sunday. So I went to New York and went up to his apartment at one P.M. He came to the door himself and he asked, "Where's your accompanist?" I didn't know anything about New York ways. I said, "Accompanist? Can't you play?" "Well, I play a little," he said. He blinked his eyes. "If you can't play it, I'll play for myself," I told him. "I'll try to play for you. I'll try," he finally said.

I put a piece on the piano. I had several things. "What is this?" he wanted to know. "This is an old Italian song,

Todd Duncan.

a classic. 'Lungi dal caro bene.'" "What?" he asked. I thought maybe he didn't understand my Italian, so I translated it for him. I was just naïve enough to do all the right things, and I didn't know I was doing the right things.

He used to tell that he'd been going around for a year and every Negro would sing either "Glory Road" or "Gwine to Heaven" or "Ol' Man River" or some Negro song. It was all right, but here comes this Negro singing an old Italian song, classic as it was. But that's what I knew and that's what I loved. I wasn't putting on any act. I was being myself.

I sang about eight bars, and I was standing beside him. He said, "Do you know this?"

"Yes, I know it."

"I want to look at your face when you sing."

So I went around in the bow of the piano, and he played it, and looked at me while I was singing—he had memorized it that quickly! I sang the same eight bars, and he stopped me and asked, "Will you be my Porgy?"

"Well," I said, "I don't know whether I could or not. I'd have to hear your music."

He laughed. "Well, I think we can arrange for you to hear some of my music. Would you come back next Sunday and sing for some other people?"

"I can't afford it," I told him, "I just can't afford to come back up here. I would like to."

He said, "Well, how much would you like? How much would it cost?"

"It would cost me thirty-five or forty dollars."

"Would you accept it from me?" He wrote out a check to me and signed it, saying, "Please accept this, and I'll expect you next Sunday at the same time."

The following Sunday, I took my wife with me with that forty dollars. We got there at one o'clock, and also waiting for the elevator was a man with striped trousers, dressed quite well—he had a cane—and there was a girl with him. "Are you this damned genius that George has got us all coming to hear?" he said. That made me mad. I said, "I beg your pardon." He said, "You'd better be God-damned good. George is pulling me out of the country. He woke us all up and got us all here to hear you." I said, "Well, that's wonderful. I certainly hope you like my singing." He was Lawrence Langner. The woman was Theresa Helburn. The whole board of the Guild—they were all there!

I was supposed to sing three or four songs. I think I sang thirty! I sang opera, I sang Negro spirituals, I sang German lieder, French chansons. We just had a wonderful time. I sang an hour, an hour and a half. Then

Todd Duncan (Porgy) and Anne Brown (Bess).

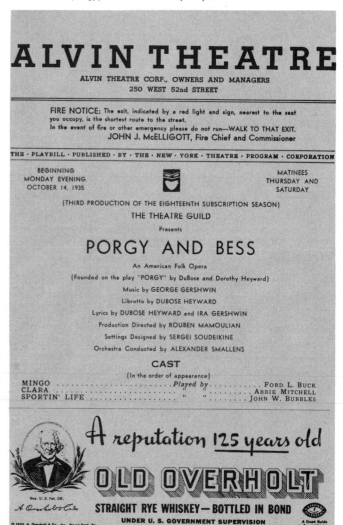

ALVIN THEATRE

ALVIN THEATRE CORP., OWNERS AND MANAGERS
250 WEST 52nd STREET

FIRE NOTICE: The exit, indicated by a red light and sign, nearest to the seat you occupy, is the shortest route to the street.
In the event of fire or other emergency please do not run—WALK TO THAT EXIT.
JOHN J. McELLIGOTT, Fire Chief and Commissioner

THE · PLAYBILL · PUBLISHED · BY · THE · NEW · YORK · THEATRE · PROGRAM · CORPORATION

BEGINNING
MONDAY EVENING
OCTOBER 14, 1935

MATINEES
THURSDAY AND
SATURDAY

(THIRD PRODUCTION OF THE EIGHTEENTH SUBSCRIPTION SEASON)
THE THEATRE GUILD
Presents

PORGY AND BESS

An American Folk Opera
(Founded on the play "PORGY" by DuBose and Dorothy Heyward)
Music by GEORGE GERSHWIN
Libretto by DUBOSE HEYWARD
Lyrics by DUBOSE HEYWARD and IRA GERSHWIN
Production Directed by ROUBEN MAMOULIAN
Settings Designed by SERGEI SOUDEIKINE
Orchestra Conducted by ALEXANDER SMALLENS

CAST
(In the order of appearance)

MINGO	Played by	FORD L. BUCK
CLARA	" "	ABBIE MITCHELL
SPORTIN' LIFE	" "	JOHN W. BUBBLES

we had some drinks and a little food. Then George said, "Now we're all going upstairs to my workroom." He called Ira and his wife across the street, and they came over, and he got out Porgy and Bess, and he and Ira stood there with their awful, rotten, bad voices and sang the whole score. Two hours we were there.

When he started the opening music, I said to myself: "All this chopsticks—it sounds awful." I looked at my wife and said quietly, "This stinks." They went on and sang "Seven, eleven," with those awful voices. He just kept playing; they kept singing. He turned around and grinned. The more they played, the more beautiful I thought the music was. By the time twenty minutes or a half hour had passed I just thought I was in heaven. These beautiful melodies in this new idiom—it was something I had never heard. I just couldn't get enough of it.

He got into the second act and he turned around to me and said, "This is your great aria. This is going to make you famous." I said, "Yes?" He said, "Listen hard." He started off—ump-pah ump-pah. And I just thought "Aria?" It was the banjo song, "I Got Plenty o' Nuthin' "—the song I've sung all over the world for nearly forty years. And to think that man knew that was the song I would sing all over the world. It was a little ditty, but so infectious and so beautiful. Well, they finally finished, and when he ended with "I'm on My Way," I was crying. I was weeping. That's the story.

The Carnegie Hall rehearsal was the first time George Gershwin ever heard his orchestration. He was very worried about that. There had been hints in different papers that he couldn't orchestrate and he didn't orchestrate—that he'd gotten others to do it for him. Now, I saw him working on the orchestration myself. I was with him every day up there, and I knew it was a lie. And he said, "Todd, what do you think? Isn't it awful what they say, and here I am working hard like a dog on it."

George was very, very easy-going—highly critical, but I never saw him lose his cool when something at a rehearsal would offend him. He would run down from the back of the theater and come either to [Rouben] Mamoulian or [Alexander] Smallens. He would write little things on a little pad of paper and after the rehearsal was over, he would come to me privately and just say, "Todd, you did this, and so and so, or sang this. Don't you think," etc.

He was upset up in Boston. My God, that opening night was killing. I think it was four hours. We performed the whole opera and we didn't get out until one o'clock or something. George didn't want one beautiful blessed note cut. He and Mamoulian and Smallens walked in the Boston Common all night long, fighting and fussing and talking about it. We spent days and days cutting. The last forty-odd pages of the opera excepting "I'm on My Way," all that last part that I sang, George Gershwin wrote for my voice. He wrote that after he met me and after he heard me. But it was just too much for one man to sing at the end of the opera....

Some nights he would be in the theater and would come backstage to my dressing room and put his head in my door and say, "Todd, thank you for 'Plenty o Nuthin' " tonight."

I GOT PLENTY O' NUTHIN'

LYRICS BY IRA GERSHWIN AND DU BOSE HEYWARD

Refrain 1:

Oh, I got plenty o' nuthin',
An' nuthin's plenty fo' me.
I got no car, got no mule, I got no misery.
De folks wid plenty o' plenty
Got a lock on dey door,
'Fraid somebody's a-goin' to rob 'em
While dey's out a-makin' more.
What for?
I got no lock on de door
(Dat's no way to be).
Dey can steal de rug from de floor,
Dat's O.K. wid me,
'Cause de things dat I prize,
Like de stars in de skies,
All are free.
Oh, I got plenty o' nuthin',
An' nuthin's plenty fo' me.
I got my gal, got my song,
Got Hebben de whole day long.
(No use complainin'!)
Got my gal, got my Lawd, got my song.

Refrain 2:

I got plenty o' nuthin',
An' nuthin's plenty fo' me.
I got de sun, got de moon, got de deep blue sea.
De folks wid plenty o' plenty,
Got to pray all de day.
Seems wid plenty you sure got to worry
How to keep de Debble away,
A-way.
I ain't a-frettin' 'bout Hell
Till de time arrive.
Never worry long as I'm well,
Never one to strive
To be good, to be bad—
What the hell! I is glad
I's alive.
Oh, I got plenty o' nuthin'
An' nuthin's plenty fo' me.
I got my gal, got my song,
Got Hebben de whole day long.
(No use complainin'!)
Got my gal, got my Lawd, got my song!

Picnic scene, "Oh, I Can't Sit Down," *Porgy and Bess.*

Crap game in Catfish Row.

RECOLLECTIONS OF ROUBEN MAMOULIAN

Noted film director Rouben Mamoulian, who had directed the original Theatre Guild production of *Porgy*, had known George Gershwin for several years before he signed a contract with the Guild to direct *Porgy and Bess* "without having heard a single note of what I was to direct."

I finally arrived in New York and on the first evening I was to hear George's score. I met George and Ira in the Gershwin apartment. All three of us were very excited. George and Ira were obviously anxious for me to like the music. As for me, I was even more anxious. You see, I loved the story of Porgy and every single character in it; I loved its changing moods, its sadness and its gaiety, its passion and its tenderness, and all the emotional richness of the Negro soul expressed in it. Porgy, the play, having been my very first production in New York, meant a great deal to me. I felt about it the way I imagine a mother feels about her first-born. If it were to be "clothed" in music, I was jealously anxious for that music to be good. It had to be good!

It was rather amusing how all three of us were trying to be nonchalant and poised that evening, yet we were trembling with excitement. The brothers handed me a tall highball and put me in a comfortable leather arm-chair. George sat down at the piano while Ira stood over him like a guardian angel. George's hands went up in the air about to strike the shining keys. Halfway down, he changed his mind, turned to me, and said, "Of course, Rouben, you must understand it's very difficult to play this score. As a matter of fact, it's really impossible! Can you play Wagner on the piano? Well, this is just like Wagner!" I assured George that I understood. Up went his nervous hands again and the next second I was listening to the opening "piano music" of the opera. I found it so exciting, so full of color, and so provocative in its rhythm that after this first piano section was over, I jumped out of my armchair and interrupted George to tell him how much I liked it. Both brothers were as happy as children to hear words of praise, though, heaven knows, they should have been used to them by then. When my explosion was over they went back to the piano, they both blissfully closed their eyes before they continued with the lovely "Summertime" song. George played with the most beatific smile on his face. He seemed to float on the waves of his own music with the Southern sun shining on him. Ira sang— he threw his head back with abandon, his eyes closed,

and sang like a nightingale! In the middle of the song George couldn't bear it any longer and took over the singing from him. To describe George's face while he sang "Summertime" is something that is beyond my capacity as a writer. Nirvana might be the word!

So it went on. George was the orchestra and sang half of the parts, Ira sang the other half. Ira was also frequently the audience. It was touching to see how he, while singing, would become so overwhelmed with admiration for his brother that he would look from him to me with half-open eyes and pantomime with a soft gesture of his hand, as if saying, "He did it. Isn't it wonderful? Isn't he wonderful?" George would frequently take his eyes away from the score and covertly watch me and my reaction to the music while pretending that he wasn't really doing it at all. It was very late into the night before we finished the opera and sometimes I think that in a way that was the best performance of it I ever heard. We all felt exultantly happy. The next morning both George and Ira had completely lost their voices. For two days they couldn't talk, they only whispered. I shall never forget that evening—the enthusiasm of the two brothers about the music, their anxiety to do it justice, their joy at its being appreciated and with it all their touching devotion for each other. It is one of those rare tender memories one so cherishes in life.

From George Gershwin,
edited and designed by Merle Armitage
(London: Longmans, Green and Co., Ltd., 1938)

Rouben Mamoulian, director of *Porgy and Bess*.

RECOLLECTIONS OF EVA JESSYE

Eva Jessye was choral director of *Porgy and Bess* and of the Eva Jessye Choir.

I met George Gershwin at the audition. My choir had just been barnstorming all through South Carolina, and for not very much money—we were barely making the train fare from town to town—and we'd come back to New York, where I was doing a radio program on South Carolina life. I'm not from South Carolina, I was born in Kansas, but we'd just been there and seen the conditions the black people were in, and I wanted to talk about it. Well, I saw this notice in Film Daily looking for a black choir; and so we all went up and we auditioned. People from the Theatre Guild were there, I remember. We did the shout "Plenty Good Room" and danced all over the stage. George Gershwin jumped up and shouted: "That's it! That's what I want!"

George didn't interfere during rehearsals; he let us do what we knew how to do. A very sad-looking man around the mouth. I remember he loved peanuts, and he was always cracking them and eating them during the times he'd come and watch us. . . . Anyway, back to the audition: afterwards he invited me up to his penthouse on 72nd Street. I remember a glassed-in flower conservatory and the three Steinways in the apartment, two downstairs for two-piano work, and one upstairs. But the first thing I noticed was a long table with several copyists busily working on the score of Porgy and Bess.

As I said, George didn't interfere much with rehearsals. He would add things and allow changes in rehearsal constantly. A lot of the gutbucket stuff he particularly liked had to be cut. And, you know, he had written in things that sounded just right, like our people. For example, near the end of the opera, at the passage "She's worse than dead, Porgy," we were doing a brush-rhythm thing with our hands, and the more longhair people who had to do with the production cut it out.

I remember one strange thing about the party after the opening. The hostess was out in the front room serving the cast members lemonade, while the "brass" was in the kitchen, drinking liquor.

George's portrait of Ruby Elzy (Serena).

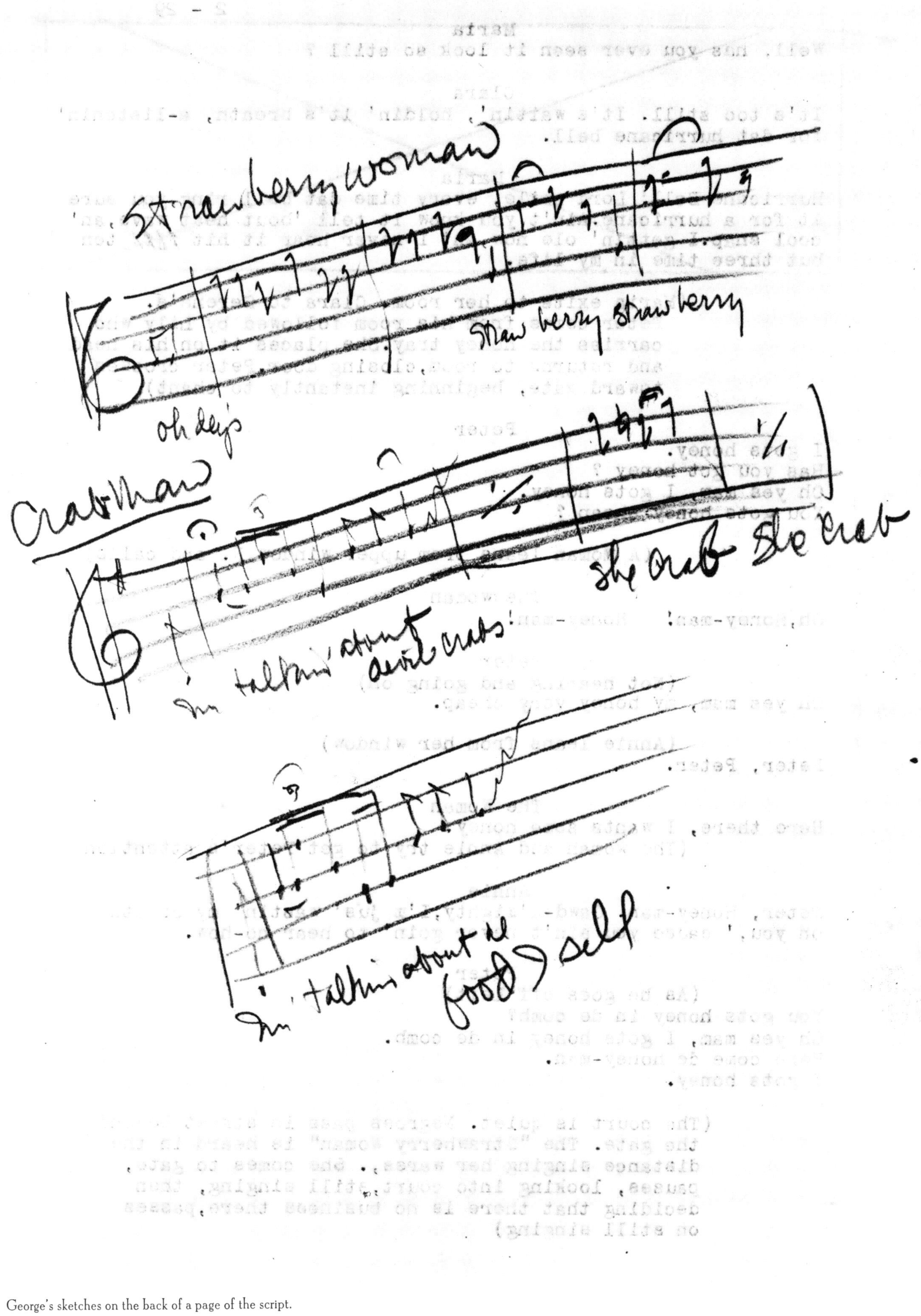

George's sketches on the back of a page of the script.

IT AIN'T
NECESSARILY SO

It ain't necessarily so,
It ain't necessarily so—
De t'ings dat yo' li'ble
To read in de Bible—
It ain't necessarily so.

Li'l David was small, but—oh my!
Li'l David was small, but—oh my!
He fought Big Goliath
Who lay down and dieth—
Li'l David was small, but—oh my!

Wadoo! Zim bam boddle-oo, zim bam boddle-oo!
Hoodle ah da wah da! Hoodle ah da wah da!
Scatty wah! Yeah!

Oh Jonah, he lived in de whale,
Oh Jonah, he lived in de whale—
Fo' he made his home in
Dat fish's abdomen—
Oh Jonah, he lived in de whale.

Li'l Moses was found in a stream,
Li'l Moses was found in a stream—
He floated on water
Till Ole Pharaoh's daughter
She fished him, she says, from dat stream.

Wadoo! Zim etc.

It ain't necessarily so,
It ain't necessarily so.
Dey tell all you chillun
De debble's a villun
But 'tain't necessarily so.

To get into hebben
Don't snap fo' a seben—
Live clean! Don't have no fault!
Oh, I takes dat gospel
Whenever it's pos'ple—
But wid a grain of salt!

Methus'lah live nine hunderd years,
Methus'lah live nine hunderd years—
But who calls dat livin'
When no gal'll give in
To no man what's nine hunderd years?

I'm preachin' dis sermon to show
It ain't nessa, ain't nessa,
Ain't nessa, ain't nessa,
Ain't necessarily so!

Encore Limerick:

'Way back in 5,000 B.C.
Ole Adam an' Eve had to flee.
Sure, dey did dat deed in
De Garden of Eden—
But why chasterize you an' me?

(Facing) Sportin' Life.

THERE'S
A BOAT DAT'S
LEAVIN' SOON
FOR NEW YORK

There's a boat dat's leavin' soon for New York.
Come wid me, dat's where we belong, sister.
You an' me kin live dat high life in New York.
Com wid me, dere you can't go wrong, sister.

I'll buy you de swellest mansion
Up on upper Fifth Avenue,
An' through Harlem we'll go struttin',
We'll go a-struttin',
An' dere'll be nuttin'
Too good for you.
I'll dress you in silks and satins
In de latest Paris styles.
All de blues you'll be forgettin',
You'll be forgettin',
There'll be no frettin'—
Jes' nothin' but smiles.

Come along wid me, dat's de place,
Don't be a fool, come along, come along.
There's a boat dat's leavin' soon for New York,
Come wid me, dat's where we belong, sister.
Dat's where we belong!

Sportin' Life lures Bess to New York.

188

RECOLLECTIONS OF KAY SWIFT

When we had the now famous party for Porgy and Bess—the last party—[Jules] Glaenzer was one of ten men all very well off, men like Bill Paley, Marshall Field, Averell Harriman, who put up the money. We had 430 people at Condé Nast's, who lent us his house and staff. I remember taking whole days making lists, sending telegrams, and there was almost nothing but acceptances. We hired a Spanish orchestra. All the men were in white tie and tails. It was the dress-up era. I was going to Philadelphia in the morning to give the first lecture on Porgy and Bess, illustrated at the piano, at the Curtis Institute. I had to make a train at eleven in the morning and it was not until seven that we all got to bed.

I remember the often-told story about [John] Bubbles. On opening night Bubbles wore an emerald-green suit he had bought at his own expense for the show. He had never worn it in rehearsals. He just sprang it that night. It would zip up the front, and he couldn't get it up and he couldn't get it down. And he had to do "Boat Dat's Leavin'" with his back to the audience. He did it beautifully, though he couldn't stand up. We had been petrified when they played his entrance music three times before he came out. I was sitting between George and Ira, and we were dying. I was digging into their arms. But nobody knew there was a stage wait because the orchestra played on without a break.

The opening was great. During the intermission we went out into the alley on the side of the Alvin and I remember Libby Holman saying, "Oh, George, it's so great I haven't stopped crying," and she was sobbing right then. Everybody was. It was so moving. The critics didn't know what hit them—they ate their words later.

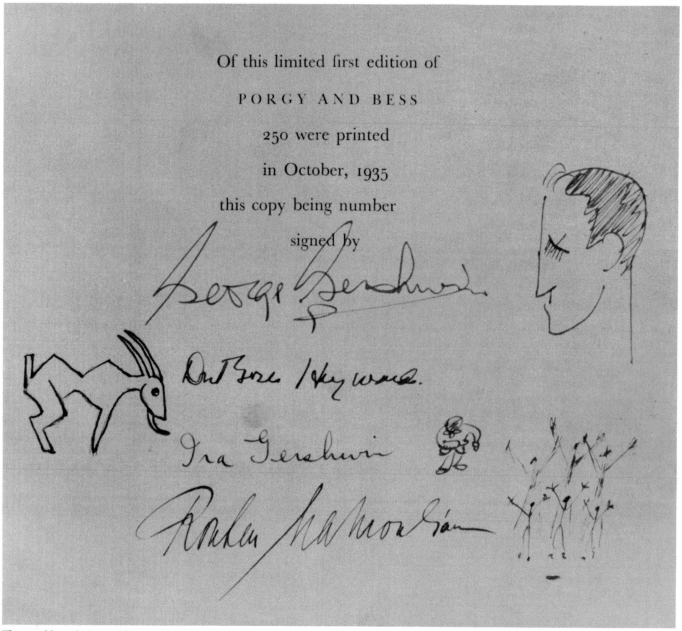

Of this limited first edition of

PORGY AND BESS

250 were printed

in October, 1935

this copy being number

signed by

The signed limited edition of the score. / (Opposite) The curtain call at the Alvin Theatre, New York, on opening night of Porgy and Bess, October 10, 1935: Todd Duncan (Porgy), Anne Brown (Bess), Rouben Mamoulian, George, Du Bose Heyward, and Warren Coleman (Crown).

George with Luigi Pirandello and Rouben Mamoulian.

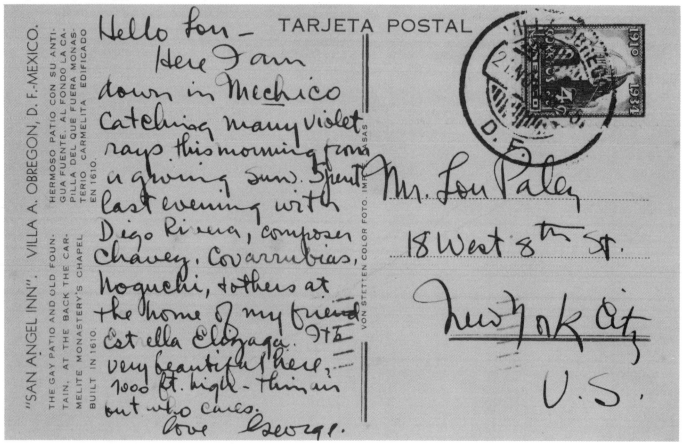

One of George's telephone doodles.

George's portrait of Diego Rivera.

One of George's telephone doodles.

Siqueiros in front of his painting of George performing in a concert hall.

ZIEGFELD FOLLIES (1936)

RECOLLECTIONS OF VERNON DUKE

Ira and I worked hard, writing and discarding dozens of songs, but somehow, perhaps owing to the performers, the score [for 1936 Ziegfeld Follies] didn't come off too impressively in the theater. Ira's writing methods were slow and soothing and very restful.... Our work sessions usually began with a family dinner with Ira and Leonore, joined by Fanny Brice or Ellen Berlin. After a long and copious meal, the company would repair to the drawing room, which housed the piano, and hectic conversation would ensue; I, on tenterhooks, would be dying to get to the piano and persuade Leonore and her guests to go elsewhere for their energetic gossip. I would shoot expressive glances at ever-placid Ira, who affected not to catch their meaning and willingly joined in the conversation. After an hour or so of this, I, totally exasperated, would invade the piano determinedly and strike a few challenging chords. This time Ira would heed my desperate call, stretch himself, emit a series of protracted sighs, say something to the effect that "one had to work so-o-o hard for a living" and more in that vein, then interrupt himself to intone the magic word: "However..." This "however" meant that the eleventh hour had struck and the period of delicious procrastination was over. Ira, sighing pathetically, would then produce a small bridge table, various writing and erasing gadgets, a typewriter and four or five books, which he seldom consulted—Roget's Thesaurus, Webster's dictionary, rhyming dictionary and the like— wipe and adjust his glasses, all these preparations at a molto adagio pace, and finally say in a resigned voice: "O.K., Dukie...play that chorus you had last night." After wrestling with last night's chorus for a half hour, Ira would embark on an ice-box-raiding expedition, with me, fearful of too long an interruption, in pursuit. There we'd stand in the kitchen, munching cheese and pickles, Ira obviously delighted with this escapist stratagem, I dutifully pretending to enjoy it too. Another sigh, another "however," then back to the piano. At 2 or 3 A.M. Ira would put away his working utensils and victoriously announce to Lee that he had completed four lines for the new chorus.

From Passport to Paris *(Boston: Little, Brown and Company, 1955)*

(Facing) Another of George's telephone doodles—framed with his signature taken from a canceled check. / Returning from Mexico, 1935.

I CAN'T
GET STARTED

MUSIC BY VERNON DUKE

Verse 1:

(He) I'm a glum one; it's explainable:
I met someone unattainable.
Life's a bore,
The world is my oyster no more.
All the papers, where I led the news
With my capers, now will spread the news:
"Superman
Turns Out to Be Flash in the Pan."

Refrain 1:

I've flown around the world in a plane;
I've settled revolutions in Spain;
The North Pole I have charted,
But can't get started with you.

Around a golf course I'm under par,
And all the movies want me to star;
I've got a house, a show-place—
But I get no place with you.

You're so supreme,
Lyrics I write of you;
Scheme
Just for a sight of you;
Dream
Both day and night of you,
And what good does it do?

When J. P. Morgan bows, I just nod;
Green Pastures wanted me to play God.
But you've got me down-hearted
'Cause I can't get started with you.

Verse 2:

(She) I'm a glum one; it's explainable:
I met someone unattainable.
Life's a bore,
The world is my oyster no more.
All the papers, where I led the news
With my capers, now will spread the news:
"Super gal
Is punchy and losing morale!"

Refrain 2:

When I sell kisses at a bazaar,
The wolves line up from nearby and far;
With kings I've à la carted—
But can't get started with you.

The millionaires I've had to turn down
Would stretch from London to New York town;
The upper crust I visit,
But say, what is it—with you?

When first we met—
How you elated me!
Pet!
You devastated me!
Yet—
Now you've deflated me
Till you're my Waterloo.

Though beauty columns ask my advice,
Though I was "Miss America" twice,
Still you've got me outsmarted
'Cause I can't get started with you.

Refrain 3:

The Himalaya Mountains I climb;
I'm written up in Fortune and Time.
I dig the 4th Dimension,
But no attention from you!

There's always "Best regards and much love"
From Mr. Lehman—you know, the Gov;
I'm there at ev'ry state ball
But behind the 8-ball with you.

Oh, tell me why
Am I no kick to you—
I,
Who'd always stick to you,
Fly—
Through thin and thick to you?
Tell me why I'm taboo.
The market trembles when I sell short;
In England I'm presented at court.
The Siamese twins I've parted—
But I can't get started with you.

Bob Hope and Fannie Brice in the *Ziegfeld Follies* of 1936.

(Facing) Eve Arden and Bob Hope introduced "I Can't Get Started"
in the *Ziegfeld Follies* of 1936.

ISLAND IN
THE WEST INDIES

MUSIC BY VERNON DUKE

Verse:

Let's both of us pack up,
Sail far from it all;
Tired having to back up
To the wall.
I know of a place where
Life really is fun—
Where days are golden
And you're beholden
To none.
Let's take passage and run!

Refrain:

Oh, there's an island down in the West Indies
Ten dollars can buy;
Away from Reuben's and from Lindy's—
'Neath a tropic,
Kaleidoscopical sky.

We'll lie around all day and just be lazy—
The world far behind;
(If that's not heaven then I'm crazy)
With no taxes
And with no axes to grind.

No traffic jams
Under the palm trees by the sea;
With breadfruit and yams
We'll never need the A&P.

In that romantic isle in the West Indies—
No airplanes above—
We'll watch the turtles at their shindies,
You an' me an'
The Caribbean
And love.

Second Ending:

We'll watch the turtles at their shindies;
Learn the lingos
Of pink flamingos,
Where nothing's immoral
'Way out on the coral,
Just you an' me an'
The Caribbean
And love.

RECOLLECTIONS OF KAY HALLE

Gloria Braggiotti and I thought it would be such fun to have a fantastic evening at Mona (Mrs. Harrison) Williams' beautiful house on Fifth Avenue. We convinced her to give an evening of music, and we had four pianos for George, Mario Braggiotti, Fats Waller, and Vernon Duke. A number of classical musicians, including Toscanini and Stokowski, were there, plus many, many friends. It was one of the most fabulous evenings.

I had been to the inaugural ceremonies of Franklin Roosevelt, and the President had said to me, "Kay, there's one thing you could do for me. Could you bring

George Gershwin to our New Year's Eve party at the White House?" Roosevelt was George's hero, and when I told George about the invitation, I thought he was going to faint. When we went down to the White House, Gloria and I stayed in the Lincoln Room, and I remember that when I met George and brought him from the diplomatic entrance to the main lobby, he stood under the chandelier and said to me, "If only my father could see me now."

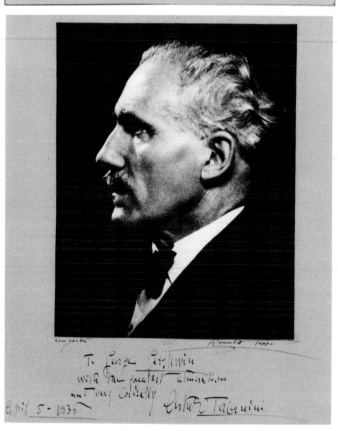

THE VOICE OF
Broadway
By Louis Sobol
White House Party!

Fifteen minutes before midnight. Franklin, Jr., steps onto the bandstand and announces a treat. "Eddie Peabody will play a few of his famous banjo solos for us." The President and his wife sit at the far end of the room opposite the bandstand and the guests form a lane from the stand to the President's chair. Little Peabody, wearing his stage uniform (red jacket and flannel trousers) addresses the President. His speech is unique and should be used in the book. "You Excellency, Mrs. President, ladies and gentlemen: I am now going to play a number which you have no doubt heard me play in the motion pictures, on the stage, with Rudy Vallee and on the Show Boat Hour over the radio." He didn't leave out a thing. He plays several numbers and gets a swell hand from the kids. Then James steps on the stand and says: "We have George Gershwin with us tonight and, inasmuch as the President has requested a number, I know he'll oblige." Gershwin plays "I Got Rhythm" and receives a tremendous ovation. He plays "Of Thee I Sing" for an encore and as he leaves the stand he shakes hands heartily with a handsome lad, Mario Braggiotti. Last year at this party Mario played "April in Paris" and he, too, went over big. Incidentally, the piano is an interesting one. It's a huge gold affair, rather gaudy, and was presented to Theodore Roosevelt in 1903 — the 100,000th piano made by Steinway.

"To George Gershwin with the greatest admiration and very cordially Arturo Toscanini, April 5, 1936."

HOLLYWOOD 1936–1937

The last year of George's life was a year of irreconcilable conflicts. He loved the California climate, thrived on hikes and tennis, and delighted in the presence of friends and family. The songwriting for films went easily and he was generally happy with the house at 1019 North Roxbury Drive that he shared with Lee and Ira. He was happy too with the garden Lee loved so much and the tennis court and swimming pool that provided relaxation.

George had many of his paintings sent from New York and began to plan concert tours in between his picture commitments. He brought Todd Duncan to California for a concert version of *Porgy and Bess*. He became quite friendly with Arnold Schoenberg, who used the Gershwin tennis court once a week. In general, around the brunches and poker parties and dinners and other gatherings with old friends like Moss Hart, Jerome Kern, Irving Berlin, Oscar Levant, Lillian Hellman, Yip Harburg, and Harold Arlen, there was a feeling that was, in George's words, "very gemütlich."

George played concerts in Seattle in December 1936; in January 1937 he performed in San Francisco with Monteux, then in Berkeley and Detroit, and back in Los Angeles on February 10 and 11, 1937, with Alexander Smallens conducting, George performed the *Concerto in F*.

At first he claimed he was not attracted by the women he met in Hollywood, but soon he found companionship with Elizabeth Allan and Simone Simon and became very much interested in Paulette Goddard, whom he met at a party Edward G. Robinson gave in honor of Stravinsky in March 1937.

Many, including his brother Ira and his friend Fred Astaire, have said it is a mistake to think that George wasn't happy in Hollywood—but they were happy there themselves, finding the life and the work very congenial. Ira, however, admitted one aspect of the life did bother George: he was less involved with the staging of his songs than he had been in New York. In the theater George had always been consulted as to how the numbers should be performed, and if there was any dissatisfaction he was happy to write new ones. In working on a film he would never know what was thought of a song until he saw the film, and several of his best songs were either not used, like "Hi-Ho," or virtually thrown away unnoticed, like "They Can't Take That Away from Me."

Others, however, saw a different side of George not only during his year in Hollywood but from the days right after the opening of *Porgy and Bess* in October 1935,

A few weeks after the opening George, with his analyst, Dr. Gregory Zilboorg, and Edward Warburg, went off to Mexico. There George hoped to paint, meet artists, and seek out new musical inspiration. But the trip was a bust, and not even the band and cast of *Porgy and Bess* who greeted the returning Grace Line ship *Santa Paula* in New York could shake George from his dissatisfaction.

George had hoped to gain inspiration from his exposure to Mexican music, but didn't. He wanted to hear Indian music, but wasn't successful there either.

Immediately after his return to New York he adapted and orchestrated a *Suite from Porgy and Bess* that was given its première by Alexander Smallens and the Philadelphia Orchestra on January 21, 1936, just six days before the national company of *Porgy and Bess* opened its brief engagement in Philadelphia. Neither George's *Suite* nor his performance of the *Concerto in F* was especially well received. Subsequent performances of the *Suite* failed to alter the original impression it made, and today it is rarely performed. The suite the public knows is the fine orchestral arrangement by Robert Russell Bennett.

Gershwin concerts in the spring and summer of 1936 continued to draw less than capacity crowds and less than enthusiastic reviews. Some critics even advised George to find something new to play, as they were tired of hearing the *Rhapsody in Blue* and the *Concerto in F* year after year. Even the July 9, 1936, Gershwin Night at Lewisohn Stadium, the scene of many of his greatest triumphs, drew only 7,000 people, far below the attendance of 12,000 to 18,000 that had greeted his previous appearances at these annual concerts. There was consolation in the fact that the concert took place on the hottest night in the history of the New York City weather bureau.

Oscar Levant, violist Otto Langley, George, Robert Russell Bennett, Fritz Reiner, Deems Taylor, and Bill Daly at Lewisohn Stadium, New York.

George left New York with a heavy heart. With him on his ride to the airport was Kay Swift, who had been close to him for a longer period than any other woman in his life. Their relationship had been severely strained by George's inability to decide one way or the other about marriage. Kay, the mother of three children, had never put any pressure on George after she had divorced her husband, James Warburg, with no commitment from George.

George's inability to resolve his dilemma over marriage, either to Kay or to anyone else, was extremely troubling to him. Marriage, of course, would mean an end to the free-wheeling bachelor life George reveled in and an assumption of responsibilities to another person that might impinge on his work.

Kay and George agreed to a year's separation during which neither one would write to the other. This was intended as a temporary solution that would allow both of them to reassess their relationship. In time, the silence was broken as each informed the other that they were seeing others. One month before the year ended, George died without having formed a lasting relationship with anyone else.

Another blow to George during 1936 was the sudden death of his close friend and musical mentor Bill Daly, who had died of a heart attack at the age of forty-nine. In George's musical life Daly had occupied a place equaled in intimacy by no one else and approximated at that time only by Kay Swift. The musical judgment of each had been indispensable to George for years, and now in Hollywood, as he prepared to greet the new year, he was without the help of either.

Creatively, George managed to go on without them. The songs he and Ira wrote for *Shall We Dance, A Damsel in Distress*, and *The Goldwyn Follies* are vintage Gershwin, revealing the brothers at the top of their form. Insouciant, witty, delectable, inspired, they are among the best George and Ira ever wrote.

Yet the emotional letdown after *Porgy and Bess*, inevitable though it was, had taken its toll, and while Hollywood had brought new economic opportunities and a comfortable life, the personal and professional disappointments of 1936 outweighed the new prosperity.

Many people who knew and loved George were sorely troubled by what they saw and heard of his emotional state. When friends of long standing like Dick Simon and Ann Ronell got married, George lamented again and again over the absurdity of his own situation: "Why can they get married and I can't?"

One woman who loved George spoke as follows: "Much as I and others loved George—and he was a sweet, wonderful man—in the end I never felt really needed for myself." Another: "George was so afraid of being hurt or rejected that he couldn't express his love for a woman in such a way that the woman he loved would come first in his life, yes, even before his music."

To one person he would say, "I want to marry," but to another he would say, "I'll never marry." Apparently he simply did not know what he would do. He assumed, and the world assumed with him, that there would always be world enough and time.

It is possible, reflects a third, that "George talked about getting married because marriage was then the accepted convention for certifying a romantic alliance. The people whom George respected believed in marriage. But if George were alive and young today, he would be like the young people whose relationships more and more obey their own inner compulsions, beginning and ending without the ceremonial hoopla which older generations felt was necessary. A lot of George's guilt and frustration was conditioned by society."

RECOLLECTIONS OF KAY SWIFT

I didn't see him for the final year of his life. He went to California in August 1936 and I never saw him after that photograph of him standing on the step of the ramp at the airport. And he had a mark around his head which was a deep groove from a straw hat that was too small for him.

George left his apartment all furnished, and Emily Paley and I went afterwards and arranged to have everything packed up and stored. When he left, he did not know how long he was going to be gone—he went for one picture and another came up afterwards and he stayed and did it. He and Ira went to the airport separately. George and I went in a taxi. We had decided we were not going to see each other or write and see how it went and if it would be a happy arrangement. We kept everything cheery and bright. He laughed and talked about the picture. We said goodbye and he walked up the ramp. And I knew for sure I'd never see him again. I didn't know why, but I knew that was all, that was it. And he stood at the top of the ramp and he waved the hat and all I could see was the groove that went around his head like an Indian headband.

At Newark Airport on August 8, 1936, prior to leaving for California.

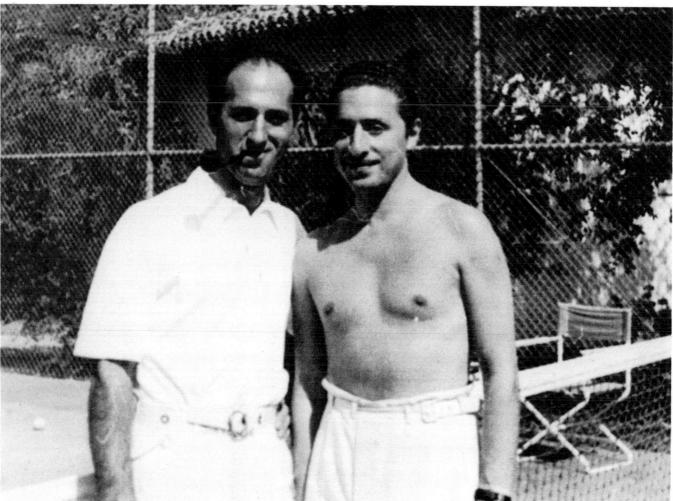

Playing tennis with Harold Arlen.

RECOLLECTIONS OF IRA GERSHWIN

In August 1936 my brother and I flew to California to work for RKO-Radio Pictures on an Astaire-Rogers film called Shall We Dance. *Before my wife found a suitable house for us, George had a piano installed in our suite at the Beverly-Wilshire Hotel in Beverly Hills. The first song we worked on was a piece not called for in the script but an idea we had for the opening of the picture:* "Fred Astaire sees on a Paris kiosk the picture-poster of Ginger Rogers, an American girl then entertaining in Paris, and immediately feels:* THIS IS SHE! *He dances through the streets, extolling to everyone the beauty and virtues of this girl whom he has never met, but whose picture he sees pasted on walls and kiosks everywhere."* When we submitted the completed song to Pandro Berman, the producer, and Mark Sandrich, the director, Mark said, "This is real $4.40 stuff and I'm crazy about it." ($4.40 was then the top price for most Broadway musicals.) When it came time to figure production costs, however, the film's budget couldn't stand the cost of the sets for this number ($55,000 in those Depression years—somewhat more than my brother and I together received for the entire score), and reluctantly the management decided to forgo "Hi-Ho!" So the song has been unknown except to a few of our friends, like Oscar Levant, Harold Arlen, and S. N. Behrman, who were around at the time, and to a few others who in the years since have learned of its existence. Like them, I feel that it's about time the song was published.*

HI-HO!

Hi-ho! Hi-ho!
At last it seems I've found her;
Now I won't be happy till my arms are around her.
Hi-ho! Ho-hi!
If a kiss she'd only throw me—oh me, oh my!
Her charm! Her smile so sweet and dimply!
I want them or I'll simply die!
Hi-ho! Hi-ho! Oh—
There's no one like her here on earth below . . .
Perhaps I'm reaching too high, hi-ho,
Hi-ho!

Please pardon me, sir,
But I'm in love with her—
And if you knew her, sir,
Then so would you
Be in love with her, too!

I beg of you, ma'am—
Look at this honey lamb;
Now that you've seen her, ma'am,
Don't you agree
No one's lovely as she?

She's lovely!
No one lovelier,
No one lovelier
Than she.

Hi-ho! Hi-ho!
For me there's none can top her;
Even if you offered Venus I wouldn't swap her.
Hi-ho! Ho-hi!
Will I ever be her Romeo? Me, oh my!
Her eyes! They thrill and then they mock you—
My heart they'll always occupy!
Hi-ho! Hi-ho! Oh—
There's no one like her here on earth below . . .
Perhaps I'm reaching too high, hi-ho.
Hi-ho!
I've got it! She's got me!
Haven't met her yet . . .
But I hope to . . . Hi-ho!

LETTER FROM GEORGE TO MABEL SCHIRMER

September 18, 1936

I miss you very much, Mabel, and wish it were possible for you to come out here. This place is just full of people you know and who love you. Of course, there are depressing moments, too, when talk of Hitler and his gang creep into the conversation. For some reason or other the feeling out here is even more acute than in the East. . . .

Our work is going along slowly because the script for the picture is not completely finished, however, with the few songs that we have, we feel that we will be ready with our part.

I saw Swing Time *out here and liked the picture very much. Although I don't think Kern has written any outstanding song hits, I think he did a very creditable job with the music and some of it is really delightful. Of course, he never really was ideal for Astaire, and I take that into consideration.*

RECOLLECTIONS OF HAROLD ARLEN

During the last year he was very often unhappy and uneasy. Lots of other people were writing well—Rodgers, Porter, others—and, of course, George liked to be king-pin. I felt that something was wrong with him one day when after a lot of us had played the piano, George said to me, "No you don't. I'm not going to follow you." I was shocked with surprise. Since we were always together in one bunch trying to help one another, there was little show of jealousy. When he acted that way, I felt uneasy. I knew something was wrong with him, and I thought it was Hollywooditis.

You know, he wanted to marry Paulette Goddard. We sat by his pool talking about it. She was a great girl, but George's life style was very free-wheeling. I knew that marriage would tie him down, so I told him that he would have to give up some of the freedom he had. He didn't say anything, because I knew—all of us knew—that he wanted to get married. But George was the kind of guy who would go first to one house and play a few songs, then go on to another house and play some more, then to another and so on. He knew he couldn't do that if he were married. Yet there was that warmth and wistfulness in him too, and it all made for great internal conflicts. So it would have been hard for George to change his life style from work, party-going, tennis, golf, long fast walks in the mountains. He always was so Goddamned excited, and the glory road had to be his.

In June, Yip and I were going back to New York to work on Hooray for What? *I went over to 1019 to say goodbye to Lee, Ira, and George. There was George sitting on the couch, but not the George I knew—not the guy who had been so full of gold, so charged with electricity, the dynamic, exciting man I'd met when I started to write for the theater. The man I saw looked spent and his face was green. He said, "Do you have to go?"*

He meant so much to me. I remember that he was the first to show me that my song "Stormy Weather" had no repeated bars. And one afternoon in Beverly Hills I came into the long room at 1019 North Roxbury and George was playing "Stormy Weather," trying to get a different harmony for it. He couldn't change it and went back to the original, but he told me that he had tried to change it not because he disliked what I had done, but just to see what might happen. That was George. He was always trying—right up to the end.

Yip Harburg and Harold Arlen.

RKO STUDIOS INC.

780 GOWER STREET, LOS ANGELES, CALIF.

REG U.S PAT OFF

October 28, 1936

Dear Mabel,

It looks as though the three Gershwins will be out here for a longer period than they first anticipated. Samuel Goldwyn is constructing a contract right now for our services for a picture to start around the fifteenth of January. And, now, RKO has piped up with talk of their option, which was originally in our agreement. They would like us to start on the next Astaire picture shortly after this contract is over. If Goldwyn doesn't have a story ready for us in about three weeks, he may put his date back so we could do the next Astaire vehicle, otherwise we go to work for Goldwyn on that date.

Naturally, I miss New York and the things it has to offer quite a good deal, and will probably miss it more as time goes on, but I must say that California has many very delightful advantages; for example, I am writing this letter on October 28, sitting in a pair of shorts with no top, in a hot sun around our pool. That sounds almost like a moving picture scenario, but it's true. We play quite a lot of tennis and the work so far seems easy. So you see, California has much to offer to the Gershwins.

I have agreed to do several concerts out here; the first taking place in Seattle on December 15, and in San Francisco on January 15, 16 and 17. Also, probably in Los Angeles late in January.

Ernest Toch and his family are out here in a house in Santa Monica. We met the other night at the big Anti-Nazi meeting which was held here. It was quite an impressive affair with many speakers, including Eddie Cantor, Gifford Cochran and several others.

HOLIDAY GREETING *by* Western Union

1936 PM 7 00

COPYRIGHTED 1936 BY WESTERN UNION TEL

```
NA348 10 SC=BEVERLYHILLS CALIF

MABEL SCHIRMER=

    DLR 31 169 EAST 78 ST=


FOR THE NEW YEAR LOVE AND KISSES HEALTH AND HAPPINESS=
    GEORGE.
```

George in Seattle for a concert, December 1936.

ten-nineteen north roxbury drive · beverly hills, california

Dear Mabel ———

I am welcoming 1937. How about you? Perhaps dear Mabel this is our year. A year that will see both of us finding that elusive something that seems to bring happiness to the lucky. The pendulum swings back, so I've heard, and it's about due to swing us back to a more satisfying state. 1936 was a year of important changes to me. They are too obvious to you to mention here. So, sweet Mabel, lift your glass high with me & drink a toast to two nice people who will, in a happy state go places this year.

SHALL WE DANCE (1937)

The road back to Hollywood in the middle 1930s was not an easy one for George and Ira. Hollywood was worried by *Porgy and Bess*, feeling that the Gershwins would be too longhair for the film industry. It took months of negotiation to convince the moguls that the composer of *Porgy and Bess* could turn out commercial tunes again.

Shall We Dance includes ballet, tap, and ballroom dancing, and Fred and Ginger walk their dogs aboard ship to an orchestral interlude by George that subtly mocks overblown Hollywood orchestrations. The film is too long but still enjoyable, while the songs, including the rejected "Hi-Ho," seem to have improved with time.

Shall We Dance (1937). Standing: dance director Hermes Pan, director Mark Sandrich, and Ira. Seated: Fred Astaire, Ginger Rogers, and George.

208

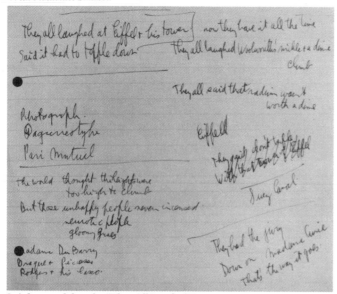

With Nathaniel Shilkret.

Ira's lyric worksheet for "They All Laughed."

THEY CAN'T TAKE THAT AWAY FROM ME

Verse:

Our romance won't end on a sorrowful note,
Though by tomorrow you're gone;
The song is ended, but as the songwriter wrote,
"The melody lingers on."
They may take you from me,
I'll miss your fond caress.
But though they take you from me,
I'll still possess:

Refrain:

The way you wear your hat,
The way you sip your tea,
The mem'ry of all that—
No, no! They can't take that away from me!

The way your smile just beams,
The way you sing off key,
The way you haunt my dreams—
No, no! They can't take that away from me!

We may never, never meet again
On the bumpy road to love,
Still I'll always, always keep
The mem'ry of—

The way you hold your knife,
The way we danced till three,
The way you've changed my life—
No! They can't take that away from me!
No, no! They can't take that away from me!

With Ginger Rogers during the filming of the production number "They All Laughed." / (Opposite) George and Simone Simon at a film preview, November 2, 1936.

LET'S CALL
THE WHOLE
THING OFF

Verse:

Things have come to a pretty pass—
Our romance is growing flat,
For you like this and the other,
While I go for this and that.
Goodness knows what the end will be;
Oh, I don't know where I'm at....
It looks as if we two will never be one.
Something must be done.

Refrain 1:

You say eether and I say eyether,
You say neether and I say nyther;
Eether, eyether, neether, nyther—
Let's call the whole thing off!

You like potato and I like po-tah-to,
You like tomato and I like to-mah-to;
Potato, po-tah-to, tomato, to-mah-to—
Let's call the whole thing off!

But oh, if we call the whole thing off, then we
*   must part.*
And oh, if we ever part, then that might break
*   my heart.*

So, if you like pajamas and I like pa-jah-mas,
I'll wear pajamas and give up pa-jah-mas.
For we know we
Need each other, so we
Better call the calling off off.
Let's call the whole thing off!

Refrain 2:

You say laughter and I say lawfter,
You say after and I say awfter;
Laughter, lawfter, after, awfter—
Let's call the whole thing off!

You like vanilla and I like vanella,
You sa's'parilla and I sa's'parella;
Vanilla, vanella, choc'late, strawb'ry—
Let's call the whole thing off!

But oh, if we call the whole thing off, then we
*   must part.*
And oh, if we ever part, then that might break
*   my heart.*

So, if you go for oysters and I go for ersters,
I'll order oysters and cancel the ersters.
For we know we
Need each other, so we
Better call the calling off off.
Let's call the whole thing off!

Refrain 3:

I say father and you say pater,
I say mother and you say mater;
Father, mother, auntie, uncle—
Let's call the whole thing off!

I like banana and you like ba-nahn-ah,
I say Havana and I get Ha-vahn-ah;
Banana, ba-nahn-ah, Havana, Ha-vahn-ah—
Never a happy medium!

Fred and Ginger in their roller-skating dance to "Let's Call the Whole Thing Off."

But oh, if we call the whole thing off, then we
*   must part.*
And oh, if we ever part, then that might break
*   my heart.*

So if I go for scallops and you go for lobster,
No more discussion—we both order lobster.
For we know we
Need each other, so we
Better call the calling off off.
Let's call the whole thing off!

THEY ALL
LAUGHED

Verse:

The odds were a hundred to one against me,
The world thought the heights were too high to climb.
But people from Missouri never incensed me:
Oh, I wasn't a bit concerned,
For from hist'ry I had learned
How many, many times the worm had turned.

Refrain 1:

They all laughed at Christopher Columbus
When he said the world was round;
They all laughed when Edison recorded sound.

They all laughed at Wilbur and his brother
When they said that man could fly;
They told Marconi
Wireless was a phony—
It's the same old cry!

They laughed at me wanting you,
Said I was reaching for the moon;
But oh, you came through—
Now they'll have to change their tune.

They all said we never could be happy,
They laughed at us—and how!
But ho, ho, ho—
Who's got the last laugh now?

Refrain 2:

They all laughed at Rockefeller Center—
Now they're fighting to get in;
They all laughed at Whitney and his cotton gin.

They all laughed at Fulton and his steamboat,
Hershey and his choc'late bar.
Ford and his Lizzie
Kept the laughers busy—
That's how people are!

They laughed at me wanting you—
Said it would be Hello! Good-bye!
But oh, you came through—
Now they're eating humble pie.

They all said we'd never get together—
Darling, let's take a bow,
For ho, ho, ho—
Who's got the last laugh—
He, he, he—
Let's at the past laugh—
Ha, ha, ha—
Who's got the last laugh now?

George and Ginger Rogers, Hollywood, 1937.

With Jerome Kern and Dorothy Fields.

With Paulette Goddard.

At work on a film score.

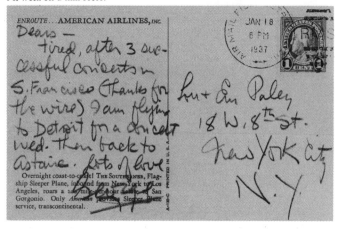

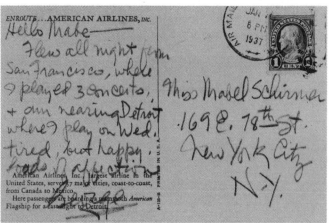

LETTER FROM
GEORGE TO MABEL SCHIRMER

March 19, 1937

Dear Mabel—

. . . our Astaire picture is about completed & in another week we have our first preview. Probably in San Diego. We are excited about it. The studio thinks it looks very good. I've spent so much time watching the first picture being shot that Ira & I are a little behind on the second one. Can you imagine that we've been on the second

Astaire picture for eight weeks already? Time has a special way of flying out here. It just zooms past. Someone once said that when time hurries by, you are happy. If that is true we've been in Heaven.

Dined at E. Robinson's the other night at a party mainly for Stravinsky. Many celebs were there. Chaplin, Goddard, Fairbanks, Dietrich, Capra & others. A grand evening. Stravinsky called Robinson in the afternoon to ask if he & [Samuel] Dushkin could play for the guests. They played of course. Eight pieces, & very interesting too. Sat next to Paulette Goddard. Mmmmmm. She's nice. Me Likee.

It is true that George Kaufman & Moss Hart have an idea for a show for Ira & myself & that they want to produce it in N.Y. sometime next season. Say around Nov. Ira & I look favorably on the idea & hope we can finish up the Goldwyn Follies in time to do the show. Even if the show doesn't materialize I shall come to New York after the Goldwyn doings.

RECOLLECTIONS OF
FRANCES GERSHWIN GODOWSKY
AND LEO GODOWSKY

Leo: George was always asking people's advice on how to compose. I remember that Schoenberg told him that the best way for "you or anybody else to improve your composing is to write variations on a theme and exhaust yourself with all the variations you can find, and when you think you have nothing else to think, start all over again." What Schoenberg told George was what any composition teacher would tell a fledgling composer.

Frankie: When we visited George in 1937 a few months before he was sick, he seemed in wonderful shape. We both were so impressed. He had such vitality and he was taking brisk walks every day. George had always been so absorbed in his work, but he had some analysis with Dr. Zilboorg, and I felt when I saw him then that he was coming into his own as a rounded person. Several times he said to us, "I don't feel I've scratched the surface. I'm out here to make enough money with movies so I don't have to think of money any more. Because I just want to work on American music: symphonies, chamber music, opera. This is what I really want to do. I don't feel I've even scratched the surface." He told Leo he wanted to start on a string quartet.

That was the last remark he made to us. We left and I never saw him again because we were in Europe when he died.

With their mother.

RECOLLECTIONS OF HENRY BOTKIN

George was insecure in so many ways, it was really unbelievable. I remember pretty often the phone would ring about five in the evening and it would be George. "Can you come over to dinner?" I would go. George would have a little dab of sour cream or something. That's all. He was always on a diet. If I hadn't come, he would have been alone. There must have been many times. You couldn't help wondering why is a guy like this in this particular condition?

The last year of his life was an awful year. Did you know about the awful loneliness he had? I remember once he came right out with it and said, "Harry, this year I've GOT to get married." Just like that. Like saying he had to write a new opera or something. The truth is George wanted the most beautiful gal, the most marvelous hostess, someone interested in music. What he wanted and demanded just didn't exist. He would have loved to have a son or a daughter or two. George was very soft. I could never get over that.

LETTER FROM GEORGE TO MABEL SCHIRMER

April 20, 1937

Dear Mabel,

I am lying comfortably on a chaise longue with a new gadget, which I have just bought, on my head. You would probably scream with laughter if you could see me. The machine is a new invention put out by the Crosley Radio Company and has been recommended by several people out here as a positive grower of hair. It's an entirely new principle and you know me for new principles. . . .

Our first Astaire picture Shall We Dance is practically ready for public gaze and if you turn on your radio you will hear the songs from it achieving a rather quick popularity. Our second Astaire opus must be finished in three weeks and then with one week's vacation we start in working for Samuel Goldwyn, so you can see that collaborators Gershwin have been extremely active and shall continue to be until the middle of September. After that, maybe New York for a few months. . . .

A DAMSEL IN DISTRESS (1937)

Box-office reports indicated that the Rogers-Astaire films had lost something of their high popularity, so Fred Astaire was teamed with Joan Fontaine in this likable but ultimately disappointing film. Quite simply, Astaire and the Gershwin songs, even backed by the effervescent George Burns and Gracie Allen, who cavort in a fun-house routine that is the film's best sequence, were not enough to make the film work.

NICE WORK IF YOU CAN GET IT

Verse:

*The man who lives for only making money
Lives a life that isn't necessarily sunny;
Likewise the man who works for fame—
There's no guarantee that time won't erase his name.
The fact is
The only work that really brings enjoyment
Is the kind that is for girl and boy meant.
Fall in love—you won't regret it.
That's the best work of all—if you can get it.*

Refrain:

*Holding hands at midnight
'Neath a starry sky . . .
Nice work if you can get it,
And you can get it—if you try.*

*Strolling with the one girl,
Sighing sigh after sigh . . .
Nice work if you can get it,
And you can get it—if you try.*

*Just imagine someone
Waiting at the cottage door,
Where two hearts become one . . .
Who could ask for anything more?*

*Loving one who loves you,
And then taking that vow . . .
Nice work if you can get it,
And if you get it—won't you tell me how?*

George Burns, Gracie Allen, and Fred Astaire do a broom dance to George's music to "Put Me to the Test." The song was not sung in *Damsel*, but years later, Ira gave the same lyric to Jerome Kern, who set it with a new tune that was used with Ira's lyric in the film *Cover Girl*.

A FOGGY DAY
(IN LONDON TOWN)

Verse:

I was a stranger in the city.
Out of town were the people I knew.
I had that feeling of self-pity:
What to do? What to do? What to do?
The outlook was decidedly blue.
But as I walked through the foggy streets alone,
It turned out to be the luckiest day I've known.

Refrain:

A foggy day in London Town
Had me low and had me down.
I viewed the morning with alarm.
The British Museum had lost its charm.
How long, I wondered, could this thing last?
But the age of miracles hadn't passed,
For, suddenly, I saw you there—
And through foggy London Town
The sun was shining ev'rywhere.

THINGS
ARE LOOKING UP

Verse:

If I should suddenly start to sing
Or stand on my head—or anything,
Don't think that I've lost my senses;
It's just that my happiness finally commences.
The long, long ages of dull despair
Are turning into thin air,
And it seems that suddenly I've
Become the happiest man alive.

Refrain:

Things are looking up!
I've been looking the landscape over
And it's covered with four leaf clover.
Oh, things are looking up
Since love looked up at me.

Bitter was my cup—
But no more will I be the mourner,
For I've certainly turned the corner,
Oh, things are looking up
Since love looked up at me.

See the sunbeams—
Ev'ry one beams
Just because of you.
Love's in session,
And my depression
Is unmistakably through.

Things are looking up!
It's a great little world we live in!
Oh, I'm happy as a pup
Since love looked up
At me.

LETTER FROM
GEORGE TO MABEL SCHIRMER

May 19, 1937

Darling Mabel,

I was delighted to get your letter and to hear that you are well and working hard and planning to sail on the twelfth of June for a trip through the Balkans, returning by the middle of July. It is also nice to know that you are planning to surprise us in California one of these days. It would be such great fun to see you and have you around—as Ira once said in a lyric, "Could you use me—for I certainly could use you." If by any chance you don't go to Europe and decide to come out here, if we have room at our place we would insist upon having you stay with us.

Ira and I have had to literally drag ourselves to work the last few days as we have just finished the second Astaire score and have to start right in on the Goldwyn Follies. Even the Gershwins can't take that kind of routine. It's too bad our contracts followed one another so closely as we both could use a month's rest. Anyway, the silver lining on this cloud is that after the Goldwyn Follies we are going to take a long vacation, come to New York and perhaps I may even go to Europe....

Give yourself a great big kiss for me and write soon.

RECOLLECTIONS OF EMIL MOSBACHER

George had a feeling for the right thing. He had compassion that was part of his being an artist. Yet in the last years George was increasingly restless. Even more than before, he needed people to share things with. He was lonely in many ways and would call me up at all hours, as I'm sure he called others, just to talk and get something off his chest.

George always had trouble with his stomach, and later, of course, George went to see a psychoanalyst. Sometimes I gave him a hard time and would try to toughen him up. I needled him by saying, "What the hell do you need this lemon and hot water at seven in the morning for? Why the hell do you need a psycho when you have all the women you could possibly want?" I used to get after him, but I never pushed him too far because each of us is different and it isn't fair to put yourself inside another person's head.

I saw George twice during the last year of his life— at the start and end of an airplane trip I took to China on an old six-passenger Martin which we had to navigate by sticking a sextant out the window. It may have been May or June when I saw him for the last time. He was finishing a movie score for Goldwyn and asked me to rent a place for him in Saratoga, New York, for August because he thought he would like to vacation there as he had many times before.

George liked to go to the races, but he didn't gamble as much as Ira did—although George did like to play roulette. But Ira really loved to gamble, and when you tell me he still enjoys his Saturday-night poker games, that makes me happy because he is a wonderful guy even if the son of a gun is twenty-four days older than I am.

I did everything I could to help Lee and Ira during the last tragic days of George's life. As soon as Lee called me, I pulled every wire I could to find first Dr. Cushing, the world's most eminent brain specialist, and, when he was unavailable, Dr. Dandy, who was considered in the same class with Cushing. On a Saturday night in July there's no one around in official Washington, but somehow I got the White House to track Dandy down in Chesapeake Bay, and then through a friend with American Airlines flew Dandy to Newark Airport so that he could fly directly to California to perform the operation. When it was too late to get him there in time for the operation, they opened up a direct line between Newark and the Cedars of Lebanon Hospital on the Coast so Dandy could follow the course of the surgery and offer advice if needed.

I don't remember going to sleep that night, but when I got Lee's call with the news we all feared but expected, I was overcome. When the numbness began to wear off, I remembered when I was with George in Charleston, South Carolina, and went with him and Du Bose Heyward from home to home where the shutters would go up and the houses looked as if they were on stilts. George would get the people in the homes to dance so hard that I thought the houses would fall down. I went to church with George, and when they passed the hat, I watched what Du Bose put in. He put in a half-dollar, so George and I did the same. On the last night we were in Charleston, I froze waiting for George at the railroad station so that we could begin our trip to Florida. It became three A.M., and while I froze I had no idea what George was doing. I didn't know what Porgy and Bess would become. All I knew that freezing December night was that I was there waiting for George because he was my friend.

Fairly late in life George took up photography and took many pictures of his friends—Lou Paley, George, and Edward G. Robinson, a time exposure.

220

Leopold Godowsky, Senior.

Lou Paley.

Emily Paley and Mabel Schirmer.

George and Irving Berlin—a time exposure.

Jules and Kendall Glaenzer.

Bill Daly.

GOLDWYN FOLLIES (1938)

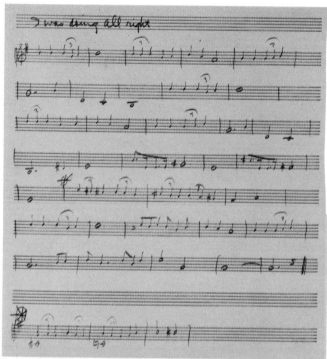

George's lead sheet for "I Was Doing All Right."

The *Goldwyn Follies* was the first American film for which George Balanchine did the choreography.

LOVE WALKED IN

Verse:

Nothing seemed to matter anymore;
Didn't care what I was headed for.
Time was standing still;
Nothing counted till
There came a knock-knock-knocking at the door.

Refrain:

Love walked right in
And drove the shadows away;
Love walked right in
And brought my sunniest day.

One magic moment,
And my heart seemed to know
That love said "Hello!"—
Though not a word was spoken.

One look, and I
Forgot the gloom of the past;
One look, and I
Had found my future at last.

One look, and I
Had found a world completely new,
When love walked in with you.

RECOLLECTIONS OF GEORGE BALANCHINE

I went to California to make my first movie in America. Samuel Goldwyn was the boss, and he arranged a conference at which I met George and Ira. My English was poor then, and Goldwyn spoke English with such an accent that we could not communicate very easily. So George Gershwin tried to be the translator, and he spoke to me like this: "Me Tarzan, you Jane." It was such crazy English, who knew what he was saying? Finally, Ira said to his brother, "George, why don't you speak a little real English?"

When I first saw George he seemed all right. He was writing songs for the film Goldwyn Follies and then we were going to do a ballet together. That would have been very enjoyable.

We met a few times and then I heard George was sick. I went to visit him and found him lying in bed in a dark room with all the shades drawn. He had a towel against his head and he obviously was in great pain. In that dark room he said to me, "It is difficult for me to work now, but I'll be all right." He knew I was trained in music, so he also said, "Do what you must. I know it will be good." He had more confidence in me than Goldwyn did then. "And when I'm all better, we'll do our ballet just the way you want it." A week later he was dead.…Ira and Vernon Duke, whom I knew from the days of Diaghilev, and I finished the score.

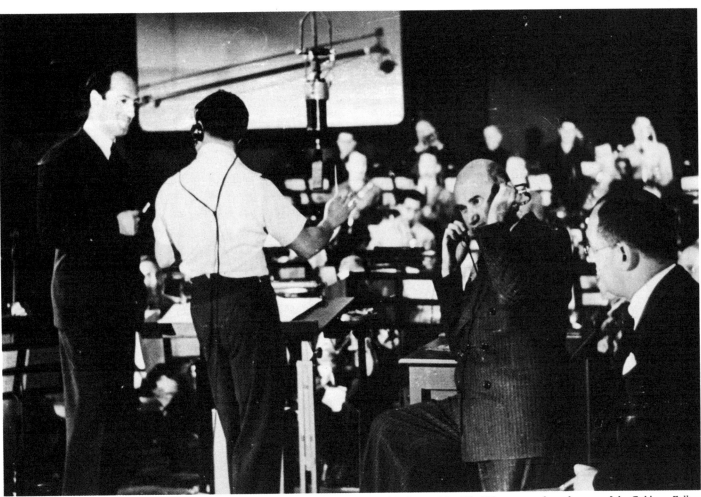

George, Samuel Goldwyn, and Ira listen while Alfred Newman conducts the score of the *Goldwyn Follies*.

Cast of the *Goldwyn Follies*: Kenny Baker and Andrea Leeds at piano; also Helen Jepson, Phil Baker, Ella Logan, Bobby Clark, the three Ritz Brothers, Vera Zorina, Charlie McCarthy, Edgar Bergen, and Adolphe Menjou. / (Overleaf) Last known photo of George Gershwin, taken at an RKO convention on June 16, 1937.

Love Is Here to Stay

"Love Is Here to Stay" was George's last song.

LOVE
IS HERE
TO STAY

Verse:

The more I read the papers,
The less I comprehend
The world and all its capers
And how it all will end.
Nothing seems to be lasting,
But that isn't our affair;
We've got something permanent—
I mean, in the way we care.

Refrain:

It's very clear
Our love is here to stay;
Not for a year,
But ever and a day.

The radio and the telephone
And the movies that we know
May just be passing fancies—
And in time may go.

But oh, my dear,
Our love is here to stay.
Together we're
Going a long, long way.

In time the Rockies may crumble,
Gibraltar may tumble
(They're only made of clay),
But—our love is here to stay.

The closing months of George's life were filled with despondency. How much of this was directly caused by his illness may never be known, but there is absolutely no evidence to support the contention that George knew, months or even years before his death, or at least had some premonition, that he was suffering from a fatal illness.

The despondency of his last months is amply attested to by people who knew him well:

John Green: "In New York George was the king of the world, the man of the hour. We all loved and revered him and appreciated his talent. When he came out to Hollywood, he was respected and admired and his friends felt as they always had felt about him, but it was not the same world at all, and that made all the difference. He would be invited to houses where there were no pianos. He would be invited to homes with pianos where people would neglect to ask him to play, or if he were asked to play, the people present did not surround and engulf and idolize him as they did in New York.

"People can be cruel everywhere, but in Hollywood these qualities are heightened. People want to be around you when you're on top and they can gore you mercilessly when you're down or they think you're down.

"When he was here George was as great a writer as ever, but he hadn't had a big success since *Of Thee I Sing* and that was in 1931. Five years is quite a stretch of time.

"When George wrote the songs for the film *Shall We Dance*, I made arrangements of them and accompanied Fred Astaire's recordings for Brunswick with my orchestra. I remember vividly when I brought the test pressings for George and Ira to hear. I went to 1019 and, as I recall, Lee, Ira, George, and George's mother were there. I put the recordings on, and when George heard 'They Can't Take That Away from Me,' he broke down, reached his hand out to me, and came close to tears. He kept saying 'Thank you' and I don't know why. That song must have meant something special to him. It was a very emotional experience for me then, and as I sit here now thirty-five years later and think about it, it still is."

Todd Duncan also recalls seeing George during the last months. "When I went out to Los Angeles in March of 1937 for Merle Armitage's concerts, I stayed at George's house. He and his agent Arthur Lyons had arranged a huge party after one of the concerts and had rented the Trocadero and invited three hundred guests. It was four thirty in the morning when George and I went home that night. When he got in the house, he said, 'Todd, you know what we went through to put on *Porgy*

and Bess because you were there. Well, if I told you I'm making more money here than ever, but I'm not happy grinding out songs for a picture, what would you think? I have plans for more ambitious works like *Porgy*, and so I will come back to New York in less than a year.'"

Henry Botkin, who was always introduced by George as "my cousin Botkin, the painter," lived with George during part of those last months, and he relates, "It was pathetic. We all tried to arouse his interest in anything, but he was so depressed and so lonely. He sat in his room for hours at a time and would put that damn contraption on his head which he originally bought to keep himself from growing balder but he later used to try to stimulate his scalp to free himself from his headaches. It was crazy.

"Then, he would try to call some of his girl friends and he would ask them to come to California or tell them to meet him in New York, but for one reason or another the ones he called turned him down.

"George started out by liking Hollywood because of the novelty of the place, but in the end he became cynical and George wasn't a cynical person. He would say, 'Harry look at this place—desert. Here they drill four holes and plant palm trees. Then they drill a bigger hole and install a swimming pool. Finally, they build a still larger, deeper hole and put up a house. It's unbelievable.'

"But it wasn't Hollywood. It would have been much the same anywhere. Hollywood made it just a little bit worse for him. There was so much stillness and unreality. George and Ira and I and my brother Ben, we all grew up in the heart of noise in big cities. George heard that noise and he found music in it and kept on finding it until he wrote his last note.

"The ending is too terrible to talk about. Who could have known? And once we knew, it was too late. It was nobody's fault. Not the doctor's, the psychoanalyst's. Not anybody's. But it is preposterous and unbelievable."

Oscar Levant: "I was at the concert the night George had a memory lapse while playing the *Concerto in F*. At one place in the *Concerto* he forgot to come in. Only Smallens, the conductor, and the orchestra, and I could really tell what happened. Because I played the piece so many times, I knew it backwards. I went backstage and said, 'George, what happened? Did I make you nervous or was Horowitz in the audience too?' He said, and he was very serious and he looked very tired, 'Oscar, I blacked out for a minute. I felt dizzy. I don't know. Was it noticeable?' I said, 'To me it was. You've been playing so many concerts and traveling so much you need a rest and maybe a checkup. So he had the checkup and it proved nothing conclusive, but when the headaches and

227

other symptoms got worse, he wouldn't allow a spinal tap. And the rest."...

George died of a brain tumor on July 11, 1937, and was buried on a rainy Thursday, July 15, 1937, after a simple funeral service attended by 3,500 persons at New York's Temple Emanu-El. Outside the synagogue a crowd of more than 1,000 gathered in the rain behind police barricades along both sides of Fifth Avenue. Hundreds had been turned away at the entrance, and policemen were forced to hold back the crowd.

Psalms were read, music by Bach, Schumann, Handel, and Beethoven was played, and Dr. Stephen Wise delivered a eulogy that described George Gershwin as the "singer of the songs of America's soul." Mayor Fiorello La Guardia headed the list of honorary pallbearers who escorted the casket from the synagogue to the strains of the *Rhapsody in Blue*. He was joined by, among others, Walter Damrosch, George M. Cohan, Edwin Franko Goldman, Gene Buck, the president of ASCAP, Vernon Duke, Al Jolson, Sam Harris, and former Mayor James J. Walker. Burial was at Hastings-on-Hudson in Westchester County.

Todd Duncan, who was at Temple Emanu-El with his wife, said that "when we came out of the synagogue, I saw a man walking with his head down in the middle of Fifth Avenue. He was walking on the white line directly between the lanes of traffic that were beginning to move again at the conclusion of the service. I looked at the man and saw that it was Al Jolson, and I watched him keep on walking, oblivious to all around him."

In the months that followed there were many eulogies and memorial concerts. (One such concert occurred on August 8 and gathered the largest crowd in the history of Lewisohn Stadium.) George's Broadway colleagues, Oscar Hammerstein and Irving Berlin, were among many who wrote heartfelt tributes. Arnold Schoenberg, one of the most influential composers of the twentieth century, spoke of George and a moving tribute was offered by Edward G. Robinson, a friend of George's from the early days of the Paley Saturday Nights.

Mourners crowd the sidewalk outside Temple Emanu-El during the funeral service for George Gershwin, July 15, 1937.

228

Outside Temple Emanu-El.

Former Mayor of New York James J. Walker.

Mayor Fiorello H. La Guardia of New York (holding Panama hat).

Al Jolson

OSCAR HAMMERSTEIN

July 1937

Our Friend wrote music
And in that mood he created
Gaiety and sweetness and beauty
And twenty-four hours after he had gone
His music filled the air
And in triumphant accents
Proclaimed to this world of men
That gaiety and sweetness and beauty
Do not die . . .
A genius differs from other men
Only in that his immortality is tangible
What he thought, what he felt, what he meant
Has been crystallized in a form of expression
A form far sturdier than the flesh and sinew of the man
But lesser beings than geniuses
Leave their marks upon this earth
And it is as a lesser being
That George Gershwin's friends knew him and loved him
We remember a young man
Who remained naïve in a sophisticated world
We remember a smile
That was nearly always on his face
A cigar
That was nearly always in his mouth
He was a lucky young man
Lucky to be so in love with the world
And lucky because the world was so in love with him
It endowed him with talent
It endowed him with character
And, rarest of all things,
It gave him a complete capacity
For enjoying all his gifts.
It was a standing joke with us
That George could not be dragged away from a piano
He loved to play the piano
And he played well
And he enjoyed his own playing
How glad we are now
That some divine instinct
Made him snatch every precious second
He could get at that keyboard
Made him drink exultantly
Of his joy-giving talent

Made him crowd every grain of gratification
He could get into his short, blessed life
Maybe the greatest thing he left us
Is this lesson
Maybe we take the good things of life
Too much for granted
Maybe we took George too much for granted
We loved him
Should we not have loved him more?
Have we ever loved him so much
As we do now?
Have we ever said so
As we do now?
We are all inadequate, muddling humans
With hearts and minds woefully unequipped
To solve the problems that beset us
We are eloquent in the recognition of our troubles
Why are we not equally eloquent
In the recognition of our blessings
As George was?
Some will want a statue erected for him
He deserves this
Some will want to endow a school of music
In his name
He deserves this
But his friends could add one more tribute:
In his honor
They could try to appreciate
And be grateful for
The good things in this world
In his honor
They could try to be kinder to one another . . .
And this would be the finest monument of all.

From George Gershwin,
edited and designed by Merle Armitage
(London: Longmans, Green and Co., Ltd., 1938)

ARNOLD SCHOENBERG

Many musicians do not consider George Gershwin a serious composer. But they should understand that, serious or not, he is a composer—that is, a man who lives in music and expresses everything, serious or not, sound or superficial, by means of music, because it is his native language. . . .

An artist is to me like an apple tree: When his time comes, whether he wants it or not, he bursts into bloom and starts to produce apples. And as an apple tree neither knows nor asks about the value experts of the market will attribute to its product, so a real composer does not ask whether his products will please the experts of serious arts. He only feels he has to say something; and says it.

It seems to me beyond doubt that Gershwin was an innovator. What he has done with rhythm, harmony, and melody is not merely style. It is fundamentally different from the mannerism of many a serious composer.... His melodies are not products of a combination, nor of a mechanical union, but they are units and could therefore not be taken to pieces....I do not know it, but I imagine he improvised them on the piano. Perhaps he gave them later the finishing touch; perhaps he spent much time to go over them again and again—I do not know. But the impression is that of an improvisation with all the merits and shortcomings appertaining to this kind of production....

I do not speak here as a musical theorist, nor am I a critic, and hence I am not forced to say whether history will consider Gershwin a kind of Johann Strauss or Debussy, Offenbach or Brahms, Lehár or Puccini.

But I know he is an artist and a composer; he expressed musical ideas; and they were new....

From George Gershwin,
edited and designed by Merle Armitage
(London: Longmans, Green and Co., Ltd., 1938)

IRVING BERLIN

I could speak of a Whiteman rehearsal
At the old Palais Royal when Paul
Played the Rhapsody that lifted Gershwin
From the "Alley" to Carnegie Hall.
I could dwell on the talent that placed him
In the class where he justly belongs,
But this verse is a songwriter's tribute
To a man who wrote wonderful songs.

His were tunes that had more than just rhythm,
For just rhythm will soon gather "corn,"
And those melodies written by Gershwin
Are as fresh now as when they were born.
As a writer of serious music,
He could dream for a while in the stars,
And step down from the heights of grand opera
To a chorus of thirty-two bars.

And this morning's Variety tells me
That the last song he wrote is a hit,
It's on top in the list of best-sellers,
And the airwaves are ringing with it.
It remains with the dozens of others,
Though the man who composed them is gone;
For a songwriter's job may be ended,
But his melodies linger on.

From George Gershwin,
edited and designed by Merle Armitage
(London: Longmans, Green and Co., Ltd., 1938)

EDWARD G. ROBINSON

It was easy to love George Gershwin, and the love and friendship he aroused in those who knew him paid great rewards. There was nothing so warming as the joy he took in the friendships he made. He was responsive to the affections of his friends in so simple and unaffected a way that even casual and transient meetings with him were enriched into unforgettable moments.

Apart from his genius in music, he had a genius for living. His absorption in music did not keep him from realizing fully all that life had to offer. His hobbies were ennobled and dignified by him above the level of hobby interest. A visit with him to an art exhibition was a galvanic experience. We would stand quietly enough before the paintings we were watching, but inwardly—and it was George, I am sure, who caused it—we felt we were fellow travelers into the very life of the picture, and partners in the inspiration of the artist who painted it.

George breathed life into everything he did: he made playing with his dog an enviable—lovingly enviable—pastime.

A round of golf with him was full of high excitement.

Parties at his home or the homes of his friends sprang to life with his presence.

All his record-breaking triumphs in the musical world were no greater than the triumphs he won in his everyday life. He took life in his stride—a gay, graceful, youthful stride. All obstacles were conquered by him with gaiety and grace.

I value above all things the memory I have of George. George—high-spirited, almost boyish—simple—unaffected—lovable—and charged with the power to make all things, great and small, absorbing and significant.

IRA

Ira and Lee returned to Beverly Hills, and Ira, seeking to assuage his grief, submerged himself in work. He finished the score he and George had begun for the *Goldwyn Follies* with the help of Vernon Duke, who worked with Ira on the music for the verses and filled out some of the harmonies where only lead sheets existed. They also wrote "Spring Again" for the score.

Of those who kept George's music alive during the years, Oscar Levant contributed as much as anyone. It was he who carried on the tradition of playing George's work at the Lewisohn Stadium concerts and at many other concerts throughout the world. Of all the artists who have recorded George's work, Levant has given us some of the greatest Gershwin recordings, especially those he did with Morton Gould of the *Second Rhapsody* and the *Variations on "I Got Rhythm."* These recordings are supreme, while his recordings of the *Rhapsody in Blue*, the *Concerto in F*, and the *Piano Preludes* are among the best ever made of these more-often recorded works.

Some time after the *Goldwyn Follies* was finished Ira persuaded himself that he would have to shake off his deep state of despondency and return to work. It was not easy. Ira recalls that "days and nights passed in a blur. Then one afternoon I got to the record player and somehow found myself putting on the Fred Astaire–Johnny Green recordings of the *Shall We Dance* score, most of which had been written in that very room less than a year before. In a few moments the room was filled with gaiety and rhythm, and I felt that George, smiling and approving, was there listening with me—and grief vanished."

Ira then managed to surprise himself by suggesting to his friend Moss Hart that they work together on a project. It was, he declared recently, "really amazing that I actually asked him for work. I have his reply to prove it. It's hard for me to believe because all my professional life I used to avoid work as much as I could." The project became *Lady in the Dark* and "I don't remember ever working harder on a musical show."

Ira kept working...

LADY IN THE DARK (1941)

Starring Gertrude Lawrence and rocketing young Danny Kaye to stardom on the strength of one song, "Tschaikowsky," *Lady in the Dark* proved that Ira had not lost his touch and was indeed able to go it alone just as he had done before he and George teamed up on a regular basis. His collaborations with Vernon Duke, Kurt Weill, Aaron Copland, Jerome Kern, Harry Warren, Arthur Schwartz, Burton Lane, and Harold Arlen confirmed Ira's status as one of the finest lyricists of our musical theater. Ira's book *Lyrics on Several Occasions* is the best book on lyrics and lyric-writing written by anyone.

After his shows *The Firebrand of Florence* (1945) and *Park Avenue* (1946) were box-office failures, he vowed never to write for Broadway again. Today he and Lee live comfortably in a house they bought in 1940 at 1021 North Beverly Drive, next door to the house which they had shared with George during the last year of his life.

One high point for Lee and Ira during recent years was the historic globe-circling journey of *Porgy and Bess* to world acclaim greater than that received by any other work of American music in our history.

Ira is still deeply concerned with George's music. He has over 100 unpublished melodies of George's and is trying to decide what to do with them. There is no question that some of them are outstanding Gershwin tunes that deserve to be known.

TSCHAIKOWSKY (AND OTHER RUSSIANS)

Verse:
Without the least excuse
Or the slightest provocation,
May I fondly introduce,
For your mental delectation,
The names that always give me brain concussion,
The names of those composers known as Russian.

Refrain:
There's Malichevsky, Rubinstein, Arensky and
*   Tschaikowsky,*
Sapelnikoff, Dimitrieff, Tscherepnin, Kryjanowsky,
Godowsky, Arteibouchefl, Moniuszko, Akimenko,
Solovieff, Prokofieff, Tiomkin, Korestchenko.
There's Glinka, Winkler, Bortniansky, Rebikoff,
*   Ilyinsky,*
There's Medtner, Balakireff, Zolotareff and
*   Kvoschinsky.*
And Sokoloff and Kopyloff, Dukelsky and Klenowsky,
And Shostakovitsch, Borodine, Gliere and
*   Nowakofski.*
There's Liadoff and Karganoff, Markievitch,
*   Pantschenko*
And Dargomyzski, Stcherbatcheff, Scriabine,
*   Vassilenko,*
Stravinsky, Rimsky-Korsakoff, Mussorgsky and
*   Gretchaninoff*
And Glazounoff and Caesar Cui, Kalinikoff,
*   Rachmaninoff,*
Stravinsky and Gretchaninoff,
Rumshinsky and Rachmaninoff,
I really have to stop, the subject has been dwelt upon
*   enough!*
(Ensemble) He'd better stop because we feel we all
*   have undergone enough!*

MY SHIP

My ship has sails that are made of silk,
The decks are trimmed with gold;
And of jam and spice
There's a paradise
In the hold.

My ship's aglow with a million pearls,
And rubies fill each bin;
The sun sits high
In a sapphire sky
When my ship comes in.

I can wait the years
Till it appears—
One fine day one spring.
But the pearls and such,
They won't mean much
If there's missing just one thing:

I do not care if that day arrives—
That dream need never be—
If the ship I sing
Doesn't also bring
My own true love to me—
My own true love to me.

COVER GIRL (1944)

LONG AGO
(AND FAR AWAY)

Verse:

Dreary days are over,
Life's a four leaf clover.
Sessions of depressions are through:
Ev'ry hope I longed for long ago comes true.

Refrain:

Long ago and far away
I dreamed a dream one day—
And now that dream is here beside me.
Long the skies were overcast,
But now the clouds have passed:
You're here at last!
Chills run up and down my spine,
Aladdin's lamp is mine:
The dream I dreamed was not denied me.
Just one look and then I knew
That all I longed for long ago was you.

THE FIREBRAND OF FLORENCE (1945)

RECOLLECTIONS OF LOTTE LENYA

I was not present when Kurt met George in Berlin in 1928, but when Kurt spoke of it later, he told me he played for George "The Alabama Song" from Mahagonny.

I met George years later, after Kurt and I came to America. One night at George's home Kurt played and I sang "Pirate Jenny." Then George turned to Kurt and said, "You know, it's funny—she sings like a hillbilly." I didn't know what that meant at the time. Kurt explained to me it wasn't meant as an insult. George was vain, but also very likable. I regret I did not get to know him better.

After George's death, Kurt and Ira got together and really got along beautifully. Ira, much more modest than George, was marvelous, adorable, kind, and understanding. The success of Lady in the Dark is well known, but they also worked together on a film, Where Do We Go from Here?, and a show, The Firebrand of Florence. In my opinion, the show was ruined by the staging of John Murray Anderson, who completely changed the character of what was, after all, the story of Benvenuto Cellini. Ira and Kurt had wanted Walter Slezak to play the Duke, and he and I would have worked very well together. But Melville Cooper was a figure from the British music hall, and in the end it seemed that either he, I, or both of us were terribly miscast. It was a great shame because The Firebrand of Florence had a lovely score, especially "Life, Love and Laughter" and "Sing Me Not a Ballad," and Where Do We Go from Here? had "Song of the Rhineland," one of the best things Ira and Kurt did together.

SING ME
NOT A BALLAD

Verse:

I am not like Circe,
Who showed men no mercy:
Men are most important in my life.
Venus, Cleo, Psyche
Are melodies in my key;
They knew how to live the high life.
Gallantry I find archaic,
Poetry I find prosaic.
Give me the man who's strong and silent:
Inarticulate—but vi'lent.

Refrain:

Sing me not a ballad,
Send me not a sonnet.
I require no ballad:
Rhyme and time are wasted on it.

Save your books and flowers;
They're not necessaries.
Oh, the precious hours
Lost in grim preliminaries!

Deck me not in jewels;
Sigh me not your sighs;
Duel me no duels;
And—please don't vocalize.

Romance me no romances;
Treasure not my glove.
Spare me your advances—
Just, oh just make love!
Spare me your advances—
Just, oh just make love!

Sam H. Harris presents

Gertrude Lawrence in

Lady in the Dark

by
Moss Hart
music by
Kurt Weill
lyrics by
Ira Gershwin

Production by
HASSARD SHORT

Musical Direction by
MAURICE ABRAVANEL

ONE LIFE TO LIVE
MY SHIP
THIS IS NEW
THE PRINCESS OF PURE DELIGHT
GIRL OF THE MOMENT
JENNY
TSCHAIKOWSKY

CHAPPELL
& CO · INC ·
RKO BUILDING
ROCKEFELLER
CENTER · N·Y·C

Fred Astaire in *The Barkleys of Broadway* (1949). Ira wrote the score for this film with Harry Warren.

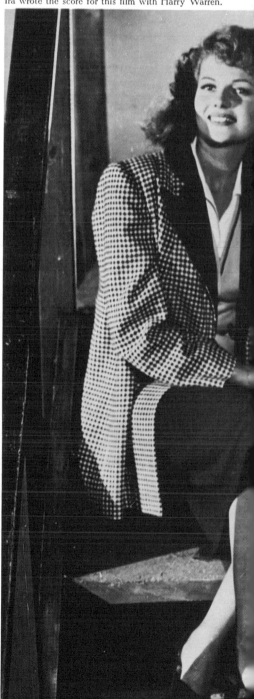

(Below) Ira and Arthur Schwartz teamed to write the score for the musical comedy *Park Avenue* (1946).

Rita Hayworth and Gene Kelly in
the film *Cover Girl* (1944).

Oscar and June Levant, shortly after their marriage in 1939. Levant was the foremost interpreter of Gershwin
music after George's death. / (Below) Gene Kelly and Oscar Levant in *An American in Paris*, the
Academy Award–winning film of 1952.

Ira with Marge Champion, André Previn, and Gower Champion. Gertrude Lawrence.

Betty Grable and Dick Haymes in the film *The Shocking Miss Pilgrim* (1946), which featured posthumous songs by George Gershwin. Kay Swift edited the tunes from George's notebooks and other sources of unused music; Ira wrote the lyrics. / (Below). Max Gordon, producer of *The Firebrand of Florence*.

Vincente Minnelli, Ira, Gene Kelly, and Arthur Freed during the filming of *An American in Paris*. (Below) At left, on platform: Gertrude Lawrence and Victor Mature. Danny Kaye is at right.

Debbie Reynolds and Bob Fosse in the film *Give a Girl a Break* (1953).

GIVE A GIRL A BREAK (1953)

RECOLLECTIONS OF BURTON LANE

I was asked to write the score for the film that turned out to be Give a Girl a Break, and when my agent, Irving Lazar, said "Who would you like to work with?" I said, "My first choice would be Ira Gershwin." He said, "Who's your second choice?" I said, "I better give you a second choice because I'm sure Ira won't take this picture, but I really prefer to do it with Ira. I would love to do something with him." And word came back a day later: Ira would love to do it, and I was thrilled.

The first day Ira and I met to work, I confessed to him that I was very nervous. I had known him for so many years, but this was the first time I'm working with him. I told him I took a pill to sort of settle my nerves. So he took out a little box of pills. He said, "I took one too." Which was sweet, whether it was true or not—it made me feel comfortable.

One of the great things about working with Ira is that he's a real pro. When Ira would have some lyrics to show me, he wouldn't have one set of lyrics. He'd have three or four. If he looked at your face and he didn't get the reaction he wanted, he'd try something else and try something else and try something else, and then he would try another one and, finally, yes, that was the one. But he never stopped trying. If you said, "Well, something isn't quite clear," he'd say, "How about this?" He never once questioned my doubts about anything, just as I never questioned anything he would say about my music.

Once he gave me a title and eight bars of lyrics, and I went home and came back the next day and I had set it. I started to play it for him, and when I finished he said, "Play it again," and when I started to play it again he was standing behind me, and at a certain moment he put his arm around me. I looked up and he was beaming. He had the biggest smile on his face. He does things without overemphasizing that make you feel right. He's wonderful. Unfortunately, it was a very bad film. The song that I set was "Applause, Applause." That was the lyric he gave me.

APPLAUSE, APPLAUSE!

MUSIC BY BURTON LANE

Verse:

When the voodoo drum is drumming
Or the humming bird is humming,
Does it thrill you? Does it fill you with delight?
To continue with our jingle:
Are you one of those who tingle:
To your shoes-ies at the blues-ies in the night?
Oh, the sounds of bugles calling
Or Niag'ra Falls a-falling
May enchant you—we will grant you that they might;
But for us on the stage, oh brother!
There's just one sound and no other;

Refrain 1:

Applause, applause!
We like applause because
It means when it is striking us
The audience is liking us.

Our work demands
You don't sit on your hands—
And if the hand's tremendous,
You send us!

We live, we thrive,
You keep us all alive
With "Bravo!" and "Bravissimo!"
We're dead if it's pianissimo.

Our quirk is work,
Is work we never shirk
In a happyland of tinsel and gauze,
Because—we like applause!

Patter Verse:

Whether you're a Swiss bell ringer
Or a crooner or a singer
Or monologist, ventriloquist or what—
Or a dog act or magician
Or a musical saw musician
Or an ingenue or pianist who is hot—
Whether you play Punchinello,
Little Eva or Othello—
Having heard the call, you've given all you've got.
And what better reward for a trouper
Than the sound we consider super?

Refrain 2:

Applause, applause!
Vociferous applause
From orchestra to gallery
Could mean a raise in salary.

Give out, give in!—
Be noisy, make a din!
(The manager, he audits
Our plaudits.)

We won renown
When opening out of town;
(In Boston and in Rockaway
They heard applause a block away)—

If we've come through,
Give credit where it's due,
And obey the theater's unwritten laws,
Because—we like applause!

RECOLLECTIONS OF HAROLD ARLEN

Ira hasn't changed since I first met him at his River-side Drive penthouse apartment about forty years ago. Oscar Levant introduced us. Ira always looked up to George and they did great work together. George was a free-wheeler, and Ira, who is a dear guy, is a Little King who loved to stay home.

In his lyric-writing, Ira is a plodder—and I don't mean that disrespectfully, I mean it in the best sense. He digs and digs and digs and digs. He edits. He goes over and over his work to change maybe only a line or just a word. I'd be sitting in the room working with him and he would walk out and I'd ask where he was going. He'd answer, "Upstairs to get typewriter ribbon; it's the only way I get exercise."

I worked both ways with Ira. When we wrote the songs for A Star Is Born, I wrote the music for "The Man That Got Away" and "Gotta Have Me Go with You" first. For "Lose That Long Face" Ira wrote the lyric first.

When I have an assignment to do sixteen songs, I do twenty-four because I always believe in giving the lyric-writer a chance to be free, and not be rigidly confined. Generally, Ira liked to hear the whole tune first. He has an excellent musical memory. I always tried to have a bundle of songs ready when I worked with him—or with anyone else, for that matter. Each collaborator reacts differently. Ira, Yipper, John [Mercer]—one musical idea might reach one of the three and turn the other two off. Sometimes I can tell in advance what kind of tune will excite each of my collaborators. But don't play bal-lads for Ira. He hates having to write ballads. He'll do them very well, but he doesn't like doing them. Sometimes, when I want to kid him, I call him up and tell him that we have a chance to do a film score—and they need five ballads.

A STAR IS BORN (1954)

THE MAN THAT GOT AWAY

The night is bitter,
The stars have lost their glitter;
The winds grow colder
And suddenly you're older—
And all because of the man that got away.

No more his eager call,
The writing's on the wall;
The dreams you've dreamed have all
Gone astray.

The man that won you
Has run off and undone you.
That great beginning
Has seen the final inning.
Don't know what happened. It's all a crazy game.

No more that all-time thrill,
For you've been through the mill—
And never a new love will
Be the same.

Good riddance, good bye!
Ev'ry trick of his you're on to.
But, fools will be fools—
And where's he gone to?

The road gets rougher,
It's lonelier and tougher.
With hope you burn up—
Tomorrow he may turn up.
There's just no let-up the live-long night and day.

Ever since this world began
There is nothing sadder than
A one man woman looking for
The man that got away . . .
The man that got away.

Judy Garland sings "The Man That Got Away" in *A Star Is Born* (1954).

(Below) Filmed in 1945.

The Firebrand of Florence (1945).

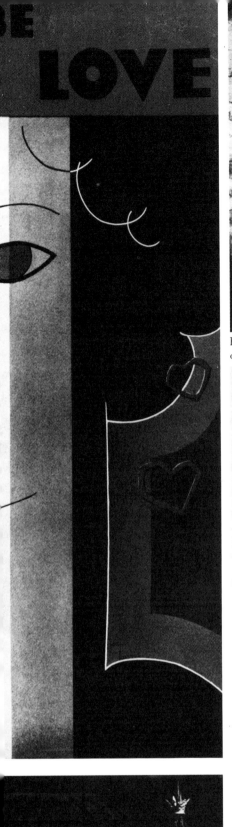

Kurt Weill. Ira and his first show was *Lady in the Dark* (1941). (Below) Fred and Ginger in *The Barkleys of Broadway*—"once more with feeling."

WHO CARES? (1970)

In February 1970 the New York City Ballet presented a forty-five-minute ballet with a score based on seventeen Gershwin songs and whimsically entitled *Who Cares?* The ballet was choreographed by the company's director, George Balanchine, who had worked with George Gershwin many years earlier in Hollywood. Balanchine created the ballet for one male soloist, three female soloists, and a corps of twenty. The work has been performed frequently and occupies a popular place in the company's repertoire.

RECOLLECTIONS OF GEORGE BALANCHINE

One night I took out my copy of George Gershwin's Song-Book *that Alajalov, the artist, had given me. The*

Jacques d'Amboise dances to "Liza."

book had his illustrations. I played the songs as they were set down in George's own arrangements and I had the idea for the ballet Who Cares? *Most of the songs are right from the book, and some are Gershwin's arrangements. On "Clap Yo' Hands" we use a recording of George himself playing.*

The people like it wherever we go because they know the songs. Melodically, George was Russian. He was a fantastic pianist with a special, personal quality. Who Cares? *is a classical ballet with American social dances, but the familiarity to the audience is through the words and the music. They know them and love them.*

George's music is so natural for dancing, so easy to work with. George is dead—how long?—thirty-five years. It's hard to believe. I remember he spoke often to me about wanting to write for the ballet. So I like to think this is George's ballet, this is the ballet we have done for him.

RECOLLECTIONS OF JACQUES D'AMBOISE

One day at rehearsal Mr. Balanchine said, "Jacques, come here! I want to do a ballet to the songs of Gershwin." That was exciting for me because when I was growing up in the Washington Heights section of New York City I was exposed to the great popular songs of Kern, Gershwin, and Berlin, and I've always liked them.

Sometimes when Mr. Balanchine suggests a ballet, it may take years before it is actually done. He has so many ideas, so many things he wants to do, that some things take longer to get started than others. But this time suddenly we were rehearsing and it went really fast.

Who Cares? *is not really tap dancing and not jazz, although it suggests and hints at both. It is a classical ballet in two parts. The first part with the corps is like an extended musical-comedy opening. The second part begins with "The Man I Love," and if the ballet contained nothing else but that one* pas de deux, *it would be wonderful.*

"Liza" and "Clap Yo' Hands" are fun because I can do different things with them every night. I try to do what I feel, and with my jazz dance training I can, in a classical ballet, do things within the framework of the ballet itself.

The music is great fun and I hope we convey that feeling. It is especially gratifying to see young kids watching the ballet and hearing the Gershwin songs. It is all new to them, and it is great that we are able to help keep his work alive.

"Here we are in 'I Got Rhythm,' really in motion, off the floor and off balance, ready to land and move in another direction"—Jacques d'Amboise.
Front row: d'Amboise and the three female soloists, Marnee Morris, Patricia McBride, and Karin von Aroldingen.

George Balanchine conferring with dancers Kay Mazzo and Jacques d'Amboise against the skyscraper backdrop of *Who Cares?*

Lee and Ira.

The songs of George and Ira Gershwin, together with George's instrumental works, represented in such quintessential fashion the spirit and outlook of that unusually creative generation of Americans who appeared in the twenties and thirties that some of their contemporaries simply refused to accept the fact of George's death.

"I don't have to believe it if I don't want to," said John O'Hara.

But time has shown that such suspension of belief is not really necessary. The music of George Gershwin did not stop with his death. It has spread and flourished in the years since then even more than it did during his lifetime. His music and the songs he wrote with Ira have proved to be touchstones that Americans and others throughout the world continue to return to as a source of musical vitality and inspiration. It can be said that the Gershwins wrote "period pieces" in that they captured a period. But, in a larger sense, their work was best described by Ira himself in the remarkably prophetic title he gave to one of their earliest collaborations—"The Real American Folk Song."

CHRONOLOGY OF SHOWS WITH THEIR SONGS

LA, LA, LUCILLE

Tryout: Nixon's Apollo Theatre, Atlantic City, April 21, 1919; National Theatre, Washington, April 27, 1919; Colonial Theatre, Boston, May 12, 1919.

Produced by Alex A. Aarons and George B. Seitz at the Henry Miller Theatre, New York, May 26, 1919. 104 performances. Music by George Gershwin. Lyrics by Arthur J. Jackson and B. G. De Sylva. Book by Fred Jackson. Directed by Herbert Gresham. Dances staged by Julian Alfred. Music conducted by Charles Previn. Cast included Janet Velie, John E. Hazzard, and Helen Clark.

MUSICAL NUMBERS

WHEN YOU LIVE IN A FURNISHED FLAT
*THE BEST OF EVERYTHING
*FROM NOW ON
MONEY, MONEY, MONEY!
*TEE-OODLE-UM-BUM-BO
*OO, HOW I LOVE TO BE LOVED BY YOU
(Lyrics by Lou Paley)
IT'S GREAT TO BE IN LOVE
*THERE'S MORE TO THE KISS THAN THE SOUND
(Lyrics by Irving Caesar)
*SOMEHOW IT SELDOM COMES TRUE
THE TEN COMMANDMENTS OF LOVE

ADDED AFTER OPENING

IT'S HARD TO TELL
*NOBODY BUT YOU

UNUSED

OUR LITTLE KITCHENETTE
*THE LOVE OF A WIFE

MORRIS GEST MIDNIGHT WHIRL

Produced by Morris Gest at the Century Grove (roof of the Century Theatre, New York), December 27, 1919. 110 performances. Music by George Gershwin. Book and lyrics by B. G. De Sylva and John Henry Mears. Staged by Julian Mitchell and Dave Bennett. Music conducted by Frank Tours. Cast included Bessie McCoy Davis, Helen Shipman, Bernard Granville, and the Rath Brothers.

MUSICAL NUMBERS

I'LL SHOW YOU A WONDERFUL WORLD
THE LEAGUE OF NATIONS

*Indicates published songs.

DOUGHNUTS
*POPPYLAND
*LIMEHOUSE NIGHTS
LET CUTIE CUT YOUR CUTICLE
BABY DOLLS

MISCELLANEOUS SONGS 1913–1919

SINCE I FOUND YOU
(George Gershwin's first known song)
(Lyrics by Leonard Praskins)†
Non-production 1913
RAGGING THE TRAUMEREI
(Lyrics by Leonard Praskins)
Non-production 1913 or 1914
TANGO
(No lyrics)
Non-production 1914
*WHEN YOU WANT 'EM, YOU CAN'T GET 'EM (WHEN YOU GOT 'EM, YOU DON'T WANT 'EM)
(George Gershwin's first published song)
(Lyrics by Murray Roth)
Non-production 1916
*MAKING OF A GIRL
(Music by Sigmund Romberg and George Gershwin)
(Lyrics by Harold Atteridge)
The Passing Show of 1916, June 22, 1916, 140 performances
MY RUNAWAY GIRL
(Lyrics by Murray Roth)
The Passing Show of 1916
*RIALTO RIPPLES
(Music by George Gershwin and Will Donaldson)
(No lyrics)
Non-production 1917
BEAUTIFUL BIRD
(Lyrics by Ira Gershwin and Lou Paley)
Non-production 1917
WHEN THERE'S A CHANCE TO DANCE
Non-production 1917 or 1918
GUSH-GUSH-GUSHING
Non-production 1918
WHEN THE ARMIES DISBAND
(Lyrics by Irving Caesar)
Non-production 1918
*YOU-OO JUST YOU
(Lyrics by Irving Caesar)
Hitchy-Koo of 1918, June 6, 1918, 68 performances
*THE REAL AMERICAN FOLK SONG (IS A RAG)
Ladies First, October 24, 1918, 164 performances
*SOME WONDERFUL SORT OF SOMEONE
(Lyrics by Schuyler Greene)
Ladies First
THERE'S MAGIC IN THE AIR
Half Past Eight, December 9, 1918, 6 performances, Syracuse, New York
THE TEN COMMANDMENTS OF LOVE
(Lyrics by Edward B. Perkins)
Half Past Eight

†Where no composer is listed, the music is by George; where no lyricist is named, the lyrics are by Ira (who is listed in most pre-1925 songs under his pseudonym, Arthur Francis). Where collaborators are involved, all names are included. Where no name is given, the song is entirely the work of the two Gershwins.

CUPID
(Lyrics by Edward B. Perkins)
Half Past Eight
HONG KONG
(Lyrics by Edward B. Perkins)
Half Past Eight
GOOD LITTLE TUNE
(Lyrics by Irving Caesar)
Non-production 1918
LITTLE THEATRE OF OUR OWN
Non-production c.1919
*LULLABY
(No lyrics)
Non-production 1919
*I WAS SO YOUNG (YOU WERE SO BEAUTIFUL)
(Lyrics by Irving Caesar and Al Bryan)
Good Morning Judge, February 6, 1919, 140 performances
*THERE'S MORE TO THE KISS THAN THE X-X-X
(Lyrics by Irving Caesar)
Good Morning, Judge
*O LAND OF MINE, AMERICA
(Lyrics by Michael E. Rourke)
Non-production 1919
*SOMETHING ABOUT LOVE
(Lyrics by Lou Paley)
The Lady in Red, May 12, 1919, 48 performances
*SWANEE
(Lyrics by Irving Caesar)
Capitol Revue ("Demi-Tasse") October 24, 1919
*COME TO THE MOON
(Lyrics by Lou Paley and Ned Wayburn)
Capitol Revue ("Demi-Tasse")

GEORGE WHITE'S SCANDALS OF 1920

Tryout: National Theatre, Washington, May 26, 1920.

Produced by George White at the Globe Theatre, New York, June 7, 1920, 134 performances. Music by George Gershwin. Lyrics by Arthur Jackson. Book by Andy Rice and George White. Staged by William Collier and George White. Music conducted by Alfred Newman. Cast included Ann Pennington, Lou Holtz, George ("Doc") Rockwell, Sascha Beaumont, Lester O'Keefe, Lester Allen, and George White.

MUSICAL NUMBERS

*MY LADY
EVERYBODY SWAT THE PROFITEER
*ON MY MIND THE WHOLE NIGHT LONG
*SCANDAL WALK
*TUM ON AND TISS ME
*THE SONGS OF LONG AGO
*IDLE DREAMS

UNUSED

MY OLD LOVE IS MY NEW LOVE
QUEEN ISABELLA

A DANGEROUS MAID

Tryout: Nixon's Apollo Theatre, Atlantic City, March 21, 1921. Closed at the Nixon Theatre, Pittsburgh, April 30, 1921. (Did not open on Broadway.)

Produced by Edgar MacGregor. Music by George Gershwin. Lyrics by Arthur Francis. Book by Charles W. Bell. Cast included Vinton Freedley, Amelia Bingham, Juliette Day (replaced by Vivienne Segal), Creighton Hale, and Juanita Fletcher.

MUSICAL NUMBERS

ANYTHING FOR YOU
*JUST TO KNOW YOU ARE MINE
*BOY WANTED
*THE SIMPLE LIFE
THE SIRENS
TRUE LOVE
*SOME RAIN MUST FALL
*DANCING SHOES

UNUSED

PIDGEE WOO
EVERY GIRL HAS A WAY

TWO LITTLE GIRLS IN BLUE

Tryout: Colonial Theatre, Boston, April 12, 1921.

Produced by A. L. Erlanger at the George M. Cohan Theatre, New York, May 3, 1921. 135 performances. Music by Vincent Youmans and Paul Lannin. Lyrics by Arthur Francis. Book by Fred Jackson. Directed by Ned Wayburn. Music conducted by Charles Previn. Cast included Madeline and Marion Fairbanks, Oscar Shaw, Fred Santley, Olin Howland, and Julia Kelety.

MUSICAL NUMBERS (See alphabetical list of songs for individual credits.)

WE'RE OFF ON A WONDERFUL TRIP
YOUR WONDERFUL U.S.A.
WHEN I'M WITH THE GIRLS
TWO LITTLE GIRLS IN BLUE
THE SILLY SEASON
*OH ME! OH MY! (OH YOU!)
*YOU STARTED SOMETHING
WE'RE OFF TO INDIA
HERE, STEWARD
*DOLLY
*WHO'S WHO WITH YOU?
*JUST LIKE YOU
THERE'S SOMETHING ABOUT ME THEY LIKE
*RICE AND SHOES
SHE'S INNOCENT
*HONEYMOON (WHEN WILL YOU SHINE FOR ME?)
I'M TICKLED SILLY

UNUSED

SUMMERTIME
HAPPY ENDING

MAKE THE BEST OF IT
LITTLE BAG OF TRICKS
SLAPSTICK
MR. AND MRS.
UTOPIA

GEORGE WHITE'S SCANDALS OF 1921

Tryout: Nixon's Apollo Theatre, Atlantic City, July 4, 1921.

Produced by George White at the Liberty Theatre, New York, July 11, 1921. 97 performances. Music by George Gershwin. Lyrics by Arthur Jackson. Book by Arthur "Bugs" Baer and George White. Staged by George White. Music conducted by Alfred Newman. Cast included Charles King, Ann Pennington, Theresa Gardella ("Aunt Jemima"), George LeMaire, Olive Vaughan, Lester Allen, Bert Gordon, and George White.

MUSICAL NUMBERS

*I LOVE YOU
*SOUTH SEA ISLES (SUNNY SOUTH SEA ISLANDS)
*DRIFTING ALONG WITH THE TIDE
*SHE'S JUST A BABY
*WHEN EAST MEETS WEST

GEORGE WHITE'S SCANDALS OF 1922

Tryout: Shubert Theatre, New Haven.

Produced by George White at the Globe Theatre, New York, August 28, 1922. 88 performances. Music by George Gershwin. Lyrics by B. G. De Sylva, E. Ray Goetz, and Arthur Francis. Book by George White, W. C. Fields, and Andy Rice. Staged by George White. Music conducted by Max Steiner. Cast included W. C. Fields, Jack McGowan, Winnie Lightner, Pearl Regay, Lester Allen, Richard Bold, Coletta Ryan, George White, Dolores Costello, and Paul Whiteman's Orchestra.

MUSICAL NUMBERS

*OH, WHAT SHE HANGS OUT (SHE HANGS OUT IN OUR ALLEY)
*CINDERELATIVES
*I FOUND A FOUR LEAF CLOVER
I CAN'T TELL WHERE THEY'RE FROM WHEN THEY DANCE
*I'LL BUILD A STAIRWAY TO PARADISE
JUST A TINY CUP OF TEA
*WHERE IS THE MAN OF MY DREAMS?
*ACROSS THE SEA (MY HEART WILL SAIL ACROSS THE SEA)
*ARGENTINA
‡BLUE MONDAY BLUES
‡HAS ANYONE SEEN MY JOE?
‡I'M GONNA SEE MY MOTHER

‡These songs were from *Blue Monday*, a brief opera that was withdrawn following the opening night.

OUR NELL

Tryout: Stamford Theatre, Stamford, Conn., November 20, 1922; Poli's Theatre, Washington, November 27, 1922.

Produced by Hayseed Productions (Ed Davidow and Rufus LeMaire) at the Nora Bayes Theatre, December 4, 1922. 40 performances. Music by George Gershwin and William Daly. Lyrics by Brian Hooker. Book by A. E. Thomas and Brian Hooker. Staged by W. H. Gilmore, Edgar MacGregor, and Julian Mason. Music conducted by Charles Sieger. Cast included Mr. and Mrs. Jimmie Barry, Olin Howland, Emma Haig, and John Merkyl.

MUSICAL NUMBERS

GOL-DURN!
*INNOCENT INGENUE BABY
THE COONEY COUNTY FAIR
NAMES I LOVE TO HEAR
*BY AND BY
MADRIGAL
WE GO TO CHURCH ON SUNDAY
*WALKING HOME WITH ANGELINE
OH, YOU LADY!
LITTLE VILLAGES

UNUSED

THE CUSTODY OF THE CHILD

THE RAINBOW

Produced by Albert de Courville at the Empire Theatre, London, April 3, 1923. 113 performances. Music by George Gershwin. Lyrics by Clifford Grey. Book by Albert de Courville, Edgar Wallace, and Noel Scott. Staged by Allan K. Foster. Music conducted by Kennedy Russell. Cast included Grace Hayes, Stephanie Stephens, Earl Rickard, Lola Raine, and Fred A. Leslie.

MUSICAL NUMBERS

*SWEETHEART (I'M SO GLAD THAT I MET YOU)
*GOOD NIGHT, MY DEAR
ANY LITTLE TUNE
MIDNIGHT BLUES
*MOONLIGHT IN VERSAILLES
*IN THE RAIN
*INNOCENT LONESOME BLUE BABY
(Lyrics by Brian Hooker and Clifford Grey)
*BENEATH THE EASTERN MOON
*OH! NINA
*STRUT LADY WITH ME

UNUSED

*SUNDAY IN LONDON TOWN
GIVE ME MY MAMMY
ALL OVER TOWN

GEORGE WHITE'S SCANDALS OF 1923

Tryout: Nixon's Apollo Theatre, Atlantic City, June 5, 1923.

Produced by George White at the Globe Theatre, New York, June 18, 1923. 168 performances. Music by George Gershwin. Lyrics by B. G. De Sylva, E. Ray Goetz, and Ballard MacDonald. Book by George White and W. K. Wells. Staged by George White. Music conducted by Charles Drury. Cast included Johnny Dooley, Winnie Lightner, Tom Patricola, Lester Allen, Richard Bold, Olive Vaughn, and Helen Hudson.

MUSICAL NUMBERS

LITTLE SCANDAL DOLLS
*YOU AND I
KATINKA
*LO-LA-LO
*THROW 'ER IN HIGH!
*LET'S BE LONESOME TOGETHER
*THE LIFE OF A ROSE
*WHERE IS SHE?
LAUGH YOUR CARES AWAY
LOOK IN THE LOOKING GLASS
*THERE IS NOTHING TOO GOOD
   FOR YOU
*(ON THE BEACH AT) HOW'VE-YOU-
   BEEN?

ADDED ON ROAD TOUR

GARDEN OF LOVE

SWEET LITTLE DEVIL

Tryout: Shubert Theatre, Boston, December 20, 1923.

Produced by Laurence Schwab at the Astor Theatre, New York, January 21, 1924. 120 performances. Music by George Gershwin. Lyrics by B. G. De Sylva. Book by Frank Mandel and Laurence Schwab. Staged by Edgar MacGregor and Sammy Lee. Music conducted by Ivan Rudisill. Cast included Constance Binney, Marjorie Gateson, Irving Beebe, Franklyn Ardell, Ruth Warren, and William Wayne.

MUSICAL NUMBERS

STRIKE, STRIKE, STRIKE
*VIRGINIA (DON'T GO TOO FAR)
*SOMEONE WHO BELIEVES IN YOU
SYSTEM
*THE JIJIBO
QUITE A PARTY
*UNDER A ONE-MAN TOP
THE MATRIMONIAL HANDICAP
JUST SUPPOSING
*HEY! HEY! LET 'ER GO!
THE SAME OLD STORY
HOORAY FOR THE U.S.A.!

UNUSED

*MAH-JONGG
*PEPITA

(YOU'RE MIGHTY LUCKY) MY LITTLE
   DUCKY
SWEET LITTLE DEVIL
BE THE LIFE OF THE CROWD

RHAPSODY IN BLUE

*Rhapsody in Blue for Jazz Band and Piano. by George Gershwin. Orchestrated by Ferde Grofé. Première: Aeolian Hall, New York, February 12, 1924—Paul Whiteman and his Palais Royal Orchestra; George Gershwin, piano.

GEORGE WHITE'S SCANDALS OF 1924

Tryout: Nixon's Apollo Theatre, Atlantic City, June 23, 1924.

Produced by George White at the Apollo Theatre, New York, June 30, 1924. 192 performances. Music by George Gershwin. Lyrics by B. G. De Sylva. Book by William K. Wells and George White. Staged by George White. Music conducted by William Daly. Cast included Winnie Lightner, Will Mahoney, Tom Patricola, the Williams Sisters, Richard Bold, Helen Hudson, and Dolores and Helene Costello.

MUSICAL NUMBERS

JUST MISSED THE OPENING CHORUS
*I NEED A GARDEN
*NIGHT TIME IN ARABY
I'M GOING BACK
*YEAR AFTER YEAR
*SOMEBODY LOVES ME
(Lyrics by B. G. De Sylva and Ballard MacDonald)
*TUNE IN (TO STATION J. O. Y.)
*MAH-JONGG
LOVERS OF ART
*ROSE OF MADRID
I LOVE YOU, MY DARLING
*KONGO KATE

PRIMROSE

Produced by George Grossmith and J. A. E. Malone at the Winter Garden Theatre, London, September 11, 1924. 255 performances. Music by George Gershwin. Lyrics by Desmond Carter and Ira Gershwin. Book by George Grossmith and Guy Bolton. Book directed by Charles A. Maynard. Dances staged by Laddie Cliff and Carl Hyson. Music conducted by John Ansell. Cast included Leslie Henson, Heather Thatcher, Vera Lennox, Percy Heming, Claude Hulbert, and Margery Hicklin.

MUSICAL NUMBERS

(Complete piano-vocal score published)
(Lyrics by Desmond Carter alone, except where indicated)

LEAVING TOWN WHILE WE MAY

TILL I MEET SOMEONE LIKE YOU
*ISN'T IT WONDERFUL
(Lyrics by Desmond Carter and Ira Gershwin)
*THE COUNTRYSIDE (THIS IS THE LIFE
   FOR A MAN)
WHEN TOBY IS OUT OF TOWN
*SOME FAR-AWAY SOMEONE
(Lyrics by Ira Gershwin and B. G. De Sylva)
THE MOPHAMS
ROSES OF FRANCE
FOUR LITTLE SIRENS
(Lyrics by Ira Gershwin)
BERKELEY SQUARE AND KEW
*BOY WANTED
(Lyrics by Ira Gershwin and Desmond Carter)
*WAIT A BIT, SUSIE
(Lyrics by Ira Gershwin and Desmond Carter)
ISN'T IT TERRIBLE WHAT THEY DID TO
   MARY QUEEN OF SCOTS
*NAUGHTY BABY
(Lyrics by Ira Gershwin and Desmond Carter)
IT IS THE FOURTEENTH OF JULY
BALLET MUSIC
I MAKE HAY WHILE THE MOON SHINES
*THAT NEW-FANGLED MOTHER OF MINE
BEAU BRUMMEL

UNUSED

THE LIVE WIRE
PEP! ZIP! AND PUNCH!

LADY, BE GOOD!

Tryout: Forrest Theatre, Philadelphia, November 17, 1924.

Produced by Alex A. Aarons and Vinton Freedley at the Liberty Theatre, New York, December 1, 1924. 330 performances. Music by George Gershwin. Lyrics by Ira Gershwin. Book by Guy Bolton and Fred Thompson. Directed by Felix Edwards. Dances staged by Sammy Lee. Music conducted by Paul Lannin. Cast included Fred and Adele Astaire, Walter Catlett, Cliff Edwards, Alan Edwards, Kathlene Martyn, with Phil Ohman and Victor Arden at the pianos.

MUSICAL NUMBERS

*HANG ON TO ME
A WONDERFUL PARTY
THE END OF A STRING
WE'RE HERE BECAUSE
*FASCINATING RHYTHM
*SO AM I
*OH, LADY, BE GOOD!
WEATHER MAN
RAINY AFTERNOON GIRLS
*THE HALF OF IT, DEARIE, BLUES
JUANITA
LEAVE IT TO LOVE
*LITTLE JAZZ BIRD
CARNIVAL TIME
SWISS MISS
(Lyrics by Ira Gershwin and Arthur Jackson)

ADDED AFTER OPENING

LINGER IN THE LOBBY
(Replaced "Weather Man" and "Rainy Afternoon
   Girls")

UNUSED

*THE MAN I LOVE
SEEING DICKIE HOME
WILL YOU REMEMBER ME?
EVENING STAR
SINGIN' PETE
THE BAD, BAD MEN

ADDED TO LONDON PRODUCTION
(Empire Theatre, April 14, 1926)

BUY A LITTLE BUTTON FROM US
(Lyrics by Desmond Carter)

*I'D RATHER CHARLESTON
(Lyrics by Desmond Carter)

SOMETHING ABOUT LOVE
(Lyrics by Lou Paley)

SHORT STORY

Short Story. A violin piece arranged by Samuel Dushkin from two unpublished Gershwin *Novelettes* for piano. Première performance by Dushkin as part of a recital at the University Club, New York, February 8, 1925.

TELL ME MORE!

Tryout: Nixon's Apollo Theatre, Atlantic City, April 6, 1925.

Produced by Alex A. Aarons at the Gaiety Theatre, New York, April 13, 1925. 100 performances. Music by George Gershwin. Lyrics by B. G. De Sylva and Ira Gershwin. Book by Fred Thompson and William K. Wells. Staged by John Harwood and Sammy Lee. Music conducted by Max Steiner. Cast included Phyllis Cleveland, Alexander Gray, Lou Holtz, Emma Haig, Esther Howard, and Andrew Tombes, with Portland Hoffa (Mrs. Fred Allen) in the chorus.

MUSICAL NUMBERS

*TELL ME MORE!
MR. AND MRS. SIPKIN
WHEN THE DEBBIES GO BY
*THREE TIMES A DAY
*WHY DO I LOVE YOU?
HOW CAN I WIN YOU NOW?
*KICKIN' THE CLOUDS AWAY
LOVE IS IN THE AIR
*MY FAIR LADY
IN SARDINIA
*BABY!
THE POETRY OF MOTION
UKULELE LORELEI

UNUSED

SHOP GIRLS AND MANNIKINS
ONCE
I'M SOMETHIN' ON AVENUE A
THE HE-MAN

ADDED TO LONDON PRODUCTION
(Winter Garden, May 26, 1925)

LOVE, I NEVER KNEW
(Lyrics by Desmond Carter)
HAVE YOU HEARD
(Lyrics by Claude Hulbert)

UNUSED (LONDON PRODUCTION)

*MURDEROUS MONTY (AND LIGHT-FINGERED JANE)
(Lyrics by Desmond Carter)

TIP-TOES

Tryout: National Theatre, Washington, November 24, 1925; Shubert Theatre, Newark, November 30, 1925; Forrest Theatre, Philadelphia, December 7, 1925; Ford's Theatre, Baltimore, December 21, 1925.

Produced by Alex A. Aarons and Vinton Freedley at the Liberty Theatre, New York, December 28, 1925. 194 performances. Music by George Gershwin. Lyrics by Ira Gershwin. Book by Guy Bolton and Fred Thompson. Directed by John Harwood. Dances staged by Sammy Lee. Music conducted by William Daly. Cast included Queenie Smith, Allen Kearns, Andrew Tombes, Harry Watson, Jeanette MacDonald, Robert Halliday, and Gertrude McDonald. Phil Ohman and Victor Arden at the pianos.

MUSICAL NUMBERS

WAITING FOR THE TRAIN
*NICE BABY
*LOOKING FOR A BOY
LADY LUCK
*WHEN DO WE DANCE?
*THESE CHARMING PEOPLE
*THAT CERTAIN FEELING
*SWEET AND LOW-DOWN
OUR LITTLE CAPTAIN
*IT'S A GREAT LITTLE WORLD
*NIGHTIE-NIGHT
TIP-TOES

UNUSED

HARLEM RIVER CHANTY
GATHER YE ROSEBUDS
DANCING HOUR
LIFE'S TOO SHORT TO BE BLUE
WE
HARBOR OF DREAMS

CONCERTO IN F

Concerto in F for Piano and Orchestra by George Gershwin. Première: Carnegie Hall, New York, December 3, 1925—The New York Symphony Society, conducted by Walter Damrosch; George Gershwin, piano.

SONG OF THE FLAME

Tryout: Playhouse, Wilmington, December 9, 1925; Poli's Theatre, Washington, December 14, 1925.

Produced by Arthur Hammerstein at the 44th Street Theatre, New York, December 30, 1925. 219 performances. Music by George Gershwin and Herbert Stothart. Book and lyrics by Otto Harbach and Oscar Hammerstein II. Directed by Frank Reicher. Musical numbers staged by Jack Haskell. Music conducted by Herbert Stothart. Cast included Tessa Kosta, Guy Robertson, Dorothy Mackaye, Greek Evans, and the Russian Art Choir.

MUSICAL NUMBERS
(Except where indicated, Gershwin and Stothart collaborated on all the songs listed here. Those by Stothart alone, as well as Russian folk songs, are unlisted.)

FAR AWAY
*SONG OF THE FLAME
WOMAN'S WORK IS NEVER DONE
*THE SIGNAL
(Music by George Gershwin)
*COSSACK LOVE SONG (DON'T FORGET ME)
TARTAR
*VODKA (DON'T GIVE ME VODKA)
*MIDNIGHT BELLS
(Music by George Gershwin)

UNUSED

*YOU ARE YOU

OH, KAY!

Tryout: Shubert Theatre, Philadelphia, October 18, 1926.

Produced by Alex A. Aarons and Vinton Freedley at the Imperial Theatre, New York, November 8, 1926. 256 performances. Music by George Gershwin. Lyrics by Ira Gershwin. Book by Guy Bolton and P. G. Wodehouse. Directed by John Harwood. Staged by Sammy Lee. Music conducted by William Daly. Cast included Gertrude Lawrence, Oscar Shaw, Victor Moore, Harland Dixon, Betty Compton, Constance Carpenter, Gerald Oliver Smith, and the Fairbanks Twins. Phil Ohman and Victor Arden at the pianos.

MUSICAL NUMBERS

THE WOMAN'S TOUCH
DON'T ASK!
*DEAR LITTLE GIRL (I HOPE YOU'VE MISSED ME)
*MAYBE
*CLAP YO' HANDS
BRIDE AND GROOM
*DO, DO, DO
*SOMEONE TO WATCH OVER ME
*FIDGETY FEET
*HEAVEN ON EARTH
(Lyrics by Ira Gershwin and Howard Dietz)
*OH, KAY!
(Lyrics by Ira Gershwin and Howard Dietz)

UNUSED

*SHOW ME THE TOWN
WHAT'S THE USE?
THE MOON IS ON THE SEA
THE SUN IS ON THE SEA
STEPPING WITH BABY
GUESS WHO
AIN'T IT ROMANTIC
BRING ON THE DING DONG DELL
WHEN OUR SHIP COMES SAILING IN

PRELUDES FOR PIANO

Preludes for Piano by George Gershwin. Première: Five Preludes were played by the composer at the Hotel Roosevelt, New York, December 4, 1926. These, plus an additional prelude, were played by Gershwin at Symphony Hall, Boston, on January 16, 1927.

STRIKE UP THE BAND
(First Version)

Tryout: Broadway Theatre, Long Branch, N.J., August 29, 1927; Shubert Theatre, Philadelphia, September 5, 1927. Closed there after two weeks.

Produced by Edgar Selwyn. Book by George S. Kaufman. Directed by R. H. Burnside. Dances staged by John Boyle. Music conducted by William Daly. Cast included Roger Pryor, Vivian Hart, Edna May Oliver, Max Hoffman, Jr., Jimmy Savo, Herbert Corthell, and Morton Downey.

MUSICAL NUMBERS

FLETCHER'S AMERICAN CHEESE CHORAL
   SOCIETY
*SEVENTEEN AND TWENTY-ONE
*TYPICAL SELF-MADE AMERICAN
MEADOW SERENADE
THE UNOFFICIAL SPOKESMAN
PATRIOTIC RALLY
*THE MAN I LOVE
*YANKEE DOODLE RHYTHM
*STRIKE UP THE BAND!
OH, THIS IS SUCH A LOVELY WAR
HOPING THAT SOME DAY YOU'D CARE
*MILITARY DANCING DRILL
HOW ABOUT A MAN LIKE ME?
HOMEWARD BOUND
THE GIRL I LOVE
THE WAR THAT ENDED WAR

FUNNY FACE

Tryout: Shubert Theatre, Philadelphia, October 11, 1927; Playhouse, Wilmington, November 14, 1927.

Produced by Alex A. Aarons and Vinton Freedley at the Alvin Theatre, New York (first show in that theater), November 22, 1927. 244 performances. Music by George Gershwin. Lyrics by Ira Gershwin. Book by Fred Thompson and Paul Gerard Smith. Directed by Edgar MacGregor. Dances staged by Bobby Connolly. Music conducted by Alfred Newman. Cast included Fred and Adele Astaire, William Kent, Victor Moore, Allen Kearns, Gertrude McDonald, and Betty Compton, Phil Ohman and Victor Arden at the pianos.

MUSICAL NUMBERS

BIRTHDAY PARTY
ONCE
*FUNNY FACE
*HIGH HAT
*'S WONDERFUL
*LET'S KISS AND MAKE UP
IN THE SWIM
*HE LOVES AND SHE LOVES
TELL THE DOC
*MY ONE AND ONLY (WHAT AM I
   GONNA DO)
SING A LITTLE SONG
BLUE HULLABALLOO
*THE BABBITT AND THE BROMIDE

UNUSED

WE'RE ALL A-WORRY, ALL AGOG
WHEN YOU'RE SINGLE
*THE WORLD IS MINE
COME ALONG, LET'S GAMBLE
IF YOU WILL TAKE OUR TIP
THE FINEST OF THE FINEST
ACROBATS
*DANCE ALONE WITH YOU (WHY DOES
   EVERYBODY HAVE TO CUT IN)
DANCING HOUR
*HOW LONG HAS THIS BEEN GOING ON?
THOSE EYES

USED IN LONDON PRODUCTION
(Princes Theatre, November 8, 1928)

LOOK AT THE DAMN THING NOW

ROSALIE

Tryout: Colonial Theatre, Boston, December 5, 1927.

Produced by Florenz Ziegfeld at the New Amsterdam Theatre, New York, January 10, 1928. 335 performances. Music by George Gershwin and Sigmund Romberg. Lyrics by P. G. Wodehouse and Ira Gershwin. Book by William Anthony McGuire and Guy Bolton. Directed by William Anthony McGuire. Numbers staged by Seymour Felix. Music conducted by Oscar Bradley. Cast included Marilyn Miller, Jack Donahue, Frank Morgan, Bobbe Arnst, Gladys Glad, Margaret Dale and Oliver McLennan.

MUSICAL NUMBERS BY GEORGE
GERSHWIN
(Those composed by Sigmund Romberg are not
   listed)

*SHOW ME THE TOWN
*SAY SO!
(Lyrics by Ira Gershwin and P. G. Wodehouse)
LET ME BE A FRIEND TO YOU
*OH GEE! OH JOY!
(Lyrics by Ira Gershwin and P. G. Wodehouse)
NEW YORK SERENADE
*HOW LONG HAS THIS BEEN GOING ON?
MERRY-ANDREW (DANCE MUSIC)

ADDED AFTER OPENING

*EV'RYBODY KNOWS I LOVE SOMEBODY
FOLLOW THE DRUM

UNUSED

*ROSALIE
*BEAUTIFUL GYPSY
*YANKEE DOODLE RHYTHM
WHEN CADETS PARADE
I FORGET WHAT I STARTED TO SAY
YOU KNOW HOW IT IS
(Lyrics by Ira Gershwin and P. G. Wodehouse)
*THE MAN I LOVE
TRUE TO THEM ALL
WHEN THE RIGHT ONE COMES ALONG

THAT'S A GOOD GIRL

Produced by Moss' Empires, Ltd., in conjunction with Jack Buchanan and United Producing Corporation, Ltd., at the London Hippodrome, June 5, 1928. 363 performances. Music by Joseph Meyer and Philip Charig. Lyrics by Douglas Furber, Ira Gershwin, and Desmond Carter. Book by Donald Furber. Directed by Jack Buchanan. Music conducted by Leonard Hornsey. Cast included Jack Buchanan. Elsie Randolph, William Kendall, Dave Fitzgibbon, and the Eight Tiller Girls.

MUSICAL NUMBERS
(Only songs with Ira Gershwin lyrics are listed)

*LET YOURSELF GO!
WHOOPEE
*CHIRP-CHIRP
WEEK END
*THE ONE I'M LOOKING FOR
*SWEET SO-AND-SO

UNUSED

DAY AFTER DAY
WHY BE GOOD?
BEFORE WE WERE MARRIED
THERE I'D SETTLE DOWN

TREASURE GIRL

Tryout: Shubert Theatre, Philadelphia, October 15, 1928.

Produced by Alex A. Aarons and Vinton Freedley at the Alvin Theatre, New York, November 8, 1928. 68 performances. Music by George Gershwin. Lyrics by Ira Gershwin. Book by Fred Thompson and Vincent Lawrence. Directed by Bertram Harrison. Dances staged by Bobby Connolly. Music conducted by Alfred Newman. Cast included Gertrude Lawrence, Clifton Webb, Mary Hay, Walter Catlett, and Paul Frawley. Chorus included Constance Cummings, Peggy Conklin, and Beryl Wallace. Phil Ohman and Victor Arden at the pianos.

MUSICAL NUMBERS

SKULL AND BONES
*I'VE GOT A CRUSH ON YOU
*OH, SO NICE
ACCORDING TO MR. GRIMES

PLACE IN THE COUNTRY
*K-RA-ZY FOR YOU
*I DON'T THINK I'LL FALL IN LOVE TODAY
*GOT A RAINBOW
*FEELING I'M FALLING
WHAT CAUSES THAT? (added after New York
  opening)
*WHAT ARE WE HERE FOR?
*WHERE'S THE BOY? HERE'S THE GIRL!

UNUSED

THIS PARTICULAR PARTY
TREASURE ISLAND
GOOD-BYE TO THE OLD LOVE, HELLO TO
  THE NEW
A-HUNTING WE WILL GO
DEAD MEN TELL NO TALES
I WANT TO MARRY A MARIONETTE

AN AMERICAN IN PARIS

An American in Paris, an orchestral tone poem by George Gershwin. Première: Carnegie Hall, New York, December 13, 1928—The Philharmonic-Symphony Society of New York, conducted by Walter Damrosch.

SHOW GIRL

Tryout: Colonial Theatre, Boston, June 24, 1929.
Produced by Florenz Ziegfeld at the Ziegfeld Theatre, New York, July 2, 1929. 111 performances. Music by George Gershwin. Lyrics by Gus Kahn and Ira Gershwin. Book by William Anthony McGuire, based on the novel by J. P. McEvoy. Dances staged by Bobby Connolly. Ballets staged by Albertina Rasch. Music conducted by William Daly. Cast included Ruby Keeler, Eddie Foy, Jr., Frank McHugh, Lou Clayton, Eddie Jackson, Jimmy Durante, Barbara Newberry, Joseph Macaulay, Nick Lucas, Harriet Hoctor, and Duke Ellington's Orchestra.

MUSICAL NUMBERS

HAPPY BIRTHDAY
MY SUNDAY FELLA
HOW COULD I FORGET
LOLITA, MY LOVE
*DO WHAT YOU DO
ONE MAN
*SO ARE YOU!
*I MUST BE HOME BY TWELVE O'CLOCK
BLACK AND WHITE
*HARLEM SERENADE
AN AMERICAN IN PARIS BLUES BALLET
HOME BLUES
FOLLOW THE MINSTREL BAND
*LIZA (ALL THE CLOUDS'LL ROLL AWAY)

UNUSED

*FEELING SENTIMENTAL
AT MRS. SIMPKIN'S FINISHING SCHOOL
ADORED ONE
TONIGHT'S THE NIGHT!
I JUST LOOKED AT YOU

I'M JUST A BUNDLE OF SUNSHINE
SOMEBODY STOLE MY HEART AWAY
SOMEONE'S ALWAYS CALLING A
  REHEARSAL
I'M OUT FOR NO GOOD REASON
  TONIGHT
HOME LOVIN' GAL
HOME LOVIN' MAN

MING TOY

Unproduced musical which Florenz Ziegfeld planned to present in 1929 with Ed Wynn as star, and Oscar Shaw and Bobbe Arnst featured. The book, by William Anthony McGuire, was adapted from the play *East Is West*, by Samuel Shipman and John B. Hymer. George and Ira Gershwin completed the following songs:

WE ARE VISITORS
*EMBRACEABLE YOU
SING SONG GIRL
*IN THE MANDARIN'S ORCHID GARDEN
IMPROMPTU IN TWO KEYS
  (INSTRUMENTAL)
CHINA GIRL
LADY OF THE MOON

MISCELLANEOUS SONGS 1920–1929

*WE'RE PALS
(Lyrics by Irving Caesar)
Dere Mable
(Tryout only) 1920
BACK HOME
(Lyrics by Irving Caesar)
Dere Mable
I DON'T KNOW WHY (WHEN I DANCE
  WITH YOU)
(Lyrics by Irving Caesar)
Dere Mable
*YAN-KEE
(Lyrics by Irving Caesar)
Non-production 1920
*OO, HOW I LOVE TO BE LOVED BY YOU
(Lyrics by Lou Paley)
Ed Wynn's Carnival, April 5, 1920
  150 performances
*WAITING FOR THE SUN TO COME OUT
The Sweetheart Shop, August 31, 1920
  55 performances
*SPANISH LOVE
(Lyrics by Irving Caesar)
Broadway Brevities of 1920, September 29, 1920
  105 performances
*LU LU
(Lyrics by Arthur Jackson)
Broadway Brevities of 1920
*SNOW FLAKES
(Lyrics by Arthur Jackson)
Broadway Brevities of 1920
ON THE BRIM OF HER OLD-FASHIONED
  BONNET
(Lyrics by E. Ray Goetz)
Snapshots of 1921, June 2, 1921, 44 performances
THE BABY BLUES
(Lyrics by E. Ray Goetz)
Snapshots of 1921

FUTURISTIC MELODY
(Lyrics by E. Ray Goetz)
Snapshots of 1921
PHOEBE
(Lyrics by Ira Gershwin and Lou Paley)
Non-production 1921
SOMETHING PECULIAR
(Lyrics by Ira Gershwin and Lou Paley)
Non-production 1921
MOLLY-ON-THE-SHORE
Non-production c.1921
*MISCHA, JASCHA, TOSCHA, SASCHA
Non-production c.1921
*MY LOG-CABIN HOME
(Lyrics by Irving Caesar and B. G. DeSylva)
The Perfect Fool, November 7, 1921
  256 performances
*NO ONE ELSE BUT THAT GIRL OF MINE
(Lyrics by Irving Caesar)
The Perfect Fool
*TOMALE (I'M HOT FOR YOU)
(Lyrics by B. G. De Sylva)
Non-production 1921
*SWANEE ROSE
(Lyrics by Irving Caesar and B. G. DeSylva)
Non-production 1921
*DIXIE ROSE
(Lyrics by Irving Caesar and B. G. DeSylva)
Non-production 1921
*THE PICCADILLY WALK
(Music by Edward A. Horan)
(Lyrics by Arthur Francis and Arthur Riscoe)
Pins and Needles, February 1, 1922, 46 performances
*DO IT AGAIN!
(Lyrics by B. G. De Sylva)
The French Doll, February 20, 1922
  120 performances
*SOMEONE
(Lyrics by Arthur Francis)
For Goodness Sake, February 20, 1922
  103 performances
*TRA-LA-LA
(Lyrics by Arthur Francis)
For Goodness Sake
*FRENCH PASTRY WALK
(Music by William Daly and Paul Lannin)
(Lyrics by Arthur Jackson and Arthur Francis)
For Goodness Sake
*FASCINATION
(Music by Louis Silvers)
(Lyrics by Arthur Francis and Schuyler Greene)
Fascination (film), released in April 1922
WHAT CAN I DO?
(Music by Maurice Yvain)
(Lyrics by Ira Gershwin and Schuyler Greene)
Non-production 1922
HUBBY
(Music by William Daly)
Non-production c.1922
*THE YANKEE DOODLE BLUES
(Lyrics by Irving Caesar and B. G. De Sylva)
Spice of 1922, July 6, 1922, 73 performances
*WHEN ALL YOUR CASTLES COME
  TUMBLING DOWN
(Music by Milton Schwarzwald)
(Lyrics by Arthur Francis)
Molly Darling, September 1, 1922, 101 performances
THE FLAPPER
(Music by George Gershwin and William Daly)
(Lyrics by B. G. De Sylva)
Non-production 1922

THAT AMERICAN BOY OF MINE
(Lyrics by Irving Caesar)
The Dancing Girl, January 24, 1923
142 performances

THE NEVADA
(Music by Joseph Meyer and William Daly)
Non-production 1923

MARY LOUISE
(Music by Richard Myers)
Non-production 1923

TELL ME IN THE GLOAMING
(Music by Irving Caesar and Niclas Kempner)
Non-production 1923

SINGING IN THE RAIN
(Music by Joseph Meyer and William Daly)
Non-production 1923

LITTLE RHYTHM, GO 'WAY
(Music by William Daly and Joseph Meyer)
Non-production 1923

*I WON'T SAY I WILL, BUT I WON'T SAY
I WON'T
(Lyrics by B. G. De Sylva and Arthur Francis)
Little Miss Bluebeard, August 28, 1923
175 performances

*HOT HINDOO
(Music by Lewis E. Gensler)
(Lyrics by Arthur Francis)
Greenwich Village Follies, September 20, 1923
131 performances

*FABRIC OF DREAMS
(Music by Raymond Hubbell)
(Lyrics by B. G. De Sylva and Arthur Francis)
Nifties of 1923, September 25, 1923, 47 performances

*AT HALF PAST SEVEN
(Lyrics by B. G. De Sylva)
Nifties of 1923

*NASHVILLE NIGHTINGALE
(Lyrics by Irving Caesar)
Nifties of 1923

*THE SUNSHINE TRAIL
(Lyrics by Arthur Francis)
The Sunshine Trail (film) Released in April 1923

*IMAGINE ME WITHOUT MY YOU (AND
YOU WITHOUT YOUR ME)
(Music by Lewis E. Gensler)
(Lyrics by Arthur Francis and Russell Bennett)
Top Hole, September 1, 1924, 104 performances

CHEERIO!
(Music by Lewis E. Gensler)
(Lyrics by Arthur Francis)
Top Hole

*I CAME HERE
(Music by Lewis E. Gensler)
(Lyrics by Marc Connelly, George S. Kaufman, and
Ira Gershwin)
Be Yourself, September 3, 1924, 93 performances

*UH-UH!
(Music by Milton Schwarzwald)
(Lyrics by Marc Connelly, George S. Kaufman, and
Ira Gershwin)
Be Yourself

*THE WRONG THING AT THE RIGHT
TIME
(Music by Milton Schwarzwald)
(Lyrics by Marc Connelly, George S. Kaufman,
and Ira Gershwin)
Be Yourself

ALL OF THEM WAS FRIENDS OF MINE
(Music by Lewis E. Gensler and Milton
Schwarzwald)
(Lyrics by Marc Connelly and Ira Gershwin)
Be Yourself

THEY DON'T MAKE 'EM THAT WAY
ANY MORE
(Music by Lewis E. Gensler and Milton
Schwarzwald)
Be Yourself

*YOU MUST COME OVER BLUES
(Music by Lewis E. Gensler)
Be Yourself
Captain Jinks, September 8, 1925, 107 performances

TURN TO THE DREAM AHEAD
(Music by Morris Hamilton)
Non-production 1924

*THE VOICE OF LOVE
(Music by Russell Bennett and Maurice Nitke)
(Lyrics by Arthur Francis)
The Firebrand, October 15, 1924, 287 performances

WHAT'S THE BIG IDEA
Non-production mid-1920's

*I WANT A YES MAN
(Music by Vincent Youmans)
(Lyrics by Ira Gershwin, Clifford Grey, and
Irving Caesar)
A Night Out
(Tryout only) 1925

*SUNNY DISPOSISH
(Music by Philip Charig)
Americana, July 26, 1926, 224 performances

*THAT LOST BARBER SHOP CHORD
Americana

*BLOWIN' THE BLUES AWAY
(Music by Philip Charig)
Americana

ASK ME AGAIN
Non-production late 1920's

THREE QUARTER BLUES
(No lyrics)
Non-production late 1920's

STRIKE UP THE BAND
(Second Version)

Tryout: Shubert Theatre, Boston, December 25, 1929.

Produced by Edgar Selwyn at the Times Square Theatre, New York, January 14, 1930. 191 performances. Music by George Gershwin. Lyrics by Ira Gershwin. Book by Morrie Ryskind (based on a libretto by George S. Kaufman). Directed by Alexander Leftwich. Dances staged by George Hale. Music conducted by Hilding Anderson. Cast included Bobby Clark, Paul McCullough, Blanche Ring, Dudley Clements, Gordon Smith, Kathryn Hamill, Helen Gilligan, Doris Carson, and Jerry Goff.

MUSICAL NUMBERS
(Complete piano-vocal score published)

FLETCHER'S AMERICAN CHOCOLATE
CHORAL SOCIETY
*I MEAN TO SAY
A TYPICAL SELF-MADE AMERICAN
*SOON
A MAN OF HIGH DEGREE
THE UNOFFICIAL SPOKESMAN
PATRIOTIC RALLY:
(a) Three Cheers for the Union!
(b) This Could Go On for Years

IF I BECAME THE PRESIDENT
*HANGIN' AROUND WITH YOU
HE KNOWS MILK
*STRIKE UP THE BAND!
IN THE RATTLE OF THE BATTLE
*MILITARY DANCING DRILL
*MADEMOISELLE IN NEW ROCHELLE
*I'VE GOT A CRUSH ON YOU
HOW ABOUT A BOY LIKE ME?
§*I WANT TO BE A WAR BRIDE
SOLDIERS' MARCH
(Unofficial March of General Holmes)
OFFICIAL RESUME
RING A DING A DING DONG DELL

UNUSED

THERE WAS NEVER SUCH A
CHARMING WAR

GIRL CRAZY

Tryout: Shubert Theatre, Philadelphia, September 29, 1930.

Produced by Alex A. Aarons and Vinton Freedley at the Alvin Theatre, New York, October 14, 1930. 272 performances. Music by George Gershwin. Lyrics by Ira Gershwin. Book by Guy Bolton and John McGowan. Directed by Alexander Leftwich. Dances staged by George Hale. Music conducted by Earl Busby (orchestra included Benny Goodman, Glenn Miller, Red Nichols, Jimmy Dorsey, Jack Teagarden, and Gene Krupa). Cast included Ginger Rogers, Allen Kearns, Ethel Merman, William Kent, and Willie Howard.

MUSICAL NUMBERS
(Complete piano-vocal score published)

THE LONESOME COWBOY
*BIDIN' MY TIME
*COULD YOU USE ME?
BRONCHO BUSTERS
*EMBRACEABLE YOU
*SAM AND DELILAH
*I GOT RHYTHM
LAND OF THE GAY CABALLERO
*BUT NOT FOR ME
*TREAT ME ROUGH
*BOY! WHAT LOVE HAS DONE TO ME!
WHEN IT'S CACTUS TIME IN ARIZONA

UNUSED

THE GAMBLER OF THE WEST
AND I HAVE YOU
SOMETHING PECULIAR
YOU CAN'T UNSCRAMBLE SCRAMBLED
EGGS

WRITTEN FOR THE 1932 FILM VERSION

*YOU'VE GOT WHAT GETS ME

DELICIOUS

Produced by Winfield Sheehan for Fox Film Corporation. Released December 3, 1931. Screenplay by Guy Bolton and Sonya Levien. Directed by David Butler. Cast

§Deleted soon after New York opening.

included Janet Gaynor, Charles Farrell, Mischa Auer, El Brendel, Raul Roulien, and Manya Roberti.

MUSICAL NUMBERS

*DELISHIOUS
DREAM SEQUENCE ("WE'RE FROM THE JOURNAL, THE WAHRHEIT, THE TELEGRAM, THE TIMES . . .")
*SOMEBODY FROM SOMEWHERE
*KATINKITSCHKA
*BLAH, BLAH, BLAH
*NEW YORK RHAPSODY (PORTION OF SECOND RHAPSODY)

UNUSED

THANKS TO YOU
YOU STARTED IT

OF THEE I SING

Tryout: Majestic Theatre, Boston, December 8, 1931.

Produced by Sam H. Harris at the Music Box, New York, December 26, 1931. 441 performances. Music by George Gershwin. Lyrics by Ira Gershwin. Book by George S. Kaufman and Morrie Ryskind. Directed by George S. Kaufman. Dances staged by George Hale. Music conducted by Charles Previn. Cast included William Gaxton, Lois Moran, Victor Moore, Grace Brinkley, George Murphy, June O'Dea, Florenz Ames, Dudley Clements, and Ralph Riggs.

MUSICAL NUMBERS
(Complete piano-vocal score published)

*WINTERGREEN FOR PRESIDENT
WHO IS THE LUCKY GIRL TO BE?
THE DIMPLE ON MY KNEE
*BECAUSE, BECAUSE
HOW BEAUTIFUL
NEVER WAS THERE A GIRL SO FAIR
SOME GIRLS CAN BAKE A PIE
*LOVE IS SWEEPING THE COUNTRY
*OF THEE I SING (BABY)
ENTRANCE OF SUPREME COURT
    JUDGES
HERE'S A KISS FOR CINDERELLA
I WAS THE MOST BEAUTIFUL BLOSSOM
HELLO, GOOD MORNING
*WHO CARES
GARCON, S'IL VOUS PLAIT
ENTRANCE OF THE FRENCH
    AMBASSADOR
*THE ILLEGITIMATE DAUGHTER
THE SENATORIAL ROLL CALL
JILTED
I'M ABOUT TO BE A MOTHER (WHO
    COULD ASK FOR ANYTHING MORE?)
PROSPERITY IS JUST AROUND THE
    CORNER
TRUMPETER, BLOW YOUR HORN

SECOND RHAPSODY

Second Rhapsody, for orchestra with piano, by George Gershwin. Première: Symphony Hall, Boston, January 29, 1932 —The Boston Symphony Orchestra, conducted by Serge Koussevitzky; George Gershwin, piano.

CUBAN OVERTURE

Cuban Overture (originally Rumba), for orchestra, by George Gershwin. Première: Lewisohn Stadium, New York, August 16, 1932—The New York Philharmonic-Symphony Orchestra, conducted by Albert Coates.

GEORGE GERSHWIN'S SONG BOOK

Piano Transcriptions of Eighteen Songs. Published September 1932 in George Gershwin's Song-Book, a volume in which the original sheet-music arrangements of "Swanee," "Nobody But You," "I'll Build a Stairway to Paradise," "Do It Again," "Fascinating Rhythm," "Oh, Lady, Be Good!" "Somebody Loves Me," "Sweet and Low-Down," "That Certain Feeling," "The Man I Love," "Clap Yo' Hands," "Do, Do, Do," "My One and Only," "'S Wonderful," "Strike Up the Band," "Liza," "I Got Rhythm," and "Who Cares?" are followed by Gershwin's own transcriptions. A special limited edition of 300 copies was published in May 1932, with each one signed by George Gershwin and by Constantin Alajalov, the book's illustrator. As a bonus, each volume included a copy of "Mischa, Jascha, Toscha, Sascha" in its first publication, with "Arthur Francis" credited as lyricist.

PARDON MY ENGLISH

Tryout: Garrick Theatre, Philadelphia, December 2, 1932; Majestic Theatre, Brooklyn, December 26, 1932.

Produced by Alex A. Aarons and Vinton Freedley at the Majestic Theatre, New York, January 20, 1933. 46 performances. Music by George Gershwin. Lyrics by Ira Gershwin. Book by Herbert Fields. Directed by John McGowan. Dances staged by George Hale. Music conducted by Earl Busby. Cast included Jack Pearl, Lyda Roberti, George Givot, Josephine Huston, Carl Randall, and Barbara Newberry.

MUSICAL NUMBERS

IN THREE QUARTER TIME
*THE LORELEI
PARDON MY ENGLISH
DANCING IN THE STREETS
*SO WHAT?
*ISN'T IT A PITY?

*MY COUSIN IN MILWAUKEE
HAIL THE HAPPY COUPLE
THE DRESDEN NORTHWEST MOUNTED
*LUCKIEST MAN IN THE WORLD
WHAT SORT OF WEDDING IS THIS?
||*TONIGHT
*WHERE YOU GO, I GO
*I'VE GOT TO BE THERE
HE'S NOT HIMSELF

UNUSED

BAUER'S HOUSE
FREUD AND JUNG AND ADLER
TOGETHER AT LAST
POOR MICHAEL! POOR GOLO!
FATHERLAND, MOTHER OF THE BAND
NO TICKEE, NO WASHEE

LET 'EM EAT CAKE

Tryout: Shubert Theatre, Boston, October 2, 1933.

Produced by Sam H. Harris at the Imperial Theatre, New York, October 21, 1933. 90 performances. Music by George Gershwin. Lyrics by Ira Gershwin. Book by George S. Kaufman and Morrie Ryskind. Directed by George S. Kaufman. Dances and ensembles staged by Von Grona and Ned McGurn. Music conducted by William Daly. Cast included William Gaxton, Lois Moran, Victor Moore, Phillip Loeb, Florenz Ames, and Ralph Riggs.

MUSICAL NUMBERS

TWEEDLEDEE FOR PRESIDENT
*UNION SQUARE
SHIRTS BY THE MILLIONS
COMES THE REVOLUTION
*MINE
CLIMB UP THE SOCIAL LADDER
CLOISTERED FROM THE NOISY CITY
*ON AND ON AND ON
DOUBLE DUMMY DRILL
*LET 'EM EAT CAKE
*BLUE, BLUE, BLUE
WHO'S THE GREATEST—?
NO COMPRENEZ, NO CAPISH, NO
    VERSTEH!
WHEN THE JUDGES DOFF THE ERMINE
UP AND AT 'EM
THAT'S WHAT HE DID
I KNOW A FOUL BALL
THROTTLE THROTTLEBOTTOM
A HELL OF A HOLE
LET 'EM EAT CAVIAR
HANGING THROTTLEBOTTOM IN THE
    MORNING

VARIATIONS ON "I GOT RHYTHM"

Variations on "I Got Rhythm," for orchestra and piano solo, by George Gershwin. Première: Symphony Hall, Boston, January 14, 1934—The Leo Reisman Symphonic Orchestra, conducted by Charles Previn; George Gershwin, piano.

|| This song is published, without lyrics, as one of Two Waltzes in C.

LIFE BEGINS AT 8:40

Tryout: Shubert Theatre, Boston, August 6, 1934.

Produced by the Messrs. Shubert at the Winter Garden, New York, August 27, 1934. 237 performances. Music by Harold Arlen. Lyrics by Ira Gershwin and E. Y. Harburg. Sketches by David Freedman. Production staged by John Murray Anderson. Dances staged by Robert Alton and Charles Weidman. Music conducted by Al Goodman. Cast included Bert Lahr, Ray Bolger, Luella Gear, Frances Williams, Brian Donlevy, and Adrienne Matzenauer.

MUSICAL NUMBERS

LIFE BEGINS
SPRING FEVER
*YOU'RE A BUILDER UPPER
MY PARAMOUNT-PUBLIX-ROXY ROSE
*SHOEIN' THE MARE
QUARTET EROTICA
*FUN TO BE FOOLED
C'EST LA VIE
*WHAT CAN YOU SAY IN A LOVE SONG?
*LET'S TAKE A WALK AROUND THE
  BLOCK
THINGS
ALL THE ELKS AND MASONS
I COULDN'T HOLD MY MAN
IT WAS LONG AGO
I'M NOT MYSELF
LIFE BEGINS AT CITY HALL

UNUSED

I KNEW HIM WHEN
I'M A COLLECTOR OF MOONBEAMS
WEEKEND CRUISE (WILL YOU LOVE ME
  MONDAY MORNING AS YOU DID ON
  FRIDAY NIGHT?)

PORGY AND BESS

Tryout: Colonial Theatre, Boston, September 30, 1935.

Produced by The Theatre Guild at the Alvin Theatre, New York, October 10, 1935. 124 performances. Music by George Gershwin. Lyrics by Du Bose Heyward and Ira Gershwin. Libretto by Du Bose Heyward, founded on the play Porgy, by Du Bose and Dorothy Heyward. Directed by Rouben Mamoulian. Music conducted by Alexander Smallens. Cast included Todd Duncan, Anne Brown, John W. Bubbles, Ruby Elzy, Warren Coleman, Abbie Mitchell, Edward Matthews, Georgette Harvey, J. Rosamond Johnson, Helen Dowdy, Ray Yeates, Ford L. Buck, and the Eva Jessye Choir.

MUSICAL NUMBERS

(Complete piano vocal score published, as well as a special limited edition of 250 copies, signed by George and Ira Gershwin, Du Bose Heyward, and Rouben Mamoulian)

*SUMMERTIME

*A WOMAN IS A SOMETIME THING
THEY PASS BY SINGING
CRAP GAME FUGUE
GONE, GONE, GONE!
OVERFLOW
*MY MAN'S GONE NOW
LEAVIN' FO' DE PROMIS' LAN'
IT TAKE A LONG PULL TO GET THERE
*I GOT PLENTY O' NUTHIN'
WOMAN TO LADY
*BESS, YOU IS MY WOMAN NOW
OH, I CAN'T SIT DOWN
*IT AIN'T NECESSARILY SO
WHAT YOU WANT WITH BESS?
TIME AND TIME AGAIN
STREET CRIES (STRAWBERRY WOMAN,
  CRAB MAN)
*I LOVES YOU, PORGY
OH, DE LAWD SHAKE DE HEAVEN
A RED HEADED WOMAN
OH, DOCTOR JESUS
CLARA, DON'T YOU BE DOWNHEARTED
*THERE'S A BOAT DAT'S LEAVIN' SOON
  FOR NEW YORK
*OH BESS, OH WHERE'S MY BESS
I'M ON MY WAY

UNUSED

THE BUZZARD SONG

SUITE FROM PORGY AND BESS

Suite from "Porgy and Bess" (Catfish Row; Porgy Sings; Fugue; Hurricane; Good Morning, Brother) by George Gershwin. Première: Academy of Music, Philadelphia, January 21, 1936—The Philadelphia Orchestra, conducted by Alexander Smallens.

ZIEGFELD FOLLIES OF 1936

Tryout: Boston Opera House, Boston, December 30, 1935.

Produced by Mrs. Florenz Ziegfeld (Billie Burke) and the Messrs. Shubert at the Winter Garden, New York, January 30, 1936. 227 performances. Music by Vernon Duke. Lyrics by Ira Gershwin. Sketches by David Freedman. Production staged by John Murray Anderson. Ballets staged by George Balanchine. Modern dances staged by Robert Alton. Music conducted by John McManus. Cast included Fannie Brice, Bob Hope, Eve Arden, Gertrude Niesen, Josephine Baker, and Harriet Hoctor.

MUSICAL NUMBERS

TIME MARCHES ON!
HE HASN'T A THING EXCEPT ME
*MY RED-LETTER DAY
*ISLAND IN THE WEST INDIES
*WORDS WITHOUT MUSIC
THE ECONOMIC SITUATION (AREN'T
  YOU WONDERFUL)
FANCY, FANCY

MAHARANEE
*THE GAZOOKA
*THAT MOMENT OF MOMENTS
SENTIMENTAL WEATHER
FIVE A.M.
*I CAN'T GET STARTED
MODERNISTIC MOE
(Lyrics by Ira Gershwin and Billy Rose)
DANCING TO OUR SCORE

UNUSED

PLEASE SEND MY DADDY BACK HOME
DOES A DUCK LOVE WATER?
I'M SHARING MY WEALTH
WISHING TREE OF HARLEM
WHY SAVE FOR THAT RAINY DAY?
HOT NUMBER
THE LAST OF THE CABBIES
THE BALLAD OF BABY FACE McGINTY
SUNDAY TAN
IT'S A DIFFERENT WORLD
SAVE YOUR YESSES
THE KNIFE-THROWER'S WIFE
*I USED TO BE ABOVE LOVE

SHALL WE DANCE

Produced by Pandro S. Berman for RKO. Released in May 1937. Music by George Gershwin. Lyrics by Ira Gershwin. Screenplay by Allan Scott and Ernest Pagano. Directed by Mark Sandrich. Music conducted by Nathaniel Shilkret. Cast included Fred Astaire, Ginger Rogers, Edward Everett Horton, Eric Blore, Jerome Cowan, and Harriet Hoctor.

MUSICAL NUMBERS

*SLAP THAT BASS
*WALKING THE DOG
(Instrumental interlude also published as
  "Promenade")
*(I'VE GOT) BEGINNER'S LUCK
*THEY ALL LAUGHED
*LET'S CALL THE WHOLE THING OFF
*THEY CAN'T TAKE THAT AWAY FROM
  ME
*SHALL WE DANCE

UNUSED

*HI-HO!
*WAKE UP, BROTHER, AND DANCE

A DAMSEL IN DISTRESS

Produced by Pandro S. Berman for RKO. Released in November 1937. Music by George Gershwin. Lyrics by Ira Gershwin. Screenplay by P. G. Wodehouse, Ernest Pagano, and S. K. Lauren. Directed by George Stevens. Music conducted by Victor Baravalle. Cast included Fred Astaire, Joan Fontaine, George Burns, Gracie Allen, Reginald Gardiner, Ray Noble, Constance Collier, and Montagu Love.

MUSICAL NUMBERS

*I CAN'T BE BOTHERED NOW
*THE JOLLY TAR AND THE MILKMAID

PUT ME TO THE TEST (Instrumental only)
*STIFF UPPER LIP
SING OF SPRING
*THINGS ARE LOOKING UP
*A FOGGY DAY (IN LONDON TOWN)
*NICE WORK IF YOU CAN GET IT

UNUSED

PAY SOME ATTENTION TO ME

GOLDWYN FOLLIES

Produced by Samuel Goldwyn. Released in February 1938. Music by George Gershwin (and Vernon Duke). Lyrics by Ira Gershwin. Screenplay by Ben Hecht. Directed by George Marshall. Music conducted by Alfred Newman. Cast included Adolphe Menjou, the Ritz Brothers, Vera Zorina, Kenny Baker, Andrea Leeds, Helen Jepson, Phil Baker, Ella Logan, Bobby Clark, Edgar Bergen, and "Charlie McCarthy."

MUSICAL NUMBERS

*LOVE WALKED IN
*I WAS DOING ALL RIGHT
*LOVE IS HERE TO STAY
*SPRING AGAIN
(Music by Vernon Duke)
* I LOVE TO RHYME

UNUSED

*JUST ANOTHER RHUMBA

LADY IN THE DARK

Tryout: Colonial Theatre, Boston, December 30, 1940.

Produced by Sam H. Harris at the Alvin Theatre, New York, January 23, 1941. 467 performances. Music by Kurt Weill. Lyrics by Ira Gershwin. Book by Moss Hart. Staged by Hassard Short. Dances staged by Albertina Rasch. Music conducted by Maurice Abravanel. Cast included Gertrude Lawrence, Danny Kaye, Victor Mature, Macdonald Carey, Bert Lytell, Natalie Schafer, and Margaret Dale.

MUSICAL NUMBERS
(Complete piano-vocal score published)

OH, FABULOUS ONE IN YOUR IVORY
    TOWER
HUXLEY
*ONE LIFE TO LIVE
*GIRL OF THE MOMENT
IT LOOKS LIKE LIZA
MAPLETON HIGH CHORALE
*THIS IS NEW
*THE PRINCESS OF PURE DELIGHT
THIS WOMAN AT THE ALTAR
THE GREATEST SHOW ON EARTH
THE BEST YEARS OF HIS LIFE
*TSCHAIKOWSKY (AND OTHER
    RUSSIANS)

*(THE SAGA OF) JENNY
*MY SHIP

UNUSED

UNFORGETTABLE
IT'S NEVER TOO LATE TO
    MENDELSSOHN
NO MATTER UNDER WHAT STAR
    YOU'RE BORN
SONG OF THE ZODIAC
BATS ABOUT YOU
THE BOSS IS BRINGING HOME A BRIDE
PARTY PARLANDO
IN OUR LITTLE SAN FERNANDO VALLEY
    HOME

THE NORTH STAR

Produced by Samuel Goldwyn. Released by RKO in October 1943. Music by Aaron Copland. Lyrics by Ira Gershwin. Screenplay by Lillian Hellman. Directed by Lewis Milestone. Cast included Walter Huston, Walter Brennan, Erich von Stroheim, Anne Baxter, Dana Andrews, Jane Withers, and Farley Granger.

MUSICAL NUMBERS

SONG OF THE FATHERLAND
VILLAGE SCENE JINGLES
*YOUNGER GENERATION
*NO VILLAGE LIKE MINE
*SONG OF THE GUERRILLAS

PROBABLY UNUSED

CAN I HELP IT?
LOADING SONG (FROM THE BALTIC TO
    THE PACIFIC)
LOADING TIME AT LAST IS OVER
WAGON SONG
WORKERS OF ALL NATIONS

COVER GIRL

Produced by Arthur Schwartz for Columbia Pictures. Released in April 1944. Music by Jerome Kern. Lyrics by Ira Gershwin. Screenplay by Virginia Van Upp. Directed by Charles Vidor. Music conducted by Morris Stoloff. Cast included Rita Hayworth, Gene Kelly, Phil Silvers, Eve Arden, Jinx Falkenburg, and Lee Bowman.

MUSICAL NUMBERS

THE SHOW MUST GO ON
WHO'S COMPLAINING?
*SURE THING
*MAKE WAY FOR TOMORROW
(Lyrics by Ira Gershwin and E. Y. Harburg)
*PUT ME TO THE TEST
*LONG AGO (AND FAR AWAY)
*COVER GIRL

UNUSED

TIME: THE PRESENT
WHAT I LOVE TO HEAR
THAT'S THE BEST OF ALL
TROPICAL NIGHT

MISCELLANEOUS SONGS 1930–1944

TODDLIN' ALONG
Nine-Fifteen Revue, February 11, 1930,
    7 performances
*I AM ONLY HUMAN AFTER ALL
(Music by Vernon Duke)
(Lyrics by Ira Gershwin and E. Y. Harburg)
The Garrick Gaieties (3rd Edition), June 4, 1930
    158 performances
*CHEERFUL LITTLE EARFUL
(Music by Harry Warren)
(Lyrics by Ira Gershwin and Billy Rose)
Sweet and Low, November 17, 1930, 184
    performances
*SWEET SO AND SO
(Music by Joseph Meyer and Philip Charig)
(Lyrics by Douglas Furker and Ira Gershwin)
Sweet and Low
*IN THE MERRY MONTH OF MAYBE
(Music by Harry Warren)
(Lyrics by Ira Gershwin and Billy Rose)
Crazy Quilt, May 19, 1931, 67 performances
*THE KEY TO MY HEART
(Music by Louis Alter)
The Social Register, November 9, 1931, 97
    performances
*TILL THEN
Non-production 1933
*KING OF SWING
(Lyrics by Albert Stillman)
Radio City Music Hall stage show 1936
I WON'T GIVE UP TILL YOU GIVE IN
    TO ME
(Lyrics by Albert Stillman)
Non-production 1936
*BY STRAUSS
The Show Is On, December 25, 1936, 237
    performances
*STRIKE UP THE BAND FOR U.C.L.A.
Non-production 1936
*ONCE THERE WERE TWO OF US
(Music by Jerome Kern)
Non-production 1938
*NOW THAT WE ARE ONE
(Music by Jerome Kern)
Non-production 1938
*NO QUESTION IN MY HEART
(Music by Jerome Kern)
Non-production 1938
*DAWN OF A NEW DAY
Song of the New York World's Fair 1939
*BABY, YOU'RE NEWS
(Music by John Green)
(Lyrics by Ira Gershwin and E. Y. Harburg)
Sticks and Stones 1939
*HONORABLE MOON
(Music by Arthur Schwartz)
(Lyrics by Ira Gershwin and E. Y. Harburg)
Non-production 1941
IF THIS BE PROPAGANDA
(Music by Harold Arlen)
(Lyrics by Ira Gershwin and E. Y. Harburg)
Non-production 1943
LET'S SHOW 'EM HOW THIS COUNTRY
    GOES TO TOWN
(No music)
Recitation verses by Ira Gershwin 1943 or 1944

THE FIREBRAND OF FLORENCE

Tryout: Colonial Theatre, Boston, February 23, 1945.

Produced by Max Gordon at the Alvin Theatre, New York, March 22, 1945. 43 performances. Music by Kurt Weill. Lyrics by Ira Gershwin. Book by Edwin Justus Mayer and Ira Gershwin, based on the former's play *The Firebrand*. Staged by John Murray Anderson. Dances staged by Catherine Littlefield. Music conducted by Maurice Abravanel. Cast included Lotte Lenya, Earl Wrightson, Melville Cooper, Beverly Tyler, and Ferdi Hoffman.

MUSICAL NUMBERS

ONE MAN'S DEATH IS ANOTHER MAN'S LIVING
COME TO FLORENCE
MY LORD AND LADIES
*THERE'LL BE LIFE, LOVE, AND LAUGHTER
*YOU'RE FAR TOO NEAR ME
ALESSANDRO THE WISE
I AM HAPPY HERE
*SING ME NOT A BALLAD
WHEN THE DUCHESS IS AWAY
I KNOW WHERE THERE'S A COZY NOOK
THE NIGHTTIME IS NO TIME FOR THINKING
DIZZILY, BUSILY
THE LITTLE NAKED BOY
MY DEAR BENVENUTO
JUST IN CASE
*A RHYME FOR ANGELA
THE WORLD IS FULL OF VILLAINS
YOU HAVE TO DO WHAT YOU DO DO
HOW WONDERFULLY FORTUNATE
LOVE IS MY ENEMY
COME TO PARIS

UNUSED

I HAD JUST BEEN PARDONED
MASTER IS FREE AGAIN

WHERE DO WE GO FROM HERE?

Produced by William Perlberg for 20th Century-Fox. Released in May 1945. Music by Kurt Weill. Lyrics by Ira Gershwin. Screenplay by Morrie Ryskind. Directed by Gregory Ratoff. Music conducted by Emil Newman. Cast included Fred MacMurray, Joan Leslie, June Haver, Anthony Quinn, Fortunio Bonanova, and Herman Bing.

MUSICAL NUMBERS

*ALL AT ONCE
WHERE DO WE GO FROM HERE?
MORALE
*IF LOVE REMAINS
*SONG OF THE RHINELAND
*THE NINA, THE PINTA, THE SANTA MARIA

UNUSED

IT HAPPENED TO HAPPEN TO ME
THAT'S HOW IT IS
WOO, WOO, WOO, WOO, MANHATTAN

RHAPSODY IN BLUE

Produced by Jesse L. Lasky for Warner Brothers. Released in September 1945. Screenplay by Howard Koch and Elliott Paul. Directed by Irving Rapper. Music directed by Ray Heindorf. Cast included Robert Alda (as George Gershwin), Herbert Rudley (as Ira Gershwin), Alexis Smith, Joan Leslie, Charles Coburn, Paul Whiteman, Al Jolson, Oscar Levant, Hazel Scott, and George White.

MUSICAL NUMBERS (In many instances performances were doubled by other artists.)

SWANEE
(Joan Leslie and Robert Alda)
'S WONDERFUL
(Ensemble)
SOMEBODY LOVES ME
(Joan Leslie and Tom Patricola)
I'LL BUILD A STAIRWAY TO PARADISE
(Ensemble)
OH, LADY, BE GOOD!
(Joan Leslie and Ensemble)
BLUE MONDAY SEQUENCE
RHAPSODY IN BLUE
(Robert Alda with Paul Whiteman's Orchestra)
THE MAN I LOVE
(Hazel Scott)
CLAP YO' HANDS
(Hazel Scott)
FASCINATING RHYTHM
(Hazel Scott)
I GOT RHYTHM
(Hazel Scott)
YANKEE DOODLE BLUES
(Hazel Scott)
LIZA
(Robert Alda)
VARIATIONS ON "I GOT RHYTHM"
(Robert Alda and Oscar Levant)
BIDIN' MY TIME
(Ensemble)
MY ONE AND ONLY
(Robert Alda)
EMBRACEABLE YOU
(Joan Leslie)
AN AMERICAN IN PARIS
(Dancers)
CUBAN OVERTURE: EXCERPT
(Orchestra)
MINE
(Robert Alda and Oscar Levant)
DELISHIOUS
(Joan Leslie)
SUMMERTIME
(Anne Brown)
LOVE WALKED IN
(Mark Stevens)
CONCERTO IN F: EXCERPT
(Oscar Levant)
RHAPSODY IN BLUE
(Oscar Levant)

PARK AVENUE

Tryout: Shubert Theatre, Philadelphia, October 7, 1946.

Produced by Max Gordon at the Shubert Theatre, New York, November 4, 1946. 72 performances. Music by Arthur Schwartz. Lyrics by Ira Gershwin. Book by Nunnally Johnson and George S. Kaufman. Directed by George S. Kaufman. Dances staged by Helen Tamiris. Music conducted by Charles Sanford. Cast included Arthur Margetson, Leonora Corbett, David Wayne, Martha Errolle, Robert Chisholm, Mary Wickes, and Ray McDonald.

MUSICAL NUMBERS

TOMORROW IS THE TIME
*FOR THE LIFE OF ME
THE DEW WAS ON THE ROSE
*DON'T BE A WOMAN IF YOU CAN
SWEET NEVADA
(Western version)
*THERE'S NO HOLDING ME
THERE'S NOTHING LIKE MARRIAGE FOR PEOPLE
HOPE FOR THE BEST
MY SON-IN-LAW
THE LAND OF OPPORTUNITEE
*GOOD-BYE TO ALL THAT

UNUSED

HEAVENLY DAY
THE FUTURE MRS. COLEMAN
SWEET NEVADA
(Waltz version)
STAY AS WE ARE
DINNER SONG

THE SHOCKING MISS PILGRIM

Produced by William Perlberg for 20th Century-Fox. Released in January 1947. Music adapted from George Gershwin's manuscripts by Kay Swift and Ira Gershwin. Lyrics by Ira Gershwin. Screenplay by George Seaton, who also directed. Music conducted by Alfred Newman. Cast included Betty Grable, Dick Haymes, Anne Revere, Allyn Joslyn, Gene Lockhart, Elizabeth Patterson, Arthur Shields, and Stanley Prager.

MUSICAL NUMBERS

SWEET PACKARD
*CHANGING MY TUNE
STAND UP AND FIGHT
*AREN'T YOU KIND OF GLAD WE DID?
*THE BACK BAY POLKA
*ONE, TWO, THREE
WALTZING IS BETTER SITTING DOWN
DEMON RUM
*FOR YOU, FOR ME, FOR EVERMORE

NOT USED

TOUR OF THE TOWN
WELCOME SONG

THE BARKLEYS OF BROADWAY

Produced by Arthur Freed for Metro-Goldwyn-Mayer. Released in May 1949. Music by Harry Warren. Lyrics by Ira Gershwin. Screenplay by Betty Comden and Adolph Green. Directed by Charles Walters. Music conducted by Lennie Hayton. Cast included Fred Astaire, Ginger Rogers, Oscar Levant, and Billie Burke.

MUSICAL NUMBERS

SWING TROT
*YOU'D BE HARD TO REPLACE
*MY ONE AND ONLY HIGHLAND FLING
WEEKEND IN THE COUNTRY
*SHOES WITH WINGS ON
MANHATTAN DOWNBEAT
*THEY CAN'T TAKE THAT AWAY FROM ME
(Music by George Gershwin)

UNUSED

CALL ON US AGAIN
THESE DAYS
THE COURTIN' OF ELMER AND ELLA
MINSTRELS ON PARADE
NATCHEZ ON THE MISSISSIP'
THE POETRY OF MOTION
SECOND FIDDLE TO A HARP
TAKING NO CHANCES ON YOU
THERE IS NO MUSIC

AN AMERICAN IN PARIS

Produced by Arthur Freed for Metro-Goldwyn-Mayer. Released in November 1951. Screenplay by Alan Jay Lerner. Directed by Vincente Minnelli. Music conducted by John Green. Cast included Gene Kelly, Leslie Caron, Oscar Levant, Georges Guetary, and Nina Foch.

MUSICAL NUMBERS

NICE WORK IF YOU CAN GET IT
(Georges Guetary and Oscar Levant)
EMBRACEABLE YOU
(Danced by Leslie Caron)
BY STRAUSS
(Georges Guetary, Gene Kelly, Oscar Levant)
I GOT RHYTHM
(Gene Kelly and French children)
LOVE IS HERE TO STAY
(Gene Kelly)
TRA-LA-LA
(Gene Kelly and Oscar Levant)
I'LL BUILD A STAIRWAY TO PARADISE
(Georges Guetary and Ensemble)
CONCERTO IN F: EXCERPT
(Oscar Levant)
'S WONDERFUL
(Georges Guetary and Gene Kelly)
LIZA
(Played by Oscar Levant)
AN AMERICAN IN PARIS
(Gene Kelly, Leslie Caron, and Dancers)

GIVE A GIRL A BREAK

Produced by Jack Cummings for Metro-Goldwyn-Mayer. Released in January 1953. Music by Burton Lane. Lyrics by Ira Gershwin. Screenplay by Albert Hackett and Frances Goodrich. Directed by Stanley Donen. Music conducted by André Previn. Cast included Marge and Gower Champion, Debbie Reynolds, Bob Fosse, and Kurt Kasznar.

MUSICAL NUMBERS

GIVE A GIRL A BREAK
NOTHING IS IMPOSSIBLE
*IN OUR UNITED STATE
*IT HAPPENS EVERY TIME
APPLAUSE! APPLAUSE!

UNUSED

ACH, DU LIEBER OOM-PAH-PAH
DREAM WORLD
WOMAN, THERE IS NO LIVING WITH YOU

A STAR IS BORN

Produced by Sidney Luft for Warner Brothers. Released in October 1954. Music by Harold Arlen. Lyrics by Ira Gershwin. Screenplay by Moss Hart, based on an earlier version by Dorothy Parker, Alan Campbell, and Robert Carson. Directed by George Cukor. Music conducted by Ray Heindorf. Cast included Judy Garland, James Mason, Jack Carson, Charles Bickford, and Tommy Noonan.

MUSICAL NUMBERS

*GOTTA HAVE ME GO WITH YOU
*THE MAN THAT GOT AWAY
TV COMMERCIAL
(Calypso)
*SWANEE
(Gershwin-Caesar, incorporated in a medley)
*HERE'S WHAT I'M HERE FOR
*IT'S A NEW WORLD
*SOMEONE AT LAST
*LOSE THAT LONG FACE

UNUSED

DANCING PARTNER
GREEN LIGHT AHEAD
I'M OFF THE DOWNBEAT

THE COUNTRY GIRL

Produced by William Perlberg for Paramount. Released in December 1954. Music by Harold Arlen. Lyrics by Ira Gershwin. Screenplay (based on the Clifford Odets play) by George Seaton, who also directed. Music conducted by Joseph J. Lilley. Cast included Bing Crosby, Grace Kelly, William Holden, and Anthony Ross.

MUSICAL NUMBERS

IT'S MINE, IT'S YOURS
(The Pitchman)

COMMERCIAL
*THE SEARCH IS THROUGH
THE LAND AROUND US
*DISSERTATION ON THE STATE OF BLISS
(Love and Learn)

KISS ME, STUPID

Produced by Billy Wilder for United Artists. Released in December 1964. Wilder also directed and wrote screenplay with I. A. L. Diamond. Music conducted by André Previn. Cast included Dean Martin, Kim Novak, Ray Walston, and Felicia Farr.

MUSICAL NUMBERS

*SOPHIA
*I'M A POACHED EGG
*ALL THE LIVELONG DAY (AND THE LIVELONG NIGHT)

WHO CARES?

Choreography by George Balanchine. Music by George Gershwin, adapted and orchestrated by Hershy Kay. Première by the New York City Ballet at the New York State Theatre on February 5, 1970. Featured dancers: Jacques d'Amboise, Patricia McBride, Marnee Morris and Karin von Aroldingen.

THE FOLLOWING SONGS ARE INCLUDED:

STRIKE UP THE BAND
SWEET AND LOW-DOWN
SOMEBODY LOVES ME
BIDIN' MY TIME
'S WONDERFUL
THAT CERTAIN FEELING
DO, DO, DO
OH, LADY, BE GOOD!
THE MAN I LOVE
I'LL BUILD A STAIRWAY TO PARADISE
EMBRACEABLE YOU
FASCINATING RHYTHM
WHO CARES
MY ONE AND ONLY
LIZA
CLAP YO' HANDS
(Danced to George Gershwin's recording)
I GOT RHYTHM

ALPHABETICAL LISTING OF SONGS

ACCORDING TO MR. GRIMES*
Ferris Hartman and ensemble,
Treasure Girl (1928)

ACH, DU LIEBER OOM-PAH-PAH
(Music by Burton Lane)
Unused / *Give a Girl a Break* (1953)

ACROBATS
Unused / *Funny Face* (1927)

ACROSS THE SEA (MY HEART WILL SAIL ACROSS THE SEA)
(Lyrics by B. G. De Sylva and E. Ray Goetz)
Richard Bold and Pearl Regay,
George White's Scandals (1922)

ADORED ONE
(Lyrics by Ira Gershwin and Gus Kahn)
Unused / *Show Girl* (1929)

A-HUNTING WE WILL GO
Unused / *Treasure Girl* (1928)

AIN'T IT ROMANTIC
Unused / *Oh, Kay!* (1926)

ALESSANDRO THE WISE
(Music by Kurt Weill)
Melville Cooper and ensemble,
The Firebrand of Florence (1945)

ALL AT ONCE
(Music by Kurt Weill)
Fred MacMurray and ensemble,
Where Do We Go from Here? (1945)

ALL OF THEM WAS FRIENDS OF MINE
(Music by Lewis E. Gensler and Milton Schwarzwald)
(Lyrics by Marc Connelly and Ira Gershwin)
Unused / *Be Yourself* (1924)

ALL OVER TOWN
(Lyrics by Clifford Grey)
Unused / *The Rainbow* (1923)

ALL THE ELKS AND MASONS
(Music by Harold Arlen)
(Lyrics by Ira Gershwin and E. Y. Harburg)
Ray Bolger and Dixie Dunbar,
Life Begins at 8:40 (1934)

ALL THE LIVELONG DAY (AND THE LONG, LONG NIGHT)
Ray Walston
Kiss Me, Stupid (1964)

"AN AMERICAN IN PARIS" BLUES BALLET
Danced by Harriet Hoctor and Albertina Rasch Girls,
Show Girl (1929)

*Where no composer is listed, the music is by George; where no lyricist is named, the lyric is by Ira (who is listed in most pre-1925 songs under his pseudonym, Arthur Francis). Where collaborators are involved, all names are included. Where no name is given, the song is entirely the work of the two Gershwins.

AND I HAVE YOU
Unused / *Girl Crazy* (1930)

ANY LITTLE TUNE
(Lyrics by Clifford Grey)
Fred A. Leslie and ensemble,
The Rainbow (1923)

ANYTHING FOR YOU
(Lyrics by Arthur Francis)
Vinton Freedley and Juanita Fletcher,
A Dangerous Maid (1921)

APPLAUSE! APPLAUSE!
(Music by Burton Lane)
Gower Champion and Debbie Reynolds,
Give a Girl a Break (1953)

AREN'T YOU KIND OF GLAD WE DID?
Dick Haymes and Betty Grable,
The Shocking Miss Pilgrim (1947)

ARGENTINA
(Lyrics by B. G. De Sylva)
Jack McGowan and ensemble,
George White's Scandals (1922)

ASK ME AGAIN
Written in late 1920s
Considered for *Goldwyn Follies* (1938)

AT HALF PAST SEVEN
(Lyrics by B. G. De Sylva)
No information in program—may have been sung by Hazel Dawn and Joe Schenck,
Nifties (1923)
(Same melody used in *Primrose* with De Sylva-Gershwin lyrics "Some Far-Away Someone")

AT MRS. SIMPKIN'S FINISHING SCHOOL
(Lyrics by Ira Gershwin and Gus Kahn)
Unused / *Show Girl* (1929)

THE BABBITT AND THE BROMIDE
Fred and Adele Astaire,
Funny Face (1927)

BABY!
(Lyrics by B. G. De Sylva and Ira Gershwin)
Emma Haig, Andrew Tombes, and ensemble,
Tell Me More! (1925)

THE BABY BLUES
(Lyrics by E. Ray Goetz)
Delyle Alda and ensemble,
Snapshots (1921)

BABY DOLLS
(Lyrics by B. G. De Sylva and John Henry Mears)
Helen Shipman and ensemble,
Morris Gest Midnight Whirl (1919)

BABY, YOU'RE NEWS
(Music by John Green)
(Lyrics by Ira Gershwin and E. Y. Harburg)
Sticks and Stones (1939)

THE BACK BAY POLKA
Allyn Joslyn, Charles Kemper, Elizabeth Patterson, Lillian Bronson, Arthur Shields, and Betty Grable,
The Shocking Miss Pilgrim (1947)

BACK HOME
(Lyrics by Irving Caesar)
Unused / *Dere Mable* (1920)

THE BAD, BAD MEN
Unused / *Lady, Be Good!* (1924)

THE BALLAD OF BABY FACE McGINTY
(Music by Vernon Duke)
Unused / *Ziegfeld Follies* (1936)

BALLET MUSIC
Primrose (1924)

BATS ABOUT YOU
(Music by Kurt Weill)
Unused / *Lady in the Dark* (1941)

BAUER'S HOUSE
Unused / *Pardon My English* (1933)

BE THE LIFE OF THE CROWD
(Lyrics by B. G. De Sylva)
Unused / *Sweet Little Devil* (1924)

BEAU BRUMMEL
(Lyrics by Desmond Carter)
Percy Heming and ensemble,
Primrose (1924)

BEAUTIFUL BIRD
(Lyrics by Ira Gershwin and Lou Paley)
Written in 1917

BEAUTIFUL GYPSY
Unused / *Rosalie* (1928)
(Same music as "Wait a Bit, Susie" from *Primrose*)

BECAUSE, BECAUSE
Ensemble,
Of Thee I Sing (1931)

BEFORE WE WERE MARRIED
(Music by Joseph Meyer and Philip Charig)
(Lyrics by Douglas Furber, Ira Gershwin, and Desmond Carter)
Unused / *That's a Good Girl* (1928)

(I'VE GOT) BEGINNER'S LUCK
Fred Astaire,
Shall We Dance (1937)

BENEATH THE EASTERN MOON
(Lyrics by Clifford Grey)
Lola Raine and ensemble,
The Rainbow (1923)

BERKELEY SQUARE AND KEW
(Lyrics by Desmond Carter)
Claude Hulbert and Margery Hicklin,
Primrose (1924)

BESS, YOU IS MY WOMAN NOW
(Lyrics by Ira Gershwin and Du Bose Heyward)
Todd Duncan and Anne Brown,
Porgy and Bess (1935)

THE BEST OF EVERYTHING
(Lyrics by Arthur J. Jackson and B. G. De Sylva)
John E. Hazzard and ensemble,
La, La, Lucille (1919)

THE BEST YEARS OF HIS LIFE
(Music by Kurt Weill)
Danny Kaye, Victor Mature, Gertrude Lawrence, and ensemble,
Lady in the Dark (1941)

BIDIN' MY TIME
The Foursome,
Girl Crazy (1930)

BIRTHDAY PARTY
Betty Compton, Gertrude McDonald, and ensemble,
Funny Face (1927)

BLACK AND WHITE
(Lyrics by Ira Gershwin and Gus Kahn)
Ensemble,
Show Girl (1929)

BLAH, BLAH, BLAH
El Brendel and Manya Roberti,
Delicious (1931)
(Previous titles: see "I Just Looked at You" and "Lady of the Moon")

BLOWIN' THE BLUES AWAY
(Music by Philip Charig)
Lew Brice, Betty Compton, Helen Morgan, Evelyn Bennett, Gay Nell, and Elizabeth Morgan/*Americana* (1926)

BLUE, BLUE, BLUE
Ensemble/*Let 'Em Eat Cake* (1933)

BLUE HULLABALLOO
Betty Compton, Gertrude McDonald, and ensemble/*Funny Face* (1927)

BLUE MONDAY BLUES
(Lyrics by B. G. De Sylva)
Jack McGowan and ensemble,
George White's Scandals (1922)

THE BOSS IS BRINGING HOME A BRIDE
(Music by Kurt Weill)
Unused / *Lady in the Dark* (1941)

BOY WANTED
(Lyrics by Arthur Francis)
Ensemble,
A Dangerous Maid (1921)
Same number (with revised lyrics by Ira Gershwin and Desmond Carter) sung by Heather Thatcher and ensemble,
Primrose (1924)

BOY! WHAT LOVE HAS DONE TO ME!
Ethel Merman/*Girl Crazy* (1930)

BRIDE AND GROOM
Sascha Beaumont, Oscar Shaw, Frank Gardiner, and ensemble,
Oh, Kay! (1926)

BRING ON THE DING DONG DELL
Unused / *Oh Kay!* (1926)

BRONCHO BUSTERS
Ensemble/*Girl Crazy* (1930)

BUT NOT FOR ME
Ginger Rogers and Willie Howard,
Girl Crazy (1930)

BUY A LITTLE BUTTON FROM US
(Lyrics by Desmond Carter)
Ensemble,
Lady, Be Good! (London production) (1926)

THE BUZZARD SONG
(Lyrics by Du Bose Heyward)
Unused in original production *Porgy and Bess* (1935)

BY AND BY
(Lyrics by Brian Hooker)
Thomas Conkey and Eva Clark,
Our Nell (1922)

BY STRAUSS
Gracie Barrie and ensemble,
The Show Is On (1936)

CALL ON US AGAIN
(Music by Harry Warren)
Unused / *The Barkleys of Broadway* (1949)

CAN I HELP IT?
(Music by Aaron Copland)
Probably unused / *The North Star* (1943)

CARNIVAL TIME
Ensemble,
Lady, Be Good! (1924)

C'EST LA VIE
(Music by Harold Arlen)
(Lyrics by Ira Gershwin and E. Y. Harburg)
Adrienne Matzenauer, Earl Oxford, Frances Comstock, Luella Gear, and Ray Bolger,
Life Begins at 8:40 (1934)

CHANGING MY TUNE
Betty Grable,
The Shocking Miss Pilgrim (1947)

CHEERFUL LITTLE EARFUL
(Music by Harry Warren)
(Lyrics by Ira Gershwin and Billy Rose)
Hannah Williams,
Sweet and Low (1930)

CHEERIO!
(Music by Lewis E. Gensler)
(Lyrics by Arthur Francis)
Unused / *Top Hole* (1924)

CHINA GIRL
Unused / Unproduced musical *Ming Toy* (1929)

CHIRP-CHIRP
(Music by Joseph Meyer and Philip Charig)
Elsie Randolph, Dave Fitzgibbon, and ensemble,
That's a Good Girl (1928)

CINDERELATIVES
(Lyrics by B. G. De Sylva)
Ensemble,
George White's Scandals (1922)

CLAP YO' HANDS
Harland Dixon, Betty Compton, Paulette Winston, Constance Carpenter, Janette Gilmore, and ensemble,
Oh, Kay! (1926)

CLARA, DON'T YOU BE DOWNHEARTED
(Lyrics by Du Bose Heyward)
Ensemble,
Porgy and Bess (1935)

CLIMB UP THE SOCIAL LADDER
Lois Moran and ensemble,
Let 'Em Eat Cake (1933)

CLOISTERED FROM THE NOISY CITY
Ralph Riggs and ensemble,
Let 'Em Eat Cake (1933)

COME ALONG, LET'S GAMBLE
Unused / *Funny Face* (1927)

COME TO FLORENCE
(Music by Kurt Weill)
Randolph Symonette, Jean Guelis, Norma Gentner, and ensemble,
The Firebrand of Florence (1945)

COME TO PARIS
(Music by Kurt Weill)
Paul Best and ensemble,
The Firebrand of Florence (1945)

COME TO THE MOON
(Lyrics by Ned Wayburn and Lou Paley)
Paul Frawley and Lucille Chalfant,
Capitol Revue ("Demi-Tasse") (1919)

COMES THE REVOLUTION
Victor Moore and ensemble,
Let 'Em Eat Cake (1933)

COMMERCIAL
(Music by Harold Arlen)
Bing Crosby,
The Country Girl (1954)

THE COONEY COUNTY FAIR
(Lyrics by Brian Hooker)
Olin Howland, Emma Haig, and ensemble,
Our Nell (1922)

COSSACK LOVE SONG (DON'T FORGET ME)
(Music by George Gershwin and Herbert Stothart)
(Lyrics by Otto Harbach and Oscar Hammerstein II)
Tessa Kosta, Guy Robertson, and ensemble,
Song of the Flame (1925)

COULD YOU USE ME?
Ginger Rogers and Allen Kearns,
Girl Crazy (1930)

THE COUNTRYSIDE (THIS IS THE LIFE FOR A MAN)
(Lyrics by Desmond Carter)
Percy Heming,
Primrose (1924)

THE COURTIN' OF ELMER AND ELLA
(Music by Harry Warren)
Unused / *The Barkleys of Broadway* (1949)

COVER GIRL
(Music by Jerome Kern)
Rita Hayworth and ensemble,
Cover Girl (1944)

CRAP GAME FUGUE
(Lyrics by Du Bose Heyward)
Ensemble,
Porgy and Bess (1935)

CUPID
(Lyrics by Edward B. Perkins)
Probably sung by Sibyl Vane,
Half Past Eight (1918)

THE CUSTODY OF THE CHILD
(Lyrics by Brian Hooker)
Unused / *Our Nell* (1922)

DANCE ALONE WITH YOU (WHY DOES EV'RYBODY HAVE TO CUT IN)
Unused / *Funny Face* (1927)
(Same music as "Ev'rybody Knows I Love Somebody" in *Rosalie*)

DANCING HOUR
Unused / *Tip-Toes* (1925)
Unused / *Funny Face* (1927)

DANCING IN THE STREETS
Ensemble,
Pardon My English (1933)

DANCING PARTNER
(Music by Harold Arlen)
Unused / *A Star Is Born* (1954)

DANCING SHOES
(Lyrics by Arthur Francis)
Vinton Freedley, Juliette Day, and ensemble,
A Dangerous Maid (1921)

DANCING TO OUR SCORE
(Music by Vernon Duke)
Rodney McLennan, Eve Arden, and ensemble,
Ziegfeld Follies (1936)

DAWN OF A NEW DAY
Song of the New York World's Fair (1939)

DAY AFTER DAY
(Music by Joseph Meyer and Philip Charig)
(Lyrics by Douglas Furber, Ira Gershwin, and Desmond Carter)
Unused / *That's a Good Girl* (1928)

DEAD MEN TELL NO TALES
Unused / *Treasure Girl* (1928)

**DEAR LITTLE GIRL
(I HOPE YOU'VE MISSED ME)**
Oscar Shaw and ensemble,
Oh, Kay! (1926)

DELISHIOUS
Raul Roulien,
Delicious (1931)

DEMON RUM
Ensemble,
The Shocking Miss Pilgrim (1947)

THE DEW WAS ON THE ROSE
(Music by Arthur Schwartz)
Leonora Corbett, Charles Purcell,
Raymond Walburn, and Robert Chisholm,
Park Avenue (1946)

THE DIMPLE ON MY KNEE
Ensemble,
Of Thee I Sing (1931)

DINNER SONG
(Music by Arthur Schwartz)
Unused / *Park Avenue* (1946)

**DISSERTATION ON THE STATE
OF BLISS (LOVE AND LEARN)**
(Music by Harold Arlen)
Bing Crosby and Jacqueline Fontaine,
The Country Girl (1954)

DIXIE ROSE
(Lyrics by Irving Caesar and B. G. De Sylva)
Featured by Al Jolson (1921)
(Same music as "Swanee Rose")

DIZZILY, BUSILY
(Music by Kurt Weill)
Gloria Story, Jean Guelis, Norma Gentner,
and ensemble,
The Firebrand of Florence (1945)

DO, DO, DO
Oscar Shaw and Gertrude Lawrence,
Oh, Kay! (1926)

DO IT AGAIN!
(Lyrics by B. G. De Sylva)
Irene Bordoni,
The French Doll (1922)
Re-introduced by Alice Delysia as
"Please Do It Again" in *Mayfair and Montmartre* (London) (1922)

DO WHAT YOU DO
(Lyrics by Ira Gershwin and Gus Kahn)
Ruby Keeler and Frank McHugh,
Show Girl (1929)

DOES A DUCK LOVE WATER?
(Music by Vernon Duke)
Unused / *Ziegfeld Follies* (1936)

DOLLY
(Music by Vincent Youmans)
(Lyrics by Arthur Francis and Schuyler Greene)
Oscar Shaw, Fred Santley, and ensemble,
Two Little Girls in Blue (1921)

DON'T ASK!
Harland Dixon and the Fairbanks Twins,
Oh, Kay! (1926)

DON'T BE A WOMAN IF YOU CAN
(Music by Arthur Schwartz)
Mary Wickes, Marthe Errolle, and Ruth
Matteson,
Park Avenue (1946)

DOUBLE DUMMY DRILL
William Gaxton and ensemble,
Let 'Em Eat Cake (1933)

DOUGHNUTS
(Lyrics by B. G. De Sylva and John Henry Mears)
Annette Bade and ensemble,
Morris Gest Midnight Whirl (1919)

**DREAM SEQUENCE (WE'RE FROM
THE *JOURNAL*, THE *WAHRHEIT*,
THE *TELEGRAM*, THE *TIMES*)**
Raul Roulien, Marvine Maazel, and
ensemble,
Delicious (1931)

DREAM WORLD
(Music by Burton Lane)
Unused / *Give a Girl a Break* (1953)

**THE DRESDEN NORTHWEST
MOUNTED**
Jack Pearl and ensemble,
Pardon My English (1933)

**DRIFTING ALONG WITH
THE TIDE**
(Lyrics by Arthur Jackson)
Lloyd Garrett and Victoria Herbert,
George White's Scandals (1921)
Also in *Mayfair and Montmartre* (London) (1922)

**THE ECONOMIC SITUATION
(AREN'T YOU WONDERFUL)**
(Music by Vernon Duke)
Eve Arden and ensemble,
Ziegfeld Follies (1936)

EMBRACEABLE YOU
Ginger Rogers and Allen Kearns,
Girl Crazy (1930)
Originally written for the unproduced
Ming Toy (1929)

THE END OF A STRING
Ensemble,
Lady, Be Good! (1924)

**ENTRANCE OF THE
FRENCH AMBASSADOR**
Florenz Ames and ensemble,
Of Thee I Sing (1931)

**ENTRANCE OF THE
SUPREME COURT JUDGES**
Ensemble,
Of Thee I Sing (1931)

EVENING STAR
Unused / *Lady, Be Good!* (1924)

EVERY GIRL HAS A WAY
(Lyrics by Arthur Francis)
Unused / *A Dangerous Maid* (1921)

**EVERYBODY SWAT THE
PROFITEER**
(Lyrics by Arthur Jackson)
Myra Cullen, Anna Green, Sascha
Beaumont, Eleanor Dana, Ruth Grey,
and Vera Colburn,
George White's Scandals (1920)

**EV'RYBODY KNOWS
I LOVE SOMEBODY**
Marilyn Miller and Jack Donahue,
Rosalie (1928)
(Added after opening. Same music as "Dance
Alone with You," dropped from *Funny Face*)

FABRIC OF DREAMS
(Music by Raymond Hubbell)
(Lyrics by B. G. De Sylva and Arthur Francis)
Joe Schenck and Hazel Dawn,
Nifties (1923)

FANCY, FANCY
(Music by Vernon Duke)
Fannie Brice and Bob Hope,
Ziegfeld Follies (1936)

FAR AWAY
(Music by George Gershwin and Herbert Stothart)
(Lyrics by Otto Harbach and Oscar Hammerstein II)
Greek Evans and the Russian Art Choir,
Song of the Flame (1925)

FASCINATING RHYTHM
Fred and Adele Astaire and Cliff
Edwards,
Lady, Be Good! (1924)

FASCINATION
(Music by Louis Silvers)
(Lyrics by Ira Gershwin and Schuyler Greene)
Theme song for film *Fascination* (1922)

**FATHERLAND, MOTHER OF
THE BAND**
Unused / *Pardon My English* (1933)

FEELING I'M FALLING
Gertrude Lawrence and Paul Frawley,
Treasure Girl (1928)

FEELING SENTIMENTAL
(Lyrics by Ira Gershwin and Gus Kahn)
Unused / *Show Girl* (1929)

FIDGETY FEET
Harland Dixon, Marion Fairbanks, and
ensemble,
Oh, Kay! (1926)

THE FINEST OF THE FINEST
Unused / *Funny Face* (1927)

FIVE A.M.
(Music by Vernon Duke)
Josephine Baker and ensemble,
Ziegfeld Follies (1936)

THE FLAPPER
(Music by George Gershwin and William Daly)
(Lyrics by B. G. De Sylva)
Non-production 1922

**FLETCHER'S AMERICAN
CHEESE CHORAL SOCIETY**
Herbert Corthell, Max Hoffman, Jr.,
Robert Bentley, and ensemble,
Strike Up the Band (first version) (1927)

**FLETCHER'S AMERICAN
CHOCOLATE CHORAL SOCIETY**
Dudley Clements, Robert Bentley,
Gordon Smith, and ensemble,
Strike Up the Band (second version)
(1930)

**A FOGGY DAY
(IN LONDON TOWN)**
Fred Astaire,
A Damsel in Distress (1937)

FOLLOW THE DRUM
Marilyn Miller and ensemble,
Rosalie (1928)
(added after opening)

FOLLOW THE MINSTREL BAND
(Lyrics by Ira Gershwin and Gus Kahn)
Eddie Jackson and band,
Show Girl (1929)

FOR THE LIFE OF ME
(Music by Arthur Schwartz)
Ray McDonald and Martha Stewart,
Park Avenue (1946)

**FOR YOU, FOR ME,
FOR EVERMORE**
Dick Haymes and Betty Grable,
The Shocking Miss Pilgrim (1947)

FOUR LITTLE SIRENS
Ensemble,
Primrose (1924)

FRENCH PASTRY WALK
(Music by William Daly and Paul Lannin)
(Lyrics by Arthur Jackson and Arthur Francis)
Charles Judels, Fred Astaire, Vinton
Freedley, and ensemble,
For Goodness Sake (1922)

FREUD AND JUNG AND ADLER
Unused / *Pardon My English* (1933)

FROM NOW ON
(Lyrics by Arthur J. Jackson and B. G. De Sylva)
Janet Velie and John E. Hazzard,
La, La, Lucille (1919)

FUN TO BE FOOLED
(Music by Harold Arlen)
(Lyrics by Ira Gershwin and E. Y. Harburg)
Frances Williams and Bartlett Simmons,
Life Begins at 8:40 (1934)

FUNNY FACE
Fred and Adele Astaire,
Funny Face (1927)

THE FUTURE MRS. COLEMAN
(Music by Arthur Schwartz)
Unused / *Park Avenue* (1946)

FUTURISTIC MELODY
(Lyrics by E. Ray Goetz)
Leo Henning, Ruth White, Gertrude
McDonald, Violet Vale, Inez and Florence
Courtney, and Gilda Gray,
Snapshots (1921)

THE GAMBLER OF THE WEST
Unused / *Girl Crazy* (1930)

GARCON, S'IL VOUS PLAIT
Ensemble,
Of Thee I Sing (1931)

GARDEN OF LOVE
(Lyrics by B. G. De Sylva)
Helen Hudson and the Tip Top Four,
George White's Scandals (1923)
(added on tour)

GATHER YE ROSEBUDS
Unused / *Tip-Toes* (1925)

THE GAZOOKA
(Music by Vernon Duke)
Bob Hope, Fannie Brice, Gertrude
Niesen, Hugh O'Connell, and ensemble,
Ziegfeld Follies (1936)

THE GIRL I LOVE
Morton Downey,
Strike Up the Band (first version) (1927)
(rewritten lyrics of "The Man I Love")

GIRL OF THE MOMENT
(Music by Kurt Weill)
Ensemble,
Lady in the Dark (1941)

GIVE A GIRL A BREAK
(Music by Burton Lane)
Debbie Reynolds, Helen Wood, Marge
Champion, and ensemble,
Give a Girl a Break (1953)

GIVE ME MY MAMMY
(Lyrics by Clifford Grey)
Unused / *The Rainbow* (1923)

GOL-DURN!
(Music by George Gershwin and William Daly)
(Lyrics by Brian Hooker)
Jimmie Barry and ensemble,
Our Nell (1922)

GONE, GONE, GONE!
(Lyrics by Du Bose Heyward)
Ensemble,
Porgy and Bess (1935)

GOOD-BYE TO ALL THAT
(Music by Arthur Schwartz)
Martha Stewart, Ray McDonald, and
ensemble,
Park Avenue (1946)

**GOOD-BYE TO THE OLD LOVE,
HELLO TO THE NEW**
Unused / *Treasure Girl* (1928)

GOOD LITTLE TUNE
(Lyrics by Irving Caesar)
Non-production c. 1918

GOOD NIGHT, MY DEAR
(Lyrics by Clifford Grey)
Grace Hayes,
The Rainbow (1923)

GOT A RAINBOW
Walter Catlett, Peggy O'Neill, Virginia
Franck, and ensemble,
Treasure Girl (1928)

GOTTA HAVE ME GO WITH YOU
(Music by Harold Arlen)
Judy Garland, Jack Harmon, and Don
McCabe,
A Star Is Born (1954)

THE GREATEST SHOW ON EARTH
(Music by Kurt Weill)
Danny Kaye and ensemble,
Lady in the Dark (1941)

GREEN LIGHT AHEAD
(Music by Harold Arlen)
Unused / *A Star Is Born* (1954)

GUESS WHO
Unused / *Oh, Kay!* (1926)
(Same music as "Don't Ask!")

GUSH-GUSH-GUSHING
Non-production 1918

HAIL THE HAPPY COUPLE
Carl Randall, Barbara Newberry, and
ensemble,
Pardon My English (1933)

THE HALF OF IT, DEARIE, BLUES
Fred Astaire and Kathlene Martyn,
Lady, Be Good! (1924)

HANG ON TO ME
Fred and Adele Astaire,
Lady, Be Good! (1924)

HANGIN' AROUND WITH YOU
Doris Carson and Gordon Smith,
Strike Up the Band (second version)
(1930)

**HANGING THROTTLEBOTTOM
IN THE MORNING**
Ensemble,
Let 'Em Eat Cake (1933)

HAPPY BIRTHDAY
(Lyrics by Ira Gershwin and Gus Kahn)
Ensemble,
Show Girl (1929)

HAPPY ENDING
(Music by Paul Lannin)
(Lyrics by Arthur Francis)
Unused / *Two Little Girls in Blue* (1921)

HARBOR OF DREAMS
Unused / *Tip-Toes* (1925)

HARLEM RIVER CHANTY
Unused / *Tip-Toes* (1925)

HARLEM SERENADE
(Lyrics by Ira Gershwin and Gus Kahn)
Ruby Keeler and ensemble,
Show Girl (1929)

HAS ANYONE SEEN MY JOE?
(Lyrics by B. G. De Sylva)
Coletta Ryan,
George White's Scandals (1922)
(Music adapted from "Lullaby"—string
quartet written in 1919)

HAVE YOU HEARD
(Lyrics by Claude Hulbert)
Leslie Henson and Claude Hulbert,
Tell Me More! (London production)
(1925)

HE HASN'T A THING EXCEPT ME
(Music by Vernon Duke)
Fannie Brice,
Ziegfeld Follies (1936)

HE KNOWS MILK
Jerry Goff, Helen Gilligan, Robert
Bentley, Dudley Clements, and ensemble,
Strike Up the Band (second version)
(1930)

HE LOVES AND SHE LOVES
Adele Astaire and Allen Kearns,
Funny Face (1927)

HEAVEN ON EARTH
(Lyrics by Ira Gershwin and Howard Dietz)
Oscar Shaw, Betty Compton, Constance
Carpenter, and ensemble,
Oh, Kay! (1926)

HEAVENLY DAY
(Music by Arthur Schwartz)
Unused / *Park Avenue* (1946)

A HELL OF A HOLE
William Gaxton and ensemble,
Let 'Em Eat Cake (1933)

HELLO, GOOD MORNING
Ensemble,
Of Thee I Sing (1931)

THE HE-MAN
(Lyrics by B. G. De Sylva and Ira Gershwin)
Unused / *Tell Me More!* (1925)

HERE, STEWARD
(Music by Vincent Youmans and Paul Lannin)
(Lyrics by Arthur Francis)
Ensemble,
Two Little Girls in Blue (1921)

HERE'S A KISS FOR CINDERELLA
William Gaxton and ensemble,
Of Thee I Sing (1931)

HERE'S WHAT I'M HERE FOR
(Music by Harold Arlen)
Judy Garland and ensemble,
A Star Is Born (1954)

HE'S NOT HIMSELF
Entire company,
Pardon My English (1933)

HEY! HEY! LET 'ER GO!
(Lyrics by B. G. De Sylva)
William Wayne and ensemble,
Sweet Little Devil (1924)

HIGH HAT
Fred Astaire and ensemble,
Funny Face (1927)

HI-HO!
Written for Fred Astaire, but unused,
Shall We Dance (1937)

HOME BLUES
(Lyrics by Ira Gershwin and Gus Kahn—set to
Homesickness Theme from *An American in Paris*)
Joseph Macauley,
Show Girl (1929)

HOME LOVIN' GAL
(Lyrics by Ira Gershwin and Gus Kahn)
Unused / *Show Girl* (1929)

HOME LOVIN' MAN
(Lyrics by Ira Gershwin and Gus Kahn)
Unused / *Show Girl* (1929)

HOMEWARD BOUND
Morton Downey and ensemble,
Strike Up the Band (first version) (1927)

**HONEYMOON (WHEN WILL YOU
SHINE FOR ME?)**
(Music by Paul Lannin)
(Lyrics by Arthur Francis)
Julia Kelety and Fred Santley,
Two Little Girls in Blue (1921)

HONG KONG
(Lyrics by Edward B. Perkins)
Probably sung by Sibyl Vane,
Half Past Eight (1918)

HONORABLE MOON
(Music by Arthur Schwartz)
(Lyrics by Ira Gershwin and E. Y. Harburg)
Non-production 1941

HOORAY FOR THE U.S.A.!
(Lyrics by B. G. De Sylva)
Franklyn Ardell, Ruth Warren, and
ensemble,
Sweet Little Devil (1924)

HOPE FOR THE BEST
(Music by Arthur Schwartz)
Martha Stewart, Marthe Errolle, Ruth
Matteson, and Mary Wickes,
Park Avenue (1946)

**HOPING THAT SOME DAY
YOU'D CARE**
Vivian Hart and Roger Pryor,
Strike Up the Band (first version) (1927)

HOT HINDOO
(Music by Lewis E. Gensler)
(Lyrics by Arthur Francis)
Unused / *Greenwich Village Follies*
(1923)

HOT NUMBER
(Music by Vernon Duke)
Unused / *Ziegfeld Follies* (1936)

HOW ABOUT A BOY LIKE ME?
Bobby Clark, Paul McCullough, Dudley
Clements, and Blanche Ring,
Strike Up the Band (second version)
(1930)

HOW ABOUT A MAN LIKE ME?
Herbert Corthell, Lew Hearn, and Edna
May Oliver,
Strike Up the Band (first version) (1927)

HOW BEAUTIFUL
Ensemble,
Of Thee I Sing (1931)

HOW CAN I WIN YOU NOW?
(Lyrics by B. G. De Sylva and Ira Gershwin)
Emma Haig and Andrew Tombes,
Tell Me More! (1925)

HOW COULD I FORGET
(Lyrics by Ira Gershwin and Gus Kahn)
Ensemble,
Show Girl (1929)

**HOW LONG HAS THIS
BEEN GOING ON?**
Unused / *Funny Face* (1927)
Bobbe Arnst,
Rosalie (1928)

**HOW WONDERFULLY
FORTUNATE**
(Music by Kurt Weill)
Beverly Tyler,
The Firebrand of Florence (1945)

**(ON THE BEACH AT)
HOW'VE-YOU-BEEN**
(Lyrics by B. G. De Sylva)
Helen Hudson and ensemble,
George White's Scandals (1923)
(Same music as "Lo-La-Lo")

HUBBY
(Music by William Daly)
Non-production c. 1922

HUXLEY
(Music by Kurt Weill)
Gertrude Lawrence, Evelyn Wyckoff,
and ensemble,
Lady in the Dark (1941)

I AM HAPPY HERE
(Music by Kurt Weill)
Melville Cooper, Ferdi Hoffman,
Earl Wrightson, Beverly Tyler, Paul Best,
Gloria Story, and ensemble,
The Firebrand of Florence (1945)

I AM ONLY HUMAN AFTER ALL
(Music by Vernon Duke)
(Lyrics by Ira Gershwin and E. Y. Harburg)
Sterling Holloway and Cynthia Rodgers,
The Garrick Gaieties (1930)

I CAME HERE
(Music by Lewis E. Gensler)
(Lyrics by Marc Connelly, George S. Kaufman,
and Ira Gershwin)
Barrett Greenwood, Dorothy Whitmore,
and ensemble,
Be Yourself (1924)

I CAN'T BE BOTHERED NOW
Fred Astaire,
A Damsel in Distress (1937)

I CAN'T GET STARTED
(Music by Vernon Duke)
Bob Hope, Eve Arden, and ensemble,
Ziegfeld Follies (1936)

**I CAN'T TELL WHERE THEY'RE
FROM WHEN THEY DANCE**
(Lyrics by B. G. De Sylva and E. Ray Goetz)
George White; danced by Mary Reed
and Myra Cullen,
George White's Scandals (1922)

I COULDN'T HOLD MY MAN
(Music by Harold Arlen)
(Lyrics by Ira Gershwin and E. Y. Harburg)
Luella Gear,
Life Begins at 8:40 (1934)

**I DON'T KNOW WHY
(WHEN I DANCE WITH YOU)**
(Lyrics by Irving Caesar)
Unused / *Dere Mable* (1920)

**I DON'T THINK I'LL FALL
IN LOVE TODAY**
Gertrude Lawrence and Paul Frawley,
Treasure Girl (1928)

**I FORGOT WHAT I STARTED
TO SAY**
Unused / *Rosalie* (1928)

I FOUND A FOUR LEAF CLOVER
(Lyrics by B. G. De Sylva)
Coletta Ryan and Richard Bold,
George White's Scandals (1922)

I GOT PLENTY O' NUTHIN'
(Lyrics by Ira Gershwin and Du Bose Heyward)
Todd Duncan and ensemble,
Porgy and Bess (1935)

I GOT RHYTHM
Ethel Merman, the Foursome,
and ensemble,
Girl Crazy (1930)

I HAD JUST BEEN PARDONED
(Music by Kurt Weill)
Unused / *The Firebrand of Florence*
(1945)

I JUST LOOKED AT YOU
(Lyrics by Ira Gershwin and Gus Kahn)
Unused / *Show Girl* (1929)
(Same music as "Blah, Blah, Blah" in *Delicious*
[1931] and "Lady of the Moon" in the unproduced
Ming Toy [1929])

I KNEW HIM WHEN
(Music by Harold Arlen)
(Lyrics by Ira Gershwin and E. Y. Harburg)
Unused / *Life Begins at 8:40* (1934)

I KNOW A FOUL BALL
Victor Moore,
Let 'Em Eat Cake (1933)

**I KNOW WHERE THERE'S
A COZY NOOK**
(Music by Kurt Weill)
Melville Cooper, Earl Wrightson,
and Beverly Tyler,
The Firebrand of Florence (1945)

I LOVE TO RHYME
Phil Baker, Edgar Bergen,
"Charlie McCarthy,"
Goldwyn Follies (1938)

269

I LOVE YOU
(Lyrics by Arthur Jackson)
Harry Rose,
George White's Scandals (1921)

I LOVE YOU, MY DARLING
(Lyrics by B. G. De Sylva)
Will Mahoney,
George White's Scandals (1924)

I LOVES YOU, PORGY
(Lyrics by Ira Gershwin and Du Bose Heyward)
Anne Brown and Todd Duncan,
Porgy and Bess (1935)

I MAKE HAY WHILE THE MOON SHINES
(Lyrics by Desmond Carter)
Heather Thatcher,
Primrose (1924)

I MEAN TO SAY
Doris Carson and Gordon Smith,
Strike Up the Band
(second version) (1930)

I MUST BE HOME BY TWELVE O'CLOCK
(Lyrics by Ira Gershwin and Gus Kahn)
Ruby Keeler and ensemble,
Show Girl (1929)

I NEED A GARDEN
(Lyrics by B. G. De Sylva)
Helen Hudson and ElmCity Four,
George White's Scandals (1924)

I USED TO BE ABOVE LOVE
(Music by Vernon Duke)
Unused / *Ziegfeld Follies* (1936)

I WANT A YES MAN
(Music by Vincent Youmans)
(Lyrics by Clifford Grey, Irving Caesar, and Ira Gershwin)
Singer uncredited,
A Night Out (1925)

I WANT TO BE A WAR BRIDE
Kathryn Hamill,
Strike Up the Band (second version)
(1930) (deleted soon after New York opening)

I WANT TO MARRY A MARIONETTE
Unused / *Treasure Girl* (1928)

I WAS DOING ALL RIGHT
Ella Logan,
Goldwyn Follies (1938)

I WAS SO YOUNG (YOU WERE SO BEAUTIFUL)
(Lyrics by Irving Caesar and Al Bryan)
Mollie King and Charles King,
Good Morning, Judge (1919)

I WAS THE MOST BEAUTIFUL BLOSSOM
Grace Brinkley,
Of Thee I Sing (1931)

I WON'T GIVE UP TILL YOU GIVE IN TO ME
(Lyrics by Albert Stillman)
Written in 1936

I WON'T SAY I WILL, BUT I WON'T SAY I WON'T
(Lyrics by B. G. De Sylva and Arthur Francis)
Irene Bordoni,
Little Miss Bluebeard (1923)

I'D RATHER CHARLESTON
(Lyrics by Desmond Carter)
Fred and Adele Astaire,
Lady, Be Good! (London production) (1926)

IDLE DREAMS
(Lyrics by Arthur Jackson)
Lloyd Garrett, Ann Pennington, and ensemble,
George White's Scandals (1920)

IF I BECAME THE PRESIDENT
Bobby Clark and Blanche Ring,
Strike Up the Band (second version) (1930)

IF LOVE REMAINS
(Music by Kurt Weill)
Fred MacMurray and June Haver,
Where Do We Go from Here? (1945)

IF THIS BE PROPAGANDA
(Music by Harold Arlen)
(Lyrics by Ira Gershwin and E. Y. Harburg)
Non-production 1943

IF YOU WILL TAKE OUR TIP
Unused / *Funny Face* (1927)

I'LL BUILD A STAIRWAY TO PARADISE
(Lyrics by B. G. De Sylva and Arthur Francis)
Winnie Lightner, Pearl Regay, Coletta Ryan, Olive Vaughn, George White, Jack McGowan, Richard Bold, Newton Alexander, and ensemble, with Paul Whiteman's Orchestra,
George White's Scandals (1922)

I'LL SHOW YOU A WONDERFUL WORLD
(Lyrics by B. G. De Sylva and John Henry Mears)
Helen Shipman and Bernard Granville,
Morris Gest Midnight Whirl (1919)

THE ILLEGITIMATE DAUGHTER
Florenz Ames and ensemble,
Of Thee I Sing (1931)

I'M A COLLECTOR OF MOONBEAMS
(Music by Harold Arlen)
(Lyrics by Ira Gershwin and E. Y. Harburg)
Unused / *Life Begins at 8:40* (1934)

I'M A POACHED EGG
Cliff Osmond and Ray Walston,
Kiss Me, Stupid (1964)

I'M ABOUT TO BE A MOTHER (WHO COULD ASK FOR ANYTHING MORE?)
Lois Moran and ensemble,
Of Thee I Sing (1931)

I'M GOING BACK
(Lyrics by B. G. De Sylva)
Will Mahoney,
George White's Scandals (1924)

I'M GONNA SEE MY MOTHER
(Lyrics by B. G. De Sylva)
Richard Bold,
George White's Scandals (1922)

I'M JUST A BUNDLE OF SUNSHINE
(Lyrics by Ira Gershwin and Gus Kahn)
Unused / *Show Girl* (1929)

I'M NOT MYSELF
(Music by Harold Arlen)
(Lyrics by Ira Gershwin and E. Y. Harburg)
Ray Bolger and ensemble,
Life Begins at 8:40 (1934)

I'M OFF THE DOWNBEAT
(Music by Harold Arlen)
Unused / *A Star Is Born* (1954)

I'M ON MY WAY
(Lyrics by Du Bose Heyward)
Todd Duncan and ensemble,
Porgy and Bess (1935)

I'M OUT FOR NO GOOD REASON TONIGHT
(Lyrics by Ira Gershwin and Gus Kahn)
Unused / *Show Girl* (1929)

I'M SHARING MY WEALTH
(Music by Vernon Duke)
Unused / *Ziegfeld Follies* (1936)

I'M SOMETHIN' ON AVENUE A
(Lyrics by B. G. De Sylva and Ira Gershwin)
Unused / *Tell Me More!* (1925)

I'M TICKLED SILLY
(Music by Vincent Youmans and Paul Lannin)
(Lyrics by Arthur Francis)
Olin Howland, Oscar Shaw, and Fred Santley,
Two Little Girls in Blue (1921)

IMAGINE ME WITHOUT MY YOU (AND YOU WITHOUT YOUR ME)
(Music by Lewis E. Gensler)
(Lyrics by Arthur Francis and Russell Bennett)
Unused /*Top Hole* (1924)

IMPROMPTU IN TWO KEYS
Instrumental possibly intended for unproduced *Ming Toy* (1929)

IN OUR LITTLE SAN FERNANDO VALLEY HOME
(Music by Kurt Weill)
Unused / *Lady in the Dark* (1941)

IN OUR UNITED STATE
(Music by Burton Lane)
Sung by Bob Fosse; danced by Bob Fosse and Debbie Reynolds,
Give a Girl a Break (1953)

IN SARDINIA
(Lyrics by B. G. De Sylva and Ira Gershwin)
Lou Holtz and ensemble,
Tell Me More! (1925)

IN THE MANDARIN'S ORCHID GARDEN
Written for unproduced musical *Ming Toy* (1929)
Introduced in recital by Eleanor Marum with Carroll Hollister at piano, Blackstone Theatre, Chicago, November 10, 1929

IN THE MERRY MONTH OF MAYBE
(Music by Harry Warren)
(Lyrics by Ira Gershwin and Billy Rose)
Ethel Norris and Tom Monroe; danced by Gomez and Winona and ensemble,
Crazy Quilt (1931)

IN THE RAIN
(Lyrics by Clifford Grey)
Fred A. Leslie, Stephanie Stephens, and ensemble,
The Rainbow (1923)

IN THE RATTLE OF THE BATTLE
Ensemble,
Strike Up the Band (second version)
(1930)

IN THE SWIM
Ensemble,
Funny Face (1927)

IN THREE-QUARTER TIME
Ruth Urban, John Cortez, and ensemble,
Pardon My English (1933)

INNOCENT INGENUE BABY
(Music by George Gershwin and William Daly)
(Lyrics by Brian Hooker)
John Merkyl and ensemble,
Our Nell (1922)

**INNOCENT LONESOME
BLUE BABY**
(Music by George Gershwin and William Daly)
(Lyrics by Brian Hooker and Clifford Grey)
Stephanie Stephens and Alec Kellaway;
danced by Ted Grant and Frances Wing,
The Rainbow (1923)
(revised version of "Innocent Ingenue
Baby")

INVALID ENTRANCE
Unused / *Funny Face* (1927)

ISLAND IN THE WEST INDIES
(Music by Vernon Duke)
Gertrude Niesen and ensemble; danced by
Josephine Baker,
Ziegfeld Follies (1936)

ISN'T IT A PITY?
George Givot and Josephine Huston,
Pardon My English (1933)

**ISN'T IT TERRIBLE WHAT THEY
DID TO MARY QUEEN OF SCOTS**
(Lyrics by Desmond Carter)
Leslie Henson and Claude Hulbert,
Primrose (1924)

ISN'T IT WONDERFUL
(Lyrics by Ira Gershwin and Desmond Carter)
Margery Hicklin and ensemble,
Primrose (1924)

IT AIN'T NECESSARILY SO
John W. Bubbles and ensemble,
Porgy and Bess (1935)

IT HAPPENED TO HAPPEN TO ME
(Music by Kurt Weill)
Unused / *Where Do We Go from Here?*
(1945)

IT HAPPENS EVERY TIME
(Music by Burton Lane)
Gower Champion; danced by Marge and
Gower Champion and ensemble,
Give a Girl a Break (1953)

IT IS THE FOURTEENTH OF JULY
(Lyrics by Desmond Carter)
Ensemble,
Primrose (1924)

IT LOOKS LIKE LIZA
(Music by Kurt Weill)
Ensemble,
Lady in the Dark (1941)

**IT TAKE A LONG PULL TO
GET THERE**
(Lyrics by Du Bose Heyward)
Edward Matthews and ensemble,
Porgy and Bess (1935)

IT WAS LONG AGO
(Music by Harold Arlen)
(Lyrics by Ira Gershwin and E. Y. Harburg)
Walter Dare Wahl and Emmett Oldfield,
Life Begins at 8:40 (1934)

IT'S A DIFFERENT WORLD
(Music by Vernon Duke)
Unused / *Ziegfeld Follies* (1936)

IT'S A GREAT LITTLE WORLD
Allen Kearns, Jeanette MacDonald,
Andrew Tombes, and Gertrude McDonald,
Tip-Toes (1925)

IT'S A NEW WORLD
(Music by Harold Arlen)
Judy Garland,
A Star Is Born (1954)

IT'S GREAT TO BE IN LOVE
(Lyrics by Arthur J. Jackson and B. G. De Sylva)
Helen Clark, John Lowe, and ensemble,
La, La, Lucille (1919)

IT'S HARD TO TELL
(Lyrics by Arthur J. Jackson and B. G. De Sylva)
Janet Velie, John E. Hazzard, Sager
Midgely, Cordelia MacDonald, Maurice
Cass, and ensemble,
La, La, Lucille (1919) (added after
opening)

**IT'S MINE, IT'S YOURS
(THE PITCHMAN)**
(Music by Harold Arlen)
Bing Crosby,
The Country Girl (1954)

**IT'S NEVER TOO LATE TO
MENDELSSOHN**
(Music by Kurt Weill)
Unused / *Lady in the Dark* (1941)

I'VE GOT A CRUSH ON YOU
Clifton Webb, Mary Hay, and ensemble,
Treasure Girl (1928)
Gordon Smith and Doris Carson,
Strike Up the Band (second version)
(1930)

I'VE GOT TO BE THERE
Carl Randall, Barbara Newberry,
and ensemble,
Pardon My English (1933)

(THE SAGA OF) JENNY
(Music by Kurt Weill)
Gertrude Lawrence and ensemble,
Lady in the Dark (1941)

THE JIJIBO
(Lyrics by B. G. De Sylva)
Ruth Warren, William Wayne,
and ensemble,
Sweet Little Devil (1924)

JILTED
Grace Brinkley, Florenz Ames,
and ensemble,
Of Thee I Sing (1931)

**THE JOLLY TAR AND THE
MILKMAID**
Fred Astaire, with Jan Duggan, Mary
Dean, Pearl Amatore, Betty Rone,
and ensemble,
A Damsel in Distress (1937)

JUANITA
Adele Astaire and ensemble,
Lady, Be Good! (1924)

JUST A TINY CUP OF TEA
(Lyrics by B. G. De Sylva)
Pearl Regay, Richard Bold, and ensemble,
George White's Scandals (1922)

JUST ANOTHER RHUMBA
Unused / *Goldwyn Follies* (1938)

JUST IN CASE
(Music by Kurt Weill)
Charles Sheldon and ensemble,
The Firebrand of Florence (1945)

JUST LIKE YOU
(Music by Paul Lannin)
(Lyrics by Arthur Francis)
Fred Santley and Marion Fairbanks,
Two Little Girls in Blue (1921)

**JUST MISSED THE OPENING
CHORUS**
(Lyrics by B. G. De Sylva)
The Williams Sisters (Dorothy and
Hannah),
George White's Scandals (1924)

JUST SUPPOSING
(Lyrics by B. G. De Sylva)
Constance Binney and Irving Beebe,
Sweet Little Devil (1924)

JUST TO KNOW YOU ARE MINE
(Lyrics by Arthur Francis)
Juliette Day,
A Dangerous Maid (1921)

KATINKA
(Lyrics by B. G. De Sylva, E. Ray Goetz, and
Ballard MacDonald)
Lester Allen and ensemble,
George White's Scandals (1923)

KATINKITSCHKA
Mischa Auer and Manya Roberti,
Delicious (1931)

THE KEY TO MY HEART
(Music by Louis Alter)
Lenore Ulric,
The Social Register (1931)

KICKIN' THE CLOUDS AWAY
(Lyrics by B. G. De Sylva and Ira Gershwin)
Phyllis Cleveland, Esther Howard,
Lou Holtz, and ensemble,
Tell Me More! (1925)

KING OF SWING
(Lyrics by Albert Stillman)
Ford L. Buck and John W. Bubbles,
Radio City Music Hall stage show (1936)

THE KNIFE-THROWER'S WIFE
(Music by Vernon Duke)
Unused / *Ziegfeld Follies* (1936)

KONGO KATE
(Lyrics by B. G. De Sylva)
Winnie Lightner, Tom Patricola,
and ensemble,
George White's Scandals (1924)

K-RA-ZY FOR YOU
Clifton Webb, Mary Hay,
and ensemble,
Treasure Girl (1928)

LADY LUCK
Ensemble,
Tip-Toes (1925)

LADY OF THE MOON
Written for the unproduced
Ming Toy (1929)
(Same music as "I Just Looked at You" dropped from *Show Girl* and "Blah, Blah, Blah" in *Delicious*)

THE LAND AROUND US
(Music by Harold Arlen)
Bing Crosby and chorus,
The Country Girl (1954)

THE LAND OF OPPORTUNITEE
(Music by Arthur Schwartz)
Arthur Margetson, Raymond Walburn, Charles Purcell, and Robert Chisholm,
Park Avenue (1946)

LAND OF THE GAY CABALLERO
Ensemble,
Girl Crazy (1930)

THE LAST OF THE CABBIES
(Music by Vernon Duke)
Unused / *Ziegfeld Follies* (1936)

LAUGH YOUR CARES AWAY
(Lyrics by B. G. De Sylva, E. Ray Goetz, and Ballard MacDonald)
Entire company,
George White's Scandals (1923)

THE LEAGUE OF NATIONS
(Lyrics by B. G. De Sylva and John Henry Mears)
Bernard Granville and ensemble,
Morris Gest Midnight Whirl (1918)

LEAVE IT TO LOVE
Adele Astaire, Alan Edwards, Kathlene Martyn, and Fred Astaire,
Lady, Be Good! (1924)

LEAVIN' FO' DE PROMIS' LAN'
(Lyrics by Du Bose Heyward)
Anne Brown and ensemble,
Porgy and Bess (1935)

LEAVING TOWN WHILE WE MAY
(Lyrics by Desmond Carter)
Ensemble,
Primrose (1924)

LET CUTIE CUT YOUR CUTICLE
(Lyrics by B. G. De Sylva and John Henry Mears)
Annette Bade and ensemble,
Morris Gest Midnight Whirl (1919)

LET 'EM EAT CAKE
William Gaxton and ensemble,
Let 'Em Eat Cake (1933)

LET 'EM EAT CAVIAR
Phillip Loeb and ensemble,
Let 'Em Eat Cake (1933)

LET ME BE A FRIEND TO YOU
Marilyn Miller and Jack Donahue,
Rosalie (1928)

LET YOURSELF GO!
(Music by Joseph Meyer and Philip Charig)
Jack Buchanan and ensemble,
That's a Good Girl (1928)

LET'S BE LONESOME TOGETHER
(Lyrics by B. G. De Sylva and E. Ray Goetz)
Richard Bold and Delyle Alda,
George White's Scandals (1923)

LET'S CALL THE WHOLE THING OFF
Fred Astaire and Ginger Rogers,
Shall We Dance (1937)

LET'S KISS AND MAKE UP
Fred and Adele Astaire and ensemble,
Funny Face (1927)

LET'S SHOW 'EM HOW THIS COUNTRY GOES TO TOWN
Recitation verses (no music) written by Ira Gershwin at the request of Secretary of the Treasury Henry Morgenthau for War Bond Drive in 1943 or 1944

LET'S TAKE A WALK AROUND THE BLOCK
(Music by Harold Arlen)
(Lyrics by Ira Gershwin and E. Y. Harburg)
Earl Oxford, Dixie Dunbar, and ensemble,
Life Begins at 8:40 (1934)

LIFE BEGINS
(Music by Harold Arlen)
(Lyrics by Ira Gershwin and E. Y. Harburg)
Earl Oxford and ensemble,
Life Begins at 8:40 (1934)

LIFE BEGINS AT CITY HALL
(Music by Harold Arlen)
(Lyrics by Ira Gershwin and E. Y. Harburg)
Bert Lahr, Luella Gear, Frances Williams, Ray Bolger, and ensemble,
Life Begins at 8:40 (1934)

THE LIFE OF A ROSE
(Lyrics by B. G. De Sylva)
Richard Bold and Marga Waldron,
George White's Scandals (1923)

LIFE'S TOO SHORT TO BE BLUE
Unused / *Tip-Toes* (1925)

LIMEHOUSE NIGHTS
(Lyrics by B. G. De Sylva and John Henry Mears)
Bessie McCoy Davis, with Mae Leslie, Margaret Morris, Peggy Fears, and Helen Lovett,
Morris Gest Midnight Whirl (1919)

LINGER IN THE LOBBY
Ensemble,
Lady, Be Good! (1924)
(added after opening)

LITTLE BAG OF TRICKS
(Music by Paul Lannin and Vincent Youmans)
(Lyrics by Arthur Francis)
Unused / *Two Little Girls in Blue* (1921)

LITTLE JAZZ BIRD
Cliff Edwards,
Lady, Be Good! (1924)

THE LITTLE NAKED BOY
(Music by Kurt Weill)
Beverly Tyler and ensemble,
The Firebrand of Florence (1945)

LITTLE RHYTHM, GO 'WAY
(Music by William Daly and Joseph Meyer)
Written in 1923

LITTLE SCANDAL DOLLS
(Lyrics by B. G. De Sylva, E. Ray Goetz, and Ballard MacDonald)
Olive Vaughn and ensemble,
George White's Scandals (1923)

LITTLE THEATRE OF OUR OWN
Written c. 1919

LITTLE VILLAGES
(Music by George Gershwin and William Daly)
(Lyrics by Brian Hooker)
John Merkyl and Mrs. Jimmie Barry,
Our Nell (1922)

THE LIVE WIRE
(Lyrics by Desmond Carter)
Unused / *Primrose* (1924)

LIZA (ALL THE CLOUDS'LL ROLL AWAY)
(Lyrics by Ira Gershwin and Gus Kahn)
Nick Lucas, Ruby Keeler, and ensemble,
Show Girl (1929)

LOADING SONG (FROM THE BALTIC TO THE PACIFIC)
(Music by Aaron Copland)
Probably unused / *The North Star* (1943)

LOADING TIME AT LAST IS OVER
(Music by Aaron Copland)
Probably unused / *The North Star* (1943)

LO-LA-LO
(Lyrics by B. G. De Sylva)
Richard Bold, Olive Vaughn, Tom Patricola, and ensemble,
George White's Scandals (1923)
(same music as "[On the Beach at] How've-You-Been")

LOLITA, MY LOVE
(Lyrics by Ira Gershwin and Gus Kahn)
Joseph Macaulay,
Show Girl (1929)

THE LONESOME COWBOY
The Foursome and ensemble,
Girl Crazy (1930)

LONG AGO (AND FAR AWAY)
(Music by Jerome Kern)
Gene Kelly and Rita Hayworth,
Cover Girl (1944)

LOOK AT THE DAMN THING NOW
Leslie Henson, Rita Page, and ensemble,
Funny Face (London production) (1928)

LOOK IN THE LOOKING GLASS
(Lyrics by B. G. De Sylva, E. Ray Goetz, and Ballard MacDonald)
Helen Hudson and ensemble,
George White's Scandals (1923)

LOOKING FOR A BOY
Queenie Smith,
Tip-Toes (1925)

THE LORELEI
Carl Randall, Barbara Newberry, and ensemble,
Pardon My English (1933)

LOSE THAT LONG FACE
(Music by Harold Arlen)
Judy Garland,
A Star Is Born (1954)

LOVE, I NEVER KNEW
(Lyrics by Desmond Carter)
Elsa MacFarlane,
Tell Me More! (London production) (1925)

LOVE IS HERE TO STAY
Kenny Baker,
Goldwyn Follies (1938)

LOVE IS IN THE AIR
(Lyrics by B. G. De Sylva and Ira Gershwin)
Ensemble,
Tell Me More! (1925)

LOVE IS MY ENEMY
(Music by Kurt Weill)
Earl Wrightson and Beverly Tyler,
The Firebrand of Florence (1945)

272

LOVE IS SWEEPING THE COUNTRY
George Murphy, June O'Dea, and ensemble,
Of Thee I Sing (1931)

THE LOVE OF A WIFE
(Lyrics by Arthur J. Jackson and B. G. De Sylva)
Unused / *La, La, Lucille* (1919)

LOVE WALKED IN
Kenny Baker,
Goldwyn Follies (1938)

LOVERS OF ART
(Lyrics by B. G. De Sylva)
Elm City Four and ensemble,
George White's Scandals (1924)

LU LU
(Lyrics by Arthur Jackson)
Edith Hallor and ensemble,
Broadway Brevities (1920)

LUCKIEST MAN IN THE WORLD
George Givot and ensemble,
Pardon My English (1933)

LULLABY
Written in 1919 as a string quartet.
Première by Juilliard Quartet in
Washington, D.C., on December 19, 1967.

MADEMOISELLE IN NEW ROCHELLE
Bobby Clark, Paul McCullough, and girls,
Strike Up the Band (second version) (1930)

MADRIGAL
(Music by George Gershwin and William Daly)
(Lyrics by Brian Hooker)
Ensemble,
Our Nell (1922)

MAHARANEE
(Music by Vernon Duke)
Josephine Baker, Rodney McLennan, and ensemble,
Ziegfeld Follies (1936)

MAH-JONGG
(Lyrics by B. G. De Sylva)
Unused / *Sweet Little Devil* (1924)
Richard Bold and ensemble,
George White's Scandals (1924)

MAKE THE BEST OF IT
(Music by Paul Lannin and Vincent Youmans)
(Lyrics by Arthur Francis)
Unused / *Two Little Girls in Blue* (1921)

MAKE WAY FOR TOMORROW
(Music by Jerome Kern)
(Lyrics by Ira Gershwin and E. Y. Harburg)
Rita Hayworth, Gene Kelly, and Phil Silvers,
Cover Girl (1944)

MAKING OF A GIRL
(Music by Sigmund Romberg and George Gershwin)
(Lyrics by Harold Atteridge)
Jack Boyle and ensemble,
The Passing Show (1916)

THE MAN I LOVE
Unused in New York. Introduced by Adele Astaire in *Lady, Be Good!* tryout 1924; sung by Vivian Hart and Roger Pryor in *Strike Up the Band* (first version) 1927; rewritten for Marilyn Miller in *Rosalie* 1928, but unused. (See also "The Girl I Love")

A MAN OF HIGH DEGREE
Bobby Clark, Paul McCullough, Dudley Clements, and ensemble,
Strike Up the Band (second version) (1930)

THE MAN THAT GOT AWAY
(Music by Harold Arlen)
Judy Garland,
A Star Is Born (1954)

MANHATTAN DOWNBEAT
(Music by Harry Warren)
Fred Astaire and ensemble,
The Barkleys of Broadway (1949)

MAPLETON HIGH CHORALE
(Music by Kurt Weill)
Ensemble,
Lady in the Dark (1941)

MARY LOUISE
(Music by Richard Myers)
Written in May 1923

MASTER IS FREE AGAIN
(Music by Kurt Weill)
Unused / *The Firebrand of Florence* (1945)

THE MATRIMONIAL HANDICAP
(Lyrics by B. G. De Sylva)
Marjorie Gateson, Ruth Warren, William Wayne, Irving Beebe, and ensemble,
Sweet Little Devil (1924)

MAYBE
Gertrude Lawrence and Oscar Shaw,
Oh, Kay! (1926)

MEADOW SERENADE
Vivian Hart and Roger Pryor,
Strike Up the Band (first version) (1927)

MERRY-ANDREW
(Instrumental)
Danced by Marilyn Miller and Jack Donahue / *Rosalie* (1928)

MIDNIGHT BELLS
(Lyrics by Otto Harbach and Oscar Hammerstein II)
Tessa Kosta,
Song of the Flame (1925)

MIDNIGHT BLUES
(Lyrics by Clifford Grey)
Lola Raine and ensemble,
The Rainbow (1923)

MILITARY DANCING DRILL
Max Hoffman, Jr., and Dorothea James,
Strike Up the Band (first version) (1927)
Ensemble,
Strike Up the Band (second version) (1930)

MINE
William Gaxton, Lois Moran, and ensemble,
Let 'Em Eat Cake (1933)

MINSTRELS ON PARADE
(Music by Harry Warren)
Unused / *The Barkleys of Broadway* (1949)

MISCHA, JASCHA, TOSCHA, SASCHA
(Lyrics by Arthur Francis)
Written c. 1921

MODERNISTIC MOE
(Music by Vernon Duke)
(Lyrics by Ira Gershwin and Billy Rose)
Fannie Brice,
Ziegfeld Follies (1936)

MOLLY-ON-THE-SHORE
Written c. 1921

MONEY, MONEY, MONEY!
(Lyrics by Arthur J. Jackson and B. G. De Sylva)
Janet Velie, John E. Hazzard, J. Clarence Harvey, Sager Midgely, Cordelia MacDonald, Maurice Cass, and ensemble,
La, La, Lucille (1919)
(subsequently replaced by "It's Hard to Tell")

THE MOON IS ON THE SEA
Unused / *Oh, Kay!* (1926)

MOONLIGHT IN VERSAILLES
(Lyrics by Clifford Grey)
Grace Hayes; danced by Ted Grant, Frances Wing, and ensemble,
The Rainbow (1923)

THE MOPHAMS
(Lyrics by Desmond Carter)
Leslie Henson, Heather Thatcher, and Thomas Weguelin,
Primrose (1924)

MORALE
(Music by Kurt Weill)
June Haver and ensemble,
Where Do We Go from Here? (1945)

MR. AND MRS.
(Music by Vincent Youmans)
(Lyrics by Arthur Francis)
Unused / *Two Little Girls in Blue* (1921)

MR. AND MRS. SIPKIN
(Lyrics by B. G. De Sylva and Ira Gershwin)
Lou Holtz and ensemble,
Tell Me More! (1925)

MURDEROUS MONTY (AND LIGHT-FINGERED JANE)
(Lyrics by Desmond Carter)
Unused / *Tell Me More!* (London production) (1925)

MY COUSIN IN MILWAUKEE
Lyda Roberti and ensemble,
Pardon My English (1933)

MY DEAR BENVENUTO
(Music by Kurt Weill)
Beverly Tyler and Earl Wrightson,
The Firebrand of Florence (1945)

MY FAIR LADY
(Lyrics by B. G. De Sylva and Ira Gershwin)
Phyllis Cleveland, Esther Howard, and ensemble,
Tell Me More! (1925)

MY LADY
(Lyrics by Arthur Jackson)
Lester O'Keefe,
George White's Scandals (1920)
Also in *Mayfair and Montmartre*, London (1922)

(YOU'RE MIGHTY LUCKY) MY LITTLE DUCKY
(Lyrics by B. G. De Sylva)
Unused / *Sweet Little Devil* (1924)
Cyril Ritchard and Madge Elliott in *The Midnight Follies* at Hotel Metropole (London) (1926)

MY LOG-CABIN HOME
(Lyrics by Irving Caesar and B. G. De Sylva)
Singer uncredited,
The Perfect Fool (1921)

MY LORD AND LADIES
(Music by Kurt Weill)
Earl Wrightson and ensemble,
The Firebrand of Florence (1945)

MY MAN'S GONE NOW
(Lyrics by Du Bose Heyward)
Ruby Elzy and ensemble,
Porgy and Bess (1935)

MY OLD LOVE IS MY NEW LOVE
(Lyrics by Arthur Jackson)
Unused / *George White's Scandals*
(1920)

MY ONE AND ONLY (WHAT AM I GONNA DO)
Fred Astaire, Betty Compton, Gertrude
McDonald, and ensemble,
Funny Face (1927)

MY ONE AND ONLY HIGHLAND FLING
(Music by Harry Warren)
Fred Astaire and Ginger Rogers,
The Barkleys of Broadway (1949)

MY PARAMOUNT-PUBLIX-ROXY ROSE
(Music by Harold Arlen)
(Lyrics by Ira Gershwin and E. Y. Harburg)
Luella Gear and Earl Oxford,
Life Begins at 8:40 (1934)

MY RED-LETTER DAY
(Music by Vernon Duke)
Cherry and June Preisser and
Duke McHale,
Ziegfeld Follies (1936)

MY RUNAWAY GIRL
(Music by Sigmund Romberg and George Gershwin)
(Lyrics by Murray Roth)
Unused / *The Passing Show* (1916)

MY SHIP
(Music by Kurt Weill)
Gertrude Lawrence,
Lady in the Dark (1941)

MY SON-IN-LAW
(Music by Arthur Schwartz)
Leonora Corbett, Martha Stewart, and
Raymond Walburn,
Park Avenue (1946)

MY SUNDAY FELLA
(Lyrics by Ira Gershwin and Gus Kahn)
Barbara Newberry and ensemble,
Show Girl (1929)

NAMES I LOVE TO HEAR
(Music by George Gershwin and William Daly)
(Lyrics by Brian Hooker)
Olin Howland, Emma Haig, Mr. and Mrs.
Jimmie Barry, and Guy Nichols,
Our Nell (1922)

NASHVILLE NIGHTINGALE
(Lyrics by Irving Caesar)
Performer uncredited; may have been sung
by Jane Greene,
Nifties (1923)

NATCHEZ ON THE MISSISSIP'
(Music by Harry Warren)
Unused / *The Barkleys of Broadway*
(1949)

NAUGHTY BABY
(Lyrics by Ira Gershwin and Desmond Carter)
Margery Hicklin and ensemble,
Primrose (1924)

THE NEVADA
(Music by Joseph Meyer and William Daly)
Written May 1923

NEVER WAS THERE A GIRL SO FAIR
Ensemble,
Of Thee I Sing (1931)

NEW YORK RHAPSODY
Orchestral music. Later developed into
concert work, *Second Rhapsody*.
Delicious (1931)

NEW YORK SERENADE
Bobbe Arnst and ensemble,
Rosalie (1928)

NICE BABY
Jeanette MacDonald, Robert Halliday,
and ensemble,
Tip-Toes (1925)

NICE WORK IF YOU CAN GET IT
Fred Astaire, Jan Duggan, Mary Dean,
Pearl Amatore, and ensemble,
A Damsel in Distress (1937)

NIGHT TIME IN ARABY
(Lyrics by B. G. De Sylva)
Richard Bold and ensemble,
George White's Scandals (1924)

THE NIGHTTIME IS NO TIME FOR THINKING
(Music by Kurt Weill)
Gloria Story, Melville Cooper, Beverly
Tyler, and ensemble,
The Firebrand of Florence (1945)

NIGHTIE-NIGHT
Queenie Smith and Allen Kearns,
Tip-Toes (1925)

THE NINA, THE PINTA, THE SANTA MARIA
(Music by Kurt Weill)
Fortunio Bonanova, Fred MacMurray,
and ensemble,
Where Do We Go from Here? (1945)

NO COMPRENEZ, NO CAPISH, NO VERSTEH!
Ensemble,
Let 'Em Eat Cake (1933)

NO MATTER UNDER WHAT STAR YOU'RE BORN
(Music by Kurt Weill)
Unused / *Lady in the Dark* (1941)

NO ONE ELSE BUT THAT GIRL OF MINE
(Lyrics by Irving Caesar)
Performer uncredited,
The Perfect Fool (1921)
(Later rewritten as "That American Boy of Mine"
in *The Dancing Girl*) (1923)

NO QUESTION IN MY HEART
(Music by Jerome Kern)
Written in 1938

NO TICKEE, NO WASHEE
Unused / *Pardon My English* (1933)

NO VILLAGE LIKE MINE
(Music by Aaron Copland)
The North Star (1943)

NOBODY BUT YOU
(Lyrics by Arthur J. Jackson and B. G. De Sylva)
Helen Clark and Lorin Raker,
La, La, Lucille (1919) (added after
opening)

NOTHING IS IMPOSSIBLE
(Music by Burton Lane)
Gower Champion, Bob Fosse, and
Kurt Kasznar,
Give a Girl a Break (1953)

NOW THAT WE ARE ONE
(Music by Jerome Kern)
Written in 1938
(companion number to "Once There Were Two
of Us")

O LAND OF MINE, AMERICA
(Lyrics by Michael E. Rourke)
One of fifteen winners in a song contest
conducted by the *New York American*
(1919)

OF THEE I SING (BABY)
William Gaxton, Lois Moran,
and ensemble,
Of Thee I Sing (1931)

OFFICIAL RESUME
Ensemble,
Strike Up the Band (second version)
(1930)

OH BESS, OH WHERE'S MY BESS
Todd Duncan, Ruby Elzy, and
Helen Dowdy,
Porgy and Bess (1935)

OH, DE LAWD SHAKE DE HEAVEN
(Lyrics by Du Bose Heyward)
Ensemble,
Porgy and Bess (1935)

OH, DOCTOR JESUS
(Lyrics by Ira Gershwin and Du Bose Heyward)
Principals and ensemble,
Porgy and Bess (1935)

OH, FABULOUS ONE IN YOUR IVORY TOWER
(Music by Kurt Weill)
Ensemble,
Lady in the Dark (1941)

OH GEE! OH JOY!
(Lyrics by Ira Gershwin and P. G. Wodehouse)
Marilyn Miller and Jack Donahue,
Rosalie (1928)

OH, I CAN'T SIT DOWN
Ensemble,
Porgy and Bess (1935)

OH, KAY!
(Lyrics by Ira Gershwin and Howard Dietz)
Gertrude Lawrence and ensemble,
Oh, Kay! (1926)

OH, LADY, BE GOOD!
Walter Catlett and ensemble,
Lady, Be Good! (1924)

OH ME! OH MY! (OH YOU!)
(Music by Vincent Youmans)
(Lyrics by Arthur Francis)
Oscar Shaw and Marion Fairbanks,
Two Little Girls in Blue (1921)

OH! NINA
(Lyrics by Clifford Grey)
Earl Rickard, the Fayre Four, and ensemble,
The Rainbow (1923)

OH, SO NICE
Gertrude Lawrence and Paul Frawley,
Treasure Girl (1928)

OH, THIS IS SUCH A LOVELY WAR
Ensemble,
Strike Up the Band (first version) (1927)

OH, WHAT SHE HANGS OUT (SHE HANGS OUT IN OUR ALLEY)
(Lyrics by B. G. De Sylva and E. Ray Goetz)
Lester Allen and ensemble,
George White's Scandals (1922)
(also published under parenthesized title)

OH, YOU LADY!
(Music by George Gershwin and William Daly)
(Lyrics by Brian Hooker)
Lora Sonderson and ensemble,
Our Nell (1922)

ON AND ON AND ON
William Gaxton, Lois Moran, and ensemble,
Let 'Em Eat Cake (1933)

ON MY MIND THE WHOLE NIGHT LONG
(Lyrics by Arthur Jackson)
Lloyd Garrett,
George White's Scandals (1920)

ON THE BRIM OF HER OLD-FASHIONED BONNET
(Lyrics by E. Ray Goetz)
Delyle Alda and ensemble,
Snapshots (1921)

ONCE
Unused / *Tell Me More!* (1925)
William Kent, Betty Compton, and ensemble,
Funny Face (1927)

ONCE THERE WERE TWO OF US
(Music by Jerome Kern)
Written in 1938
(companion number to "Now That We Are One")

THE ONE I'M LOOKING FOR
(Music by Joseph Meyer and Philip Charig)
(Lyrics by Ira Gershwin and Douglas Furber)
Jack Buchanan and Elsie Randolph,
That's a Good Girl (1928)

ONE LIFE TO LIVE
(Music by Kurt Weill)
Gertrude Lawrence and Danny Kaye,
Lady in the Dark (1941)

ONE MAN
(Lyrics by Ira Gershwin and Gus Kahn)
Barbara Newberry,
Show Girl (1929)

ONE MAN'S DEATH IS ANOTHER MAN'S LIVING
(Music by Kurt Weill)
Randolph Symonette,
The Firebrand of Florence (1945)

ONE, TWO, THREE
Dick Haymes and ensemble; danced by Betty Grable and Dick Haymes,
The Shocking Miss Pilgrim (1946)

OO, HOW I LOVE TO BE LOVED BY YOU
(Lyrics by Lou Paley)
Helen Clark and Lorin Raker,
La, La, Lucille (1919)
(subsequently replaced by "Nobody But You")
Unused / *Ed Wynn's Carnival* (1920)

OUR LITTLE CAPTAIN
Queenie Smith and ensemble,
Tip-Toes (1925)

OUR LITTLE KITCHENETTE
(Lyrics by Arthur J. Jackson and B. G. De Sylva)
Unused / *La, La, Lucille* (1919)

OVERFLOW
(Lyrics by Du Bose Heyward)
Ensemble,
Porgy and Bess (1935)

PARDON MY ENGLISH
Lyda Roberti and George Givot,
Pardon My English (1933)

PARTY PARLANDO
(Music by Kurt Weill)
Unused / *Lady in the Dark* (1941)

PATRIOTIC RALLY
Ensemble,
Strike Up the Band (both versions) (1927 and 1930)

PAY SOME ATTENTION TO ME
Unused / *A Damsel in Distress* (1937)

PEP! ZIP! AND PUNCH!
(Lyrics by Desmond Carter)
Unused / *Primrose* (1924)

PEPITA
(Lyrics by B. G. De Sylva)
Unused / *Sweet Little Devil* (1924)

PHOEBE
(Lyrics by Ira Gershwin and Lou Paley)
Written in August 1921

THE PICCADILLY WALK
(Music by Edward A. Horan)
(Lyrics by Arthur Francis and Arthur Riscoe)
Harry Pilcer (probably),
Pins and Needles (1922)

PIDGEE WOO
(Lyrics by Arthur Francis)
Unused / *A Dangerous Maid* (1921)

PLACE IN THE COUNTRY
Paul Frawley, Norman Curtis, and ensemble,
Treasure Girl (1928)

PLEASE SEND MY DADDY BACK HOME
(Music by Vernon Duke)
Unused / *Ziegfeld Follies* (1936)

THE POETRY OF MOTION
(Lyrics by B. G. De Sylva and Ira Gershwin)
Willie Covan and Leonard Ruffin,
Tell Me More! (1925)

THE POETRY OF MOTION
(Music by Harry Warren)
Unused / *The Barkleys of Broadway* (1949)

POOR MICHAEL! POOR GOLO!
Unused / *Pardon My English* (1933)

POPPYLAND
(Lyrics by B. G. De Sylva and John Henry Mears)
Bernard Granville, Helen Shipman, and ensemble,
Morris Gest Midnight Whirl (1919)

THE PRINCESS OF PURE DELIGHT
(Music by Kurt Weill)
Gertrude Lawrence,
Lady in the Dark (1941)

PROSPERITY IS JUST AROUND THE CORNER
William Gaxton and ensemble,
Of Thee I Sing (1931)

PUT ME TO THE TEST
(Music by George Gershwin; Ira Gershwin's lyrics not sung)
Danced by Fred Astaire, George Burns, and Gracie Allen,
A Damsel in Distress (1937)

PUT ME TO THE TEST
(Music by Jerome Kern)
Gene Kelly; danced by Gene Kelly, Rita Hayworth, and ensemble,
Cover Girl (1944)
(Kern composed an entirely new melody to Ira's unused lyrics, which had been written for George's music in *A Damsel in Distress*)

QUARTET EROTICA
(Music by Harold Arlen)
(Lyrics by Ira Gershwin and E. Y. Harburg)
James McColl, Brian Donlevy, Ray Bolger, and Bert Lahr,
Life Begins at 8:40 (1934)

QUEEN ISABELLA
(Lyrics by Arthur Jackson)
Unused / *George White's Scandals* (1920)

QUITE A PARTY
(Lyrics by B. G. De Sylva)
Ensemble,
Sweet Little Devil (1924)

RAGGING THE TRAUMEREI
(Lyrics by Leonard Praskins)
Written c.1913 or 1914

RAINY AFTERNOON GIRLS
Ensemble,
Lady, Be Good! (1924)

THE REAL AMERICAN FOLK SONG (IS A RAG)
Hal Ford,
Ladies First (1918)
(Nora Bayes sang the song on the tryout tour)

A RED HEADED WOMAN
Warren Coleman,
Porgy and Bess (1935)

A RHYME FOR ANGELA
(Music by Kurt Weill)
Melville Cooper and ensemble,
The Firebrand of Florence (1945)

RIALTO RIPPLES
(Music by George Gershwin and Will Donaldson)
Piano rag solo (1917)

RICE AND SHOES
(Music by Vincent Youmans)
(Lyrics by Schuyler Greene and Arthur Francis)
Oscar Shaw, Fred Santley, and ensemble,
Two Little Girls in Blue (1921)

RING A DING A DING DONG DELL
Ensemble,
Strike Up the Band (second version)
(1930)

ROSALIE
Unused / *Rosalie* (1928)

ROSE OF MADRID
(Lyrics by B. G. De Sylva)
Richard Bold and ensemble,
George White's Scandals (1924)

ROSES OF FRANCE
(Lyrics by Desmond Carter)
Esme de Vayne and ensemble,
Primrose (1924)

'S WONDERFUL
Adele Astaire and Allen Kearns,
Funny Face (1927)

SAM AND DELILAH
Ethel Merman and ensemble,
Girl Crazy (1930)

THE SAME OLD STORY
(Lyrics by B. G. De Sylva)
Constance Binney and ensemble,
Sweet Little Devil (1924)

SAVE YOUR YESSES
(Music by Vernon Duke)
Unused / *Ziegfeld Follies* (1936)

SAY SO!
(Lyrics by Ira Gershwin and P. G. Wodehouse)
Marilyn Miller and Oliver McLennan,
Rosalie (1928)

SCANDAL WALK
(Lyrics by Arthur Jackson)
Ann Pennington and ensemble,
George White's Scandals (1920)

THE SEARCH IS THROUGH
(Music by Harold Arlen)
Bing Crosby,
The Country Girl (1954)

SECOND FIDDLE TO A HARP
(Music by Harry Warren)
Unused / *The Barkleys of Broadway*
(1949)

SEEING DICKIE HOME
Unused / *Lady, Be Good!* (1924)

THE SENATORIAL ROLL CALL
Victor Moore and ensemble,
Of Thee I Sing (1931)

SENTIMENTAL WEATHER
(Music by Vernon Duke)
Cherry and June Preisser and
Duke McHale,
Ziegfeld Follies (1936)

SEVENTEEN AND TWENTY-ONE
Dorothea James and Max Hoffman, Jr.,
Strike Up the Band (first version) (1927)

SHALL WE DANCE
Fred Astaire; danced by Astaire, Ginger
Rogers, and ensemble,
Shall We Dance (1937)

SHE'S INNOCENT
(Music by Vincent Youmans and Paul Lannin)
(Lyrics by Arthur Francis)
Ensemble,
Two Little Girls in Blue (1921)

SHE'S JUST A BABY
(Lyrics by Arthur Jackson)
Ann Pennington and ensemble,
George White's Scandals (1921)

SHIRTS BY THE MILLIONS
Lois Moran and Florenz Ames,
Let 'Em Eat Cake (1933)

SHOEIN' THE MARE
(Music by Harold Arlen)
(Lyrics by Ira Gershwin and E. Y. Harburg)
Adrienne Matzenauer and ensemble,
Life Begins at 8:40 (1934)

SHOES WITH WINGS ON
(Music by Harry Warren)
Fred Astaire,
The Barkleys of Broadway (1949)

SHOP GIRLS AND MANNIKINS
(Lyrics by B. G. De Sylva and Ira Gershwin)
Unused / *Tell Me More!* (1925)

SHOW ME THE TOWN
Unused / *Oh, Kay!* (1926)
Bobbe Arnst and ensemble,
Rosalie (1928)

THE SHOW MUST GO ON
(Music by Jerome Kern)
Ensemble,
Cover Girl (1944)

THE SIGNAL
(Lyrics by Otto Harbach and Oscar Hammerstein II)
Tessa Kosta, Guy Robertson, and
ensemble,
Song of the Flame (1925)

THE SILLY SEASON
(Music by Vincent Youmans and Paul Lannin)
(Lyrics by Arthur Francis)
Emma Janvier, Oscar Shaw, Fred Santley,
and ensemble,
Two Little Girls in Blue (1921)

THE SIMPLE LIFE
(Lyrics by Arthur Francis)
Juliette Day,
A Dangerous Maid (1921)

SINCE I FOUND YOU
(Lyrics by Leonard Praskins)
George Gershwin's earliest song, c. 1913

SING A LITTLE SONG
Ritz Quartet, Phil Ohman and Victor
Arden, and ensemble,
Funny Face (1927)

SING ME NOT A BALLAD
(Music by Kurt Weill)
Lotte Lenya and quartet,
The Firebrand of Florence (1945)

SING OF SPRING
Jan Duggan and ensemble,
A Damsel in Distress (1937)

SING SONG GIRL
Unused / Unproduced *Ming Toy* (1929)

SINGIN' PETE
Unused / *Lady, Be Good!* (1924)

SINGING IN THE RAIN
(Music by Joseph Meyer and William Daly)
Written in 1923

THE SIRENS
(Lyrics by Arthur Francis)
Ensemble,
A Dangerous Maid (1921)

SKULL AND BONES
Ensemble,
Treasure Girl (1928)

SLAP THAT BASS
Fred Astaire and unidentified singer,
Shall We Dance (1937)

SLAPSTICK
(Music by Paul Lannin)
(Lyrics by Arthur Francis)
Unused / *Two Little Girls in Blue* (1921)

SNOW FLAKES
(Lyrics by Arthur Jackson)
Edith Hallor,
Broadway Brevities (1920)

SO AM I
Alan Edwards and Adele Astaire,
Lady, Be Good! (1924)

SO ARE YOU!
(Lyrics by Ira Gershwin and Gus Kahn)
Eddie Foy, Jr., and Kathryn Hereford,
Show Girl (1929)

SO WHAT?
Jack Pearl and Josephine Huston,
Pardon My English (1933)

SOLDIERS' MARCH (UNOFFICIAL MARCH OF GENERAL HOLMES)
(Instrumental)
Strike Up the Band (second version)
(1930)

SOME FAR-AWAY SOMEONE
(Lyrics by Ira Gershwin and B. G. De Sylva)
Percy Heming and Margery Hicklin,
Primrose (1924)
(Same melody as "At Half Past Seven" from
Nifties) (1923)

SOME GIRLS CAN BAKE A PIE
William Gaxton, Grace Brinkley, and
ensemble,
Of Thee I Sing (1931)

SOME RAIN MUST FALL
(Lyrics by Arthur Francis)
Juliette Day,
A Dangerous Maid (1921)

SOME WONDERFUL SORT OF SOMEONE
(Lyrics by Schuyler Greene)
Nora Bayes,
Ladies First (1918)

SOMEBODY FROM SOMEWHERE
Janet Gaynor,
Delicious (1931)

SOMEBODY LOVES ME
(Lyrics by B. G. DeSylva and Ballard MacDonald)
Winnie Lightner to Tom Patricola;
ensemble,
George White's Scandals (1924)

SOMEBODY STOLE MY HEART AWAY
(Lyrics by Ira Gershwin and Gus Kahn)
Unused / *Show Girl* (1929)

SOMEHOW IT SELDOM COMES TRUE
(Lyrics by Arthur J. Jackson and B. G. De Sylva)
Janet Velie,
La, La, Lucille (1919)

SOMEONE
(Lyrics by Arthur Francis)
Helen Ford, Vinton Freedley, and ensemble,
For Goodness Sake (1922)

SOMEONE AT LAST
(Music by Harold Arlen)
Judy Garland, James Mason, and ensemble,
A Star Is Born (1954)

SOMEONE TO WATCH OVER ME
Gertrude Lawrence,
Oh, Kay! (1926)

SOMEONE WHO BELIEVES IN YOU
(Lyrics by B. G. De Sylva)
Constance Binney and Irving Beebe,
Sweet Little Devil (1924)

SOMEONE'S ALWAYS CALLING A REHEARSAL
(Lyrics by Ira Gershwin and Gus Kahn)
Unused / *Show Girl* (1929)

SOMETHING ABOUT LOVE
(Lyrics by Lou Paley)
Adele Rowland and Donald MacDonald,
The Lady in Red (1919)
(Also in British production of *Lady, Be Good!*) (1926)

SOMETHING PECULIAR
(Ira Gershwin and Lou Paley)
Written c. 1921

SOMETHING PECULIAR
Unused / *Girl Crazy* (1930)

SONG OF THE FATHERLAND
(Text of V. Lebedevsky-Kumach adapted by Ira Gershwin)
(Music of I. Dunayevsky transcribed by Aaron Copland)
The North Star (1943)

SONG OF THE FLAME
(Music by George Gershwin and Herbert Stothart)
(Lyrics by Otto Harbach and Oscar Hammerstein II)
Tessa Kosta, Greek Evans, and Russian Art Choir,
Song of the Flame (1925)

SONG OF THE GUERRILLAS
(Music by Aaron Copland)
The North Star (1943)

SONG OF THE RHINELAND
(Music by Kurt Weill)
Ensemble,
Where Do We Go from Here? (1945)

SONG OF THE ZODIAC
(Music by Kurt Weill)
Unused / *Lady in the Dark* (1941)

THE SONGS OF LONG AGO
(Lyrics by Arthur Jackson)
Lester O'Keefe and ensemble,
George White's Scandals (1920)

SOON
Jerry Goff and Helen Gilligan,
Strike Up the Band (second version) (1930)

SOPHIA
Ray Walston; reprised by Dean Martin and ensemble,
Kiss Me, Stupid (1964)
(Music adapted from "Wake Up Brother and Dance")

SOUTH SEA ISLES (SUNNY SOUTH SEA ISLANDS)
(Lyrics by Arthur Jackson)
Charles King and Ann Pennington,
George White's Scandals (1921)
(Also used in *Mayfair and Montmartre*, London) (1922)

SPANISH LOVE
(Lyrics by Irving Caesar)
Hal van Rensellaer,
Broadway Brevities (1920)

SPRING AGAIN
(Music by Vernon Duke)
Kenny Baker,
Goldwyn Follies (1938)

SPRING FEVER
(Music by Harold Arlen)
(Lyrics by Ira Gershwin and E. Y. Harburg)
Frances Williams,
Life Begins at 8:40 (1934)

STAND UP AND FIGHT
Anne Revere, Betty Grable, Dick Haymes, and ensemble,
The Shocking Miss Pilgrim (1946)

STAY AS WE ARE
(Music by Arthur Schwartz)
Unused / *Park Avenue* (1946)

STEPPING WITH BABY
Unused / *Oh, Kay!* (1926)

STIFF UPPER LIP
Gracie Allen; danced by Fred Astaire, George Burns, and Gracie Allen,
A Damsel in Distress (1937)

STREET CRIES (STRAWBERRY WOMAN, CRAB MAN)
(Lyrics by Du Bose Heyward)
Helen Dowdy and Ray Yeates,
Porgy and Bess (1935)

STRIKE, STRIKE, STRIKE
(Lyrics by B. G. De Sylva)
Marjorie Gateson, Rae Bowdin, and ensemble,
Sweet Little Devil (1924)

STRIKE UP THE BAND!
Max Hoffman, Jr., and ensemble,
Strike Up the Band (first version) (1927)
Jerry Goff and ensemble,
Strike Up the Band (second version) (1930)

STRIKE UP THE BAND FOR U.C.L.A.
Special lyrics, rewritten in 1936

STRUT LADY WITH ME
(Lyrics by Clifford Grey)
Grace Hayes; danced by Jack Edge, Ted Grant, Frances Wing, Fred A. Leslie, and ensemble,
The Rainbow (1923)

SUMMERTIME
(Music by Paul Lannin)
(Lyrics by Arthur Francis)
Unused / *Two Little Girls in Blue* (1921)

SUMMERTIME
(Lyrics by Du Bose Heyward)
Abbie Mitchell,
Porgy and Bess (1935)

THE SUN IS ON THE SEA
Unused / *Oh, Kay!* (1926)

SUNDAY IN LONDON TOWN
(Lyrics by Clifford Grey)
Unused / *The Rainbow* (1923)

SUNDAY TAN
(Music by Vernon Duke)
Unused / *Ziegfeld Follies* (1936)

SUNNY DISPOSISH
(Music by Philip Charig)
Arline and Edgar Gardiner,
Americana (1926)

THE SUNSHINE TRAIL
(Lyrics by Arthur Francis)
Theme song to promote the silent film
The Sunshine Trail (1923)

SURE THING
(Music by Jerome Kern)
Rita Hayworth and ensemble,
Cover Girl (1944)

SWANEE
(Lyrics by Irving Caesar)
Muriel DeForrest,
Capitol Revue ("Demi-Tasse") (1919)
(Subsequently—probably late 1919—Al Jolson popularized "Swanee" in a Sunday-night show at the Winter Garden, New York, and then in a touring company of his revue *Sinbad* during 1920)

SWANEE ROSE
(Lyrics by Irving Caesar and B. G. De Sylva)
Featured by Al Jolson (1921)
(Same music as "Dixie Rose")

SWEET AND LOW-DOWN
Harry Watson, Lovey Lee, Amy Revere, and ensemble,
Tip-Toes (1925)

SWEET LITTLE DEVIL
(Lyrics by B. G. De Sylva)
Unused / *Sweet Little Devil* (1924)

SWEET NEVADA (WALTZ VERSION)
(Music by Arthur Schwartz)
Unused / *Park Avenue* (1946)

SWEET NEVADA (WESTERN VERSION)
(Music by Arthur Schwartz)
Leonora Corbett, David Wayne, and ensemble,
Park Avenue (1946)

SWEET PACKARD
Ensemble,
The Shocking Miss Pilgrim (1946)

SWEET SO-AND-SO
(Music by Joseph Meyer and Philip Charig)
(Lyrics by Douglas Furber and Ira Gershwin)
Jack Buchanan and ensemble,
That's a Good Girl (1928)
Hannah Williams and Jerry Norris,
Sweet and Low (1930)

SWEETHEART (I'M SO GLAD THAT I MET YOU)
(Lyrics by Clifford Grey)
Lola Raine and Elsie Mayfair,
The Rainbow (1923)

SWING TROT
(Music by Harry Warren)
Fred Astaire and Ginger Rogers,
The Barkleys of Broadway (1949)

SWISS MISS
(Lyrics by Arthur Jackson and Ira Gershwin)
Fred and Adele Astaire,
Lady, Be Good! (1924)

SYSTEM
(Lyrics by B. G. De Sylva)
Constance Binney, Marjorie Gateson,
and Ruth Warren,
Sweet Little Devil (1924)

TV COMMERCIAL (CALYPSO)
(Music by Harold Arlen)
Judy Garland,
A Star Is Born (1954)

TAKING NO CHANCES ON YOU
(Music by Harry Warren)
Unused / *The Barkleys of Broadway*
(1949)

TANGO
Piano solo performed by George Gershwin
in his first appearance as pianist-composer
at the Finley Club, Christadora House,
147 Avenue B, New York, March 21, 1914

TARTAR
(Music by George Gershwin and Herbert Stothart)
(Lyrics by Otto Harbach and Oscar Hammerstein II)
Greek Evans and the Russian Art Choir,
Song of the Flame (1925)

TEE-OODLE-UM-BUM-BO
(Lyrics by Arthur J. Jackson and B. G. De Sylva)
Janet Velie, J. Clarence Harvey,
and ensemble,
La, La, Lucille (1919)

TELL ME IN THE GLOAMING
(Music by Irving Caesar and Niclas Kempner)
Written May 1923

TELL ME MORE!
(Lyrics by B. G. De Sylva and Ira Gershwin)
Alexander Gray and Phyllis Cleveland,
Tell Me More! (1925)

TELL THE DOC
William Kent and ensemble,
Funny Face (1927)

**THE TEN COMMANDMENTS
OF LOVE**
(Lyrics by Edward B. Perkins)
Probably sung by Sibyl Vane,
Half Past Eight (1918)

**THE TEN COMMANDMENTS
OF LOVE**
(Lyrics by Arthur J. Jackson and B. G. De Sylva)
John E. Hazzard, Janet Velie,
and ensemble,
La, La, Lucille (1919)

THANKS TO YOU
Unused / *Delicious* (1931)

THAT AMERICAN BOY OF MINE
(Lyrics by Irving Caesar)
Sally Fields,
The Dancing Girl (1923)
(Rewritten version of "No One Else But That Girl
of Mine" in *The Perfect Fool*) (1921)

THAT CERTAIN FEELING
Queenie Smith and Allen Kearns,
Tip-Toes (1925)

**THAT LOST BARBER SHOP
CHORD**
Louis Lazarin and male quartet,
Americana (1926)

THAT MOMENT OF MOMENTS
(Music by Vernon Duke)
Gertrude Niesen and Rodney McLennan;
danced by Harriet Hoctor,
Ziegfeld Follies (1936)

**THAT NEW-FANGLED MOTHER
OF MINE**
(Lyrics by Desmond Carter)
Leslie Henson,
Primrose (1924)

THAT'S HOW IT IS
(Music by Kurt Weill)
Unused / *Where Do We Go from Here?*
(1945)

THAT'S THE BEST OF ALL
(Music by Jerome Kern)
Unused / *Cover Girl* (1944)

THAT'S WHAT HE DID
Victor Moore, Phillip Loeb,
and ensemble,
Let 'Em Eat Cake (1933)

THERE I'D SETTLE DOWN
(Music by Joseph Meyer and Philip Charig)
(Lyrics by Douglas Furber, Ira Gershwin and
Desmond Carter)
Unused / *That's a Good Girl* (1928)

THERE IS NO MUSIC
(Music by Harry Warren)
Unused / *The Barkleys of Broadway*
(1949)

**THERE IS NOTHING TOO GOOD
FOR YOU**
(Lyrics by B. G. De Sylva and E. Ray Goetz)
Richard Bold, Helen Hudson,
and ensemble,
George White's Scandals (1923)

**THERE WAS NEVER SUCH A
CHARMING WAR**
Unused / *Strike Up the Band*
(second version) (1930)

**THERE'LL BE LIFE, LOVE, AND
LAUGHTER**
(Music by Kurt Weill)
Earl Wrightson and ensemble,
The Firebrand of Florence (1945)

**THERE'S A BOAT DAT'S LEAVIN'
SOON FOR NEW YORK**
John W. Bubbles and Anne Brown,
Porgy and Bess (1935)

THERE'S MAGIC IN THE AIR
Probably sung by Sibyl Vane,
Half Past Eight (1918)

**THERE'S MORE TO THE KISS
THAN THE X-X-X**
(Lyrics by Irving Caesar)
Mollie King,
Good Morning, Judge (1919)
(Same song, retitled "There's More to the Kiss
than the Sound," was sung by Helen Clark and
ensemble in *La, La, Lucille* (1919)

THERE'S NO HOLDING ME
(Music by Arthur Schwartz)
Ray MacDonald and Martha Stewart,
Park Avenue (1946)

**THERE'S NOTHING LIKE
MARRIAGE FOR PEOPLE**
(Music by Arthur Schwartz)
Leonora Corbett, Marthe Errolle, Ruth
Matteson, Mary Wickes, Arthur
Margetson, Robert Chisholm, Charles
Purcell, and Raymond Walburn,
Park Avenue (1946)

**THERE'S SOMETHING ABOUT ME
THEY LIKE**
(Music by Vincent Youmans)
(Lyrics by Arthur Francis and Fred Jackson)
Olin Howland,
Two Little Girls in Blue (1921)

THESE CHARMING PEOPLE
Queenie Smith, Andrew Tombes, and
Harry Watson,
Tip-Toes (1925)

THESE DAYS
(Music by Harry Warren)
Unused / *The Barkleys of Broadway*
(1949)

THEY ALL LAUGHED
Ginger Rogers,
Shall We Dance (1937)

**THEY CAN'T TAKE THAT AWAY
FROM ME**
Fred Astaire,
Shall We Dance (1937)
(Re-introduced by Fred Astaire in *The Barkleys
of Broadway*) (1949)

**THEY DON'T MAKE 'EM THAT
WAY ANY MORE**
(Music by Lewis E. Gensler and Milton
Schwarzwald)
Unused / *Be Yourself* (1924)

THEY PASS BY SINGING
(Lyrics by Du Bose Heyward)
Todd Duncan,
Porgy and Bess (1935)

THINGS
(Music by Harold Arlen)
(Lyrics by Ira Gershwin and E. Y. Harburg)
Bert Lahr,
Life Begins at 8:40 (1934)

THINGS ARE LOOKING UP
Fred Astaire; danced by Fred Astaire
and Joan Fontaine,
A Damsel in Distress (1937)

THIS IS NEW
(Music by Kurt Weill)
Gertrude Lawrence and Victor Mature,
Lady in the Dark (1941)

THIS PARTICULAR PARTY
Unused / *Treasure Girl* (1928)

THIS WOMAN AT THE ALTAR
(Music by Kurt Weill)
Ensemble,
Lady in the Dark (1941)

THOSE EYES
Unused / *Funny Face* (1927)

THREE-QUARTER BLUES
(Instrumental)
Written in late 1920's

THREE TIMES A DAY
(Lyrics by B. G. De Sylva and Ira Gershwin)
Alexander Gray and Phyllis Cleveland,
Tell Me More! (1925)

THROTTLE THROTTLEBOTTOM
Phillip Loeb and ensemble,
Let 'Em Eat Cake (1933)

THROW 'ER IN HIGH!
(Lyrics by B. G. De Sylva and E. Ray Goetz)
Winnie Lightner and Lester Allen,
George White's Scandals (1923)

TILL I MEET SOMEONE LIKE YOU
(Lyrics by Desmond Carter)
Claude Hulbert and Vera Lennox,
Primrose (1924)

TILL THEN
Non-production 1933

TIME AND TIME AGAIN
(Lyrics by Du Bose Heyward)
Ruby Elzy and ensemble,
Porgy and Bess (1935)

TIME MARCHES ON!
(Music by Vernon Duke)
Rodney McLennan and ensemble,
Ziegfeld Follies (1936)

TIME: THE PRESENT
(Music by Jerome Kern)
Unused / *Cover Girl* (1944)

TIP-TOES
Queenie Smith and ensemble,
Tip-Toes (1925)

TODDLIN' ALONG
Nan Blackstone,
9:15 Revue (1930)
(same song as "The World Is Mine" from
Funny Face)

TOGETHER AT LAST
Unused / *Pardon My English* (1933)

TOMALE (I'M HOT FOR YOU)
(Lyrics by B. G. De Sylva)
Featured by Al Jolson (1921)

TOMORROW IS THE TIME
(Music by Arthur Schwartz)
Ensemble,
Park Avenue (1946)

TONIGHT
George Givot and Josephine Huston,
Pardon My English (1933)
(one of the *Two Waltzes in C* for piano)

TONIGHT'S THE NIGHT!
(Lyrics by Ira Gershwin and Gus Kahn)
Unused / *Show Girl* (1929)

TOUR OF THE TOWN
Unused / *The Shocking Miss Pilgrim*
(1946)

TRA-LA-LA
(Lyrics by Arthur Francis)
Marjorie Gateson and John E. Hazzard,
For Goodness Sake (1922)
(re-introduced by Gene Kelly and Oscar Levant
in the film *An American in Paris*)

TREASURE ISLAND
Unused / *Treasure Girl* (1928)

TREAT ME ROUGH
William Kent and ensemble,
Girl Crazy (1930)

TROPICAL NIGHT
(Music by Jerome Kern)
Unused / *Cover Girl* (1944)

TRUE LOVE
(Lyrics by Arthur Francis)
Juliette Day and Vinton Freedley,
A Dangerous Maid (1921)

TRUE TO THEM ALL
Unused / *Rosalie* (1928)

TRUMPETER, BLOW YOUR HORN
Ensemble,
Of Thee I Sing (1931)

TSCHAIKOWSKY (AND OTHER RUSSIANS)
(Music by Kurt Weill)
Danny Kaye and ensemble,
Lady in the Dark (1941)

TUM ON AND TISS ME
(Lyrics by Arthur Jackson)
Ann Pennington and ensemble,
George White's Scandals (1920)

TUNE IN (TO STATION J.O.Y.)
(Lyrics by B. G. De Sylva)
Winnie Lightner and ensemble,
George White's Scandals (1924)

TURN TO THE DREAM AHEAD
(Music by Morris Hamilton)
Written in June 1924

TWEEDLEDEE FOR PRESIDENT
Ensemble,
Let 'Em Eat Cake (1933)

TWO LITTLE GIRLS IN BLUE
(Music by Vincent Youmans)
(Lyrics by Arthur Francis)
The Fairbanks Twins
(Madeline and Marion),
Two Little Girls in Blue (1921)

A TYPICAL SELF-MADE AMERICAN
Herbert Corthell, Roger Pryor,
and ensemble,
Strike Up the Band (first version) (1927)
Dudley Clements, Jerry Goff,
and ensemble,
Strike Up the Band (second version)
(1930)

UH-UH!
(Music by Milton Schwarzwald)
(Lyrics by Marc Connelly, George S. Kaufman,
and Ira Gershwin)
Queenie Smith and Jack Donahue,
Be Yourself (1924)

UKULELE LORELEI
(Lyrics by B. G. De Sylva and Ira Gershwin)
Emma Haig and ensemble,
Tell Me More! (1925)

UNDER A ONE-MAN TOP
(Lyrics by B. G. De Sylva)
Ruth Warren and William Wayne,
Sweet Little Devil (1924)

UNFORGETTABLE
(Music by Kurt Weill)
Unused / *Lady in the Dark* (1941)

UNION SQUARE
Ensemble,
Let 'Em Eat Cake (1933)

THE UNOFFICIAL SPOKESMAN
Lew Hearn, Herbert Corthell,
and ensemble,
Strike Up the Band (first version) (1927)
Bobby Clark and ensemble,
Strike Up the Band (second version)
(1930)

UP AND AT 'EM
Ralph Riggs and ensemble,
Let 'Em Eat Cake (1933)

UTOPIA
(Music by Vincent Youmans)
(Lyrics by Arthur Francis)
Unused / *Two Little Girls in Blue* (1921)

VILLAGE SCENE JINGLES
(Music by Aaron Copland)
The North Star (1943)

VIRGINIA (DON'T GO TOO FAR)
(Lyrics by B. G. De Sylva)
Constance Binney and ensemble,
Sweet Little Devil (1924)

VODKA
(Music by George Gershwin and Herbert Stothart)
(Lyrics by Otto Harbach and Oscar Hammerstein II)
Dorothy Mackaye and ensemble,
Song of the Flame (1925)

THE VOICE OF LOVE
(Music by Russell Bennett and Maurice Nitke)
(Lyrics by Arthur Francis)
Unused / *The Firebrand* (1924)

WAGON SONG
(Music by Aaron Copland)
Probably unused / *The North Star* (1943)

WAIT A BIT, SUSIE
(Lyrics by Ira Gershwin and Desmond Carter)
Margery Hicklin, Percy Heming,
and ensemble,
Primrose (1924)
(same music as "Beautiful Gypsy" dropped from
Rosalie) (1928)

WAITING FOR THE SUN TO COME OUT
(Lyrics by Arthur Francis)
Helen Ford, Joseph Lertora, and ensemble,
The Sweetheart Shop (1920)

WAITING FOR THE TRAIN
Ensemble,
Tip-Toes (1925)

WAKE UP, BROTHER, AND DANCE
Unused / *Shall We Dance* (1937)

WALKING HOME WITH ANGELINE
(Lyrics by Brian Hooker)
Olin Howland, Emma Haig,
and ensemble,
Our Nell (1922)

WALKING THE DOG (published as PROMENADE)
(Instrumental)
Promenaded by Fred Astaire and
Ginger Rogers,
Shall We Dance (1937)

WALTZING IS BETTER SITTING DOWN
Dick Haymes and Betty Grable,
The Shocking Miss Pilgrim (1946)

THE WAR THAT ENDED WAR
Ensemble,
Strike Up the Band (first version) (1927)

WE
Unused / *Tip-Toes* (1925)

WE ARE VISITORS
Written for the unproduced *Ming Toy*
(1929)
Part of the music (with new lyrics) was
used in the patter chorus of "Love Is
Sweeping the Country" in *Of Thee I Sing*
(1931)

WE GO TO CHURCH ON SUNDAY
(Lyrics by Brian Hooker)
Ensemble,
Our Nell (1922)

WEATHER MAN
Ensemble,
Lady Be Good! (1924)

WEEK END
(Music by Joseph Meyer and Philip Charig)
Ensemble,
That's A Good Girl (1928)

WEEK-END CRUISE (WILL YOU LOVE ME MONDAY MORNING AS YOU DID ON FRIDAY NIGHT?)
(Music by Harold Arlen)
(Lyrics by Ira Gershwin and E. Y. Harburg)
Unused / *Life Begins at 8:40* (1934)

WEEKEND IN THE COUNTRY
(Music by Harry Warren)
Fred Astaire, Ginger Rogers, and Oscar Levant,
The Barkleys of Broadway (1949)

WELCOME SONG
Unused / *The Shocking Miss Pilgrim* (1946)

WE'RE ALL A-WORRY, ALL AGOG
Unused / *Funny Face* (1927)

WE'RE HERE BECAUSE
Patricia Clarke, Gerald Oliver Smith, and ensemble,
Lady, Be Good! (1924)

WE'RE OFF ON A WONDERFUL TRIP
(Music by Vincent Youmans and Paul Lannin)
(Lyrics by Arthur Francis)
George Mack and ensemble,
Two Little Girls in Blue (1921)

WE'RE OFF TO INDIA
(Music by Vincent Youmans and Paul Lannin)
(Lyrics by Arthur Francis)
Ensemble,
Two Little Girls in Blue (1921)

WE'RE PALS
(Lyrics by Irving Caesar)
Louis Bennison,
Dere Mable (1919)

WHAT ARE WE HERE FOR?
Gertrude Lawrence, Clifton Webb, and ensemble,
Treasure Girl (1928)

WHAT CAN I DO?
(Music by Maurice Yvain)
(Lyrics by Ira Gershwin and Schuyler Greene)
Written in August 1922 (English lyrics for French melody "Avec le sourire")

WHAT CAN YOU SAY IN A LOVE SONG?
(Music by Harold Arlen)
(Lyrics by Ira Gershwin and E. Y. Harburg)
Josephine Houston and Bartlett Simmons,
Life Begins at 8:40 (1934)

WHAT CAUSES THAT?
Clifton Webb, Mary Hay, and ensemble,
Treasure Girl (1928) (added after New York opening)

WHAT I LOVE TO HEAR
(Music by Jerome Kern)
Unused / *Cover Girl* (1944)

WHAT SORT OF WEDDING IS THIS?
Ensemble,
Pardon My English (1933)

WHAT YOU WANT WITH BESS?
(Lyrics by Du Bose Heyward)
Anne Brown and Warren Coleman,
Porgy and Bess (1935)

WHAT'S THE BIG IDEA?
Written in mid-1920s

WHAT'S THE USE?
Unused / *Oh, Kay!* (1926)

WHEN ALL YOUR CASTLES COME TUMBLING DOWN
(Music by Milton E. Schwarzwald)
(Lyrics by Arthur Francis)
Mary Milburn,
Molly Darling (1922)

WHEN CADETS PARADE
Unused / *Rosalie* (1928)

WHEN DO WE DANCE?
Allen Kearns, Gertrude McDonald, and Lovey Lee,
Tip-Toes (1925)

WHEN EAST MEETS WEST
(Lyrics by Arthur Jackson)
Charles King and Victoria Herbert,
George White's Scandals (1921)
(also used in *Mayfair and Montmartre*, London) (1922)

WHEN I'M WITH THE GIRLS
(Music by Vincent Youmans)
(Lyrics by Arthur Francis)
Oscar Shaw and ensemble,
Two Little Girls in Blue (1921)

WHEN IT'S CACTUS TIME IN ARIZONA
Ginger Rogers and ensemble,
Girl Crazy (1930)

WHEN OUR SHIP COMES SAILING IN
Unused / *Oh, Kay!* (1926)

WHEN THE ARMIES DISBAND
(Lyrics by Irving Caesar)
Written for Henry Ford's Peace Ship during World War I, probably 1918

WHEN THE DEBBIES GO BY
(Lyrics by B. G. De Sylva and Ira Gershwin)
Esther Howard and ensemble,
Tell Me More! (1925)

WHEN THE DUCHESS IS AWAY
(Music by Kurt Weill)
Charles Sheldon, Melville Cooper, Gloria Story, and ensemble,
The Firebrand of Florence (1945)

WHEN THE JUDGES DOFF THE ERMINE
Ralph Riggs and ensemble,
Let 'Em Eat Cake (1933)

WHEN THE RIGHT ONE COMES ALONG
Unused / *Rosalie* (1928)

WHEN THERE'S A CHANCE TO DANCE
Written in 1917 or 1918

WHEN TOBY IS OUT OF TOWN
(Lyrics by Desmond Carter)
Leslie Henson and ensemble,
Primrose (1924)

WHEN YOU LIVE IN A FURNISHED FLAT
(Lyrics by Arthur Jackson and B. G. De Sylva)
Janet Velie, J. Clarence Harvey, and M. Rale,
La, La, Lucille (1919)

WHEN YOU WANT 'EM, YOU CAN'T GET 'EM (WHEN YOU GOT 'EM, YOU DON'T WANT 'EM)
(Lyrics by Murray Roth)
George Gershwin's first published song —1916

WHEN YOU'RE SINGLE
Unused / *Funny Face* (1927)

WHERE DO WE GO FROM HERE?
(Music by Kurt Weill)
Where Do We Go from Here? (1945)

WHERE IS SHE?
(Lyrics by B. G. De Sylva)
Tip Top Four and ensemble,
George White's Scandals (1923)

WHERE IS THE MAN OF MY DREAMS?
(Lyrics by B. G. De Sylva and E. Ray Goetz)
Winnie Lightner,
George White's Scandals (1922)

WHERE YOU GO, I GO
Lyda Roberti and Jack Pearl,
Pardon My English (1933)

WHERE'S THE BOY? HERE'S THE GIRL!
Gertrude Lawrence, Phil Ohman, Victor Arden, and ensemble,
Treasure Girl (1928)

WHO CARES
William Gaxton and Lois Moran,
Of Thee I Sing (1931)

WHO IS THE LUCKY GIRL TO BE?
Grace Brinkley and ensemble,
Of Thee I Sing (1931)

WHOOPEE
(Music by Joseph Meyer and Philip Charig)
The Eight Tiller Girls and ensemble,
That's a Good Girl (1928)

WHO'S COMPLAINING?
(Music by Jerome Kern)
Phil Silvers and ensemble,
Cover Girl (1944)

WHO'S THE GREATEST—?
William Gaxton and ensemble,
Let 'Em Eat Cake (1933)

WHO'S WHO WITH YOU?
(Music by Vincent Youmans)
(Lyrics by Arthur Francis)
Oscar Shaw and Marion Fairbanks,
Two Little Girls in Blue (1921)

WHY BE GOOD?
(Music by Joseph Meyer and Philip Charig)
(Lyrics by Douglas Furber, Ira Gershwin and Desmond Carter)
Unused / *That's a Good Girl* (1928)

WHY DO I LOVE YOU?
(Lyrics by B. G. De Sylva and Ira Gershwin)
Esther Howard, Lou Holtz, and ensemble,
Tell Me More! (1925)

WHY SAVE FOR THAT RAINY DAY?
(Music by Vernon Duke)
Unused / *Ziegfeld Follies* (1936)

WILL YOU REMEMBER ME?
Unused / *Lady, Be Good!* (1924)

WINTERGREEN FOR PRESIDENT
Ensemble,
Of Thee I Sing (1931)

WISHING TREE OF HARLEM
(Music by Vernon Duke)
Unused / *Ziegfeld Follies* (1936)

A WOMAN IS A SOMETIME THING
(Lyrics by Du Bose Heyward)
Edward Matthews and ensemble,
Porgy and Bess (1935)

WOMAN, THERE IS NO LIVING WITH YOU
(Music by Burton Lane)
Unused / *Give a Girl a Break* (1953)

WOMAN TO LADY
(Lyrics by Du Bose Heyward)
Todd Duncan, Anne Brown, J. Rosamond Johnson, and ensemble,
Porgy and Bess (1935)

THE WOMAN'S TOUCH
Betty Compton, Constance Carpenter, and ensemble,
Oh, Kay! (1926)

WOMAN'S WORK IS NEVER DONE
(Music by George Gershwin and Herbert Stothart)
(Lyrics by Otto Harbach and Oscar Hammerstein II)
Dorothy Mackaye and ensemble,
Song of the Flame (1925)

A WONDERFUL PARTY
Ensemble,
Lady, Be Good! (1924)

WOO, WOO, WOO, WOO, MANHATTAN
(Music by Kurt Weill)
Unused / *Where Do We Go from Here?* (1945)

WORDS WITHOUT MUSIC
(Music by Vernon Duke)
Gertrude Niesen; danced by Harriet Hoctor,
Ziegfeld Follies (1936)

WORKERS OF ALL NATIONS
(Music by Aaron Copland)
Unused / *The North Star* (1943)

THE WORLD IS FULL OF VILLAINS
(Music by Kurt Weill)
Melville Cooper and ensemble,
The Firebrand of Florence (1945)

THE WORLD IS MINE
Unused / *Funny Face* (1927)
(same song as "Toddlin' Along
in *9:15 Revue*) (1930)

THE WRONG THING AT THE RIGHT TIME
(Music by Milton Schwarzwald)
(Lyrics by George S. Kaufman, Marc Connelly, and Ira Gershwin)
Be Yourself (1924)

YAN-KEE
(Lyrics by Irving Caesar)
Written in 1920

THE YANKEE DOODLE BLUES
(Lyrics by Irving Caesar and B. G. De Sylva)
Georgie Price,
Spice (1922)

YANKEE DOODLE RHYTHM
Jimmy Savo, Ruth Wilcox, Max Hoffman, Jr., and Dorothea James,
Strike Up the Band (first version) (1927)
Unused / *Rosalie* (1928)

YEAR AFTER YEAR
(Lyrics by B. G. De Sylva)
Richard Bold and Helen Hudson,
George White's Scandals (1924)

YOU AND I
(Lyrics by B. G. De Sylva, E. Ray Goetz, and Ballard MacDonald)
Beulah Berson and ensemble,
George White's Scandals (1923)

YOU ARE YOU
(Music by George Gershwin and Herbert Stothart)
(Lyrics by Otto Harbach and Oscar Hammerstein II)
Unused / *Song of the Flame* (1925)

YOU CAN'T UNSCRAMBLE SCRAMBLED EGGS
Unused / *Girl Crazy* (1930)

YOU HAVE TO DO WHAT YOU DO DO
(Music by Kurt Weill)
Earl Wrightson, Melville Cooper, Paul Best, Lotte Lenya, Ferdi Hoffman, and Marion Green,
The Firebrand of Florence (1945)

YOU KNOW HOW IT IS
(Lyrics by Ira Gershwin and P. G. Wodehouse)
Unused / *Rosalie* (1928)

YOU MUST COME OVER BLUES
(Music by Lewis E. Gensler)
Unused / *Be Yourself* (1924)
Arthur West and Marion Sunshine,
Captain Jinks (1925)

YOU STARTED IT
Unused / *Delicious* (1931)

YOU STARTED SOMETHING
(Music by Vincent Youmans)
(Lyrics by Arthur Francis)
Fred Santley and Madeline Fairbanks,
Two Little Girls in Blue (1921)

YOU'D BE HARD TO REPLACE
(Music by Harry Warren)
Fred Astaire,
The Barkleys of Broadway (1949)

YOUNGER GENERATION
(Music by Aaron Copland)
The North Star (1943)

YOU-OO JUST YOU
(Lyrics by Irving Caesar)
Adele Dixon,
Hitchy-Koo (1918)

YOUR WONDERFUL U.S.A.
(Music by Paul Lannin)
(Lyrics by Arthur Francis)
Olin Howland and Julia Kelety,
Two Little Girls in Blue (1921)

YOU'RE A BUILDER-UPPER
(Music by Harold Arlen)
(Lyrics by Ira Gershwin and E. Y. Harburg)
Ray Bolger, Dixie Dunbar, and ensemble,
Life Begins at 8:40 (1934)

YOU'RE FAR TOO NEAR ME
(Music by Kurt Weill)
Earl Wrightson and Beverly Tyler,
The Firebrand of Florence (1945)

YOU'VE GOT WHAT GETS ME
Eddie Quillan and Arline Judge,
Girl Crazy (first film version) (1932)

DISCOGRAPHY OF ORIGINAL CAST RECORDINGS AND STUDIO RE-CREATIONS

COMPILED BY MILES KREUGER
10″ 78 RPM RECORDINGS UNLESS
OTHERWISE NOTED

SINBAD (1918)

SWANEE
Al Jolson
Columbia   A 2884
Note: This record was made January 8, 1920,
long after the Broadway production had closed.

SWANEE
Al Jolson, Orchestra Conducted by Carmen Dragon
[not in show]
Decca   23470. Reissued on Decca DL 9035
(12″ LP).

While Jolson's recordings of "Swanee" are not
original cast recordings, they are among the most
important Gershwin recordings ever made.

SCANDALS (1920)

SONGS OF LONG AGO
Lester O'Keefe with mixed quartet
Brunswick   2046

GEORGE WHITE'S SCANDALS (1922)

I'LL BUILD A STAIRWAY TO PARADISE
Paul Whiteman and His Orchestra
Victor   18949. Reissued on RCA Victor LPV-555
(12″ LP).

I FOUND A FOUR LEAF CLOVER
Paul Whiteman and His Orchestra
Victor   18950

GEORGE WHITE'S SCANDALS (1923)

THE LIFE OF A ROSE
Charles Dornberger and His Orchestra
Victor   19151

LITTLE MISS BLUEBEARD (1923)

I WON'T SAY I WILL (BUT I WON'T
   SAY I WON'T)
Irene Bordoni
Victor   19199

RHAPSODY IN BLUE (Concert, 1924)

Original acoustic recording
George Gershwin, piano, with Paul Whiteman and
His Concert Orchestra
Victor   55225 (12″)

Electric re-recording
George Gershwin, piano, with Paul Whiteman and
His Concert Orchestra
Victor   35822 (12″). Reissued on RCA Victor
LPV-555 (12″ LP)

ANDANTE FROM RHAPSODY IN BLUE
George Gershwin, piano solo
Columbia   50107-D (12″), 7192-M (12″)

GEORGE WHITE'S SCANDALS (1924)

SOMEBODY LOVES ME
Isabelle Patricola [not in show] assisted by
Tom Patricola
Vocalion   14866

PRIMROSE (London, 1924)

WHEN TOBY IS OUT OF TOWN
Leslie Henson
English Columbia   9001 (12″)

THAT NEW-FANGLED MOTHER OF MINE
Leslie Henson
English Columbia   9001 (12″)

BOY WANTED
Heather Thatcher and chorus
English Columbia   9002 (12″)

MARY, QUEEN OF SCOTS
Leslie Henson and Claude Hulbert
English Columbia   9002 (12″)

I MAKE HAY WHILE THE MOON SHINES
Heather Thatcher and chorus
English Columbia   9003 (12″)

THE MOPHAMS
Leslie Henson, Heather Thatcher, and
Thomas Weguelin
English Columbia   9003 (12″)

I'LL HAVE A HOUSE IN BERKELEY
   SQUARE (BERKELEY SQUARE AND KEW)
Margery Hicklin and Claude Hulbert
English Columbia   9004 (12″)

NAUGHTY BABY
Margery Hicklin and chorus
English Columbia   9004 (12″)

SOME FARAWAY SOMEONE
Percy Heming and Margery Hicklin
English Columbia   9005 (12″)

Selections:
I'LL HAVE A HOUSE IN BERKELEY
   SQUARE (BERKELEY SQUARE AND KEW)
TILL I MEET SOMEONE LIKE YOU
THAT NEW-FANGLED MOTHER OF MINE
SOME FARAWAY SOMEONE
BOY WANTED
I MAKE HAY WHILE THE SUN SHINES
NAUGHTY BABY
ISN'T IT WONDERFUL?
WAIT A BIT, SUSIE

   Winter Garden Theatre Orchestra
English Columbia   9006 (12″)

THE COUNTRYSIDE
Percy Heming
English Columbia   9007 (12″)

WAIT A BIT, SUSIE
Percy Heming
English Columbia   9007 (12″)

LADY, BE GOOD! (1924)

FASCINATING RHYTHM, introducing
   SO AM I
Carl Fenton s Orchestra [not in show], piano
passages by Victor Arden and Phil Ohman
Brunswick   2790

FASCINATING RHYTHM
Cliff Edwards
Perfect   11560

OH, LADY, BE GOOD!
Cliff Edwards
Perfect   11564

OH, LADY, BE GOOD!
Fred Astaire, Granz All-Stars
Mercury   MG C-1004 (12″ LP)
The Astaire Story

OH, LADY, BE GOOD!
Fred Astaire, Orchestra conducted by David Rose
Choreo   A/AS-1 (12″ LP)
Three Evenings with Fred Astaire

OH, LADY, BE GOOD!
Fred Astaire, Orchestra conducted by
Elliot Lawrence
Daybreak   DR 2009 (12″ LP)
'S Wonderful, 'S Marvelous, 'S Gershwin

OH, LADY, BE GOOD!
Fred Astaire, Orchestra directed by Pete King
Kapp   KL-1165, KS-3049 (12″ LP) *Now*

FASCINATING RHYTHM
Fred Astaire, Granz All-Stars
Mercury   MG C-1003 (12″ LP)
The Astaire Story

FASCINATING RHYTHM
Fred Astaire, Orchestra conducted by David Rose
Choreo   A/AS-1 (12″ LP)
Three Evenings with Fred Astaire

FASCINATING RHYTHM
Fred Astaire, Orchestra conducted by
Elliot Lawrence
Daybreak   DR 2009 (12″ LP)
'S Wonderful, 'S Marvelous, 'S Gershwin
Note: See also London production, 1926.

TELL ME MORE (1925)

THREE TIMES A DAY
Alexander Gray
Columbia   368-D

TELL ME MORE
Alexander Gray
Columbia   368-D

TIP-TOES (1925)

LOOKING FOR A BOY, introducing
   SWEET AND LOW-DOWN
Phil Ohman and Victor Arden with Their Orchestra
Brunswick   3035

THAT CERTAIN FEELING, introducing
    WHEN DO WE DANCE
Phil Ohman and Victor Arden with Their Orchestra
Brunswick 3035
Note: See also London production, 1926.

SONG OF THE FLAME (1925)

SONG OF THE FLAME
Tessa Kosta assisted by Russian Art Choir
Columbia 618-D

COSSACK LOVE SONG
Tessa Kosta assisted by Russian Art Choir
Columbia 618-D

LADY, BE GOOD! (London, 1926)

FASCINATING RHYTHM
Fred and Adele Astaire,
George Gershwin at the piano
English Columbia 3969

THE HALF OF IT DEARIE BLUES
Fred Astaire, George Gershwin at the piano
English Columbia 3969

HANG ON TO ME
Fred and Adele Astaire,
George Gershwin at the piano
English Columbia 3970

I'D RATHER CHARLESTON
Fred and Adele Astaire,
George Gershwin at the piano
English Columbia 3970

SO AM I
Adele Astaire and George Vollaire,
Empire Theatre Orchestra conducted by J. Heuvel
English Columbia 3979

SWISS MISS
Fred and Adele Astaire,
Empire Theatre Orchestra conducted by J. Heuvel
English Columbia 3979

OH, LADY, BE GOOD
William Kent, Empire Theatre Orchestra
conducted by J. Heuvel
English Columbia 3980

FASCINATING RHYTHM
Buddy Lee
English Columbia 3981

OH, LADY, BE GOOD
Buddy Lee
English Columbia 3981

Note: Above selections reissued on 12" LP
Lady, Be Good!, World Record Club Limited
H 124, Monmouth-Evergreen MES-7036.

TIP-TOES (London, 1926)

LOOKING FOR A BOY
George Gershwin, piano solo
English Columbia 4065

SWEET AND LOW-DOWN
George Gershwin, piano solo
English Columbia 4065

THAT CERTAIN FEELING
George Gershwin, piano solo
English Columbia 4066

WHEN DO WE DANCE?
George Gershwin, piano solo
English Columbia 4066

Note: Above selections reissued on 12" LP, World
Record Club Limited
SH 144, Monmouth-Evergreen MES-7037

LOOKING FOR A BOY
Dorothy Dickson
English Columbia 4078

WHEN DO WE DANCE?
Allen Kearns, Peggy Beatty and Chorus
English Columbia 4078

SWEET AND LOW-DOWN
Laddie Cliff, Peggy Beatty and Chorus
English Columbia 4079

THESE CHARMING PEOPLE
Dorothy Dickson, Laddie Cliff and John Kirby
English Columbia 4079

IT'S A GREAT LITTLE WORLD
Laddie Cliff and Chorus
English Columbia 4080

NICE BABY
Evan Thomas, Vera Bryer and Chorus
English Columbia 4080

NIGHTIE-NIGHT
Dorothy Dickson and Allen Kearns
English Columbia 9129 (12")

THAT CERTAIN FEELING
Dorothy Dickson and Allen Kearns
English Columbia 9129 (12")

Note: Above selections reissued on 12" LP
Tip-Toes/Wildflower, Monmouth-Evergreen
MES 7052.

OH, KAY! (1926)

DO, DO, DO
Gertrude Lawrence
Victor 20331

SOMEONE TO WATCH OVER ME
Gertrude Lawrence
Victor 20331

CLAP YO' HANDS, introducing
    FIDGETY FEET
Phil Ohman and Victor Arden with
Their Orchestra
Brunswick 3377

DO, DO, DO, introducing SOMEONE
    TO WATCH OVER ME
Phil Ohman and Victor Arden with
Their Orchestra
Brunswick 3377

MAYBE
Virginia Rea and Franklyn Baur [not in show] with
Phil Ohman and Victor Arden at the pianos
Brunswick 3381

SOMEONE TO WATCH OVER ME
Virginia Rea and Franklyn Baur [not in show] with
Phil Ohman and Victor Arden at the pianos
Brunswick 3381

DO, DO, DO (part of medley including
"Limehouse Blues," "You Were Meant for Me")
Gertrude Lawrence
His Master's Voice C 2835 (12")

Reissued on 12" LP. Monmouth-Evergreen
MES 7043

SOMEONE TO WATCH OVER ME
(part of medley including "Cup of Coffee,"
"Wild Thyme," "Experiment")
Gertrude Lawrence
His Master's Voice C 2835 (12")
Reissued on 12" LP. Monmouth-Evergreen
MES 7043

SOMEONE TO WATCH OVER ME
Gertrude Lawrence
Decca 28266

DO, DO, DO
Gertrude Lawrence
Decca 28267

Studio re-creation with Barbara Ruick, Jack Cassidy,
Allen Case, Roger White, Orchestra conducted
by Lehman Engel
Columbia CL 1050, OL 7050, OS 2550 (12" LP)

Note: See also London production, 1927, and
revival, 1960.

PRELUDES FOR PIANO (Concert, 1926)

Preludes Numbers 1, 2 and 3
George Gershwin at the piano
Columbia 50107-D (12"), 7192-M (12")

OH, KAY! (London, 1927)

CLAP YO' HANDS
George Gershwin, piano solo
English Columbia 4538,
American Columbia 809-D

DO, DO, DO
George Gershwin, piano solo
English Columbia 4538,
American Columbia 809-D

MAYBE
George Gershwin, piano solo
English Columbia 4539,
American Columbia 812-D

SOMEONE TO WATCH OVER ME
George Gershwin, piano solo
English Columbia 4539,
American Columbia 812-D

DO, DO, DO
Gertrude Lawrence and Harold French,
His Majesty's Theatre Orchestra conducted by
Arthur Wood
English Columbia 4617

CLAP YO' HANDS
Claude Hulbert and Chorus, His Majesty's
Theatre Orchestra conducted by Arthur Wood
English Columbia 4617

SOMEONE TO WATCH OVER ME
Gertrude Lawrence, His Majesty's Theatre
Orchestra conducted by Arthur Wood
English Columbia 4618

MAYBE
Gertrude Lawrence and Harold French,
His Majesty's Theatre Orchestra conducted by
Arthur Wood
English Columbia 4618

Note: English Columbia 4617 and 4618 reissued on
Monmouth-Evergreen MES 7043 (12" LP).

FUNNY FACE (1927)

'S WONDERFUL
Victor Arden and Phil Ohman and Their
Orchestra, vocal refrain by Johnny Marvin
[not in show]
Victor   21114

FUNNY FACE
Victor Arden and Phil Ohman and Their
Orchestra, vocal refrain by Johnny Marvin
[not in show]
Victor   21114

Selections:

'S WONDERFUL
MY ONE AND ONLY
HE LOVES AND SHE LOVES
FUNNY FACE
'S WONDERFUL
FUNNY FACE
Victor Arden and Phil Ohman and Their
Orchestra with male chorus
Victor   35918 (12″)

'S WONDERFUL
Fred Astaire, Granz All-Stars
Mercury   MG C-1001 (12″ LP)
The Astaire Story

'S WONDERFUL
Fred Astaire, Orchestra conducted by
Elliot Lawrence
Daybreak   DR 2009 (12″ LP)
'S Wonderful, 'S Marvelous, 'S Gershwin

FUNNY FACE
Fred Astaire, Orchestra conducted by David Rose
Choreo   A/AS-1 (12″ LP)
Three Evenings with Fred Astaire
Note: See also London production, 1928, and
film, 1957.

THAT'S A GOOD GIRL (London, 1928)

CHIRP-CHIRP
Elsie Randolph
English Columbia   4952

SWEET SO-AND-SO
Jack Buchanan
English Columbia   4952

THE ONE I'M LOOKING FOR
Jack Buchanan and Elsie Randolph
English Columbia   9462 (12″)

Note: Above second and third selections reissued on
The Debonair Jack Buchanan: Music for Pleasure,
MFP 1160 (12″ LP).

TREASURE GIRL (1928)

FEELING I'M FALLING
Victor Arden and Phil Ohman and Their
Orchestra, vocal refrain by Lewis James
[not in cast]
Victor   21795

GOT A RAINBOW
Victor Arden and Phil Ohman and Their
Orchestra, vocal chorus
Victor   21795

I'VE GOT A CRUSH ON YOU
Gertrude Lawrence
Decca   28266

Studio re-creation of five songs from *Treasure Girl*
with Betty Comden, piano by Richard Lewine
Ava   A-26 (12″ LP) *Remember These*

AN AMERICAN IN PARIS (1928)

Concert Work
Victor Symphony Orchestra under the direction of
Nathaniel Shilkret (Celeste Passage played by
George Gershwin)
Victor   35963 and 35964 (12″)

FUNNY FACE (London, 1928)

'S WONDERFUL and FUNNY FACE
George Gershwin, piano solo
English Columbia   5109

MY ONE AND ONLY
George Gershwin, piano solo
English Columbia   5109

HIGH HAT
Fred Astaire and Chorus, Orchestra conducted
by Julian Jones
English Columbia   5173

MY ONE AND ONLY
Fred Astaire, Orchestra conducted by Julian Jones
English Columbia   5173

FUNNY FACE
Fred and Adele Astaire, Orchestra conducted by
Julian Jones
English Columbia   5174

THE BABBITT AND THE BROMIDE
Fred and Adele Astaire, Orchestra conducted by
Julian Jones
English Columbia   5174

'S WONDERFUL
Adele Astaire and Bernard Clifton, Orchestra
conducted by Julian Jones
English Columbia   5175

HE LOVES AND SHE LOVES
Adele Astaire and Bernard Clifton, Orchestra
conducted by Julian Jones
English Columbia   5175

TELL THE DOC
Leslie Henson and Male Quartet, Orchestra
conducted by Julian Jones
English Columbia   9592 (12″)

Note: Pianists Jacques Fray and Mario Braggiotti
are featured on recordings conducted by Julian
Jones. All above recordings reissued on 12″ LP,
Funny Face, World Record Club Limited SH 144.
Monmouth-Evergreen MES-7037.

SHOW GIRL (1929)

LIZA
Al Jolson
Brunswick   4402

LIZA
Al Jolson, Orchestra conducted by Morris Stoloff
Decca   24109. Reissued on Decca DL-9036
(12″ LP).

STRIKE UP THE BAND (1930)

STRIKE UP THE BAND!
Red Nichols and His
"Strike Up the Band" Orchestra
Brunswick   4695

SOON
Red Nichols and His
"Strike Up the Band" Orchestra
Brunswick   4695

MADEMOISELLE IN NEW ROCHELLE
Bobby Clark and Paul McCullough,
George Gershwin at the piano
20th Fox   Fox   5013 (12″ LP)
George Gershwin at the Piano

GIRL CRAZY (1930)

EMBRACEABLE YOU
Loring "Red" Nichols and His Orchestra,
vocal refrain by Dick Robertson [not in show]
Brunswick   4957

I GOT RHYTHM
Loring "Red" Nichols and His Orchestra,
vocal refrain by Dick Robertson [not in show]
Brunswick   4957, 6711

BIDIN' MY TIME
The Foursome
Brunswick   4996

BIDIN' MY TIME
The Foursome
Decca   2880

I GOT RHYTHM
Ethel Merman, Orchestra conducted by
Jay Blackton
Decca   24453

I GOT RHYTHM (part of medley with
Mary Martin)
Ethel Merman, Orchestra conducted by
Jay Blackton [not in show]
Decca DU 999 (12″)

I GOT RHYTHM
Ethel Merman, The Buddy Cole Quartet
[not in show]
Decca   DX-153 (12″ LP) *Ethel Merman—
a musical autobiography*

EMBRACEABLE YOU
Ethel Merman, The Buddy Cole Quartet
[not in show]
Decca   DX-153 (12″ LP) *Ethel Merman—
a musical autobiography*

I GOT RHYTHM
Ethel Merman, Billy May Orchestra
Reprise   R 6032 (12″ LP) *Merman...Her Greatest*

SAM AND DELILAH
Ethel Merman, Billy May Orchestra
Reprise   R 6032 (12″ LP) *Merman...Her Greatest*

BUT NOT FOR ME
Ethel Merman, Billy May Orchestra
Reprise   R 6032 (12″ LP) *Merman...Her Greatest*

I GOT RHYTHM
Ethel Merman, Billy May Orchestra
Reprise   R9-6062 (12″ LP) *Merman in Vegas*

I GOT RHYTHM
Ethel Merman, Stanley Black and The London
Festival Orchestra
London   XPS-901 (12″ LP) *Merman Sings Merman*

EMBRACEABLE YOU
Ginger Rogers, Jack Marshall Orchestra
Citel   CLP-201, CSP-2201 (12″ LP) *Hello, Ginger!*

BUT NOT FOR ME
Ginger Rogers, Jack Marshall Orchestra
Citel   CLP-201, CSP-2201 (12″ LP) *Hello, Ginger!*

Studio re-creation with Mary Martin, Louise
Carlyle, Eddie Chappell, Orchestra conducted by
Lehman Engel
Columbia   ML 4475, CL 822, OL 7060, OS 2560
(12″ LP)
Note: See also films, 1943 and 1965 (called
When the Boys Meet the Girls).

PORGY AND BESS (1935)

I GOT PLENTY O' NUTHIN'
Leo Reisman and His Orchestra [not in show],
vocal refrain by Edward Matthews
Brunswick   7562

IT AIN'T NECESSARILY SO
Leo Reisman and His Orchestra [not in show],
vocal refrain by Edward Matthews
Brunswick   7562

SELECTIONS
Lawrence Tibbett, Helen Jepson [not in show],
Orchestra and Chorus conducted by
Alexander Smallens
Victor   C-25 (12″ Set of 4),
RCA Camden   CAL 500 (12″ LP)
Note: This recording was personally supervised by
the composer.

I GOT PLENTY O' NUTHIN'
Todd Duncan
Musicraft   468

OH BESS, OH WHERE'S MY BESS
Todd Duncan
Musicraft   468

Studio re-creation with Lawrence Winters, Camilla
Williams, Inez Matthews, Warren Coleman, Avon
Long, Orchestra conducted by Lehman Engel,
J. Rosamond Johnson Chorus
Columbia   Set SL-162, OSL-162,
Odyssey 32560018 (Three 12″ LP's)

Studio re-creation with above cast (excerpts from
above)
Columbia   ML 4766, OL 4766, CL 922 (12″ LP)

Studio re-creation with Leontyne Price, William
Warfield, McHenry Boatwright, Orchestra
conducted by Skitch Henderson
RCA Victor   LM/LSC-2679 (12″ LP)

Studio re-creation with Brock Peters, Margaret Tynes,
Theresa Merritte, Joseph Crawford, William
Dillard, Miriam Burton, Orchestra conducted by
Paul Belanger
Musical Masterpiece Society   M2035-OP22
(12″ LP)

Studio re-creation with Lawrence Winters, Isabelle
Lucas, Ray Ellington, Barbara Elsy, Pauline
Stevens, Orchestra conducted by Kenneth Alwyn
Heliodor   H/HS 25052 (12″)
Note: See also revivals, 1942 and 1953, and film,
1959.

SHALL WE DANCE (Film, 1937)

(I'VE GOT) BEGINNER'S LUCK
Fred Astaire, Johnny Green and His Orchestra
[not in film]
Brunswick   7855

THEY CAN'T TAKE THAT AWAY
   FROM ME
Fred Astaire, Johnny Green and His Orchestra
[not in film]
Brunswick   7855

THEY ALL LAUGHED
Fred Astaire, Johnny Green and His Orchestra
[not in film]
Brunswick   7856

SLAP THAT BASS
Fred Astaire, Johnny Green and His Orchestra
[not in film]
Brunswick   7856

LET'S CALL THE WHOLE THING OFF
Fred Astaire, Johnny Green and His Orchestra
[not in film]
Brunswick   7857

SHALL WE DANCE
Fred Astaire, Johnny Green and His Orchestra
[not in film]
Brunswick   7857

LET'S CALL THE WHOLE THING OFF
Fred Astaire, Granz All-Stars
Mercury   MG C-1001 (12″ LP) *The Astaire Story*

THEY ALL LAUGHED
Fred Astaire, Granz All-Stars
Mercury   MG C-1001 (12″ LP) *The Astaire Story*

THEY CAN'T TAKE THAT AWAY
   FROM ME
Fred Astaire, Granz All-Stars
Mercury   MG C-1004 (12″ LP) *The Astaire Story*

THEY CAN'T TAKE THAT AWAY
   FROM ME
Fred Astaire, Orchestra conducted by Pete King
Kapp   KL-1165/KS-3049 (12″ LP) *Now*

THEY ALL LAUGHED
Fred Astaire, Orchestra conducted by Pete King
Kapp   KL-1165/KS-3049 (12″ LP) *Now*

THEY CAN'T TAKE THAT AWAY FROM ME
Fred Astaire, Orchestra conducted by David Rose
Choreo   A/AS-1 (12″ LP) *Three Evenings with
Fred Astaire*

THEY ALL LAUGHED
Fred Astaire, Orchestra conducted by David Rose
Choreo   A/AS-1 (12″ LP) *Three Evenings with
Fred Astaire*

LET'S CALL THE WHOLE THING OFF
Fred Astaire, Orchestra conducted by David Rose
Choreo   A/AS-1 (12″ LP) *Three Evenings with
Fred Astaire*

THEY CAN'T TAKE THAT AWAY FROM ME
Fred Astaire, Orchestra conducted by
Elliot Lawrence
Daybreak   DR 2009 (12″ LP) *'S Wonderful,
'S Marvelous, 'S Gershwin*

THEY ALL LAUGHED
Fred Astaire, Orchestra conducted by
Elliot Lawrence
Daybreak   DR 2009 (12″ LP) *'S Wonderful,
'S Marvelous, 'S Gershwin*

LET'S CALL THE WHOLE THING OFF
Fred Astaire, Orchestra conducted by
Elliot Lawrence
Daybreak   DR 2009 (12″ LP) *'S Wonderful,
'S Marvelous, 'S Gershwin*

A DAMSEL IN DISTRESS
(Film, 1937)

I CAN'T BE BOTHERED NOW
Fred Astaire, Ray Noble and His Orchestra
Brunswick   7982

A FOGGY DAY
Fred Astaire, Ray Noble and His Orchestra
Brunswick   7982

THINGS ARE LOOKING UP
Fred Astaire, Ray Noble and His Orchestra
Brunswick   7983

NICE WORK IF YOU CAN GET IT
Fred Astaire, Ray Noble and His Orchestra
Brunswick   7983

A FOGGY DAY
Fred Astaire, Granz All-Stars
Mercury   MG C-1004 (12″ LP) *The Astaire Story*

NICE WORK IF YOU CAN GET IT
Fred Astaire, Granz All-Stars
Mercury   MG C-1002 (12″ LP) *The Astaire Story*

A FOGGY DAY
Fred Astaire, Orchestra conducted by David Rose
Choreo   A/AS-1 (12″ LP) *Three Evenings with
Fred Astaire*

NICE WORK IF YOU CAN GET IT
Fred Astaire, Orchestra conducted by David Rose
Choreo   A/AS-1 (12″ LP) *Three Evenings with
Fred Astaire*

A FOGGY DAY
Fred Astaire, Orchestra conducted by Pete King
Kapp   KL-1165, KS-3049 (12″ LP) *Now*

A FOGGY DAY
Fred Astaire, Orchestra conducted by
Elliot Lawrence
Daybreak   DR 2009 (12″ LP) *'S Wonderful,
'S Marvelous, 'S Gershwin*

GOLDWYN FOLLIES
(Film, 1938)

LOVE WALKED IN
Kenny Baker
Decca   1795

LOVE IS HERE TO STAY
Ella Logan
Brunswick   8064

I WAS DOING ALL RIGHT
Ella Logan
Brunswick   8064

LADY IN THE DARK (1941)

SELECTIONS
Gertrude Lawrence
Victor   P-60 (Set of 3). Reissued on RCA Victor
LRT 700 (10″ LP) and RCA Victor LPV-503
(12″ LP).

TSCHAIKOWSKY
Danny Kaye, Orchestra conducted by
Maurice Abravanel
Columbia   36025

JENNY
Danny Kaye, Orchestra conducted by
Maurice Abravanel
Columbia   36025

THE PRINCESS OF PURE DELIGHT
Danny Kaye, Orchestra conducted by
Maurice Abravanel
Columbia   36042

MY SHIP
Danny Kaye, Orchestra conducted by
Maurice Abravanel
Columbia   36042

IT'S NEVER TOO LATE TO MENDELSSOHN
Danny Kaye, Orchestra conducted by
Maurice Abravanel
Columbia   36163

ONE LIFE TO LIVE
Danny Kaye, Orchestra conducted by
Maurice Abravanel
Columbia   36163

JENNY
Gertrude Lawrence
Decca   28269

Studio re-creation with Risë Stevens, Adolph Green,
John Reardon, Orchestra conducted by
Lehman Engel
Columbia   OL 5990, OS 2390 (12" LP)
Danny Kaye selections reissued on *Danny Kaye
Entertains*, Columbia   CL 6249 (10" LP) and
Pure Delight, Harmony   HL 7012 (12" LP).

PORGY AND BESS (Revival, 1942)

SELECTIONS Volume One
Todd Duncan, Anne Brown, Eva Jessye Choir,
Orchestra conducted by Alexander Smallens
Decca   A-145 (12" Set of 4), DU-739 (12" Set
of 4), 9-17 (45 rpm Set of 4), DL 7006 (10" LP)

SELECTIONS Volume Two
Todd Duncan, Anne Brown, Edward Matthews,
Helen Dowdy, William Woolfolk, Avon Long,
Eva Jessye Choir, Orchestra conducted by
Alexander Smallens
Decca   A-283 (Set of 3)

SELECTIONS Volume Three
Leo Reisman and His Orchestra [not in show],
Avon Long, Helen Dowdy
Decca   A-351 (Set of 3)
Note: Volumes One and Two combined on Decca
DL 8042, DL 79024.

GIRL CRAZY (Film, 1943)

SELECTIONS
Judy Garland, Mickey Rooney, Orchestra
conducted by Georgie Stoll
Decca   A-362 (Set of 3), DL 5412 (10" LP)

COVER GIRL (Film, 1944)

LONG AGO AND FAR AWAY
Gene Kelly, Orchestra conducted by Morris Stoloff
Colpix   CP 503 (12" LP) *Soundtracks, Voices and
Themes from Great Movies*

THE FIREBRAND OF FLORENCE (1945)

SING ME NOT A BALLAD
Lotte Lenya, Orchestra conducted by Maurice
Levine [not in show]
Columbia   KL 5229 (12" LP) *September Song*

WHERE DO WE GO FROM HERE (Film, 1945)

SONG OF THE RHINELAND
THE NINA, THE PINTA, AND THE SANTA
  MARIA
WOO, WOO, WOO, WOO, MANHATTAN
  (INDIAN SONG)
Ira Gershwin vocal, Kurt Weill piano.
Heritage   H-0051 (12" LP) issued in 1953 under
the title *Tryout—Private Rehearsal Recordings of
Kurt Weill and Ira Gershwin*

THE SHOCKING MISS PILGRIM (Film, 1946)

FOR YOU, FOR ME, FOR EVERMORE
Dick Haymes, Judy Garland [not in film]
Decca   23687

AREN'T YOU KIND OF GLAD WE DID?
Dick Haymes, Judy Garland [not in film]
Decca   23687

THE BARKLEYS OF BROADWAY (Film, 1949)

MY ONE AND ONLY HIGHLAND FLING
Fred Astaire, Ginger Rogers, Lennie Hayton and
MGM Orchestra
MGM   50016

YOU'D BE HARD TO REPLACE
Fred Astaire, Lennie Hayton and MGM Orchestra
MGM   50016

THEY CAN'T TAKE THAT AWAY FROM ME
Fred Astaire, Lennie Hayton and MGM Orchestra
MGM   50017

SHOES WITH WINGS ON
Fred Astaire, Lennie Hayton and MGM Orchestra
MGM   50017
Note: Above recordings originally packaged in
two-disc folder L-8.

AN AMERICAN IN PARIS (Film, 1951)

Original Soundtrack Album
Gene Kelly, Leslie Caron, Georges Guetary,
Johnny Green and MGM Orchestra
MGM   MGM 93 (Set of 4), E-93 (10" LP),
X-93 (45 Extended Play) and MGM MS-552
(12" LP)

OF THEE I SING (Revival, 1952)

Original Cast Album
Jack Carson, Paul Hartman, Jack Whiting,
Lenore Lonergan, Betty Oakes, Florenz Ames
Capitol   S 350 (12" LP)

A STAR IS BORN (Film, 1954)

Original Soundtrack Album
Judy Garland
Columbia   BL 1201 (12" LP), CL 1101 (12" LP)
and Harmony 11366 (12" LP)

LADY IN THE DARK (Television Production, 1954)

Original Cast Album
Ann Sothern, Carleton Carpenter
RCA Victor   LM-1882 (12" LP)

THE COUNTRY GIRL (Film, 1954)

Selections
Bing Crosby
Decca   ED 2201 (45 EP), DL 5556 (10" LP)
with *Little Boy Lost*

FUNNY FACE (Film, 1957)

Original Soundtrack Album
Fred Astaire, Audrey Hepburn, Kay Thompson
Verve   MGV-15001 (12" LP)

PORGY AND BESS (Film, 1959)

Original Soundtrack Album
Robert McFerrin, Adele Addison,
Sammy Davis, Jr., Pearl Bailey
Columbia   OL 5410/OS 2016 (12" LP)

OH, KAY! (Revival, 1960)

Original Cast Album
David Daniels, Marti Stevens, Bernie West
20th Fox   4003/SFX 4003 (12" LP)

WHEN THE BOYS MEET THE GIRLS (Film, 1965)

Original Soundtrack Album
Connie Francis, Harve Presnell, Louis Armstrong,
Herman's Hermits
MGM   E/SE-4334 (12" LP)

OF THEE I SING (Television, 1972)

Original Soundtrack Album
Carroll O'Connor, Jack Gilford, Cloris Leachman,
Michele Lee
Columbia   S 31763

PIANO ROLLOGRAPHY

COMPILED BY MICHAEL MONTGOMERY

A rollography is a list or annotated classification of an artist's piano-roll recordings. What follows constitutes all known piano rolls recorded by George Gershwin. As first published in *Record Research* in 1962, it was the most complete listing of Gershwin's piano rolls ever compiled. As new information has come to light and old errors have been corrected, it has been possible to expand, update, and refine the old listing into a far more comprehensive listing of Gershwin rolls.

In general, the months and years shown above the roll titles are the dates the rolls were released for public sale. A roll was probably recorded two or three months prior to its release. Neither the order of release nor the numerical order of the rolls is an infallible indication of the order in which the rolls were recorded. The information presented here has been drawn from many sources—notably, the roll labels, company catalogs and bulletins, and trade journals. The name in parentheses under a roll title is usually the name of the composer, although sometimes the lyricist's name is also included.

George Gershwin is a recording artist on all of these rolls, but he is not the sole artist on all of the rolls. Occasionally, he recorded with other roll artists, among them: Rudolph O. Erlebach (15 rolls), Edwin E. Wilson (6 duets), and Cliff Hess (1 duet). (One source also lists Muriel Pollock on a duet.)

In his early years as a roll artist for the Standard Music Roll Company, Gershwin recorded "Perfection" rolls under three pseudonyms (James Baker, Fred Murtha, and Bert Wynn) in addition to the recordings under his own name. It is not known, however, if all rolls bearing the names of James Baker, Fred Murtha, and Bert Wynn were recorded by George Gershwin, but nevertheless all such known rolls are listed here.

Gershwin began to make piano rolls in late 1915, and most of his earliest rolls were hand-played rolls on the "Perfection" label of the Standard Music Roll Company. The individual rolls retailed from 24 to 30 cents. With the help of Felix Arndt, composer of "Nola" and a leading roll artist, Gershwin began to record for the Aeolian Company, the giant of the American piano-roll business, in early 1916. More than 100 of his more than 125 rolls were made as an Aeolian artist.

"Metro-Art," "Universal Uni-Record," "Universal Song Roll," "Mel-O-Dee," "Universal," and "Duo-Art" are all Aeolian brand names. The Universal rolls could be played on any player piano, while the others all had special features that in essence led to a more faithfully reproduced piano sound with more subtleties and nuances.

Aeolian also leased their rolls to the Wilcox & White Company, of Meriden, Connecticut, which brought out many Gershwin rolls, after their original Aeolian release, under such labels as "Angelus-Voltem," "Artrio-Angelus," and "Angelus." In addition, George made at least one roll for the Welte-Mignon Company.

In some instances the retail prices of rolls are indicated after the catalog number. A Song Roll included words along the side of the roll to enable people to sing along with the roll.

During 1973 an attempt is being made to locate every known George Gershwin piano roll and to reissue them on long-playing records. The importance of this undertaking is emphasized by the fact that, since Gershwin made relatively few recordings on disc, his piano rolls constitute the largest and most significant legacy of his performing style.

Special thanks are offered to many individuals who assisted in the preparation of this rollography:

Collector Jack Edwards of Maspeth, New York, who graciously lent me his vast collection of original catalog material.

Agatha Kalkanis, Director of the Music and Performing Arts Division of the Detroit Public Library, for providing information on the release dates of the Duo-Art rolls from 1923 on.

Other collectors who have been particularly helpful include Bill Burkhardt, Grand Rapids, Michigan; Trebor Tichenor, St. Louis, Missouri; George Blau, Atlanta, Georgia; and Alvin Johnson, Farmersburg, Iowa.

1916

JANUARY

BRING ALONG YOUR DANCING SHOES
(Kahn and Le Boy)   Fox Trot Arrangement
Played by George Gershwin
"Perfection"   86585

KANGAROO HOP
(Morris)   Fox Trot
Played by George Gershwin
"Perfection"   86595

MARCH

"Latest Popular Songs—Some Being Adapted for Both Singing and Dancing"
GIVE A LITTLE CREDIT TO YOUR DAD
(Vincent)   One and Two Step Arrangement
Played by Bert Wynn
"Perfection"   86625

YOU CAN'T GET ALONG WHEN YOU'RE
   WITH 'EM OR WITHOUT 'EM
(Fischer)   Fox Trot Song
Played by Fred Murtha
"Perfection"   86626

THE LETTER THAT NEVER REACHED
   HOME
(Gottler)   March Song
Played by Bert Wynn
"Perfection"   86629

AT THE FOUNTAIN OF YOUTH
(Jentes)   One and Two Step Arrangement
Played by George Gershwin
"Perfection"   86630

"Dance Music"
BANTAM STEP
(Jentes)   A Raggy Fox Trot
Played by George Gershwin
"Perfection"   86632

"Latest Popular Songs"
WHEN YOU'RE DANCING THE OLD
   FASHIONED WALTZ
(Von Tilzer)
Played by George Gershwin
"Perfection"   86634

GOOD-BYE, GOOD-LUCK, GOD BLESS
   YOU
(Ball)   Waltz Ballad
Played by James Baker
"Perfection"   86637

I GAVE MY HEART AND HAND TO
   SOMEONE IN DIXIELAND
(Lange)
Played by Fred Murtha
"Perfection"   86641

APRIL

"Latest Popular Songs"
SIAM, HOW LONESOME I AM
(Fischer)
Played by Fred Murtha
"Perfection"   86656

DOWN WHERE THE SWANEE RIVER
   FLOWS (From *Robinson Crusoe, Jr.*, Winter
Garden, 1916)
(Von Tilzer)
Played by George Gershwin
"Perfection"   86663

WAKE UP AMERICA
(Glogau)   March Song
Played by Fred Murtha
"Perfection"   86667

"Dance Music"
HONKY TONKY (DOWN IN HONKY
   TONKY TOWN)
(McCarron)   One Step
Played by George Gershwin
"Perfection"   86671

MAY

OH JOE WITH YOUR FIDDLE AND BOW
(Donaldson)   Fox Trot
Played by George Gershwin
"Perfection"   86703

INTERNATIONAL FOX TROT—
   A NOVELTY MEDLEY OF FAMILIAR
   MELODIES
(Platzmann)
Played by Fred Murtha
"Perfection"   86705

NAT'AN! NAT'AN! TELL ME FOR WHAT
ARE YOU WAITIN', NAT'AN?
(Kendis)   Fox Trot Arrangement
Played by Bert Wynn
"Perfection"   86711

SOME GIRLS DO AND SOME GIRLS
DON'T
(Jentes)   Fox Trot Arrangement
Played by George Gershwin
"Perfection"   86712

ARRAH GO ON I'M GONNA GO BACK TO
OREGON
(Grant)   One Step Arrangement
Played by George Gershwin
"Perfection"   86713

"Dances and Marches"
CHINESE BLUES
(Gardner)   Fox Trot
Played by Bert Wynn
"Perfection"   86717

WHEN YOU'RE DANCING THE OLD
FASHIONED WALTZ
(Albert Von Tilzer)
Played by George Gershwin
Metro-Art   202668 $.45
Universal Uni-Record   202669 $.45

YOU CAN'T GET ALONG WITH 'EM OR
WITHOUT 'EM
(Fred Fischer)   Fox Trot
Played by George Gershwin
Metro-Art   202676 $.40
Universal Uni-Record   202677 $.40

BANTAM STEP
(Harry Jentes)   Fox Trot
Played by George Gershwin
Metro-Art   202684 $.50
Universal Uni-Record   202685 $.50

JUNE

"Latest Popular Songs"
I WAS NEVER NEARER HEAVEN IN MY
LIFE
(Snyder)   Ballad
Played by Fred Murtha
"Perfection"   86727

AND THEY CALLED IT DIXIELAND
(Whiting)   One Step Arrangement
Played by George Gershwin
"Perfection"   86736

"Latest Dances"
PASTIME RAG
(Matthews)   A Slow Drag
Played by Fred Murtha
Note: This is Matthews' "Pastime Rag No. 3"
"Perfection"   86738

"Hebrew Music" ("Standard Rolls For June")
DAS PINTELE YUD
(Perlmutter and Wohl)
Played by Georoge (sic) Gershwin
"Perfection"   (# not shown)

GOTT UN SEIN MISHPET IS GERECHT
(Meyerowitz)
Played by Georoge (sic) Gershwin
"Perfection"   (# not shown)

Note: These two titles are included in Arto Roll
No. 86378—"Hebrew Popular Songs—Medley," a
roll that retailed for $1.10, and is shown in Arto
catalogs of this period as "Played by Baltuck." In
the medley they comprise selections 5 and 4, respec-
tively.

WHEN VERDI PLAYS THE HURDY-GURDY
(Walter Donaldson)
Played by George Gershwin
Metro-Art   202712 $.45
Universal Uni-Record   202713 $.45

OH! PROMISE ME THAT YOU'LL COME
BACK TO ALABAM'
(George W. Meyer)
Played by George Gershwin

Metro-Art   202714 $.40
Universal Uni-Record   202715 $.40

Note: MA202716/Un202717 is not played by
George Gershwin.

SAIL ON TO CEYLON
(Herman Paley)
Played by George Gershwin
Metro-Art   202718 $.50
Universal Uni-Record   202719 $.50

Note: The above 3 rolls were released by Aeolian
in the same month that Uni-Record issued the roll
of "Maple Leaf Rag" played by Scott Joplin.

JULY

"Latest Dances"
WALKIN' THE DOG
(Brooks)   Dance, New Dance Fox Trot Arrange-
ment
Played by George Gershwin
"Perfection"   86753

Note: No George Gershwin rolls were released in
July by Aeolian.

AUGUST

COME ON TO NASHVILLE TENNESSEE
(Walter Donaldson)   Fox Trot
Played by George Gershwin
"One of the latest vaudeville hits. A sure winner."
Metro-Art   202852 $.40
Universal Uni-Record   202853 $.40

YOU'RE A DOG-GONE DANGEROUS GIRL
(Clark & Monaco)   Fox Trot
Played by George Gershwin
"One of the big successes featured by Al Jolson in
his latest Winter Garden production."
Metro-Art   202854 $.40
Universal Uni-Record   202855 $.40

SEPTEMBER

WHEN YOU WANT 'EM YOU CAN'T GET
'EM
(George Gershwin)   Fox Trot
Played by George Gershwin
Metro-Art   202864
Universal Uni-Record   202865

Note: This was George Gershwin's first published
song.

HONOLULU BLUES
(James V. Monaco)   Fox Trot
Played by George Gershwin
Metro-Art   202864
Universal Uni-Record   202873

I WAS NEVER NEARER HEAVEN IN MY
LIFE
(Ted Snyder)
Played by George Gershwin
Metro-Art   202902
Universal Uni-Record   202903

RIALTO RIPPLES
(George Gershwin)   Fox Trot
Played by George Gershwin
Metro-Art   202934
Universal Uni-Record   202935

Note: This was George Gershwin's first published
instrumental number, written in collaboration with
Will Donaldson.

DECEMBER

TIDDLE-DE-WINKS
(Melville Morris)   Fox Trot
Played by George Gershwin
Metro-Art   203052
Universal Uni-Record   203053

I'M DOWN IN HONOLULU LOOKING
THEM OVER
(Irving Berlin)
Played by George Gershwin

Metro-Art   203054 $.40
Universal Uni-Record   203055

1917

JANUARY

Aeolian Song Rolls were first introduced in January 1917. All ended in odd numbers, and George
Gershwin played the entire first month's output.

SOMEWHERE THERE'S A LITTLE
COTTAGE STANDING
(Music—Marshall, Lyric—Sunshine)   Saxophone
Arrangement
Played by George Gershwin   (Assisted by R. O.
Erlebach)
"A great song with a wonderful melody and a
master lyric. One that leaves a lingering impression
that guarantees applause and enchore [sic]."
Universal Song Roll   2001 $.60

MAMMY'S LITTLE COAL BLACK ROSE
(Music—Whiting, Lyric—Egan)
Played by George Gershwin
"A wonderful song by the writers of 'And They
Called It Dixieland.' It has a delightful melody
and an appealing lyric."
Universal Song Roll   2005 $.60
Later issued as Mel-O-Dee 2005

JUST A WORD OF SYMPATHY
(Music—Alstyne, Lyric—Kahn)
Played by George Gershwin
"A brand new ballad hit by the writer of 'Mem-
ories.'"
Universal Song Roll   2007 $.60
Later issued on Mel-O-Dee 2007

IF YOU'LL COME BACK TO MY GARDEN
OF LOVE
(Music—Gumble, Lyric—Murphy)
Played by George Gershwin
"This beautiful song is just commencing to reach
the height of popularity. Both the words and the
music are bound to please."
Universal Song Roll   2009 $.60
Later issued on Mel-O-Dee 2009

HOW IS EVERY LITTLE THING IN DIXIE?
(Music—Gumbel [sic], Lyric—Yellen)
Played by George Gershwin
"A great fast song by the writers of numerous hits.
A splendid roll for dancing."
Universal Song Roll   2013 $.60
Later issued on Mel-O-Dee 2013

FEBRUARY

Note: The two George Gershwin song rolls issued
in February 1917 have serial numbers that fit in
numerically among the five rolls issued in January.

WHOSE PRETTY BABY ARE YOU NOW?
(Music—Egbert Van Alstyne, Lyric—Gus Kahn)
Saxophone Arrangement
Played by George Gershwin. Assisted by R.E.O.
[sic]
"The answer song to the popular 'Pretty Baby' is
here offered in Saxophone arrangement. The lyric
is a humorous one, and the roll is also arranged for
dancing purposes."
Universal Song Roll   2003 $.75
Later issued on Mel-O-Dee 2003
Also issued on Angelus 6001 in April 1917

IT'S A CUTE LITTLE WAY OF MY OWN
(from Follow Me)
(Music—Harry Tierney, Lyric—Held & Bryan)
Played by George Gershwin
"The individual song success from Anna Held's
latest musical comedy offering, Follow Me."
Universal Song Roll   2011 $.75
Later issued on Mel-O-Dee 2011

MARCH

'WAY DOWN IN IOWA I'M GOING TO
HIDE AWAY
(George Meyer)
Played by George Gershwin
"One of the popular song hits of the day which is
meeting with great favor."

Metro-Art 203072 $.40
Universal 203073
Angelus Voltem 1535

HESITATION BLUES
(Middleton and Smythe) Fox Trot
Played by George Gershwin
"One of the best known blues ever written, here
played with much swing and pep."
Metro-Art 203074 $.40
Universal Uni-Record 203075
Angelus Voltem 1525
Artrio-Angelus 7695 $1.75

APRIL

WHERE THE BLACK-EYED
 SUSANS GROW
(Whiting and Radford)
Played by George Gershwin
Universal Song Roll 2079 $.80
Later issued on Mel-O-Dee 2079

BECAUSE YOU'RE IRISH
(Van Alstyne and Kahn)
Played by George Gershwin
Universal Song Roll 2081 $.75
Angelus 6011

SHE'S DIXIE ALL THE TIME
(Tierney and Bryan)
Played by George Gershwin
Universal Song Roll 2083 $.75
Angelus 6017

MAY

I WONDER WHY (from Love o' Mike)
(Kern) Fox Trot
Played by George Gershwin
Metro-Art 201208 $.50
Universal 201209

HAVANOLA (HAVE ANOTHER)
(Frey) Fox Trot
Played by George Gershwin
Metro-Art 203098 $.50
Universal 203099

BUZZIN' THE BEE
(Wendling and Wells) Fox Trot
Played by George Gershwin
Metro-Art 203184 $.50
Universal 203185

Note: May 1917 was the month that Aeolian first
introduced its rolls played by James P. Johnson:
"After Tonight," a duet with William H. Farrell,
"Caprice Rag," and "Steeplechase Rag."

JULY

AIN'T YOU COMIN' BACK TO DIXIELAND?
(Richard Whiting) Jass-Fox Trot
Played by Erlebach & Gershwin
Universal Song Roll 2205
Duo-Art 1545 $1.25
Artrio-Angelus 7745 $1.75

ROLLING IN HIS LITTLE ROLLING CHAIR
(Halsey K. Mohr) Jass-Fox Trot E-Flat
Played by Gershwin & Erlebach
Universal Song Roll 2257 $.80

AUGUST

LILY OF THE VALLEY
(Anatol Friedland) Jass-Fox Trot
Played by Gershwin & Erlebach
Universal Song Roll 2293 $.80
Later issued on Mel-O-Dee 2293
Angelus Voltem 6051 9/17
Duo-Art 1547 9/17 $1.25

FOR YOUR COUNTRY AND MY
 COUNTRY
(Irving Berlin) Jass-One Step
Played by Gershwin & Erlebach
Universal Song Roll 2307 $1.00
Angelus Voltem 6051 9/17
Duo-Art 1543 $1.25

MELE HULA
(William H. Tyers) Fox-Trot
Played by George Gershwin
Metro-Art 203198
Universal 203199

SEPTEMBER

YOU'RE A GREAT BIG LONESOME BABY
(Richard Whiting) Fox Trot
Played by George Gershwin
Universal Song Roll 2529 $.80

SWEETEST LITTLE GIRL IN TENNESSEE
(Harry Carroll) Jass-Fox Trot
Played by Gershwin & Wilson
Universal Song Roll 2333 $.80

STORY BOOK BALL
(George Perry) Jass-Fox Trot
Played by Gershwin & Erlebach
Universal Song Roll 2337 $.75
Later issued on Mel-O-Dee 2337

HUCKLEBERRY FINN
(Joe Young) Jass-Fox Trot
Played by Wilson & Gershwin
Metro-Art 203224 $.50
Universal 203225

SOME SWEET DAY
(Abe Olman) Jass-Fox Trot
Played by Gershwin & Erlebach
Metro-Art 203232 $.50
Universal 203233

CHU-CHIN-CHOW (from Follies 1917)
(Dave Stamper) Jass-Fox Trot
Played by Gershwin & Wilson
Metro-Art 203238 $.50
Universal 203239
Artrio-Angelus 7769 $2.00

The Artrio-Angelus issue of this roll appears in a
medley as follows:

CHINESE MEDLEY Fox Trot
(Berlin, Smith & Stamper)
Introducing: (1) "From Here to Shanghai"; (2)
"While the Incense is Burning"; (3) "Chu-Chin-
Chow." Jazz Arrangements
Played by Youmans, Erlebach, Wilson, Nelson &
Gershwin
(from the original Artrio-Angelus catalog)

OCTOBER

I'VE GOT THE NICEST LITTLE HOME IN
 DIXIE
(Walter Donaldson) Jass-Fox Trot
Played by Gershwin & Wilson
Universal Song Roll 2385 $.80
Angelus 6082

WHEN IT'S ALL OVER
(Kerry Mills) Jass-One Step
Played by Erlebach & Gershwin
Universal Song Roll 2393 $.80
Angelus 6088

WHOSE LITTLE HEART ARE YOU
 BREAKING NOW
(Irving Berlin) Fox Trot
Played by Gershwin & Wilson
Universal Song Roll 2411 $.80

SOME SUNDAY MORNING
(Richard Whiting) Saxophone-Fox Trot
Played by Gershwin & Erlebach
Universal Song Roll 2413 $1.00
Later issued on Mel-O-Dee 2413
Also issued on Duo-Art 1566 $1.25

Note: On the above roll, the Duo-Art catalog calls
it a "Fox Trot" while the label of the Universal
Song Roll reads "Saxophone Drag."

SOUTHERN GALS
(Albert Gumble) Fox Trot
Played by Gershwin & Wilson
Universal Song Roll 2417 $.80

MY FAULTLESS PAJAMA GIRL
(Louis H. Fischer) Fox Trot

Played by Gershwin & Erlebach
Metro-Art 203248 $.50
Universal 203249

RUBY RAG
(Harry Ruby) Fox Trot
Played by Gershwin & Erlebach
Metro-Art 203256 $.50
Universal 203257

JAZAMINE
(Harry Akst) Fox Trot
Played by George Gershwin
Metro-Art 203262 $.50
Universal 203263

NOVEMBER

MR. JAZZ HIMSELF
(Irving Berlin) Jass-Fox Trot
Played by Gershwin & Erlebach
"Irving Berlin's latest effort. The jazziest of all jazz
songs."
Universal Song Roll 2529 $.80
Later issued on Mel-O-Dee 2529

HELLO WISCONSIN
(Harry Ruby) Fox Trot
Played by George Gershwin
"The prize-winning novelty song of the season."
Universal Song Roll 2543 $.80

SO LONG SAMMY
(Albert Gumble) One Step
Played by George Gershwin
"The latest of war songs has made a hit with the
boys in 'Khaki.'"
Universal Song Roll 2553 $.80
Angelus 6098

DECEMBER

MY SWEETIE
(Irving Berlin)
Played by George Gershwin
Universal Song Roll 2567 $.80
Angelus 6107 (12/17)

THE BRAVEST HEART OF ALL
(Whiting) Fox Trot—Key of E flat
Played by Wynn
SingA Word Roll 53 Full # Unk.
"Perfection" 87113

Note: The above roll is credited as having been
"Played by Bert Wynn" but whether it is Gershwin
may never be determined, even if a copy of the roll
is discovered. Though he was an exclusive Aeolian
artist by this time, Gershwin may have returned to
Standard to visit and cut a roll for them for old
times' sake; or this might have been a number he
recorded the previous year that wasn't issued until
December 1917; or some other Standard pianist
might have recorded it at this time and used Gershwin's old pseudonym. We list it here because it
seems to be the only "Bert Wynn" roll issued by
Standard after Gershwin left in mid-1916. It is very
likely a genuine Gershwin item.

1918

JANUARY

THE PICTURE I WANT TO SEE
(from Miss 1917)
(Kern) Fox Trot
Played by George Gershwin
Metro-Art 203334 $.55
Universal 203335
Artrio-Angelus 7807 $1.50

THE LAND WHERE THE GOOD SONGS
GO (from Miss 1917)
(Kern) Jass-Fox Trot
Played by Gershwin & Erlebach
Metro-Art 203336 $.55
Universal 203337
Angelus Voltem (Number Unknown) (1/18)
Duo-Art 1590 $1.25 (7/18)

Note: George Gershwin was the rehearsal pianist
for Miss 1917.

FEBRUARY

SOME SWEET DAY
(Abe Olman)   Jass-Fox Trot
Played by Gershwin & Erlebach
Universal Song Roll   2685 $.85
Angelus   6150
Artrio-Angelus   7768 $1.75

Note: This roll was first released in September 1917
as an instrumental roll, at a price of $.50.

SEPTEMBER

GARDEN OF MY DREAMS
(from *Follies 1918*)
(Dave Stamper)   E-flat
Played by George Gershwin
Universal Song Roll   3085 $1.00

LITTLE TUNE, GO AWAY
(from *Rock-a-Bye Baby*)
(Jerome D. Kern)   Fox Trot   Key D
Played by George Gershwin
Universal Song Roll   3087 $1.00

WHEN I HEAR A SYNCOPATED TUNE
(from *Follies 1918*)
(Louis A. Hirsch)   Fox Trot   Key G
Played by George Gershwin
Universal Song Roll   3091
Angelus   6259

Note: George Gershwin was rehearsal pianist for
both the *Ziegfeld Follies of 1918* and *Rock-a-Bye
Baby*.

1919

APRIL

Note: All of the George Gershwin rolls for this
month except "Girl of My Heart" are from the
musical comedy *Oh, My Dear!*

I'D ASK NO MORE
(Louis A. Hirsch)   Key C
Played by George Gershwin
Universal Song Roll   3259 $1.00
Later issued on Mel-O-Dee 3259

YOU NEVER KNOW
(Louis A. Hirsch)   E-flat
Played by George Gershwin
Universal Song Roll   3261 $1.00
Later issued on Mel-O-Dee 3261
Angelus   6365   (4/19)

CITY OF DREAMS
(Louis A. Hirsch)   E-flat
Played by George Gershwin
Universal Song Roll   3263 $1.00
Later issued on Mel-O-Dee 3263

I WONDER WHETHER
(Louis A. Hirsch)   E-flat
Played by George Gershwin
Universal Song Roll   3265 $1.00
Later issued on Mel-O-Dee 3265
Angelus   6359   (4/19)

GIRL OF MY HEART
(from *Somebody's Sweetheart*)
(Buffano)   E-flat
Played by George Gershwin
Universal Song Roll   3267 $1.00
Later issued on Mel-O-Dee 3267
Angelus   6355   (4/19)

LAND WHERE JOURNEYS END
(Louis A. Hirsch)   A-flat
Played by George Gershwin
Universal Song Roll   3271
Later issued on Mel-O-Dee 3271

OH, MY DEAR—FOX TROT MEDLEY
(Louis A. Hirsch)
Introducing: (1) I Wonder Whether; (2) You
Never Know; (3) I'd Ask No More; (4) The Land
Where Journeys End; (5) City of Dreams; (6) I
Wonder Whether
Played by George Gershwin
Metro-Art   203518 $1.00

Universal   203519
Angelus Voltem   1602   (4/19)
Artrio-Angelus   7958 $1.75

SEPTEMBER

TEE-OODLE-UM-BUM-BO
(from *La, La, Lucille*)
(Gershwin)   One Step
Played by George Gershwin
Universal Song Roll   3517
Later issued on Mel-O-Dee 3517
Duo-Art Song Roll   10023
Artrio-Angelus   8033 $1.50

Note: This roll was reissued in 1972 on Klavier
KS-122 Stereo, *George Gershwin Plays Gershwin
& Kern*.

OCTOBER

FROM NOW ON (from *La, La, Lucille*)
(George Gershwin)   Fox Trot   Key G
Played by George Gershwin
Universal Song Roll   3543 $1.25
Artrio-Angelus   8044 $1.50

NOBODY BUT YOU (from *La, La, Lucille*)
(George Gershwin)   One Step   E-flat
Played by George Gershwin
Universal Song Roll   3549 $1.25
Later issued on Mel-O-Dee 3549
Artrio-Angelus   8045 $1.50

I WAS SO YOUNG, YOU WERE SO
   BEAUTIFUL (from *Good Morning, Judge*)
(George Gershwin)   Ballad Key G
Played by George Gershwin
Universal Song Roll   3557 $1.25
Later issued on Mel-O-Dee 3557
Duo-Art Song Roll   10033
Artrio-Angelus   8047 $1.50

Note: This roll was reissued in 1972 on Klavier
KS-122 Stereo, *George Gershwin Plays Gershwin
& Kern*.

EXACT DATE UNKNOWN
BUT PROBABLY 1919

FIRST ROSE OF SUMMER
(Jerome Kern)   Fox Trot
Played by George Gershwin, composer of *La, La,
Lucille*
Welte-Mignon   3966A

Note: This very rare roll surfaced in 1972 at an
auction. The paper width is 12-7/8″ (all other
Gershwin rolls listed here are 11-1/4″ wide) and
it can be played only on a special player piano having a Welte reproducing system that can accommodate rolls of this width. Like Aeolian's Duo-Art,
this Welte roll is designed with extra perforations
along each edge to reproduce the artist's exact performance of the original recording on a Welte player. Other artists who made Welte rolls of this size
were Negro pianists James Reese Europe and Ford
Dabney (who produced several duet rolls) and
Hughie Woolford, a New York musician and long-
time friend of Eubie Blake. These rolls were apparently recorded in Poughkeepsie, New York.
George Gershwin may have recorded other rolls for
Welte, but as of this time, none are known.

1920

FEBRUARY

COME TO THE MOON
(Gershwin)   Fox Trot
Played by George Gershwin
Mel-O-Dee   3701

SWANEE
(Gershwin)   One Step
Played by George Gershwin
Mel-O-Dee   3707
Duo-Art   1649

MARCH

LIMEHOUSE NIGHTS (from *Century Whirl*)
(Gershwin)   One Step
Played by George Gershwin
Mel-O-Dee   3739
Duo-Art   1654
Artrio-Angelus   8105 $1.50

POPPY LAND (from *Century Whirl*)
(Gershwin)
Played by George Gershwin
Mel-O-Dee   3741
Artrio-Angelus   8108 $1.50

Note: The show's actual title was *Morris Gest
Midnight Whirl*.

JUNE

LEFT ALL ALONE AGAIN BLUES
(from *Night Boat*)
(Kern)   Fox Trot
Played by George Gershwin
Mel-O-Dee   3845
Duo-Art   1664
Artrio-Angelus   8139 $1.50

WHOSE BABY ARE YOU? (from *Night Boat*)
(Kern)   One Step
Played by George Gershwin
Mel-O-Dee   3853
Duo-Art   1667

Note: The show's actual title was *The Night Boat*;
lyrics were by Anne Caldwell.

Note: In the *Music Trade Indicator* for June 19,
1920 (pp. 34–35), appeared the following article,
headed "A GRAND, A ROLL—AND PEN-
NINGTON—Dancer Cavorts Atop a Weber
Grand to Tune of Mel-O-Dee Roll—LISTEN!—
New York, June 16":
   "Perhaps—no unquestionably—the liveliest bit of
tabasco in that whole saucepan of jazz and Mel-O-
Dee, the scandals [*sic*] of 1920 is Miss Ann Pennington.
   "From her feet up Ann is 'tres bien' but no small
part of her success in the *Scandals of 1920* is her
'dancing piano.' No! The piano doesn't really
dance. Ann dances on the roof of a Weber Grand
to the tune of a Mel-O-Dee Roll in the cleverest
stunt of this year's Scandal.
   "Dancing on a piano may be a common stunt,
but—you don't know the half of it. This piano is an
orchestra and dance floor both. And some orchestra!!
   "When Ann gets anything in her head you
can't stop it—it goes right to her feet and George
White knows enough not to stop Ann's feet; what
is more Ann always insists on the best.
   "'Cause: Ann's idea—
   "Result: George White went to the Aeolian
Company and told them his story. They took a
Weber Grand Electric Player Piano and made a
special dancing top.
   "Then they called in George Gershwin, that ever
ready, ever tuneful pianist who makes Mel-O-Dee
rolls exclusively for the Aeolian Company. George
just ran his fingers up and down the keys and turned
out a real, regular, Pennington Mel-O-Dee Special.
   "All you need do is to see Scandals of 1920 to
realize that the best dance team this year is Ann
Pennington, the dancing piano, and her Mel-O-Dee
orchestra. They are the hit of the Scandals and
Ann says, 'Don't thank me, thank Aeolian and
George and Mel-O-Dee!' "

   It is possible that the roll mentioned above was
a special roll made for Ann Pennington's use in
the show, as described, and not one of the three
regular-issue rolls listed next. It is also possible that
the roll referred to is "Scandal Walk."

AUGUST

ON MY MIND THE WHOLE NIGHT LONG
(from *Scandals of 1920*)
(Gershwin)   Blues-Fox Trot
Played by George Gershwin
Metro-Art   203576
Universal   203577
Artrio-Angelus   8167 $1.50

IDOL [SIC] DREAMS (from *Scandals of 1920*)
(Gershwin) Fox Trot
Played by George Gershwin
Mel-O-Dee 203579
Artrio-Angelus 8168 $1.50

SCANDAL WALK (from *Scandals of 1920*)
(Gershwin) Fox Trot
Played by George Gershwin
Mel-O-Dee 203583
Artrio-Angelus 8169 $1.50

SEPTEMBER

WHISPERING
(Schonberger) Fox Trot, Key E-flat
Played by George Gershwin
"A splendid arrangement of this latest Pacific Coast
hit."
Mel-O-Dee 4007 $1.25
Artrio-Angelus 2013 $1.75
(Song Roll, with Words)

OCTOBER

SWEETHEART SHOP SELECTION
comprising (1) WAITING FOR THE SUN TO
     COME OUT; (2) DIDN'T YOU?; (3) IS
     THERE ANY LITTLE THING I CAN DO?;
     (4) MY CARAVAN
(Felix and Gershwin)
Played by George Gershwin
"This new musical- comedy which has met with
great success in Chicago and is soon due for a New
York run [*sic*]."
Mel-O-Dee 203733 $1.25

Note: The labels on some rolls list tune (2) as (4)
and vice versa.

Note: The *Music Trade Indicator*, August 14, 1920,
p. 33, carried this article, headed "MEL-O-DEE'S
LATEST HIT": "The song hit from the Musical
Show, '*The Sweetheart Shop*,' now playing at the
Illinois Theater in Chicago, is '*Waiting for the Sun
to Come Out*,' written by George Gershwin, star
pianist of the Mel-O-Dee Company. This number
has proved so popular in Chicago that the Mel-O-
Dee Company are bringing out a special roll from
the '*Sweetheart Shop*' because of the unusual call.
Mr. Gershwin is also responsible for the music in
'*George White's Scandals of 1920*.'"

A YOUNG MAN'S FANCY
(The music box number from *What's in a Name*)
(Music by Milton Ager) Fox Trot, Key E-flat
Played by George Gershwin
"Mr. Gershwin has played a music box effect in
this roll that is somewhat startling. It makes a won-
derful fox-trot and is used by dance orchestras
from coast to coast."
Mel-O-Dee 203737 $.85
(Instrumental)
Mel-O-Dee 4083 (11/20)
(Song Roll)
Artrio-Angelus 8025 $1.50
(Instrumental)

DECEMBER

WHEN THE RIGHT LITTLE GIRL
     COMES ALONG (from *Jim-Jam-Jems*)
(Hanley) One-Step, Key of E-flat
Played by George Gershwin
Mel-O-Dee 3985 $1.25

DARLING
(Schoenberger) Fox-Trot
Played by Gershwin & Hess
Mel-O-Dee 4109 $1.25

Note: Cliff Hess, well-known songwriter, was also a
Mel-O-Dee staff pianist. While the bulletin shows
the composer here as "Schoenberger," the roll label
lists it as "Schonberg."

IF A WISH COULD MAKE IT SO
(from *Tickle Me*)
(Stothart) Fox-Trot, Key of E-flat
Played by George Gershwin
Mel-O-Dee 4117 $1.25

SINGING THE BLUES
(Conrad & Robinson) Fox-Trot, Key of E-flat
Played by George Gershwin
Mel-O-Dee 4133 $1.25
Artrio-Angelus 2027 $1.75
(Song Roll with Words)

SWEET LITTLE STRANGER
(from *Jim-Jam-Jems*)
(Hanley) Fox-Trot, Key of E-flat
Played by George Gershwin
Mel-O-Dee 4135 $1.25

WAITIN' FOR ME
(Pinkard) Fox-Trot, Key of E-flat
Played by George Gershwin
Mel-O-Dee 4139 $1.25

1921

JANUARY

JUST SNAP YOUR FINGERS AT CARE
(from *Greenwich Village Follies*, 1920)
(Silvers) Fox-Trot, Key G
Played by George Gershwin
Mel-O-Dee 4151 $1.25

ROCK-A-BYE LULLABYE MAMMY
(Donaldson) Fox-Trot, Key G
Played by George Gershwin
Mel-O-Dee 4165 $1.25
Duo-Art 1705

Note: This roll was reissued on Klavier KS-122
Stereo, *George Gershwin Plays Gershwin & Kern*.

GRIEVING FOR YOU
(Gold) Fox-Trot, Key F
Played by George Gershwin
Mel-O-Dee 4167 $1.25
Duo-Art 1702
Artrio-Angelus 2030 $1.75
(Song Roll, with Words)

I'M A LONESOME LITTLE RAINDROP
(Hanley) Fox-Trot, Key E-flat
Played by George Gershwin
Mel-O-Dee 4179 $1.25
Artrio-Angelus 2031 $1.75
(Song Roll, with Words)

MARCH

MAKE BELIEVE
(Shilkret) Fox-Trot, E-flat
Played by George Gershwin
Mel-O-Dee 4267 $1.25
Duo-Art 1718 (George Gershwin "Assisted by
Muriel Pollock," a Mel-O-Dee Recording pianist)

WHIP-POOR-WILL
(Kern) Fox Trot, B-flat
Played by George Gershwin
Mel-O-Dee 4275 $1.25
Duo-Art 1719

Note: This roll was reissued on Klavier KS-122
Stereo, *George Gershwin Plays Gershwin & Kern*.

EXACT DATE UNKNOWN POSSIBLY MAY 1921

DRIFTING ALONG WITH THE TIDE
(from *George White's Scandals of 1921*)
(George Gershwin) Fox Trot and Song Roll
Played by George Gershwin
Duo-Art 17445 $1.25

Note: This roll is listed in Duo-Art's July 1, 1922,
Catalog, its 1924 General Catalog, and its 1927
Dance Music Supplement.
This roll was reissued on Klavier KS-122 Stereo,
George Gershwin Plays Gershwin & Kern.

1925

MAY

RHAPSODY IN BLUE, PART II:
     ANDANTINO AND FINALE
(George Gershwin)

Played by George Gershwin
Duo-Art 68787 $1.75

Note: It is almost certain that Gershwin recorded
both Parts I and II of the *Rhapsody in Blue* at this
time, but for some reason the company decided to
issue only the second part. The Duo-Art Number
68777 was never assigned to a roll, so it is quite
possible that Duo-Art 68777 was contemplated for
Rhapsody in Blue, Part I. Part I was issued in
January 1927.

JULY

KICKIN' THE CLOUDS AWAY (from *Tell Me
More*)
(George Gershwin)
Played by George Gershwin
Mel-O-Dee 47014 $1.00
Duo-Art 713122 $1.25

Note: The Duo-Art Monthly Bulletin for July 1925
describes the roll as follows: "George Gershwin
himself has here recorded one of his newest popular hits—one of the numbers that have made *Tell
Me More* a great musical comedy success. This is a
snappy Fox-Trot with a great dance tune and an
abundance of real Gershwin harmonies."

SEPTEMBER

SO AM I (from *Lady, Be Good!*)
(George Gershwin) Ballad B-flat
Played by George Gershwin
Mel-O-Dee 47056 $1.00
Duo-Art 102625 $1.25
(With Words)

Note: The Duo-Art Monthly Bulletin for September 1925 describes the roll as follows: "One of the
popular hits of one of Broadway's outstanding musical-comedy successes of the year, *Lady, Be Good!*
This is a ballad setting in George Gershwin's best
style of a clever and pretty little duet, the words of
which are by Ira Gershwin."

Note: Reissued on Klavier KS-122 Stereo, *George
Gershwin Plays Gershwin & Kern*.

1926

APRIL

SWEET AND LOW-DOWN
(from *Tip-Toes*)
(George Gershwin) Fox-Trot
Arranged and Played by George Gershwin
Duo-Art 713214 $1.25
Mel-O-Dee 47175 $1.00

Note: Reissued on Klavier KS-122 Stereo, *George
Gershwin Plays Gershwin & Kern*.

THAT CERTAIN FEELING
(from *Tip-Toes*)
(George Gershwin) Fox-Trot
Arranged and Played by George Gershwin
Duo-Art 713216 $1.25
Mel-O-Dee 47178 $1.00
These are almost certainly the last piano rolls re-
corded by George Gershwin. The April 1926 Duo-
Art Monthly Bulletin describes them as follows: "In
'Sweet and Low-Down' and 'That Certain Feeling'
George Gershwin himself has recorded in his indi-
vidualistic and inimitable style the two big Fox-Trot
hits from his very successful new musical comedy,
Tip-Toes. These are special arrangements made by
Mr. Gershwin exclusively for the Duo-Art Piano—
and they are winners."

1927

JANUARY

RHAPSODY IN BLUE, PART I
(George Gershwin)
Arranged and Played by George Gershwin
Duo-Art 70947 $1.75

Note: Although this roll was issued in 1927, it was
probably recorded in 1925 at the same time that
Gershwin recorded Part II.

BIBLIOGRAPHY

I. BOOKS BY AND ABOUT THE GERSHWINS

Armitage, Merle. *George Gershwin.* New York: Longmans, Green & Co., 1938.

Armitage, Merle. *George Gershwin: Man and Legend.* New York: Duell, Sloan and Pearce, 1958.

Duke, Vernon. *Passport to Paris.* Boston: Little, Brown & Co., 1955.

Durham, Frank. *DuBose Heyward: The Man Who Wrote Porgy.* Columbia: University of South Carolina Press, 1954.

Ewen, David. *The Story of George Gershwin.* New York: Henry Holt & Co., 1943.

Ewen, David. *George Gershwin: His Journey to Greatness.* New York: Prentice-Hall, 1970.

Gershwin, George. *George Gershwin's Song Book.* New York: Simon and Schuster, 1932.

Gershwin, George and Ira. *The George and Ira Gershwin Song Book.* New York: Simon and Schuster, 1960.

Gershwin, Ira. *Lyrics on Several Occasions.* New York: Alfred A. Knopf, 1959. Paperback edition, New York: The Viking Press, 1973.

Goldberg, Isaac. *George Gershwin.* New York: Simon and Schuster, 1931; Supplemented by Edith Garson, New York: Frederick Ungar Publishing Co., 1958.

Jablonski, Edward, and Lawrence D. Stewart. *The Gershwin Years.* New York: Doubleday & Co., 1958. Revised 1973.

Levant, Oscar. *A Smattering of Ignorance.* New York: Doubleday & Co., 1940.

Payne, Robert. *Gershwin.* London: Robert Hale, 1960.

Rosenfeld, Paul. *Discoveries of a Music Critic.* New York: Harcourt Brace & Co., 1936.

Rushmore, Robert. *The Life of George Gershwin.* New York: Crowell-Collier Press, 1966.

II. GENERAL WORKS

Astaire, Fred. *Steps in Time.* New York: Harper & Bros, 1959.

Baral, Robert. *Revue.* New York: Fleet Publishing Co., 1962.

Blesh, Rudi, and Harriet Janis. *They All Played Ragtime.* New York: Alfred A. Knopf, 1950.

Burton, Jack. *Blue Book of Broadway Musicals.* New York: Century House, 1952.

Burton, Jack. *Blue Book of Hollywood Musicals.* New York: Century House, 1953.

Burton, Jack. *Blue Book of Tin Pan Alley.* New York: Century House, 1950.

Chase, Gilbert, *America's Music.* New York: McGraw-Hill Book Co., 1955.

Croce, Arlene. *The Fred Astaire & Ginger Rogers Book.* New York: Outerbridge & Lazard, 1972.

Ewen, David. *The New Complete Book of the American Musical Theater.* New York: Holt, Rinehart & Winston, 1970.

Ewen, David. *The Story of America's Musical Theater.* New York: Chilton Co., 1961.

Farnsworth, Marjorie. *The Ziegfeld Follies.* New York: Bonanza Books, 1956.

Goldberg, Isaac. *Tin Pan Alley.* New York: John Day Co., 1930. Introduction by George Gershwin.

Green, Stanley. *Ring Bells! Sing Songs!* New York: Arlington House, 1971.

Green, Stanley. *The World of Musical Comedy.* New York: Grosset & Dunlap, 1960; Revised, New York: A. S. Barnes, 1968.

Handlin, Oscar. *The Uprooted.* Boston: Little, Brown & Co., 1951.

Higham, Charles. *Ziegfeld.* Chicago: Henry Regnery, 1972.

Jablonski, Edward. *Harold Arlen: Happy with the Blues.* New York: Doubleday & Co., 1961.

Kazin, Alfred. *On Native Grounds.* New York: Harcourt, Brace & Co., 1942.

Kimball, Robert. *Cole.* New York: Holt, Rinehart & Winston, 1971.

Kimball, Robert, and William Bolcolm. *Reminiscing with Sissle and Blake.* New York: The Viking Press, 1973.

Knox, Donald. *The Magic Factory.* New York: Praeger Publishers, 1973.

Lawrence, Gertrude. *A Star Danced.* New York: Doubleday & Co., 1945.

Levant, Oscar. *Memoirs of an Amnesiac.* New York: G. P. Putnam's Sons, 1965.

Levant, Oscar. *The Unimportance of Being Oscar.* New York: G. P. Putnam's Sons, 1968.

Lewine, Richard, and Alfred Simon. *Encyclopedia of Theatre Music.* New York: Random House, 1961.

Lewine, Richard, and Alfred Simon. *Songs of the American Theater.* New York: Dodd, Mead, 1973.

Mellers, Wilfrid. *Music in a New Found Land.* New York: Alfred A. Knopf, 1965.

Merman, Ethel, and Pete Martin. *Who Could Ask for Anything More?* New York: Doubleday & Co., 1955.

Parks, Melvin. *Musicals of the 1930's.* Published privately by the Museum of the City of New York, 1966.

Richman, Harry, and Richard Gehman. *A Hell of a Life.* New York: Duell, Sloan and Pearce, 1966.

Rischin, Moses. *The Promised City: New York's Jews 1870–1914.* Cambridge: Harvard University Press, 1962.

Schuller, Gunther. *Early Jazz: Its Roots and Musical Development.* New York: Oxford University Press, 1968.

Seldes, Gilbert. *The 7 Lively Arts.* New York: Harper & Bros., 1924.

Smith, Cecil. *Musical Comedy in America.* New York: Theatre Arts, 1950.

Stearns, Marshall W. *The Story of Jazz.* New York: Oxford University Press, 1956.

Stearns, Marshall and Jean. *Jazz Dance.* New York: The Macmillan Co., 1968.

Teichmann, Howard. *George S. Kaufman: An Intimate Portrait.* New York: Atheneum, 1972.

Thomson, Virgil. *American Music Since 1910.* New York: Holt, Rinehart & Winston, 1970.

Wilder, Alec. *American Popular Song.* New York: Oxford University Press. 1972.

Contributors to production
Tony Clark: Editor
Lesley Krauss: Production Editor
Harry Ford: Production Director
Delos D. Rowe Associates: Mechanical Preparation
Carl S. Barile: Designer's Production Assistant

The text of this book is set
in Intertype Egmont and Intertype Bodoni Modern
Typesetting by The Composing Room, Inc., New York City,
under the direction of Al Sloves
Platemaking, printing and binding by Kingsport Press, Inc.,
Kingsport, Tennessee
Paper manufactured by S.D. Warren Company, Portland, Maine
Cloth manufactured by Joanna Western Mills Company, Chicago